MONEY AND BANKING

MONEY AND BANKING

DONALD T. SAVAGE
University of Maine at Orono

A WILEY/HAMILTON PUBLICATION
Santa Barbara New York London Sydney Toronto
John Wiley & Sons

This book was designed by Sally
Thompson, copyedited by Brian Williams
and set in 10 point Times Roman by
Skil-Set Typographers. Illustrations
were prepared by Etcetera Graphics
and the cover was
designed by John Alexander. Production
was supervised by Chuck Pendergast
and Jean Varven.

Library of Congress Cataloging in Publication Data

Savage, Donald T
Money and banking.

"A Wiley/Hamilton publication."
Includes bibliographies and index.
1. Finance. 2. Money. 3. Banks and banking.
4. Credit. 5. International finance. I. Title.
HG173.S26 332 76-56134
ISBN 0-471-75519-2

Printed in the United States of America.

10 9 8 7 6 5 4 3 2 1

To Pat

CONTENTS

ABOUT THE AUTHOR

Donald T. Savage is an Associate Professor of Economics at the University of Maine at Orono. He teaches graduate and undergraduate courses in Money and Banking and Macroeconomics. Prior to teaching at the University of Maine, he taught at Clark University. For the academic year 1976–1977, Professor Savage is on leave from the University of Maine and is employed by the Division of Research and Statistics of the Board of Governors of the Federal Reserve System. The opinions expressed in this book, however, are those of the author and do not necessarily reflect those of the Board of Governors of the Federal Reserve System.

Professor Savage earned his undergraduate degree at the University of Massachusetts (Amherst) and his graduate degrees at the University of Wisconsin (Madison). He is a member of the American Economics Association and the American Finance Association.

Professor Savage was co-author of *Economics in American Society* (with Dr. John A. Orr) and principle author of Savage, et.al., *The Economics of Environmental Improvement*.

PREFACE

The undergraduate course in Money and Banking has changed a great deal in the past decade, and so have the kind of students enrolling in it. Throughout the United States, economics enrollments have increased and more nonmajors are taking intermediate level economics courses. This book is intended to meet the needs of interested nonmajors as well as the needs of economics and business students. Thus, it presents the traditional basic material of a Money and Banking course and integrates that background with a consideration of newer issues such as credit allocation systems.

The topical coverage of the book, which is organized in four parts, is as follows:

Chapter 1 is an introductory chapter that describes the scope of Money and Banking and relates monetary objectives to more general social objectives. The chapter also introduces the student to many domestic and international monetary and financial problems.

Part 1, composed of Chapters 2 through 6, discusses money, financial institutions, and the regulation of the monetary system. Special emphasis is given to the development of the financial system, the expansion of Electronic Funds Transfer Systems, and changes in the regulation of financial institutions. *The Report of the President's Commission on Financial Structure and Regulation* is reviewed and the 1975 *Financial Institutions and the Nation's Economy (FINE) Discussion Principles* are described.

Part 2, which includes Chapters 7 through 15, discusses monetary theory and policy. It begins with an extensive discussion of macroeconomic objectives, measurement systems, and tradeoffs, explains the money supply expansion process, examines the classical macroeconomic model, and develops the quantity theory of money. Chapters 10 and 11 present a traditional Keynesian macroeconomic system.

The coverage of macroeconomic theory is a clear and concise graphical and algebraic presentation of the basics, with relatively few theoretical embellishments. Reviews of early drafts of the manuscript revealed that most instructors have their own definite theoretical tastes and preferences. Thus, I decided that the best approach would be to develop conventional basic models—the Keynesian cross and the IS-LM model—upon which each instructor could build. While the models can stand alone in a relatively nontheoretical course, they can be used as the basis for the development of additional theory concepts according to time availability, class interests, theory backgrounds, and instructor preferences.

Chapter 12 is devoted to the development of modern monetarist analysis. The works of Professor Milton Friedman (and his critics) are covered in considerable depth, and the monetarist work done at the Federal Reserve Bank of St. Louis is described in some detail. Although this book is not intended to compete in the developing market for monetarist-oriented textbooks, it allocates a greater than average amount of space to the monetarist contributions.

Chapters 13 and 14 discuss the formulation and conduct of monetary policy. Chapter 15 examines the ability of monetary policy to cope with recession and inflation. Coverage of the history of monetary policy is limited; particular historical episodes are described throughout the text, but there is no systematic year-by-year treatment of past policy.

Part 3, comprising Chapters 16 through 19, considers the allocation of credit in the American economy. This is an interesting and controversial new topic. In spite of several years of Congressional interest, very little work has been published on this subject.

The first three chapters examine the effects of the market, government credit programs, and monetary policy on the allocation of credit. Flow of Funds data are used to study the allocation of credit between various uses and users. In Chapter 19, several possible credit allocation systems are examined. An appropriate amount of emphasis is placed on the problems associated with any attempt to change the allocation of credit.

The international monetary system is the subject of Part 4. The Balance of Payments accounting system is explained, and alternative measures of surplus and deficit are examined. Major emphasis is placed on floating and pegged exchange-rate systems. The decisions made at the 1976 Jamaica meetings of the IMF interim committee are incorporated into the analysis. Several international monetary problems receive substantial attention, with a concentration on the problems of the American dollar. The international monetary implications of the food and energy crises of the 1970s are also considered.

In each part of the book I have attempted to emphasize the importance of on-going changes in problems, theory, institutions, and policy. There is a clear recognition of the fact that economists do not have all the answers to society's monetary problems.

The development of this book from the initial idea to the final product required the assistance of many people. Mr. P. J. Wilkinson, Wiley/Hamilton's Economics Editor, provided continuing guidance in the development of the manuscript and selected an outstanding group of reviewers. The reviewers were: Kenneth W. Hollman, University of Mississippi; Michael Klein, Indiana University; James T. Lucas, Virginia Polytechnic Institute and State University; Marvin E. Rozen, Pennsylvania State University; William Shropshire, Emory University; Barry Siegel, University of Oregon; Samuel Skogstad, Georgia State University; Robert Sorenson, University of Missouri at St. Louis; Frederick Strobel, Kalamazoo College; James L. Weatherby, Jr., University of Texas.

All the reviewers were extremely helpful. Each one examined the manuscript from a different point of view and made unique suggestions. Each reviewer was very careful and perceptive and was responsible for significant improvements in the manuscript. I adopted nearly all their suggestions and appreciate their well-considered comments and corrections.

My wife also made a very significant contribution to the production of the final manuscript. She labored along with me day and night in the process of organizing, editing, reviewing, proofreading, and correcting the work. Her attention to writing style and clarity of exposition has greatly improved the book.

Finally, I want to thank Miss Frances Walsh and Mrs. Jean Everett for their typing assistance. Their patient typing of several drafts of the book and many pages of messy handwritten copy is greatly appreciated.

Donald T. Savage

Orono, Maine
January 1977

MONEY AND BANKING

1

THE MONETARY SYSTEM AND SOCIAL OBJECTIVES

Student: I'll be needing a student loan in order to return to college in the fall.

Banker: I'm sorry, but we're not making any new student loans this year.

Student: Well, in that case, I'll have to go to work and will be needing a car to commute.

Banker: I'm sure you'll be happy with our auto loan terms.

The student in this fictional, but certainly not impossible, scene has learned a lesson in the allocation of scarce resources. He undoubtedly also formed some fairly strong opinions about the banking system and social priorities. Perhaps, when he is able to return to college, the memory of this incident will motivate him to take a course in money and banking. When he attends the initial class his first question might well be: "Why would the bank grant me an auto loan but not a tuition loan? The car would have contributed to air pollution, but the tuition loan would have increased my ultimate contribution to society and my future income tax payments to the government." He has become concerned with the American financial system and its relationship to social objectives. This concern is also a good issue with which to begin a book about money and banking.

American society has many economic and social objectives. Some of them have been written into law, others are less specifically formulated. The first include laws against monopolies (such as the Sherman Act of 1890) or promoting full employment (such as the Employment Act of 1946). The second, less specific objectives include "a high standard of living" and "an efficient allocation of resources."

But except in very general terms, it is difficult to specify social objectives. For example, how are "a high standard of living" or "full employment" defined? Even if a goal is defined, how is it to be achieved? If the achievement methods are available, who is to be responsible for attaining the goal? What will happen if the goal is not reached or if its achievement interferes with the attainment of another desirable goal? The value of any goal, new or old, must be questioned.

As with other economic arrangements, monetary institutions and policies exist for the purpose of achieving the economic and social objectives of the society. While the objectives of money and banking may not be as controversial as other social objectives, implementation of the specific objectives may be more controversial. For example, it is easy to argue that financial institutions should allocate credit in a socially desirable way, but would everyone agree that student tuition loans should have priority over home loans? No, it depends on whether you're a student or a potential homeowner.

Money and Banking and General Social Objectives

Four major subject areas are considered in this book: (1) money and financial institutions; (2) the relationship between money and the level of economic activity and prices; (3) the allocation of credit; and (4) the international monetary system.

In each area, economists are concerned with specific aspects of economic theory, the development and functioning of institutions, and policy-making procedures. The analysis must also consider general objectives to be achieved in each subject area, the present mechanisms for achieving the objectives, past economic performance and possible improvements. This introduction outlines the four subject areas.

Money and Financial Institutions

All but the most primitive societies need a monetary system and financial institutions. If the exchange of goods between members of the society is going to advance beyond the level of barter — the exchange of goods for goods — there must be some instrument or commodity that people are willing to accept in exchange for goods and services. The specific form that money takes in a given society is not important; the important question is whether people are willing to give up goods in exchange for the monetary unit. Colored beads may not look like money to you and me, but they were used to buy Manhattan Island. A piece of paper called the Reichsmark may have looked like money, but in post–World War I Germany so many Reichsmarks were printed that people became unwilling to exchange goods for this money and the money lost its purchasing power.

Coin and paper currency conform to our mental image of money and are useful in small face-to-face transactions. However, they are less efficient for large transactions or for transactions between people who live many miles apart. Especially in its metallic forms, money is difficult to transport and cash is subject to theft. Thus, modern economies use a second type of money, balances in checking accounts. A check — essentially an order to the bank to transfer funds from your account to that of the person named on your check—is easier to send long distances and more difficult for a thief to use.

Financial institutions also are concerned with the borrowing and lending of funds. Your brother may wish to save part of his income for his old age; you may wish to buy a new home but not have sufficient savings. You could borrow your brother's savings and agree to repay him in the future. Although arrangements of this type are used, in a complex society it is often difficult to bring together borrowers and lenders. Thus, financial institutions serve as intermediaries and tailor both saving and borrowing to individual needs. These financial intermediaries provide different forms of savings accounts and different types of loans. The institution also provides diversification because the saver lends to an institution rather than to an individual and the institution spreads its risk by lending to many different borrowers.

The monetary and financial systems can survive only as long as they are trusted by the public. The monetary unit provided by the government must be generally acceptable. The purchasing power of money must be reasonably stable over time, because people will not accept a currency that is rapidly declining in value. There must be a sufficient supply of money to carry on transactions, but the supply must be controlled so that the monetary unit will maintain its purchasing power.

The social consequences of public loss of confidence in the banking system are disastrous, as demonstrated by the widespread bank failures of the 1930s. The public could not discriminate between soundly managed and poorly managed banks, and a rumor that a bank could not pay cash to its depositors caused the depositors to try to withdraw their funds. The resulting massive withdrawals exhausted the bank's short-run ability to pay cash and forced it to close. The establishment of federal deposit insurance was an important step in restoring public confidence in the financial system, and removed the cause of massive sudden withdrawals of funds. Public confidence is maintained by governmental examination and regulation of financial institutions.

Money, Economic Activity, and Prices

This second major part of the text analyzes the relationships (a) between money and the level of economic activity and (b) between money and prices. As later chapters indicate, economists have varying opinions relative to the connections between money, output, and prices; however, nearly all believe that some important relationships do exist and that the objective is to control the money supply so that society can avoid the economic and social costs of recession and inflation.

A recession — technically defined as two consecutive three-month periods of decline in the level of output of goods and services — results from the failure to employ all available units of labor and capital. The total cost of a recession is much more than lost economic output. Costs include the personal losses of restricted entry into the labor market, interrupted careers, lost savings, job relocations, mental anguish, family problems, and reduced worthwhile private and public investments.

An inflation — defined as a sustained rapid increase in prices — also imposes social costs. For example, retired people and others on fixed incomes lose purchasing power. Those holding assets such as money, savings deposits, and bonds also lose. Debtors gain from inflation; for example, the home buyer with a long-term mortgage repays dollars that have less purchasing power than the dollars he borrowed. Attempts to control inflation also involve social costs; the high interest rates associated with anti-inflationary policies restrict home purchases and deter new housing construction.

To provide a rising standard of living, a meaningful job for all, and relative price stability requires an understanding of the relationships between money, economic activity, and prices.

The Allocation of Credit

Economics is generally defined as the science of the allocation of scarce resources. Credit, like goods and services, can be allocated by the market, by government plan, or by some combination of market and nonmarket systems. In the United States the market is the primary credit allocation mechanism, although in recent years the government has increasingly intervened in the market to divert credit to particular uses.

One may question whether these present market mechanisms and systems of government intervention are working as desired. Is credit being made available to finance the desired mix of output at appropriate interest rates? Perhaps less credit should be available for automobile purchases and more credit should be available for energy-producing investments. How does society determine that some credit uses or users should receive more credit at lower interest rates and others should receive less credit at higher interest rates? Can the government determine the appropriate allocation of credit and devise systems to bring about this allocation of credit? These questions are explored in Part III of the text.

The International Monetary System

Part IV of this book considers the institutions of international finance, exchange rate systems, and the conflicts between domestic and international economic objectives.

Over the past two decades the financial systems of the developed nations have become increasingly integrated. The United States has opened its credit and capital markets to foreign borrowers, lenders, and investors; American firms are increasingly borrowing, lending, and investing in the capital markets of other nations.

If money is to flow between nations — either for trade or for investment — there must be a set of international institutions to provide for the conversion of one nation's currency into another nation's currency. Without these mechanisms and institutions, the world would lose the opportunity to obtain the gains from international trade and capital mobility.

International finance also involves some social concerns because of the relationship between international economic policy and domestic economic policy. The pursuit of a given domestic policy may require a country to sacrifice an international economic objective; for example, expanded domestic employment may increase the demand for imported goods and produce a balance of trade deficit (imports greater than exports). Or, pursuit of a given international objective may require the country to sacrifice a domestic goal; for example, the desire to avoid a balance of trade deficit may lead policy makers to reject policies that would expand domestic employment. Obviously, choosing between domestic and international economic goals can be difficult.

Meeting Social Objectives: A Preliminary Evaluation

How well are present institutions and policies meeting these four social objectives? Although the answer is often a matter of opinion, some general statements can be made.

Money and Financial Institutions

As the next chapter indicates, the establishment of a generally acceptable American medium of exchange proved to be very difficult. The failure to develop a true uniform national currency early in American history caused problems for both the public and the banking system. Only in this century has the currency problem been eliminated.

From a domestic viewpoint, the Great Depression of the 1930s brought the American financial system so close to total collapse that it became necessary to make many changes. Today, in spite of a few well-publicized bank failures, the American financial system remains extremely stable. The institution of bank deposit insurance and the supervision of financial institutions by state and federal government agencies has reduced the number of bank failures, and now such failures are usually the result of very bad management or criminal behavior.

Financial stability has not been obtained without costs. Some critics argue that the desire for stability has reduced competition between financial institutions. To protect his depositors' funds, the potential banker must obtain a charter from the state or federal government and must demonstrate that the market can profitably support a new bank without causing financial hazard to the existing financial institutions. Limiting entry to create stability limits competition, increases the cost

TABLE 1–1 1960–1974 Unemployment Rates (percentages adjusted to conform to United States definitions)

YEAR	UNITED STATES	CANADA	FRANCE	GREAT BRITAIN	ITALY	JAPAN	WEST GERMANY
1960	5.5	7.0	2.5	2.0	4.3	1.7	0.8
1961	6.7	7.1	1.9	1.9	3.7	1.5	0.5
1962	5.5	5.9	1.8	2.8	3.2	1.3	0.4
1963	5.7	5.5	2.1	3.5	2.7	1.3	0.5
1964	5.2	4.7	1.6	2.5	3.0	1.2	0.3
1965	4.5	3.9	2.0	2.2	4.0	1.2	0.3
1966	3.8	3.6	2.1	2.4	4.3	1.4	0.3
1967	3.8	4.1	2.7	3.8	3.8	1.3	1.0
1968	3.6	4.8	3.2	3.7	3.8	1.2	1.2
1969	3.5	4.7	2.8	3.7	3.7	1.1	0.7
1970	4.9	5.9	2.5	3.1	3.5	1.2	0.5
1971	5.9	6.4	2.8	3.8	3.5	1.3	0.7
1972	5.6	6.3	2.8	4.3	4.0	1.4	0.9
1973	4.9	5.6	2.7	3.0	3.8	1.3	1.0
1974	5.6	5.4	3.1	3.0	3.1	1.4	2.1

SOURCE: Constance Sorrentino, "Unemployment in the United States and Seven Foreign Countries," *Monthly Labor Review,* September 1970, p. 14., and Joyanna Moy and Constance Sorrentino, "Unemployment in Nine Industrial Nations, 1973–1975," *Monthly Labor Review,* June 1975, p. 12.

of financial services, and increases the profits of the existing institutions. Some would argue that the gains from increased competition would more than offset the losses that might result from bank failures.

Money, Economic Activity, and Prices

The American price and employment record has been mixed. The post–World War II period has been marked by continued inflation and periodic recessions. While the problems of inflation and unemployment appeared to be almost solved in the early 1960s, the Vietnam war era gave rise to a new round of inflation. Recession, inflation, food shortages, and energy price rises followed and continued into the latter half of the 1970s. The record in Tables 1–1 and 1–2 indicate that the United States has experienced less inflation and more unemployment than have most other developed nations.

As a result of John Maynard Keynes' pioneering work in the 1930s[1] there is now less fear of massive depression and hyperinflation. Yet, the tools of macroeconomics have not been able to bring about the desired degree of price and

[1]See John Maynard Keynes, *The General Theory of Employment, Interest, and Money* (New York: Harcourt, Brace and Company, 1936).

TABLE 1–2 Percent Increase in Consumer Price Indexes, 1960–1975

YEAR	*UNITED STATES*	*CANADA*	*FRANCE*	*GREAT BRITAIN*	*ITALY*	*JAPAN*	*WEST GERMANY*
1960	1.6	1.1	3.5	1.1	2.2	3.7	1.3
1961	0.9	0.5	3.3	3.4	2.2	5.3	2.3
1962	1.2	1.2	4.9	4.3	4.6	6.9	3.1
1963	1.2	1.8	4.8	1.9	7.4	8.5	3.0
1964	1.4	1.8	3.4	3.2	6.0	3.9	2.3
1965	1.8	2.5	2.5	4.8	4.5	6.7	3.4
1966	2.8	3.7	2.7	3.9	2.4	5.1	3.5
1967	2.6	3.5	2.6	2.5	3.2	4.0	1.4
1968	4.2	4.2	4.6	4.7	1.3	5.4	1.5
1969	5.4	4.5	6.4	5.4	2.6	5.2	2.7
1970	5.9	3.3	5.3	6.4	5.0	7.6	3.7
1971	4.3	2.9	5.5	9.5	5.0	6.3	5.3
1972	3.3	4.8	5.9	6.8	5.6	4.9	5.5
1973	6.2	7.6	7.3	8.3	10.4	11.7	6.9
1974	11.0	10.9	13.7	16.0	19.4	23.2	7.0
1975	9.1[a]	10.4[b]	11.3[b]	24.5[b]	16.1[c]	11.5[b]	5.7[b]

[a]Full year. [b]January–November data. [c]January–September data.

SOURCE: Calculated from *1976 Economic Report of the President,* p. 282.

employment stability. Part of the remaining work to be done in this area involves the resolution of the role of money in the process of income and price level determination.

The Allocation of Credit

Assuming other factors constant, the credit worthiness of the borrower, rather than the social value of the use of the borrowed funds, determines the interest rate charged on a loan. Credit worthiness may or may not reflect the observer's judgment of the social value of the use of the credit. For example, the loan to expand a hospital may carry a higher interest rate than the loan to build a factory to produce the ultimate gadget because the factory may be a much better credit risk than the hospital.

This comparison involves a value judgment; it implies that society places more value on the gadget than on the hospital. One who argues that the hospital should be able to borrow at a lower rate than the gadget factory is implying that either society's priorities are wrong or that the market system of credit allocation is not correctly reflecting society's true preferences. The economist cannot change society's priorities, but if the market is not reflecting society's preferences, the economist should consider alternative systems of credit allocation.

The partial attempts by government to influence credit distribution have not been uniformly successful. Controls placed on the use of credit for securities purchases have worked well, and the stock market speculator is now less able to purchase securities on borrowed money. However, home mortgage credit is another story. While some of the programs designed to increase the average person's ability to own his own home have expanded home ownership in the United States, mortgage interest-rate ceilings often restrict the flow of credit to housing during periods of high interest rates.

Major impacts on credit allocation have resulted from the design of American income tax laws. Most states and municipalities can borrow funds at a lower interest rate than can the federal government, even though the federal government — which can both tax and create money — cannot go bankrupt. However, the holder of state and municipal bonds does not have to pay federal income taxes on the interest received. For the high-income investor, a nontaxable 5 percent return on a state or local government bond may be better than an 8 percent taxable return on a federal government bond.

The deductibility of interest payments is another tax effect on the allocation of credit. The housing industry benefits from the fact that the homeowner can deduct the interest he pays on his mortgage debt. This is a form of subsidy to the homeowner and changes the allocation of housing between apartments and single-family dwellings.

Problems in the allocation of credit arise during the various stages of the business cycle. For some borrowers, an upswing in business activity and the concomitant rising interest rates mean that credit is more difficult to obtain. The housing industry and state and local governments appear to be affected by high interest rates more than other credit-using sectors of the economy.

No government agency has any extensive authority to control the distribution of credit among alternative users or uses. The Federal Reserve System is able to control the total quantity of bank credit but, with minor exceptions, resists assuming overall responsibility for the allocation of credit. The market is responsible for credit allocation, and, if there are imperfections in the market's operation, relatively little is done to compensate for these imperfections. However, the market's allocation of credit, even if it is not perfect, may be better than any alternative allocation system. Thus, alternative methods of credit allocation should be examined to determine if the allocation system can be improved.

The International Monetary System

The Bretton Woods system of relatively fixed currency exchange rates, devised at the end of World War II, functioned quite well for many years. In the postwar period, trade between nations expanded at rapid rates, the wartime currency exchange controls were dismantled, and tariffs were reduced. All forms of international commerce prospered free of the prewar instabilities.

A system of fixed (or pegged) exchange rates between currencies provided the stability necessary for economic recovery from the Depression of the 1930s and

World War II. However, the pegged exchange rate system did not contain an efficient mechanism for changing currency prices. Each nation was expected to maintain the price of its currency at a given level with respect to the American dollar. Frequently, domestic economic policies had to be sacrificed in order to maintain a nation's exchange rate. The pegged exchange rate system also depended on the stability of the American dollar, which was the strongest currency at the end of World War II. However, the devaluations of the American dollar in 1971 and 1973 forced economists to take an entirely new look at the international monetary system. When the dollar was no longer the strongest currency, the inherent problems of the system were recognized and the need for change was clear.

Beginning in August 1971, the international monetary system entered a transitional period. The two devaluations of the dollar and the suspension of the right of foreign governments to convert dollars to gold resulted in the eventual adoption of a system of floating exchange rates. The rate of exchange between two currencies is now a function simply of the supply of and demand for each currency. This new exchange rate system, adopted unofficially in 1973, became the official system in 1976. Floating exchange rates appear to be working reasonably well but can only be evaluated over a longer time period.

Conclusion

The four subject areas introduced in this chapter are examined in more detail in the remaining chapters of the book. In each part the reader should consider the theory, processes, and problems involved in attempting to achieve society's goals.

PART I

MONEY AND FINANCIAL INSTITUTIONS

These next five chapters examine the financial structure of the American economy. Chapter 2 describes the functions and supply of money. Chapter 3 discusses the economic functions of American financial institutions and the role of the major institutions. Chapters 4 and 5 concentrate on the key role of the commercial banking system as the center of the payments mechanism and as the vehicle for the transmission of monetary policy. Chapter 6 reviews the many aspects of regulation of the financial system.

The objectives of Part I are to provide an understanding of the following:

1. general information relative to the American money supply;
2. the major types of financial institutions and their functions;
3. the regulatory processes that govern the operation of financial institutions; and
4. background information for the subsequent analysis of monetary policy.

2

MONEY: ITS FUNCTIONS AND SUPPLY

This chapter considers the economic significance of money. The four main questions are: (1) What does society expect money to do? (2) How has society selected a monetary system? (3) How did the United States select a monetary unit? (4) How does an economist measure the supply of money?

What Does Money Do?

This section is concerned with the four functions of money. Money is a medium of exchange, a unit of account, a standard of deferred payment, and a store of value.

A Medium of Exchange

The basic function of money is to serve as a *medium of exchange*. Alternatively, money can be described as *generalized purchasing power*. The traditional definition, which stresses this particular function, is: money is anything that is generally acceptable as a medium of exchange. The concept of money as a medium of exchange means that the item selected to be "money" can be used to obtain other goods and services.

Any economic system in which the trading of goods and services is to rise above the level of barter needs a monetary unit as a medium of exchange. Barter represents the oldest method of trading but has definite limitations as an economy develops. In an economic system without specialization and division of labor, each person produces nearly all that he consumes. He has no need for the goods produced by others and thus has no need for a medium of exchange. If this solitary producer and consumer does not produce all the goods he wants to consume, he needs a method for exchanging his goods for the goods produced by others. Barter is the first possible solution to this problem. The solitary producer — a farmer, in this case — trades the goods that he has grown for other items. For example, he trades eggs for flour at the local general store. This solution works fine as long as the local store owner wants eggs, but if he does not, the farmer must find someone else who does and who will give the farmer either flour or something else that can be traded to the store owner in exchange for flour.

The problem with the barter system is the need for a *double coincidence of wants*. For barter to be possible, each party to the transaction must want the product that the other person has to offer. While the barter system will operate as long as there are sufficient double coincidences of wants within the market system, the odds of finding coinciding wants decrease as the number of people and the number of products increase. Thus, in a more complex system, the farmer may trade his eggs to the shoemaker for a pair of shoes, trade the shoes to the butcher for a pound of meat, and then trade the meat to the store owner for the flour. Obviously, this becomes very complex and time consuming for all concerned. Each person has specialized in the production of one item and must find others willing to take that item in exchange for various other goods and services. Thus, the stage is set for the introduction of a medium of exchange or an item of generalized purchasing power as a means of reducing the costs of carrying out the exchange of goods.

The requirements for the medium of exchange are fairly flexible, and some rather strange things have served as a medium of exchange. The most specific requirement is that the item selected to be money must be widely accepted as the medium of exchange. All parties must explicitly or implicitly agree that transactions will be conducted with this item. If this agreement is enforced by the government, the item selected as the medium of exchange becomes *legal tender,* which means that the item *must* be accepted for the payment of all private and public debts. The government will accept the legal tender in payment of taxes, and sellers must accept the legal tender in exchange for goods and services. Through the power of the state, therefore, the money is made *generally acceptable in exchange for goods and services.*

The item chosen to serve as the medium of exchange should possess other desirable characteristics. Money should be immediately recognizable as money and yet be difficult to counterfeit. All modern economies go to great lengths to make their money both recognizable and to prevent the production of "funny money." Money should be portable, so that it can be easily carried on one's person or otherwise transported, and durable, so that it does not quickly wear out or physically depreciate in value as it changes hands or is stored. Money should be divisible so that small purchases can be made easily and so that sellers can make change. Finally, money must be homogeneous; that is, all units of a given denomination must be of equal value in exchange.

A Unit of Account

Money also serves as a *unit of account*, which means simply that accounting records are kept in terms of this unit and prices are denominated in terms of the unit. The dollar serves as a unit of account in the United States because prices are expressed in terms of dollars and financial records are kept in dollars.

As a unit of account, the monetary unit serves as a common denominator for the expression of the relative prices of goods. Under the barter system of exchange, the value of each good has to be expressed in terms of the number of units of each and every good. Thus, there would be a series of prices for eggs in terms of a certain number of bushels of wheat per dozen eggs, a certain number of pounds of salt per dozen eggs, and so forth for all goods. Similarly, there would have to be exchange ratios between salt and each of the other goods and between flour and each of the other goods. Obviously, the whole problem is simplified greatly by stating all prices in terms of the one unit of account.

The item that serves as a unit of account does not necessarily have to be, although it usually is, a medium of exchange. Before the recent decimalization of the currency, the English expressed many prices, especially those of personal services and higher priced goods, in terms of guineas. (A guinea was 21 shillings or 1 pound plus 1 shilling). However, there had not been any coin or paper guinea in circulation for many years.

Standard of Deferred Payment

The monetary unit also serves as a *standard of deferred payment;* debts are denominated in terms of the monetary unit. Alternatively, debts could be expressed in terms of a good. For example, debts could be expressed in terms of dozens of eggs. The problem with the use of one good as a measure of indebtedness is that its value may change between the time the debt is incurred and the time of repayment. Assume a farmer loans his neighbor one dozen eggs for one year. The neighbor agrees to repay with one dozen eggs in a year. At the time the loan is made, the farmer could have traded his one dozen eggs for one bushel of wheat. The price of wheat is one dozen eggs at the time the loan is made. Owing to an increase in the chicken population during the period of the indebtedness, the price of eggs falls so that at the time of debt repayment the one dozen eggs will only trade for one-half bushel of wheat. The lender is receiving repayment in a commodity (eggs) that no longer buys the same amount of other goods (wheat) as could have been purchased at the time the loan was made. The system has worked against the creditor. If the chicken population had decreased, the debtor would have been the one taking the loss on the transaction.

The expression of debts in terms of the monetary unit is an attempt to avoid the type of problem that arose in the egg loan. Money is generalized purchasing power and should not fluctuate in value in a way that unfairly penalizes either the creditor or the debtor. The value of the debt, instead of being expressed in terms of a specific commodity that can fluctuate in price, is expressed in terms of general purchasing power.

Store of Value

The *store of value* function of money means that money should serve as an efficient means for the holder of purchasing power to transfer that purchasing power into some future time period. This fourth function of money presents the most problems. Money not spent today should be able to purchase an equivalent quantity of goods in any future time period. If the monetary unit is able to purchase more units of goods in the future time period, it has *appreciated* in value. However, if the quantity of goods that can be purchased with a unit of money decreases over time, the monetary unit has *depreciated*.

While the monetary unit should serve as the most efficient store of value, its failures in this regard have led wary individuals to use other goods as stores of value. Precious metals, jewels, and objects of art have frequently served the store of value function better than the official monetary unit.

The failure of a nation's money supply to serve as an efficient store of value may arise from a number of sources. First, a commodity money such as eggs may physically depreciate — rot or otherwise decline in value — both as a commodity and as a monetary unit. Second, the purchasing power of the monetary unit may decline as a result of an increase in the supply of the monetary unit relative to the supply of other goods. While the causes of inflation — the decline in the purchasing power of money — are complex, the traditional cause of changes in the purchasing power of money arose from changes in the supply of the monetary unit. Assume, for example, a monetary system using gold nuggets as a medium of exchange. There are given quantities of gold nuggets and other goods. Suddenly, a new gold mine is discovered and the gold miners have an increased supply of nuggets to spend for goods. Assuming the supply of other goods is constant, prices will rise as the holders of the new money compete with other consumers for the available goods. Finally, money's failure to serve as a satisfactory store of value may be attributable to a loss of public confidence in the future general acceptability of the monetary unit. If the public believes that the item serving as money will not be an acceptable medium of exchange in the future, they will attempt to rid themselves of money. The flight from money to goods will bid up prices and thus reduce money's purchasing power.

Establishing A Monetary System

Now that the functions of money have been described, the next step is to consider the ways societies have gone about selecting a monetary unit to perform these functions. The selection of the item designated "money" was originally determined by custom and usage and in modern societies is decided by the government. The options available to society are either a *metallic-based system* (a variation of the gold system) or a *paper currency system*. These systems and some variations are discussed below.

Metallic-Based Systems

Historically, gold and/or silver served as money, with gold being more widely used than silver. These metals received the approval of the state to serve as money long after they were assigned the role by society. The reasons for the selection of precious metals as money did not rest upon any complex economic model. First, gold was, and continues to be, in limited supply; annual additions to the world's stock of gold are relatively small. Thus, its value was stable and it served as a good store of value. Second, gold possessed the characteristics of an efficient unit of exchange — portability, divisibility (by melting it down), durability, and resistance to counterfeiting. Third, gold had alternative uses to serving as money. Decorative, religious, artistic, and industrial uses of gold are still common. Finally, gold and silver are both relatively soft metals and even with the relatively primitive technologies of past millennia these metals could easily be worked into coins. Thus, gold and/or silver became endowed with monetary as well as nonmonetary value.

The earliest forms of metallic money were not refined; raw nuggets of gold served as money as recently as the days of the development of the American West. However, gold in its nugget form was not a good currency because each unit of gold was of a different weight and degree of fineness. Each person receiving gold in this form would have to weigh and assay each nugget; the units of currency lacked uniformity.

The Gold Coin Standard A much better solution to the use of gold as money is represented by the gold coin standard. As the name implies, gold circulates as currency in the form of coins having a given weight, fineness, and shape. Thus, the value of a coin is easily recognizable and the problem of nonstandardized shapes is eliminated.

Under the gold coin standard, the mint stands ready to transform gold bullion into coins of an equal value. Thus, the value of gold as money is maintained equal to the value of gold as a metal. In addition, gold can be imported, exported, or melted into bullion.

The first problem of the gold standard is that the supply of gold or other precious metals does not necessarily expand in relation to the needs of an expanding economy for a growing money supply. The supply of gold available for use as money depends on the nation's natural endowment of gold mines, the current rate of production (determined by technology, the costs of the factors of production, the price of gold, and the export or import of gold as a result of international trade balances). None of these factors operate automatically to increase the supply of monetary metals as the economy expands. Second, the circulation of gold as money results in losses owing to the normal wearing of the coins or to their debasing by people removing part of the gold and then passing the coins at their regular face value. Third, the demand for gold as money must compete with the demand for gold for nonmonetary uses — commercial, industrial, and ornamental.

The Gold Bullion Standard The gold bullion standard is another variation of the gold standard. The monetary unit is again defined in terms of a fixed quantity of gold; however, instead of the gold being circulated as coins, paper money convertible into gold is used as the hand-to-hand currency. This system has the virtues of avoiding the losses resulting from the circulation of gold coins and conserving the domestic supply of gold for the settlement of international payments.

Under the gold bullion standard, paper currency can be converted into gold bullion. The standard bullion unit currently in use weighs 400 ounces. At the last official price of gold of $42.22 per ounce (which was set in 1973), a gold brick was worth $16,888. The free market price of gold has risen to approximately $130 per ounce, and a brick would be worth $52,000. In 1976, the use of an official price of gold was eliminated by international agreement.

The supply of currency under a gold bullion standard may or may not be equal to the supply of gold. The paper money issued as claims against the gold may be fully or partially backed by gold. Thus, the monetary authority may actually hold $1 worth of gold for each paper dollar or it may hold only some portion of a dollar's worth of gold behind each paper dollar. If the monetary authority is able to vary the percentage of gold backing of the currency, the rigidity of the link between the money supply and the gold supply is reduced.

Until August 1971, the United States operated on a limited, or international, gold bullion standard. The dollar was convertible into gold only by foreign central banks. Thus, the dollar had international, but not domestic, convertibility. The suspension of gold convertibility in 1971 eliminated a basic feature of the post–World War II international monetary system.

The Gold Exchange Standard A third variation of the gold standard is the gold exchange standard. The gold exchange standard bases the monetary reserves of one nation on the holdings of claims against another nation on the gold bullion standard. While the United States operated on the international gold bullion standard, other nations held dollars as international backing for their currency. The dollars represented a claim against the American gold supply. Therefore, instead of directly holding gold, other nations based their monetary systems on that which was — or was thought to be — convertible into gold.

The major problem with the gold exchange standard, which had become very obvious by August 1971, is the pyramiding of money supplies on a fixed quantity of gold. The nation on the gold bullion standard uses its gold as the basis for its domestic currency. The nation on the gold exchange standard uses as its reserves the domestic currency of the nation on the gold bullion standard. Thus, the limited gold supply of the gold bullion country is the ultimate base for two nations' currency supplies. As the amount of currency based on the gold supply grows, the possibility of complete conversion diminishes until the claims against the gold far exceed the supply of gold. As the ratio of claims against gold to the supply of gold increases, the holders of the claims become increasingly worried about the value of their conversion rights. Some convert and reduce the gold available to the others; this makes other holders of claims increasingly concerned about their ability to convert. If everyone tries to convert, the system collapses and the holder of the gold must suspend conversion.

The problems of the gold standard, the shortage of gold, and the desire of nations to avoid the domestic policies that were required by the gold standard led to the increasing detachment of money from gold.

Paper Currency Systems

Early paper money systems had a long tradition of problems. Historically, inconvertible paper currency frequently was overissued to finance the deficits of the government — often to support war efforts — and became generally unacceptable as a medium of exchange. This inconvertible paper currency is called *fiat* money because it exists only on the basis of the government's decree that it is money.

The basic need for a paper money system arises out of the problems of the gold standard. Limitations on the supply of gold and the failure of the supply of gold to increase in proportion to the growth of the demand for money make a paper money supply necessary. In addition, when gold has been the international medium of exchange, domestic paper money systems permitted a nation to centralize its gold supply for settling international trade balances.

There are a wide variety of possible paper money systems. Assuming domestic convertibility of the paper money, conversion may be permitted in any amount or may be limited to conversion into large quantities of bullion. Under both systems, the money-issuing agency may hold either sufficient gold to convert all of the outstanding paper money or may hold gold equal only to some fraction of the paper money.

With full backing of the paper currency by gold, the expansion of the money supply is restricted by the growth of gold holdings. With fractional backing, conversion is possible when only a few desire to convert but impossible when all money holders desire to convert to gold. If too many people attempt to convert, there is not sufficient gold to go around and the government must suspend convertibility. Naturally, the suspension of convertibility decreases confidence in that nation's money supply, economy, and government.

A nonconvertible paper currency may also be either fully backed by gold or partially backed by gold, even though conversion is not permitted. In either case, the issuance of the paper currency is limited by the gold stock unless changes in the percentage of gold backing are permitted.

The final step in the breaking of the link between gold and currency is the *managed inconvertible paper money system*. Although currency is not convertible, the quantity of money is limited by intelligent management. Under a managed system, a government agency controls the supply of money in order to ensure that the money maintains its value and continues to be an acceptable medium of exchange.

Do We Need Gold?

The problems involved in linking money to a precious metal lead to the question, can a monetary system — both domestic and international — be constructed without reliance on gold or other metals? The answer is yes—the world's money supply does not need to be tied to gold.

Domestically, there is no need for gold convertibility of the currency. The gold coin standard was eliminated for the reasons stated previously. Gold is limited in supply and does not serve well as a circulating medium. As economic history indicates, the requirement that paper money be convertible into gold did not serve to prevent the overissuance of paper money. Seldom have shortages of gold restrained expansion of the domestic paper money supply. The needs of the economy for a larger money supply have resulted either in decreases of the paper currency/gold ratio or suspension of convertibility.

Faith in the domestic currency supply rests not on the basis of convertibility into gold and silver but on the faith of the populace in the money-issuing authority. If the people believe that the government is following sound policies with respect to the control of the money supply, confidence in the value and future acceptability of the money will be maintained regardless of the existence or nonexistence of conversion rights. Thus, an inconvertible form of money is only as good as the management process that controls its supply.

On the international level, the question of convertibility of currencies into gold was different because of tradition, the number of countries involved, a greater belief in the ability of gold to act as a restraint on money supply expansion, and the lack of agreement on a different international monetary system.

The issue of alternative international monetary systems is covered in the last part of this book, but it is already clear that the role of gold has decreased on the international level. Until 1971, the American dollar could be converted into gold by foreign monetary authorities. The price of the dollar was defined in terms of gold and most foreign currencies had fixed prices in terms of dollars. The suspension of dollar convertibility in 1971 eventually forced a change in the world monetary system.

In 1973, most nations moved unofficially to the floating exchange rate system, in which the price of one nation's currency (in terms of units of another nation's currency) is determined by the market forces of supply and demand. This system can be described as an international fiat system because currencies are not convertible into gold.

In 1976, when the floating exchange rate system became the official international system, the monetary role of gold was further reduced. The International Monetary Fund (the major international agency concerned with world monetary cooperation) decided to sell part of the gold it holds as a result of the payment of membership quotas by participating nations. It now seems certain that gold is to become just another commodity, both domestically and internationally; however, some individuals and national monetary agencies will continue to hold part of their assets in gold.

American Monetary Standards

The early American monetary systems were based on the systems of the European colonial powers. The colonies used various foreign currencies as well as ad hoc currency systems including kegs of tobacco and wampum. The first formal monetary standard was defined by the Coinage Act of 1792. This act selected the dollar as the monetary unit and defined the dollar in terms of both gold and silver. The original definition of the dollar was 24.75 grains of fine gold and 371.25 grains of fine silver; in terms of the relative prices of the two metals, 15 ounces of silver equalled 1 ounce of gold. The mint stood ready to accept metal and mint coins at those rates.

The adoption of a bimetallic standard was not the best of choices because the world price ratio of the two metals did not remain equal to the United States' mint ratio. The price of gold increased on world markets so that 1 ounce of gold became equal to 15 ½ ounces of silver. Thus, there was an incentive to export gold to the world market rather than to bring gold to the U.S. mint. Gold could be sold on the world market for 15 ½ ounces of silver and the silver could then be delivered to the mint for coinage. Gold flowed out of the country and the domestic money supply was composed mainly of silver.

The example of the above paragraph illustrates an old economic principle known as *Gresham's Law,* which states that bad money (overvalued money) drives out good money (undervalued money). In the silver and gold bimetallism case, the price of gold in terms of silver was set too low (gold was undervalued) and gold went out of circulation.

The Coinage Acts of 1834 and 1837 changed the mint ratio between gold and silver to a ratio of 16 ounces of silver equalled 1 ounce of gold. This ratio represented an overcorrection, and gold replaced silver as the predominant metal. This shift to gold was reinforced by the increased availability of gold as the western areas of the nation yielded new gold supplies.

The need for funds during the War Between the States led the government to issue "greenbacks," which were not convertible into either gold or silver. Naturally, gold coins were preferred to the unbacked paper currency and coins were hoarded while the greenbacks were used for transactions purposes — again showing Gresham's Law in operation. During and immediately after the Civil War, neither of the nation's paper currencies — greenbacks or bank notes — were convertible into gold.

Resumption of gold convertibility took place in 1879. The period from 1879 to 1900 was marked by a long conflict on the question of whether the United States should be on a gold standard or whether silver should also be a major monetary metal. The peak of the conflict came in the 1896 presidential election campaign between Willian Jennings Bryan and William McKinley. McKinley's victory, in spite of Bryan's famous "Cross of Gold" speech, resulted in American adoption of the gold standard.

The gold coin standard lasted until the Great Depression of the 1930s, when under President Franklin Roosevelt's administration the nature of the monetary system was substantially changed. Gold was withdrawn from general circulation, currency conversion into gold ceased, and the United States went onto an international gold bullion ". . . standard that, until August 1971, allowed . . ." foreign central banks to convert dollars into gold. At present the United States is on a managed, inconvertible currency system, and although the dollar is still officially defined in terms of gold, conversion is impossible for either foreign or domestic holders of dollars. The right of individuals to own gold was restored in 1975, and Americans can buy gold just as they can purchase other commodities on the free market. Still, the restoration of the right to hold gold did not reestablish conversion.

The American Money Supply

Throughout American history, the money supply of the United States has changed considerably. Although gold coins, and some silver coins, circulated for most of the period, the history of paper money is more interesting.

Attempts to issue paper money date back to the colonial period. Various colonies issued paper currency with different forms of backing. The Massachusetts colony issued paper currency backed by land. Some of these early paper currency issues were redeemable, but many were not redeemable, were overissued, and could not be exchanged for goods and services at their par value. Such abuses led England to prevent the issuance of currency in the British-controlled colonies.

The first paper currency issue of the independent nation, called the *continental,* was issued to finance the War of Independence. This was the first of several paper currency disasters. While the intention was that the continental currency would be convertible to gold eventually, it was not convertible and its market value in terms of gold deteriorated rapidly as greater and greater quantities of currency were printed and as the odds of an American victory fluctuated. At the end of the war the currency was nearly worthless and was never made convertible.

The First Bank of the United States (1791–1811) and the Second Bank of the United States (1816–1836) both issued bank notes, paper currency issued by a bank rather than by the government. The notes were liabilities of the issuing bank and were convertible into gold or silver. Both the First and the Second Bank held adequate metallic reserves to ensure conversion and the notes met the test of acceptability in exchange for goods and services. Had the Second Bank of the United States survived its political opponents, the American monetary system would have been spared many problems. However, the Jacksonian Democrats, desiring a larger money supply and lower interest rates and fearing a banking monopoly, opposed the continued operation of the Second Bank and its charter expired.

With the Second Bank of the United States eliminated, the state banks had the field of bank note issuance all to themselves and the "wildcat banking era" began. Until the Civil War, the nation's paper currency supply consisted of bank notes issued by hundreds of different state-chartered banks. These paper currencies varied in quality from state to state and bank to bank. Although the currency was redeemable in *specie* (gold coin), the requirements for specie reserves and the soundness of bank management fluctuated greatly. Many banks overissued currency and failed when attempts were made to convert the currency to specie. Some of the less honorable banks issued paper currency in populated urban areas but required that redemption requests be made at a branch located in a distant, inconvenient location. To the extent that holders of the currency were deterred from attempting to redeem their currency, the bank was able to continue the overissuance of notes.

Given the large number of note-issuing banks and the range of quality of notes, a $1 note issued by one bank was not necessarily as good as a $1 note issued by another bank. Thus, units of the money supply having the same face value did not have the same value in exchange. Bankers found it necessary to establish exchange ratios between various bank notes. The exchange value of a note was dependent not just on its face value but also on the market's appraisal of the management and reserves of the issuing bank.

In some areas of the country, systems were designed to maintain the market value of bank notes at their face value. In New York State, for instance, the banks established an insurance fund to protect the holders of notes issued by New York banks. If a New York bank failed, note holders were compensated from the insurance fund. In Massachusetts, the Suffolk Bank of Boston acted to protect the quality of note issue in the New England area by encouraging other banks to maintain redemption funds in specie at the Suffolk Bank. The Suffolk Bank also used the threat of massive redemption demands to discourage other banks from overissuing notes. Thus, while some bank notes were perfectly acceptable and circulated at face value, others were overissued and of dubious quality.

The problems of the era of state bank note issue led to the establishment, during the Civil War, of the National Banking System. The federal government began chartering banks and regulating note issuance. The issuance of notes by the state banks was quickly terminated by the imposition of a tax on bank notes. The tax destroyed the profitability of note issuance for the state banks and the newly established national banks were given a monopoly of note issuance.

Determined to establish a sound system of bank note issuance, the federal government imposed uniform reserve requirements to ensure the safety and convertibility of national bank notes. A national bank could issue notes up to 90 percent of the maturity value or market value (whichever was less) of government bonds owned by the bank and deposited with the newly created federal office of the Comptroller of the Currency. In addition, the national banks were required to maintain a redemption fund.

The high uniform reserve requirements guaranteed the quality of national bank notes and overcame the problems of the state bank note system. While the principle was good, the ability to issue national bank notes was dependent upon the continued existence of government debt. During the post–Civil War period, the government attempted to reduce the national debt, and in so doing, reduced the supply of bonds available as security for national bank notes. Thus, the supply of national bank notes could not grow to accommodate the growing nation's demand for money. After 1935, national bank notes were no longer issued and their retirement was begun.

During the Civil War, the government began issuing United States notes, the so-called "greenbacks." At the time of issuance, the greenbacks were non-redeemable, but in 1879 they were made convertible into gold. The greenbacks are still part of the circulating currency of the nation, although the amount outstanding, mostly in the form of $100 bills, is limited.

Silver certificates were the next of the major American paper currencies. The discovery of silver in the West and political pressure from the Western politicians led to government purchase of silver under the Bland-Allison Act of 1878. The price of silver was supported by the government, and the silver was minted into coins. However, the public's demand for these coins was not sufficient to keep all of the silver dollars in circulation and therefore in 1886 the government began issuing silver certificates, which were redeemable in silver. Additional silver certificates were authorized by the Sherman Silver Purchase Act of 1890. This act was repealed in 1893, and in recent years the last of the silver certificates were retired and replaced by Federal Reserve notes.

Gold certificates, backed by the gold holdings of the U.S. Treasury, were issued from 1879 until the United States ended domestic gold convertibility in 1933. These certificates were convertible into gold.

The newest source of paper money in the United states is the *Federal Reserve note*. The Federal Reserve Act of 1913 empowered the Federal Reserve Banks to issue notes, and today these obligations of the Federal Reserve System constitute the major portion of the circulating paper currency. Originally, the Federal Reserve Banks were required to hold reserves in the form of gold, gold certificates, eligible paper (assets of commercial banks which can be used by the banks as security for loans from the Federal Reserve Banks), and government securities. The gold reserve requirement was lowered over time and eliminated in 1968 so that more gold would be available for the payment of foreign obligations. Of course, after 1933, the Federal Reserve notes were not convertible into gold and the Federal Reserve held gold certificates issued by the Treasury rather than gold itself. The Federal Reserve still holds $11.6 billion of gold certificates but cannot obtain the gold represented by the certificates; the certificates no longer have any significant effect on the money supply.

The present currency supply of the United States consists primarily of obligations of the Federal Reserve System, with minor quantities of other forms of currency that are in the process of retirement—national bank notes and greenbacks. All growth in the supply of paper currency is in the form of Federal Reserve notes.

The measurement of the money supply of the United States includes more than currency and coin. These elements of the money supply have been overshadowed in importance by demand deposits.

How Much Money is There?

In spite of the long history of monetary analysis, there is no completely acceptable definition of the supply of money. Although clearly the definition must include coins and paper money in circulation, the problem begins with the inclusion of various types of bank deposits.

Bank deposits are of two basic types: demand deposits and time deposits. *Demand deposits* are balances in checking accounts. Your checking account is a demand deposit because the bank must immediately honor your request (demand) to withdraw funds from your checking account. A *time deposit* adds a time factor to the terms of the bank deposit. The time factor may be either a requirement that the funds remain on deposit for some fixed period of time or a legal requirement that the depositor give the bank advance notice of his intention to withdraw funds.

Both demand deposits and time deposits are accepted by commercial banks. A commercial bank is often defined as a banking institution that can accept demand deposit accounts. It can also be defined as a bank that can accept both demand and time deposits from both businesses and individuals and can engage in both business and consumer lending. Other institutions, such as savings banks, have more limited deposit and lending powers. Which of these deposits, at which institutions, should be included in the money supply?

Demand deposits are counted as part of the supply of money because they meet the means of payment test; they are generally acceptable in exchange for goods and services. Their general acceptability is somewhat less than that of coin and currency, as anyone knows who has tried to cash a check away from home. Checks, however, are a standard method of making payments.

Approximately 25 billion checks are written each year in the United States. While the vast majority of small transactions is made in cash, checks account for all of the large transactions. Coin and currency are used for the large number of small daily transactions—such as the purchase of coffee and the newspaper in the morning—but General Motors would not, of course, pay for the construction of a new assembly plant in cash.

The most common definition of the money supply[1] is *coin and currency circulating outside the commercial banking system plus demand deposits other than deposits held by the Federal government and deposits by one commercial bank in another commercial bank.* This is the M_1 definition of the money supply or the narrowly defined money supply. The M_1 definition of the money supply is used throughout this book unless otherwise noted.

Beyond the inclusion of coin, currency, and demand deposits in the definition, the going becomes more difficult. Only these three items meet the test of "generally acceptable in exchange for goods and service." Nevertheless, an

[1]For a complete definition of items included and excluded, see tables on the supply of money in any monthly issue of the *Federal Reserve Bulletin*.

TABLE 2–1 The Money Supply, December 1975

DEFINITION	MONEY SUPPLY (BILLIONS OF DOLLARS)
M_1	303.4
M_2	668.4
M_3	1093.6

SOURCE: *Federal Reserve Bulletin,* May 1976, p. A12.

argument can be made that other assets that can be easily converted into the means of payment also should be included in the definition.

The standard M_1 definition of the money supply does not include time deposits. Thus, a checking account balance is counted as money, but a savings account is not. To the individual, these two assets are easy substitutes for each other. Assuming that one has a savings account and a checking account at the same bank, one can transfer the balance from the savings account to the checking account. While one cannot go into the grocery store and present one's savings account passbook to pay for the groceries, it is relatively easy to go to the bank, transfer funds from savings to checking, and then write a check to pay for the groceries. Some economists therefore argue that the easy conversion of time deposits to demand deposits or to cash indicates that time deposits at commercial banks should be included in the definition of the money supply. The M_2 definition of the money supply includes *commercial bank time deposits,* as well as *coin, currency, and demand deposits*.

Extending the logic for the inclusion of time deposits at commercial banks, a case can be made that other assets should be included in the definition of the money supply. For example, deposits at mutual savings banks and savings and loan associations are not much more difficult to convert into cash or demand deposits than are time deposits at commercial banks. One must go to the savings and loan association to withdraw funds and then either spend the money or deposit the funds in a checking account at a commercial bank. However, there are significant differences between time deposits at commercial banks and savings deposits at mutual savings banks and savings and loan associations. For example, time deposits at commercial banks include temporarily idle corporate deposits, which are much more likely to be converted to demand deposits than is the long-term savings account of an individual at a savings and loan association. The M_3 definition of the money supply includes *deposits at mutual savings banks and savings and loan associations, as well as commercial bank time deposits, coin, currency, and demand deposits*.

One must accept a definition of the money supply before asking the question, how much money is there? Table 2–1 presents data on the size of the money supply as of December 1975, according to the three definitions.

The logic of the M_2 and M_3 definitions of the money supply leaves the door open for further definitions of the money supply. There are other assets that are not directly a means of payment but can be converted easily into a means of payment. Thus, once the definition of the money supply is extended beyond M_1, the logical stopping point is not obvious. For example, the next possible asset that could be included in a potential M_4 definition of the money supply would be short-term federal government bonds, called Treasury bills. *Treasury bills* are a perfectly safe, short-term asset that can be sold without difficulty in the government bond markets and that fluctuate relatively little in price. The process of converting treasury bills into the ultimate means of payment is somewhat more complex than converting a time deposit into a demand deposit. An organized market exists for Treasury bills and the seller can obtain the proceeds from the sale of bills within a short period of time. Thus, perhaps these shortest term government securities should be counted as part of the supply of money.

If the standards for inclusion of assets in the definition of the money supply are relaxed to allow the inclusion of Treasury bills, a good case can be made for the inclusion of short-term commercial paper. *Commercial paper* is short-term debt issued by the largest and safest of major corporations. Although commercial paper does not have the complete safety of government debt, it is an income producing asset in which firms can invest idle funds for short periods of time.

The plot of this discussion should be clear now. As the standards for inclusion in the definition of money are gradually relaxed, there is no logical stopping point. Everything is eventually convertible into the ultimate means of payment. A house can be sold but the uncertainty of the sale price and the length of time required to obtain cash would be arguments against the inclusion of houses in the money supply.

One further problem of defining the money supply—how about credit cards? Do BankAmericard or Master Charge count in the supply of money? No. Credit cards are simply evidence that the holder of the card will pay his bill when he receives the statement from his bank. Thus, credit cards, rather than being money, are simply a way of promising to pay money in the future.

To reiterate the point made earlier, for the purposes of this book *the term "money supply" normally refers to coin, currency, and demand deposits*. The M_2 definition reappears in Chapter 12.

The problem of defining the money supply will continue in the future; changes in the financial system may force a redefinition of money. The definition of the money supply is reconsidered in conjunction with the discussion of other financial institutions in the next chapter.

REVIEW QUESTIONS

1. Why do the problems of barter increase as the number of products available in the economy increases?

2. What are the functions of money? Why would gold coins be a better form of money than gold nuggets?

3. Most currencies do not serve as a perfect store of value. If you held $100 in a savings account for the past year and received 5¼ percent interest, how much purchasing power would you have lost? What would your real (after interest and inflation) return on your savings have been?

4. Define Gresham's Law. How did the workings of Gresham's Law change the American money supply in the late 1700s and early 1800s?

5. Assume the price of the metal in a given coin increases so that the value of the metal is greater than the monetary value of the coin. What would Gresham's Law predict would happen?

6. What were the problems of paper currencies issued by state-chartered banks before the Civil War? How were these problems corrected by the establishment of the National Banking System?

7. What is the difference between a demand deposit and a time deposit?

8. What are the differences between the M_1, M_2, and M_3 definitions of the money supply?

9. How would one expect the widespread use of credit cards to affect the demand for cash? The demand for demand deposit balances?

10. Describe the various forms of the gold standard.

SUGGESTED READINGS

M. L. Burstein, *Money.* Cambridge, Mass.: Schenkman Publishing Co., 1963, chaps. I, II, IV-C.

Milton Friedman and Anna Schwartz, *A Monetary History of the United States, 1867–1960*. Princeton, N.J.: Princeton University Press, 1963.

Bray Hammond, "Banking Before the Civil War," in Deane Carson, ed. *Banking and Monetary Studies*. Homewood, Ill.: Richard D. Irwin, 1963, pp. 1–14.

Benjamin J. Klebaner, *Commercial Banking in the United States: A History.* Hinsdale, Ill.: Dryden Press, 1974.

Herman E. Krooss, ed., *Documentary History of Banking in the United States*. New York: Chelsea House Publishing Co., 1969.

Lewis Mandell, *Credit Card Use in the United States,* Institute for Social Research, Univerity of Michigan, Ann Arbor, 1972.

D. H. Robertson, *Money.* Chicago: University of Chicago Press, 1964, chaps. I–IV.

Hugh Rockoff, "The Free Banking Era: A Reexamination," *Journal of Money, Credit and Banking,* Ohio State University Press, Columbus, May 1974, pp. 141–167.

3

FINANCIAL INSTITUTIONS

There is a vast network of financial institutions—depository and nondepository, public and private—related to the achievement of social objectives. This chapter discusses the major financial institutions in the American economy. First, the key public institution, the Federal Reserve System, is described. Next, the functions of private financial institutions are analyzed. Third, the major types of deposit-accepting institutions and their sources and uses of funds are studied and the key role of the commercial bank is established. Finally, there is an examination of the implications of some probable changes in the financial system.

The Federal Reserve System

The Federal Reserve System was established in 1914 to be the nation's central bank. The original role of a central bank was to serve as a banker's bank or as a *lender of last resort;* the central bank's function was to lend to commercial banks in a time of monetary crisis. American monetary history is replete with examples of the banking system's inability to meet demands for the conversion of deposits to currency. The conversion problem was especially severe for the large city banks because banks outside the major cities held their reserves in the form of deposits at the major city banks. When these country banks all withdrew their deposits in order to expand their lending or to meet their deposit outflows, the ability of the urban banks to meet the demand was limited. The urban banks then had to attempt to convert their assets to cash and reduce their lending to meet the deposit outflows, and in some cases they were unable to meet all the demands for currency.

In those days, no mechanism existed to expand the total supply of currency in a period of large-scale conversions from deposits to currency. In technical terms, the currency was *inelastic*. The Federal Reserve System, therefore, was created to provide an elastic currency that would expand and contract in response to the economy's needs for currency.

The designers of the Federal Reserve System sought to establish a lending institution that could convert the assets of the commercial banks into currency. In a time of crisis, a bank could pledge its assets to a Federal Reserve Bank in exchange for a loan of a new type of currency, called Federal Reserve notes, from the Federal Reserve Bank. By this mechanism, the bank could meet deposit outflows.

The Federal Reserve Banks

The Federal Reserve Act of 1913 provided for the establishment of 12 Federal Reserve Banks to serve 12 geographical regions of the United States. Federal Reserve Banks, by district, are as follows: Boston (First District); New York (Second); Philadelphia (Third); Cleveland (Fourth); Richmond, Va. (Fifth); Atlanta (Sixth); Chicago (Seventh); St. Louis (Eighth); Minneapolis (Ninth); Kansas City, Mo. (Tenth); Dallas (Eleventh); and San Francisco (Twelfth). Branches of the Federal Reserve Banks are located in other cities.

The provision of several regional banks instead of one central bank, as was the custom in other countries, recognized regional variations in the demand for and supply of credit. A national money market had not developed when the Federal Reserve System was instituted.

Nationally chartered banks were required to join the Federal Reserve Bank in their district, but membership was made optional for state-chartered banks. All member banks were required to purchase stock, in proportion to their capital, in the Federal Reserve Bank in their district. Member commercial banks still must hold Federal Reserve Bank stock. The Federal Reserve Bank stock cannot be sold or transferred, pays a limited dividend, and is returned to the Federal Reserve Bank if the member bank leaves the System. Federal Reserve stock is a very minor part of a member bank's assets.

Each Federal Reserve Bank is managed by a president elected by the Bank's directors. Three types of directors are selected to govern each Federal Reserve Bank. Three Class A directors, all bankers, are elected by the member banks in that district to represent small, medium, and large banks. The member banks also elect three Class B directors from the business community in the district. Three Class C directors are appointed by the Board of Governors of the Federal Reserve System in Washington, D.C., to represent the public.

Although the role of the individual Federal Reserve Bank in the making of monetary policy has declined over time, it performs six key functions in the economic system:

1. It maintains the payments mechanism. As described later in the chapter, the check clearing process is conducted through the Federal Reserve Banks. The Banks also provide coin and currency, as needed, to the commerical banks.

2. It lends to member banks. (This is called *discounting.)* This was the original function of the Federal Reserve Banks, and it is still important. Each Federal Reserve Bank establishes a discount rate and evaluates loan requests from member banks. Changes in the discount rate must be approved by the Board of Governors of the Federal Reserve System. In recent years, the discount rate has been maintained and changed on a national basis.

3. It participates in making monetary policy. The presidents of the Federal Reserve Banks attend Federal Open Market Committee meetings. These meeting

result in the formulation of American monetary policy. The president of the Federal Reserve Bank of New York is a permanent member of the Federal Open Market Committee. Four other seats on the Committee rotate among the other eleven Reserve Bank presidents.

4. It supervises member banks. Each Federal Reserve Bank is involved in examining member banks and has an input into decisions relative to bank mergers and holding company operations in its district.

5. It acts as the fiscal agent of the Treasury. A Federal Reserve Bank plays a role in the mechanics of selling and paying federal debt obligations. The Treasury maintains its checking account with the Federal Reserve System.

6. Each Federal Reserve Bank is involved in economic research. Most conduct research of particular regional interest and promote the economic development of their region.

The Board of Governors of the Federal Reserve System

The Board of Governors of the Federal Reserve System, based in Washington, D.C., is the major unit of the Federal Reserve System. The seven members of the Board are appointed by the President of the United States and must be confirmed by the U.S. Senate. The governors serve a 14-year term on the Board.

The major responsibility of the Board of Governors is the formulation of monetary policy. The Board can approve or disapprove of discount rate changes proposed by Reserve Banks and establishes the level of reserves that member banks must hold against deposits. All seven governors are members of the Federal Open Market Committee, which controls open market operations (the purchase or sale of government debt by the Federal Reserve System).

Four other functions performed by the Board and its staff are the following:

1. They supervise member banks, make decisions on some bank mergers, and regulate bank holding companies.

2. They consult on federal macroeconomic policy matters. The Board, especially the chairman, advises the President and Congress on macroeconomic policy.

3. They set policy and coordinate activities carried out by the Federal Reserve Banks. Supervision of fiscal agency functions, the check clearing process, general guidelines for discounting, and other activities conducted through the Banks are under the control or influence of the Board.

4. They conduct economic research. The staff of the Board is involved in economic research relative to monetary policy and other areas of interest to the Federal Reserve System.

The Independence of the Federal Reserve System

The Federal Reserve System has a unique position as a governmental organization. Although originally established with private funds, it is independent of both the government and the banks. Two aspects of this independence are important. First, the Federal Reserve System is independent in policy making. Although the President of the United States appoints and the Senate confirms the members of the Board of Governors, the Board members cannot be removed except for malfeasance. Therefore, the President cannot dictate monetary policy decisions. Unless there are deaths or resignations, one seat on the Board becomes vacant every two years and a new President may have a long wait before he can appoint a majority of the governors. The benefit of this arrangement is the protection of policy making from political influence. The cost is the possibility that the views and policy decisions of the Federal Reserve System may be at odds with the goals of the Administration and the Congress. No mechanism exists to guarantee the coordination of monetary policy with other Federal macroeconomic policies.

Besides policy making independence, the Federal Reserve System has financial independence; indeed, it is a profit maker, and the interest on its approximately $90 billion portfolio of government bonds provides adequate income to finance operations. Being financially independent means that the System does not have to go to Congress for operating funds. Instead, the System pays its expenses and a dividend on its stock, builds up its surplus, and then transfers the remaining income to the Treasury as interest on Federal Reserve notes. This payment now amounts to over $5 billion per year. The Federal Reserve System argues that financial independence is necessary to maintain policy-making independence. Otherwise, appropriations could be used as a lever to force a policy satisfactory to a Congressional committee or President.

The Federal Reserve System's role in the economy is described in greater detail in later chapters as matters involving the specific functions of the System are considered.

Functions of Financial Institutions

Institutions grow and change in response to real or perceived needs for services, and financial institutions are no different. The major functions of financial institutions, described in the following sections, are: providing payment mechanisms, financial intermediation, allocating credit, and transmitting monetary policy.

Providing Payments Mechanisms

The first function of the financial system is the provision of a variety of fast and efficient mechanisms for the transfer of funds between economic units and between places.

Distributing Coin and Currency When the consumer uses coin or currency to pay for something, he or she seldom gives any thought to where the money comes from. How does the public obtain currency for making payments? The commercial banking system and the Federal Reserve System provide the distribution network

TABLE 3–1 Check Clearing with Both Accounts in the Same Bank

COLLEGETOWN BANK		
Assets	*Liabilities*	
	Demand Deposit Accounts of:	
	College Student	−$10.00
	Sam's Grocery	+$10.00
	Capital	

for coin and currency. Assume that a shoe store needs additional cash to make change. The firm obtains this cash from its bank by drawing upon its demand deposit account. Where does the bank go for its cash? The member bank obtains currency and coin by drawing on its reserve account at the Federal Reserve Bank in its district, or by borrowing from the Federal Reserve. Banks that are not members of the Federal Reserve System obtain cash through the member banks.

The Federal Reserve System supplies coin and currency as the needs of the economy and the public's demand for cash change over time. Normally this mechanism works smoothly. If the public needs added cash, they draw on bank balances and the banks draw on their Federal Reserve balances. Reduced needs for coin and currency result in inflows to the banks and to the Federal Reserve System. This system seldom breaks down, but in the mid-1960s a coin shortage developed. The mints could not keep the Federal Reserve System supplied with a sufficient quantity of coins to satisfy the needs of the public.

Check Clearing The second part of the payments mechanism is the checking account (demand deposit) system. Most large transactions are conducted by check, and, since World War II the spread of personal checking accounts has resulted in a great growth in the number of checks being written each year.

Given the huge number of checks written, the demand deposit mechanism operates very efficiently. Consider what happens when you write a check for $10 on your account at Collegetown Bank to pay for food at Sam's Grocery. The process of clearing the check depends on a number of factors. The four examples start with simple assumptions and work up to the most complex situations. The bank balance sheets are simplified and time lags in the check clearing process are ignored.

CASE I: YOU AND THE GROCER HAVE ACCOUNTS AT THE SAME BANK.

This is the easiest case. The simplified balance sheet for Collegetown Bank in Table 3–1 illustrates the transaction. The grocer deposits your check in his account. The bank adds the amount of the check to the grocer's account and subtracts that amount from your account. Note in Table 3–1 that the checking

TABLE 3–2 Check Clearing Between Two Local Banks

COLLEGETOWN BANK

Assets	*Liabilities*
Clearinghouse balance −$10.00	Demand deposits of College student −$10.00
	Capital

THE FIRST NATIONAL BANK OF COLLEGETOWN

Assets	*Liabilities*
Clearinghouse balance +$10.00	Demand deposits of Sam's Grocery +$10.00
	Capital

accounts are liabilities of the bank; the bank owes you the money in your account. Your checking account balance is your asset and the bank's liability.

CASE II: YOU AND THE GROCER HAVE ACCOUNTS AT DIFFERENT LOCAL BANKS.

This case is different because two local banks are now involved. In most communities having two or more banks there is a local or regional check clearinghouse at which the banks settle balances between themselves.

In this case, Sam's Grocery deposits your check in The First National Bank of Collegetown. At the end of the day, First National brings to the clearinghouse your check and all other checks drawn on local banks and deposited at First National. At the clearinghouse, First National presents the checks drawn on other banks and accepts the checks drawn on it and presented by other banks. The net difference between the value of checks presented for collection by The First National Bank of Collegetown and the checks presented to it by other banks results in each bank either receiving funds from, or paying funds to, the clearinghouse.

The balance sheet entries for the college student's check are illustrated in Table 3–2.

Next, assume a clearinghouse with three banks, as shown in Table 3–3.

Collegetown Bank has presented $25,000 in checks drawn on other banks and has been presented with $30,000 in checks by these banks. Collegetown Bank owes the clearinghouse $5,000. The First National Bank of Collegetown has presented $25,000 worth of checks and has been presented with $15,000 in checks. This bank is owed $10,000 by the clearinghouse. Suburban State Bank presented $15,000 and has been presented with $20,000; Suburban owes the clearinghouse $5,000. The $10,000 owed to the clearinghouse ($5,000 each by

TABLE 3–3 Clearinghouse Example

	CHECKS DRAWN ON:			
CHECKS PRESENTED BY:	*Collegetown Bank*	*F.N.B. of Collegetown*	*Suburban State Bank*	*Total*
Collegetown Bank	$ —	$10,000	$15,000	$25,000
F.N.B. of Collegetown	20,000	—	5,000	25,000
Suburban State Bank	10,000	5,000	—	15,000
	30,000	15,000	20,000	

Collegetown and Suburban) is equal to the amount owed by the clearinghouse to First National Bank of Collegetown ($10,000). Each bank settles with the clearinghouse for the day's activity. The checks go back to the bank on which they were written and are deducted from customer accounts.

CASE III: YOU AND THE GROCER HAVE ACCOUNTS AT BANKS IN DIFFERENT CITIES IN THE SAME FEDERAL RESERVE DISTRICT. Assume in this case that Sam's Grocery is part of a regional chain of groceries which maintains its checking account in another city in the same Federal Reserve District as Collegetowns'. For purposes of illustration, assume Collegetown is in Maine and the grocer's bank, State Bank of Hartford, is in Hartford, Connecticut. Both Collegetown Bank and State Bank of Hartford are members of the Federal Reserve Bank of Boston. As members of the Federal Reserve, both banks are required to hold reserve balances, equal to a given percentage of their deposits, at the Federal Reserve Bank of Boston. The reserves held by the banks provide the vehicle for clearing checks.

You write a $10 check against your account at Collegetown Bank to Sam's Grocery. Sam's Grocery sends the check to its home office in Hartford. The home office deposits your check in its checking account at State Bank of Hartford. Sam's Grocery now has greater deposits in its checking account. State Bank of Hartford sends the check to the Federal Reserve Bank of Boston and receives credit for the check in the form of an increase in its reserves at the Federal Reserve Bank. The Federal Reserve Bank of Boston decreases the reserve balance of the bank on which the check was drawn, Collegetown Bank. The check is then sent to Collegetown Bank, which in turn decreases the balance in your checking account. Thus, the clearing of the check has been accomplished merely by a transfer of reserves between the banks by the Federal Reserve Bank. This example is presented in Table 3–4 (intermediate entries in each balance sheet have been omitted).

What happens if a bank is not a member of the Federal Reserve System? It has two options. First, it can be a *clearing* member of the Federal Reserve System. A bank may hold a small balance at the Federal Reserve Bank in its district so that

TABLE 3–4 Check Clearing Between Banks in the Same Federal Reserve District

STATE BANK OF HARTFORD

Assets	*Liabilities*
Reserves at Federal Reserve Bank of Boston +$10.00	Demand deposits of Sam's Grocery +$10.00
	Capital

COLLEGETOWN BANK

Assets	*Liabilities*
Reserves at Federal Reserve Bank of Boston −$10.00	Demand deposits of College student −$10.00
	Capital

FEDERAL RESERVE BANK OF BOSTON

Assets	*Liabilities*
	Reserves of State Bank of Hartford +$10.00
	Reserves of Collegetown Bank −$10.00
	Capital

checks drawn against the bank can be cleared. The balance required to be a clearing member is much smaller than would be required as reserves if the bank were a full member of the Federal Reserve System. Second, the nonmember bank can clear through a member bank. In this arrangement, checks drawn on the nonmember bank clear through the Federal Reserve Bank *as if* they were drawn on the member bank. The nonmember bank maintains an account at the member bank and checks cleared through the member bank's reserve account are charged against the nonmember's deposits at the member bank.

CASE IV: YOU AND SAM'S GROCERY HAVE BANKS IN DIFFERENT FEDERAL RESERVE DISTRICTS.

This case is the most complex because two Federal Reserve Banks are involved. You continue to maintain your checking account with the Collegetown Bank, and Collegetown Bank is a member bank in the Boston Federal Reserve District. Sam's Grocery, in this example, is a national chain and all checks are sent to the home office in Chicago. The home office maintains the chain's bank account at the Last National Bank of Chicago. Last National is a member of the Federal Reserve System and holds required reserves at the Federal Reserve Bank of Chicago. While there are several entries to be made, the process is not as complex as it first appears.

Your check is deposited at the Last National Bank of Chicago and Sam's

TABLE 3–5 Clearing Between Banks in Different Federal Reserve Districts

LAST NATIONAL BANK OF CHICAGO

Assets	*Liabilities*
Reserves at Federal Reserve Bank of Chicago +$10.00	Demand deposits of Sam's Grocery +$10.00
	Capital

FEDERAL RESERVE BANK OF CHICAGO

Assets	*Liabilities*
Balance at Interdistrict Settlement Fund +$10.00	Reserves of Last National Bank of Chicago +$10.00
	Capital

INTERDISTRICT SETTLEMENT FUND

Assets	*Liabilities*
	Balance of Federal Reserve Bank of Chicago +$10.00
	Balance of Federal Reserve Bank of Boston −$10.00
	Capital

FEDERAL RESERVE BANK OF BOSTON

Assets	*Liabilities*
Balance at Interdistrict Settlement Fund −$10.00	Reserves of Collegetown Bank −$10.00
	Capital

COLLEGETOWN BANK

Assets	*Liabilities*
Reserves at Federal Reserve Bank of Boston −$10.00	Demand deposits of College student −$10.00
	Capital

Grocery has a larger checking account balance. The Last National Bank collects on the check by submitting it for clearance to the Federal Reserve Bank of Chicago and receiving reserve credit. The Federal Reserve Bank of Chicago receives a credit at the Interdistrict Settlement Fund (explained below), adds to the reserves of the Last National Bank, and sends the check to the Federal Reserve Bank of Boston. The Federal Reserve Bank of Boston records a loss in its balance at the Interdistrict Settlement Fund, decreases the reserves of Collegetown Bank, and sends the check to Collegetown Bank. Collegetown Bank records its loss of reserves and decreases the balance in your account. Table 3–5 presents simplified entries to record this transaction.

In the course of the day, a Federal Reserve Bank receives from its member commercial banks checks drawn on banks in each of the other Federal Reserve Districts. The Federal Reserve Bank totals the value of the checks originating in each of the other districts and submits the totals to the Interdistrict Settlement Fund. The Interdistrict Settlement Fund calculates the balance owed to or owed by each Federal Reserve Bank. The settlement of net clearing balances between the Federal Reserve Banks is accomplished by a redistribution of the assets of the Federal Reserve System between the Federal Reserve Banks.

In any of these examples, if your check bounces (you do not have sufficient funds in your account to cover the check), your bank sends the check back through the clearing process. The firm to which you wrote the check receives it back from its bank and they will contact you.

Other Parts of the Payments Mechanism Various other less important parts of the payments system are also operated through the commercial banking system and other financial institutions. For instance, travelers checks, certified checks, and cashiers checks are all sold by banks, and in recent years bank credit cards, such as Master Charge and BankAmericard, have become important to the payments system.

The Future of the Payments Mechanism The high and rising costs of operating the check clearing system have created pressures for the development of a less expensive means of transferring funds. In the next several years, radical changes in the payments system will evolve as newly developed electronic systems are put into operation. The general term for the new payments system is *Electronic Funds Transfer Systems* (EFTS), which are made possible by the miniaturization of electronic components.

One aspect of EFTS is the point-of-sale terminal. This type of system can connect the seller of goods to the banks of both the seller and the buyer. For example, the grocery store clerk could collect for the consumer's purchases by activating an electronic system that would check the balance in the shopper's account, deduct the amount of the purchase from that account, and add the amount of the purchase to the grocery store's bank account. The advantages of this system are the reduction in check clearing costs, the immediate availability of the money to the store, and the elimination of bad check losses. Problems include the questions of who will own this electronic system, who can use it, and what controls are needed to avoid its fraudulent use.

Another aspect of EFTS is the direct deposit to bank accounts of paychecks and other income receipts. For example, each employee of a firm could have his paycheck deposited directly to his checking or savings account at any bank. The employer would send a computer tape to each designated institution, and the banks would read the payments tape and credit funds to the various employees' accounts. Direct depositing of payments is already used by some firms, and Social Security recipients can elect to have their checks deposited directly to their accounts.

In addition, the same type of system can be used to make payments out of depositors' accounts. Utility bills and other recurring payments such as mortgages and car payments can be deducted from depositor accounts and the computer tape sent to the utility company and lending institutions.

Also, under EFTS, remote computer terminals can perform the functions of a branch office. Using a computer terminal located in a store or other public place, the depositor can transfer funds between savings and checking accounts, make deposits and cash withdrawals, or activate a line of credit. Some terminals are unmanned and others are manned by personnel of the host store or financial institution.

Under rules issued by the Comptroller of the Currency in 1975, a national bank can establish remote terminals within 50 miles of its home office. Beyond the 50-mile radius the facility must be shared with a local financial institution.

Development of off-premises terminals brings up a host of problems. Should all institutions have access to any terminal on a cost-sharing basis? Or can one bank have exclusive rights to the terminal it installs in a grocery store? Who regulates the use of these terminals? What impact will terminals of out-of-state banks have on full-service branches of local banks?

A reasonable argument can be made that these terminals are really branches of banks and as such should be controlled under Federal and state branch-banking laws. In October 1976, the U.S. Supreme Court allowed to stand lower court rulings that classified off-premises terminals as branches subject to branch banking restrictions.

The growth of EFTS promises future cost savings. Once the equipment is purchased the cost per transaction is very low. The reduction of paperwork costs in the check clearing process, the potential reduction of bad check losses, and the opportunity for increased competition create great incentives to adopt the new technology. Inevitably, technology will advance to the point at which a super computer system will link all banks together and the consumer will be able to use any terminal, or his telephone, to transfer funds from his account to the bank account of any person or business firm in the nation.

As this system develops, watch for a number of issues to create controversy. First, who is going to own the EFTS system and how will costs be distributed among users? Second, how will the regulatory process be adapted to control a nationwide EFTS system? Third, what effect will the system have on the use of checks, coin, and currency? Finally, how will development of EFTS create pressures for change in the powers of various financial institutions?

Financial Intermediation

Financial institutions perform a role as intermediaries between savers and borrowers. In exchange for the saver's funds, the financial institutions issue claims in the form of various types of deposit accounts. The institutions lend the funds to borrowers in exchange for claims on the borrowers—various types of loan agreements. Specialization in the issuance or acceptance of various types of claims differentiates the various financial institutions.[1]

The depository financial institution is a device that brings together savers and borrowers. Although loans could be provided directly from savers to borrowers, this solution presents at least five problems. First, direct loans commit both the lender and the borrower for a fixed period of time. If the lender wants his money back before the loan matures, he cannot obtain the funds unless he finds another lender willing to buy the loan. Second, the amount the lender wants to lend must correspond to the amount the borrower wants to borrow. Third, the lender must possess the expertise necessary to evaluate the soundness of the loan and the credit worthiness of the borrower. Fourth, the direct loan may result in the lender putting all of his eggs in one basket—he may not have sufficient funds to spread his risk around by making a number of loans. Fifth, continued savings would result in a continuing need to find borrowers. If a consumer saved $25 per month and no institutions existed, each month the saver would have to find someone to borrow the $25 if he wished to receive interest on his money.

The need for financial intermediaries, operating between savers and borrowers, is clear from the disadvantages of the direct-lending solution. The savings institution collects the savings of a large number of people and makes a large number of loans to various individuals. The risk is spread over many loans, the officers of the institutions develop lending expertise, and cash holdings permit any given depositor to withdraw his funds. Thus, indirect lending through institutions reduces the risk and costs and increases the flexibility of the individual saver and borrower.

The Saving Aspect The consumer may employ his savings in a great variety of ways; the major types of financial assets held by consumers are listed in Table 3–6.

Demand deposits as part of the payments mechanism have already been described. Holding demand deposits is not very attractive because the banks are prohibited from paying interest on demand deposit accounts.

The traditional major alternative to a demand deposit is a savings account at a commercial bank, savings bank, savings and loan association, or credit union. The familiar passbook savings account is a form of time deposit because the institution can, by law, force the depositor to give advance notice, usually one month, of his intention to withdraw funds. In practice this legal restriction on the right to immediate withdrawal from savings accounts has not been exercised since the 1930s.

In the late 1960s and the 1970s, financial institutions placed increased emphasis on attracting time deposits, and *certificates of deposit* (CDs), ranging in size from $1,000 to over $100,000, became an important form of time deposit.

[1]The classic article on the importance of financial intermediaries in the monetary process is John G. Gurley and Edward S. Shaw, "Financial Intermediaries and the Saving-Investment Process," *Journal of Finance,* May 1956, pp. 257–276.

TABLE 3–6 Personal Holdings of Financial Assets, December 31, 1975[p]

	BILLIONS OF DOLLARS[a]	
Deposits and currency	973.9	
Demand deposits and currency		187.1
Time and savings accounts		786.8
Debt securities	295.2	
U.S. government securities		119.6
State and local government bonds		71.6
Corporate and foreign bonds		62.2
Mortgages		40.6
Commercial paper		1.2
Equity securities	618.7	
Investment company shares		45.8
Other corporate shares		572.9
Other	577.2	
Life insurance reserves		164.9
Pension fund reserves		369.0
Security credit		5.0
Miscellaneous assets		38.3
Total financial assets	2464.9	

[p]Preliminary data. Includes households, personal trusts and nonprofit organizations.
[a]Detail may not add to totals due to rounding.

SOURCE: Division of Research and Statistics, Board of Governors of the Federal Reserve System.

Large certificates (over $100,000) are typically issued to corporations, and the depositor can transfer ownership of the certificates to another holder. Smaller certificates cannot normally be sold by the original depositor. The certificate of deposit specifies that the depositor will keep his money in the bank for a given period of time, ranging from 30 days to over six years.

The maximum interest rate payable on time deposits is regulated by the Federal Reserve's *Regulation Q*. No interest can be paid on demand deposits, although in practice the consumer is paid for the use of his money by receiving checking account services at a price less than the cost of those services. It costs the bank money to service a checking account, but in most cases there is no charge for a checking account. The difference between the bank's cost of providing this service and what the customer pays for the service is a hidden interest payment.

On time deposits, the Regulation Q maximum interest rate varies with the maturity period of the deposit. The passbook savings account pays the lowest rate; interest rates on CDs are scaled upwards from the passbook rate. For time deposits of over $100,000 there is no maximum legal rate, and the rate paid on large CDs fluctuates as market interest rates change. Thus, the larger the deposit and the longer the time period of the deposit agreement, the higher the interest rate. On small denomination certificates of deposit, one can retrieve one's funds before the end of the agreed-upon period; however, the interest rate drops to the basic passbook rate and three months' interest is forfeited.

The direct relationship between the length of the deposit period and the maximum interest rate payable makes sense from the point of view of both the institution and the saver. The saver has more options for the use of his funds and is rewarded for agreeing to give up control of his funds for a longer period of time. The institution, knowing that these funds will be available for its use for an extended period of time, can commit the funds to longer term uses.

Controls over the maximum rate of interest payable on all forms of deposits were established in the 1930s to prevent banks from paying excessive rates of interest to attract deposits. The regulators feared that banks, in competing for deposits, would push up interest rates to very high levels and to earn the money to pay these high rates of interest would have to make risky, high interest rate loans. By controlling interest rate competition and keeping maximum rates relatively low, banks would be protected from having to assume excessive risk and would be less likely to fail. Today, the existence of Regulation Q is defended on the grounds that, by holding interest rates low at those institutions that finance home purchases, home mortgage rates are lowered and therefore home ownership is fostered.

Thus, by the regulation of interest rates payable on deposits, the saver is prevented from earning as high a return as he could earn in the absence of Regulation Q. In periods of high interest rates, the consumer's loss may be quite significant; in periods of low interest rates, the difference is zero or relatively small.

However, when regulations exist, so do ways around regulations. First, if the savings and loan association cannot pay a rate competitive with rates being paid on other assets of equal risk, there is an incentive to find another use for one's funds. In the late 1960s and the early 1970s, for instance, savings institutions were paying about 5¼ percent on passbook savings and knowledgeable savers had better alternatives. The withdrawal of funds from institutions in order to take advantage of higher yielding opportunities is termed *financial disintermediation*.

New alternatives, free from Regulation Q interest rate ceilings, attracted the savers' money away from financial institutions. Small purchases of government and corporate bonds by individuals increased rapidly as the gap between savings account interest rates and bond interest rates grew. Money market mutual funds were created so that people with small amounts of money could, in effect, pool their funds to purchase high-yielding assets.

Financial disintermediation, which was very prevalent in 1966, 1969, and 1974, created problems for the financial institutions. Their lending activities had to be restricted, and in some cases the great outflow of deposits threatened the existence of the institutions. The institutions attempted to prevent such outflows by encouraging the purchase of certificates of deposit, but even these were not competitive with interest rates on other debt securities.

The lesson of these periods of financial disintermediation is that the consumer is becoming more sophisticated and will seek out the best rate for his money. If the financial institutions cannot pay, or are not permitted to pay, a competitive rate on deposits, they will not be able to survive.

The Lending Aspect Both business and consumer borrowing from financial institutions have changed since World War II. The development of installment lending and the entry of more institutions into the installment-lending field have increased the ratio of consumer debt to consumer income. The growth of consumer debt has caused concern among those who question the consumers' ability to meet their installment obligations. The ability to meet debt payments continues as long as government policy maintains reasonably full employment and rising income levels, but long periods of very high unemployment and depressed incomes could create widespread debt repayment problems.

The second change in consumer lending is the gradual lengthening of the average term of home mortgages. Twenty years was once the outside limit on the length of a mortgage, but now the 30-year mortgage is common. Also, there has been a gradual decrease in the minimum down payment requirement for a home loan.

Business borrowing from financial institutions has also changed since 1945. Whereas banks traditionally loaned to businesses on a short-term basis—mainly less than one year—there has been a substantial growth in longer term loans to businesses. The banking system now has a more stable source of funds than in the prewar period and can lend to business firms for 5- or 10-year periods.

Financial Markets Intermediation between buyers and sellers of financial assets is a major function of the total network of financial institutions. Although a complete survey of the various financial institutions is not necessary for the purposes of this book, the activities of some of these institutions should be noted. Some institutions deal in newly issued securities, called the *primary market,* and some provide facilities for the resale of already existing assets, the *secondary market.*

THE PRIMARY MARKETS

The primary market for debt securities consists of two groups—direct lending institutions and security underwriting firms. Direct lending institutions, such as commercial banks and savings and loan associations, buy the borrower's note (his promise to pay at some point in the future) or the note of a business firm or government. They deal directly with the borrower—the consumer or the business firm. The second group, security underwriting firms, also called investment bankers, purchase new issues of corporate and government securities from the issuer of the securities and then resell the securities to investors. To make the corporation's securities competitive with those of other comparable issuers, the investment banker works with the corporation to determine the type of securities to be sold and the terms to be offered. Terms must be generous enough to attract buyers but must also reflect the corporation's desire to avoid paying more than is necessary.

After the terms of the new issue of bonds are negotiated between the underwriter and the issuer of securities, the underwriter buys the entire issue of securities from the corporation. The underwriter now must distribute the securities to individuals and institutions. Thus, the underwriter is a middleman, an intermediary, between the security issuer and the ultimate holder of the bonds. This transaction is a negotiated underwriting of a security issue.

Two alternative methods of issuing securities are also used frequently—*competitive bidding* and *direct placement*. In some cases, the issuer of the debt establishes the terms of the security issue and then invites competitive bids for the securities from various underwriters or groups of underwriters. Competitive bidding is usually required on issues of state or municipal government bonds. With direct placement, the issuer of the securities may negotiate directly with a large financial institution, such as a large pension fund or insurance company, which buys the entire issue of securities for its own investment portfolio.

THE SECONDARY MARKETS.
The secondary market, the market for already existing rather than new bonds or stocks, contains a wide variety of types of institutions and types of securities. The secondary markets increase the liquidity of financial assets. Those assets for which there are active secondary markets can be sold rapidly at published prices determined by supply and demand.

The best known of the secondary markets are the various stock exchanges—the New York Stock Exchange, the American Stock Exchange, and the various smaller regional exchanges. These markets exist as a place for brokers to meet to execute the buying and selling orders of their customers. On a good day, 20 million shares of common stock may change hands on the New York Stock Exchange alone. The existence of the exchanges provides the holder of those issues of stock that are traded on the exchange with a ready market for the sale of his stock. Shares of common stock of small, less well-known companies are usually handled in the over-the-counter market. The over-the-counter market is a network of dealers who maintain an inventory of certain stocks in which they specialize and who buy and sell from their inventory. A dealer holds an inventory and the investor buys the stock from the dealer; a broker acts as a middleman in finding someone who will sell the stock to the investor.

Less well known, but more important for a study of money and banking than the stock market institutions, are the government bond dealers. Several large New York firms specialize in dealing in government debt. These dealers purchase the debt of governments, either as it is issued or from investors and other dealers, and offer to buy and/or sell the debt to other investors, institutions, or dealers. The dealers maintain inventories of various maturities of bonds of many governmental units and buy and sell from these inventories. Of course, in the process of their trading they hope to make a profit. Other similar firms specialize in dealing in corporate bonds.

Another secondary market, important for monetary policy, is the Federal Funds market. The Federal Funds market is a private market for the borrowing (called a *purchase*) and lending (called a *sale*) of excess bank reserves. A bank holding greater reserves than are required by government regulation can lend those excess reserves to a bank that does not hold sufficient reserves to meet legal requirements. The loan of the reserves may be arranged through either a bank or a Federal Funds dealer.

For many types of loans, there are no, or only poorly developed, secondary markets. In making some types of loans, the lending institution knows that it has only limited opportunities to sell the loan before maturity.

Why are there either no or only limited secondary markets for loans such as consumer installment loans, home mortgages, and small business loans? The answer hinges on the nature of these loans, lack of knowledge, and the high cost of obtaining knowledge. Suppose a bank for some reason wants to find another lender to take over your car loan. Those who might potentially purchase this loan do not know you, your credit worthiness, or the condition of your mortgaged car, and the cost of obtaining this information would be high—especially in relation to the amount of the loan. Even though the interest would be higher on your car loan than on General Motors bonds, the cost of obtaining necessary information about you as opposed to GM probably offsets the interest rate differential. General Motors' credit rating can easily be obtained from financial publications, and the cost of obtaining that information can be spread over the purchase of hundreds of thousands of dollars of General Motors bonds. To purchase $100,000 of car loans, on the other hand, would require many credit investigations.

Therefore, small loans, loans to borrowers with unknown credit ratings, and loans secured by property of unknown worth are difficult for the financial institution to resell. The federal goverment has attempted to foster the development of an active secondary market in home mortgages, but its efforts have not been completely successful.

Making a loan for which there is no good secondary market means that the lender is locked into this loan until the borrower repays the loan or defaults. Thus, the institution holding assets for which there is no active secondary market has less flexibility in reallocating funds than does an institution holding assets for which there is an active secondary market.

Allocating Credit

The financial system performs part of the process of allocating credit between various end uses and between various borrowers. Given that the supply of credit is limited, rationing methods are necessary. The financial institutions perform the rationing function on both a price and a nonprice basis.

On the price basis, credit is allocated through the charging of interest. Interest is the price of credit to the consumer, business, or government that seeks to borrow. An appropriate interest rate is established for each individual loan. In a situation of nonprice rationing, the bank may be willing to make car loans at 10 percent (the price is fixed) but will judge each loan application on its own merits. Applications from low-risk applicants are accepted at 10 percent and applications from high-risk applicants are rejected. In this case, the price is set and the quantity is rationed on the basis of appraised credit worthiness.

The credit allocation process is also influenced by the fact that different institutions specialize (either by choice or as a result of the regulatory process) in certain types of loans. Thus, if the flow of savings deposits to savings and loan associations decreased suddenly, there would be less credit available for home mortgage loans because mortgages are the speciality of the savings and loan associations.

Many other factors affecting the allocation of credit are considered in Part III. However, the key role of the various financial institutions in the allocation process must be emphasized.

Transmitting Monetary Policy

The final function of financial institutions is the transmission of monetary policy from those who make the policy—the Federal Reserve System—to those who are affected by and must react to the policy, consumers and business firms. In Part II of this book this transmission process is considered both in theoretical terms and in real-world policy-making terms.

At this point, a few comments are needed to indicate the general scope of the process. The actions of the Federal Reserve System affect both the ability of the financial institutions to make loans and the terms on which loans are made. Changes in lending activity, or the prices charged by the financial institutions, affect the borrowing and spending decisions of the consumer, business, and governmental sectors of the economy. Thus, the financial institutions, to varying degrees, are the instruments by which monetary policy has its effects on the level of economic activity.

The key to the Federal Reserve's control over the lending ability of financial institutions is the power of the Federal Reserve to create additional, or destroy existing, commercial bank reserves. By taking away reserves from the commercial banking system, the Federal Reserve is able to restrict the funds available for lending by the banks. By supplying new reserves to commercial banks, more funds are made available for lending. This process of credit creation is described in detail in later chapters.

Major Depository Institutions

This section focuses on the specific functions performed by the four major depository institutions in the American economy—the commercial banks, savings and loan associations, mutual savings banks, and credit unions. The activities of each type of institution are considered in terms of the institution's sources and uses of funds.

Commercial Banks

The distinguishing feature of the commercial bank is its key role in the payments mechanism. The commercial bank is the center of the payments system because the demand deposit liabilities of the commercial bank are the major part of the economy's money supply. In addition, commercial banks are the major source of coin and currency and will be at the center of any future Electronic Funds Transfer System.

The commercial banking system is also preeminent in the process of transmitting monetary policy and serves as a savings depository, lender, and credit allocator. None of the other financial institutions participate in all of these functions and no other type of institution is as important in the overall functioning of the financial system.

There are over 14,400 commercial banks in the United States and these banks operate over 28,000 offices. Deposits in all but a few very small banks are insured by the Federal Deposit Insurance Corporation (FDIC).

Sources of Funds The commercial bank's major sources of funds, as shown on the right-hand side of the simplified balance sheet in Table 3–7 are demand deposits, time and savings deposits, and capital. Demand deposits were traditionally the largest single source of funds but the pressures of high loan demand since the mid-1960s have increased the banks' interest in competing for time deposits. In addition, high interest rates on other assets have encouraged depositors to minimize demand deposit holdings.

Note that the smallest major source of funds for commercial banks is capital. The capital account represents mainly the revenues from the sale of stock when the bank was incorporated, subsequent stock sales, and retained earnings. Bank capital accounts have never been a major source of funds but the ratio of capital to total sources of funds has declined in recent years.

Uses of Funds The left-hand side of Table 3–7 illustrates the division of the bank's assets. The largest portion of assets is devoted to loans; loans are the major source of income for the commercial bank.

The cash assets of the commercial bank include vault cash, cash items in the process of collection (that is, going through the clearing process), and reserves that the banks are required to hold either as deposits in other banks or as deposits at a Federal Reserve Bank.

The securities categories include both federal government debt issues—mainly short-term Treasury bills—and other longer term bonds issued by federal,

TABLE 3–7 Sources and Uses of Funds—All Commercial Banks, December 31, 1975

ASSETS (uses of funds)			*LIABILITIES AND CAPITAL (sources of funds)*		
	Millions of dollars[a]	*Percent of total assets*[a]		*Millions of dollars*[a]	*Percent of total liabilities and capital*[a]
Cash assets	128,270	13.4	Liabilities	889,900	92.9
U.S. Treasury securities	84,220	8.8	Demand deposits	323,110	33.7
Other securities	145,070	15.1	Time deposits	458,660	47.8
Loans	542,090	56.6	Borrowing	58,100	6.1
Other assets	58,760	6.1	Other	50,030	5.2
			Capital	68,510	7.1
Total assets	958,410	100.0	Total liabilities and capital	958,410	100.0

[a] Detail may not add to total due to rounding.

SOURCE: *Federal Reserve Bulletin*, March 1976, p. A14.

state, and local governments and by corporations. The Treasury bills are held as a short-term asset that can be sold easily to meet reserve needs, and the longer term debt is held as a source of income.

The balance sheet of the commercial bank is examined in greater detail in Chapters 4 and 5.

Savings and Loan Associations

The savings and loan association is a more specialized institution than the commercial bank. Two basic functions are performed by the nation's 5,000-plus associations: the accumulation of savings and the granting of mortgage loans. Most savings and loan associations are mutual institutions; as mutuals, they are not operated for the profit of stockholders but are owned by the depositors. The institution's earnings are distributed as interest (frequently called *dividends*) to the depositors. However, federally chartered savings and loan associations can be organized as stockholder-owned, private profit-making businesses; some states also permit stockholder-owned associations. Nearly 700 associations, principally in California, Texas, Ohio, and Illinois, are profit-making enterprises.[2]

Savings and loan associations can be established according to either state laws or federal laws. Federal or state insurance plans cover 97 percent of the deposits in savings and loan associations.[3] The federal insuring agency is the Federal Savings and Loan Insurance Corporation (FSLIC).

Sources of Funds Table 3–8 indicates the sources and uses of funds by savings and loan associations. On the sources of funds side, the overwhelming item is savings deposits. The savings deposits are divided between regular passbook accounts (about 44 percent) and longer term accounts, such as certificates of deposit, earning in excess of the regular passbook rate (about 56 percent).[4]

Uses of Funds On the uses of funds side of the balance sheet in Table 3–8, the specialization of savings and loan associations becomes apparent. Most of the assets are invested in mortgages; of the total mortgages, over 81 percent are one- to four-family home mortgages.[5] In 1974, nearly 48 percent of mortgage credit outstanding on one- to four-family, nonfarm home mortgages was held by savings and loan associations.[6]

The degree of specialization of savings and loan associations permits the

[2]*Savings and Loan Fact Book,* United States League of Savings Institutions, Chicago, 1975, pp. 13, 96.

[3]Ibid., p. 13.

[4]Ibid., p. 100.

[5]Ibid., p. 90.

[6]Ibid., p. 87.

TABLE 3–8 Sources and Uses of Funds—All Savings and Loan Associations, December 31, 1975

ASSETS (uses of funds)			*LIABILITIES AND NET WORTH (sources of funds)*		
	Millions of dollars[a]	*Percent of total assets*[a]		*Millions of dollars*[a]	*Percent of total liabilities and net worth*[a]
Cash and investment securities	30,900	9.1	Savings capital	286,042	84.5
Mortgages	278,693	82.4	Borrowed money	20,730	6.1
Other assets	28,802	8.5	Other liabilities	11,846	3.5
			Net worth	19,776	5.8
Total assets	338,395	100.0	Total liabilities and net worth	338,395	100.0

[a]Detail may not add to total due to rounding.

SOURCE: *Federal Reserve Bulletin,* March 1976, p. A31.

development of expertise in the area of home financing, but it also creates problems in the management of this type of institution. The average mortgage is a relatively long-term instrument; in recent years, 25- to 30-year mortgages have become increasingly common. Thus, the loan portfolio of the typical savings and loan association turns over very slowly. Once a loan is made at a given interest rate, the savings and loan association is committed for a long time unless the house is sold or the mortgagor prepays or defaults. The average return on the loan portfolio is relatively stable; each year some loans made at past interest rates are fully paid and new loans are made at current interest rates. In a period of rising interest rates, the return on new mortgages rises but the average rate on all mortgages increases only slightly.

The rate of return received by the savings and loan association on its loan portfolio limits the dividend payable to depositors. Given that the average portfolio return does not increase as fast as market interest rates rise, depositors have an incentive to withdraw their funds and invest in higher yielding assets. Thus, the institution is losing funds at a time when opportunities exist to lend at high rates. The institution that borrows short (the depositors can withdraw their funds easily with no notice) and lends long (makes long-term loans) is exposed to losses of funds in rising interest rate periods and inflows of funds when market interest rates fall more rapidly than the average yield on the institution's portfolio.

Mutual Savings Banks

The mutual savings bank, as the name implies, is a depositor-owned institution organized to attract savings deposits. Most mutual savings banks were established in the middle to late 19th century to promote thrift among the working classes. There are now 480 savings banks with total assets of nearly $110 billion. The savings bank movement, however, has not been a national phenomenon; 435 of the 480 mutual savings banks are located in just six states—Massachusetts, New York, Connecticut, Maine, New Hampshire, and New Jersey. Only 11 other states and Puerto Rico have one or more mutual savings banks.

In the states having the majority of mutual savings banks, these are extremely important institutions. In those states, almost half of all savings deposits are held in mutual savings banks,[7] and savings banks hold over one-half of the combined mortgage holdings of mutual savings banks, commercial banks, and savings and loan associations.[8] Of total mortgage debt outstanding nationwide, 10.9 percent is held by savings banks as opposed to the 36.3 percent held by savings and loan associations.[9]

[7] *1975 National Fact Book of Mutual Savings Banks,* National Association of Mutual Savings Banks, New York, 1975, p. 46.

[8] Ibid., p. 55.

[9] Ibid., p. 52.

Sources of Funds The sources and uses of funds by mutual savings banks are presented in Table 3–9. As the table indicates, regular savings deposits are the major source of funds. The growth of longer term time deposits has not been as rapid at mutual savings banks as at savings and loan associations. Deposits at all mutual savings banks are insured by either the Federal Deposit Insurance Corporation or by state-operated insurance funds. The mutual savings banks attract funds mainly from relatively small savers; the average regular deposit account is only $3,882.[10]

The mutual savings banks are gradually winning the power to offer personal checking accounts. In New England mutual savings banks are permitted to accept interest-bearing deposits subject to withdrawal or transfer by check. The check is called a *negotiable order of withdrawal,* and the interest-bearing account is called a NOW account. Clearly, the trend seems to be in the direction of allowing mutual savings banks and savings and loan associations to offer some form of personal checking account services.

Uses of Funds As Table 3–9 indicates, the major use of funds by mutual savings banks is residential mortgage lending. The lending and investing powers of the mutual savings banks are usually greater than those of the savings and loan associations, although the specific limitations vary from state to state. The lending of the savings bank does not have to be as totally related to home financing as does the lending of savings and loan associations, and the mutual savings banks have wider powers to invest in corporate securities.

The mutual savings bank industry, which has a more diversified loan portfolio than does the savings and loan industry, has not suffered from financial disintermediation to the same extent as the savings and loan associations. However, net deposit gains have been smaller during periods of general financial disintermediation.

Credit Unions

Over 29 million people are members of credit unions in the United States, and savings accounts in credit unions total over $27 billion.

Credit unions are different from other forms of depository institutions in a number of ways. First, credit unions are membership organizations. Over half of the nearly 23,000 credit unions in the United States are organized on an occupational basis; their membership is restricted to the employees of a given enterprise. Other typical units served by credit unions include residential areas, educational organizations, professional associations, and governmental units. Thus, the credit union begins with a common bond between the members.

[10]Ibid., p. 17.

TABLE 3–9 Sources and Uses of Funds—All Mutual Savings Banks, December 31, 1975

ASSETS (uses of funds)	*Millions of dollars*[a]	*Percent of total assets*[a]	*LIABILITIES AND NET WORTH (sources of funds)*	*Millions of dollars*[a]	*Percent of total liabilities and reserves*[a]
Cash and government bonds	7,144	5.9	Deposits	109,796	90.7
Corporate and other securities	29,505	24.4	Other liabilities	2,770	2.3
Mortgage loans	77,127	63.7	General reserve accounts	8,433	7.0
Other loans	4,028	3.3			
Other assets	3,195	2.6			
Total assets	120,999	100.0	Total liabilities and reserves	120,999	100.0

[a] Detail may not add to total due to rounding.

SOURCE: *Federal Reserve Bulletin,* March 1976, p. A30.

Second, the typical credit union is relatively small; average assets per credit union were about $1.4 million in 1974. Sixty-two percent of all credit unions had assets of less than $500,000. Therefore, the average credit union is much smaller than the average commercial bank, savings and loan association, or mutual savings bank.[11]

Third, the operation of many credit unions depends on the voluntary provision of some services and facilities. The donated labor of the members, who serve on loan committees and as officers, lowers costs. In addition, the physical facilities of the employer may be made available at little or no cost. The unit that represents the bond between the credit union members probably subsidizes a substantial portion of total operating costs as part of the total fringe-benefit package available to the employees.

Fourth, the common bond between the members of the credit union may result in lower loan losses than would be experienced by other types of institutions. The member who defaults on his loan from the credit union is reducing the return on the savings of his co-workers; both he and they may look upon this differently from defaulting on a loan from an impersonal financial institution. On the other hand, the risk of loan defaults may be increased by the fact that all the members of the credit union are affected by the same economic forces. If the members have the bond of common employment in a given firm, the ability to repay loans depends on the economic fortunes of that firm.

Fifth, the operation of many credit unions, especially the smaller ones, is by relatively untrained personnel. The officers of the credit union are often drawn from the membership and probably do not possess any training or experience in managing a financial intermediary. Although advice from state or national organizations is available and on-the-job training is acquired, the officers' primary work experience and training are usually in other areas.

Finally, the lending process is probably less impersonal than at other financial institutions. Especially in a small group, the members of the loan committee are the friends and co-workers of the loan applicant. While they may be in a better position to judge his willingness and ability to repay the loan than the loan officers of a commercial bank, personal factors may influence the loan decision.

Low interest rates, resulting from cost savings, make the credit union an attractive place to seek a consumer loan. Other advantages of borrowing at a credit union include locational convenience (frequently in the same location as the borrower's place of work) and the convenience of payroll-deduction installment payments. The major advantages of saving at a credit union are a higher rate of return on savings, convenience, and payroll deductions.

A detailed balance sheet for all credit unions is not available, but the

[11]All statistical information on credit unions is from *Credit Union National Association Yearbook,* Credit Union National Association, Madison, Wis., 1975. Data includes only those credit unions reporting to the national association.

sources and uses of funds are easily identified. The major source of funds is the savings of members. The uses of funds run the full range of consumer lending—auto loans, home repair loans, vacation loans, and other personal loans.

The Changing Financial System

Financial institutions are changing and continued change is likely. This section introduces some studies of the financial system and examines some of the implications of proposed changes.

Studies of the Financial System

The 1971 *Report of the President's Commission on Financial Structure and Regulation*[12] recommended many changes in financial institutions. These and others contained in the United States Treasury's proposed *Financial Institutions Act of 1975*[13] are, at this writing, pending in the Congress. Similar studies done in various states have resulted in significant changes in state banking laws.

The Report of the President's Commission—called the Hunt Commission Report after its chairman, Reed O. Hunt—stressed the necessity for greater competition in financial markets and more flexibility for various types of institutions to provide a wider range of services. For example, the commission stated that "greater flexibility and operational freedom in the financial structure will improve the allocation of resources to the nation's economic and social needs."[14] No institution would be forced to give up its traditional specialization, but those institutions desiring to diversify their activities would be free to do so.

The report also stressed that two types of institutions providing the same service should be regulated in the same manner so that neither had an unfair advantage. For example, it argued that savings and loan associations and savings banks should be permitted to offer checking account services. However, under present regulations, deposits in commercial bank checking accounts are subject to significantly higher reserve requirements than are deposits at the thrift institutions. If thrift institutions were permitted to offer checking accounts with their present reserve requirements, the thrift institutions would have a large competitive advantage over commercial banks. Thus, the Hunt Commission concluded, thrift institutions should be permitted to accept checking account deposits only if these accounts were subject to the same reserve requirements as demand deposits at commercial banks.[15]

[12]*The Report of the President's Commission on Financial Structure and Regulation*, U.S. Government Printing Office, December 1971.

[13]U.S. Department of the Treasury, *The Financial Institutions Act of 1975*, March 19, 1975.

[14]*The Report of the President's Commission on Financial Structure and Regulation*, op. cit., p. 8.

[15]Ibid., pp.65–68.

As mentioned, the savings and loan industry has specialized heavily in home mortgage lending and so has suffered from an inability to attract and retain funds during periods of high interest rates. To a lesser extent, these same problems have affected the mutual savings banks.

The Hunt Commission recommended these problems be attacked in two ways. First, it suggested ways the thrift institutions might be allowed to diversify their lending activity—for example, empowering those not already permitted to do so to make limited purchases of equity (ownership) interests in housing programs, to make secured and unsecured consumer loans, to make construction loans, to make mobile home loans, and to invest in high grade public and private bonds. This diversification would make the industry less dependent on the housing industry and would shorten the average maturity of the thrift industry's loan portfolio.[16]

Second, the commission suggested that thrift institutions would be able to attract a more stable source of funds by issuing their own bonds, and would be permitted to "offer a wider variety of time and savings deposits and certificates of deposit, varying with respect to interest rate, withdrawal power, and maturity."[17]

Attracting a greater proportion of total sources of funds on some basis other than passbook savings is necessary for the thrift institutions to avoid repetition of the 1966, 1969, and 1974 periods of financial disintermediation. Longer term deposit arrangements provide a higher degree of certainty for both the financial institution and the saver.

The Hunt Commission recommendations would also force greater competition for deposits. While the Commission would retain the prohibition against paying interest on demand deposits, Regulation Q ceiling interest rates on time and savings deposits would be phased out over time.

Further recommendations of the Hunt Commission would permit changes in the ownership of financial institutions. Thrift institutions could convert to commercial banks, mutually owned commercial banks could be chartered, and mutually owned thrift institutions could convert to stock ownership.

The recommendations of the Hunt Commission and the subsequent Treasury recommendations, if enacted into law, would bring about substantial changes in the legal forms of organization and the powers of the various types of financial institutions. All the recommendations stress the need for more competition between institutions and thus appear to be beneficial to the consumer and the economy.

In late 1975, the House Banking, Currency and Housing Committee of the U.S. Congress released a series of discussion principles, entitled *Financial Institutions and the Nation's Economy (FINE) Discussion Principles,* to serve as the basis for the committee's analysis of proposed changes in the financial system.[18] Like

[16]Ibid., pp. 31–34.

[17]Ibid., p. 33.

[18]*Financial Institutions and the Nation's Economy (FINE) Discussion Principles,* 94th Cong., 1st Sess., Committee on Banking, Currency and Housing, House of Representatives, November 1975.

the recommendations of the Hunt Commission, the FINE principles included a call for a five-year phase-out of Regulation Q, charter conversions, greater lending and investing powers for thrift institutions, and checking account powers for thrift institutions. The discussion principles added trust services to the list of suggested new powers for thrift institutions. To increase competition in the financial industry, the principles implied that chartering requirements should be less restrictive.[19]

Institutional Change, EFTS, and the Money Supply

The development of Electronic Funds Transfer Systems is one of the forces creating pressures for changes in the deposit powers of the thrift institutions. The savings banks and the savings and loan associations want to offer checking account services. If the EFTS payments system were restricted to commercial banks, imagine what would happen to the savings and loan association if all paychecks were deposited in commercial bank checking accounts by employers. The employees could then withdraw money from these accounts, transfer funds to savings accounts and pay bills from remote terminals, and what reason would they have to come to the savings and loan associations? Perhaps, they would gain a slightly higher interest rate on their savings, but would that be sufficient to offset the convenience of dealing with the commercial bank through its branches and terminals? Obviously, then, mutual savings banks and savings and loan associations wish to be part of the EFTS. To be fully competitive, the thrift institutions must be able to offer some form of checking accounts, whether they are called demand deposits or NOW accounts.

If checking account powers are extended to thrift institutions, and NOW accounts spread to many states, the definition of the money supply will have to be modified to include all deposits subject to transfer by check.

Even without the extension of checking account powers, the traditional distinctions between demand deposits and time deposits will be reduced and will require changes in the definition of the money supply. Assume your savings and loan association has a terminal in your local supermarket so that you can make withdrawals to pay for your groceries. The deposits being withdrawn are savings deposits, but they are really serving the function of demand deposits except that no check is used. Alternatively, if the terminal in the supermarket was owned by your commercial bank, you could transfer funds from savings to checking and then use the demand deposits to pay for the groceries. In both of these cases, the savings account is not really different from a checking account in terms of depositor access.

The development of EFTS and the eventual spread of NOW accounts and checking accounts at thrift institutions will force the inclusion of all depository institutions in the EFTS and may require the redefinition of the money supply into the M_3 definition, which includes all commercial bank and thrift institution deposits except large certificates of deposit.

[19]Ibid., pp.1–4.

Institutions, types of deposits, and the legal powers of institutions are all undergoing a period of rapid change. The financial institutions of the mid-1980s will be significantly different from those of the mid-1970s. It is to be hoped that the change will bring greater competition and lower costs of financial services to business and consumers.

REVIEW QUESTIONS

1. Define the role of a financial intermediary.

2. List the functions of (**a**) a commercial bank, (**b**) a mutual savings bank, (**c**) a savings and loan association, (**d**) a credit union.

3. Construct T accounts such as those in the chapter and illustrate the entries which would be necessary to clear your check drawn on the Fourth National Bank of Atlanta and sent to a store in Dallas, Texas, in settlement of your account.

4. Most banks today do not impose service charges on personal checking accounts. How can the bank provide this seemingly free service and yet make a profit?

5. Describe the organization of a Federal Reserve Bank and the organization of the Board of Governors of the Federal Reserve System.

6. What is the difference between a mutually owned and a stockholder-owned financial institution? Does this make a difference to the depositor? What are the rights of a depositor-owner of a mutual institution in your state?

7. In what ways do the suggestions of the Hunt Commission and the FINE Discussion Principles seek to increase competition in the provision of financial services?

8. Why do commercial banks allocate a smaller proportion of their funds to home mortgages than do mutual savings banks and savings and loan associations?

9. What would be the possible costs and benefits to society of removing all ceilings on interest rates payable on time deposits? Of removing the prohibition against paying interest on demand deposits?

10. What forces motivated the banks to encourage the use of certificates of deposit in the 1960s?

SUGGESTED READINGS

George J. Benston, "Savings Banking and the Public Interest," *Journal of Money, Credit and Banking,* vol. IV, no. 1, part II, Ohio State University Press, Columbus, February 1972, pp. 133–226.

The Federal Reserve System: Purposes and Functions, Board of Governors of the Federal Reserve System, Washington, D.C., 1974.

Katharine Gibson, "The Early History and Initial Impact of NOW Accounts," *New England Economic Review,* Federal Reserve Bank of Boston, January–February 1975, pp. 17–26.

Doris E. Harless, *Nonbank Financial Institutions,* Federal Reserve Bank of Richmond, Richmond, Va., October 1975.

Robert E. Knight, "The Changing Payments Mechanism: Electronic Funds Transfer Arrangements," *Federal Reserve Bank of Kansas City Monthly Review,* July–August 1974, pp. 10–20.

Herman E. Krooss and Martin R. Blyn, *A History of Financial Intermediaries.* New York: Random House, 1971.

Donald A. Leonard, "State Laws Affect the Pace of New Bank Charters," *Federal Reserve Bank of Philadelphia Business Review,* September 1974, pp. 7–11.

Jean M. Lovati, "The Changing Competition Between Commercial Banks and Thrift Institutions for Deposits," *Federal Reserve Bank of St. Louis Review,* July 1975, pp. 2–8.

James B. Ludtke, *The American Financial System,* 2nd ed. Boston: Allyn and Bacon, 1968.

Murray E. Polakoff et al., *Financial Institutions and Markets.* Boston: Houghton Mifflin, 1970.

Roland I. Robinson, "The Hunt Commission Report: A Search for Politically Feasible Solutions to the Problems of Financial Structure," *Journal of Finance,* American Finance Association, New York, September 1972, pp. 765–777.

Roland I. Robinson and Dwayne Wrightsman, *Financial Markets: The Accumulation and Allocation of Wealth.* New York: McGraw-Hill Book Company, 1974.

4

THE COMMERCIAL BANKING SYSTEM: LIABILITIES

While all financial intermediaries are important to the overall functioning of the economic system, the commercial banking system is critical and requires special attention. This detailed analysis is important because, as explained in Chapter 3, the commercial banking system is at the heart of the process by which payments are made, credit is allocated, and monetary policy is conducted. The specific task of this chapter is to consider the liabilities and the capital accounts of the commercial banking system.

Commercial Bank Deposit Liabilities

The liabilities and capital side of the balance sheet of the commercial banking system is presented in Table 4–1. As indicated in Chapter 3, deposits are the major liabilities of the commercial banking system. Demand deposits account for 33.3 percent of total liabilities and capital, and time deposits account for 47.8 percent of total liabilities and capital.

Demand Deposits

The ability to accept deposits subject to withdrawal or transfer by check is a major distinguishing feature of the commercial bank. The commercial bank is unique in that its demand deposit liabilities are used as the means of payment. Table 4–1 indicates the ownership of demand deposits by various types of holders. As would be expected, the largest proportion of demand deposits is held by individuals, partnerships, and corporations.

The demand deposits of the United States Government represent funds from tax collections that have not yet been transferred to the Treasury's checking account at the Federal Reserve System. In order to avoid large fluctuations in the

TABLE 4–1 Liabilities and Capital of all Commercial Banks, June 30, 1975

	MILLIONS OF DOLLARS	*PERCENT OF TOTAL LIABILITIES AND CAPITAL*
Demand deposits	309,726	33.27
Mutual savings banks	1,279	0.14
Other individuals, partnerships, and corporations	232,079	24.93
U.S. government	3,117	0.33
States and political subdivisions	18,217	1.96
Foreign governments, central banks, etc.	1,555	0.17
Commercial banks in U.S.	34,345	3.69
Banks in foreign countries	6,957	0.75
Certified and officers' checks, etc.	12,176	1.31
Time and savings deposits	444,936	47.79
Savings deposits	151,744	16.30
Accumulated for personal loan payments	338	0.04
Mutual savings banks	648	0.07
Other individuals, partnerships, and corporations	219,489	23.57
U.S. government	492	0.05
States and political subdivisions	48,219	5.18
Foreign governments, central banks, etc.	13,445	1.44
Commercial banks in U.S.	8,449	0.91
Banks in foreign countries	2,111	0.23
Total deposits	754,662	81.05
Federal Funds purchased and securities sold under agreements to repurchase	56,529	6.07
Other liabilities for borrowed money	5,891	0.63
Other liabilities	38,450	4.13
Total liabilities	855,533	91.89
Minority interest in consolidated subsidiaries	5	0.00
Total reserves on loans/securities	8,963	0.96
Total capital accounts	66,557	7.15
Capital notes and debentures	4,347	0.47
Equity capital	62,210	6.68
Preferred stock	50	0.00
Common stock	15,176	1.63
Surplus	25,968	2.79
Undivided profits	20,053	2.15
Other capital reserves	963	0.10
Total liabilities, reserves, minority interest, capital accounts	931,057	100.00

SOURCE: *Federal Reserve Bulletin,* November 1975, p. A17.

supply of money when consumers and businesses are making tax payments, the Treasury temporarily deposits checks for the payment of taxes back into the banks on which the checks were drawn. The volume of deposits does not change, just the ownership of the deposits. As the Treasury needs the funds to pay its bills, funds are transferred from the banks to the Treasury's account at the Federal Reserve System.

A large portion of total demand deposits are deposits of commercial and savings banks. These interbank deposits are termed *correspondent balances*. Most of these deposits represent the reserves of banks that are not members of the Federal Reserve System. If a bank is not a member of the Federal Reserve System, state regulations govern the holding of reserves against deposits. These non-member banks hold a large portion of their reserves in the form of deposits in larger urban banks.

The urban banks compete actively for the reserve deposits and other working balances of smaller banks. *Correspondent banking* offers a variety of specialized services to the smaller banks and is the major point of contact between the small bank and the national money markets. The small bank typically receives portfolio investment advice, economic forecasting services, a market for the sale of excess reserves, securities transaction services, trust advisory services, and the participation of the urban bank in loans too large to be made by the small bank.

Both the urban and rural bank gain by the correspondent relationship. The small bank obtains specialized services that it could not afford to provide for itself, and the large bank obtains the noninterest-bearing demand deposits. Before the institution of the Federal Reserve System, correspondent banking relationships were the major means of holding reserves. With most larger banks now members of the Federal Reserve System, correspondent balances are less important to monetary policy; however, they continue to be the major form of reserve holding for small, rural nonmember banks.

Time Deposits

Time deposits are the largest source of funds in Table 4–1. The time deposit component of the commercial bank balance sheet has increased very significantly in the last 25 years. The data in Table 4–2 indicate the growing importance of time deposits and the growing portion of large certificates of deposit within the time deposit category. In 1951, time deposits equalled only 40 percent of demand deposits. By 1975, time deposits were 204 percent of demand deposits. Even if the value of large certificates of deposit is subtracted from total time deposits, time deposits in 1975 equalled 167 percent of demand deposits.

The growth in the importance of time deposits to commercial banks represents a number of factors. First, rising interest rates have made the holders of funds more anxious to minimize demand deposit balances and switch temporarily idle funds into time deposit accounts. Second, the high loan demand for much of

TABLE 4–2 Demand and Time Deposits 1951–1975 (billions of dollars)

YEAR	DEMAND DEPOSITS	TOTAL TIME DEPOSITS	LARGE CDs
1951	96.5	38.2	
1953	101.1	44.5	
1955	107.4	50.0	
1957	107.6	57.4	
1959	114.5	67.4	
1961	119.1	82.7	2.8
1963	124.1	112.0	9.6
1965	134.9	146.3	16.2
1967	146.5	183.1	20.5
1969	162.7	194.5	11.0
1971	182.7	271.2	33.5
1973	209.9	364.5	63.8
1975[p]	222.6	454.5	83.3

[p]preliminary.

SOURCE: *1976 Economic Report of the President,* p. 231.

the period encouraged the commercial banks to compete with the thrift institutions for savings deposits. The development of new forms of time deposits, such as the small consumer certificate of deposit, increased the holding of time deposits. Finally, rising income levels have made possible greater consumer savings. These savings were placed in interest-bearing deposits, rather than in checking accounts.

Nondeposit Liabilities

Although demand and time deposits represent over 88 percent of the liabilities of the banking system, other liabilities have grown in importance as high levels of loan demand have provided the banks with the incentive to develop increasingly exotic sources of funds. This section of the chapter briefly considers the traditional and new sources of funds and the Federal Reserve System's attempts to regulate the banks' search for funds.

The Federal Funds Market

The lending and borrowing of excess bank reserves in the Federal Funds market permits a more complete utilization of the reserves available to the banking system. The bank with more reserves than necessary to meet legal minimum reserve requirements can loan its excess reserves to another bank that does not have its required level of reserves. The loan is effected by the transfer of reserves on the books of the Federal Reserve System. Most of the trading in Federal Funds is between commercial banks, but mutual savings banks and savings and loan associations can also participate in the market.

The typical Federal Funds loan places the reserves into the reserve account of the borrowing bank overnight (when checks are being cleared and reserve balances calculated) and returns the reserves to the lending bank the next day. The other basic Federal Funds loan is for the weekend; longer term arrangements are gradually developing. The *Federal Funds rate,* the interest rate on these loans, is a relatively sensitive indicator of the supply of and demand for reserves within the banking system.

The Federal Funds market originated in the 1920s, but was not needed during the 1930s and 1940s because of the large quantity of excess reserves made available to the banking system. Few banks needed to borrow and most bank borrowing was from the Federal Reserve Banks. However, during the late 1950s and the 1960s, the use of the Federal Funds market expanded as periods of tight money became more frequent. As more banks tried to maximize earnings by minimizing their holdings of nonearning reserves, the need for the market increased.

A bank that always holds substantial excess reserves never needs to borrow; however, the bank is losing the income that could be earned by lending or investing the excess reserves. On the other hand, holding only the bare minimum amount of reserves exposes the bank to the risk of falling below the minimum level of reserves and having to borrow. Smaller banks typically hold excess reserves and are sellers of Federal Funds, while large urban banks attempt to minimize the holding of reserves and are buyers of reserves. Especially in periods of high interest rates, small banks sell their excess reserves in the Federal Funds market. Although the total quantity of reserves available to the banking system is not changed by the operation of the Federal Funds market, the existing supply of reserves is reallocated between banks.

The Federal Reserve Bank Discount Window

Another source of funds for member commercial banks is borrowing from the Federal Reserve Banks. The process by which member commercial banks borrow from a Federal Reserve Bank is called *discounting,* and the rate charged the borrowing bank by the Federal Reserve is called the *discount rate*.

Borrowing at the Federal Reserve discount window involves a pledge of assets (usually Treasury bills) by the borrowing bank. The proceeds of the loan usually take the form of an increase in the borrowing bank's reserve account. The traditional term of the discount loan is 15 days, although loans can be renewed.

Lending to commercial banks by the Federal Reserve Banks is the oldest part of American monetary policy. The Federal Reserve System was established as a lender of last resort to provide short-term liquidity to the banking system. If a bank was experiencing a run on deposits and could not convert its assets to cash, the Federal Reserve Bank would loan Federal Reserve notes to the bank on the security of the bank's assets. The Federal Reserve notes would enable the bank to meet deposit outflows while liquidating its assets.

Over time, the function of the discounting process changed and discounting now serves to provide the banks with short-term credit. An advance of reserves to a bank is not intended to be a long-term loan but is designed to provide the bank with time to adjust its asset and liability structure so that reserve requirements can be met without the need to borrow.

Unlike borrowing in the Federal Funds market, borrowing from the Federal Reserve Banks requires that the member bank apply for the loan. Discounting is a privilege, rather than a right, and the Federal Reserve Banks exercise administrative supervision over borrowing banks.

In 1973, the Federal Reserve expanded the discounting process to permit seasonal lending to member banks and emergency lending to member and nonmember financial institutions. In some cases, banks experience regular strong seasonal loan demands. A bank specializing in crop financing, for instance, would need large quantities of reserves during the growing period and much lower reserves after the crops were harvested and loans were repaid. In these cases, the bank could prearrange to borrow given amounts of reserves during the period of high loan demand. This type of credit is not the traditional adjustment credit but provides the bank with the ability to meet the credit needs of its customers.

Emergency credit to members and nonmembers is permitted under the strict supervision of the Federal Reserve Banks. When conditions threaten the stability of one part of the financial system, all parts are threatened. The Federal Reserve System recognizes its obligation to maintain the solvency and liquidity of the entire financial system and can provide reserves to a member bank that is in danger of failing, to an endangered nonmember financial institution, or to a member bank that in turn lends to the endangered nonmember institution. Thus, the Federal Reserve System became the lender of last resort, not just to member institutions, but to the entire financial system.

The Eurodollar Market

The Eurodollar market is a market in dollar-denominated deposits in foreign countries. Even though one is dealing with a German bank, deposits, withdrawals, and checks can be in terms of dollars, rather than marks. During the 1960s, the balance of payments deficits of the United States and the growth of multinational corporations led to an increase in foreign dollar holdings. Because the American dollar is the medium of exchange for many transactions not involving Americans, Eurodollar accounts grew rapidly.

In recent years most large American banks have opened branches or subsidiaries in other major nations. In part, these branches are intended to finance foreign trade and assist in the foreign activities of the banks' American customers.

However, the branches also serve to collect deposits of Eurodollars. The dollars held as deposits in the foreign branches can then be loaned by the foreign branch to the American home office. The home office then has another source of funds to support its own lending operations.

Initially, this system of obtaining funds was very attractive. As a loan between branches of the same bank, the funds were not classified as deposits and were not subject to reserve requirements. Thus, there was an incentive for a bank to encourage its customers to make deposits in foreign branches rather than in the American home office. The home office could then borrow the money from its foreign branch and avoid the American reserve requirement. In addition, it was easier to compete for deposits through the foreign branch because Regulation Q interest rate ceilings did not apply.

However, all good things come to an end and this case was no exception. The Federal Reserve System recognized that the borrowing of Eurodollar deposits by American banks from their foreign branches was a way around Regulation Q and the reserve requirements. These "borrowings" were reclassified as deposits and subjected to reserve requirements. The reclassification increased the cost of these funds to the bank and reduced activity in the market. However, even with the loopholes plugged, the Eurodollar market continues to be a very active market and provides banks with an added source of funds.

Repurchase Agreements

The repurchase agreement is another short-term source of funds for the large commercial bank. The bank sells a given asset to a customer, usually a business firm or other financial institution, with the agreement that on a given date the bank will buy the asset back at a given price. The difference between the price at which the bank sells the asset and the price at which it buys back the same asset represents the yield on the transaction for the temporary owner of the asset. Of course, the difference between the buying and the selling price can be made sufficiently large to yield a rate of return in excess of the Regulation Q ceilings on interest rates on deposits.

Both loans and securities may be transferred by repurchase agreements. If the buyer of the asset has an account at the selling bank, the bank's deposits decrease by the amount of the transaction; the buyer uses his deposits to pay for the asset. The decreased level of deposits permits the bank to hold a lower level of required reserves.

If the purchaser of the asset pays with a check on an account at another bank, the check-clearing process results in a reserve gain for the selling bank. Thus, during the period of the transaction, the bank's reserve position is improved. When the asset sold with a repurchase agreement is a loan, the funds are treated as deposits by the Federal Reserve and reserve requirements apply; repurchase agreements on securities are not considered as deposits and the funds are not subject to reserve requirements.

Bank Holding Company Commercial Paper

Commercial paper is short-term debt sold by business corporations. The sale of commercial paper has long been a standard method of raising funds. A large portion of commercial paper outstanding is sold by financing subsidaries of major corporations, such as General Motors Acceptance Corporation, and by finance companies, such as Household Finance Corporation.

However, in the late 1960s, bank holding companies[1] and nonbank subsidiaries of bank holding companies began selling commercial paper at high competitive market rates of interest. The funds raised by the sale of the paper were either deposited in the holding company's bank or were used for repurchase agreements with the holding company's bank. Thus, the nonbank part of the holding company was used to raise funds for the bank. The Federal Reserve reacted by imposing reserve requirements on the transaction between the holding company affiliate, which sold the commercial paper, and the commercial bank.

In periods of high loan demand, the bankers have a great incentive to develop innovative methods of raising funds. Fund sources that are not subject to reserve requirements and Regulation Q are preferred. Few banks are involved in any of the more exotic ways of raising funds; only very large and very aggressive banks are operating in Eurodollars, repurchase agreements, or holding company commercial paper. More banks use the Federal Reserve discount mechanism and the Federal Funds market, but even these traditional sources of funds are utilized heavily by only a relatively small proportion of banks.

The Capital Account and Loss Reserves

Two other important items are on the sources of funds side of the balance sheet. First, total reserves on loans and securities—loss reserves—are entered in Table 4–1 as approximately 1 percent of total funds. The purpose of these reserve accounts is to retain funds in the bank to absorb possible losses on loans and securities.

The bank's total capital account is the final source of funds. The capital account, the difference between assets and liabilities, is relatively small. Few nonfinancial businesses could operate with such a small capital account. In recent years, the capital account has declined as a proportion of total sources of funds. This decline has created some concern among bank regulators who fear that the gap between assets and liabilities is becoming too narrow.

One factor causing the declining capital ratio is inflation. Inflation increases the average size of bank loans and the average working balances held in checking accounts. However, the only capital account item that increases with

[1] A bank holding company is a corporation organized for the purpose of holding stock in one or more commercial banks. The holding company does not do a banking business; it owns banks. For a full discussion of bank holding companies, see Chapter 6.

inflation is undivided profits. Unless undivided profits grow very rapidly, the ratio of capital to total sources of funds declines.

The traditional sources of capital for the commercial banks have been common stock and retained earnings. Given the heavy debt structure represented by deposits and other liabilities, the use of borrowed funds as a source of capital was not widespread. However, in recent years, the use of debt capital has been increasing. The most common form of debt is debentures (unsecured bonds) subordinated to deposit liabilities. The subordinated feature means that in the event of the failure of the bank, the depositors would receive priority over the bondholders in the distribution of the bank's assets.

In the late 1960s, many banks sold short-term capital notes as a means of attracting funds. While the banks considered these notes as additions to the capital account, depositors tended to regard them as a deposit paying a rate in excess of the Regulation Q ceiling. The Federal Reserve System took the same point of view and classified capital notes as deposits subject to reserve requirements and Regulation Q, unless the terms of the capital notes were clearly those of a bond rather than those of a deposit. Notes, or bonds, continue to be used by banks as a source of capital. One bank has innovated with the introduction of floating rate notes—the interest rate paid on the bank's notes fluctuates with current market interest rates.

Most banks currently need new equity capital. Bank earnings have not increased sufficiently to maintain the equity portion of the capital account. In many cases, new sales of common stock present problems. Except for a very small proportion of banks, organized securities markets for bank stock do not exist. Prices of bank stocks, relative to per-share profits, are typically low; investors seldom regard bank stocks as glamorous investments. In addition, many smaller banks are owned by a small group of investors and the sale of new stock would dilute control of the bank. However, in spite of the problems involved, most banks will have to find new equity capital in the near future.

The Management of Liabilities

Having considered the various sources of funds available to the commercial bank, the next step is to define and describe two alternative approaches to managing the liabilities side of the balance sheet. The approaches can be described as passive and aggressive.

The *passive approach* to liability management, which is followed by most financial institutions, limits the bank to the lending or investing of those funds received as a result of the normal amount of advertising and new business solicitation. Most banks do not use the more sophisticated methods of obtaining nondeposit funds. The typical small bank probably issues small denomination certificates of deposit and may buy Federal Funds, but it does not utilize the more sophisticated methods of fund raising employed by the very large banks.

By taking the passive approach to liability management, the bank must manage its portfolio of loans and securities within the limitations imposed by the liability side of the balance sheet. In a period of high loan demand, the main options of the bank are either to redistribute assets or improve the terms on which deposits are attracted. Given Regulation Q ceilings, the deposit-expanding option offers only limited opportunities. On the asset side of the balance sheet, some loan commitments cannot be terminated, and liquid asset holdings can be reduced only so far without endangering the bank. Therefore, in a period of high loan demand, this type of bank is restrained from making all possible profitable loans. New good-risk borrowers must be turned down and/or credit must be rationed to long-standing customers.

The bank following an *aggressive approach* to liability management would deemphasize the cost of borrowed or deposited funds and emphasize meeting all loan demands (at interest rates reflecting the high cost of funds). The development of all the newer sources of nondeposit funds reflects the attempts of the larger aggressive banks to avoid having to restrict lending in a period of high loan demand.

The management of liabilities also implies decisions at the margin relative to the lowest cost sources of additional funds. Faced with various sources of funds for various periods of time at various interest rates, management must attempt to select the cost-minimizing method of financing its lending activities. If all sources of funds were obtained for the same term at the same interest rate, decisions would be easy. Naturally, this is not the normal situation. For example, a bank could sell certificates of deposit with a six-month maturity or could buy Federal Funds every day for six months. Which is the lowest cost alternative? The CD offers a known interest cost for the period; the daily rate on Federal Funds fluctuates. If interest rates rise during the period, the Federal Funds option will prove to be more expensive; declining interest rates would have made the Federal Funds option less expensive.

The time period over which the funds are needed is another variable to be considered. Assume that the bank obtains funds by the sale of CDs for six months at a 7 percent interest cost to meet current loan demands. Then suppose the economy slows down and loan demand decreases. The bank is paying 7 percent for funds that are no longer needed for lending and ends up investing the money in short-term securities at 5 percent.

Thus, the search for deposit and nondeposit funds involves some critical judgments relative to future cost of funds, lending opportunities, and the general level of business activity. These decisions are obviously more critical to the bank that takes a more aggressive posture toward seeking funds.

The attraction of funds provides the raw material for the operation of the bank. Once obtained, money must be employed at returns high enough to cover the cost of the funds, the other expenses of the bank, and a return to the stockholders. The management of assets is examined in the next chapter.

REVIEW QUESTIONS

1. Explain correspondent banking. How does this help the large bank? the small bank? Why was correspondent banking especially important before the establishment of the Federal Reserve System?

2. How does the Federal Funds market work? How does the market provide for a more efficient utilization of the total quantity of reserves available to the banking system?

3. Explain how the Federal Reserve discount window serves as a lender of last resort.

4. What are the functions of the bank's capital account? What factors have operated to reduce capital as a source of funds?

5. Explain liability management.

6. How did Eurodollar borrowings enable banks to evade reserve requirements and Regulation Q?

7. What is commercial paper? Why would a bank holding company, rather than a bank, sell commercial paper?

8. A bank sells a loan to a business firm under a repurchase agreement. The business is not a depositor at the bank. How does this transaction affect the bank's deposit and reserve positions?

9. What forces motivated the banks to develop new nondeposit sources of funds in the 1960s and 1970s?

10. Why did the Federal Reserve System impose controls on nondeposit sources of funds?

SUGGESTED READINGS

Howard D. Crosse, *Management Policies for Commercial Banks*. Englewood Cliffs, N.J.: Prentice-Hall, 1962.

Arnold Dill, "Liability Management Banking: Its Growth and Impact," *Federal Reserve Bank of Atlanta Monthly Review,* February 1971, pp. 22–31.

Donald M. DePamphilis, "The Short-Term Commercial Bank Adjustment Process and Federal Reserve Regulation," *New England Economic Review,* May–June 1974, pp. 14–21.

"The Eurodollar Market: The Anatomy of a Deposit and Loan Market, Part I: Market Structure," *Federal Reserve Bank of Cleveland Economic Review,* March 1970, pp. 3–19.

"The Eurodollar Market: Part II: Interest Rate Relationships," *Federal Reserve Bank of Cleveland Economic Review,* April 1970, pp. 3–18.

"The Eurodollar Market: Part III: Some Implications," *Federal Reserve Bank of Cleveland Economic Review,* May 1970, pp. 3–14.

Benjamin M. Friedman, "Regulation Q and the Commercial Loan Market in the 1960s," *Journal of Money, Credit and Banking,* Ohio State University Press, Columbus, August 1975, pp. 277–296.

Lucille S. Mayne, "Supervisory Influence on Bank Capital," *Journal of Finance,* American Finance Association, New York, June 1972, pp. 637–651.

Edward J. McCarthy, *Reserve Position: Methods of Adjustment,* Federal Reserve Bank of Boston, 1971.

John J. Mingo, "Regulatory Influence on Bank Capital Investment," *Journal of Finance,* American Finance Association, New York, September 1975, pp. 1111–1121.

Jimmie R. Monhollon and Glenn Picou, eds., *Instruments of the Money Market,* Federal Reserve Bank of Richmond, Va., 1974.

Stuart A. Schweitzer, "Bank Liability Management: For Better or for Worse?" *Federal Reserve Bank of Philadelphia Business Review,* December 1974, pp. 3–12.

Ronald D. Watson, "Banking on Debt for Capital Needs," *Federal Reserve Bank of Philadelphia Business Review,* December 1974, pp. 17–28.

5

THE COMMERCIAL BANKING SYSTEM: ASSETS

This chapter continues the analysis of the commercial banking system by examining the asset side of the balance sheet shown in Table 4–1. The various types of assets held by commercial banks are studied and the relationship between these assets and the bank's goals of liquidity, solvency, and profitability are analyzed.

Liquidity, Solvency, and Profitability

The process of commercial bank asset-management must ensure that the institution remains liquid, solvent, and profitable. In this section, each of these terms is defined and related to the asset structure of the commercial bank.

Liquidity

Liquidity is the ability to pay cash on demand. I can take cash out of my checking account at any time I desire and the bank must honor my request to withdraw funds. Likewise, liquidity requires that the bank be able to meet adverse check clearing balances from its reserve holdings at a Federal Reserve Bank or at a correspondent bank.

Most of the deposit liabilities of the commercial banks are subject to withdrawal either without notice or on prior-notice terms (which are normally waived). Thus, the commercial bank must be able to meet the demands for payment or close its doors.

The degree of need for liquidity depends upon the expectation of loss of deposits. If all depositors appeared at the same moment to withdraw all their funds, no institution could meet the demand for cash. The normal expectation is that while some depositors will be withdrawing funds and writing checks against their accounts, other depositors will be adding to their accounts and depositing checks drawn on other banks. There may be weekly, monthly, or seasonal patterns of deposit receipts and withdrawals, but these fluctuations can be anticipated and assets arranged so that cash and reserves are available to meet large negative clearing balances.

The cash and clearing balance needs vary as the composition of total deposits changes. Demand deposits represent funds that businesses and individuals expect to spend in the relatively near future; savings deposits represent funds reserved for future use. The rate of deposit turnover is lower for savings deposits than for demand deposits. For this reason, the cash and other liquid asset needs of the commercial banks are much higher than the liquidity needs of the thrift institutions.

Solvency

Protection of solvency is a second aspect of asset management. An institution is solvent as long as the cash value of its assets is greater than the value of its liabilities. The threat to solvency is much greater for financial institutions than it is for other types of businesses. As the balance sheets for the various institutions in Chapter 3 indicate, the capital accounts, the difference between assets and liabilities, are not very large. For a typical commercial bank, if the value of assets decreased by more than 7 or 8 percent, liabilities would be greater than assets and the bank would be insolvent. Thus, the institution cannot afford to assume a great deal of risk in its asset accounts.

The risk of deterioration in the market value of a bank's assets can arise from a number of factors. One is a decrease in the market value of securities. Loan accounts present a second and a greater degree of risk. Loans may decrease in value because of poor lending policies, such as the lending institution's failure to accurately judge the borrower's ability to repay. Alternatively, factors beyond the control of both lender and borrower, such as a recession, may reduce the borrower's ability to repay his loan.

A failing institution may be illiquid but solvent, or insolvent but liquid. The doors close if demands to withdraw cannot be met even though the eventual liquidation of assets would provide sufficient funds to satisfy the claims of all depositors. Many insolvent but liquid banks were able to survive the bank panics of the 1930s because, although these banks would have been found insolvent upon examination, they had maintained sufficient liquidity to meet all withdrawal demands and maintained the confidence of their depositors.

Profitability

The growth of the commercial bank requires profitability. An operating loss decreases the retained earnings portion of the capital account. The lower the value of the capital account, the smaller the margin between assets and liabilities and the greater the danger of insolvency. If the institution achieves an equal increase in

TABLE 5–1 Assets of All Commercial Banks, June 30, 1975

	MILLIONS OF DOLLARS	*PERCENT OF TOTAL ASSETS*
Cash bank balances, items in process	128,716	13.82
Currency and coin	10,102	1.08
Reserves with Federal Reserve Banks	26,890	2.89
Demand balances with U.S. banks	34,278	3.68
Other balances with U.S. banks	5,727	0.62
Balances with banks in foreign countries	2,296	0.25
Cash items in process of collection	49,422	5.31
Total securities held (book value)	212,058	22.78
U.S. Treasury	68,191	7.32
Other U.S. government agencies	33,882	3.64
States and political subdivisions	101,472	10.90
All other securities	8,513	0.91
Federal Funds sold and securities resale agreements	38,841	4.17
Other loans	496,990	53.38
Real estate loans	131,445	14.12
Loans to domestic and foreign banks	11,155	1.20
Loans to other financial institutions	32,413	3.48
Loans on securities to brokers and dealers	5,534	0.59
Other loans for purchase/carry securities	3,836	0.41
Loans to farmers	19,071	2.05
Commercial and industrial loans	178,993	19.22
Loans to individuals	101,816	10.94
All other loans	12,726	1.37
Other assets	54,453	5.85
Total assets	931,057	100.00

SOURCE: *Federal Reserve Bulletin,* November 1975, p. A16.

assets and liabilities but does not earn increased profits, the relative size of the capital account declines. To maintain the relative size of the capital account, new funds must be obtained. Dividends to stockholders can be decreased to accumulate retained earnings but, in the long run, new stockholders can be attracted only if the bank is able to pay a competitive dividend. Unless the profit outlook of the institution is reasonably bright, funds are difficult and expensive to obtain.

The assets of the bank must be allocated so that all three objectives—liquidity, solvency, and profitability—can be achieved. Unfortunately, there is some conflict between these objectives. For example, the perfectly liquid and solvent institution would hold all of its assets as vault cash, but this policy would produce no income and the institution would soon go out of business. At the other extreme, high interest rate, high-risk loans might appear to be a very profitable course of action, but if many of the loans were not repaid the institution would also become insolvent and be forced to close. Thus, the assets of the institution must be distributed so that profits are maximized within the constraints of maintaining liquidity and solvency.

The Assets of the Commercial Bank

The asset side of the commercial banking system's balance sheet, presented in Table 5–1, can be divided into three categories: cash items, securities, and loans. Each category is discussed below.

The Cash Items

Cash items account for nearly 14 percent of the total assets of the commercial banking system. The items in this category are largely self-explanatory. They include the cash on hand, balances at other banks, balances at the Federal Reserve Banks, and items being cleared through the check clearing mechanism.

The cash items are the first line of liquidity protection for the banking system. All of these items are, or can quickly become, currency to meet deposit outflows, or reserves to cover adverse clearing balances. Clearly, coin and currency are most readily available to the bank; however, a bank can draw upon its balances at other banks in a relatively short time. Items in the process of collection will result in either increases in the bank's reserve account at a Federal Reserve Bank or in larger correspondent balances at another commercial bank. Reserves at a Federal Reserve Bank provide a limited degree of liquidity. As deposits fall, required reserves fall—but reserves are only a fraction of deposits.

While cash items represent a relatively large portion of the asset portfolio, they contribute practically nothing to the bank's income. Only the small amount of (see Table 5–1) "other balances with U.S. banks," which includes time deposits, would earn any return. The other items are nonearning assets. Thus, for reasons of liquidity and to meet regulations of the states and the Federal Reserve System, the commercial bank must forego income on a significant portion of total assets. Some services are received as a result of holding correspondent balances and reserves at the Federal Reserve Banks, but these services would not represent a high return on the assets.

The proportion of cash items to total assets in Table 5–1 is low relative to historical standards. In recent years the high interest rates and the high loan demand have encouraged banks to minimize the volume of nonearning assets. For purposes of comparison, the ratio of cash items to total assets was 20.25 percent in

1960, 16.25 percent in 1970, and 13.82 percent in 1975.[1] There is no magic number that can be cited as the minimum percentage of cash assets but, given legal reserve requirements and the need for working cash balances, the prospects for further compression of the cash ratio seem limited.

The Securities Account and Liquidity

Securities, the second major category of assets in Table 5–1, account for 22.78 percent of total assets. Security holdings perform two important functions in the bank's portfolio. Short-term securities provide liquidity, and longer term securities provide income.

The major short-term security held by the banks is the Treasury bill. The Treasury bill is the shortest term debt security sold by the federal government. Each week a new issue of Treasury bills is sold with a maturity of 91 days in the future. Each Thursday an issue of bills, sold 91 days in the past, matures and the holders are repaid. This process of paying off maturing debt by selling a new issue of debt is called *refunding* the debt.

Treasury bills perform three valuable functions in the bank's portfolio. First, Treasury bills serve as the major source of secondary reserves for the bank. They are the second line of liquidity defense behind the cash items. In the event of a cash drain, Treasury bill holdings are liquidated as the supply of cash items decreases. Treasury bills are highly liquid and can be sold easily through large money-market banks or government securities dealers. Commercial paper also serves as a secondary reserve asset, but Treasury bills are the major asset backing up the cash items as a protector of liquidity.

Second, by holding Treasury bills, the bank can tailor the maturity of its security portfolio to its expected cash needs. At any time, there are 13 issues of 91-day Treasury bills outstanding in the market. There is an issue maturing this Thursday, next Thursday, two weeks from Thursday, and so forth. In addition, Treasury bills of maturities other than the standard 91-day variety are also sold regularly by the Treasury. There are bills with 26-week maturities and 1-year maturities.[2] Given the great variety of maturities available, the bank currently holding excess cash and expecting an increase in the demand for loans in 6 weeks can invest the cash in the issue of bills scheduled to mature in 6 weeks. When the loan demand appears, the Treasury bills will be maturing and funds will be available.

Treasury bills provide income to the bank. While the yield is not as high as that which can be obtained from loans or longer term securities, the combination of yield and liquidity protection makes bills an attractive holding.

[1] *Federal Reserve Bulletin,* November 1975, p. A14. Ratios for 1960 and 1970 are end-of-year values. Ratio for 1975 is as of June 30, 1975.

[2] For a complete listing of the maturities, yields, and prices of U.S. Treasury bills, see the financial pages of a major newspaper.

Holders of Treasury bills are compensated in a different manner than are the holders of most other debt instruments. On bonds, for example, the holder of the bond is paid interest at a fixed percentage of the face value of the bond. Thus, a 20-year $1,000 utility company bond with an interest rate of 8 percent would promise the holder of the bond $80 per year (8 percent of $1,000) each year for 20 years. Treasury bills, on the other hand, are sold without any provision for the payment of interest to the holder. The bills are sold at a discount (at an amount less than the maturity value), and the holder's return takes the form of the difference between the purchase price of the bill and the selling price or the maturity value.

Treasury bills are sold on an auction basis. The government determines the quantity to be sold at a given week's auction and sells the bills to the highest bidders. Each interested institution or individual submits a bid for the quantities they would buy at various prices. The bids are ranked, with the highest bidders receiving the quantity for which they bid at the price they bid and lower bids being accepted until the entire issue is sold. The return received by the successful bidder is the difference between the price paid and the $1,000 maturity value. If a buyer bids $950 for a $1,000 bill and his bid is accepted, his return, assuming he holds the bill to maturity, is $50. If he sells before the maturity date, his return depends upon the market value at the time he sells.

The auctioning of bills is a very competitive process, and the spread between the highest bid and the lowest accepted bid is very narrow. The return on the holding of bills, the *bill rate,* varies sharply over time and is watched by the financial community as a key indicator of the degree of monetary ease or restraint.

Short-term securities provide a higher degree of liquidity to the bank than do long-term securities, for three reasons.

First, the short-term security is closer to maturity and the holder can always receive the face value of his bond by waiting for the bond to mature.

Second, the volume of trading is greater in the short-term debt market than in longer term markets because (a) the banks use the short-term market to adjust their liquidity positions and (b) the Federal Reserve System, in the process of conducting monetary policy, buys and sells short-term debt.

Third, the relationship between interest rates, time to maturity, and bond prices is such that the price of short-term securities fluctuates less than the price of long-term securities. Some examples of the relationships between bond prices, interest rates, and time to maturity are given below.

The Relationship Between Interest Rates and Bond Prices There are three general rules to remember in the analysis of the relationship between bond prices and interest rates.

1. The price of an outstanding bond moves inversely to changes in the level of interest rates. Rising interest rates mean declining bond prices, and falling interest rates mean rising bond prices.

2. Equal degrees of risk bring equal degrees of reward. The bonds issued by two firms with equal credit ratings should sell at prices that provide the bondholder with the same return regardless of which bond he holds.

3. A dollar next year is not the same as a dollar today. Given a choice, the rational person would rather have a dollar today than a dollar tomorrow. The dollar today can be spent today or can be loaned out at interest; its value is greater than the value of a dollar to be received in the future. Thus, today's value of a dollar to be received in the future is less than today's value of a dollar received today.

An example of present and future values will set the stage for the later discussion of bond prices. Would you give me a dollar today in return for my promise to repay you one year from now? Even if you were sure of my willingness and ability to repay you, this would not be a good deal for you. You are giving up the opportunity to earn a year's interest on the dollar. Thus, you will charge me for the use of your money—say an interest rate of 8 percent per year. Thus, at the end of one year, I pay you $\$1.00 + 0.08\ (\$1.00) = \$1.08$ or, simplifying, I pay you $1.08\ (\$1.00) = \$1.08$.

Now consider a more complex example. Suppose I borrow $100 and promise to pay you $100 a year from now. After taking my IOU you decide that you would rather have cash now than one year from now, and so you try to sell my $100 IOU. You find that all potential buyers refuse to give up $100 today for $100 one year from today because they have more gainful uses for their money. Finally, a friend agrees to take the IOU off your hands at a price that will yield him a 10 percent rate of return on his money. To determine the appropriate price, divide the face value of the $100 IOU by 1 plus the desired rate of return on the investment:

$$\frac{\$100}{1 + 0.10} = \frac{\$100}{1.10} = \$90.91$$

If your friend gives you $90.91 for my $100.00 IOU and he holds the IOU until I pay the $100.00, he will receive a 10 percent rate of return on his money. In more technical language, $90.91 is the present value of $100 to be received in one year applying an interest rate of 10 percent.

Now, consider a hypothetical bond issued by ABC Corporation with a face or maturity value of $1,000. ABC promises to pay the holder of the bonds an annual interest rate of 5 percent. Five percent is the coupon interest rate. The bonds have a 21-year maturity—that is, at the end of the 21 years the corporation will redeem the bonds and pay the holder $1,000. Thus, the person who buys one of these bonds for $1,000 is being promised the following deal: each year the ABC Corporation will pay him $50 in interest—the coupon rate of interest of 5 percent times the $1,000 face value of the bond—and after 21 years ABC will pay $1,000. The purchaser of the bond is giving up $1,000 today for a future stream of payments that is as follows:

Year:	*1*	*2*	*3*	. . .	*20*	*21*	*21*
Payment:	$50	$50	$50	. . .	$50	$50	$1,000

The investor is giving up $1,000 today in exchange for 21 annual payments of $50 each and a payment of $1,000 in 21 years. Mathematically, ABC is offering investors a stream of future payments that, when discounted by the interest rate demanded for this type of risk (5 percent), is equal to the price ($1,000) of the bond. Thus,

$$\$1{,}000 = \frac{\$50}{(1+0.05)^1} + \frac{\$50}{(1+0.05)^2} + \frac{\$50}{(1+0.05)^3} + \cdots + \frac{\$50}{(1+0.05)^{21}} + \frac{\$1{,}000}{(1+0.05)^{21}}$$

The ABC bond example is complicated because of the number of years involved in the transaction. Just as a dollar today is worth more than a dollar one year from now, a dollar one year from now is worth more than a dollar two years from now. The discount factor is raised to powers to calculate the lower present value of the payments to be received in the more distant future. For example, the $50 interest payment to be received in one year has a present value of

$$\frac{\$50}{(1+0.05)^1} = \$47.62$$

because $47.62 deposited at 5 percent for one year would be worth $50. The $50 interest payment to be received in two years has a present value of

$$\frac{\$50}{(1+0.05)^2} = \$45.35$$

because $45.35 deposited at 5 percent compounded annually for two years would be $50. The $1,000 to be received when the bond matures in 21 years has a present value of

$$\frac{\$1{,}000}{(1+0.05)^{21}} = \$358.94$$

Having established the price of a bond as the sum of the present values of a stream of future interest payments and the principle repayment, the next problem is to examine the cause of bond price fluctuations. Fluctuations in the price of bonds occur because the terms of the bond contract are established at the time the bonds are issued and do not change during the life of the bond contract. Thus, the holder of an ABC bond will receive the agreed-upon $50 per year regardless of interest rate fluctuations during the 21 years.

Assume that after one year passes, bonds are issued by Corporation XYZ for a 20-year period. XYZ's credit rating is equal to that of the ABC Corporation. However, during the past year, market interest rates have increased and XYZ must promise to pay a 6 percent coupon rate of interest. XYZ sells its bonds at $1,000 by promising a stream of payments of

Year:	*1*	*2*	*3*	. . .	*20*	*20*
Payment:	$60	$60	$60	. . .	$60	$1,000

The ABC bonds are now 20 years from maturity and will pay $50 interest per year for 20 years. Would an investor rather receive \$50 or \$60 per year for the next 20 years? Naturally, investors would prefer \$60. So the market price of the ABC bonds must change to make the \$50 payment on the ABC bonds competitive with the \$60 payment on the XYZ bonds. The new market price of the ABC bonds will be equal to the sum of the stream of the remaining fixed payments discounted by the *current* interest rate of 6 percent. Thus,

$$\begin{aligned}\text{Market price of ABC bonds} &= \frac{\$50}{(1 + 0.06)^1} + \frac{\$50}{(1 + 0.06)^2} + \frac{\$50}{(1 + 0.06)^3} + \\ &\quad \ldots + \frac{\$50}{(1 + 0.06)^{20}} + \frac{\$1{,}000}{(1 + 0.06)^{20}} = \$885.30\end{aligned}$$

By paying \$885.30 for the ABC bonds an investor would receive the same 6 percent return on his money as the investor who pays \$1,000 for the XYZ bonds. Thus, as interest rates rose, the price of the outstanding ABC bonds had to fall in order to make the relatively low, fixed interest payment competitive with the higher return an investor could receive on newly issued bonds.

The investor holding ABC bonds when interest rates increase has two options. First, he can continue to hold the bonds and accept the 5 percent return. When the bonds mature he will receive \$1,000. Second, he can sell the bonds before maturity at a price determined by the relationship between 5 percent and the current level of interest rates. If interest rates had fallen during the period after the issuance of the ABC bonds, the price of the ABC bonds would have risen above the \$1,000 face value because the payments stream would have been superior to that of newly issued bonds offering lower rates of return.

Bond Prices and Time to Maturity The range of possible bond price fluctuations increases as the time to maturity increases. The price of a one-year bond will not change as much with a given change in market interest rates as the price of a bond with 20 years to maturity. For example, the market price of the ABC bond decreased from \$1,000 to \$885.30 as the market rate of interest increased from 5 to 6 percent. The price of a one-year bond with a coupon rate of interest of 5 percent would have decreased to \$990.57 as the interest rate increased to 6 percent. The difference in the degree of price fluctuation is due to the variation in the number of periods over which the effect of a change in the interest rate is compounded.

To summarize, the short-term security, such as Treasury bills or short-term commercial paper, serves the liquidity needs of the commercial bank. Because the prices of these securities do not fluctuate with changes in interest rates as much as the price of long-term securities, the bank can count on being able to liquidate short-term securities with a minimum amount of loss.

The Securities Account and Income

Securities are not as profitable for a bank as loans, but in periods of low loan demand the securities account becomes a more important contributor to profitability.

The major types of securities held for income by the commercial bank are (a) medium and longer term federal government bonds, (b) debt obligations of various federal government agencies that borrow separately from the U.S. Treasury, such as the Federal Land Bank and the Government National Mortgage Association; and (c) bonds issued by states, cities, towns, school districts and other governmental units.

The Risks In this category of securities holdings, the bank assumes two types of risk. The first is that the issuer of bonds will default on the payment of either interest or principal. Clearly the bank desires to minimize this risk. The small size of the capital account limits the ability to accept losses on the securities account. Thus, the bank restricts its purchases of bonds to highly rated issues that have low default risks. In addition, holdings are diversified between bonds of various borrowers.

Second, the bank accepts an interest rate risk. In a period of high interest rates and a high demand for loans, the market value of the bank's bond portfolio will usually be below the purchase price of the bonds. Most likely, the bonds were purchased during periods of low loan demand and low interest rates. The bank originally bought the bonds with funds not needed to service its loan customers. Then, when loan demand increases, interest rates rise and bond prices decline. The funds to meet the loan demand must be obtained by selling securities at a loss. While the loans are more attractive for the bank than continuing to hold the bonds, a loss must be taken before the money is available for lending. To some extent, the bank may feel "locked in" to its bonds by the desire to avoid taking a loss but the strength of the *lock-in effect* decreases as the interest rate on loans increases.

The Incentives The major incentive for the holding of longer term bonds is the after-tax yield. Banks, like wealthy individuals, often receive a higher after-tax yield by holding state and local government bonds (on which the interest is not subject to federal income taxes) than by holding federal government bonds (on which the interest is taxable).

CALCULATING BEFORE-TAX YIELD.
The before-tax yield on a bond is obtained most easily by consulting bond tables. Bond tables relate the yield on a bond, the market price of the bond, the coupon rate of interest, and the time to maturity of the bond. If the other three variables are known, the yield to maturity can be looked up in the bond tables.

Some newspaper listings of bond prices also state the yield to maturity which an investor would obtain if he purchased a given bond and held that bond to its maturity date. The market prices of major actively traded bonds are published in many newspapers. Bond prices are quoted as if the maturity value of a bond were \$100 instead of \$1,000. Thus, a bond listed as selling for 88⅜ sold for \$883.75. Bond prices, like stock prices, are quoted in terms of eighths of a dollar rather than in decimals. Newspaper listings include the name of the issuer of the bond, the coupon rate of interest, the maturity date, the range of prices at which sales took place on a given day, and the yield to maturity.

The third method of calculating yield is the do-it-yourself method. A simple, if not perfectly accurate, formula provides an approximation of yield to maturity. The yield to maturity is the average annual percentage return that a holder would receive if he bought the bond at the current market price and held the bond until it matured. That is,

$$\text{Yield to maturity} = \frac{\text{annual interest payment} + \text{discount (or minus premium)/years to maturity}}{\text{(purchase price} + \text{maturity value)/2}}$$

An investor reads in the bond listings of his newspaper that DEF bonds maturing in 20 years and bearing a coupon rate of 5 percent are selling for 88½. He would like to have a rough but quick approximation of the return he would receive if he bought this bond and held it for 20 years. The values are:

Annual interest payment (5% of \$1,000) = \$50.00
Discount (\$1,000 – \$885.00) = \$115.00
Years to maturity = 20 years
Purchase price = \$885.00
Maturity price = \$1,000.00

and the calculation is:

$$\text{Yield to maturity} = \frac{\$50 + (\$115/20)}{(885 + \$1{,}000)/2} = \frac{\$55.75}{\$942.50} = 5.91\%$$

Two simplifying but technically incorrect assumptions are made in the formula. First, in the numerator, the assumption is made that one-twentieth of the discount is received each year. This is not the case; the \$115 is only received when the bond matures at its face value of \$1,000. Second, in the denominator, the formula obtains the average amount that the investor has invested in the bond over 20 years. The price on the day of the purchase is \$885 and the price the instant before redemption is \$1,000. These two values are averaged to obtain a rough measure of the amount that is invested in the bond. The true value of the investment could only be calculated in retrospect by averaging all of the daily market values of the bond over the 20 years. The average annual return in the numerator is then divided by the average amount invested to obtain the yield to maturity.

As a second example of the formula, assume the same DEF bond is selling at 104. Now the buyer must pay a premium—a price in excess of the maturity value—to purchase the bond. The yield to maturity calculation is:

$$\text{Yield to maturity} = \frac{\$50 - (\$40/20)}{(\$1{,}040 + \$1000)/2} = \frac{\$48}{\$1020} = 4.71\%$$

In this case, one twentieth of the premium of \$40—the difference between the purchase price of \$1,040 and the maturity value of \$1,000—is subtracted from the

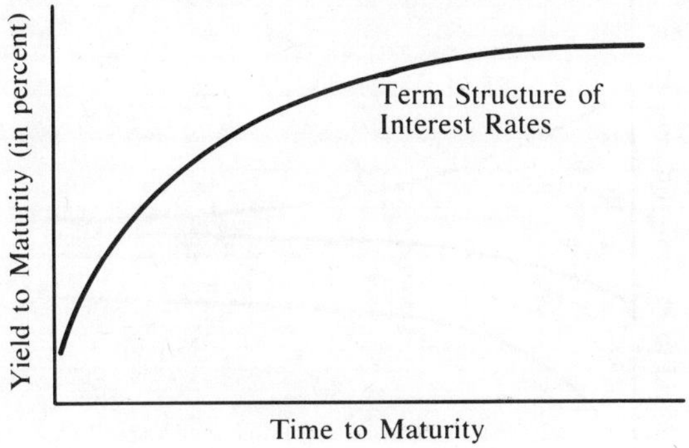

FIGURE 5–1 Hypothetical Term Structure of Interest Rates Curve

annual interest payment. Paying the higher price for the bond lowers the yield to maturity to 4.71 percent.

THE TERM STRUCTURE OF INTEREST RATES.
The relationship between the yield on bonds and the time to maturity of those bonds is called the *term structure of interest rates*. The term structure of interest rates is a key factor in the management of the bank's bond portfolio.

Assume that the yield on each of the various issues of federal government debt is calculated. Government debt maturities range from Treasury bills about to mature to long-term bonds maturing after the turn of the next century. A table is made up listing the yield on each issue of bonds and the length of time to maturity of that issue. Then the yield and the time to maturity of each issue are entered on a graph such as Figure 5–1. Plotting a line through the points, a curve representing the current term structure of interest rates for federal government debt is obtained. The curve represents the yield that could be obtained from holding various maturities of federal government debt.

The term structure of interest rates on government debt may take various shapes, such as curves *A, B,* and *C* in Figure 5–2. Curve *A* is the low-interest-rate curve; short-term, intermediate-term, and long-term rates are all relatively low. Under curve *A* conditions, the bank would be encouraged to buy longer term securities, or to "move out the yield curve," to obtain added income. As the bank increases the average maturity of its debt holdings in order to obtain a higher yield, the exposure to the interest rate risk increases. Note also that curve *A* would be favorable to the process of intermediation at both commercial banks and other financial institutions; short-term interest rates are low relative to long-term rates. The bank can obtain short-term deposits from its customers at low cost and invest the funds long term at a high yield.

Curve *B* represents an intermediate level of interest rates. The short-term rate is much higher than in curve *A,* and there is relatively little difference between

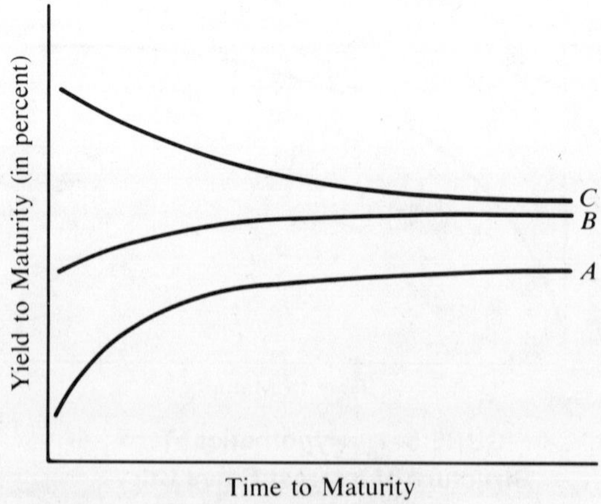

FIGURE 5–2 Hypothetical Term Structure of Interest Rates Curves

short- and long-term rates. The bank would not increase its current income by purchasing longer term securities. Looking at the intermediation process, short-term interest rates are nearly as high as long-term rates, and the bank would have more difficulty attracting funds.

Curve *C* represents very high interest rates; the short-term rate is extremely high and the bank can obtain the highest current yield by investing in short-term governments. Long-term interest rates are also higher than in the other examples. The bank, in making its investment decision, must also consider the reinvestment problems. The high short-term rates are attractive, but what will interest rates be when these short-term securities mature and the funds are reinvested? Interest rates may be even higher and the bank would be able to do better the next time; however, interest rates may be lower at the time of reinvestment and the bank would earn a smaller return. Perhaps, the bank should move out the yield curve, accept the somewhat lower longer term interest rate, and be secure in the knowledge that it will earn that rate for a long period of time regardless of what happens to short-term rates.

Curve *C* represents financial disintermediation. The high short-term interest rates would encourage depositors to withdraw funds from the banks. They could earn a high short-term return by directly investing the funds in short-term securities that would be nearly as liquid as deposits.

Why does the term structure of interest rates take these different shapes at various times? There are two major theories that attempt to explain the shape of the yield curve. The first is the *expectations theory.*[3] According to the expectations theory, the yield on a long-term bond is equal to the average of the expected yields

[3]David Meiselman, *The Term Structure of Interest Rates* (Englewood Cliffs, N.J.: Prentice-Hall, 1962).

on an equivalent series of short-term bonds. For example, the investor should obtain the same rate of return on a one-year government bond as he would expect to receive from buying four sequential issues of three-month government bonds during the year. The yield on the one-year bond becomes a function of what the market expects the average yield to be on the four issues of three-month bonds. Likewise, the yield on a 25-year government bond would be the average of the expected yields on the next 100 issues of three-month Treasury bills.

If investors expected that their return would be higher by holding the one-year bond than by buying four consecutive issues of three-month bonds, investors would switch from three-month bonds to one-year bonds. The return on one-year bonds would go down (the higher demand increases the price and lowers the yield). The return on three-month bonds would go up as the lower demand decreased the price and increased the yield. Substitution between the two alternatives maintains the equality of the expected returns.

On curve *A* in Figure 5–2, the current short-term interest rate is low. Investors, however, expect that the average of future short-term interest rates will be higher than the current short-term interest rate. Thus, on curve *A,* the current long-term rate, reflecting investor expectations, is higher than the current short-term rate.

On curve *C,* the current short-term rate is very high. Investors expect that the average of future short-term interest rates will be lower than the current short-term rate. Thus, on curve *C,* the current long-term rate, reflecting investor expectations, is lower than the current short-term rate.

The key concept is that any long-term interest rate is an average of the market's expectation of yields on a series of short-term interest rates over an equivalent period of time.

The alternative theory of the term structure of interest rates is the *segmented market theory,* [4] which states that there are three relatively separate securities markets—for short-term debt, intermediate debt, and long-term debt. Buyers and sellers of bonds are not completely free to move between the three sectors of the market. By law, regulation, custom, or the needs of their industry, each borrower and lender concentrates most of his borrowing or lending activity in one given segment of the debt market. Therefore, the short-term interest rate is determined by the supply and demand for short-term funds, the intermediate-term interest rate by the supply and demand for intermediate-term funds, and the long-term interest rate by the supply and demand for long-term funds.

The term structure of interest rates is a product of the price determination process in each of the three markets and represents the peculiarities of supply and demand in each market. For example, on curve *A* in Figure 5–2, the supply of short-term funds may be great relative to the demand for short-term funds, and the

[4]John M. Culbertson, "The Term Structure of Interest Rates," *Quarterly Journal of Economics,* November 1957, pp. 485–517.

short-term rate is low. However, the supply of long-term funds is low relative to the demand for long-term funds, and the long-term interest rate is high. On curve C in Figure 5–2, short-term funds are scarce relative to the demand, and the short-term rate is very high; the supply of long-term funds is large relative to the demand for long-term funds, and the long-term interest rate is relatively low.

Some long-term lenders will move into the short end of the market when short-term interest rates are especially high relative to long-term rates, and some short-term lenders will move into the long end of the market when long-term interest rates are especially high. However, the theory assumes that each type of lender and borrower remains attached to one basic segment of the market.

Regardless of which theory of the term structure of interest rates is correct, the analysis points up the decision-making problems of the managers of the bank's income-producing portfolio. The added yield, which may be obtained by moving out the term structure curve, must be balanced against the interest rate risk.

Bank Loans

Table 5–1 indicates that over 53 percent of the banking system's funds are allocated to loans. To the banker, this is the most important activity of the bank; the loan portfolio generates the bulk of the bank's profits.

The variety of loans made by the typical commercial bank is indicated in the condensed balance sheet of Table 5–1. Other financial institutions, businesses, farmers, and consumers are all in debt to the commercial banking system. The commercial banking system is the major source of commercial and industrial loans, loans to other financial institutions, and securities loans. Commercial banks are relatively less important as home mortgage lenders.

While the loan account is important as a source of profit to the commercial bank, it does not provide liquidity and represents the greatest threat to solvency. Most loans on the books of the commercial bank are relatively illiquid. The degree of liquidity varies with the time to maturity of the loan and the possibility of selling the loan to another lender. On these standards, the liquidity of commercial bank loans varies substantially from loan to loan. For example, loans to security brokers and dealers are frequently *call* loans and can be terminated or "called" by the bank on relatively short notice. At the other extreme, loans on real estate are typically of a longer maturity. The transferability of a loan to another lender, either by the sale of the loan contract or by cancelling the loan with a subsequent loan being made by another lender, varies with the existence, or nonexistence, of a secondary market in the particular type of loan.

The degree of liquidity of the typical loan portfolio has decreased over time as other assets have taken over the function of providing liquidity to the bank's asset account. Fifty years ago, most bank loans were based on the *commercial credit theory,* or *real bills doctrine,* of bank lending. These theories reasoned that the function of the bank was to provide short-term self-liquidating credit; the use of the loan proceeds should generate funds for the repayment of the loan. For example, a crop-financing loan to a farmer would be self liquidating, because funds would be available to repay the loan when the crop was harvested and sold. Loans to retailers to finance the expansion of inventories before heavy selling seasons would also meet the self-liquidating requirement. These types of loans were also real bills in that they financed "real" business activity.

The commercial credit theory of bank lending was based on the pre-Depression needs of the banking system. First, the loan portfolio of the bank had to contribute to the bank's liquidity. The theory predominated in a period in which threats to liquidity, arising from runs on the banks, were very real. The bank had to be prepared to liquidate its assets quickly in the event of a run. Second, the present variety of highly marketable securities did not exist in the pre–World War II period. The modern bank has a variety of assets that can be held for liquidity, and, therefore, does not need the same degree of liquidity in its loan account. To state it oversimply, Treasury bills today provide liquidity protection, while the loan account provides the profits. Before the development of assets such as Treasury bills, the loan account had to perform both functions.

After the reforms of the 1930s provided greater stability to the banking system and the growth of government debt provided an abundant supply of highly liquid assets, the lending activity of the commercial banking system became more diversified. Since World War II, a variety of types of loans, which would have been considered "unsound" by pre-Depression standards, have been developed.

One new type of commercial bank loan is the *consumer installment loan*. Before the war, few consumers had very extensive dealings with commercial banks. However, over the last three decades the commercial banks have become more consumer oriented. As part of this new orientation, installment lending has expanded, residential real estate lending has increased, and credit cards and other forms of automatic consumer lending have been devised. Most of these loans are not self-liquidating loans; a car loan will not lead to the provision of funds for the repayment of the loan (unless the car is used for business purposes). However, the bank is more concerned with the repayment capacity of the borrower, rather than any self-liquidating features of the loan. Does the borrower have sufficient income to meet the payments? Do his other expenses leave a margin for the car payments? Does he have other debts? Is his income stable? What is his past credit record? These are important questions to the lender.

Security may be required for the consumer loan but security is not as important as the measure of repayment ability. While the bank wants the right to repossess your car for nonpayment, it really does not want to have to repossess, of course. The repossession process is complicated, slow, and expensive. The bank is not and does not want to be in the business of selling used cars.

The reduced emphasis on loan liquidity has also changed the process of lending to business firms. While the banks still make crop-financing loans and inventory loans, the business loan portfolio includes more long-term lending to business firms. The business term loan is now a common form of lending. A term loan has a maturity of at least one year but is frequently as long as 10 years. As with the consumer loan, the standard criteria for granting loans place greatest emphasis on the ability of the firm to generate sufficient income to repay the loan. Increasing amounts of short-term business lending provide for relatively automatic loan renewals. While this continuous short-term borrowing is technically different from a term loan, the effect is basically the same.

Interest Rates on Loans From the point of view of the potential borrower, at least nine factors influence the interest rate on a loan.

1. One variable is the cost of money to the lender. The bank must obtain funds to make loans and must pay a competitive price to secure those funds. Clearly, the bank cannot pay 10 percent for deposits and make loans at 5 percent. To continue in operation, the bank must cover its cost of money, its operating costs, and a normal profit.
2. Opportunity costs are important. By lending to one person, the bank gives up the opportunity of lending to another loan applicant. If all other factors are equal, the bank lends to the borrower willing to pay a higher interest rate.
3. The degree of competitiveness in a given market has an impact on the interest rate. The wider the borrower's options between numbers and types of institutions, the better are his chances of obtaining the lowest possible interest rate on a given type of loan.
4. The type of loan and the level of loss experience influence interest rates. An installment payment loan involves more processing cost than a personal loan and loss rates are higher. Higher default rates and higher credit-granting and processing costs increase lending rates.
5. The rate on a particular loan is influenced by the degree of risk represented by the individual borrower. Each loan application represents a unique set of circumstances and special types of risk that may influence the loan decision.
6. Usury statutes may limit the rate of interest which can be charged on a given loan, especially on loans to consumers. In this case, the effect of a low ceiling rate of interest may be the denial of loans to high-risk applicants.
7. The value of collateral pledged by the borrower may influence the interest rate. However, the interest rate–collateral relationship varies from case to case, and in many instances the financially strong borrower is able to borrow without specific collateral at a rate lower than is charged to a weaker borrower with pledged collateral.
8. The size of the loan may influence the interest rate. Credit investigation and loan processing costs are relatively fixed costs. On a small loan, the interest rate may be higher; as the size of the loan increases, the fixed costs per dollar loaned decrease and the interest rate required to cover costs decreases.

9. The maturity of the loan and the current term structure of interest rates influence the cost of credit.

After all this, however, there is still only one way a borrower can be assured of obtaining the best interest rate—shop around among financial institutions.

The Prime Rate Of all of the various interest rates charged by banks on loans to the many different types of borrowers, the most attention is paid to the prime rate. In a way, this attention is misdirected because most banks make very few loans at the prime rate. The *prime rate* is that rate charged by commercial banks on short-term loans to large businesses with the highest credit rating. Very few firms qualify to borrow at the prime rate.

In August 1975, the prime rate fluctuated between 7½ and 7¾ percent, but the average rate on all short-term business loans at 35 money market centers was 8.22 percent. The average interest rate on loans over $1 million was 8 percent.[5]

THE PROBLEMS OF ASSET MANAGEMENT

The examination of the asset portion of the balance sheet of the commercial banking system in Table 5–1 indicates that the banks' assets are allocated between cash items, securities, and loans. The cash items represent working funds such as vault cash and immediate liquidity items that provide little income. The security account provides a source of secondary liquidity through the holding of short-term debt and provides income through the holding of longer term federal, state, and local government debt. The loan account provides short- and longer term funds to businesses and consumers and provides the largest portion of the bank's income.

The obvious basic problem of bank asset management is to allocate the available funds so as to maximize profits without endangering the solvency or the liquidity of the institution. Making riskier loans may increase current income, but at the same time it increases the prospect of higher loan loss rates. Moving funds from short-term liquid assets to longer term securities increases income, but it also poses the possible future danger of having to liquidate the longer term securities at a loss in order to meet deposit outflows or future loan demands.

An overly conservative lending policy, as evidenced by a low loan/asset ratio, may ensure the institution's future liquidity and solvency but lowers the profitability of the institution. In addition, by not meeting the loan needs of its market areas, the bank is risking the loss of customers to its more aggressive competitors or is helping to build a case for a new bank to argue for permission to enter the area to better serve the credit needs of the community. Therefore, the bank

[5] *Federal Reserve Bulletin,* December 1975, p. A26.

must walk the line between threats to liquidity and solvency on the one hand and threats to profitability on the other hand.

Given that the bank is an on-going institution, 100 percent of assets cannot be reallocated daily. Adjustments in the use of funds can only be made at the margin as bonds mature, loans are repaid, and cash items fluctuate. Thus, at the margin, the bank must make daily decisions about asset management. Should funds from maturing Treasury bills be used to purchase a new issue of bills or should the funds be used to expand the higher yielding consumer installment loan portfolio? Should funds being received as payments on installment loans be used to make new installment loans or should the funds be used to meet the loan demands of business customers with long-standing ties to the bank? What is the current term structure of interest rates on securities and loans?

At this point, it should become clear that the problems of asset management and liability management are not independent of each other. The individual bank's ability to meet loan demands is related to the ability to attract funds from depositors or other sources. Changes on one side of the balance sheet require changes on the other side. An outflow of deposits forces a contraction of lending or investing activity, and a deposit inflow permits an expansion of lending or investing activity.

In establishing terms on which the bank will attempt to attract deposits, concern must be given to the profitable employment of these funds on the asset side of the balance sheet. It is not profitable to pay a high interest rate for funds and then lend the funds at low interest rates. Likewise, the bank does not maximize profits if it fails to attract all the funds that could be profitably employed by the loan department.

Thus, liability and asset management are joint activities, and the success of the bank depends upon its ability to attract and employ funds with constant attention to the alternative sources, uses, costs, and returns from various activities.

REVIEW QUESTIONS

1. Carefully define and distinguish between liquidity and solvency. What types of assets protect the bank's liquidity? What assets endanger the bank's solvency?

2. How does the objective of profitability conflict with the goals of liquidity and solvency?

3. Why are the liquidity needs of a commercial bank greater than the liquidity needs of a savings and loan association?

4. Describe the term structure of interest rates. How are the various-shaped yield curves related to financial intermediation.

5. What are the two functions of securities in the commercial bank's portfolio?

6. Why do bond prices decrease as interest rates increase? How can this phenomenon result in the bank feeling locked into its securities portfolio?

7. Explain asset management and its relationship to liability management.

8. A $1,000 bond maturing in 12 years bears a 4 percent coupon interest rate and sells for 92½. What is the yield to maturity?

9. Describe Treasury bills and the process by which Treasury bills are sold. Why are they important in bank asset management?

10. How has the commercial bank's loan portfolio changed in the post–World War II period?

SUGGESTED READINGS

W. F. Mackara, "The ABC's of the Prime Rate," *Federal Reserve Bank of Atlanta Monthly Review,* July 1974, pp. 100–105.

Edward W. Reed, Richard V. Cotter, Edward K. Gill, and Richard K. Smith, Jr., *Commercial Banking*. Englewood Cliffs, N.J.: Prentice-Hall, 1976.

Roland I. Robinson, *The Management of Bank Funds,* 2nd ed. New York: McGraw-Hill Book Company, 1962.

Robert P. Shay, "Factors Affecting Price, Volume and Credit Risk in the Consumer Finance Industry," *Journal of Finance,* American Finance Association, New York, May 1970, pp. 503–515.

Paul F. Smith, "Pricing Policies on Consumer Loans at Commercial Banks," *Journal of Finance,* American Finance Association, New York, May 1970, pp. 517–525.

William T. Terrill and William J. Frazer, Jr., "Interest Rates, Portfolio Behavior, and Marketable Government Securities," *Journal of Finance,* American Finance Association, New York, March 1972, pp. 1–35.

Ronald D. Watson, "Bank Bond Management: The Maturity Dilemma," *Federal Reserve Bank of Philadelphia Business Review,* March 1972, pp. 23–29.

6

THE REGULATION OF FINANCIAL INSTITUTIONS

A discussion of financial institutions would not be complete without an examination of the regulatory process. While all financial institutions are regulated by governments—both federal and state—this discussion covers only those institutions that accept deposits from the public. Thus, there is no coverage of the regulation of the securities markets by the Securities and Exchange Commission. The main emphasis is on the regulation of the commercial banking system, with some attention also given to the thrift institutions.

The Objectives of Regulation

Historically, the overriding concern of the regulatory process was the prevention of bank failures. Prior to the development of federal deposit insurance, a bank failure meant a loss not only to the owners of the bank but also to the depositors.

Bank failures came both as isolated incidents and in great national waves. During the period 1864–1896, for instance, 1,234 banks failed. These failures were not evenly distributed in time. Only one bank closed in 1870, but in 1893, 261 failures occurred.[1]

The years of massive bank failures were yet to come. In 1921, 23,045 banks were operating.[2] Failures accounted for the disappearance of 5,411 banks between 1921 and 1930. From 1930 through 1933, 8,812 banks failed; almost half of these failures took place in 1933.[3]

Runs on banks were common prior to the inception of deposit insurance but have been infrequent since 1934. Many of the banks that closed during the Great

[1]John M. Chapman and Ray B. Westerfield, *Problems in Banking, Money and Credit* (New York: Ronald Press Co., 1927), p. 663.

[2]Ross M. Robertson, *The Comptroller and Bank Supervision*, Office of the Comptroller of the Currency, Washington, D.C., 1968, p. 98.

[3]Ibid., p. 125.

Depression closed not because they were poorly managed or were holding worthless assets, but because rumors or fears about a given bank, or banks in general, led to demands for cash that could not be met in the short run. Given time, a bank could liquidate its assets and pay its depositors but cash holdings were not sufficient to meet sudden unexpected demands to withdraw funds.

In 1934, the institution of the Federal Deposit Insurance Corporation's program for insuring deposits and weeding out unsound banks increased confidence in the banking system and lowered the failure rate to only 61 banks. The failure rate fluctuated between 17 and 84 banks per year through 1942. Between 1942 and 1975 less than 10 banks per year failed;[4] in 1974, 13 banks failed.

The data on bank failures indicate the high degree of instability that characterized the American banking system prior to the establishment of the FDIC. Given the traditional problem of bank failures, the first concern of bank regulation has been the safety of the banking system. The prevention of loss to the depositors is foremost in the minds of most bank regulators. Prior to the FDIC, a bank failure meant that the depositors lost part or all of their deposits. Upon the liquidation or reorganization of the bank, the depositors usually recovered some portion of their deposits but, of course, receiving only, say, 20 percent of one's life savings is not satisfactory to most people.

The institution of deposit insurance has changed the public's attitude toward bank failures. Prior to 1934, the mere hint that something was wrong with a bank could lead to lines of depositors waiting to withdraw their money. Today, the failure of a bank does not cause the same amount of panic—except among the stockholders. The public knows that deposits are insured—although there is a maximum amount of insurance coverage per account—and that the FDIC will make up any losses, with only slight inconvenience to the depositors. While only nationally chartered banks are required to belong to FDIC, nearly all banks do belong. There are only 253 uninsured commercial banks, and they hold only 1.75 percent of total commercial banking assets.

The failures of the United States National Bank of San Diego in 1973 and the Franklin National Bank of New York City in 1974 caused some general concern over the liquidity and solvency of the banking industry and some concern about specific practices of these banks; however, they did not generate any widespread loss of confidence in the banking system. Unlike the typical case prior to 1934, the failure of these two banks did not lead to panic withdrawals of deposits from other banks.

As is usually the case, the FDIC arranged a "shotgun wedding" between the failing banks and other banks. The marriage partner took over, by merger, the deposit liabilities and the sound assets of the failed bank and used branch offices of the failed bank to open its own branches. The customers of the failed bank became

[4] *1974 Annual Report of the Federal Deposit Insurance Corporation,* Washington, D.C., 1975, p. 245.

the customers of the acquiring bank and business went on as usual. In forced mergers of this sort, the FDIC acquires the questionable assets of the failed bank and provides cash to the acquiring bank to make up the difference between the sound assets received and the deposit liabilities assumed.

Although the problem of bank failures has been contained, the major proportion of the total regulatory effort is still directed toward the protection of the liquidity and solvency of the banking system. However, the regulators are gradually giving greater emphasis to a second objective—namely, the preservation and promotion of a competitive financial system.

To an extent, the goals of a high degree of safety and a high degree of competitiveness conflict. A monopoly bank would be the safest bank. Being the only bank, the monopolist would make only the safest loans, would never lose deposits to competitors, and would earn monopoly profits sufficient to attract all necessary capital. However, from earliest American history, the control of all credit by a monopoly bank has been feared. At the other extreme, the model of perfect competition relies upon entry into the industry and exit from the industry (including exit via failure) to maintain prices at the normal profit level. Clearly, a trade-off must be made between the degree of competition permitted and the achievement of other regulatory objectives. Each new entrant into a banking market increases competition and increases the possibility that an existing firm will be unable to survive the new competition. The problem of the regulator is to seek a balance between an adequate degree of competition and protection of the stability of the banking system.

The Regulators

Regulatory responsibility is not centralized in any one office but is divided between a collection of federal and state agencies.

State Regulation

Regulation on the state level is conducted by an agency headed by a bank commissioner, superintendent, or department head. The responsibilities of the state banking agency normally are as follows:

1. It examines financial institutions chartered by the state. Depending on the state, the examination will be a more or less detailed audit of accounts, a determination that all listed assets actually exist, a check for evidence of fraud or other wrongdoing, a determination of compliance with the laws of the state, and an examination of the soundness of the assets of the institution.

2. It is responsible for structural changes in the financial system. The banking agency must approve the formation of new state-chartered banks and the

opening or closing of branch offices (if branches are permitted by state law), and it has input into structural decisions made by other regulatory agencies.

3. It regulates the powers of financial institutions. In some, but not all, states, the bank commissioner has discretionary authority to permit given institutions to undertake new activities not specifically authorized by statute but considered by the commissioner to be in the public's interest.

4. It wields general powers to protect the interest of the public, such as regulating small loan companies, and enforcing truth-in-lending laws, usury laws, and other state laws that regulate the financial system.

While the general powers of state regulatory agencies provide a basis for overall regulation, the emphasis in most states has been on the examination of banks. The desire to maintain a safe banking system is the major goal of most state bank regulators.

Federal Regulation

On the federal level, three agencies—the Federal Reserve System, the Comptroller of the Currency, and the Federal Deposit Insurance Corporation—have responsibilities in the regulation of commercial banks. Each of these agencies examines the subgroup of banks coming under its jurisdiction. The Federal Reserve System examines member banks, the Comptroller of the Currency examines national banks, and the FDIC examines insured banks. Thus, a nationally chartered, insured, Federal Reserve System member bank could be examined by all three agencies. In practice, the federal and state agencies cooperate in conducting bank examinations so that duplication is reduced and the banks are not being examined continuously.

Mutual savings banks are not nationally chartered, so there is no specific federal supervising agency. However, those mutual savings banks that choose to belong to the FDIC and/or the Federal Reserve System are supervised by those agencies.

Those savings and loan associations that are chartered by the federal government are supervised by the Federal Home Loan Bank Board and its insuring branch, the Federal Savings and Loan Insurance Corporation. State-chartered savings and loan associations and all mutual savings banks are supervised by the state banking agencies.

Many proposals have been made to consolidate the regulation of financial institutions into one federal agency. However, resistance to change has always prevailed. *The Financial Institutions and the Nation's Economy (FINE) Discussion Principles* suggested the creation of a Federal Depository Institutions Commission, which would assume responsibility for the regulation of all federally insured financial institutions. This new superagency would regulate, insure, and examine all commercial banks, mutual savings banks, savings and loan associations, and credit unions now insured by any federal government agency. The agency would have responsibilities to maintain both the soundness and the competitiveness of financial institutions. To preserve a role for state regulators, the federal agency could delegate some of its powers to state banking authorities.[5]

The present division of powers between supervisory agencies is very apparent in the regulation of the structure of the banking industry. The next section describes the process of regulating the chartering of banks, branch banking, bank mergers, and bank holding companies.

Regulating the Structure of the Banking Industry

Economists believe that the structure of an industry affects the performance of that industry. For example, theory indicates that the perfect monopolist will restrict output and increase price to achieve maximum profits. The structure of the industry (only one firm) affects behavior (output and pricing decisions).

In banking, society desires a competitive environment consistent with the avoidance of bank failures. The achievement of this goal requires regulatory concern with all changes in the competitive pattern and the constraints within which the individual bank operates. The regulator must be concerned with new bank formations, branching, mergers, and holding company formations and acquisitions. These structural changes are considered in the following sections.

Bank Entry

The formation of a new commercial bank is the first part of the examination of banking structure. The establishment of a new bank requires a charter from either the state banking commissioner or from the Administrator of National Banks in the Office of the Comptroller of the Currency, which is in the U.S. Treasury Department.

The existence of a dual chartering system—bank incorporation by both state and federal authorities—results from the historical development of American banking. The opposition to a national banking system was expressed in the battle between President Andrew Jackson and the Second Bank of the United States. Jackson's victory resulted in the withdrawal of the federal government from bank chartering until the Civil War era. In the interim, bank formation was controlled by the various states. In some states, banks were chartered by a regulatory process; in other states they were chartered by individual acts of the state legislature. As indicated in the discussion of the money supply in Chapter 2, the quality of state banks and the extent to which they were regulated varied widely between states. In 1863 and 1864, the federal government established the national banking system to

[5] *Financial Institutions and the Nation's Economy (FINE) Discussion Principles,* 94th Cong., 1st Sess., Committee on Banking, Currency and Housing, November 1975, pp. 11–13.

provide stable banks and a uniform currency. The tax placed on the note issue of the state banks was expected to result in the demise of state banks. However, not all state banks converted to national charters, although those banks that did not convert ceased issuing notes. Thus, there remains both a state banking system and a national banking system. Today neither type of bank can issue notes, and the powers of state-chartered and nationally chartered banks are very similar.

The existence of dual chartering means that the incorporators of a proposed new bank can select their primary regulator. That is, the regulated are allowed to select their regulator! The decision as to which type of charter to seek depends on several considerations. One is whether the current state bank commissioner in the state of incorporation is more likely to grant the charter than is the Comptroller of the Currency. Another is whether the potential bankers believe membership in the Federal Reserve System would be beneficial.

If the bank receives a national charter, membership in the Federal Reserve System is required; with a state charter, membership in the Federal Reserve System is optional. The major benefit of being a member is the ability to borrow reserves from the Federal Reserve Banks; the major cost is maintaining the high level of reserve requirements imposed by the Federal Reserve. The ultimate decision-making variable appears to be the comparison of state reserve requirements with those of the Federal Reserve System. Each state determines, by statute, the level and form of reserves that must be held by state-chartered banks. In some states, requirements are low; one state (Illinois) imposes no minimum requirements. In a few states, state requirements are even higher than the Federal Reserve's requirements, which gives banks the incentive to belong to the Federal Reserve System.

The reserve requirements imposed by the Federal Reserve specify percentages of demand and time deposits which must be held as nonearning deposits at a regional Reserve Bank. To the bank, this may mean that 10 to 22 percent of its demand deposits are held as reserves and produce no income. If the state requires only a 10 percent requirement and allows a portion of that 10 percent to be held as income-producing liquid assets, the cost of belonging to the Federal Reserve System is very high; unless the bank plans to use the Federal Reserve's services very heavily, membership is not profitable.

Some banks consider membership in the Federal Reserve System of prestige value, even though the costs of membership are high. In addition to general prestige, the eligibility of bank executives to serve on committees or boards of the regional Federal Reserve Banks may be worth the cost of membership.

The FINE suggestions would require all federally insured depository institutions to hold reserves at the Federal Reserve Banks. Nearly all financial institutions would thereby become member banks, bear the costs, and receive the benefits, of membership.[6] In the past, nonmember institutions have vigorously resisted being forced to belong to the Federal Reserve System.

[6]Ibid., pp. 2–3.

TABLE 6–1 Bank Charter and Membership, June 30, 1975 (by numbers of banks)

	NUMBER OF BANKS	*PERCENT*
National member	4,730	32.5
State member	1,064	7.3
State nonmember	8,779	60.2
Total	14,573	100.0

SOURCE: *Federal Reserve Bulletin,* November 1975, pp. A14–A15.

The current breakdown of bank charters, according to numbers of banks, is shown in Table 6–1. In Table 6–2, the assets of banks in each membership group are presented. Table 6–1 indicates that only 32.5 percent of all banks are nationally chartered. Most banks have chosen state charters. However, Table 6–2 indicates that 77 percent of total commercial bank assets are held by members of the Federal Reserve System.

Typically, the smaller banks have found that membership in the Federal Reserve System does not provide sufficient benefits to outweigh the costs of meeting higher reserve requirements. The larger banks tend to use the Federal Reserve System's services more extensively and have opted for membership in spite of the usually higher reserve requirements.

Once the regulatory agency has been decided upon, the incorporators must then convince that agency to award them the charter. This process is by no means easy. Those forming the bank must satisfy the agency's requirements in three general areas:

1. They must show that the proposed management has the ability to operate a bank, is honest, and would inspire public confidence in the bank.

2. They must show that the public need and convenience would be served by the establishment of the proposed bank.

3. They must show that the bank would be able to achieve profitability within a reasonable period of time.

Naturally, the existing banks in the market area of the proposed bank will oppose the granting of a new charter. Not wanting a new competitor, they will lobby formally and informally against granting the charter.

The applicants for a charter will argue that they would provide more, better, and cheaper services to the community than are being provided by the existing banks. They will also argue that their entry would not have a significant adverse effect on the existing banks because the community has an unsatisfied demand for credit and banking facilities. Opponents of the new charter will, of course, argue that they are providing all banking services and credit needed by the community, that granting a new charter will produce excessive competition, which

TABLE 6–2 Bank Charter and Membership, June 30, 1975 (by assets in millions of dollars)

	ASSETS (millions of dollars)	*PERCENT*
National member	536,836	57.7
State member	179,787	19.3
State nonmember	214,434	23.0
Total	931,057	100.0

SOURCE: *Federal Reserve Bulletin,* November 1975, pp. A14–A15.

would mean that none of the banks would be able to earn a profit and so one or more banks might fail.

The banking agency must then decide whether the public need and convenience would be served by granting the new bank charter. Many people believed that the country was "overbanked" at the start of the 1930s as a result of too liberal bank chartering. After the experience of the 1930s, the bias swung in the opposite direction and, in an attempt to increase the safety of the system, chartering became overly restrictive. Only in the early 1960s did the recognition of the need for greater competition result in an increased level of approved applications for new bank charters.

As Table 6–3 indicates, recent years have witnessed an increase in new chartering activity on both the state and federal levels. The formation of new banks has not been distributed evenly between states. A large portion of the new banks are located in those states that prohibit or limit branch banking. If existing banks are not free to enter a new market area, new banks are formed to operate either as independent entities or as parts of holding companies. Thus, the next topic to be considered is the influence of branch banking on the development of the structure of the banking industry.

Branch Banking

Each state establishes the limitations, if any, on branching by banks headquartered in that state. The national banking laws of the 1860s did not provide for branches to be established by nationally chartered banks; the fear of a large national bank with many branches still persisted. The national banks operated under a competitive handicap in those states that allowed state banks to operate branch offices. The McFadden Act of 1927 and the Banking Act of 1933 removed this competitive handicap by permitting national banks in a given state to branch to the same geographical extent as state banks could branch. Thus, state limitations on branching apply to both state-chartered and nationally chartered banks.

TABLE 6–3 New Bank Charters, by Decade

	NATIONAL	*STATE*	*TOTAL*
1936–1945	55	480	535
1946–1955	156	705	861
1956–1965	663	1023	1686
1966–1975	465	1651	2116

SOURCES: Data for 1936–1955 are found in Ross M. Robertson, *The Comptroller and Bank Supervision,* Office of the Comptroller of the Currency, Washington, D.C., 1968, pp. 128–129. Annual data for 1956–1975 are found in the *Federal Reserve Bulletin.*

The degree of branch banking permitted by the various states ranges from *unit banking* (an absolute prohibition of branching) to full statewide branching. Between these extremes are a variety of schemes for permitting the establishment of branches within regions of the states. Common examples are branching within the county in which the home office is located, branching in home and adjacent counties, branching within a limited radius of the home office, and branching within market areas of the state.

Nationally, the data on branch banking indicate that of 14,936 commercial and mutual savings banks, only 5,477 operate one or more branch offices. However, those 5,477 banks have a total of 29,886 branches, of which 10,304 are in the head office city, 9,213 are in the head office county, 5,415 are in contiguous counties, and 4,954 are in noncontiguous counties.

However, these national data do not tell the whole story, for there are also differences in state banking laws. For example, in California, 131 commercial banks operate 3,459 branches. On the other extreme, Wyoming has 74 commercial banks and no branches (except for one limited office serving a government facility). Illinois has 1,203 commercial banks and only 186 branches, all but one of which are in the home office city.[7] Thus, there are wide variations in branching laws throughout the United States.

Proponents of large-scale branch banking claim there are at least eight advantages:

1. Large institutions will develop, which are able to achieve the economies of scale.

2. Large institutions are able to provide specialized services that could not be provided by smaller unit banks.

3. Banking services can be provided in communities that are large enough

[7] All data on branch banking are from *Federal Reserve Bulletin,* April 1975, pp. A76–A77.

to support a branch office but not large enough to support the home office of a unit bank.

4. Large institutions can pay wages sufficiently high to attract qualified specialists in particular subareas of the financial business.

5. There is greater competition in an area that might support only one unit bank but can support two or three branches of different branch banking organizations.

6. Large institutions can serve the public need and convenience by locating branches in suburban areas, shopping centers, and places other than the typical downtown location of the main office.

7. Loan risks are diversified over a wider geographical area.

8. Funds can be reallocated from areas having high deposit potential and low loan demand to areas having low deposit potential and high loan demand.

Opponents of the growth of branch banking also have eight arguments:

1. Branch banking, they say, leads to the domination of the banking industry by a small number of very large banks, which may not, in fact, compete very vigorously with each other.

2. The branch office manager's primary loyalty is to the branch bank's home office. Therefore, he is less concerned with community development than is the president of a locally based unit bank.

3. The branch office may siphon funds out of the community by lending the community's deposits in areas served by other branch offices.

4. The development of the large branch-banking system forces the unit bank to either close or sell out to a branch-banking organization. The branch bank entering an area served by a unit bank can underprice its services at that branch office and cover the losses with profits earned by other offices. The unit bank, totally dependent on business from that one area, is unable to meet the price competition and is forced out of business.

5. Correspondent banking relationships between the small unit bank and large urban banks enable the unit bank to supply all the services provided by the large branch bank.

6. The economies of scale claimed by the branch banks are in fact associated with bank size; therefore, with a large institution these economies are reduced by the expense of maintaining many offices.

7. The branch office cannot make decisions as rapidly as the local unit bank because important decisions must be referred to the home office by the local branch manager.

8. The branch office does not provide all services at all branches, and the consumer must go to the head office to obtain the claimed extra services of the branch banking organization.

Still, when all the evidence relative to branch banking is evaluated, the claims of the advocates of expanded branch banking stand up better than those of its opponents.[8] While all the studies cannot be cited here, a number of points seem clear:

1. The population per banking office is much lower in states that allow branch banking than in unit-banking states. Using the availability of banking offices as a measure of the extent to which the financial system is meeting the needs and convenience of the public provides a point in favor of branching.

2. The widespread development of branch banking in other countries has not reduced the competitiveness of commercial banking. Countries such as Canada and England have only a handful of major banks, each with thousands of branches countrywide.

3. There is no evidence that the growth of branch banking has really hurt unit banks. The well-managed unit bank can survive and prosper in an environment of extensive branch banking.

4. The existence of branch banking has provided a market for the sale of small unit banks. The owner of a small bank who desires to sell out finds that he can obtain a better price for his bank when branch banking is permitted. The branch banks are looking for new offices and have the capital to purchase the small unit bank.

5. The trend toward suburbanization provides impetus to the branching movement. The central-city bank wants to follow its customers from downtown to the suburbs and to the shopping centers. The provision of banking facilities at all locations necessary to meet the public needs and convenience demands some degree of branch banking.

Regardless of how strong various economic arguments may be, they are frequently lost in the intense political battles that surround proposals to change state branch-banking laws. No issue is more likely to divide bankers. The large city banks desire a liberalization of branching legislation so that they can expand their market area. The suburban and rural unit banks, fearful of an invasion by the large city banks, want to protect their traditional market areas. The outcome of this struggle may depend upon relative political strength in the state legislatures. Thus, the impetus of branch banking should be increased as the one-man-one-vote decisions of the U.S. Supreme Court reduce the traditional rural domination of many state legislatures.

Even where state laws permit branch banking, a bank cannot open a branch office when or where it wants. The opening of a new branch is regulated in a manner similar to the chartering of a new bank. The bank applying for permission to open a branch office must demonstrate that the new office will serve the needs

[8]For a recent survey of the evidence on branch banking, see G. G. Gilbert and W. A. Longbrake, "The Effects of Branching by Financial Institutions on Competition, Productive Efficiency and Stability: An Examination of the Evidence," *Journal of Bank Research,* vol. 4, no. 3 (Autumn 1973), pp. 154–167.

TABLE 6–4 State Branching Laws[a]

	NUMBER OF STATES
Allow statewide branching	22
Allow limited branching	15
Allow no branching	14

[a]Table includes District of Columbia.

SOURCE: Division of Research and Statistics, Board of Governors of the Federal Reserve System, September 1975. Includes approved changes effective in 1976 and 1977.

and convenience of the public and not endanger the existence of other banking offices in the same market area. Opponents of the new branch—the unit banks and other banks having branches in the area—have their opportunity to oppose the granting of permission to establish a new branch.

The trend seems to be in favor of larger banks with increasing numbers of branches. Recent changes in branching laws are less restrictive. However, it will be many years before statewide branch banking is permitted in all states. The present division of states according to the permissible degree of branching is presented in Table 6–4.

Future policy decisions will have to be made on the issue of interstate branching. At present, there are only a handful of bank branches operating in states other than their home-offfice state. In many cases, the restriction of interstate branching divides natural market areas. For example, much of northern New Jersey is within the natural market area of New York City. However, the New York City banks cannot branch into New Jersey and the New Jersey banks cannot branch into New York. Likewise, the New York City banks cannot follow their customers to the residential areas of Connecticut.

Given the increasing sophistication of communications equipment, there is no reason why one bank could not manage a nationwide system of branch offices. The pressure for nationwide branching is still somewhat in the future, but it will arise as banks find their opportunities for branching geographically limited by state boundaries.

Nationwide branching would open a whole new set of opportunities for branching and for mergers. The smaller banks would face not only the existing competition from the relatively larger banks in their own state but also competition from the large out-of-state banks. However, the impact of allowing Bank of America, Chase Manhattan Bank, or First National City Bank to branch freely within the nation might fall less on the small rural bank than on the intermediate size banks in the urban centers of various states. One can more easily imagine Chase Manhattan opening a branch in Boston or Atlanta than in Fort Kent, Maine, or Rhinelander, Wisconsin. Similarly, it is doubtful that Wells Fargo would open a branch in Norman, Oklahoma, or Oskaloosa, Iowa.

The FINE discussion principles suggested permitting interstate branching by all federally insured depository institutions under the supervision of the proposed Federal Depository Institutions Commission. In those states where branch banking is not permitted, banks could only branch into cities having populations in excess of 2 million people. In order to preserve competition, interstate branching systems could not be formed via bank mergers.[9]

For large business customers, the existence of interstate branching would not make much difference. The large corporation is not tied to borrowing from large local banks and already seeks its credit on a nationwide basis. The real increase in banking alternatives would be most noticeable for the consumer whose volume of business does not justify trips to New York, Chicago, or San Francisco. Resistance to changes in branching laws may result in interstate branching being delayed until after an Electronic Funds Transfer System has accomplished the same objectives.

Bank Mergers

The third point at which the structure of the banking industry is regulated is the merger of two or more banks. Between 1950 and 1974, nearly 3,500 bank mergers took place.[10] In most mergers, the smaller bank was acquired by the larger bank and the offices of the smaller bank became branch offices of the larger, acquiring bank. Mergers are to be expected because as businesses grow the size of banks must also increase. Otherwise, the banks would not be large enough to meet the credit needs of business.

Mergers, like all other banking activities, are regulated by the banking authorities. The basic framework for the control of bank mergers is provided by the Bank Merger Act of 1960, which divided the regulation of mergers between the three Federal banking agencies on the basis of the membership of the bank resulting from the merger. Thus, if the surviving bank is to be an insured, state nonmember bank of the Federal Reserve System, approval of the merger is sought from the Federal Deposit Insurance Corporation. If the resulting bank is to be a state bank belonging to the Federal Reserve, the Federal Reserve System would consider the merger application. Finally, if the surviving bank is to be a national bank, the Comptroller of the Currency becomes the governing agency in the merger process. In each case, the agency is required to seek an opinion from the U.S. Department of Justice relative to the expected impact of the proposed merger on competition.

The Bank Merger Act established a series of banking factors to be consid-

[9] *Financial Institutions and the Nation's Economy (FINE) Discussion Principles,* op. cit., p. 3.

[10] Calculated from annual table, "Number of Banking Offices in the United States," *Federal Reserve Bulletin,* February issues, 1951–1975.

ered by the regulatory agencies in conjunction with the competitive factors. The banking factors include the financial history and condition of each of the banks involved, the adequacy of their capital structures, future earnings prospects, the management of the banks, and the needs and convenience of the community.

The application and interpretation of the Bank Merger Act involved a great deal of litigation relative to the relationship between the antitrust laws and the Bank Merger Act. For example, if the relevant agency determines that the positive benefits of the banking factors outweigh any negative factors in terms of loss of competition, can the merger be attacked under the Sherman and Clayton antitrust acts? The answer is yes. The 1963 Philadelphia National Bank case established that bank mergers, even though approved by the banking agencies, could be challenged under Section 7 of the Clayton Act. This section prohibits mergers that would have the effect of substantially reducing competition or tending to create a monopoly. In 1964, the First National Bank of Lexington (Kentucky) case established that bank mergers could be prohibited under Section 1 of the Sherman Antitrust Act, which prohibits monopolies.

Under the 1966 Amendments to the Bank Merger Act, should the Justice Department believe that a proposed merger would reduce competition or tend to create a monopoly, suit must be brought within 30 days of the approval of the merger by the banking agencies. If the merger is challenged, the banks cannot merge until the courts decide whether the proposed merger would violate the antitrust laws.

In the past few years, the merger movement has slowed down to approximately 100 mergers per year. There are at least two reasons for this slowdown. First, many of the banks that were good merger candidates have already been acquired by other banks. During the heavy merger years, the typical acquired bank was relatively small—too small to achieve economies of scale, too small to provide sizable loans to businesses, too small to obtain new capital for expansion, and too small to provide for management succession. A frequently used justification for merger was the advanced age of the management of the bank to be acquired. Thus, merger became a way for aging bank owners and managers to retire and shift their estates from relatively illiquid bank stock to other assets.

Second, the merger process usually resulted in the offices of the acquired bank becoming branches of the acquiring bank. Thus, the limitations placed on branch banking have tended to limit the possibilities for mergers. Finally, growing concentration in many banking markets reduced the possibility that mergers would be approved by the regulatory agencies and not be challenged in court by the Justice Department.

Bank Holding Companies

The slowdown in the merger movement coincided with the growth of the bank holding company. The *holding company* is a device to bring two or more banks, or a bank and other related businesses, under the control of one corporation. The system is fairly simple. Assume Bank A desires to form a holding company. A new corporation called United Bankshares (an assumed name) is formed. The stockholders of Bank A swap their stock for an equal proportion of United Bankshares stock. Now, United Bankshares owns the stock of Bank A, and the former stockholders of Bank A are the stockholders of United Bankshares. United Bankshares is a bank holding company; it owns a bank but does not itself do a banking business.

United Bankshares next arranges a stock swap with the stockholders of Bank B. Bank B is now owned by United Bankshares and the former stockholders of Bank B now hold stock in United Bankshares. Obviously, any number of banks can be brought into the holding company group. The banks in the holding company may operate as completely independent units under their original names or may be given a name that identifies their membership in the holding company group.

There are three economic incentives for forming bank holding companies.

1. There may be economies in the joint use of certain facilities. For example, each of the banks in the holding company may be too small to afford its own computer facilities, so the holding company forms a computing subsidiary and all the banks in the holding company share its use and cost, with unneeded computer time being sold to other firms.

2. The holding company device provides a way around restrictive state branching laws. While the major bank in the holding company may be prohibited from branching into a given area, the acquisition of a bank in that area by the holding company is legal. Thus, holding companies have tended to grow most rapidly in those areas where branching is restricted. Although the number of banks has not decreased, as it would have if mergers and branching had been allowed, the concentration of banking has increased as more and more previously independent banks are brought into holding company operations.

3. The holding company movement has permitted banks to diversify into operations related to banking. While banking law has always attempted to keep banking a separate line of commerce and prevent diversification, the holding company provides a way around these prohibitions. The holding company, not the bank, is entering other businesses.

Diversification by bank holding companies involves some dangers. In general, the problems center around the maintenance of "arm's length" relationships between the subsidiary bank and other subsidiaries of the holding company. Assume the holding company owns ABC Computer Service Corporation. Will ABC Computer receive preferential treatment from ABC Bank? How will the competitive pattern of the computer service business be affected if other computer service companies have to pay higher interest rates because they are not affiliated with bank holding companies? Secondly, assume ABC Computer Service Corporation falls upon bad times and is in danger of failing. Will ABC Bank be pressured by ABC Holding Company to lend funds to the computer service company on terms that the bank would not give to an unaffiliated computer service company?

The bank may be forced to accept a loan risk greater than it would normally accept and endanger its own solvency.

Legislation regulating holding companies was passed by Congress in 1956 under the Bank Holding Company Act. This act placed the responsibility for the control of holding companies with the Federal Reserve System, so that both the formation of a bank holding company and each acquisition of a bank or other business are subject to the approval of the Board of Governors of the Federal Reserve. Most of the criteria and mechanisms for the approval of holding company acquisitions are similar to those of the merger approval process. The Federal Reserve must consider both the banking factors and the competitive factors in making its decisions. As with bank mergers, holding company acquisitions can be challenged by the Justice Department under antitrust laws.

The competitive factors in the holding company process are more difficult to judge. In many cases, the bank that is being acquired by the holding company is not competitive with those banks already owned by the holding company. Prohibitions against branching may prevent the banks in the holding company from branching into the market area of the new acquisition. However, there could be competition between the banks if branching laws were changed, or elsewhere if branching is permitted but has not yet occurred. The issue of potential competition has yet to be established conclusively in the courts.

The 1970 amendments to the Bank Holding Company Act brought one-bank holding companies under coverage of the law and provided for supervision of the nonbanking activities of all bank holding companies. The Federal Reserve was charged with the responsibility for developing a "laundry list" of permissible activities for bank holding companies. The list of permissible activities includes only those activities closely related to banking. Some permissible activities include ownership of companies that hold property for the banks in the holding company group, provide computer services to the banks and others, and underwrite credit life insurance sold by the banks in the holding company group.

Table 6–5 indicates the importance of holding companies on a state-by-state basis. Note the wide variation in the percentage of banking offices operated by banks in bank holding companies in the various states. As expected, there are more bank holding companies operating more banks in the unit banking states than in the branch banking states.

Regulating the Powers of the Banking System

In addition to regulating the structure of the banking system, bank regulations also cover the sources and the uses of funds of the banking system. Both the goal of preventing bank failures and the goal of promoting competition are affected by the regulation of the means by which banks attract funds and the subsequent use of the funds. Many of these regulations have been discussed previously and are only briefly cited at this point.

TABLE 6–5 Banking Offices and Assets of Banks in Holding Company Groups, December 31, 1974[a]

BRANCHING CLASS	NUMBER OF BANK HOLDING COMPANIES	NUMBER OF BANKS OWNED BY BANK HOLDING COMPANIES	OFFICES OF BANKS IN BANK HOLDING COMPANIES AS A PERCENTAGE OF ALL COMMERCIAL BANK OFFICES	ASSETS OF BANKS IN BANK HOLDING COMPANIES AS A PERCENTAGE OF ALL COMMERCIAL BANK ASSETS
Statewide branching states				
Alaska	2	1	5.8	9.5
Ariz.	5	6	59.2	54.6
Calif.	43	46	85.1	93.8
Conn.	9	14	58.7	71.8
D.C.	5	3	31.2	23.1
Del.	4	3	23.6	15.9
Hawaii	2	2	65.1	69.0
Idaho	5	5	54.2	53.4
Maine	7	26	70.4	72.0
Md.	14	24	64.3	74.5
N.C.	10	13	60.5	72.3
N.J.	21	63	47.4	54.9
Nev.	3	3	68.1	64.8
Oreg.	5	6	67.5	81.6
R.I.	10	10	90.8	96.2
S.C.	7	8	46.9	53.9
S. Dak.	29	41	45.1	60.9
Utah	9	15	74.8	81.3
Va.	21	121	73.1	79.4
Vt.	3	3	20.0	26.9
Wash.	6	10	54.6	69.4
Limited branching states				
Ala.	15	63	47.3	57.7
Ga.	30	40	35.1	58.9
Ind.	32	29	23.2	38.2
Ky.	8	9	13.1	21.4
La.	16	17	17.1	36.7
Mass.	33	70	74.6	88.9
Mich.	45	101	53.6	72.6
Miss.	4	4	10.9	26.1
N.H.	6	17	26.0	37.5
N. Mex.	10	28	53.4	68.1
N.Y.	46	124	76.3	88.6
Ohio	37	138	46.8	63.4
Pa.	26	28	36.4	59.3
Tenn.	17	72	43.6	63.9
Wis.	62	156	28.2	52.9
Unit banking states				
Ark.	21	23	14.2	21.0
Colo.	75	144	47.4	79.6
Fla.	62	448	63.4	80.5
Ill.	161	157	14.3	62.9
Iowa	147	179	31.3	42.0
Kans.	136	135	24.9	35.2
Minn.	111	231	33.0	71.5
Mo.	98	235	39.5	70.6
Mont.	32	65	43.7	68.4
Nebr.	140	138	35.1	58.0
N. Dak.	20	48	31.0	42.5
Okla.	63	61	15.6	49.6
Texas	93	235	18.7	58.5
W. Va.	9	9	4.6	4.5
Wyo.	22	35	46.7	57.5

[a] States assigned to branching groups according to *Federal Reserve System* classifications as of September 1975.

SOURCE: "Banking Offices and Deposits of Banks in Holding Company Groups," *Federal Reserve Bulletin,* June 1975, pp. A76–78.

Raising Funds

The most significant limitations on the ability to raise funds are the traditional prohibition against demand deposit accounts at thrift institutions and the prohibition against paying interest on checking account balances. Regulation Q ceilings on interest rates payable on time deposits also restrict competition for funds. In addition, the difference between Regulation Q ceilings applicable to thrift institutions and those applicable to commercial banks create differences in the ability to attract funds.

New methods of obtaining funds bring new forms of regulation in their wake. Eurodollar borrowings, repurchase agreements, and holding company commercial paper all developed as unregulated sources of funds. However, regulations soon were developed to reclassify these borrowings as deposits subject to reserve requirements.

Thus, regulation and law cover both the terms on which funds can be obtained and the maximum interest rate that can be paid for deposits.

Uses of Funds

The employment of funds by financial institutions has also been regulated closely. These regulations have taken a variety of forms:

1. Certain institutions have been limited in the types of loans that can be made. For example, thrift institutions are usually prohibited from making business loans, or at least limited in their ability to do so.

2. The maximum size of a loan may be limited by either a fixed dollar ceiling or a specified percentage of the institution's capital. Most commercial bank regulations limit the maximum loan to a given borrower to 10 percent of the bank's capital and surplus.

3. The purchase of securities by financial institutions has been regulated by the use of either a legal list or the prudent man rule. The *legal list* has declined in use, but was once a popular method of controlling the security investments of some types of institutions—especially mutual savings banks. The state banking department would list specific securities eligible for purchase by institutions subject to the legal list requirement. The use of the legal list approach naturally was designed to prevent the regulated institutions from investing in securities below the quality levels considered appropriate by the banking authorities. The *prudent man rule* does away with the listing of specific eligible securities and places the burden of selection on the institution rather than on the regulator. The test of eligibility is whether a "prudent" man would invest in a particular security.

4. In some cases, regulations limit the maximum term of given types of loans. Limits on the term to maturity of loans increase the institution's liquidity.

5. The specification of a given level and form of reserves to protect the liquidity and solvency of an institution has placed limits on the lending ability of financial intermediaries.

6. Regulations specifying the percentage of downpayment or purchaser equity have been used to control the purchase of consumer-durable goods and common stock. Again, these regulations have been used both to protect the institution and to limit these types of borrowing.

Banking regulators, then, have attempted to preserve the liquidity and solvency of the financial system by controlling the methods by which funds are both obtained and used. The questions that remain, however, are whether the regulators have gone too far in this process and whether the effect of detailed regulation has been to restrict competition.

Competition in Banking

The regulation of financial institutions is designed to protect the liquidity and solvency of the institutions and at the same time maintain competition in the industry. Thus, some attention should be given to the measurement of competition in the provision of financial services.

There are a number of problems in studying competition. First, one must determine the nature of the services rendered by the industry. Each particular service may be provided by one or more of the various types of institutions. For example, to analyze competition in savings accounts the analysis of concentration ratios should include data from commercial banks, mutual savings banks, savings and loan associations, and credit unions. However, to study competition in commercial and industrial loans, one can confine the analysis to commercial banks, because the other financial institutions do not normally make commercial or industrial loans. Therefore, for each service, a given subset of institutions should be included in the analysis.

Second, the definition of the market within which competition is to be measured varies with the nature of the service being provided. For the very large commercial loan, the market is nationwide. Banks from all over the country compete for the business of large firms with good credit ratings. However, for the consumer's car loan the market is basically local, because the consumer cannot afford to shop nationwide for the loan and the lender cannot afford to investigate the credit worthiness of consumers outside his market area. Thus, the loan size, the availability of knowledge of the borrower's credit rating, and the cost of obtaining information determine the relevant market within which to measure market concentration.

Data on the concentration of commercial banking are presented in Table 6–6. The data are presented in terms of the 100 largest banking organizations (either bank holding companies or banks). The national data indicate that in 1957 the 100 largest banking organizations held 48.2 percent of total commercial bank deposits, and in the period 1957–1973 that share changed very little.

TABLE 6–6 Percent of Total Domestic Deposits Held by the 100 Largest Banking Organizations, 1957–1973

YEAR	*PERCENT OF DEPOSITS HELD BY 100 LARGEST BANKING ORGANIZATIONS*
1957	48.2
1961	49.4
1966	49.3
1968	49.0
1973	47.0

SOURCE: Samuel H. Talley, "The Impact of Holding Company Acquisitions on Aggregate Concentration in Banking," *Staff Economic Studies,* No. 80, Board of Governors of the Federal Reserve System, Washington, D.C., 1974, p. 6.

The state data on concentration are presented in Table 6–7. In the table the states are subdivided by branching classification, whether they permit statewide branching, limited branching, or unit banking. The average proportion of deposits held by the five largest banking organizations is highest in those states permitting statewide branch banking and lowest in the unit banking states.

The interpretation of concentration data is always hazardous. The existence of high concentration ratios in the statewide branching states does not necessarily mean that banking is less competitive in those states than in the unit-banking states. A state might have only five banking organizations, but each organization might have a branch or subsidiary in each town in the state and these five banks would compete vigorously. Alternatively, each town in the state could have one unit bank functioning as a local monopolist.

In recent years, the analysis of banking concentration data is further complicated by the growth of holding companies. Thus, while data were traditionally presented on a bank basis, data must now be developed in a manner that treats each holding company group as if it were one bank. However, in some cases, the holding company affiliates compete as though they were independent banks.

Finally, the analysis has considered only commercial banks. Many of the services offered by commercial banks are also offered by other financial institutions. With the expected expansion of the powers of thrift institutions, the degree of competition in the provision of many bank services should increase.

In summary, banking appears to be a relatively competitive industry on the national level and in most states. In some states, however, questions can be raised relative to the existing degree of concentration. Local and regional monopoly situations can still exist—especially in unit banking states. The power of existing monopolies is reduced in importance both by the ability of larger customers to deal

TABLE 6–7 Percent of Statewide Deposits Held by Five Largest Banking Organizations, 1957–1973

Statewide branching	*1957*	*1973*
Alaska	81.5	87.9
Ariz.	98.6	94.7
Calif.	76.5	75.6
Conn.	49.3	61.3
D.C.	73.4	88.8
Del.	86.6	92.0
Hawaii	N.A.	89.2
Idaho	85.2	87.9
Maine	38.8	69.9
Md.	51.9	61.3
Nev.	100.0	97.0
N.C.	42.4	68.1
Oreg.	91.4	83.1
R.I.	98.2	92.7
S.C.	50.6	56.1
S. Dak.	42.9	49.3
Utah	78.8	72.0
Va.	28.0	50.7
Vt.	29.1	54.9
Wash.	74.4	76.2
Limited branching	*1957*	*1973*
Ala.	41.5	45.1
Ga.	50.7	47.7
Ind.	27.4	25.1
Ky.	32.3	29.7
La.	40.3	28.1
Mass.	57.3	62.9
Mich.	52.9	46.9
Miss.	25.7	33.4
N.H.	34.7	40.1
N.J.	22.5	29.3
N. Mex.	56.6	63.6
N.Y.	52.3	55.4
Ohio	35.3	33.3
Pa.	36.3	33.4
Tenn.	40.1	42.1
Wis.	31.5	32.9
Unit banking	*1957*	*1973*
Ark.	24.2	21.0
Colo.	41.0	47.6
Fla.	21.0	31.7
Ill.	42.5	41.3
Iowa	20.8	18.5
Kans.	19.8	13.2
Minn.	63.7	57.4
Mo.	38.8	32.8
Mont.	58.4	52.8
Nebr.	40.3	31.8
N. Dak.	53.1	49.8
Okla.	41.1	28.7
Texas	26.4	25.3
W. Va.	24.6	17.5
Wyo.	48.1	45.0

SOURCE: Samuel H. Talley, "The Impact of Holding Company Acquisitions on Aggregate Concentration in Banking," *Staff Economic Studies,* No. 80, Board of Governors of the Federal Reserve System, Washington, D.C., 1974 pp. 15–16.

with banks outside the area and by the threat of new entry if high profits are achieved.

The Profitability of Commercial Banking

In a regulated industry, the level of profitability achieved may indicate the impact of the regulatory process. Regulation may reduce the profits of the industry to such a low level that growth is impossible. Alternatively, the regulatory process may, by limiting entry and competition, guarantee high profits for the regulated firms.

In banking, the traditional emphasis on liquidity and solvency could lead to too little competition among the existing banks. Protected against real or potential competition, the existing firms could earn greater than normal profits. Table 6–8 examines the profits of all insured commercial banks for the years 1965–1974. Profit data for all manufacturing corporations are included for comparison. Naturally, the aggregate data conceal the degree of variation in profits between individual banks.

The data in Table 6–8 do not seem to indicate that the banks have, as a group, earned exorbitant profits. A return of 11% or less hardly seems to be a high return on capital. Given the years covered by Table 6–8, the rate of return on capital may be above the long-run profit level. All the years covered in the table were years of high loan demand. Loans are the greatest income producers for the banks and income is higher in a period of high loan demand. In addition, the years covered in the table were high-interest-rate years. In a period in which high-grade corporate bonds—involving very minimal risk—were yielding 8 to 9 percent and ordinary savings accounts were paying over 5 percent, the return on capital earned by the banking system does not appear to be too high.

Thus, examination of the aggregate data does not confirm the hypothesis that the overall regulatory process works to the great advantage of the banks. Those who look at the high interest rates charged by the banks during this period and assume that the banks must be making great profits are simply neglecting the fact that while loan rates were relatively high, the cost of the funds to the banks was also unusually high.

Conclusion

This chapter has indicated the concerns of the regulatory process for the maintenance of liquidity, solvency, and competition in the banking industry, and the various ways society has organized the regulatory process to achieve these goals. Trends indicate that the future emphasis will be toward a greater amount of freedom for the individual institution to expand its powers and be competitive in more markets. On an aggregate basis, greater relative emphasis is being placed on competition as opposed to the traditional concerns of banking safety. Society and bank regulators finally may have recovered from the national banking trauma of

TABLE 6–8 The Profitability of Insured Banks

Year	After-tax net income	Total assets	Total capital	Net income/ total assets (percent)	Net income total capital (percent)	After-tax profits/equity all manufacturing corporations (percent)
	THOUSANDS OF DOLLARS					
1965	2,514,733	357,214,409	28,820,861	0.70	8.72	13.0
1966	2,684,340	387,113,663	30,850,686	0.69	8.70	13.4
1967	3,141,858	421,128,433	32,876,674	0.74	9.55	11.7
1968	3,425,938	468,213,101	35,332,148	0.73	9.69	12.1
1969	4,334,567	516,325,000	38,215,000	0.83	11.34	11.5
1970	4,816,939	542,255,000	47,239,000	0.88	10.19	9.3
1971	5,212,217	601,390,000	50,980,000	0.86	10.22	9.7
1972	5,628,482	676,721,000	56,125,000	0.83	10.03	10.6
1973	6,555,188	774,031,000	62,274,000	0.85	10.53	12.8
1974	7,067,444	868,407,000	68,691,000	0.81	10.29	14.9

SOURCES: Banking data from *Federal Reserve Bulletin,* May issues 1966–1973 and June issues 1974–1975; manufacturing data from *1976 Economic Report of the President,* p. 261.

the 1930s and realized that higher degrees of competition can be achieved without any significant loss of safety.

Is the Financial System Meeting Social Objectives?

In general it is difficult to criticize the present American financial system in terms of the topics considered in this part of the book. By general measure, the system is working well:

1. The chronic problem of bank failures, which plagued the financial system for so long, has apparently been solved. The system has achieved the basic stability that is a precondition for all other objectives.

2. The system appears, with increasing success, to be able to weather various periods of strain, such as prolonged periods of extremely high interest rates. The problems of disintermediation which threatened the system in 1966 and 1969 seemed to have been less threatening in 1974.

3. The system shows continued ability to develop new methods of meeting the financial needs of the economy. The development of new forms of lending and new methods of attracting funds are evidence of flexibility and adaptability. The outlook is for greater amounts of innovation as methods of providing for the widespread use of electronic transfer of funds come closer to reality.

4. Although the merger and holding company movements present the threat of reduced competition, procedures to control these trends are in effect and represent some degree of restraining power.

5. The gradual movement toward nationwide banking represents the hope of increasing competition over time. Although the banking system has traditionally been regulated on a state-by-state basis, more banks perform some functions on a national basis and eventually it may be possible to measure competition in all banking services on a national basis.

6. The problem of providing an acceptable means of payment is solved. The dollar is completely acceptable domestically, and though its international value is no longer as stable as it once was, the dollar remains a basic international currency. However, maintaining the stable purchasing power of the dollar—the store of value function—continues to be a problem. This problem is discussed in Part II.

7. The noncommercial bank financial intermediaries, which experienced more disintermediation difficulties than the commercial banks, appear to be adjusting to continued high interest rates. The recommendations of the Hunt Commission should provide more stable thrift institutions.

The major remaining problem areas appear in the next three parts of the book; however, the financial structure seems to be in good shape and on the verge of achieving new and more progressive institutional arrangements for meeting the needs of the economy and the general public.

REVIEW QUESTIONS

1. How is banking regulated in your state? Are the majority of banks federally chartered or state-chartered? To what extent does state law permit branch banking?

2. Why is the responsibility for bank regulation divided between so many state and federal agencies? What are the costs and benefits of this division?

3. What factors enter the decision to grant a new bank charter?

4. How are applications for bank mergers and bank holding-company acquisitions judged?

5. Why are the nonbanking activities of bank holding companies restricted?

6. What are the costs and benefits of prohibiting interstate branch banking?

7. What forces tended to create the bank merger movement? What forces encouraged the growth of bank holding companies?

8. Why is the measurement of concentration in the banking industry difficult? Has there been an increase or decrease in concentration in your state? What factors can you suggest which would account for any change in concentration?

9. Unrestricted chartering of banks would increase competition but might increase the number of bank failures. Has society reached the right tradeoff between stability and competition?

10. A great deal of insight into the regulation of mergers and holding company acquisitions can be obtained by reading the decisions in specific cases. The *Federal Reserve Bulletin* publishes an analysis of most cases handled by the Board of Governors. Read some recent cases and isolate the factors considered in the Board's decision.

SUGGESTED READINGS

Paul S. Anderson and Robert W. Eisenmenger, "Structural Reform for Thrift Institutions: The Experience in the United States and Canada," *New England Economic Review,* Federal Reserve Bank of Boston, July–August 1972, pp. 3–17.

Frederick W. Bell and Neil B. Murphy, *Costs in Commercial Banking: A Quantitative Analysis of Bank Behavior and Its Relation to Bank Regulation,* Federal Reserve Bank of Boston, April 1968.

Edward G. Boehne, "Falling Fed Membership and Eroding Monetary Control: What Can Be Done?" *Federal Reserve Bank of Philadelphia Business Review,* June 1974, pp. 3–15.

Samuel B. Chase, Jr. and John J. Mingo, "The Regulation of Bank Holding Companies," *Journal of Finance,* American Finance Association, New York; May 1975, pp. 281–292.

Donnie L. Daniel, William A. Longbrake, and Neil B. Murphy, "The Effect of Technology on Bank Economies of Scale for Demand Deposits," *Journal of Finance,* American Finance Association, New York; March 1973, pp. 131–146.

Edward C. Gallick, "Bank Size and Profitability," *Federal Reserve Bank of Kansas City Monthly Review,* January 1976, pp. 11–16.

Leon Korobow and David P. Stuhr, "Toward Early Warning of Changes in Banks' Financial Condition: A Progress Report," *Federal Reserve Bank of New York Monthly Review,* July 1975, pp. 157–165.

Brenton C. Leavitt, "Bank Supervision in a Dynamic Environment," *New England Economic Review,* Federal Reserve Bank of Boston, November–December 1974, pp. 24–28.

Policies for a More Competitive Financial System, Federal Reserve Bank of Boston, June 1972.

Charles D. Salley, "Concentration in Banking Markets: Regulatory Numerology or Useful Merger Guideline?" *Federal Reserve Bank of Atlanta Monthly Review,* November 1972, pp. 186–193.

The material studied in Part II is a critical part of a money and banking text, and the controversial material covered in this section is of great importance for the management of the economic system. The principal concern is: how does money affect other economic variables? Related questions are: how can the supply of money be controlled? what is affected by changing the supply of money? can monetary policy contribute to the elimination of recession and inflation? what are the problems involved in the use of monetary policy?

Chapter 7 examines the macroeconomic objectives of American society and the relationship of these objectives to the use of monetary policy. Major questions include the issue of tradeoffs among the economic goals and between economic and noneconomic goals.

The coverage of monetary theory begins in Chapter 8, with an analysis of the process by which the money supply is changed. Chapters 9 through 11 present pre-Keynesian and Keynesian macroeconomic theory. Chapter 12 discusses the present-day dissenters from the Keynesian tradition—the monetarist group led by Milton Friedman of the University of Chicago. All of these chapters examine theories of the relationship between money and the level of economic activity.

The last three chapters, 13 through 15, examine monetary policy—the making of the policy, the methods of conducting the policy, and the results of the policy.

The chapters in this part of the text are somewhat more complex than those in other parts of the book, and the reader is urged to follow the various theoretical analyses with considerable care.

7

MACROECONOMIC MEASURES AND OBJECTIVES

Full employment, the maximum rate of economic growth, and stable prices are all generally accepted macroeconomic goals. These goals are more readily obtainable by the efficient use of monetary management. The theoretical relationships between money and these macroeconomic objectives are the major concern of this part of the book. This chapter examines the goals, questions the definitions of these goals, and describes the possible need to establish tradeoffs among the economic goals and between economic and noneconomic goals. Credit allocation and international balance of payments goals are given less attention here because they are covered in Parts III and IV.

The Measurement of Macroeconomic Well-being

The analysis of the relationship between monetary policy and macroeconomic goals requires an understanding of the measurement systems used by economists to evaluate the performance of the economy. Three general measurement processes are covered in this section of the chapter—the measures of output, prices, and employment.

The development of high-quality economic data is a prerequisite for the establishment of an informed macroeconomic policy. Only very general policy measures can be suggested if there are no data on either the actual performance or the best potential performance of the economy. Larger errors of measurement can be tolerated if the economy is far from a target, but small errors may be disastrous when the economy is close to the target. If the unemployment rate is estimated to be 25 percent of the labor force, an estimating error of plus or minus 10 percent of the labor force is acceptable, because the appropriate policy measures are the same whether the true rate of unemployment is 15 percent or 35 percent—either unemployment rate would call for massive expansionary macroeconomic policies. However, as policy makers attempt to deal with smaller deviations from targets,

PART II

MONEY, ECONOMIC ACTIVITY, AND PRICES

the need for more accurate data increases. If a true unemployment rate of 3 percent were estimated to be 8 percent, an overly expansionary policy would be adopted. If a 3 percent rate were estimated when the true rate was 8 percent, appropriate policies to reduce unemployment would not be adopted.

The availability of an extensive supply of data on the performance of the economy is a post–World War II phenomenon. Much of the available data for the years prior to the war have been collected and published in the postwar period. Bureaucrats and economists have always been data collectors, but much of the data for early periods of American history is a by-product of the functioning of specific industries or government agencies. For example, price level data collected by the Department of Labor extend back to World War I.

The Gross National Product and Its Components

The *national income accounting system* is a result of the pioneering work of the Harvard economist Simon Kuznets. In 1941, the publication of Kuznets' *National Income and Its Components, 1919–1938*[1] made available comprehensive data for the post–World War I period and established a framework for the collection and publication of future data. Today, the Department of Commerce is responsible for collecting and publishing the national income accounting data.

The most generally used measure of macroeconomic activity is the Gross National Product (GNP). *Gross National Product* is the sum of the market values of all final goods and services produced in a given period of time. A few clarifying points relative to this definition are required:

1. GNP measures the market value of goods and services produced. Thus, goods are valued at their selling prices and inflation increases the level of GNP unless a correction is made to remove the effect of higher prices.

2. GNP includes only *final* goods and services. Goods are counted as they are sold to the ultimate user. Coal sold to the consumer to heat his home is a final use of the coal and is counted. Coal sold to make steel, which will become part of a car, is not counted. The value of the coal going to make steel is counted, along with all other components of the car, when the car is sold to the consumer. If this were not the case, many items would be counted more than once and GNP would be overstated.

3. GNP measures production for a given time period. Only goods and services produced in that time period are counted. The subsequent resale of existing goods does not affect GNP.

Equally important are some of the conventions that are employed in determining what is, and what is not, included in GNP computations. Normally, goods that do not pass through the marketplace are not included. Therefore, work

[1] Simon Kuznets, *National Income and Its Components, 1919–1938,* National Bureau of Economic Research, New York, 1941.

TABLE 7–1 Major Measures of Income and Output (billions of dollars)

	GROSS AND NET NATIONAL PRODUCT AND NATIONAL INCOME, 1929–1975			*DISPOSITION OF PERSONAL INCOME, 1929–1975*			
Year	*Gross National Product*	*Net National Product*	*National Income*	*Personal Income*	*Disposable Personal Income*	*Total Consumption*	*Personal Saving*
1929	103.1	95.2	86.8	85.9	83.3	79.1	4.2
1933	55.6	48.6	40.3	47.0	45.5	46.5	−.9
1939	90.5	83.2	72.6	72.8	70.3	67.7	2.6
1940	99.7	92.2	81.1	78.3	75.7	71.8	3.8
1945	211.9	200.7	181.5	171.1	150.2	120.7	29.6
1950	286.2	262.3	236.2	226.1	205.5	192.0	10.8
1955	399.3	364.0	328.0	308.8	273.4	253.7	14.9
1960	506.0	458.3	412.0	399.7	349.4	324.9	17.1
1965	688.1	630.6	566.0	537.0	472.2	430.2	30.3
1970	982.4	891.6	798.4	801.3	685.9	618.8	50.6
1975[p]	1499.0	1346.4	1209.5	1246.0	1076.8	963.2	89.6

[p]preliminary.

SOURCE: *1975 Economic Report of the President*, pp. 264–268, and *1976 Economic Report of the President*, pp. 183–187.

that a plumber does on his own plumbing does not count and services performed by housewives in their own homes are not counted. The full value of the loaf of bread purchased in the store is counted, but only the value of the purchased ingredients is counted if the loaf of bread is baked at home. Part of the reason for the exclusion of items not passing through the marketplace is the lack of data on prices. What is the true value of the housewife's services in her own home? Some transactions that do not pass through the marketplace are given estimated values. Thus, if a farmer consumes part of his own crop, that portion is counted as if it had been sold. The rental value of owner-occupied homes is counted; everyone is a renter in the national income accounting system.

The lack of data is also responsible for the exclusion of illegal activities. While illegal activities generate income and employment and often satisfy needs, these economic functions do not generate official data for inclusion in the GNP tables.

Gross National Product, in the first column of Table 7–1, does not allow for the physical depreciation of productive facilities. Part of the year's production is necessary to replace that portion of the stock of machinery and factories which was worn out during the year. It is extremely difficult to estimate a given year's decline in the value of the stock of productive facilities. Physical deterioration is one problem and obsolescence is a second problem. Equipment, which is still physically capable of producing output, may be rendered obsolete by the introduction of new technology. The firm may no longer be able to operate profitably using the old equipment even though the equipment is in mint condition. The Department of Commerce attempts to measure depreciation in the national income accounts; the subtraction of the *capital consumption allowance* (depreciation) from the value of GNP results in a second major measure of economic activity, *Net National Product* (NNP). NNP is simply GNP minus the depreciation allowance.

From Net National Product to National Income The NNP is refined further to obtain a measure of National Income *(Y)*. *National Income* measures the income attributable to the factors of production—land, labor, and capital. The differences between NNP and Y are necessary to adjust for values that are included (or excluded) from NNP but do (or do not) become part of National Income. To Net National Product:

Add subsidies less current surplus of government enterprises. Government enterprises include various governmental activities that are similar to private businesses, such as a municipal water system or a state-owned electric company. Assume that the municipal water system operates at a loss and the loss is made up by the local government out of general tax revenues. The sale of water (counted in GNP and NNP) does not include all factor payments included in National Income. The factor payments are increased to the appropriate level by adding the city's subsidy to the water system.

TABLE 7–2 Two Ways of Calculating National Income

FIRST METHOD:

GNP
− Capital consumption allowance
= Net National Product
+ Subsidies less current surplus of government enterprises
− Indirect business taxes
− Business transfer payments
− Statistical discrepancy
= National Income

SECOND METHOD:

Compensation of employees
    wages and salaries
    supplements
+ Business and professional income and inventory valuation adjustment
+ Income of farm proprietors
+ Rental income of persons
+ Corporate profits and inventory valuation adjustment
+ Net interest
= National Income

Subtract indirect business taxes. The prices of some of the products in NNP include tax payments that are the income of the government rather than income for the factors of production. Sales and excise taxes are important in this category.

Subtract business transfer payments. Some of the revenues of businesses do not become returns to the factors of production. Typical items included in this category are bad debt losses, charitable contributions, and contest prizes. While these are reentered later as income accruing to people, they are not factor income and are excluded at this point.

Subtract statistical discrepancy. Nothing is perfect and that includes the National Income Accounting data collection process. The discrepancy is calculated here to reconcile this estimate of National Income with the estimate of National Income which can be obtained by summing the incomes received by all of the factors of production. If National Income, the return to the factors of production, is estimated both by working down from GNP and by adding up factor incomes, a statistical discrepancy entry must be made so that the two estimates are equal. The two ways of calculating National Income are illustrated in Table 7–2.

From National Income to Disposable Personal Income National Income is income attributable to the factors of production, but it is not all available for consumer spending. In addition, people receive some income that is not a result of providing factor services. To move from National Income to *Disposable Personal Income* requires additional adjustments:

Subtract corporate profits and inventory valuation adjustment. Corporate profits are not available for consumer spending and are subtracted out at this stage. The inventory valuation adjustment is designed to remove from corporate profits the effects of inflation (or deflation) on business inventories.

Subtract contributions for social insurance. Both employees and employers must pay various types of social insurance taxes. Social Security taxes (Old Age and Survivors Insurance) are the largest part of this item.

Subtract wage accruals less disbursements. This minor item, having a zero value most of the time, adjusts for the fact that some wages that have been earned have not been paid to the wage earner at the end of the accounting period and some wages that have been paid have not yet been earned.

Add government transfer payments to persons. A *transfer payment* is a payment for which no current services are rendered. Included in this category would be Social Security payments to retired people or other eligible recipients, welfare payments, unemployment compensation, and veterans benefits. These important components of income available for consumer spending are not received as a reward for supplying factor services.

Add interest paid by government (net) and by consumers. Interest payments by the government (net of interest paid to the government) and by consumers (except for interest on residential mortgages) are not considered part of National Income because they are not related to current productive activity. Interest on the government debt involves payments for past borrowings. Interest paid by consumers is mainly for the purchase of consumption goods rather than productive assets. Even though these interest payments are not part of National Income, they are part of the income available to the recipients of the interest payments.

Add dividends. Corporate profits were subtracted previously because corporate profits per se are not income to people. However, a portion of corporate profits is paid out as dividends to stockholders and is available for people to consume or save.

Add business transfer payments. The business transfer payments that were subtracted previously because they were not part of factor incomes are part of the income available for people to spend and are added back at this point.

Finally, after all of these adjustments, there is a measure of *Personal Income*—that sum of money available to consumer spending units. However, not all of one's income can be consumed. First, income taxes must be paid. Therefore, the value of Personal Income in Table 7–1 is reduced by the amount of personal income tax liabilities. The remaining income measure is Disposable Personal Income. Disposable income can be consumed or saved.

All of the major income measures provide information relative to the performance of the economy. Gross National Product can also be examined by looking at the various types of spending. This view of GNP is presented in Table 7–3. The major categories of expenditures on output are (a) personal consumption expenditures, (b) gross private domestic investment, (c) net exports of goods and services, and (d) government purchases of goods and services.

The components of GNP—consumption, investment, government spend-

TABLE 7–3 Gross National Product (billions of dollars)

ITEM	*1929*	*1933*	*1941*	*1950*	*1970*	*1971*	*1972*	*1973*	*1974*	*1975*[p]
Gross National Product	103.1	55.6	124.5	286.2	982.4	1063.4	1171.1	1306.3	1406.9	1499.0
Personal consumption expenditures	77.2	45.8	80.6	192.0	618.8	668.2	733.0	808.5	885.9	963.2
Durable goods	9.2	3.5	9.6	30.8	84.9	97.1	111.2	122.9	121.9	127.7
Nondurable goods	37.7	22.3	42.9	98.2	264.7	277.7	299.3	334.4	375.7	410.0
Services	30.3	20.1	28.1	63.0	269.1	293.4	322.4	351.3	388.3	425.5
Gross private domestic investment	16.2	1.4	17.9	53.8	140.8	160.0	188.3	220.5	212.2	183.3
Fixed investment	14.5	3.0	13.4	47.0	137.0	153.6	178.8	203.0	202.5	197.5
Nonresidential	10.6	2.4	9.5	27.1	100.5	104.1	116.8	136.5	147.9	148.7
Structures	5.0	.9	2.9	9.3	37.7	39.3	42.5	49.0	54.4	52.6
Producers' durable equipment	5.6	1.5	6.6	17.8	62.8	64.7	74.3	87.5	93.5	96.1
Residential structures	4.0	.6	3.9	19.9	36.6	49.6	62.0	66.5	54.6	48.8
Change in business inventories	1.7	−1.6	4.5	6.8	3.8	6.4	9.4	17.5	9.7	−14.2
Net exports of goods and services	1.1	.4	1.3	1.9	3.9	1.6	−3.3	7.4	7.7	21.5
Exports	7.0	2.4	5.9	13.9	62.5	65.6	72.7	101.5	144.2	147.3
Imports	5.9	2.0	4.6	12.0	58.5	64.0	75.9	94.2	136.5	125.8
Government purchases of goods and services	8.5	8.0	24.8	38.5	218.9	233.7	253.1	269.9	301.1	330.9
Federal	1.3	2.0	16.9	18.7	95.6	96.2	102.1	102.0	111.7	123.1
National defense	—	—	13.8	14.0	73.5	70.2	73.5	73.4	77.4	84.0
Other	—	—	3.1	4.7	22.1	26.0	28.6	28.6	34.3	39.2
State and local	7.2	6.0	7.9	19.8	123.2	137.5	151.0	168.0	189.4	207.8

[p]preliminary.

SOURCES: *1975 Economic Report of the President,* pp. 249, 252–253, and *1976 Economic Report of the President,* pp. 171, 181, 190.

ing, and net exports—are the critical values upon which economic policy has its effects, and in later chapters the forces affecting each of these components are examined. In addition, the effect of policy measures on each component of GNP is discussed. The objective is to attain an actual level of GNP which is as close as possible to the maximum potential level of GNP.

Price Levels

The second measurement problem is the determination of indices of prices. As indicated previously, GNP measures the market value of all currently produced goods and services. Thus, GNP can increase not only because more goods are produced but also because the price of a fixed quantity of output has increased. Usually, each year's increase in GNP results partly from an increase in physical output and partly from an increase in the price level.

There are methods of correcting *nominal GNP* (GNP uncorrected for price changes) to obtain *real GNP* (GNP after correcting for changes in prices). The price index for correcting GNP is the *implicit GNP deflator*. Specific indices of prices are also available to deflate (remove the effect of price changes from) most of the major components of GNP. Nominal GNP, the implicit GNP deflator, and real GNP in 1972 prices are presented in Table 7–4.

The numerator of the GNP deflator is the summation (Σ) of the products obtained by multiplying the number of units of each currently produced item by the current price of that item. The denominator is the summation of the products obtained by multiplying the number of units of each currently produced item by the base period price of each currently produced item. Symbolically,

$$\frac{\sum p_1 q_1}{\sum p_0 q_1} \times 100 = \text{Implicit GNP deflator}$$

where p_1 = current prices
p_0 = base period prices
q_1 = current output
Σ = summation of price time's quantity

As an example, assume that the economy's total output consists of 50 units of one all-purpose item. The miracle item sold at \$500 per unit in the 1960 base period and currently sells at \$750 per unit. The implicit price deflator would be

$$\frac{\$750 \times 50}{\$500 \times 50} \times 100 = 150$$

The numerator of the equation is the current GNP, and the denominator is what the GNP would have been in 1960 if 1960's output had been 50 units of the all-purpose item. Thus, it is assumed that the price of the item in 1960 would have been \$500 per unit if 50 units had been produced that year. In the deflating process,

TABLE 7–4 GNP in Current Dollars and 1972 Dollars (billions of dollars)

YEAR	GNP CURRENT DOLLARS	GNP DEFLATOR	GNP 1972 DOLLARS
1946	209.6	44.06	475.7
1947	232.8	49.70	468.3
1948	259.1	53.13	487.7
1949	258.0	52.59	490.7
1950	286.2	53.64	533.5
1951	330.2	57.27	576.5
1952	347.2	58.00	598.5
1953	366.1	58.88	621.8
1954	366.3	59.69	613.7
1955	399.3	60.98	654.8
1956	420.7	62.90	668.8
1957	442.8	65.02	680.9
1958	448.9	66.06	679.5
1959	486.5	67.52	720.4
1960	506.0	68.67	736.8
1961	523.3	69.28	755.3
1962	563.8	70.55	799.1
1963	594.7	71.59	830.7
1964	635.7	72.71	874.4
1965	688.1	74.32	925.9
1966	753.0	76.76	981.0
1967	796.3	79.02	1007.7
1968	868.5	82.57	1051.8
1969	935.5	86.72	1078.8
1970	982.4	91.36	1075.3
1971	1063.4	96.02	1107.5
1972	1171.1	100.00	1171.1
1973	1306.3	105.92	1233.4
1974	1406.9	116.20	1210.7
1975[p]	1499.0	126.35	1186.4

[p]preliminary.

SOURCE: *1976 Economic Report of the President*, pp. 171–172, 174.

today's level of production is valued in terms of the prices that prevailed in an earlier base period.

The GNP deflator is the most comprehensive of the government's price indices and is the index referred to each quarter in the government's announcement of the level of GNP and the division of the change in GNP between output changes and price changes. If you are required to do any statistical work that involves adjusting data for price changes, attempt to find that price index which is most appropriate for the series of data. A bit of searching turns up a large collection of price indices for specific components of GNP and for other economic series.

The *Consumer Price Index* (CPI) is better known than the GNP deflator. The CPI attempts to measure the cost of living for urban clerical and wage earners, but the CPI is applied generally as the index for determining changes in the cost of living for all consumers. The CPI is constructed differently from the GNP deflator. The series is based on a representative market basket of goods and services which would be purchased by the urban clerical or wage earner with a wife and two children. Once the typical collection of goods and services for this typical family is selected, each of the goods and services is priced for the base period and for each subsequent period. The relationship between the base period prices and the prices in later periods produces the consumer price index.

Mathematically, the CPI is constructed as

$$\frac{\sum p_1 q_0}{\sum p_0 q_0} \times 100 = \text{Consumer Price Index}$$

where p_1 = current prices
p_0 = base period prices
q_0 = base period quantity of goods
Σ = summation of price times quantity

In constructing the CPI, the market basket of goods is held constant from year to year. In the GNP deflator, the current output of goods and services is used as the output measure.

The consumer price index and some of its components are presented in Table 7–5. The base period is 1967 and the price index is calculated in terms of 1967 being equal to 100. The table indicates not only the continuous upward trend in the CPI but also the variation in rates of price increase for different components of the total market basket.

There are a number of major problems with the CPI. First there is the question of representativeness. Does the collection of goods in the typical market basket truly reflect the purchasing patterns of a given individual? No, for probably no single consumer allocates his purchases in the exact proportions assumed in the market basket.

Second, the market basket, once selected, stays constant for 10 years. Every decade the market basket is revised to reflect changes in purchasing patterns. If 1,000 gallons of heating oil were included in the base period, the typical consumer is assumed to use 1,000 gallons of oil each year regardless of changes in the price of oil. However, theory indicates that quantity demanded decreases as price increases. The typical consumer, faced with a doubling of the price of oil, probably will not use as much oil as he did in the base period. The CPI does not recognize these economizing efforts and overstates the actual increase in the cost of living until the market basket is revised.

Third, the market basket, once established for the next decade, does not take into account changes in the quality or availability of goods. For example, assume an index was constructed on the basis of 1967 consumption patterns. The market basket assumed a man would purchase three white-cotton long-sleeve shirts a year. When in 1975 an attempt was made to price those shirts to compute

TABLE 7–5 Consumer Price Indices by Expenditure Classes, 1929–1975, for Urban Wage Earners and Clerical Workers (1967 = 100)

YEAR	ALL ITEMS	FOOD	HOUSING TOTAL	HOUSING RENT	APPAREL AND UPKEEP	TRANSPORTATION	MEDICAL CARE	PERSONAL CARE	READING AND RECREATION	OTHER GOODS AND SERVICES
1929	51.3	48.3	—	76.0	48.5	—	—	—	—	—
1933	38.8	30.6	—	54.1	36.9	—	—	—	—	—
1939	41.6	34.6	52.2	56.0	42.4	43.0	36.7	40.3	45.3	46.9
1940	42.0	35.2	52.4	56.2	42.8	42.7	36.8	40.2	46.1	48.3
1945	53.9	50.7	59.1	58.8	61.5	47.8	42.1	55.1	62.4	56.9
1950	72.1	74.5	72.8	70.4	79.0	68.2	53.7	68.3	74.4	69.9
1952	79.5	84.3	78.7	76.2	85.3	77.3	59.3	75.6	76.9	76.6
1954	80.5	82.8	81.7	83.2	84.5	78.3	63.4	76.6	76.9	79.8
1956	81.4	82.2	83.6	85.9	85.8	78.8	67.2	81.1	77.8	81.0
1958	86.6	88.5	87.7	89.1	87.5	86.0	73.2	86.9	83.9	84.4
1960	88.7	88.0	90.2	91.7	89.6	89.6	79.1	90.1	87.3	87.8
1962	90.6	89.9	91.7	94.0	90.9	92.5	83.5	92.2	91.3	89.1
1964	92.9	92.4	93.8	95.9	92.7	94.3	87.3	94.5	95.0	92.0
1965	94.5	94.4	94.9	96.9	93.7	95.9	89.5	95.2	95.9	94.2
1966	97.2	99.1	97.2	98.2	96.1	97.2	93.4	97.1	97.5	97.2
1967	100.0	100.0	100.0	100.0	100.0	100.0	100.0	100.0	100.0	100.0
1968	104.2	103.6	104.2	102.4	105.4	103.2	106.1	104.2	104.7	104.6
1969	109.8	108.9	110.8	105.7	111.5	107.2	113.4	109.3	108.7	109.1
1970	116.3	114.9	118.9	110.1	116.1	112.7	120.6	113.2	113.4	116.0
1971	121.3	118.4	124.3	115.2	119.8	118.6	128.4	116.8	119.3	120.9
1972	125.3	123.5	129.2	119.2	122.3	119.9	132.5	119.8	122.8	125.5
1973	133.1	141.4	135.0	124.3	126.8	123.8	137.7	125.2	125.9	129.0
1974	147.7	161.7	150.6	130.6	136.2	137.7	150.5	137.3	133.8	137.2
1975	161.2	175.4	166.8	137.3	142.3	150.6	168.6	150.7	144.4	147.4

SOURCE: *1976 Economic Report of the President,* p. 220.

the index value, it was found that few stores carried white-cotton shirts, that they were mainly selling permanent-pressed colored print polyester shirts, which cost twice as much as the old shirts but had the advantage of not requiring ironing. Thus, the market basket had become out of date; it was measuring the prices of some items that no one was buying. Thus, the introduction of new products, changes in tastes, and improvements in old products all make the market basket less representative. By the end of the decade, the market basket may be very obsolete.

Thus, while the consumer price index plays an important role in the economy, unless you are the typical person assumed in the market basket, the CPI is not an accurate measure of your cost of living. Despite the limitations, the economic impact of the CPI is tremendous. The announcement of an increase in the index makes consumers feel less well-off, triggers automatic wage increases for many workers, causes other workers to demand higher wages, and causes government policy makers to reconsider their positions.

The other major price index is the *Wholesale Price Index* (WPI), which measures changes in the prices of both farm and industrial goods at the wholesale level. Specialized indices measure changes in the prices of basic raw materials, capital equipment, and other components of the total collection of intermediate goods.

The Wholesale Price Index usually moves in advance of the CPI. If the wholesale prices of steel, rubber, and glass all increase, you can be sure that retail car prices will rise in the future as car makers pass their higher materials costs on to the car buyer.

Employment and Unemployment Data

The third collection of data relative to the macroeconomic performance of the economy relates to employment and unemployment. One of the objectives of macroeconomic policy is to provide full employment. To accommodate the growth of the labor force and maintain full employment requires an annual expansion of the number of available jobs. Table 7–6 provides the basic data on unemployment. Various series of data record unemployment rates for different socioeconomic groups.

The first basic problem encountered in the calculation of unemployment is the definition of the labor force. Only those in the labor force can be unemployed. Clearly, if one is not working and indicates that he does not want a job, he is not part of the labor force and should not be counted as unemployed. The government should not change its macroeconomic policies in this case. Thus, to be counted as unemployed one must be both out of work and actively seeking employment. However, if a person would like a job but has been so discouraged by past efforts to find one that he is no longer looking for a job, he has technically left the labor force and is not counted as being unemployed. Thus, the data on unemployment, as

TABLE 7–6 Selected Unemployment Rates, 1948–1975 (percent)

		BY AGE AND SEX			BY COLOR		BY SELECTED GROUPS			
Year	*All workers*	*Both sexes 16–19 years*	*Men 20 years and over*	*Women 20 years and over*	*White*	*Negro and other races*	*Household heads*	*Married men*	*Full-time workers*	*Blue-collar workers*
1948	3.8	9.2	3.2	3.6	3.5	5.9	—	—	—	4.2
1949	5.9	13.4	5.4	5.3	5.6	8.9	—	3.5	5.4	8.0
1950	5.3	12.2	4.7	5.1	4.9	9.0	—	4.6	5.0	7.2
1952	3.0	8.5	2.4	3.2	2.8	5.4	—	1.4	2.5	3.6
1954	5.5	12.6	4.9	5.5	5.0	9.9	—	4.0	5.2	7.2
1956	4.1	11.1	3.4	4.2	3.6	8.3	—	2.6	3.7	5.1
1958	6.8	15.9	6.2	6.1	6.1	12.6	—	5.1	7.2	10.2
1960	5.5	14.7	4.7	5.1	4.9	10.2	—	3.7	—	7.8
1961	6.7	16.8	5.7	6.3	6.0	12.4	—	4.6	6.7	9.2
1962	5.5	14.7	4.6	5.4	4.9	10.9	—	3.6	—	7.4
1963	5.7	17.2	4.5	5.4	5.0	10.8	3.7	3.4	5.5	7.3
1964	5.2	16.2	3.9	5.2	4.6	9.6	3.2	2.8	4.9	6.3
1965	4.5	14.8	3.2	4.5	4.1	8.1	2.7	2.4	4.2	5.3
1966	3.8	12.8	2.5	3.8	3.4	7.3	2.2	1.9	3.5	4.2
1967	3.8	12.8	2.3	4.2	3.4	7.4	2.1	1.8	3.4	4.4
1968	3.6	12.7	2.2	3.8	3.2	6.7	1.9	1.6	3.1	4.1
1969	3.5	12.2	2.1	3.7	3.1	6.4	1.8	1.5	3.1	3.9
1970	4.9	15.2	3.5	4.8	4.5	8.2	2.9	2.6	4.5	6.2
1971	5.9	16.9	4.4	5.7	5.4	9.9	3.6	3.2	5.5	7.4
1972	5.6	16.2	4.0	5.4	5.0	10.0	3.3	2.8	5.1	6.5
1973	4.9	14.5	3.2	4.8	4.3	8.9	2.9	2.3	4.3	5.3
1974	5.6	16.0	3.8	5.5	5.0	9.9	3.3	2.7	5.1	6.7
1975	8.5	19.9	6.7	8.0	7.8	13.9	5.8	5.1	8.1	11.7

SOURCE: *1976 Economic Report of the President*, p. 199.

published by the government, are biased downward by the existence of discouraged workers—those who have given up looking for a job.

The size of the labor force, given the discouraged worker problem, varies with the rate of unemployment. As the demand for labor increases during periods of prosperity, previously discouraged workers reenter the labor force. As the demand for labor falls during a recession, discouraged workers drop out of the labor force. This variation in the size of the labor force is especially important for the employment of teenagers and secondary family workers. Married males and other self-supporting persons cannot normally afford to drop out of the labor force.

The second major problem with the employment goal is the definition of full employment. What is full employment? The hypothetical goal of every last member of the labor force being employed is probably not obtainable nor even desirable. At any time, some people are out of work by choice, are in the process of moving from one job to another, or have left a job to search for a better job. Given a relatively high level of per capita savings, people can afford to be "between jobs." The person who devotes more time to searching for the right job is apt to be better satisfied with his new job than the person who takes the first job that comes along. The extra time out of work may be a good investment if it results in a better-paying position. Prosperity may increase this transitory unemployment by creating both the savings necessary to finance the additional search time and the optimistic feeling that the perfect job can be found by extra searching. In the highly mobile American economy, a substantial portion of total unemployment is composed of people who are between jobs.

Another part of unemployment, which may be called structural unemployment, results not from a lack of general demand for labor but from a disparity between the skills demanded by employers and the skills possessed by the unemployed. As product demands change and the methods of production change, the composition of the demand for labor changes. Some skills are in greater demand and others are in lesser demand. The buggywhip makers are out of work while the auto makers are looking for assembly line engineers. As skills become less general and more specialized, this type of unemployment problem increases. If one has spent a large part of a lifetime becoming an economist and is unemployed, it is no consolation to know that there is a shortage of brain surgeons. Structural unemployment presents more difficult policy problems. Expanding the level of aggregate demand does not make economists into brain surgeons. If skills are somewhat less specific than the economist–brain surgeon example, an expansion of demand creates the incentives for employers to train or retrain workers to perform new tasks. However, the accommodation of the skill distribution of the labor supply to the current composition of demand for labor usually requires governmental manpower training programs.

Third, some unemployment results from the personal characteristics of the job seeker. Although much of this unemployment is the result of prejudice and is illegal, problems of this type exist and unfortunately will probably continue to exist in various subtle ways regardless of all the antidiscrimination laws passed.

How can an applicant actually prove that a job was denied him because his hair was too long, he walked in an effeminate way, his skin color was wrong, or other grounds on which the personnel manager may care to discriminate? Ability to perform the job should be the only qualification but, especially if there are several qualified applicants, selection on the basis of other factors is possible.

Unemployment that results from discrimination does yield to an expansion of total demand. When the supply of labor is very limited and production is restricted because of the need for more workers, one cannot afford to exercise one's biases. Therefore, those most likely to be subject to discriminatory hiring practices probably have more to gain from a high level of demand for labor than will ever be gained from equal opportunity employment regulations.

Fourth, underemployment also presents measurement and policy problems. Some people, trained for highly skilled and highly paid jobs, may be unable to find employment in their field and may be forced to accept low-paying jobs that do not utilize their skills and training. In addition, some workers who desire full-time employment may be able to find only part-time jobs.

Finally, unemployment may result simply from a lack of aggregate demand for goods and services. The expansion of aggregate demand through monetary and fiscal policies can eliminate this form of unemployment. Specific policies of increasing knowledge of job opportunities, worker training and retraining, labor mobility, and antidiscrimination policies are needed for the other types of unemployment.

Thus, there are two questions—what is full employment, and how much of the unemployment that exists at any time can be eliminated by monetary and fiscal policy? Neither question has a satisfactory answer. The U.S. government's target level of full employment varies over time (and appears to vary with the existing level of unemployment). When unemployment is high, the acceptable level of unemployment seems to increase. When unemployment is low and falling, there is always the challenge of lowering the acceptable rate and doing still better. The American target is always higher than would be acceptable in other developed industrial nations. An unemployment rate of 4%, which might be acceptable in the United States, would bring down the government in most European nations. In part, the difference between European unemployment rates and American rates is accounted for by differences in measurement; however, as Table 1–1 in Chapter 1 indicated, the American unemployment rate is higher even when the European data are adjusted to the American measuring system. The definition of full employment is related to the definition of price stability; tradeoffs between these goals are covered in the next section.

Tradeoffs Between Economic Goals

The attainment of the various macroeconomic goals is complicated by the fact that some of the goals require policy measures opposite to those measures required to achieve other goals. Two goals — maximum economic growth and full employment — require generally expansionary monetary and fiscal policies. Low interest rates, higher rates of expansion of the money supply, and deficits in the government budget are suggested policies to attain these goals. However, the goals of stable prices and international balance of payments equilibrium generally require high interest rates, lower rates of growth of the money supply, and a government budget that is either in balance or in surplus. Thus, the complete attainment of one set of goals may require the acceptance of a relative failure to achieve the other set of goals. If both sets of goals cannot be achieved simultaneously, the determination of an acceptable compromise becomes the controversial problem. For example, is a combination of a 5 percent unemployment rate and a 4 percent inflation rate preferable to a 6 percent unemployment rate and a 3 percent inflation rate? Those secure in their employment and vulnerable to inflation would choose the higher level of unemployment and lower level of inflation. Naturally, those more vulnerable to unemployment would make the opposite choice.

The Phillips Curve

The analysis of tradeoffs concentrates on the relationship between inflation and unemployment. The original empirical work on this subject was performed by the British economist A. W. Phillips,[2] and the concept of the Phillips curve has become a fixture of economic analysis. Phillips' article dealt with the 1861–1957 relationship between the level of unemployment and the rate of increase of money wages in Great Britain. The relationship, as expected, illustrated that wages increased less when unemployment rates were high and that the rate of increase of wages accelerated at lower unemployment levels. The lower the level of unemployment, the greater the amount of wage increase which is required to obtain a further reduction in the unemployment rate.

The plotting of data on wage rate changes and unemployment levels indicated that the rate of increase in wage rates was also a function of the direction of change of the unemployment rate. Thus, for a given level of unemployment, the rate of increase of wages was higher if unemployment was falling than if unemployment was rising. Behavioral expectations of labor and management would provide logical support to this finding. Labor will request, and management will grant, a higher rate of wage increase if economic conditions are improving. If economic conditions are deteriorating, labor will be more restrained in its demands and management will be more resistant to labor's demands.

Although the original Phillips curves were drawn in terms of the rate of wage increase and the level of unemployment, the analysis can be extended to use the rate of increase of prices instead of the rate of increase of wages. Given that

[2] A. W. Phillips, "The Relationship Between Unemployment and the Rate of Change of Money Wage Rates in the United Kingdom, 1861–1957," *Economica*, vol. 25 (November 1958), pp. 283–299.

changes in the level of prices are closely associated with changes in wages and assuming a relatively constant rate of change of labor productivity, the price variable can be substituted for the wage variable.

An American Phillips curve, using the rate of increase of the GNP deflator as the price variable, is presented in Figure 7–1. One problem with the data for the Phillips curve is immediately apparent. The curve fitted through the points prior to 1970 lies well to the left of the curve fitted to all of the data points. For the 1970s, the tradeoff between inflation and unemployment appears to have worsened; a higher rate of inflation is associated with any given level of unemployment. Are the observations for the early 1970s merely deviations from the curve caused by some special factor or do these observations represent a permanent rightward shift of the curve?

Five questions can be raised relative to the Phillips curve analysis. The first is, what is the basic logic of constructing a relationship of this sort? The implications are (1) that there is a causal link between unemployment levels and rates of price increase such that policies that result in a given level of unemployment "cause" a given rate of price increase, and (2) that all other factors and all changes in the economy are so unimportant that a 1974 unemployment rate equal to the 1954 unemployment rate would result in the same inflation rate in 1974 as in 1954.

Second, if one admits to the influence of other variables in the analysis, which variables are important? The influence of the direction of movement of the unemployment rate has already been mentioned. In addition, the rate of increase in productivity may be of importance. At any given rate of unemployment, the rate of increase of prices will be lower if productivity (output per man-hour) is rising rapidly than if productivity is declining or increasing very slowly. Also, conditions within subsectors of the labor market may influence the rate of increase of wages and prices. Assume two submarkets for labor. In one market, the demand for labor is very high relative to the supply and wages increase very sharply. In the other market, demand is low and wages do not increase. The average rate of wage increase in this case would be greater than the average rate of wage increase if demand and supply conditions were the same in each submarket and wages increased moderately in each submarket. Profit levels are another factor that may be important. If employer profits are high, management may agree to labor's demands for larger wage increases at any level of unemployment.

Third, what policies would be appropriate to shift the tradeoff curve to the left? The answer to this question depends upon the factors considered important on the previous list. If productivity is the key variable, increases in productivity would help move the curve. If submarket differences are the key, increased labor mobility would help to reduce the differences between demand and supply conditions in the various submarkets.

Fourth, can policy makers "hit" any desired target on a tradeoff curve? An announced policy of achieving a given low level of unemployment regardless of the cost in terms of price increases may create inflationary expectations and result in an actual rate of inflation larger than would be suggested by the historical data.

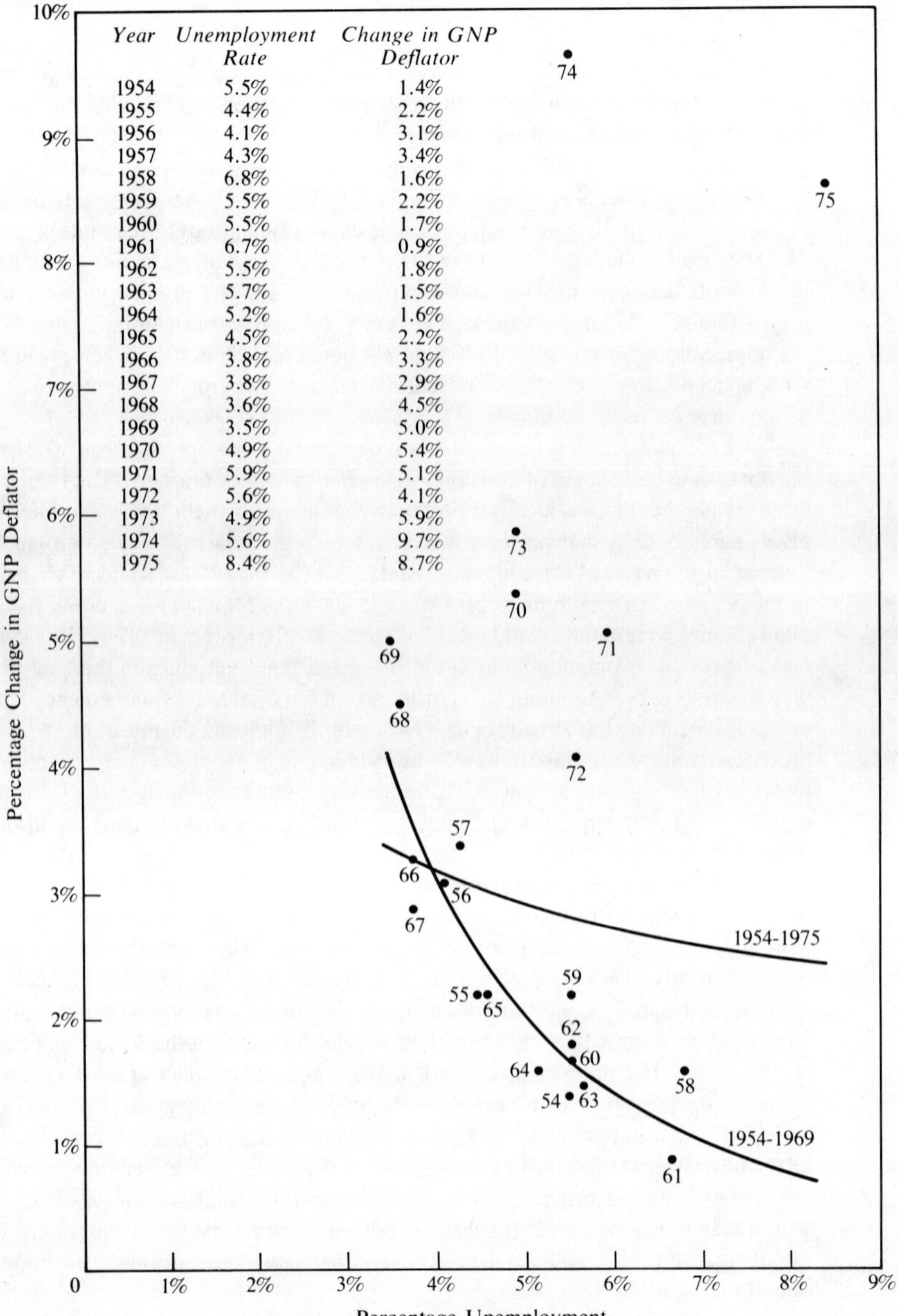

SOURCE. *1976 Economic Report of the President,* pp. 175, 199.

FIGURE 7–1 The United States' Tradeoff Between Unemployment and Inflation, 1954–1975

Fifth, is there a normal rate of unemployment, determined in the labor market, which macroeconomic policy cannot change in the long run? Some economists, such as Professor Milton Friedman of the University of Chicago, think so. Short term reductions in the unemployment rate can be achieved by accepting a higher rate of inflation but, in the long run, the Phillips curve is a straight line perpendicular to the horizontal axis of the diagram. This Phillips curve would imply that the given rate of unemployment is consistent with any rate of inflation. A discussion of the Friedman analysis is presented in Chapter 12.

There is sufficient doubt about the validity of the simple Phillips curve analysis that the cautious analyst would be well advised not to place a great amount of reliance on these historical relationships.

Even if a tradeoff relationship between unemployment and inflation can be established empirically, the question remains as to the most desirable position on the curve. Obviously, both unemployment and inflation involve social costs. The costs to those who are unemployed are more obvious and concentrated than the costs of inflation; inflation hits those who are unable to adjust their money incomes upward as the price level advances.

What are the socioeconomic costs and benefits of different unemployment-inflation tradeoffs? From the point of view of those who would accept a higher rate of inflation as the price of a lower level of unemployment, the benefits would be as follows:

1. The incidence of poverty would be reduced as more people, especially minorities and disadvantaged workers, become gainfully employed.

2. There would be greater job mobility for the employed. The opportunities to move into better positions are greater when the economy is closer to full employment.

3. Skill development would be encouraged. In a period of full employment, the incentives for business to upgrade the skills of the labor force are increased.

4. Social problems associated with unemployment and poverty would be reduced. Crime and violence should decline as the standard of living improves and the despair of unemployment and poverty is eliminated.

Those who stress the evils of inflation, and are willing to accept unemployment in order to lower the inflation rate, cannot disagree with the value of reducing unemployment but argue that inflation has its own bad effects:

1. Although an easy money policy may temporarily reduce the unemployment rate, eventually the maintenance of the lower rate of unemployment will require an unacceptable rate of inflation.

2. Inflation is a cruel tax on those who do not have the ability to adjust to rapidly rising prices. Those on fixed incomes or those who hold their wealth in fixed-dollar assets, such as bonds, lose purchasing power. Inflation redistributes wealth from the small, uninformed saver to the sharp speculator.

3. Eventually inflation requires anti-inflationary policies that may be so strong that they result in economic collapse and extremely high levels of unemployment.

4. Inflation causes resources to be diverted from real productive activity to devising ways to escape the impact of inflation.

5. Inflation destroys the incentives for saving and investing.

Part of the argument between these two groups depends on the ability to control the rate of inflation. Those whose fear of inflation is great believe that inflation, once begun, will continue at ever-growing rates. Those who are less worried about inflation tend to believe that a stable tradeoff can be made and "a little more" inflation can be accepted without an inevitable rush into hyperinflation.

In terms of tradeoffs between inflation and growth, the arguments of the anti-inflation forces would remain essentially unchanged. The arguments of those who would accept more inflation in the hope of more growth would argue the following points:

1. Inflation reduces the real value of corporate and personal debt and thus increases the ability to spend on new productive or consumer goods.

2. Inflation increases money profits and money income. To the extent that people suffer from money illusion, inflation stimulates spending. The term *money illusion* refers to a person's perception of his economic well-being as his money income and the price level change. If both his income and consumer prices double and he thinks he is better off, he suffers from money illusion. If he realizes that his costs have gone up by the same proportion as his income and that he is no better off, he does not suffer from money illusion.

3. The prospect of inflation increases the attractiveness of current spending. By buying now one avoids a higher future cost and contributes to total demand and the growth of GNP.

4. The prospect of inflation makes capital investment more attractive. As the firm evaluates the market for the goods to be produced by a machine purchased today, the prospect of rising product prices makes the investment more attractive.

5. Rapid growth makes economic readjustments easier to bear. If the economy is growing rapidly, resources that are no longer in demand for one use find alternative uses. Those who are displaced by automation, or by a declining demand for their product, can more easily find alternative employment in a rapidly expanding economy.

6. Rapid growth also produces the previously cited benefits of low levels of unemployment and produces a higher standard of living and a reduction of poverty.

The employment and growth advocates have answers to the objectives raised by those who are willing to lower employment and growth rates in order to prevent inflation. The main argument, cited earlier, is that the rate of inflation can be increased without causing an exploding cycle of greater and greater rates of inflation. In addition, the argument can be made that inflation protection can be provided for those who would suffer from inflation. Cost of living adjustments can be inserted into pension plans, Social Security benefits, wage contracts, and even into bond contracts. The idea of *indexing* all factor and transfer payments to the cost of living would minimize the impact of inflation and reduce the cost of obtaining the benefits of a higher rate of economic growth and a lower level of unemployment. However, to the staunchest opponents of inflation, the acceptance of indexing would represent a surrender in the war against inflation.

The International Tradeoff

The whole problem of tradeoffs between prices, growth, and employment comes together in the discussion of the international balance of trade. (A balance of trade equilibrium is defined here simply as a condition in which the value of a nation's exports of goods and services is equal to the value of its imports of goods and services.) Exporting goods is important to most national economies. The United States exports a far lower percentage of its goods and services (about 10 percent of GNP) than do other nations. Exports provide employment for domestic workers in export-related industries; the increased volume of production in those industries allows for the achievement of potential economies of scale. In addition, exports provide the foreign exchange earnings to purchase those goods that can be produced more efficiently in other nations.

The demand for a nation's export goods is a function of the income level in other nations and/or the price of the export goods relative to the price of competing goods from other countries. In some cases, the demand for export goods is highly income-elastic (for example, the demand for French wines increases as American incomes increase). In other cases, the demand is more sensitive to prices (for example, the international demand for American steel depends on American steel prices relative to steel prices in other nations). Therefore, if a nation seeks to expand production and employment in its export industries, inflation must be avoided.

The level of the nation's imports is also affected by control, or lack of control, of price levels. If domestic prices rise more rapidly than foreign prices, consumers and business firms will shift from domestic goods to imported goods. Thus, rapidly rising domestic prices discourage exports and encourage imports; the balance of trade position deteriorates on both sides.

Control of the domestic price level is the key to achieving an export-import balance or an export surplus. However, holding back inflation may require measures that increase unemployment and lower the rate of economic growth. An economy that must maintain a high level of exports may be forced to accept strong anti-inflation policies.

For the United States, the relatively low importance of exports in total production has reduced the severity of national-international tradeoffs. However, international considerations have influenced policy making. At times, interest rates have been higher than would have been necessary for purely domestic policy purposes. The devaluations of the dollar in 1971 and 1973 evidenced the need for American concern with the international competitiveness of American-made goods.

In summary, none of the economic goals are absolutes. The attainment of a given goal, or goals, may require some sacrifice in terms of obtaining alternative economic goals. As should be clear from the discussion, the precise quantitative magnitude of potential tradeoffs has not been established to the satisfaction of all.

A Second Set of Goal Tradeoffs

Beyond the basic employment, growth, price stability, and balance of payments equilibrium goals, there are two other economic and noneconomic goals that have the potential for conflicting with these four basic macroeconomic goals. They are the maintenance of economic freedom, and the maintenance of the quality of life.

Maintaining Economic Freedom

The freedom of the marketplace has a high value to Americans. The ability to negotiate for the sale of one's labor services, to decide what to produce, how to produce, to whom to sell and at what price are all characteristics of the capitalistic economic system. Challenges to these traditional rights bring strong responses from the affected individuals or firms. Two examples illustrate the problem.

The strike of the National Football League Players' Association in the summer of 1974 revolved around the players' opposition to rules that bound them to a given club and limited their right to negotiate with other clubs. The claimed advantages of the draft are that the system distributes talent more evenly among the teams and produces a better competitive balance among the teams. If a player could negotiate with all clubs, the club having the most money would have all the best players, would always win, and the fans would lose interest in the game. The claimed disadvantage is that the system places the player in the position of having no alternatives; he is dealing with a monopsonist buyer (a single buyer) of his services. The players claim this lowers the income they can earn in their short playing career. There is some logic to both sides of the argument, and we will not make an attempt here to judge the weight of the evidence.

Another case cited as an infringement on the traditional rights of contract resulted from the 1974 crude oil allocation rules. The major oil companies, which had integrated their operations and assured themselves of having sufficient supplies of crude oil, were forced to share their crude oil with independent firms that had traditionally undercut the prices charged by the majors. Lack of forced sharing would have driven the independents out of business and led to further concentration of the industry. Again, we will make no attempt to judge the merits of each side's arguments.

In a more macroeconomic context, the use of wage and price controls in the 1971–1973 period placed a limit on traditional economic freedom. Although some argued that these limitations were necessary in order to reduce inflation, the contribution of the controls is questionable. Some would also affirm that, in the long run, extensive controls over wages and prices will be necessary to avoid inflation. Thus, the time may come when even greater limitations on wage- and price-setting behavior will be considered as the necessary tradeoff for price stability.

To an even greater extent, all of the macroeconomic goals could probably be achieved more easily by converting to a system of minimum economic freedom. The completely planned economy, controlled by the government, might have substantial advantages in achieving these goals. Everyone would have a job, investment would be oriented toward growth-producing areas, prices and wages would be dictated, and international trade would be controlled by the state. If the system could be managed perfectly, the macroeconomic objectives would be accomplished. Not only would this type of system restrict economic freedom in the consumption and production of goods, but it would run the risk of failing to allocate resources in the most efficient manner. The complexity of the resource allocation process is the source of continuing problems in the centrally managed economy. In the relatively uncontrolled economic system, resource allocation decisions are made mainly by the market system. The periodic failures of the market system to attain the macroeconomic goals have resulted, since Keynes, in the use of monetary and fiscal policies. However, even when government did not stand ready to correct unemployment problems, few were ready to discard the market system for a planned economy.

Maintenance of Quality of Life

The second tradeoff issue involves the maintenance of the quality of life. GNP measures the production of goods and services but does not evaluate the contribution these goods and services make to human welfare and happiness. Four specific cases deserve comment in this regard.

First, many of the goods included in total GNP do not directly increase human well-being but serve (or are supposed to serve) as deterrents to threats to our well-being. Nationally, we spend billions of dollars on national defense. The large standing army and massive spending on ever more sophisticated weapons technology does not increase our physical well-being and some even question whether all the spending does indeed serve to deter attacks upon our future welfare. On a more local level, large amounts are spent to prevent crime.

Second, one can question whether the increased material standard of living really increases our sense of well-being. Are we as a nation actually happier with today's collection of goods and services than were our grandparents with a much more limited array of goods? If we are, the social statistics do not seem to indicate any increase in general happiness—the self-defrosting refrigerator, for instance, doesn't seem to have lowered the divorce rate.

Third, the quality of the physical environment has been the victim of the rush to obtain more and more goods. The production of goods resulted in the joint production of "bads"—environmental pollution. The production of pollution along with the production and consumption of goods resulted in the rapid deterioration of air and water quality and the waste of natural resources. Only in the past few years, as the impact of this environmental pollution has become more and more obvious to the senses, has the nation realized the necessity for making drastic changes in the methods of producing goods. Now there are those who fear that the environment may again be sacrificed in a quest for energy self-sufficiency.

The statement of the environmental problem in terms of either more goods or a better environment has been overdramatized by many, and the overdramatization may have been necessary to begin the process of protecting the earth's physical environment. However, there is some tradeoff required between more goods and a better environment. Air and water pollution abatement requirements force firms to spend expensive capital on waste treatment facilities rather than on equipment for the expansion of production. The installation of catalytic converters on 1975 automobiles raised the cost of cars to the consumer and, all other things being equal, left him with less disposable income to buy other goods and services. Thus, mechanisms have been set up to require the producer or user of goods to bear the costs of protecting or cleaning up the natural environment. In technical terms, the negative externalities are being internalized. The air pollution costs, which the owner of a car could impose on society, are no longer accepted by society and the automobile owner must pay for a catalytic converter. Society's costs are now the consumer's costs.

Some items that are not included in the GNP do contribute to human welfare. Over time society has chosen to have increased amounts of leisure time rather than more goods. The gradual decline in the average work-week reflects this substitution of leisure for goods and services. However, the value of leisure to the consumer is not reflected in the GNP accounting system. The wife working in the home, rather than in a factory, results in fewer goods being produced; the impact of this situation on human welfare is not reflected in standard economic data.

Finally, changes in the quality of goods are not fully reflected in the value of GNP unless the higher quality results in a higher price. The substitution of safety for gadgetry in the construction of an automobile should increase social welfare. If the value of the omitted gadgets is equal to the value of added structural steel, neither the price of the car nor the value of GNP is changed. The contribution to GNP of a given item may fall while the quality is improving if the price of the product also falls. The improvement of electronic calculators and the simultaneous rapid decline in the price of calculators is an example of quality improvement and price decline. In other cases, the contribution to GNP, the price, stays the same but the quality of goods declines. The durability of many items seems to decrease over time; these quality decreases are not always reflected in lower selling prices.

The National Income accounting measuring system is far from perfect as a means of measuring national welfare. Macroeconomic measures to increase measured GNP may not increase national welfare. However, pending the development of better quantitative measures of prosperity, GNP and its components will continue to be the policy objectives, and the tradeoffs between GNP and welfare will continue to be assessed on a relatively nonquantified basis.

Fortunately, efforts are under way to construct better measures of national welfare. The Nordhaus-Tobin Measure of Economic Welfare (MEW)[3] is the most notable of these attempts. MEW measures a sustainable level of output and lowers GNP to make allowance for the added capital requirements necessary for growth. MEW takes out of GNP allowances for "regrettables," such as national defense expenditures, which do not increase the welfare of households. MEW includes the value of leisure and goods that do not pass through the marketplace. Disutilities, such as environmental pollution, are subtracted out of GNP in arriving at MEW.

The development of added macroeconomic measures, such as MEW, is to be encouraged. While policy measures will continue to be based primarily on standard GNP concepts, the concerns expressed by MEW must not be neglected.

REVIEW QUESTIONS

1. Why is the rapid availability of high-quality data on the performance of the economy critical to the achievement of economic goals?

2. Why can National Income be measured directly by adding all factor payments or indirectly by starting with GNP and making additions and subtractions?

3. What problems are encountered in measuring unemployment?

4. What does the Phillips curve purport to measure? How valid is this method of analysis? What reasons can be offered to explain the substantial deviations from the curve in 1970–1975?

5. How does the Consumer Price Index differ from the Gross National Product Deflator?

6. What tradeoffs may be necessary between domestic and international economic goals?

7. In what ways is GNP not a good measure of economic well-being? Are there other factors that could be added to the Nordhaus-Tobin Measure of Economic Welfare?

8. What are the costs of recession? of inflation?

9. What types of unemployment are least apt to be reduced by an expansion of aggregate demand for goods and services?

10. Define the following terms: (**a**) indexing, (**b**) money illusion, (**c**) disposable personal income, (**d**) labor force, (**e**) national income.

[3]William Nordhaus and James Tobin, "Is Growth Obsolete?" *Economic Growth*, 50th Anniversary Colloquium, vol. 5, (National Bureau of Economic Research, New York, 1972).

SUGGESTED READINGS

William I. Abraham, *National Income and Economic Accounting*. Englewood Cliffs, N.J.: Prentice-Hall, 1969.

Robert J. Flanagan, "The U.S. Phillips Curve and International Unemployment Rate Differentials," *American Economic Review,* March 1973, pp. 114–131.

Robert Lekachman, *National Income and the Public Welfare*. New York: Random House, 1972.

Robert A. McMillan, "A Reexamination of the 'Full Employment' Goal," *Federal Reserve Bank of Cleveland Economic Review,* March–April 1973, pp. 3–17.

Arthur M. Okun, *Equality and Efficiency: The Big Tradeoff*. Washington, D.C.: Brookings Institution, 1975.

Sheldon W. Stahl, "The Phillips Curve: A Dilemma for Public Policy, Inflation versus Unemployment," *Federal Reserve Bank of Philadelphia Business Review,* January 1969, pp. 11–17.

Frederick R. Strobel, "GNP and Economic Welfare," *Federal Reserve Bank of Atlanta Monthly Review,* June 1974, pp. 74–79.

Richard M. Young, "Inflation and the Distribution of Income and Wealth: Are the Poor Really Hurt?" *Federal Reserve Bank of Philadelphia Business Review,* September 1973, pp. 16–25.

8

THE COMMERCIAL BANKING SYSTEM AND THE MONEY SUPPLY

Monetary policy requires that the central bank have the power to control the supply of money. Although economists may disagree with regard to the process by which changes in the supply of money affect other economic variables, the need for mechanisms to change the supply of money is universally recognized. This chapter describes the methods by which the money supply is altered under different types of monetary systems. After a brief coverage of the methods of changing the money supply used prior to the development of modern central banking, the analysis focuses on the techniques used by the Federal Reserve System to expand or contract the American money supply.

Gold, the Printing Press, and the Money Supply

Under the international gold coin standard, all money was in the form of gold and the control of the domestic supply of money was at least one step removed from the government. Increases in the supply of gold coins could arise from three sources. The first source of new money was the mining of new gold and the delivery of the gold to the mint to be processed into coins. However, most countries produced little or no gold; additions to the money supply from this source were never very large.

The second source of added money was the conversion of nonmonetary gold to gold coin. The holder of gold jewelry, gold art objects, and other forms of nonmonetary gold could have the gold melted down and minted into coins. Conversely, the money supply could decrease if gold coins were converted to other gold products.

The third, and major, cause of a change in the supply of money under the gold coin standard was international transactions. International trade was the primary determinant of changes in the domestic supply of money because exporters received gold in payment for exports and importers used gold to pay for imported goods. If exports exceeded imports, the supply of gold in the nation increased; if imports were greater than exports, the national gold supply declined. Thus, the nation's international trade position produced changes in the supply of money.

Fluctuations in the supply of money resulting from the export-import position of the nation imposed a monetary policy whether or not the nation had a central bank or governmental monetary authority. A country experiencing a balance of payments deficit was gradually drained of its gold holdings, and money became increasingly scarce until the balance of trade position improved and gold flowed back into the nation.

In a gold-based paper money system, the change in the supply of gold could have an even greater effect on the supply of money. If the money supply consisted of gold coins and paper money, the paper money was convertible into gold and each bank issuing paper money was required to hold reserves equal to some fraction of the bank's outstanding paper currency. In this system, the outflow of gold removed money from circulation in a multiple of the value of the gold outflow. For example, assume a bank was required to hold gold equal to 10 percent of the value of its outstanding convertible paper money. If each dollar's worth of gold was currently being used to back \$10 worth of paper money, the loss of a dollar's worth of gold resulted in a \$10 contraction of the maximum paper money supply. Under the convertible paper money system, the reversal of the gold outflow became increasingly imperative.

The alternatives to reversing the gold outflow were the production of more gold, a reduction of the percentage of gold reserves behind the paper currency, and the suspension of the gold convertibility of paper money. Each of these alternatives presented problems. Gold production was limited by resource endowments and mining technology. Reducing the percentage of gold backing reduced public confidence in the ability of the banks to convert and increased the public's desire to convert paper money to gold. Given the fractional reserve system, conversion attempts rapidly reduced the banks' gold stocks and led to the suspension of conversion.

As described in Chapter 2, the United States, under the National Banking System, permitted the nationally chartered banks to issue money backed by the banks' holdings of government bonds. The volume of notes was a function of the volume of government debt. As the government paid off its Civil War debts, the supply of national bank notes had to be contracted. Instead of using the supply of government debt as a means of controlling the growth of the supply of money, the desire to retire the debt prevailed and the quantity of national bank notes contracted.

A fiat money system is another traditional method of changing the money supply. This system requires only a treasury department and a printing press. The money supply consists of inconvertible paper money and changes in the supply of money are dictated by the size of the government's deficit. If the government does not cover its expenditures with tax revenues, new money is printed and used to pay remaining bills. Today, most governments borrow to meet their deficits; prior to the development of government bond markets, the money supply was expanded to cover the excess of expenditures over tax receipts. History records many examples of the overuse of the printing press. Most great inflations, such as the post–World War I inflation in Germany, resulted from the overissuance of fiat money.

The Central Bank, the Commercial Bank, and the Money Supply

In a modern developed economy, the supply of money is controlled by a central bank. The American central bank, the Federal Reserve System, changes the supply of money by changing the supply of reserves available to the commercial banking system. A complete understanding of the methods of money supply control is critical to the understanding of monetary theory and policy.

The Balance Sheet of the Federal Reserve System

An understanding of the monetary control process begins with the examination of the balance sheet of the Federal Reserve System. Table 8–1 presents a condensed balance sheet and the following paragraphs explain the various accounts.

Assets

GOLD CERTIFICATE ACCOUNTS

Prior to the 1933 suspension of private gold ownership in the United States, the Federal Reserve held gold. In 1933, the Federal Reserve surrendered its gold to the Treasury and the gold was replaced with gold certificates. When the Treasury sells gold, the process of clearing the buyer's check reduces bank deposits and bank reserves. The Treasury's deposits at the Federal Reserve increase as the check is credited to the Treasury's checking account at the Federal Reserve. The Treasury uses its added deposits at the Federal Reserve to retire gold certificates held by the Federal Reserve.

SDR ACCOUNT

Special Drawing Rights (SDRs) are issued by the International Monetary Fund (IMF) to expand the world's supply of international reserves. The Treasury receives the SDRs from the IMF and deposits these SDRs with the Federal Reserve. In exchange, the Treasury receives a credit in its international exchange stabilization account at the Federal Reserve. The exchange stabilization account is included under Foreign and other deposits on the liability side of the Federal Reserve System's balance sheet. The function of SDRs and the exchange stabilization account are covered in Part IV of this book.

TABLE 8–1 Consolidated Statement of Condition of All Federal Reserve Banks, December 31, 1975

	MILLIONS OF DOLLARS			
Total assets	120,402			
Gold certificate accounts		11,599		
SDR account		500		
U.S. government and government agency securities		94,124		
Member bank borrowing		211		
Acceptances		1,126		
Cash items in process of collection		9,183		
Cash		347		
Other assets		3,312		
Liabilities and capital	120,402			
Liabilities		118,544		
Federal Reserve notes			77,159	
Deposits			34,780	
Member bank reserves				26,052
Treasury				7,285
Foreign and other				1,443
Deferred availability cash items			5,495	
Other liabilities and accrued dividends			1,110	
Capital accounts		1,858		

SOURCE: *Federal Reserve Bulletin,* February 1976, p. A10.

U.S. GOVERNMENT AND GOVERNMENT AGENCY SECURITIES

These debt securities of the federal government and various federal government agencies are the major assets of the Federal Reserve System. The Federal Reserve may purchase securities outright or may buy them under repurchase agreements. Under a repurchase agreement, the seller agrees to repurchase the securities at a given future date and price.

MEMBER BANK BORROWING

This entry represents borrowing at the discount window by banks belonging to the Federal Reserve System.

ACCEPTANCES

Acceptances are a result of the financing of international trade. A commercial bank "accepts" a draft by a foreign exporter drawn upon a domestic importer. The bank agrees to pay when payment becomes due. Acceptances are bought and sold in the market and the Federal Reserve can purchase these assets just as they buy and sell government securities.

CASH ITEMS IN THE PROCESS OF COLLECTION

This entry represents checks in the process of collection for which the Federal Reserve has not yet received payment from the banks on which the checks were drawn.

CASH
This is currency held by the Federal Reserve other than the Federal Reserve's holdings of its own Federal Reserve notes.

Liabilities

FEDERAL RESERVE NOTES
Federal Reserve notes comprise the major portion of the circulating currency of the nation and are a liability of the Federal Reserve System.

DEPOSITS
Deposits at the Federal Reserve include member bank reserve deposits, the general checking account balance of the United States Treasury, balances of foreign governments and foreign central banks, the exchange stabilization account, and nonmember banks' check clearing balances.

DEFERRED AVAILABILITY CASH ITEMS
This balance represents checks in the clearing process for which the Federal Reserve has not yet granted reserve credit.

OTHER LIABILITIES AND ACCRUED DIVIDENDS
This includes miscellaneous liabilities and dividends due to be paid on the Federal Reserve stock held by member banks.

Capital Accounts Capital accounts include the paid-in capital of the Federal Reserve Banks and the accrued surplus from retained earnings.

The Provision of Additional Reserves

There are a variety of methods by which the reserves available to the banking system can change or be changed. For the moment, two methods can be assumed: discounting and open market operations.

Discounting Assume that the Fail-Proof National Bank applies for a loan from the Federal Reserve Bank in its district. The Federal Reserve Bank examines the application and grants the loan request. The proceeds of the loan, $1,000, are given to the bank in the form of an increase in its reserve account. The changes in the balance sheet of the bank and the balance sheet of the Federal Reserve System are illustrated in Table 8–2 using simple T accounts.

The key point of the operation is the fact that the total supply of reserves available to the banking system has increased. Fail-Proof National Bank gained reserves and no bank lost reserves.

TABLE 8–2 Effects of a Discount Window Loan

FEDERAL RESERVE BANK		FAIL-PROOF NATIONAL BANK	
Assets	*Liabilities*	*Assets*	*Liabilities*
Loans +$1,000	Member bank deposits (reserves) +$1,000	Reserves +$1,000	Borrowing from Federal Reserve +$1,000
	Capital		Capital

Open Market Operations The purchase or sale of government securities by the Federal Reserve System is termed *open market operations* and is the primary method used by the Federal Reserve to control the size of the money supply.

To begin the process, assume that a government securities dealer decides to liquidate $100 of its holdings of government debt. The buyer of these securities happens to be the Federal Reserve System. The securities dealer receives a check from the Federal Reserve in payment for the securities and deposits the check from the Federal Reserve in its checking account at Fail-Proof National Bank. Fail-Proof sends the check through the check clearing process and receives $100 of reserve credit at the Federal Reserve. The simplified balance sheet changes are illustrated in Table 8–3.

The key point in the illustration of open market operations is that the Federal Reserve, when paying for the government securities, created new reserves for Fail-Proof National Bank. Unlike the cases of check clearing illustrated in Chapter 3, the transaction did not result in a reserve loss at any other commercial bank. Fail-Proof has gained reserves, but no other bank has lost reserves; Fail-Proof's gain is a net addition to the reserves available to the banking system. Balance sheets for Fail-Proof National Bank, both before and after the open market

TABLE 8–3 Open Market Purchase of Government Securities

SECURITIES DEALER		FAIL-PROOF NATIONAL BANK		FEDERAL RESERVE BANK	
Assets	*Liabilities*	*Assets*	*Liabilities*	*Assets*	*Liabilities*
Demand deposits +$100	Capital	Reserves at Federal Reserve Bank +$100	Demand deposits +$100	Government bonds +$100	Reserves of Fail-Proof National Bank +$100
Government bonds −$100			Capital		Capital

TABLE 8–4 The Effect of Open Market Operations on Fail-Proof National Bank

BEFORE				*AFTER*			
FAIL-PROOF NATIONAL BANK				*FAIL-PROOF NATIONAL BANK*			
Assets		*Liabilities*		*Assets*		*Liabilities*	
Securities	$2,500	Demand		Securities	$2,500	Demand	
Loans	2,000	deposits	$5,000	Loans	2,000	deposits	$5,100
Reserves	1,000	*Capital*	500	Reserves	1,100	*Capital*	500
	$5,500		$5,500		$5,600		$5,600

operations, are presented in Table 8–4 to show the gain of deposits and reserves. The balance sheets are simplified and assumed numbers are used for the various accounts.

The Money Supply Expansion Process

The open market operation in Tables 8–3 and 8–4 forms the basis for the illustration of the expansion process. To begin the analysis, the following assumptions are made:

1. All money is held as demand deposits (checking account balances at commercial banks).
2. Time, and other forms of bank deposits, do not exist.
3. All commercial banks hold reserve balances at the Federal Reserve banks in an amount equal to 20 percent of demand deposits.
4. Each commercial bank is holding reserves equal to exactly 20 percent of demand deposits, does not desire to hold any excess reserves (more than 20 percent), and is not permitted to hold less than the required percentage of reserves.
5. All banks have additional lending opportunities.

Applying these assumptions to Fail-Proof National Bank, Fail-Proof held exactly the required amount of reserves against its demand deposits before the open market operation. After the open market operation, Fail-Proof has excess reserves. Required reserves are $1,020 ($5,100 × 0.20) and total reserves are $1,100. Thus, excess reserves are $80 ($1,100 –$1,020). The general rule of these money supply expansion models is that the bank can increase its holdings of loans or securities by an amount equal to its excess reserves.

Assume that a potential borrower approaches the bank for an $80 loan. He passes the bank's credit investigation and receives a loan of $80. The bank adds the proceeds of the loan, $80, to the borrower's checking account at the bank. In other words, the bank creates $80 of demand deposits for the borrower. The bank adds the new loan to its loan portfolio; the new balance sheet position of the bank is portrayed in Table 8–5.

TABLE 8–5

FAIL-PROOF NATIONAL BANK			
Assets		*Liabilities*	
Securities	$2,500	Demand deposits	$5,180
Loans	2,080		
Reserves	1,100	*Capital*	500
	$5,680		$5,680

The step illustrated in Table 8–5 is only an intermediate step, because the borrower has not borrowed in order to hold additional demand deposit balances; he intends to spend the proceeds of the loan. Therefore, assume that the borrower uses the funds to have repairs made on his car and he pays $80 to Joe's Garage. Joe receives the $80 check and deposits the check in his checking account at the Commerce National Bank. Commerce National Bank submits the check to the Federal Reserve System to be cleared and in the normal process receives $80 of reserve credit. Fail-Proof National Bank loses $80 of reserves as a result of the check clearing process. Fail-Proof records its $80 reserve loss and subtracts $80 from the deposit account of the borrower. These transactions are summarized in Table 8–6.

After all the transactions have taken place, the final balance sheet of Fail-Proof National Bank is presented in Table 8–7. The net effect on Fail-Proof has been an increase in demand deposits of $100 (the securities dealer's deposit), an increase in reserves of $20, and an increase in loans of $80. The emphasis now shifts to Commerce National Bank; the effects on Commerce's balance sheet are illustrated by additions and subtractions and balance sheet details are omitted.

TABLE 8–6

Check of borrower drawn on account at Fail-Proof National Bank	→	Joe's Garage	→	Joe's account at Commerce National Bank	→
Federal Reserve Bank	→	Reserve credit to Commerce National Bank	→	Reserve loss to Fail-Proof National Bank	→
Fail-Proof National Bank decreases its reserve account and the demand deposit account of the borrower					

TABLE 8–7

FAIL-PROOF NATIONAL BANK

Assets		*Liabilities*	
Securities	$2,500	Demand deposits	$5,100
Loans	2,080		
Reserves	1,020	*Capital*	500
	$5,600		$5,600

When the $80 check drawn on Fail-Proof is deposited in Commerce Bank by Joe's Garage and is cleared through the Federal Reserve, the changes in Commerce Bank's balance sheet are as shown in Table 8–8. Assuming that Commerce was exactly meeting the 20 percent reserve requirement before these changes, the bank now has $80 of additional reserves for only $80 of additional demand deposits. Commerce has excess reserves of $64 because only $16 of added reserves is needed to meet the reserve requirement on the added $80 of demand deposits. Therefore, following the general rule, Commerce can lend out its $64 of excess reserves.

TABLE 8–8

COMMERCE NATIONAL BANK

Step 1	Reserves +$80	Demand deposits +$80

Assuming a borrower is found, Commerce grants a loan for $64 and credits the proceeds to the demand deposit account of the borrower. These transactions are recorded as Step 2 in Table 8–9. Next, the borrower spends the proceeds of the loan by drawing a check on his account at Commerce to the order of Speedy Appliance Repair Service. Speedy Appliance Repair Service deposits the check in its account at Grand National Bank. The clearing of the check results in the transfer of $64 of

TABLE 8–9

COMMERCE NATIONAL BANK

Step 1	Reserves +$80	Demand deposits +$80
Step 2	Loans +$64	Demand deposits +$64

TABLE 8–10

COMMERCE NATIONAL BANK		
Step 1	Reserves +$80	Demand deposits +$80
Step 2	Loans +$64	Demand deposits +$64
Step 3	Reserves −$64	Demand deposits −$64

reserves from Commerce to Grand National Bank. The subsequent reduction of the borrower's deposits and Commerce's reserves are shown in Step 3 of Table 8–10.

The net effect of the series of transactions on the balance sheet of Commerce National Bank is illustrated in Table 8–11. Commerce National Bank received added deposits of $80 (the deposit of Joe's Garage) and has met the 20 percent reserve requirement by increasing its reserve deposits by $16. The other $64 was used to make an added loan.

So far, the added $100 of reserves provided by the Federal Reserve's purchase of securities has resulted in an increase in demand deposits of $244 ($100 by the securities dealer, $80 by Joe's Garage, and $64 by Speedy Appliance Repair). Loans have expanded by $144 ($80 loaned out by Fail-Proof and $64 loaned out by Commerce). However, the process goes beyond this point. When Commerce National Bank lost $64 of reserves and deposits in Step 3 of Table 8–10, Grand National Bank gained deposits and reserves of $64.

Grand National Bank, having added deposits and added reserves of $64, is in a position to lend its excess reserves of $64 – ($64 × 0.20) = $51.20. Table 8–12 illustrates the receipt of $64 of added deposits and reserves in Step 1, the granting of a loan and creation of new demand deposits of $51.20 in Step 2, and the loss of reserves and reduction of deposits of $51.20 in Step 3. The net effect on Grand National Bank is a $64 increase of deposits, an increase of loans of $51.20, and an increase of reserves of $12.80.

Grand National's loss of reserves in Step 3 results in a reserve gain for another bank and the process continues. However, at this point, a summary table

TABLE 8–11

COMMERCE NATIONAL BANK		
Assets		*Liabilities*
Loans	+$64	Demand deposits +80
Reserves	+$16	
		Capital

TABLE 8–12

	GRAND NATIONAL BANK	
Step 1	Reserves +$64.00	Demand deposits +$64.00
Step 2	Loans +$51.20	Demand deposits +$51.20
Step 3	Reserves −$51.20	Demand deposits −$51.20

saves going through more detail. In Table 8–13, the net effect on each bank in the process is summarized and the total changes over an infinite number of banks are calculated.

As Table 8–13 indicates, the total change in the money supply, equal in this case to the change in demand deposits, has been $500. The original addition of $100 of reserves has resulted in a multiple expansion of the money supply. Each bank in the sequence has used its new reserves to increase its lending activity. As a result, total loans have increased by $400. The $100 of reserves provided by the Federal Reserve has become required reserves for the $500 of new demand deposits.

The process of contraction of the money supply is the reverse of the expansion process. In the contraction case, the Federal Reserve System sells $100 of securities and the security dealer pays for the securities by check. The Federal Reserve collects on the $100 check by decreasing the reserve account of the bank

TABLE 8–13 Summary Table of Deposit Expansion Process

BANK	*CHANGE IN DEMAND DEPOSITS*	*CHANGE IN RESERVES*	*CHANGE IN LOANS*
Fail-Proof National	$100.00	$20.00	$80.00
Commerce National	80.00	16.00	64.00
Grand National	64.00	12.80	51.20
Bank *A*	51.20	10.24	40.96
Bank *B*	40.96	8.19	32.77
Bank *C*	32.77	6.55	26.22
Bank *D*	26.22	5.24	20.98
Bank *E*	20.98	4.20	16.78
Bank *F*	16.78	3.36	13.42
Bank *G*	13.42	2.68	10.74
Bank *H*	10.74	2.15	8.59
Bank *I*	8.59	1.72	6.87
	↓	↓	↓
	∞	∞	∞
	$500.00	$100.00	$400.00

on which the check is drawn. The security dealer has \$100 more government securities and \$100 less demand deposits. The security dealer's bank loses \$100 of demand deposits and loses \$100 of reserves. The bank now has a deficiency in its reserve account at the Federal Reserve. The \$100 deposit loss reduced required reserves by \$20; the total reserve loss was \$100. The bank is \$80 deficient in its reserve account.

The usual reaction to a reserve deficiency is to liquidate short-term government securities because loans cannot be easily sold and most loans cannot be called in before maturity. Thus, the bank sells \$80 of securities to an investor. The investor pays by check and when the bank clears the check through the Federal Reserve, it receives \$80 of reserve credit. However, the investor's bank has now lost \$80 of deposits and \$80 of reserves; the investor's bank has a \$64 reserve shortage because total reserves declined \$80 and required reserves declined \$16. This bank must now sell \$64 of securities to restore its reserve balance, and a third bank loses reserves. The process continues until bank security holdings have decreased by \$400 and demand deposits have decreased by \$500.

Under the original assumptions, a formula can be developed for the expansion of demand deposits. The added reserves were the monetary base on which the added demand deposits were constructed. Thus

$$\Delta\text{Reserves} = \Delta\text{demand deposits} \times \text{reserve requirement}$$

or

$$\Delta R = \Delta DD \times RR_{DD}$$

where

ΔR = change in reserves available to the banking system
ΔDD = change in demand deposits
RR_{DD} = reserve requirement on demand deposits

To derive the change in demand deposits, start with

$$\Delta R = \Delta DD \times RR_{DD}$$

and divide both sides of the equation by $1/RR_{DD}$ to obtain

$$\Delta DD = \Delta R \times \frac{1}{RR_{DD}}$$

Using the numbers of Table 8–13,

$$\$500 = \$100 \times \frac{1}{0.20}$$

This simple model of expansion of the supply of demand deposits makes clear the impact of a change in the reserve requirement. An increase in the reserve requirement decreases the maximum possible expansion of deposits resulting from a given reserve increase. The example of an expansion of demand deposits of \$500 resulting from an increase in reserves of \$100 assumed a reserve requirement of 20 percent. If the reserve requirement had been 25 percent, the maximum quantity of new demand deposits would have been \$400.

Public Asset Preferences The example of expansion of the money supply in Table 8–13 assumed that all money was held in the form of demand deposits. However, this is clearly not a good assumption. Some of the expansion of the money supply will be in the form of an expansion of cash holdings, and some will be in the form of added holdings of demand deposits. In addition, depositors will convert some of the new demand deposits into time deposits.

The conversion of demand deposits into cash or time deposits reduces the amount of reserves available to support new demand deposits. If the public increases its cash holdings, the banks must draw down reserves in order to meet the cash withdrawals. If depositors convert demand deposits into time deposits, reserves that were previously supporting the expansion of demand deposits must be used as reserves for time deposits.

Allowing for the holding of cash and time deposits, reserves are now divided so that

$$\Delta R = (\Delta DD \times RR_{DD}) + (\Delta TD \times RR_{TD}) + \Delta CC$$

where $\Delta TD =$ change in dollars of time deposits
$RR_{TD} =$ reserve requirement on time deposits
$\Delta CC =$ change in coin and currency outstanding

The equation for the change in demand deposits now becomes[1]

$$\Delta DD = \Delta R \left[\frac{1}{RR_{DD} + \left(\frac{\Delta TD}{\Delta DD} \times RR_{TD} \right) + \frac{\Delta CC}{\Delta DD}} \right]$$

The change in demand deposits becomes a function of the change in reserves, the increase in time deposits desired by the public for each added dollar of demand deposits $\Delta TD/\Delta DD$, and the increase in coin and currency desired by the public for each added dollar of demand deposits $\Delta CC/\Delta DD$.

To illustrate the workings of the equation, assume

$\Delta R =$ \$100 (added reserves)
$RR_{DD} =$ 0.20 (reserve requirement on demand deposits)
$RR_{TD} =$ 0.04 (reserve requirement on time deposits)
$\frac{\Delta TD}{\Delta DD} =$ 0.25 (the amount of added time deposits desired by the public for each added dollar of demand deposits)
$\frac{\Delta CC}{\Delta DD} =$ 0.29 (the amount of added coin and currency desired by the public for each added dollar of demand deposits)

[1]The derivation is

$$\Delta R = (\Delta DD \times RR_{DD}) + (\Delta TD \times RR_{TD}) + \Delta CC$$

Multiply both sides of the equation by $\frac{1}{\Delta R \times \Delta DD}$, so that

$$\frac{1}{\Delta DD} = \frac{1}{\Delta R} \left[RR_{DD} + \left(\frac{\Delta TD}{\Delta DD} \times RR_{TD} \right) + \frac{\Delta CC}{\Delta DD} \right]$$

Invert so that

$$\Delta DD = \Delta R \left[\frac{1}{RR_{DD} + \left(\frac{\Delta TD}{\Delta DD} \times RR_{TD} \right) + \frac{\Delta CC}{\Delta DD}} \right]$$

Solving for ΔDD,

$$\Delta DD = \$100 \left[\frac{1}{0.20 + (0.25 \times 0.04) + 0.29} \right]$$

$$\Delta DD = \$100 \left(\frac{1}{0.50} \right)$$

$$\Delta DD = \$200$$

In this example, the change in assets resulting from the $100 increase in reserves is

ΔDD = $200
ΔCC = $58 (29% of the amount of the increase in demand deposits)
ΔTD = $50 (25% of the increase in demand deposits)

The change in the supply of money is the sum of the change in demand deposits and the change in coin and currency or $258.

Restating the reserve use equation,

$$\Delta R = (\Delta DD \times RR_{DD}) + (\Delta TD \times RR_{TD}) + \Delta CC$$

and substituting the results of the example

$$\$100 = (\$200 \times 0.20) + (\$50 \times 0.04) + \$58$$
$$\$100 = \$40 + \$2 + \$58$$

The $100 increase in reserves was used in the following way:

$40 = required reserves for an additional $200 of demand deposits
$ 2 = required reserves for an additional $50 of time deposits
$58 = increase in coin and currency outstanding

Excess Reserves Thus far, the assumption has been that all reserves supplied by the central bank have been used by the commercial banks to expand the money supply. The commercial banking system has not desired to hold more than the minimum quantity of reserves. This assumption is not necessary to the analysis. To incorporate the holding of excess reserves, *XR,* the reserve use equation is expanded. The new equation is

$$\Delta R = (\Delta DD \times RR_{DD}) + (\Delta TD \times RR_{TD}) + \Delta CC + \Delta XR$$

The new equation for the expansion of demand deposits is

$$\Delta DD = \Delta R \left[\frac{1}{RR_{DD} + \left(\frac{\Delta TD}{\Delta DD} \times RR_{TD} \right) + \frac{\Delta CC}{\Delta DD} + \frac{\Delta XR}{\Delta DD}} \right]$$

All terms are the same in the new expansion equation except for the addition of $\Delta XR/\Delta DD$, which measures the change in excess reserves held by the member banks for each $1 change in demand deposits.

Assuming that the other variables have the same values as in the previous example and that the banks desire to hold \$0.10 of excess reserves for each additional dollar of demand deposits, the change in demand deposits resulting from an additional \$100 of reserves is

$$\Delta DD = \$100 \times \left[\frac{1}{0.20 + (0.25 \times 0.04) + 0.29 + 0.10}\right]$$

$$\$166.67 = \$100\left(\frac{1}{0.6}\right)$$

The change in demand deposits of \$166.67 plus a change in coin and currency of \$48.33 (0.29 × \$166.67) results in a total change in the money supply of \$215. The change in time deposits is \$41.67 (0.25 × \$166.67). As would be expected, the holding of excess reserves resulted in a smaller change in the money supply than in the previous example.

Returning to the reserve use equation,

$$\Delta R = (\Delta DD \times RR_{DD}) + (\Delta TD \times RR_{TD}) + \Delta CC + \Delta XR$$

and substituting the results of the example,

$$\$100 = (\$166.67 \times 0.20) + (\$41.67 \times 0.04) + \$48.33 + \$16.67$$
$$\$100 = \$33.33 + \$1.67 + \$48.33 + \$16.67$$

The \$100 increase in reserves was used in the following manner:

\$33.33 = required reserves for the additional \$166.67 of demand deposits
\$ 1.67 = required reserves for the additional \$41.67 of time deposits
\$48.33 = increase in coin and currency outstanding
\$16.67 = excess reserves (0.10 of added demand deposits)
\$100.00

Who Controls Changes in the Money Supply?

Having examined the mechanical process by which changes in the money supply occur, the next question is, who controls these changes? The changes in the money supply are a result of the preferences and interaction of the Federal Reserve System, the commercial banks, and the public.

The role of the Federal Reserve is clear from the examples in the previous sections. The Federal Reserve controls the supply of reserves available to the banking system. Unless the Federal Reserve supplies added reserves, there is a limit to the amount by which the public and the commercial banks can expand the money supply.

Besides controlling the supply of reserves available to the banking system, the Federal Reserve controls the reserve requirements on demand and time deposits. Changes in reserve requirements affect the maximum possible change in demand deposits resulting from a given amount of added reserves. As reserve requirements on either demand or time deposits are increased, a smaller proportion of funds is available to make new loans and create new demand deposits. If reserve requirements are decreased, the maximum possible expansion of the money supply is increased, although the banks do not have to use the excess reserves to expand the money supply. They may hold excess reserves.

The Federal Reserve's influence on the money supply expansion process goes beyond these direct influences. By varying the terms on which banks can offer demand and time deposit accounts to the public, the Federal Reserve influences the form in which the public chooses to hold its wealth. For example, by increasing Regulation Q ceilings, the Federal Reserve can increase the desire of the public to hold time deposits. Likewise, permitting the banks to pay interest on demand deposits would probably encourage people to hold more demand deposits and less cash; reducing the value of $\Delta CC/\Delta DD$ would increase the maximum quantity of demand deposits which could result from a given quantity of reserves.

The behavior of the public is the second influence on the expansion potential of a given quantity of reserves. By changing their relative holdings of coin and currency, demand deposits, and time deposits, the public can change the results of the demand deposit expansion process. A desire to hold a relatively larger amount of coin and currency drains reserves from the commercial banking system and limits the ability of the banks to expand demand deposits. As indicated previously, the public's choice between currency, demand deposits, and time deposits depends heavily on the terms that the banks offer (or are permitted to offer) on deposit accounts.

Finally, the behavior of the banks affects the expansion that can take place as a result of the provision of new reserves by the Federal Reserve System. Within the limits established by the Federal Reserve, the banks select the terms on which they will accept deposits. Even though the Federal Reserve allows banks to pay a given rate of interest on time deposits, the banks do not have to pay that rate. Therefore, the expansion of deposits depends on the banks' willingness and ability to utilize the powers provided by the Federal Reserve System.

The ability of the banking system to vary the quantity of excess reserves is the most potentially destabilizing factor in the expansion process. Although the Federal Reserve System can create additional reserves for the banking system, it cannot force the banks to use these added reserves to expand the money supply. The multiplier relationship between reserves and the money supply decreases if the banks desire to hold additional excess reserves. Even though the central bank may be creating additional reserves, monetary expansion does not take place if the banks merely add the new reserves to their excess reserve holdings.

Two possible explanations can be used to justify the holding of excess reserves. First, uncertainty about the stability of the banking system may cause an increase in bank holdings of excess reserves. This factor was especially important before World War II. The periodic monetary panics and waves of bank failures frightened the banks into holding excess reserves.

In the present context, the interest rate is probably the more important determinant of the holding of excess reserves. As interest rates rise, the opportunity cost of holding excess reserves rises. Excess reserves provide no income to the bank, and high interest rates encourage banks to utilize their excess reserves. Alternatively, the banks can lend their excess reserves, through the Federal Funds market, to banks that will utilize the reserves. Thus, the value of the money expansion multiplier should increase as interest rates rise and the opportunity cost of holding excess reserves increases.

Factors Changing the Effective Quantity of Bank Reserves

The quantity of reserves available to the member banks can be changed by a large number of factors. Some of these factors are policy variables such as open market operations and discounting; other factors result from nonpolicy influences on the supply of reserves. This section presents an analysis of the various factors that change bank reserves.

On a very short-term basis, the weekly publication (each Friday) of member bank reserve changes is the best key to current policy analysis. However, one week's change in member bank reserve levels does not mean a policy change. One must be careful to avoid reading too much into this statement.

The format of the weekly statement of member bank reserve changes presented in this section follows the format of the Federal Reserve System. Various newspapers publish the statement in slightly different forms.

The member bank reserve statement is framed in terms of factors supplying reserves to the banking system and factors absorbing the reserves of the banking system. The statement of factors supplying and absorbing reserves is presented in Table 8–14. The table also presents the net change in each item from the previous week's statement.

The basis of the statement of member bank reserve changes is the balance sheet of the Federal Reserve System presented in Table 8–1. The statement of member bank reserve changes developed in this section is for the same date as the balance sheet in Table 8–1 so that figures can be transferred directly from Table 8–1 to the new statement.

The Factors Supplying Reserve Funds

Comparing Table 8–14 with Table 8–1 indicates that nearly all of the items on the asset side of the balance sheet of the Federal Reserve System supply reserve funds to the banking system. The major policy items, changes in the Federal Reserve's holdings of government securities and changes in Federal Reserve loans to member banks, were the source of added reserves to the banks in the money supply expansion models. The same reasoning applies to the other items transferred from the asset side of the Federal Reserve balance sheet to the list of items supplying reserves. The differences are covered in the following subsections.

TABLE 8–14 Changes in Member Bank Reserves, December 31, 1975

	DECEMBER 31, 1975 (millions of dollars)		CHANGE FROM PREVIOUS WEEK (millions of dollars)	
FACTORS SUPPLYING RESERVE FUNDS				
U.S. government securities (including U.S. agency securities)	94,124		− 335	
Bought outright		92,789		+ 12
Held under repurchase agreements		1,335		−347
Loans (member bank borrowing)	211		−1,052	
Float	3,688		−1,168	
Acceptances	1,126		+ 156	
Other Federal Reserve assets	3,312		− 54	
Gold stock	11,599		0	
Special drawing rights	500		0	
Treasury currency outstanding	10,218		+ 119	
Total factors supplying reserve funds	124,778		−2,334	
FACTORS ABSORBING RESERVE FUNDS				
Currency in circulation	86,547		− 61	
Treasury cash	483		+ 49	
Deposits in Federal Reserve (other than member bank reserves)	8,728		+1,059	
Treasury deposits		7,285		+794
Foreign and other deposits		1,443		+265
Other Federal Reserve liabilities and capital	2,968		− 503	
Member bank reserves	26,052		−2,878	
Total factors absorbing reserve funds	124,778		−2,334	

SOURCE: *Federal Reserve Bulletin,* February 1976, pp. A2–A3.

Float Float is a new item. The entry for float is obtained by subtracting the liability entry "deferred availability cash items" from the asset entry "cash items in process of collection." *Float* is created as a result of the check clearing process. The asset item represents checks in the process of collection for which the Federal Reserve has not yet decreased bank reserve accounts. The banks on which these checks were drawn have not yet lost reserves. Deferred availability cash items are checks for which the Federal Reserve has not yet granted added reserve credit to the banks depositing the checks.

If all checks deposited in Federal Reserve Banks resulted in instantaneous gains and losses of reserves, float would be zero. Normally, the volume of float is relatively predictable. The Federal Reserve System is able to make reasonably accurate forecasts of the volume of float for a given day. If the Federal Reserve forecasts that a rise in the level of float on a given day would produce an excessive increase in total reserves available to the banking system, open market sales of government securities can be employed to remove these extra reserves from the banking system. Problems with the level of float arise when something happens to disrupt the normal check clearing process. Equipment breakdowns and transportation delays can rapidly increase the level of float. For example, assume a Federal Reserve Bank's computing equipment breaks down. The adding to and subtracting from bank reserve accounts stop and float moves unpredictably.

Treasury Currency Outstanding Treasury currency outstanding is a factor supplying reserves to the banking system. However, Treasury currency outstanding does not appear on the balance sheet of the Federal Reserve System. The outstanding Treasury currency is coin, United States notes, and silver certificates. Additions to Treasury currency outstanding supply reserve funds because the currency can be deposited in the banking system and become part of member bank reserves.

Cash The entry of cash on the balance sheet of the Federal Reserve System, Table 8–1, is subtracted in moving to the list of factors supplying reserve funds. The cash holdings of the Federal Reserve are holdings of Treasury currency. The fact that the Federal Reserve is holding the currency means it is not in circulation and is not a factor supplying reserves to the banking system.

In summary,

Total factors supplying reserves = total assets of Federal Reserve
– deferred availability cash items
– cash + Treasury currency out-
– standing

Factors Absorbing Reserve Funds

Except for the first two entries, the list of factors absorbing reserve funds is the same as the items on the liabilities and capital side of the balance sheet of the Federal Reserve System. Decreases in any of these items would provide added reserves for member banks. For example, if the Treasury spent part of its deposits at the Federal Reserve banks, the funds would become deposits of businesses and individuals in commercial banks, and the banks would receive added reserve credit when the Treasury's checks were cleared.

Currency in Circulation Currency in circulation absorbs reserve funds. If people desired to hold smaller amounts of currency, the excess currency would flow into the banks and the banks would turn the currency into the Federal Reserve and obtain reserve credit. Conversely, if people desire to hold more currency, the banks obtain more currency for the public by drawing against their reserve deposits at the Federal Reserve banks.

The figure for currency in circulation is calculated by adding the value of Federal Reserve notes outstanding and the value of Treasury currency. From this total, the cash asset item on the Federal Reserve's balance sheet and the Treasury cash item are subtracted. These two subtractions are necessary because the cash is not outstanding; this cash is held by the Federal Reserve or the Treasury.

Treasury Cash The cash holdings of the Treasury are added as a factor absorbing reserves. Although this item was subtracted in the calculation of currency outstanding because it is held by the Treasury, it does absorb reserves. If the Treasury reduced its holdings of cash, reserves would be expanded.

Member Bank Reserves The key result of the whole process is the effect of all of the other variables on the level of member bank reserves.

Interpretation of the Table

Making a policy interpretation from the information in Table 8–14 is difficult and risky. Over time, weekly changes in member bank reserves indicate trends resulting from business cycle factors, seasonal patterns of reserve availability, or monetary policy.

With a given week's data, one is most interested in the changes in government securities holdings and changes in the supply of member bank reserves. The observer can determine, for example, whether the Federal Reserve used open market operations to offset changes in the level of float or whether the Federal Reserve permitted a change in float or changes in currency outstanding to change the level of bank reserves. In general, one should examine the policy variables and the nonpolicy factors and attempt to determine the Federal Reserve's policy from the reaction of the Federal Reserve to changes in the nonpolicy factors such as changes in the level of float or changes in the Treasury's balance. If the Federal Reserve does not want changes in these items to affect policy, open market operations are used. However, the failure to offset an increase in the Treasury's deposits at the Federal Reserve indicates that the Federal Reserve is permitting the increase in the Treasury's account to absorb bank reserves.

A Recapitulation

Given the importance of the full understanding of the process by which the supply of money is changed, it may be helpful to give a brief recapitulation of the major points of the chapter:

1. The maximum possible expansion or contraction of the supply of money is a multiple of a change in the supply of reserves available to the banking system.

2. The expansion process begins with the bank initially receiving new reserves and proceeds through other banks as the excess reserves are used by each bank for the expansion of loans or security holdings.

3. The maximum possible expansion of the supply of demand deposits depends upon the level of reserve requirements for demand and time deposits; the desires of the public to hold coin, currency, and time deposits in preference to holding demand deposits; and the desire of the banking system to hold excess reserves.

4. The availability of reserves to make possible the expansion of the supply of demand deposits is influenced by the policies of the Federal Reserve with respect to open market operations, discounting, and reserve requirements.

5. Other factors, all of which are summarized in the table of factors supplying and absorbing reserves, affect the level of reserve availability unless offset by the use of open market operations or other policy measures.

REVIEW QUESTIONS

1. Using *T* accounts, illustrate the effect on the reserves of the banking system of the repayment by a bank of a discount window loan from a Federal Reserve Bank. Illustrate the effect of an open market sale of government securities by the Federal Reserve System.

2. List and briefly describe the major assets and liabilities of the Federal Reserve System.

3. Using the equations derived in the chapter, calculate the changes in demand deposits, time deposits, and currency under the following set of assumptions:

a. reserves increase by $1,000,
b. the currency/demand deposit ratio is 0.22,
c. the time deposit/demand deposit ratio is 0.20,
d. the excess reserve/demand deposit ratio is 0.05,
e. the reserve requirement on demand deposits is 0.12,
f. the reserve requirement on time deposits is 0.05.

(To check your work, the change in the M_1 measure of the money supply is $3,050.)

4. In Question 3, how are the added reserves of $1,000 distributed between added cash holdings, added excess reserve holdings, added reserves for demand deposits, and added reserves for time deposits?

5. Assume that the desire of the banking system to hold excess reserves increases from $0.05 to $0.10 per added $1 of demand deposits. How are the values in Question 3 changed?

6. How is the money supply calculated in Question 3 changed if the public desires to hold $0.25 additional currency for each $1 of added demand deposits?

7. List the major factors supplying and absorbing reserves available to the banking system.

8. Consult a newspaper and study the Federal Reserve's weekly statement of factors supplying and absorbing reserves. Can you interpret any policy change from this statement?

9. Using the example begun in Table 8–3, assume the Federal Reserve System sold $100 of securities. Work through the analysis of Table 8–3 through Table 8–13, assuming that each bank reacts to its reserve loss by selling securities.

10. Review the impacts of the public, the commercial banks, and the Federal Reserve System on the money supply process.

SUGGESTED READINGS

Albert E. Burger, "The Relationship Between Monetary Base and Money: How Close?" *Federal Reserve Bank of St. Louis Review,* October 1975, pp. 3–8.

Albert E. Burger, "Revision of the Monetary Base," *Federal Reserve Bank of St. Louis Review,* April 1975, pp. 23–28.

Willard T. Carleton and William R. Bryan, "Deposit Expansion and Federal Reserve-Banking System Interaction: A Micro Unit Simulation," *American Economic Review,* December 1971, pp. 901–915.

Arline Hoel, "A Primer on Federal Reserve Float," *Federal Reserve Bank of New York Monthly Review,* October 1975, pp. 245–253.

Modern Money Mechanics: A Workbook on Deposits, Currency and Bank Reserves, Federal Reserve Bank of Chicago, 1975.

Robert H. Rasche, "A Review of Empirical Studies of the Money Supply Mechanism," *Federal Reserve Bank of St. Louis Review,* July 1972, pp. 11–19.

9

PRE-KEYNESIAN MONETARY THOUGHT

The study of the theoretical relationship between money and other economic variables is nearly as old as recorded history. Although the full historical treatment of monetary thought is more appropriately included in a History of Economic Thought course, this chapter will focus on the major schools of thought. Most attention will be given to the development of the classical model, the quantity theory of money, and the 20th-century challenges to these venerable theories.

The Mercantilists and Money

The mercantilist school of thought was predominant in the period of the growth of nation-states and survived until the attack on mercantilism associated with the 1776 publication of Adam Smith's *An Inquiry into the Nature and Causes of the Wealth of Nations*. The mercantilists, who were interested in the development of the fortunes of the nation-state, tended to be very concerned with the acquisition of gold bullion by a nation and so proposed policies aimed at fostering the inflow of gold bullion and preventing its outflow.

The inflow of bullion into the mercantilist state was important not only for basic economic reasons but also for building the strength and financial resources of the state. The state with large reserves was able to consolidate its position in a changing world and had the wealth to protect itself militarily. In many cases, the mercantilists made the error of confusing wealth in the form of bullion with wealth in the form of productive capital goods.

The mercantilists were concerned with the balance of trade of the nation. They realized that this was the source of bullion imports and many went so far as to argue that the export of bullion should be prohibited.

During the mercantilist period, a relationship was observed between the quantity of money in circulation and the level of prices. The inflow of gold bullion from the Western Hemisphere during the years of exploration and exploitation drastically expanded the supply of bullion and resulted in price increases in all of Western Europe.

The mercantilists also recognized that the increase in the supply of money would have an effect on the volume of output. John Maynard Keynes, in his "Notes on Mercantilism" in *The General Theory of Employment, Interest, and Money,* argued that the mercantilist objective of promoting an inflow of gold was an efficient policy for that period. The nation had no direct controls over the rate of interest. However, an inflow of gold, by increasing the supply of money, lowered interest rates and stimulated business investment.[1] However, it is doubtful that any of the mercantilist writers saw this more subtle effect of the increase in the quantity of bullion. The mercantilists' belief that the inflow of gold would affect the level of output was stated in much more general terms.

The Specie Flow Mechanism

In general, the mercantilists did not have a full understanding of the relationship between the flow of gold bullion and the balance of trade. They frequently overlooked the fact that their nationalistic trade protection policies, if followed by all nations, would be self-defeating. Obviously, all nations could not be exporting more than they were importing and all could not be experiencing an inflow of gold. One nation's inflow had to be another nation's outflow.

The English philosopher, David Hume, drew together the thoughts of the mercantilists and developed the relationships between gold flows and prices. Hume is not classified as a mercantilist but is more in the tradition of Adam Smith; however, his writings preceded Smith's.[2]

Hume's analysis of the gold flow mechanism recognized that an inflow of gold, owing to a balance of trade surplus, increased the money supply and the level of prices. The rise in the level of prices made domestic goods less competitive in international markets and led to a decline in exports. At the same time, the higher domestic prices created an incentive for people to substitute imported goods for domestically produced goods. Thus, exports decreased and imports increased. The balance of trade shifted from surplus to deficit and gold flowed out of the country.

For the nation experiencing a balance of trade deficit, the process worked in the opposite direction. The export of bullion led to a fall in price levels and stimulated the exportation of goods. The combination of higher exports and lowered imports reversed the balance of trade deficit and led to gold inflows. Thus, both a balance of trade surplus and a balance of trade deficit were transitory phenomena which, owing to the effect of bullion flows on prices, would be eliminated over time. The specie flow mechanism was developed further by David Ricardo in the early 1800s.

[1]John M. Keynes, *The General Theory of Employment, Interest, and Money* (New York: Harcourt, Brace and Company, 1936), pp. 336–337.

[2]The collected economic essays of David Hume and an interpretation of his work are available in Eugene Rotwein, ed., *The Economic Writings of David Hume* (Edinburgh: Nelson, 1955). See his essays "Of Money" and "Of the Balance of Trade."

The Classical Period

The classical economists, loosely defined to cover most people from Adam Smith (late 1700s) to W. S. Jevons (about 1870), were concerned mainly with questions that today are classified as microeconomic issues. The theories of value and distribution were carefully developed within the context of a laissez faire economic system.

The theory of money and topics classified as macroeconomic concerns were not the major areas of interest to most of the classical economists. Except for the dissenters to the classical tradition, led by Karl Marx, classical macroeconomic thought centered around two concepts: the quantity theory of money and Say's Law. Points at which classical economists diverged from these concepts can be found in the literature,[3] but these two very critical ideas predominated in discussions of public policy until the Keynesian revolution.

Say's Law

Say's Law (John Baptiste Say, 1767–1832) is a cornerstone of classical thinking about macroeconomic problems. Stated in its most basic form, *Say's Law* argues that "supply creates its own demand." To the classical economist, and in a strictly accounting framework, the production of goods creates income sufficient to purchase the goods produced. As illustrated in Chapter 7, the value of output is equal to the value of incomes produced.

Assuming a purely barter economy with no money introduced into the model, the operation of the classical system is easily developed. In the primitive economy, with specialization of production and trade between individuals, the act of producing goods is equivalent to the demanding of goods. The harvester of coconuts is working to gather more coconuts because he expects to be able to trade the coconuts he does not consume for goods produced by other individuals. His supply of goods is a reflection of his demand for goods. If he did not desire the goods produced by other individuals, he would not bother gathering more coconuts and would sun himself under the coconut tree. In more formal terminology, if he did not want to consume other people's output, he would not produce goods and would instead increase his leisure. The fact that he chooses leisure reduces both the demand for and the supply of goods.

The Real Sector of the Classical Model

The classical model, viewing aggregate supply as creating aggregate demand, goes on to illustrate that unemployment does not represent an equilibrium condition of the economy. The coconut gatherer is not unemployed when he lies under

[3]See B. A. Corry, *Money, Saving and Investment in English Economics, 1800–1850* (London: Macmillan & Co., 1962).

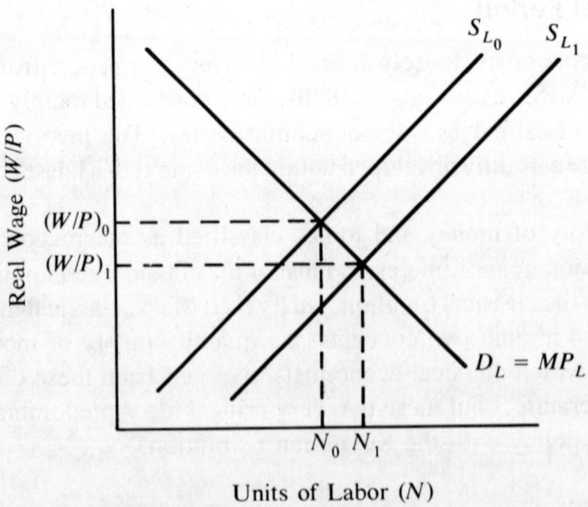

FIGURE 9–1 The Classical Labor Market

the tree; he has chosen leisure in preference to the added goods and services that could be obtained if he gathered more coconuts. If supply creates its own demand, then all that is required for a full employment level of aggregate demand is a full employment level of aggregate supply. If people are out of work and desire more goods, they will seek employment, push down wages, increase output, and generate incomes sufficient to purchase the additional output. Thus, there is no reason for the persistence of unemployment.

The classical model of the labor market presented in Figure 9–1 is such that unemployment is eliminated by wage flexibility. The supply of labor is represented by a curve S_{L0} sloping upward to the right in terms of the *real wage*, W/P (the wage in money terms, W, adjusted for the price level, P). At higher real wages, more units of labor are supplied to employers. A rise in the real wage is required to increase the quantity of labor supplied because people must be induced to substitute work, and the goods to be obtained from the income earned, for leisure.

The derivation of the demand for labor curve in terms of the real wage is more complex. Assume a fixed supply of capital and other factors of production except labor. Table 9–1 presents a basic analysis of the demand for labor. Column (2) presents the number of units of output which could be produced with each alternative number of units of labor in column (1). As the number of units of labor increases, the volume of output increases. Column (3) presents the marginal product of labor (*MPL*). The *marginal product of labor* is the amount of added output resulting from the employment of an additional unit of labor. For example, with 2 units of labor, output is 30 units; with 3 units of labor, output is 38 units. The marginal product of the third unit of labor is 8 units. The marginal product of labor declines as the number of units of labor increases because of the law of diminishing returns to the variable factor.

TABLE 9–1 The Demand for Labor

(1) UNITS OF LABOR	(2) UNITS OF OUTPUT	(3) MARGINAL PRODUCT OF LABOR (MPL)	(4) PRICE OF OUTPUT (P) ($)	(5) VALUE OF MARGINAL PRODUCT (VMP) ($)	(6) MONEY WAGE (W) ($)
1	20	20	5	100	20
2	30	10	5	50	20
3	38	8	5	40	20
4	44	6	5	30	20
5	48	4	5	20	20
6	50	2	5	10	20

In column (4), the price of the product is stated as $5 per unit. The firm is producing under conditions of perfect competition so that increases in the level of output have no effect on the price of the product. Column (5) measures the value to the firm of the marginal product of added units of labor and is obtained by multiplying column (3) by column (4). The value of the marginal product *(VMP)* of added units of labor declines because of the effect of diminishing marginal returns.

Column (6) presents data on the money wage that must be paid in order to attract added units of labor. Assume that the firm is operating in a perfectly competitive labor market so that all desired units of labor can be hired at the going wage of $20. The profit-maximizing rule for the firm is to hire all units of labor for which the value of the marginal product is equal to or greater than the money wage. Comparing columns (5) and (6) in Table 9–1 indicates that the value of the marginal product of the first 5 units of labor is equal to or greater than the wage that must be paid to each of these units of labor. Thus, the firm will hire 5 units of labor. The sixth unit of labor produces $10 worth of added product and would have to be paid $20. Hiring the sixth unit of labor would not be profitable.

To move from the rule that the firm hires all units of labor for which the value of the marginal product is equal to or greater than the wage to the format desired for further analysis, one adjustment is required. At this point,

$$\text{Value of marginal product} = \text{money wage}$$

or

$$VMP = W$$

However, the value of the marginal product is equal to the marginal product (MP) times the price (P), so it can be written

$$VMP = W \quad \text{or} \quad MP \times P = W$$

Dividing both sides of this identity by price (P), yields

$$MP = \frac{W}{P}$$

In the final formulation, the rule is that the firm hires units of labor up to the point at which the marginal product of labor (MP) is equal to the real wage of labor (W/P).

The diagram of the labor market is presented in Figure 9–1. The demand for labor function represents the marginal product of labor and indicates the number of units of labor which would be hired at each real wage. Given that additional units of labor result in a lower marginal product, more units of labor are hired only at a lower real wage. The demand for labor curve and the supply of labor curve determine the level of employment, N_0, and the equilibrium real wage $(W/P)_0$.

In classical economics, Figure 9–1 takes care of the unemployment problem. Those not working at the real wage $(W/P)_0$ prefer leisure to the going real wage. An increasing labor force would result in more units of labor being supplied at each possible real wage (a shift to the right of the supply of labor curve to S_{L1}), a decline in the real wage to $(W/P)_1$, and an increase in the units of labor employed from N_0 to N_1.

In a technical sense, unemployment could result only if wages were "sticky" and the real wage remained at $(W/P)_0$ while the true equilibrium real wage was $(W/P)_1$. If the wage of $(W/P)_0$ were maintained while the equilibrium wage declined to $(W/P)_1$, then the quantity of labor supplied would exceed the quantity of labor demanded, and some people who were willing to work would be unable to find employment. However, assuming that the unemployed workers would lower their wage demands in order to obtain employment, wages would be forced down to the new equilibrium level.

The persistence of classical thinking in this regard continued right through the Great Depression of the 1930s. To many observers, the solution for the vast unemployment of the 1930s was to bring about a lowering of wages.

In summary, unemployment to the classical economists was self-correcting. Supply and demand in the free market would take care of the problem. A decrease in the demand for a specific product would create unemployment for the producers of that item. The classical economist reasoned that these workers would quickly learn the lessons of the marketplace and switch to the production of an alternative good. All problems were self-correcting!

The second part of the production portion of the classical model of the economy provides the relationship between employment and output. Given a fixed (in the short run) supply of the other factors of production, the quantity of output is a function of the quantity of labor employed. The relationship between employment and output is illustrated in Figure 9–2. The lower part of Figure 9–2 is identical to Figure 9–1. The hypothetical scales on the horizontal axes of the two parts of Figure 9–2 are the same, so that the given quantity of employment determined in the lower portion can be transferred vertically to the upper portion.

In Figure 9–2, once the quantity of employment (N) is determined in the lower diagram, reference to the production function in the upper diagram provides the level of output (O) on the vertical axis. The output curve is sloped to indicate the influence of diminishing returns to the variable factor of production, labor. The demand for labor curve, the marginal product of labor, is derived from the slope of

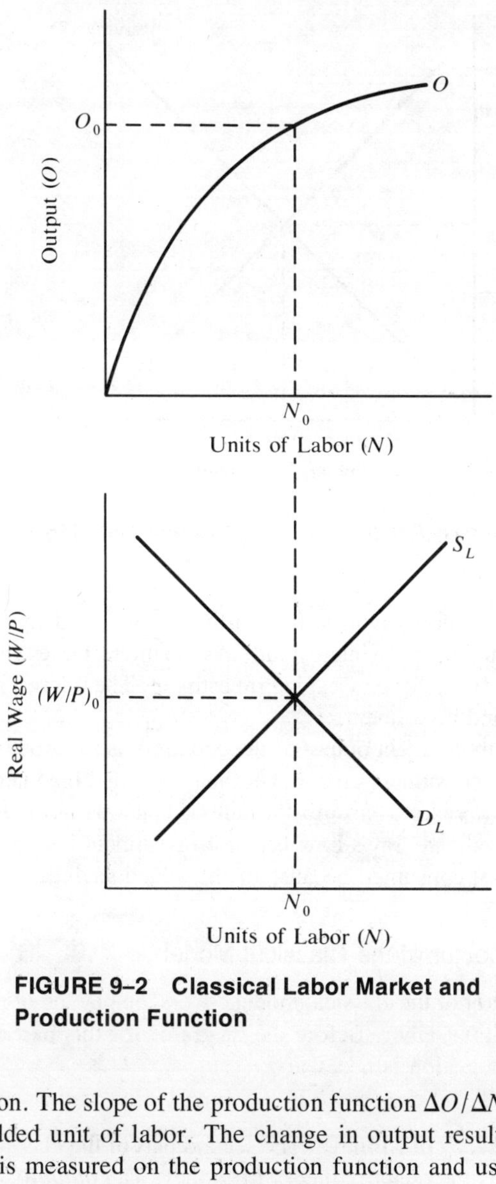

FIGURE 9–2 Classical Labor Market and Production Function

the output function. The slope of the production function $\Delta O / \Delta N$ is the marginal product of an added unit of labor. The change in output resulting from a unit change in labor is measured on the production function and used to derive the demand for labor curve in the lower half of Figure 9–2.

The two parts of Figure 9–2 cover the components of the real sector that are to be used for the development of the classical model. However, the real sector also includes the determination of the rate of interest. In Figure 9–3, the classical model of the interest rate is presented.

In Figure 9–3, the supply of saving is a function of the interest rate, i. At

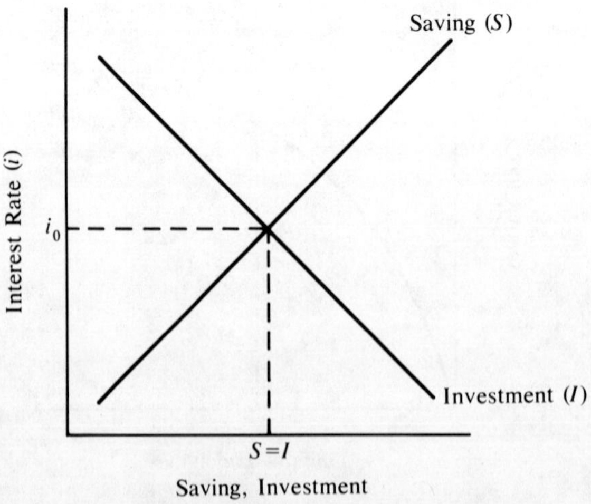

FIGURE 9–3 Classical Interest Rate Model

higher interest rates, more saving will be forthcoming. The demand for investment funds is also a function of the interest rate. As the interest rate falls, entrepreneurs will borrow more funds for new capital investment. The interest rate fluctuates to equalize saving and investment.

The full employment output of the economy is absorbed by consumption and investment. If consumers save, rather than consume, the interest rate declines and investment increases to absorb the output that was not consumed. Greater saving did not invalidate Say's Law because investment increased to absorb the output that was not consumed because of the added saving.

The Monetary Sector of the Classical Model

The monetary sector of the classical model covers the placing of money price tags on goods and units of labor. Before the diagrams for this part of the model are drawn, some explanation is necessary.

The Quantity Theory of Money The second part of the classical model, along with Say's Law, is the quantity theory of money. The *quantity theory of money* raised to its highest level states that a change in the supply of money leads to an equal proportionate change in the level of prices. Thus, if the money supply is doubled, the average level of prices also doubles. The influence of increases in the supply of money on prices was recognized early in economic history and appeared in various forms from the European age of exploration to the 1930s.

The quantity theory begins with the *equation of exchange*, which is stated in terms of four variables. The four variables are

M = the supply of money
V = velocity, the rate of turnover of the money supply, or the number of times the average unit of money is used per time period to purchase output
P = the average price of a unit of output
O = units of output

The equation of exchange states the truism that the quantity of money times the number of times the average unit of money is spent on output is equal to the average price of a unit of output times the number of units of output. Thus,

$$M \times V = P \times O$$

In this form, the equation of exchange states that the purchases of output, MV, are equal to the sales of output, PO. There is no arguing with that proposition! Using some simple numbers, if the money supply consists of 100 units of money and the average unit is spent on output five times in a year, the purchase of output is \$500. Because purchases and sales must be equal, the product of P and O must also be \$500. Assume 50 units of output are produced and the average price per unit of output is \$10; 50 units times a price of \$10 per unit produces the required \$500. At this point there is no theory.

The equation of exchange becomes a theory of economic behavior when assumptions are made about the variables in the model. The first question is, what effect will a change in the quantity of money have on the level of output? Classical economists had an easy answer to that question—the quantity of money has no effect on the level of output. The quantity of output is determined by the labor market and the production function. The real forces determined the level of output and only a change in the real forces could change the level of output.

The second question is, what effect do changes in the quantity of money have on the level of velocity? To consider this relationship, the classical attitude toward the holding of money must be explored.

Money, in the typical classical sense, was an economic tool that permitted society to avoid the problems of barter. Money was not an important participant in the determination of real variables. Money was important for its value as a medium of exchange, but the holding of money for its own sake was an act of economic irrationality.

Why would people hold money? The holder of money receives no interest. By holding money, the irrational man incurred an opportunity cost; he was losing the return that could be generated by the profitable employment of that money. The only rational reason for holding money was to spread out one's purchasing power over the period between paydays. A person could spend all of his income at the moment that he was paid but, more likely, would hold some cash to spend over the days remaining until the next payday. However, by the day on which the next pay was due, the consumer's cash balance would be zero. Money, the classical economists thought, was necessary to avoid bartering problems and to bridge the gap between paydays, but there was no other incentive to hold money.

The supply of money in the economy moved between the business sector and the factors of production. On payday, the factors of production received money from the business sector and as consumers gradually spent their incomes, the money flowed back to business firms. The next payday, the process began all over again. Neither business firms nor the income receivers held any idle cash balances.

The rate of turnover of the supply of money is a function of the length of the pay period. Assume that factors of production are paid once a month and spend their incomes evenly over the month so that they have zero cash holdings at the moment before the next payday. In this system, an average dollar is spent on output 12 times a year, once each month. The income velocity, the turnover of money against output, is 12. Alternatively, this average dollar changes hands 24 times a year—12 times as factor payments and 12 times as payments for output. The transactions velocity measure, 24, is a second measure of velocity and becomes important later in the chapter.

According to the quantity theory of money, the rate of turnover of money against output does not change as the quantity of money changes. The average dollar is exchanged for goods once a month and changes hands twice a month. A change in the length of the payment period would change velocity, but the quantity of money would have no effect on the rate of turnover of money. Therefore, velocity and output would remain constant as the supply of money changed. If the two sides of the equation of exchange were to be equal, changes in the quantity of money must lead to changes in the level of prices.

Taking a simple numerical example, assume

M = \$100 (money supply)
V = 12 (number of times each dollar is spent on output)
P = \$20 (price per unit of output)
O = 60 (units of output per year)

so that

$$\$100 \times 12 = \$20 \times 60$$

If both V and O are held constant (are not affected by a change in the quantity of money), then an increase in the quantity of money by 50 percent to \$150 leads to an increase in prices of 50 percent to \$30, so that

$$\$150 \times 12 = \$30 \times 60$$

The assumption of the quantity theory of money permits the development of a monetary sector of the classical model. In Figure 9–4, the two parts of Figure 9–2 are reproduced, along with a third sector that represents the operation of the quantity theory of money. The curve in the new diagram is a rectangular hyperbola; the product of O times P at all points on the curve is a constant. By the equation of exchange, the product of P times O must be equal to the product of M times V. P is plotted on the horizontal axis and O on the vertical axis. For example, using the

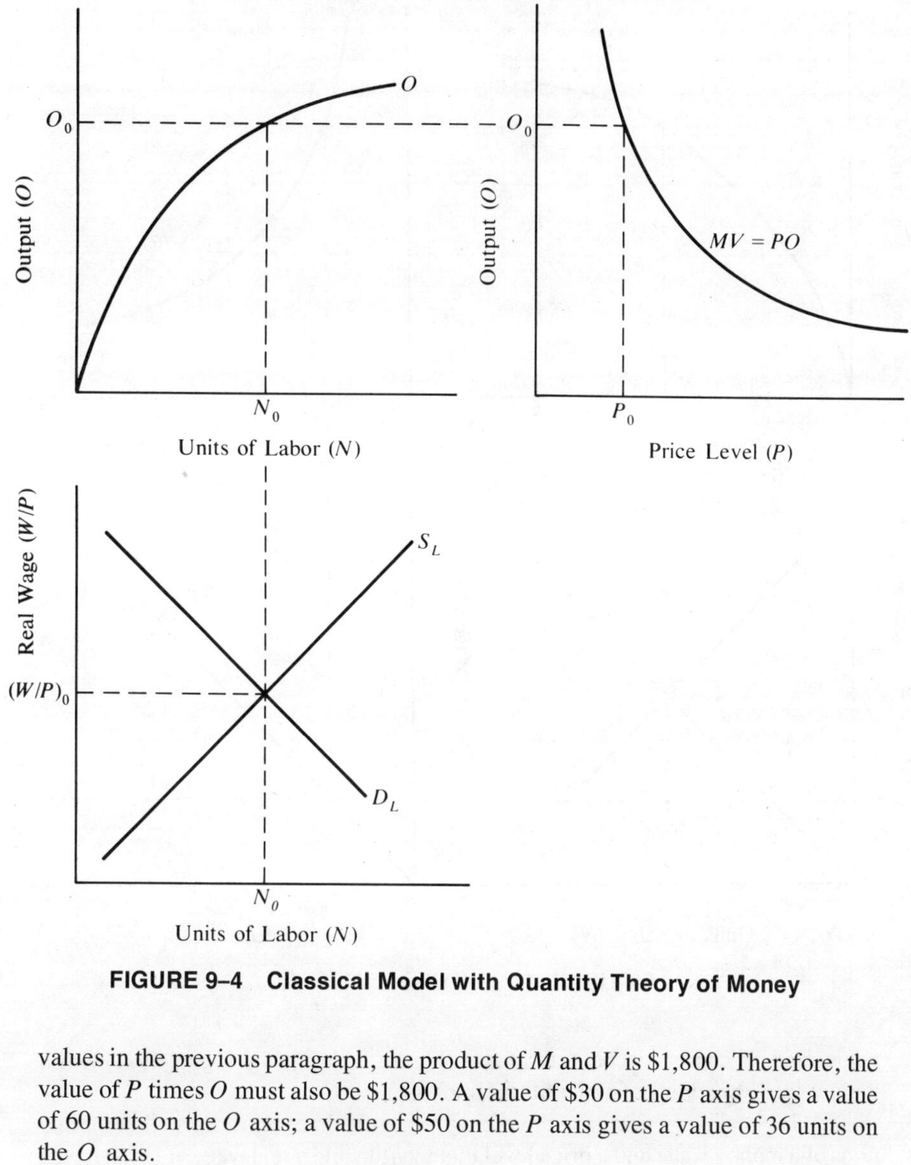

FIGURE 9–4 Classical Model with Quantity Theory of Money

values in the previous paragraph, the product of M and V is \$1,800. Therefore, the value of P times O must also be \$1,800. A value of \$30 on the P axis gives a value of 60 units on the O axis; a value of \$50 on the P axis gives a value of 36 units on the O axis.

The level of output, determined by the production function, is brought into the new sector in Figure 9–4 and the value of the price level is determined on the horizontal axis of the quantity theory diagram. Having determined the price level, only one additional diagram is necessary to complete this classical model. The real wage has been determined in the labor market diagram and the price level in the quantity theory diagram. The value of the money wage, W, is now the only missing

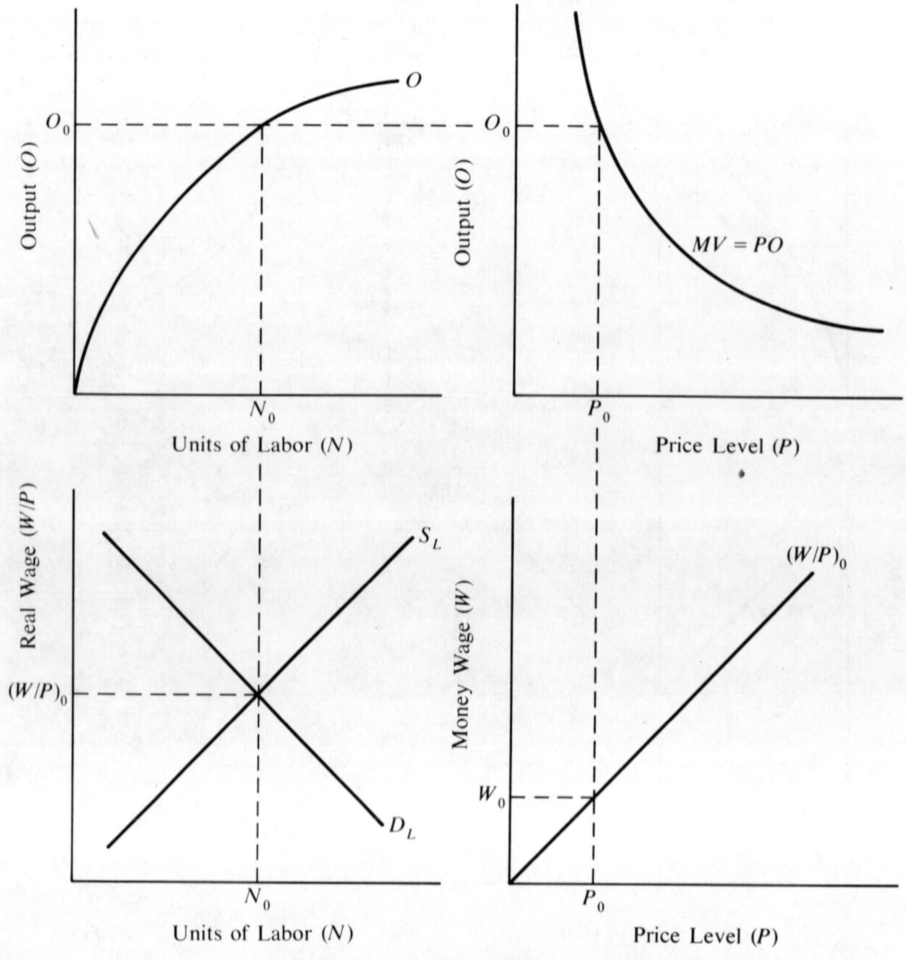

FIGURE 9–5 Full Classical Model

value, and W can easily be determined. Figure 9–5 repeats Figure 9–4 with a money wage quadrant completing the model.

The real wage vector in the money wage quadrant represents all combinations of a money wage and a price level that would yield a real wage of $(W/P)_0$, the real wage determined in the labor market. For example, if the real wage is to be \$10, this real wage could be produced by a money wage of \$20 and a price level of 2, a money wage of \$25 and a price level of 2.5, etc. All combinations of a money wage and a price level which yield a \$10 real wage are illustrated on the vector in the wage quadrant. Given the price level, P_0, and the real wage, $(W/P)_0$, the appropriate money wage, W_0, is determined.

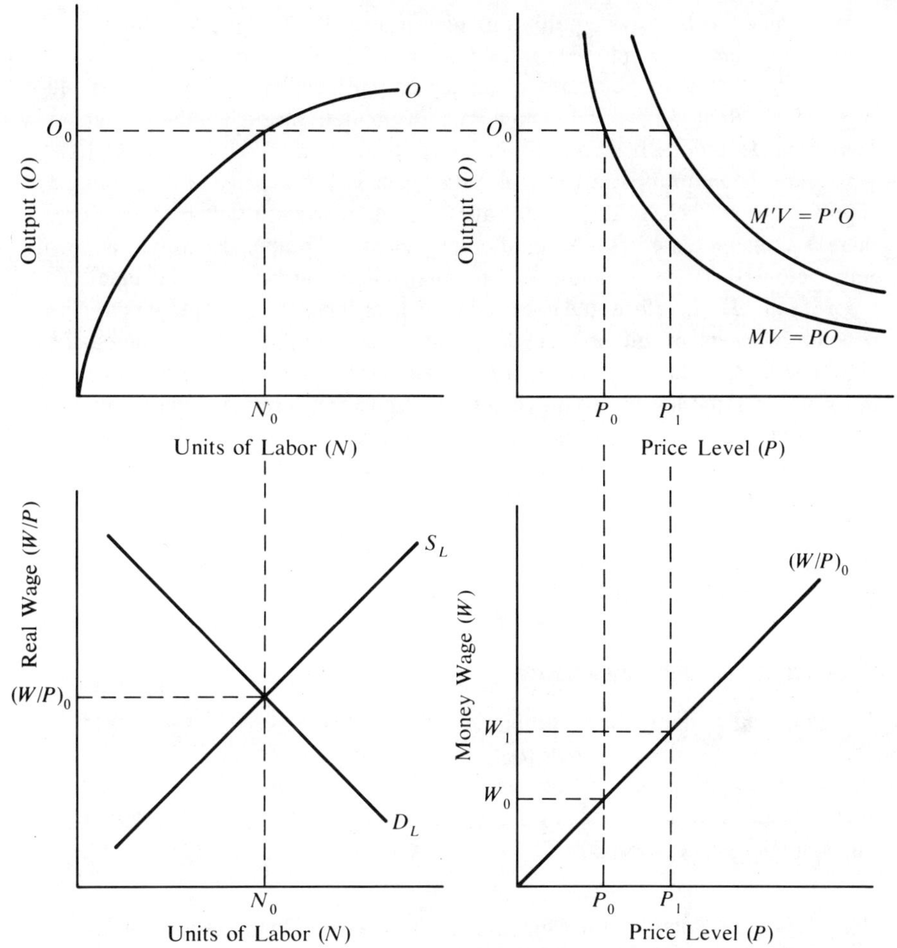

FIGURE 9–6 Classical Model with Change in the Money Supply

All the key variables—the level of employment, the real wage, the level of output, the level of prices, and the money wage—are now determined. The next major point is to examine the effect of a change in the supply of money.

In Figure 9–6, a change in the supply of money is introduced. The effect is diagrammed as a shift to the right of the *MV* curve in the upper right-hand quadrant. The product of the new money supply and the original level of velocity produces the new rectangular hyperbola illustrated in the diagram as $M'V = P'O$. Output remains constant and the effect of the money supply change is to increase the level of prices from P_0 to P_1. The new price level in the upper right-hand quadrant is brought down to the money wage quadrant and a new money wage, W_1, is determined. The new equilibrium real wage, $(W/P)_1$, is equal to the old *equilibrium real wage,* $(W/P)_0$.

The change in the supply of money only affects the money wage and the price level. Real wages and output remain at their original values after any temporary deviations from equilibrium have been worked out. The most likely temporary deviation is a fall in real wages because an expansion of the money supply increases prices faster than wages. As the real wage falls below $(W/P)_0$, there is some increase in the level of employment and output. However, at a real wage below $(W/P)_0$, the quantity of labor demanded is greater than the quantity of labor supplied. Therefore, the excess demand for labor leads employers to compete for workers by bidding up the money wage until the excess demand is eliminated at the old real wage of $(W/P)_0$. Therefore, any effects of the change in the supply of money on employment or output are purely transitory and are eliminated as the system comes back to equilibrium.[4]

Money served as a medium of exchange and determined the absolute level of prices in the classical system but did not affect the value of the real variables. A government advised by the classical economists did not have to worry too much about the macroeconomic aspects of the system. The economy would work toward full employment automatically.

Fisher and the Quantity Theory

The traditional quantity theory of money received its finest and last major exposition in the 1911 book *The Purchasing Power of Money* by Irving Fisher.[5] Fisher's presentation of the quantity theory is in terms of *transactions* rather than output, and the velocity measure is the average rate of turnover of money for transactions. The symbolic theory becomes $MV = PT$, in which

M = the supply of money
V = the number of times the average dollar is used in transactions in a given time period
P = the average price of transactions
T = the number of transactions

A transaction is any exchange of goods or services for money. In terms of the earlier analysis of velocity, both the spending of money for output and the payment of the factors of production are transactions.

The contribution of Fisher to the quantity theory of money is important for

[4]For a comprehensive treatment of the classical model, see Gardner Ackley, *Macroeconomic Theory* (New York: Macmillan Company, 1961), chap. 5–8, and Edward Shapiro, *Macroeconomic Analysis,* 3rd ed. (New York: Harcourt Brace Jovanovich, 1974), chap. 17.

[5]Irving Fisher, *The Purchasing Power of Money* (New York: The Macmillan Company, 1911).

two reasons. First, Fisher presented a perfectly rigid relationship between changes in the supply of money and changes in prices. A given change in the supply of money leads to an equal proportionate change in the level of prices. Second, Fisher argued that changes in the supply of money do not affect velocity or output.

Fisher's factors determining the volume of trade (output) are

1. conditions affecting producers, such as geographic differences in natural resource endowments, the extent of the division of labor in production, the development of production technology, and the stock of productive capital goods;
2. the demands of consumers resulting from the variety of human desires for goods; and
3. other factors, such as the development of the transportation industry, the extent of free trade, the confidence of the business community, and the nature of the monetary system.[6]

None of these factors would be affected by a change in the quantity of money.

In his consideration of the determinants of velocity, Fisher produced a similar list of nonmonetary factors that control the rate of turnover of the money supply. These factors include

1. habits of consumers with regard to the use of credit, the use of checks, and saving or hoarding;
2. the characteristics of the payments system relative to the regularity and frequency with which payments are made and the difference between the timing of the receipt and use of funds; and
3. other causes such as the density of the population and the efficiency of the transportation system.[7]

Changes in the supply of money are not on Fisher's list of factors determining velocity and the reader is led to Fisher's conclusion that price changes are equal in proportion to changes in the supply of money.

The Cambridge Cash Balance Equation

The Marshallian tradition, which produced great advances in price theory, did not produce equivalent improvements in the theory of money. Alfred Marshall and his contemporaries at Cambridge University continued to work on the basis of Say's Law and to accept the basic logic of the quantity theory of money.

The Cambridge cash balance equation modified the quantity theory to the extent of presenting the quantity theory as a theory of the demand for money. The basic form of the equation was

$$M = kPO$$

[6]Ibid., pp. 74–79.
[7]Ibid., pp. 79–89.

where k represents the proportion of the value of output that consumers and producers desire to hold in the form of cash.[8] The value of k is simply the reciprocal of V. Assuming that people desire to hold a given percentage k of the value of output in the form of money, an increase in the supply of money will have the usual effect—an increase in the level of prices, with k and O remaining constant.

Keynes, in his early writings, was heavily influenced by the classical tradition of his teachers at Cambridge. However, over time, his opinions relative to the stability of k began to change and as he worked toward *The General Theory* he gradually recognized that the proportion of income that would be held as cash balances would depend in part on the level of interest rates. The influence of interest rates on the demand for money became an important part of *The General Theory* and is considered in the next chapter.

Pre-Keynesian Monetary Policy

Assuming that changes in the supply of money affect the level of prices rather than the level of employment and output, what are the functions of monetary policy?

First, monetary policy could serve as a means of protecting the nation's gold supply. Tighter credit and higher interest rates could attract investment funds into the nation. Prior to 1931, the policy of the Bank of England was oriented toward the maintenance of England's gold reserves, and it was generally believed that increases in the interest rate would attract funds to the London money makets.

Control of the money supply would also reinforce the operations of the specie flow mechanism. A decline in the supply of money, whether resulting from the outflow of gold or from the reduction of the supply of paper money convertible into gold, would help lower the price of domestic goods in domestic and world markets.

The control of the supply of money by the banking authority could also be used to control the supply of credit. Overexpansion of credit could be prevented by the use of monetary policy. On the other hand, a liquidity crisis could be avoided or corrected by the existence of a central bank (or a private bank performing central banking functions) that would be a lender of last resort to the banking system. If one bank was willing and able to lend to the other banks when the demand for currency conversion or the withdrawal of deposits grew to crisis proportions, panic in the monetary system could be averted and the need to suspend currency conversion could be avoided.

The Bank of England came to perform the role of lender of last resort in England by the mid-1800s, and the original function of the Federal Reserve System was to lend to the commercial banks in times of financial panic. The early

[8]Alfred Marshall, *Money, Credit, and Commerce* (London: Macmillan & Co., 1923), pp. 44–46.

development of central banking functions in England is described in Walter Bagehot's classic 1873 work, *Lombard Street*.[9]

By the beginning of the 20th century, the impact of changes in the supply of money on the rate of interest was beginning to be recognized as an important economic variable. The works of Knut Wicksell, the Swedish neoclassical economist, had a major impact on monetary writings.

Wicksell, while holding to the classical belief in the influence of the quantity of money on the level of prices, increased the sophistication of monetary analysis. In the basic quantity theory of money, the growth in the money supply was assumed to arise from inflows of gold or creation of new money by the government. Wicksell, more than his predecessors, recognized the role of the banking system in the process of money creation.

In the Wicksellian analysis, there are two interest rates—the market rate of interest and the natural rate of interest. The market rate of interest is the cost of borrowing funds and is what we would today call "the rate of interest." The natural rate of interest is determined, as in the classical model, by the productivity of capital (determining the demand for investment funds) and the saving function (reflecting the willingness of savers to forego consumption).

If the market rate of interest is equal to the natural rate of interest, saving is equal to investment and prices are stable. The problem arises when the market and natural rates of interest are different. A gap between the market rate and the natural rate of interest is likely because the natural rate cannot be observed directly and is likely to fluctuate over time.

Assume that the productivity of capital increases so that the natural rate of interest rises above the market rate of interest. If the banks have no excess reserves, and no other factors in the money-expansion equation change, the money supply cannot increase. There is more saving and investment and less consumption because of the higher natural rate of interest. Investment spending is substituted for consumption spending. Price levels do not change because the supply of money does not change. Competition for the fixed available supply of money bids the market rate of interest up to equality with the natural rate of interest.

However, if the banks have excess reserves available and the central bank does not intervene, the outcome may be different. Given that the natural rate of interest is greater than the market rate of interest, there is an incentive for business to borrow from the banks and expand their investment spending. The demand for capital goods is now equal to the sum of saving and the new bank loans. The money supply has increased and prices are bid up as firms attempt to divert additional resources to their investment projects and consumers attempt to maintain their consumption. The introduction of the new money into the system has created demands for goods greater than the supply of goods because the demand for

[9]Walter Bagehot, *Lombard Street* (New York: Scribner, Armstrong & Co., 1873). Also available in a new edition with an introduction by Frank Genovese (Homewood, Ill.: Richard D. Irwin, 1962).

investment goods has exceeded the supply of saving by an amount equal to the new money created. Price increases continue as long as the banks are willing and able to lend at a rate less than the natural rate of interest. However, the process should be self-limiting because the banks, as they gradually reduce their holdings of excess reserves, should increase the market interest rate until it is equal to the natural rate of interest. In addition, the rising price of capital goods should lower the profitability of investment and reduce the investment demand.

The Wicksellian mechanism should also work when the market rate of interest is greater than the natural rate. In this case, the cost of borrowing from the banks is greater than the return on capital and firms should be led to reduce their borrowing and thereby decrease the money supply. The decline in the investment demand for goods should result in falling prices and the decreased demand for borrowing should lower the market rate of interest.[10]

If the objective of the central bank is to hold the price level constant, an appropriate monetary policy requires the central bank to change the supply of excess reserves and prevent the monetary creation that would lead to increasing prices or the monetary contraction that would lead to falling prices.

Assume that the banks hold excess reserves and that their holdings of excess reserves are, as suggested in Chapter 8, an inverse function of the interest rate. The natural rate of interest rises above the market rate of interest, business loan demand increases, and market interest rates begin to rise. At higher interest rates, the banks desire to use their excess reserves to make added loans. The central bank should absorb these excess reserves and prevent the expansion of the money supply and the rise in prices.

If the natural rate of interest falls below the market rate of interest, business loan demand decreases and market interest rates fall. The banks' demand for excess reserves increases. The central bank should supply added reserves so that the higher bank demand for excess reserves is accommodated without a contraction of the money supply.

The Wicksellian analysis broke new ground in macroeconomic writing and had a great deal of influence on Keynes' early writings. In the Wicksellian analysis, the saving and investment equality so important to the later Keynesian analysis was developed, but Wicksell was unable to break away completely from the hold of Say's Law and the quantity theory of money.

Keynesian Objections To Classical Thought

The general outline of the state of monetary theory prior to the 1936 publication of Keynes' *The General Theory of Employment, Interest, and Money* reveals the persistence of Say's Law and the quantity theory of money. Both of these ideas

[10] Knut Wicksell, *Lectures on Political Economy,* vol. 2 (New York: The Macmillan Company, 1935), pp. 205–208.

presented obstacles to the development of theories that could more accurately explain the conditions of the real world.

Objections to Say's Law

A number of objections can be raised to the concept of Say's Law. The assumption that the economy can be in equilibrium only at full employment is the most vulnerable part of the classical system. The industrialized world suffered through recessions and depressions during the entire period of the dominance of classical thought; the deviations from full employment were considered by the classical economists to be temporary and self-correcting. However, the Great Depression of the 1930s revealed the invalidity of the theory of the self-correcting system. The Keynesian argument that the economy could be in a position of equilibrium at either full employment or at less than full employment was a recognition of the realities of the world. Although the production of goods creates sufficient income in an accounting sense for the purchase of those goods by income recipients, there is no guarantee that the full employment supply of goods will indeed be produced.

Second, the ability of the government to increase the level of output and employment—denied by the traditional classical method of thinking—received a theoretical justification from the Keynesian analysis. The classical economists argued against the use of government fiscal policy in the form of public works jobs for the unemployed. Traditional classical theory taught that these programs, if financed by the expansion of the money supply, would be inflationary and, if financed by taxation, would merely transfer income from the taxpayers to the unemployed. The level of output in the private sector would decline as the public sector expanded; the net output gain would be zero. In addition, if the government were to employ the unemployed, this action would delay the decline in wages that was necessary to restore full employment. If full employment was to be restored, wages must fall and government make-work employment would only postpone this necessary decline.

Even before the publication of *The General Theory,* the debate over public employment programs had begun. A colleague of Keynes, R. F. Kahn,[11] had argued the value of governmental employment creation in England. Kahn's argument was essentially that, given high levels of unemployment, the government employment program would not bid up wages and would provide purchasing power for the workers. As the workers employed by the government spent this income, they would create added demand for goods and result in workers being employed in the private sector of the economy. Kahn recognized what Keynes later came to call the *multiplier effect of spending,* but Kahn was not able to quantify the relationship.

Although Kahn's argument was correct, the idea of using government

[11]R. F. Kahn, "The Relation of Home Investment to Unemployment," *Economic Journal,* vol. 41 (June 1931), pp. 173–198.

deficits to stimulate employment did not work its way into official policy-making circles until well into the Great Depression. Some of the American classical economists did attempt to convince President Herbert Hoover of the need for deficit spending and expansion of the money supply.[12] However, the idea of the annually balanced budget was firmly established, and the Congress passed a substantial tax increase in 1932 because government spending had increased and the Depression had lowered tax revenues. Changes in the thinking of economists came earlier than changes in the conventional political wisdom.

The correction of unemployment via a decline in wages and prices, the classical hope for a return to full employment, was considered by Keynes to have only limited possibilities. What are the effects of a general reduction in wages and prices? First, an equal percentage reduction of wages and prices does not change the level of real wages. However, the real value of money assets is changed. The classical economists argued that the rise in the real value of money and other dollar assets would encourage greater spending. Keynes argued that the real burden of debt would also increase and would lead to reduced spending. A person holding cash and bonds of equal money value to his liabilities would not be affected by a change in the price level, but a person with heavy debts would have great difficulty paying those debts if his money income fell.

To illustrate the problems posed by a change in price levels, assume you earn $20,000 a year and the Consumer Price Index is 100. You have a $50,000 mortgage on your home. Now prices and wages decline by 50 percent, so that your income is $10,000 per year and the CPI is 50. In real terms, your income is unchanged. However, you are much worse off because the mortgage on your house is fixed and you must make the same dollar payments to the lender even though you have only half as many dollars of income. On the other hand, the lender's purchasing power is increased because he is receiving a constant number of dollars per month and the real purchasing power of those dollars has doubled. Thus, debtors lose and creditors win. The classical forces countered this example with the argument that the largest debtor was the government and that government spending would not be affected by changes in the real value of government debt.

A second problem area relative to the general reduction of wages and prices is the effect on expectations. If consumers and employers expect that further reductions in wages and prices are forthcoming, consumers have an incentive to postpone purchases pending further price declines and employers have an incentive to postpone hiring pending greater declines in wages. Thus, the fall in wages and prices may decrease purchasing and hiring and lead to further falls in wages and prices.

A third effect of a reduction in wages and prices is the impact on the nation's export position. The fall in wages and prices should increase exports and decrease imports, unless the deflationary policy is followed by similar policies in other nations.

[12]For a discussion of the efforts of the Chicago economists to influence policy, see J. Ronnie Davis, "Chicago Economists, Deficit Budgets, and the Early 1930s," *American Economic Review,* June 1968, pp. 476–482.

Fourth, a reduction in the level of wages and prices would lead to a reduction of the transaction demand for money. In the Keynesian mechanism, this could be a favorable result, leading to a fall in the rate of interest and an increase in the level of investment.

In summary, Keynes saw some good resulting from the classical policy of permitting wages and prices to decline, but on net he believed that this mechanism would decrease the level of aggregate demand for goods and services and lower the level of employment.

Keynes also objected to the saving and investment mechanism employed by the classical economists. The argument that saving and investment determined the interest rate, as illustrated in Figure 9–3, was false, Keynes maintained. Keynes continued to employ an investment function similar to the one assumed by the classical economists, but he argued that saving, rather than being a function of the interest rate, was a function of the level of income. This point seems obvious today; if one doesn't have any income, one cannot save regardless of how high interest rates go! The level of income, rather than the interest rate, is the major determinant of saving.

After attacking the determination of the interest rate by the forces of saving and investment, Keynes argued that the interest rate is determined by the supply of, and demand for, money. This analysis is presented in the next chapter.

Say's Law assumes that all unemployment is voluntary in nature and results from the unwillingness of the unemployed to accept jobs at the level of real wages that would produce full employment. Keynes argued that there could be involuntary unemployment and that a portion of the labor force could be unable to find jobs even if they were willing to work for less than the current real wage. A deficiency of total demand could reduce the demand for labor so that all workers could not be employed even if they were willing to work at reduced real wages.

Finally, the classical model assumes a line of causation that is the reverse of that employed by Keynes. In the classical tradition, the demand for labor (determined by the marginal product of labor) and the supply of labor determined employment, output, and the income available to purchase the output. In the Keynesian mechanism, aggregate demand determines the level of output, which determines the level of employment, which determines the marginal product of labor. The classical mechanism overemphasized the supply side; the Keynesian analysis emphasizes the demand side and assumes that supply will respond to changes in demand as long as there is less than full employment.

Problems in the Quantity Theory of Money

The quantity theory of money leaves a great deal to be desired. The latter-day quantity theorists, such as Milton Friedman, use the quantity theory under quite different assumptions than those of Irving Fisher. The Friedman version of the quantity theory is covered in Chapter 12.

The quantity theory makes four assumptions that are troublesome.

First, the theory assumes a full employment output or transactions level.

But Fisher's list of variables determining the level of output is not complete. While these variables do influence output, they do not guarantee a full employment level of output. Once the Say's Law assumption relative to output is eliminated, output can assume any level, and the effect of changes in the supply of money can fall on either the volume of output or the level of prices. Thus, Keynes concluded that the quantity theory relationship between changes in money and changes in prices held only after the system had achieved full employment.

Second, the assumption that money serves only as a medium of exchange is also doubtful. Certainly the holding of transactions balances is the most important motive for the holding of money. However, there are other reasons why people hold money. Keynes' alternative reasons for the holding of money are explained in the next chapter.

Third, the assumption of a constant level of velocity is questionable. If money is held for other than transactions motives, the rate of turnover of the money supply may be affected by changes in the rate of interest. Given that interest is not earned on the holding of money, people should be led to hold less money when interest rates increase. A reduction in the holding of money, a decrease in k in the Cambridge equation, is equivalent to an increase in V in the Fisher equation. If data on velocity, defined as $V = GNP/M$, are plotted against the interest rate, the results support the view that velocity and interest rates are related.

Fourth, the quantity theory assumes that price levels respond passively to changes in the money supply, and that prices do not themselves affect the level of other variables in the equation. However, changes in prices may affect the level of other variables. For example, a rise in prices may create expectations of further price rises and lead people to reduce their holdings of money. A rush to reduce money holdings produces a rise in the level of V. Thus P, rather than changing passively, may lead to a change in another variable in the equation. Under the gold standard, a fall in the level of prices increased the profitability of producing gold; a decline in P could lead to an increase in the supply of money.

If none of the variables in the quantity theory of money can be considered as a constant and if the price level, rather than being passive, can have feedback effects on the other variables, the usefulness of the equation is drastically reduced. Even Keynes' admission that the quantity theory would apply at full employment is questionable. However, the quantity theory, thought to have been discarded in the period after the publication of *The General Theory,* recovered in the 1960s in a new form under the influence of Milton Friedman.

In Defense of the Classical Economists

The description and criticisms of the classical method of thought contained in this chapter are the usual interpretations of classical writing and are patterned on the formulation of classical thought attacked by Keynes. However, the classical response to this line of criticism is that Keynes was attacking a "straw man" and that the classical economists were not as rigid as Keynes argued. The implication was that Keynes overcriticized classical theory in order to clear the way for the introduction of his method of analysis. Corry, in a defense of the classical model, writes:

He built a straw man: a system of economic thinking that had not merely divorced the theory of money from the theory of output, but had never married them; a system that denied the influence of the quantity of money on the rate of interest; a system that believed in the equality of aggregate demand and aggregate supply at all levels of output and employment. The fact of the matter is that these simple pictures, of orthodox and unorthodox alike, give a woefully inadequate account of the actual situation.[13]

Many of the problems of the classical analysis can be traced to the fact that much basic classical reasoning was couched in terms of a single agricultural commodity—wheat or corn—rather than in money terms. The model of saving and investment had its origin in this type of analysis. Saving was represented as the amount of the annual crop not consumed but held as seed for the next year's crop and for the support of the farmer during the next growing period. The crop withheld was both saving and investment. No wonder it was easy for the classical economists, even if money price tags were placed on he crop, to reason that saving and investment would be equal.

On the effect of changes in the supply of money on price levels, Corry quotes Hume as arguing that an increase in the supply of money would lead to the employment of unused factors of production before the increase in the supply of money would lead to higher prices. Other classical economists at various points made similar statements. Corry's case is that the classical economists were generalizing when they wrote that the level of output would be determined by nonmonetary factors and that the stronger statements of the classical economists should not be interpreted out of context.[14]

Corry's comprehensive and interesting analysis of the classical school aside, the fact remains that the economists trained in the classical tradition did not have a workable solution for the problems that descended upon the world during the 1930s. The problem of the Great Depression proved to be too much for classical analysis, and after several years of waiting for the market system to restore full employment, economists and governments were ready for new and different policy solutions. Keynes appeared with a new school of thought and provided a hope for better results.

Keynes, by the time of the 1936 publication of *The General Theory of Employment, Interest and Money*, was a well-established economist. As a book, *The General Theory* is not one of his better written books and its interpretation and reinterpretation have occupied economists ever since its publication. The ideas and

[13]Corry, op. cit., p. 9.
[14]Ibid., pp. 40–41.

methodology have been worked into a new conventional wisdom. Keynes' work was not readily accepted in the period immediately following the publication of the book. Many critics of *The General Theory* objected to the conclusions and policy prescriptions of the book because they challenged, especially in the United States, the idea of a balanced government budget and justified an increased role for government in the economy.

The next two chapters present a conventional outline of the Keynesian and post-Keynesian models that serve as the framework of modern macroeconomic analysis.

REVIEW QUESTIONS

1. Define Say's Law. Why did Say's Law automatically produce full employment?

2. Draw the classical four-sector model. Illustrate the effect of a decrease of the money supply.

3. Using the basic four-sector classical model, illustrate the effects of a shift to the right of the supply of labor curve.

4. The classical economists believed that the increase of real wages would result from the addition of capital and increases in the productivity of labor. Illustrate the effects of an increase in the productivity of labor. (Changes are required in the production function, the demand for labor function, and the real wage vector.)

5. Explain the quantity theory of money. How did Fisher use this theory to argue that changes in the supply of money would lead to equal proportionate changes in prices?

6. What is the difference between income velocity and transactions velocity?

7. Explain Wicksell's analysis of the natural and the market rate of interest.

8. Why did Keynes believe that a reduction of wages and prices would not lead to an increase in the level of economic activity?

9. What are the classical arguments against the use of fiscal policy to stimulate the economy?

10. How were savings and investment brought to equality in the classical analysis?

SUGGESTED READINGS

William J. Baumol, *Economic Dynamics*, 2nd ed. New York: Macmillan Company, 1959, chap. 2.

Gary S. Becker and William J. Baumol, "The Classical Monetary Theory: The Outcome of the Discussion," *Economica*, November 1952, pp. 355–376.

James L. Cochrane, *Macroeconomics Before Keynes*, Glenview, Ill.: Scott, Foresman and Co., 1970.

Edwin Dean, editor, *The Controversy Over the Quantity Theory of Money*. Boston: D. C. Heath and Co., 1965.

Everett E. Hagen, "The Classical Theory of the Level of Output and Employment," in M. G. Mueller, ed., *Readings in Macroeconomics*, 2nd ed. New York: Holt, Rinehart and Winston, 1971.

Lawrence R. Klein, *The Keynesian Revolution*, 2nd ed. New York: Macmillan Company, 1966, chap. 1–2.

Don Patinkin, "Price Flexibility and Full Employment," *American Economic Review*, September 1948, pp. 543–564.

10

THE BASIC KEYNESIAN MODEL OF INCOME

The Keynesian theory of income determination is a theory of aggregate demand. The level of aggregate demand for goods and services determines the level of output, national income, and employment. The Keynesian analysis eliminates the classical assumption of a self-correcting, full employment equilibrium economy. Aggregate demand and aggregate supply may be equal at any level of employment. The goal of public policy is to ensure a level of aggregate demand such that aggregate demand and aggregate supply are equal at the full employment level of aggregate supply.

In the first section of this chapter, the components of aggregate demand are combined into a basic nonmonetary Keynesian model of the level of national income. The analysis is constructed on a step-by-step basis, using both graphic and algebraic analyses. The second section of the chapter presents the derivation of the interest rate and the relationship between the interest rate and the level of investment. All of the concepts developed in this chapter are combined in Chapter 11 to form a more complete model of national income determination.

A Basic National Income Model

In any Keynesian model, the level of national income is a function of the level of aggregate demand. The components of aggregate demand are consumption, investment, government spending, and net exports; these variables represent spending by consumers, businesses, governments, and foreigners. In this first basic model, the supply and demand for money do not enter into the income determination process.

Consumption

The largest single portion of aggregate demand is consumer demand for goods and services. The concept of the consumption function, the relationship between consumption and income, is attributable to Keynes. Some Keynesian analysts

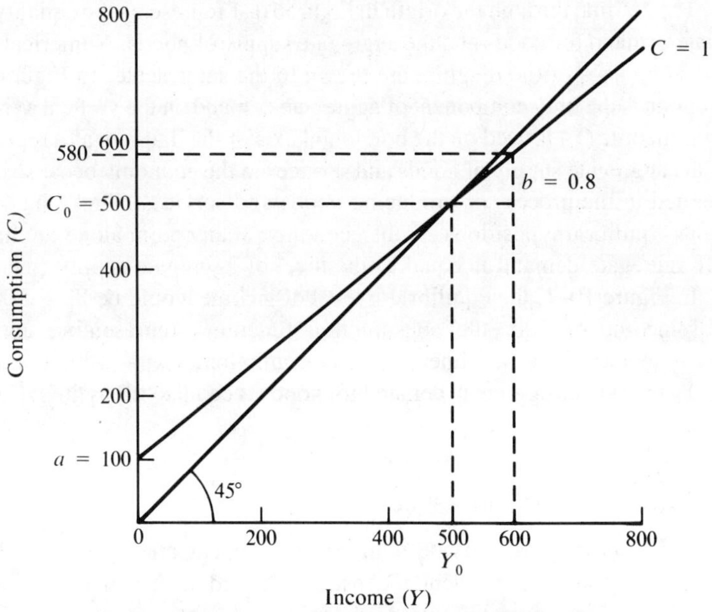

FIGURE 10-1 The Consumption Function

consider the theory of the consumption function to be Keynes' single most important contribution to economic analysis.

The basic Keynesian consumption function, now called the *absolute income hypothesis*, states simply that the level of consumption is a function of the level of income and can be written as

$$C = a + bY$$

where C = the dollar value of consumption
a = a constant indicating the amount of consumption spending at a zero level of income
b = the *marginal propensity to consume* (MPC), the increase in consumption per dollar increase in income
Y = the amount of income

The basic Keynesian consumption function is presented in Figure 10–1. In this figure, the value of a is \$100; at a zero income level, people would consume (presumably out of past saving) \$100 of output; b, the slope of the consumption function, indicates that the increase of consumption per unit increase of income is 0.8. For every dollar increase of income, consumption increases by \$0.80. At $Y = 500$, $C = 500$; but at $Y = 600$, $C = 580$. The consumption function is $C = 100 + 0.8Y$.

The 45° line through the origin in Figure 10–1 represents the equality of the aggregate demand for goods and the aggregate supply of goods. Numerical values along the two axes of the diagram are drawn to the same scale. In Figure 10–1, consumption is the only component of aggregate demand on the vertical axis of the diagram. Income (Y) is used on the horizontal axis of the diagram as a representation of the aggregate supply of goods and services in the economy because income is generated in the process of producing goods and services. Thus, the 45° line represents equilibrium positions for the economy; at any point along the line, the level of aggregate demand is equal to the level of aggregate supply (income).

In Figure 10–1, the equilibrium level of income would be $Y_0 = 500$. At a level of income of 500, the consumption function—representing aggregate demand—intersects the 45° line. Thus, consumption, $C_0 = 500$, is equal to income $Y_0 = 500$; the aggregate demand for goods is equal to the aggregate supply of goods.

Gross Private Domestic Investment

The components of gross private domestic investment are producers' durable equipment and structures, residential construction, and the net change in business inventories. Business expenditures on producers' durable equipment and structures, the formal term for expenditures on plant and machinery, are the major part of total investment.

All of the components of total investment are relatively unstable over the course of the business cycle. The critical role of fluctuations in investment has long been recognized. For example, Keynes wrote in *The General Theory*, "it is not so easy to revive the marginal efficiency of capital, determined, as it is, by the uncontrollable and disobedient psychology of the business world."[1]

While business expenditures on plant and equipment vary sharply during periods of economic expansion and contraction, fluctuations in residential construction and changes in business inventories are also important. Changes in the level of business inventories have been one of the traditional major sources of business instability—especially in less severe business recessions. Business inventories are increased during periods of economic expansion and add to the level of aggregate demand. During recessions, firms reduce production in order to lower their holdings of finished goods and goods in process.

The net change in inventories may be either intended or unintended investment. The firm may desire to increase its inventories; this is intended inventory investment. Alternatively, the firm's holdings of inventories may increase because sales have failed to meet expectations; unintended inventory investment has taken place.

The analysis of investment is a complex process involving the examination of the inducements to invest (the expectation of profits) and the cost of investment

[1] J. M. Keynes, *The General Theory of Employment, Interest, and Money,* (New York: Harcourt, Brace and Company, 1936), p. 317.

(the cost of obtaining the funds to carry out investment projects). This analysis is undertaken in the next major section of this chapter.

In this section of the chapter, the model of national income determination is simplified by considering investment to be an exogenously determined variable. An *exogenously determined* variable has a value that is determined outside of the model instead of by the operation of the model. For the purposes of the model, the exogenously determined variable has an assigned value that does not change as a result of the operation of the model. By contrast, an *endogenously determined* variable has a value that is determined by the workings of the model. For example, if investment is stated to be 10 units in a given model, that means investment is being assigned an exogenously determined value. No equation or model is presented to explain why investment is 10 units. However, if investment is defined as 10 percent of total income, investment is endogenous; as the level of income changes, investment changes. The level of investment is established by the operation of the income-determination model.

Assume a simple model in which the only components of aggregate demand are consumption and investment. Investment is given an exogenously determined value, $I = I_0$. The basic model for the determination of the level of income is

$$Y = C + I \tag{1}$$
$$C = a + bY \tag{2}$$
$$I = I_0 \tag{3}$$

Equation (1) is the income identity. Income is equal to the sum of consumption demand and investment demand. Equation (2) defines consumption by the usual Keynesian consumption function. Equation (3) gives the fixed value of investment, I_0.

To solve for the equilibrium level of income using these equations, substitute the values of consumption and investment into the income identity, so that

$$Y = a + bY + I_0 \tag{4}$$

Solving for Y,

$$Y - bY = a + I_0 \tag{5}$$
$$Y(1 - b) = a + I_0 \tag{6}$$
$$Y = (a + I_0)\left(\frac{1}{1-b}\right) \tag{7}$$

The value $\frac{1}{1-b}$ in Equation (7) is the multiplier in this model. b is the value of the marginal propensity to consume in the consumption function, $C = a + bY$. Assuming simple numbers, an example illustrates the idea. Assume that $C = 70 + 0.6Y$ and $I_0 = 10$. Using these values in Equation (7),

$$Y = (70 + 10)\left(\frac{1}{1 - 0.6}\right) = \frac{80}{0.4} = 200$$

Income is equal to 200 units, consumption is 190, and investment is 10.

TABLE 10–1 The Investment Multiplier (dollars)

CHANGE IN INCOME	*CHANGE IN CONSUMPTION*	*CHANGE IN SAVING*
10.00	6.00	4.00
6.00	3.60	2.40
3.60	2.16	1.44
2.16	1.30	0.86
1.30	0.78	0.52
0.78	0.47	0.31
0.47	0.28	0.19
↓	↓	↓
∞	∞	∞
25.00	15.00	10.00

Changes in Investment and the Multiplier Changes in the level of investment are important because these changes have a multiplier effect on the level of income. The level of income changes by an amount greater than the change in the level of investment. Assuming again that demand is composed of only consumption and investment and that the exogenously determined level of investment increases from $I_0 = 10$ to $I_0 = 20$, the new equilibrium level of income becomes

$$Y = (70 + 20)\left(\frac{1}{1 - 0.6}\right) = \frac{90}{0.4} = 225$$

Increasing investment by 10 units caused an increase of income of 25 units. The multiplier (m) is 2.5, or $\left(\frac{1}{1 - 0.6}\right)$, and the change in the level of income is $\Delta Y = \Delta I(m)$, or $25 = 10(2.5)$.

Why does the change of investment cause income to change by a multiple of the change in investment? The reason is simple. The $10 investment expenditure caused incomes to rise by $10 because the factors of production which produced the investment good received $10 of added income. Those receiving the added $10 of income spend $6 and save $4 of the added income; the marginal propensity to consume additional income is 0.6 and the *marginal propensity to save* (MPS) is 0.4.

The $6 of added consumption by the producers of the investment good is added income for a second set of factors of production. This second group of income recipients consumes six-tenths of their income gain ($3.60) and saves four-tenths ($2.40). Their consumption expenditures become added income for a third group of factors of production who also increase their consumption and saving according to the MPC and the MPS.

This process continues for an infinite number of rounds. Each group's spending becomes income for the next group, and each subsequent group increases its spending by a fraction of the increase in its income. The multiplier process is illustrated in Table 10–1. After an infinite number of rounds, the initial change in investment of \$10 has led to a change in income of \$25, a change in consumption of \$15, and a change in saving of \$10. Note that using a higher marginal propensity to consume would have produced a larger multiplier value and the change in the level of income would have been larger.

In the example in Table 10–1, the level of income increased by an amount sufficient to generate added saving equal to the amount of added investment. Saving and investment must be equal at the equilibrium level of income. Saving is a *leakage* from the flow of spending; saving represents income that is not spent on consumption. Investment is an addition to, or an *injection* into, the basic flow of consumption spending. If the leakage from the spending stream (saving) is greater than the injection into the spending stream (investment), the level of income declines. If the leakage from the spending stream (saving) is less than the injection into the spending stream (investment), the level of income increases. Only when the leakages and injections are equal is the level of income constant (in equilibrium).

The income determination process also can be illustrated graphically. In Figure 10–2, the analysis begins with the construction of the axes. Income (aggregate supply) is plotted on the horizontal axis; aggregate demand and the components of aggregate demand are plotted on the vertical axis. The same scale is used on both axes so that the 45° line represents the equality of aggregate demand and aggregate supply.

Next, a consumption function is plotted with the values $C = 70 + 0.6Y$. Consumption and income are equal at an income level of $Y = 175$. The income level can be determined both on the graph and by solving for Y in the equations

$$Y = C$$
$$C = a + bY$$
$$Y = a + bY$$
$$Y - bY = a$$
$$Y = a\left(\frac{1}{1-b}\right)$$

$$\text{or} \qquad 175 = 70\left(\frac{1}{1-0.6}\right)$$

In Figure 10–2, the saving function is added to the diagram. The saving function is $S = -a + (1-b)Y$ and is plotted with a vertical intercept of –70 units and a slope of 0.4. If income is zero, the level of saving is $-a$, or -70. Saving is zero when consumption and income are both equal to 175, and saving increases 0.4 units for each one unit increase in income.

The addition of investment to the diagram requires two steps. First, investment of 10 units is added to the consumption function in Figure 10–2. The new aggregate demand function, $C + I$, lies 10 units above the consumption function at all levels of income. The $C + I$ function intersects the aggregate demand equals aggregate supply line at $Y = 200$. As was determined in the

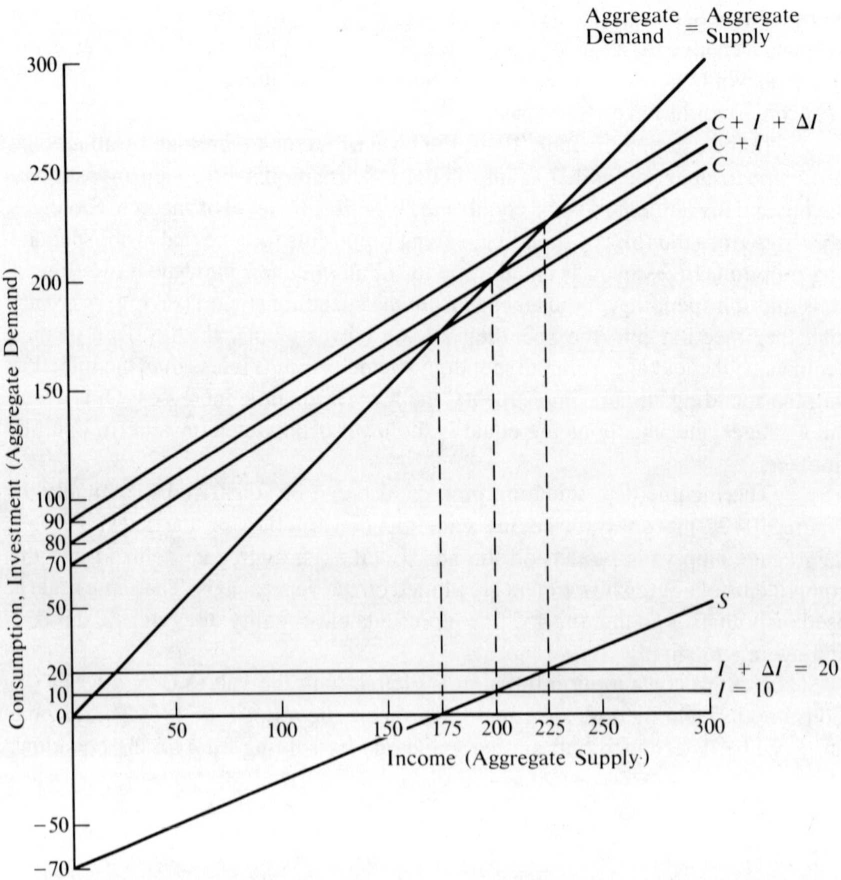

FIGURE 10–2 Income Determination: Consumption, Investment, and Change in Investment

multiplier example, the equilibrium level of income increased 25 units as a result of the addition of 10 units of investment.

Second, the 10 units of investment are plotted independent of the consumption function by measuring up 10 units from the origin of the graph. Investment equals 10 units regardless of the level of income; the investment function is a straight line parallel to the horizontal axis. Note that saving equals investment at the equilibrium level of income of 200 units.

Adding a second 10 units of investment is simply a repetition of the process. The aggregate demand function moves up another 10 units to $C + I + \Delta I$, and the investment function moves up 10 units to $I + \Delta I$ in Figure 10–2. As expected, at the equilibrium level of income of 225 units, aggregate demand equals aggregate supply and saving equals investment.

Government Spending and Taxes

Government spending is the third component of aggregate demand. In most basic income determination models, the level of government spending is an exogenously determined variable. The Congress and the Administration, rather than this model, determine the level of government spending.

The Addition of Government Spending The addition of government spending to the income determination model presents no new problems. The mathematical solution requires adding government spending (G) to the income identity, which becomes $Y = C + I + G$, and assigning a value to government spending, $G = G_0$. Therefore,

$$Y = C + I + G \tag{1}$$
$$C = a + bY \tag{2}$$
$$I = I_0 \tag{3}$$
$$G = G_0 \tag{4}$$

and substituting Equations (2) through (4) into (1),

$$Y = a + bY + I_0 + G_0 \tag{5}$$

Solving for Y,

$$Y - bY = a + I_0 + G_0 \tag{6}$$
$$Y(1 - b) = a + I_0 + G_0$$

so that

$$Y = (a + I_0 + G_0)\left(\frac{1}{1 - b}\right)$$

The multiplier applicable to the addition of government spending is the same, $1/(1 - b)$, as the investment multiplier.

The addition of government spending of 20 units to the graphical model of Figure 10–2 also presents no new problems. The final step of Figure 10–2 is reproduced in Figure 10–3, except that $I + \Delta I$ is simplified to I; the total level of investment is 20. Government spending of 20 units is added to the $C + I$ function, which becomes $C + I + G$. The 20 units of government spending also are added to I in the saving and investment analysis, so that $I + G = S$.

The 20-unit increase in government spending has the expected multiplier effect on income in Figure 10–3. The aggregate demand equals aggregate supply equilibrium occurs at 275 units of income; saving is equal to the sum of investment and government spending at 275 units of income. Government spending, like investment, is an injection into the income stream and increases the level of income by a multiple of the increase in government spending.

Increasing government spending is an instrument of fiscal policy. Fiscal policy involves changing the level of government spending and/or taxes in order to change the level of income. If income is at a less than full employment level, increasing government spending moves the economy toward the full employment income level. Owing to the multiplier relationship, the increase in government

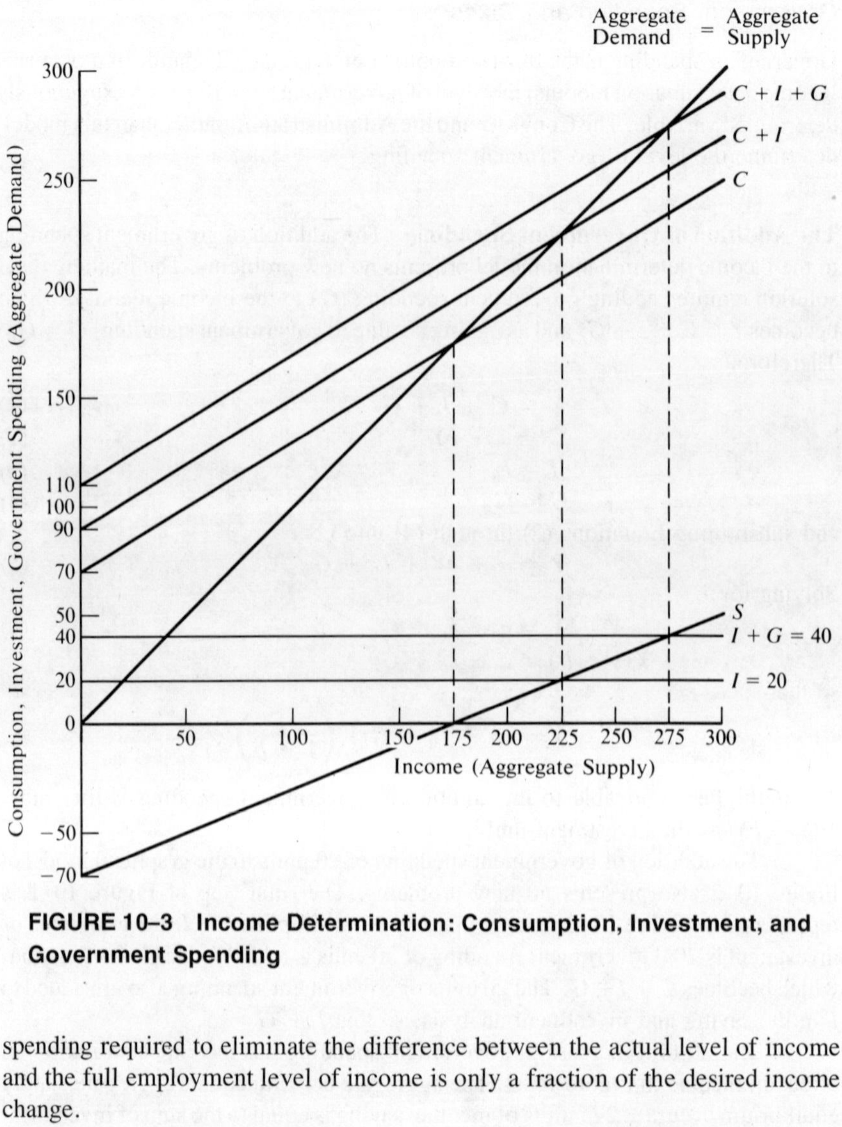

FIGURE 10–3 Income Determination: Consumption, Investment, and Government Spending

spending required to eliminate the difference between the actual level of income and the full employment level of income is only a fraction of the desired income change.

The Addition of Taxes Unfortunately, taxes tend to come along with government expenditures. The addition of taxes to the model requires that taxes be viewed as a force reducing spending and income in the economy. Like saving, taxes represent a leakage from the flow of expenditures. People do not spend income paid in taxes or allocated to saving.

To add taxes to the algebraic model, some assumptions must be made. First taxes reduce the levels of both consumption and saving. The burden of the tax payment falls on consumption and saving according to the values of the marginal propensity to consume and the marginal propensity to save. In the example used, the assumption has been that consumers spend 60 percent of increases in their income (MPC = 0.6) and save 40 percent of increases in their income (MPS = 0.4). Second, the addition of taxes requires rewriting the consumption function so that consumption and saving are functions of *disposable,* or after-tax, income. Thus, the consumption function becomes $C = a + bYd$ and $Yd = Y - T$. Third, a tax function is required. For simplicity at this point, assume that taxes are exogenous, so that $T = T_0$.

The algebraic model of the system now becomes:

$$Y = C + I + G \qquad (1)$$
$$C = a + bYd \qquad (2)$$
$$Yd = Y - T \qquad (3)$$
$$I = I_0 \qquad (4)$$
$$G = G_0 \qquad (5)$$
$$T = T_0 \qquad (6)$$

Substituting (6) into (3) and then (3) into (2) gives

$$C = a + b(Y - T_0) \qquad (7)$$

Then substituting (4), (5), and (7) into (1) gives

$$Y = a + b(Y - T_0) + I_0 + G_0$$

and

$$Y = a + bY - bT_0 + I_0 + G_0$$

and solving for Y yields

$$Y - bY = a - bT_0 + I_0 + G_0$$
$$Y = (a - bT_0 + I_0 + G_0)\left(\frac{1}{1 - b}\right)$$

Note that although a change in investment or government spending changes the level of income according to the multiplier of $\left(\frac{1}{1-b}\right)$, the tax variable is preceded by b in the income equation. The tax decreased spending only by the amount of the marginal propensity to consume times the tax, bT. The effect of adding the tax is given by the equation

$$\Delta Y = \Delta T_0 \times \left(\frac{-b}{1 - b}\right)$$

and the value of the tax multiplier is $-b/(1 - b)$. The tax multiplier has a lower numerical value than the government spending multiplier because only a portion of taxes comes out of consumption. The remainder of the tax comes out of saving and reduces another form of nonspending. Assuming an MPC of 0.6, the government spending multiplier is 2.5, or $\left(\frac{1}{1-0.6}\right)$ and the tax multiplier is –1.5, or $\left(\frac{-0.6}{1-0.6}\right)$.

The difference between the government spending multiplier and the tax multiplier leads to the rule of the balanced budget multiplier. According to the balanced budget multiplier, an equal change in both government spending and

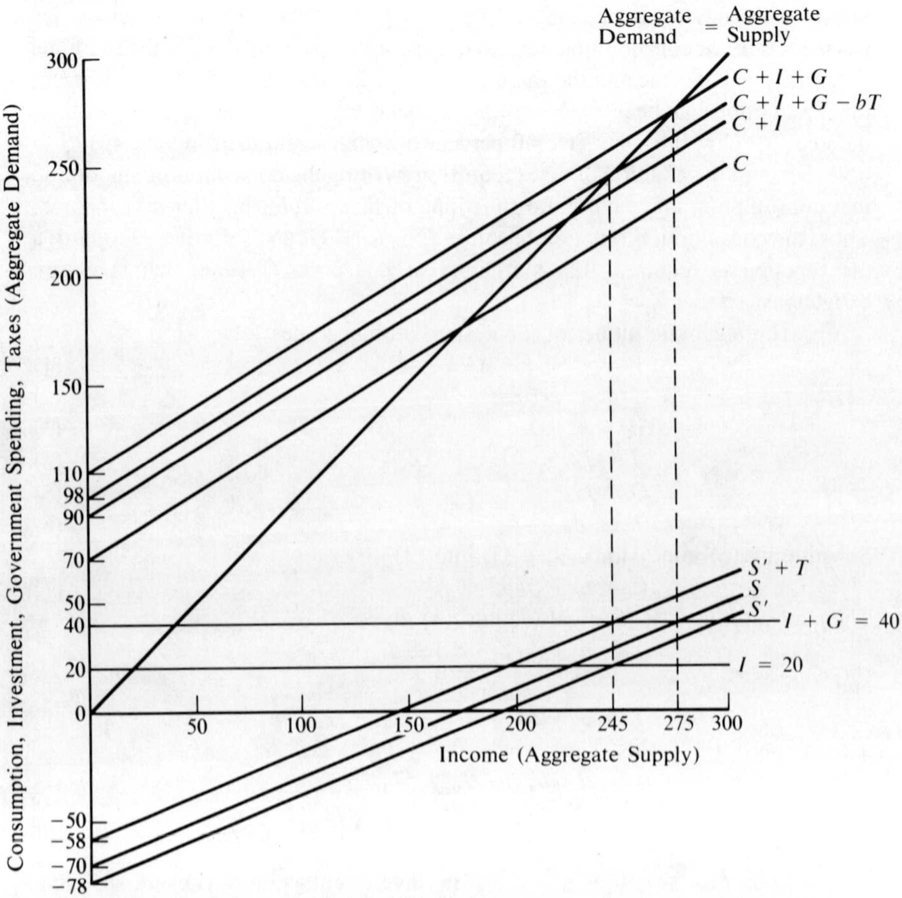

FIGURE 10–4 Income Determination: The Addition of Taxes

taxes changes the level of income by the same amount. If the government spending multiplier is 2.5 and the tax multiplier is –1.5, an increase in both government spending and taxes of \$100 increases income by \$100. The expansionary force is $\Delta Y = \Delta G \times 2.5$, or \$250, and the contractionary force is $\Delta Y = \Delta T \times -1.5$, or –\$150. The balanced budget multiplier has a value of one in basic aggregate demand models of this type; in the real world, relationships are more complex and the balanced budget multiplier value is not necessarily one.

Adding taxes to the diagrammatic version of the model requires three adjustments. Assume that taxes of 20 units are added to the model in Figure 10–3. The result of the addition of $T = 20$ is illustrated in Figure 10–4. First, the aggregate demand curve, $C + I + G$, is lowered by 12 units; it becomes $C + I + G - bT$ to reflect the fact that consumption is lowered by the value of the marginal propensity to consume times the tax, 0.6×20, or 12. Second, the saving function is lowered from S to S' to reflect the reduction in saving resulting from the impact of taxes on saving. The saving function is reduced by the marginal propensity to save times the tax, 0.4×20, or 8. Third, the amount of the tax is added to the new saving function to produce the $S' + T$ function. Taxes, a leakage from the spending stream, are added to saving so that the sum of the leakages can be compared with the sum of the additions to the spending flow, investment and government spending. At the new equilibrium level of income of 245 units, the sum of saving and taxes is equal to the sum of investment and government spending.

Note that the balanced budget multiplier was applied in Figure 10–4. The equilibrium level of income after the addition of government spending of 20 units and taxes of 20 units is 245. The equilibrium level of income before the addition of either taxes or government spending was 225 units.

Exports and Imports

The introduction of the foreign sector into the model adds little new in the way of complication. Exports and imports can be treated as either exogenous or endogenous variables. In the present model, both exports (X) and imports (IM) are treated as exogenously determined.

The algebraic model is expanded from its previous version to

$$\begin{aligned} Y &= C + I + G + (X - IM) \\ C &= a + bYd \\ Yd &= Y - T \\ I &= I_0 \\ G &= G_0 \\ T &= T_0 \\ X &= X_0 \\ IM &= IM_0 \end{aligned}$$

Following the usual steps of solving for Y,

$$Y = a + bY - bT_0 + I_0 + G_0 + X_0 - IM_0$$

and

$$Y = (a - bT_0 + I_0 + G_0 + X_0 - IM_0)\left(\frac{1}{1 - b}\right)$$

The multiplier for exports is the same as the investment and government spending multiplier. The multiplier for imports is of the same numerical value but has a negative sign. Export demand is an added source of demand and increases the income level. Imports do *not* increase domestic income; incomes are generated in the countries that produced the goods. Imports would not appear in the aggregate demand function at all except for the fact that consumption, investment, and government spending all include some purchases of foreign-made goods. The subtraction of imports is necessary to take the imported content out of the other items in the aggregate demand equation.

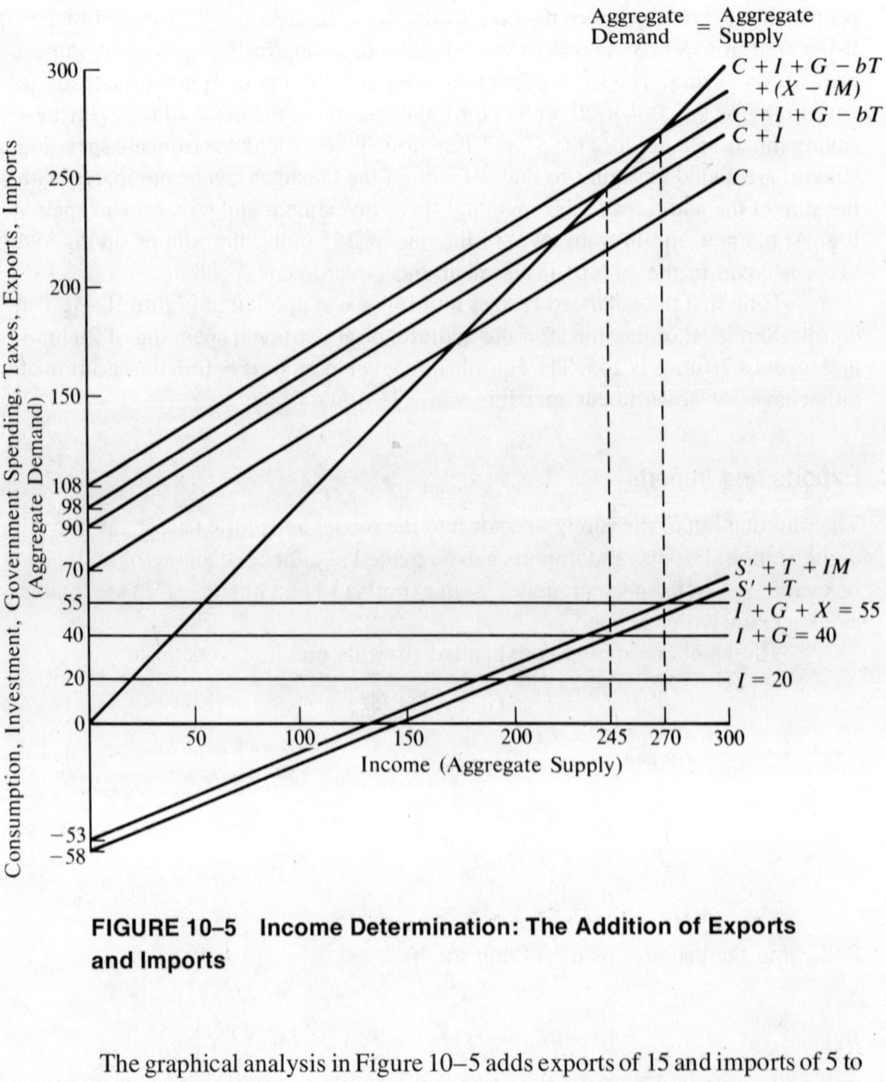

FIGURE 10–5 Income Determination: The Addition of Exports and Imports

The graphical analysis in Figure 10–5 adds exports of 15 and imports of 5 to the analysis of Figure 10–4. In Figure 10–5, the aggregate demand function shifts upwards 10 units to $C + I + G - bT + (X - IM)$. In the saving-investment analysis, exports of 15 are added to the $I + G$ function, which becomes $I + G + X$, and imports of 5 are added to the $S' + T$ function, which becomes $S' + T + IM$. At the new equilibrium level of income of 270 units, the sum of saving plus taxes plus imports is equal to the sum of investment plus government spending plus exports.

The final equilibrium level of income of 270 is 25 units larger than the level of income before the addition of exports and imports. The change in income was equal to net exports $(X - IM)$ times the multiplier of 2.5.

A Final Basic Model

Assume the following model:

$$Y = C + I + G + (X - IM)$$
$$C = a + bYd$$
$$Yd = Y - T$$
$$T = T_0 + tY$$
$$I = I_0$$
$$G = G_0$$
$$X = X_0$$
$$IM = IM_0$$

This model differs slightly from the previous models. The level of taxes, T, is an exogenously determined fixed sum, T_0, plus a percentage, t, of income.

To solve for C, substitute the value of T into the equation $Yd = Y - T$, so that $Yd = Y - T_0 - tY$. Substituting the value of Yd into the consumption function, $C = a + b(Y - T_0 - tY)$, or $C = a + bY - bT_0 - btY$. Next, the exogenously determined values of the components of aggregate demand, C, I, G, X, and IM, are substituted into the income determination equation, so that

$$Y = a + bY - bT_0 - btY + I_0 + G_0 + X_0 - IM_0$$

Clearing the Y terms to the left-hand side,

$$Y - bY + btY = a - bT_0 + I_0 + G_0 + X_0 - IM_0$$

Factoring Y from the left-hand side,

$$Y(1 - b + bt) = a - bT_0 + I_0 + G_0 + X_0 - IM_0$$

Dividing both sides by $(1 - b + bt)$,

$$Y = (a - bT_0 + I_0 + G_0 + X_0 - IM_0)\left(\frac{1}{1 - b + bt}\right)$$

The multiplier for this model is

$$\left(\frac{1}{1 - b + bt}\right)$$

Assuming Some Numbers If assumed numbers are assigned to the model, various policy effects can be illustrated. The following initial values of the variables are assumed:

a (the vertical intercept of the consumption function) = 22.5
b (the marginal propensity to consume after tax income) = 0.75
T_0 (the lump sum tax which is not affected by income) = 30

$$\begin{aligned} t \text{ (the tax rate as a percentage of income)} &= 0.2 \\ I_0 \text{ (investment)} &= 60 \\ G_0 \text{ (government spending)} &= 130 \\ X_0 \text{ (exports)} &= 25 \\ IM_0 \text{ (imports)} &= 15 \end{aligned}$$

Substituting the assumed values into the income equation,

$$Y = [22.5 - 0.75(30) + 60 + 130 + 25 - 15]\left[\frac{1}{1 - 0.75 + 0.75(0.2)}\right]$$

$$Y = 200\left(\frac{1}{0.4}\right) = 500$$

To calculate those variables that were not exogenously determined, start by determining the value of taxes. The tax function is $T = 30 + 0.2Y$; at $Y = 500$, taxes are $30 + 0.2(500)$, or 130. Income after taxes is 370. The consumption function indicates that consumers spend $22.5 + 0.75Yd$. Yd is 370, and thus consumption is 300.

Checking the income determination equation,

$$\begin{aligned} C &= 300 \\ +I &= 60 \\ +G &= 130 \\ +X &= 25 \\ -IM &= \underline{-15} \\ Y &= 500 \end{aligned}$$

The sum of the additions to the income stream from investment, government spending, and exports should be equal to the leakages from spending for saving, taxes, and imports. Thus,

$$\begin{aligned} I &= 60 & S &= 70 \\ G &= 130 & T &= 130 \\ X &= \underline{25} & IM &= \underline{15} \\ & \ 215 & & \ 215 \end{aligned}$$

Note that the comparable individual items in the additions and leakages lists are not equal; it is only necessary that the totals be equal. In this case, saving is larger than investment, but an excess of exports over imports compensates for the difference. The example was designed so that government spending and taxes would be equal.

The Basic Multipliers. The multiplier for the change of all variables except taxes is $\left(\frac{1}{1 - b + bt}\right)$. Given the assumed numbers, the multiplier is 2.5. For a change in the lump sum tax, T_0, the multiplier is $\left(\frac{-b}{1 - b + bt}\right)$, or -1.875.

The Policy Measures

Assume that the full employment level of income in the economy is 550 and the actual level of income, as derived, is 500. Income must be increased by 50 units. The first alternative is to increase investment, government spending, or exports by 20 units. A 20-unit increase in any of these variables would increase the level of income by 50 units because the multiplier is 2.5. Assume a government spending increase of 20 units. The income determination equation becomes

$$Y = [22.5 - 0.75(30) + 60 + \underline{150} + 25 - 15]\left[\frac{1}{1 - 0.75 + 0.75(0.2)}\right]$$

$$Y = 220\left(\frac{1}{0.4}\right) = 550$$

The endogenous variables in the equation are changed when government spending is increased from 130 to 150. The additions and leakages from the spending stream at Y = 550 are:

$$\begin{aligned} I &= 60 & S &= 80 \\ G &= 150 & T &= 140 \\ X &= \underline{25} & IM &= \underline{15} \\ & 235 & & 235 \end{aligned}$$

Again, the total additions and total leakages are equal. Although government spending was increased by 20 units, the deficit in the government's budget is only 10 units because tax collections, which are geared to the level of income, increased as the level of income was increased by the added government spending.

A second alternative policy measure is to leave government spending unchanged at 130 and to decrease the level of the fixed tax, T_0. If this tax is reduced from 30 to 3.333, the level of income increases to 550. The income determination equation for this change is

$$Y = [22.5 - 0.75\underline{(3.333)} + 60 + 130 + 25 - 15]\left[\frac{1}{1 - 0.75 + 0.75(0.2)}\right]$$

$$Y = 220\left(\frac{1}{0.4}\right) = 550$$

The additions and leakages are

$$\begin{aligned} I &= 60 & S &= 86.667 \\ G &= 130 & T &= 113.333 \\ X &= \underline{25} & IM &= \underline{15.0} \\ & 215 & & 215.000 \end{aligned}$$

The reduction of the lump sum tax from 30 to 3.333, a decrease of 26.667, increased the level of income by the required 50 units. However, the deficit in the government's budget is only 16.667. Tax collections increased by 10 units as the level of income increased by 50 units.

The third and final change is a reduction of the marginal tax rate, t. By lowering t, the level of income can be increased. Assuming the income equation is written with the original values, except that t is lowered to $t = 0.151515$,

$$Y = [22.5 - 0.75(30) + 60 + 130 + 25 - 15]\left[\frac{1}{1 - 0.75 + 0.75(0.151515)}\right]$$

$$Y = 200\left(\frac{1}{0.363636}\right) = 550$$

The additions and leakages in this case are

$$\begin{array}{rlrl} I = & 60 & S = & 86.667 \\ G = & 130 & T = & 113.333 \\ X = & \underline{25} & IM = & \underline{15.0} \\ & 215 & & 215.000 \end{array}$$

The deficit in the government's budget is 16.667 units. The decline in tax collections from the *original* 500 units of income was from 130 to 105.7575, a revenue loss of 24.2425. However, income increased by 50 units and 0.151515 of this increase, or 7.57575, was paid as taxes. The net between the loss of 24.2425 and the gain of 7.5757 is the deficit of 16.667.

Summary This is one of the many possible models that can be constructed, and you should experiment with basic models of this type. At this point, the analysis can be summarized in a few key points:

1. Income is a function of aggregate demand.
2. Aggregate demand is the sum of consumption, investment, government expenditures, and net exports (exports minus imports). Increases in these variables increase income.
3. Changes in the level of demand have multiplier effects on the level of income. The three basic multipliers are the expenditure multiplier (for government spending, investment, and exports minus imports), the tax multiplier, and the balanced budget multiplier.
4. At the equilibrium level of income, the sum of the additions to spending, $I + G + X$, are equal to the subtractions from the level of spending, $S + T + IM$.
5. The objective is to maintain the level of demand at the full employment level. The level of demand can be changed by variations in government spending and taxes.

Thus far, the analysis has been simplified by assuming that investment is exogenously determined and that the supply of and demand for money does not affect the analysis. In the next two sections, these assumptions are removed.

Investment and the Interest Rate

In the basic models developed in the previous section, the level of investment was assumed to be exogenously determined. Assumed numbers for the level of investment were used in the examples and no information was provided about the source of the numbers. In this section, an investment model is constructed, an interest rate model is developed and the two models are combined to determine the level of investment.

The Marginal Efficiency of Investment

The starting point for a discussion of investment activity is the analysis of the marginal efficiency of capital, and the best place to begin that analysis is with a single firm. Assume a firm is considering a series of possible investment projects. Each project involves certain costs and holds out the expectation of future profits. The objective is to rank all possible investment projects, select those projects that hold out the promise of a high rate of return on investment, and eliminate from consideration all projects that do not promise to earn the minimum acceptable rate of return.

Assume that the first project suggested for consideration by the investment committee is the purchase of a new stamping machine for the stamping department of the factory. The cost of the machine, the only easily determined variable in the entire analysis, is $1,000. During the five-year life of the machine, the firm must recapture the $1,000 investment and earn a return on the invested funds. Therefore, the committee must estimate the revenue from the sale of the machine's output and all of the costs associated with producing and selling the product (except the depreciation of the machine). After subtracting expected costs from expected sales revenue, it is determined that the firm can expect to receive $300 per year after costs. The return of $300 per year for five years represents the funds necessary to repay the $1,000 investment and provide the firm with a return on its investment.

The next question is, what rate of return will the firm receive if it invests $1,000 now and receives a payback of $300 per year for five years? It is necessary to solve for r, the rate of return, in the following equation:[2]

$$\$1{,}000 = \frac{\$300}{(1+r)^1} + \frac{\$300}{(1+r)^2} + \frac{\$300}{(1+r)^3} + \frac{\$300}{(1+r)^4} + \frac{\$300}{(1+r)^5}$$

The calculation of the rate of return on an investment project involves the same type of analysis used in the bond price calculations in Chapter 5. In each case,

[2]The general form of the equation is

$$\text{Cost} = \frac{\text{return in year 1}}{(1+r)^1} + \frac{\text{return in year 2}}{(1+r)^2} \ldots + \frac{\text{return in year } n}{(1+r)^n}$$

TABLE 10–2 Costs and Expected Returns on Investment Projects

PROJECT	*COST (dollars)*	*EXPECTED RATE OF RETURN (percent)*
A	15,000	20
B	20,000	16
C	5,000	14
D	10,000	12
E	25,000	8

future returns are being given present values. In the bond example, the price of the bond was derived as a function of various interest rates; in capital investment examples, the cost of the investment is known and the problem is to solve for the rate of return represented by the future payments.

Solving for r, a rate of return of 15.24 percent is found to equalize the cost of the project with the present value of future returns. Thus, it is determined that if the firm invests in this machine, it will, over five years, recoup its $1,000 investment and earn a 15.24 percent annual rate of return on its funds.

An expected rate of return is calculated for each of the investment projects under consideration. Then the projects are ranked on the basis of the expected rate of return. The *expected* should be emphasized, because all of these calculations are based on expectations with regard to the selling price of the product, the costs of production, and the life of the machine. Assume the firm is considering five investment projects and these projects have costs and expected rates of return as presented in Table 10–2. Having calculated the rates of return on the five projects and ranked the projects according to their rates of return, the investment committee must decide which projects should be undertaken and which should be rejected.

If the firm is willing to invest only in those projects that yield 20 percent or more, it will invest in project *A*, and its total investment will be $15,000. As the firm reduces its minimum acceptable rate of return, more projects are accepted and investment increases. If the firm is willing to accept 16 percent or better, it will invest in projects *A* and *B*, and investment will be $35,000; if 14 percent is acceptable, investment will be $40,000. The amounts that would be invested at the various minimum acceptable expected rates of return are presented in Figure 10–6.

The relationship between the minimum acceptable expected rate of return and the amount of investment in Figure 10–6 is called the *marginal efficiency of capital* function. Usually this function is drawn as a smooth line, but in this case the function is not smooth because there is only one firm with a finite number of investment projects.

The example in Table 10–2 describes the details of the investment decision-making process for one firm. It is necessary to conceptualize the aggregation of similar marginal efficiency of capital functions for all firms in order to construct a total investment demand function. In moving from the micro (one firm)

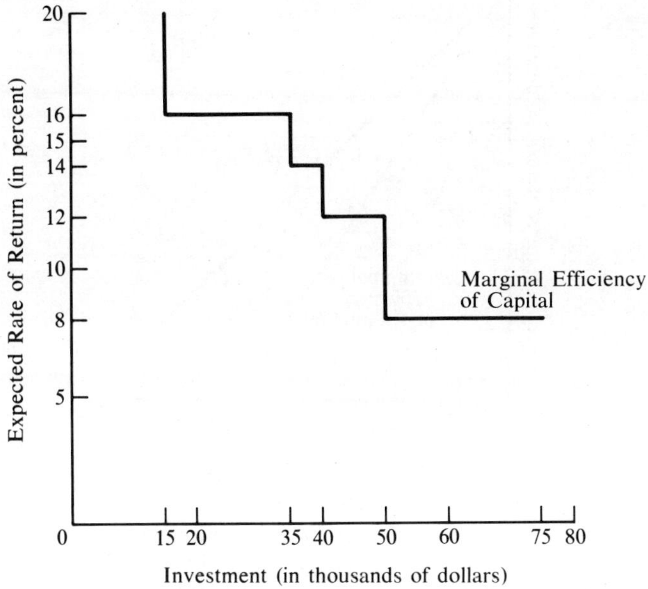

FIGURE 10–6 Marginal Efficiency of Capital Function

level to the macro (all firms) level, one change is made. On the macro level, a *marginal efficiency of investment* (MEI) function is preferable to the marginal efficiency of capital (MEC) function.

The difference between the marginal efficiency of capital function and the marginal efficiency of investment function involves more than the simple aggregation process. The MEI function recognizes the fact that the total level of investment demand may affect the expected rate of return on individual investment projects. If all firms desire to increase their investment activity at the same time, and the capital goods industries are operating near capacity output, the prices of plant and equipment increase. The increase in capital goods prices lowers the rate of return on investment projects.

The difference between the MEC and the MEI increases as the level of investment increases. The theoretical relationship is illustrated in Figure 10–7. At a very low level of investment, the capital goods industries are operating well below capacity. The excess capacity tends to prevent increases in the price of capital goods. Thus, at low levels of investment, the MEC and the MEI are nearly identical. However, as the demand for investment goods increases, the excess capacity in the capital goods industries is eliminated and the prices of capital goods increase more rapidly. As the prices of capital goods increase, the rate of return on investment projects declines and the difference between the marginal efficiency of

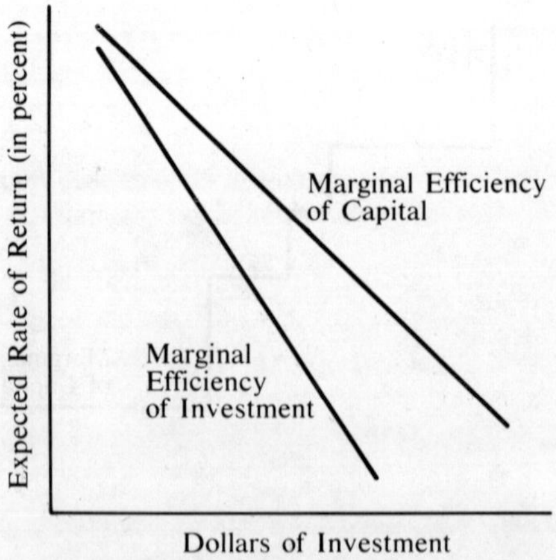

FIGURE 10–7 The Marginal Efficiency of Capital and the Marginal Efficiency of Investment

capital and the marginal efficiency of investment increases. In subsequent analyses, the MEI is used to represent the demand for investment goods.

The Interest Rate

Having constructed an MEI function as the demand for investment goods in terms of the minimum acceptable expected rate of return, the next problem is the selection of a minimum acceptable rate of return. In the most basic model, the interest rate is used as the minimum acceptable rate of return.

Assume that the firm will invest in all projects that offer an expected rate of return equal to, or greater than, the cost of investment funds. Borrowing funds at 8 percent and investing in projects yielding 7 percent is a losing proposition. Alternatively, if the firm can borrow at 8 percent, the failure to invest in a project yielding 9 percent would violate the rules of profit maximization.

Using the rate of interest as the cutoff rate for the acceptance or rejection of investment projects is an oversimplification because the firm has many sources of funds. Each source of funds has a cost. The basic internal sources of funds are depreciation allowances and retained earnings. These are not costless sources of funds, even though no one must be paid interest on their use. The cost of internally generated funds is the opportunity cost to the stockholders. The stockholders could be receiving these funds as dividends and reinvesting the dividends in an alternative income-producing asset. In addition to the internal sources of funds, the firm uses external funds that require payment of dividends to stockholders or interest to creditors or bondholders. Thus, the firm must determine the cost of each alterna-

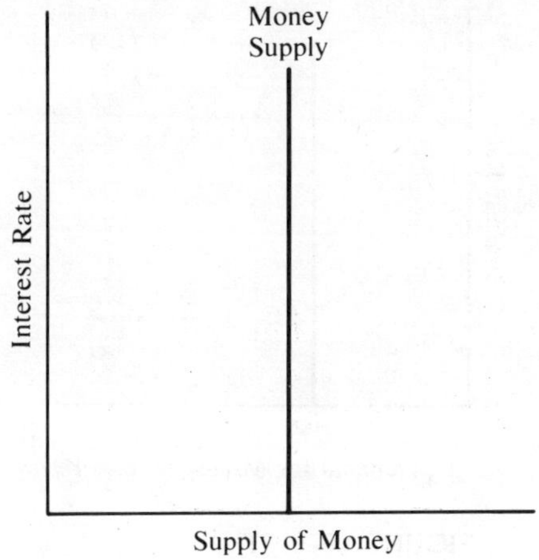

FIGURE 10–8 The Supply of Money

tive source of funds and select that source, or combination of sources, that provides funds to the firm at the lowest cost. The interest rate serves as a simple, convenient proxy for the cost of all the sources of funds available to the firm.

The basic Keynesian interest rate is determined by the demand for and the supply of money. Unlike the classical interest rate, which was determined by saving and investment, the Keynesian interest rate is determined by the supply of and demand for money. Interest is the price of money and, like all prices, is determined by supply and demand.

The Supply of Money The supply of money in terms of the interest rate is taken as a constant value. Given the quantity of reserves provided by the central bank and the values for the money supply expansion model, a fixed quantity of money is available. In Figure 10–8, the supply of money has zero interest elasticity. This is the conventional presentation. However, if a higher interest rate induces the banks to hold fewer excess reserves, higher interest rates should result in a larger money supply. Under this assumption, the supply of money function would slope upwards to the right.

The Demand for Money The demand for money is somewhat more involved than the supply of money. Keynes presents three demands for money: transactions, precautionary, and speculative.

I. TRANSACTIONS DEMAND FOR MONEY

The transactions demand for money is the basic demand for money. This demand for money was recognized by the classical economists. This is a demand to hold

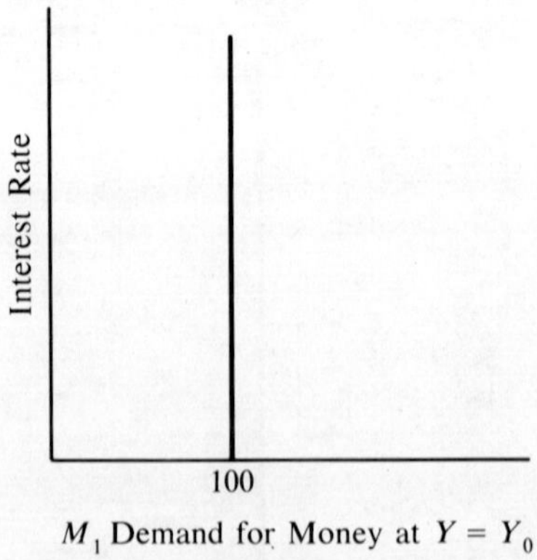

FIGURE 10–9 The Transactions and Precautionary Demands for Money

money as a medium of exchange in order to bridge the gap between the receipt of income and the making of payments. Consumers hold money in order to spread out expenditures over the period between paychecks. The business firm holds money in order to pay the factors of production. The transactions demand for money is a demand to hold money to make expected, routine, normal expenditures.

II. PRECAUTIONARY DEMAND FOR MONEY

The second demand—the precautionary demand—is, as the name implies, the holding of money to make unexpected payments. A simple example illustrates the difference between transactions and precautionary demands for money. Say you are planning to drive from New York to California and are trying to estimate your need for money. You calculate all the known costs: meals, lodgings, gas, oil, tolls, and so on. Your demand for money to cover these costs is a transactions demand. However, there is a chance that, halfway across the country, the rear end will fall out of the car and you will be faced with a large repair bill. To cover this risk, you have a precautionary demand for money. You don't expect the rear end to fall out—it never did before—but there is a chance that this or some other unexpected need for funds will arise.

Both the transactions demand and the precautionary demand for money are considered to be functions of the level of income. In the graphical analysis, these demands are combined as the M_1 demand for money. In Figure 10–9, the M_1 demand for money, at a given level of income, $Y = Y_0$, is drawn with the assumption that this demand for money is perfectly inelastic with respect to the rate of interest.

In Figure 10–9, at the assumed level of income, the M_1 demand for money

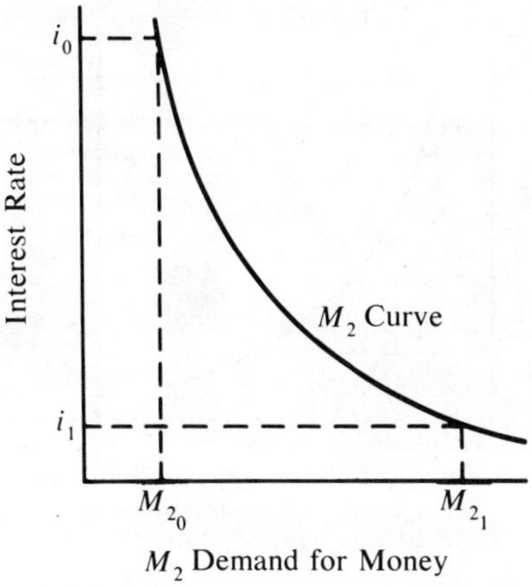

FIGURE 10–10 The Speculative Demand for Money

is 100 units regardless of the rate of interest. For higher levels of income, the transactions and precautionary demands would be higher. The rate of interest does not affect these demands for money in a basic model. However, there are theoretical and empirical reasons to believe that high interest rates lead individuals and businesses to reduce their money demands. Under this assumption, the M_1 demand curve would bend backwards towards the vertical axis as the interest rate increases.

III. SPECULATIVE DEMAND FOR MONEY

The speculative demand for money is the demand for money to be held as an asset in preference to holding some other asset. The classical economists argued that the rational man would never hold money as an asset because he could always do better by holding an interest-bearing asset. However, Keynes deviated from classical thought and presented the case for an asset demand for money. The demand for speculative balances, the asset demand for money, is an inverse function of the interest rate. The speculative demand for money curve, the M_2 curve, is illustrated in Figure 10–10.

The easiest way to think of the speculative demand for money is in terms of an investor faced with the alternative of holding either money or bonds. At the interest rate i_0 in Figure 10–10, why would the rational investor hold only a small amount of speculative balances and hold the remainder of his funds in bonds? There are three elements to the answer:

1. At i_0, interest rates are relatively high and the opportunity cost of holding cash is very high. The amount of interest that would be lost by holding cash leads the investor to hold less cash and more bonds.

2. At i_0, the return to the bond investor is high relative to the cost of switching from cash to bonds. Most of the costs of purchasing bonds—the

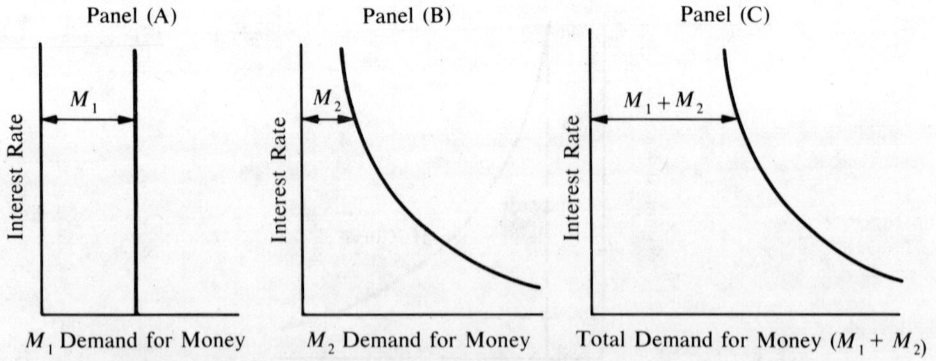

FIGURE 10–11 Combining the M_1 and M_2 Demands for Money

brokerage cost, information-seeking costs, and time costs of the transaction—are the same regardless of the interest rate. At a high interest rate, all of these costs are quickly recovered by the investor.

3. At i_0, the price of the bonds is relatively low. Recall that there is an inverse relationship between interest rates and bond prices. At a high interest rate, the bond purchaser is buying low. He hopes that as interest rates decline to more normal levels in the future, bond prices will rise and he will receive a capital gain.

By contrast, at i_1, the investor holds a relatively large portion of his funds in cash rather than in bonds for three reasons:

1. At i_1, interest rates are low and the opportunity cost of holding money is low. Little is lost by holding money.

2. At i_1, the fixed costs of switching from cash to bonds are high relative to the return to be earned on the bonds. Effort and expense are required to earn a relatively low interest rate.

3. At i_1, bond prices are high. The investor fears that interest rates will rise to more normal levels, bond prices will fall, and he will incur a capital loss.

Thus, the hypothetical investor divides his asset holdings between money and bonds on the basis of opportunity cost, return versus cost of switching, and the possibility of a change in the value of the asset.

To derive the total demand for money, the M_1 demand of Figure 10–9 is added to the M_2 demand of Figure 10–10. The total demand for money, $M_1 + M_2$, is presented in Figure 10–11. The derivation of the total demand for money in Figure 10–11 is simply a horizontal summing of the M_1 and M_2 demands.

The next step is to combine the total demand for money in panel (C) of Figure 10–11 with the supply of money in Figure 10–8. This final combination determines the interest rate in Figure 10–12. As with all prices, the price of money, the interest rate i_0, is determined by the intersection of demand and supply curves in Figure 10–12. Changes in the interest rate can be brought about by

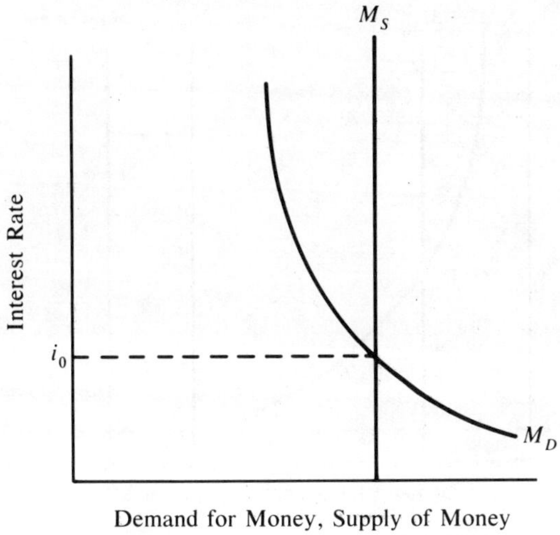

FIGURE 10–12 The Interest Rate

changing the supply of money in Figure 10–12. If the demand for money curve remains constant and the supply of money is increased, the equilibrium interest rate declines.

One further basic problem needs to be introduced at this point. Keynes argued that the demand for money curve could become parallel to the horizontal axis at a very low rate of interest. This concept is known as the *liquidity trap* and is illustrated in Figure 10–13. The liquidity trap area of the demand for money curve is based on the assumption that the factors explaining the shape of the speculative demand curve become so strong that investors are unwilling to hold additional bonds. The opportunity cost is so low, the switching cost is so high relative to the return, and the possibility of a capital loss is so great that people prefer added cash to added bonds.

The liquidity trap concept implies a limit on the ability of the monetary authority to change interest rates. In Figure 10–13, the original money supply is M_{S_0} and the interest rate is i_0. As the money supply increases to M_{S_1} the rate of interest declines to i_1. However, an increase in the money supply from M_{S_1} to M_{S_2} does not decrease the interest rate. The liquidity trap has been reached and the increase in the money supply from M_{S_1} to M_{S_2} has been added to speculative holdings; no part of this increase in the money supply has been used to purchase bonds.

Summary The demand for money is composed of three demands—transactions, precautionary, and speculative. The first two are stated as a function

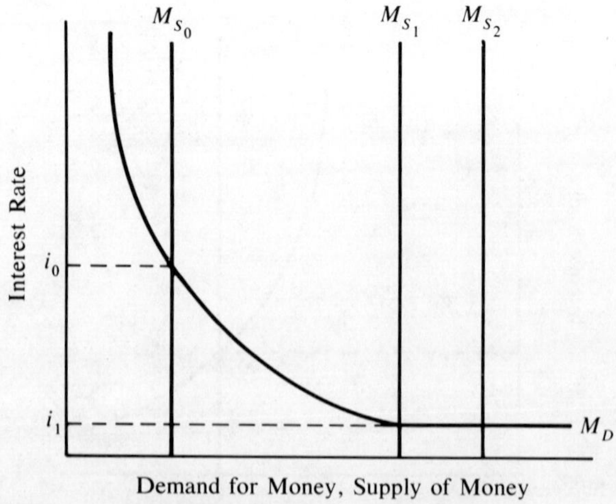

FIGURE 10–13 The Liquidity Trap

of the level of income; the third is stated as a function of the interest rate. The total demand for money and the supply of money determine the interest rate. Finally, the concept of the liquidity trap suggests that there may be a "floor" to the rate of interest and that after a point further increases in the supply of money do not reduce the interest rate.

Combining the Marginal Efficiency of Investment and the Interest Rate

The determination of the level of investment requires combining the marginal efficiency of investment curve and the interest rate model. In Figure 10–14, the supply and demand for money in panel (A) determine the interest rate; the interest rate serves as the cutoff rate in the marginal efficiency of investment analysis and the level of investment is determined in panel (B).

The liquidity trap produces a floor to the rate of interest. Once the money supply has increased to M_{S_1} and the interest rate has been reduced to i_1, further increases in the money supply do not lower the interest rate. Given these conditions, investment could not increase beyond the level I'.

The combination of the interest rate analysis and the marginal efficiency of investment function determines the level of investment. This value of investment is then added to the simple Keynesian model of aggregate demand. Thus, the line of causation of income determination begins with the supply and demand for money determining the interest rate. The interest rate and the marginal efficiency of investment function determine the level of investment. The level of investment and the other components of aggregate demand determine the level of income, output, and employment.

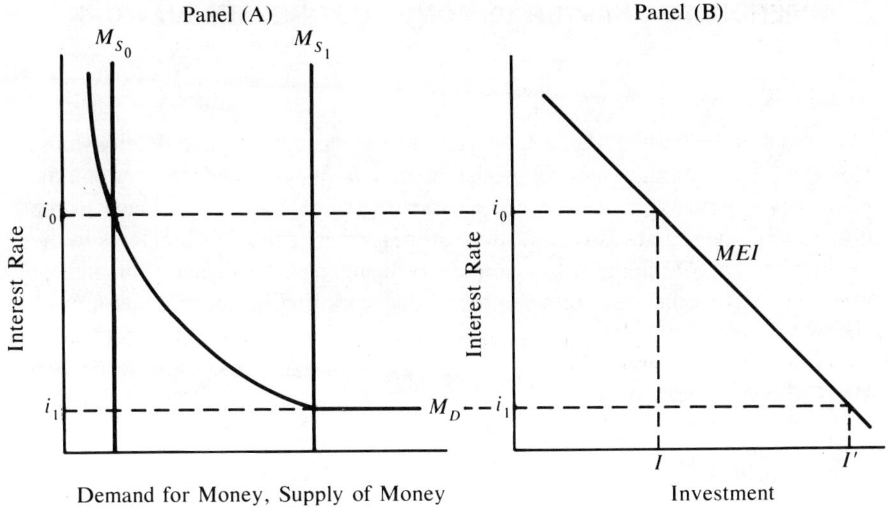

FIGURE 10–14 The Money Supply, the Interest Rate, and the Level of Investment

The addition of the material in this section adds a new tool of macroeconomic policy, monetary policy. By increasing the supply of money in panel (A) of Figure 10–14, the central bank can lower the interest rate and increase the level of investment. Assuming the normal multiplier relationships, the level of income increases.

A Final Problem

The basic model outlined in this chapter suffers from a feedback problem. Assume that a level of income is determined in the manner outlined in the previous two paragraphs. Then the level of government spending is increased and the level of income increases. The increase in the level of income increases the transactions demand for money. The increase in the demand for money increases the interest rate and decreases the level of investment. The decrease in the level of investment decreases the level of income, which again changes the transactions demand for money.

Each change in a component of aggregate demand changes income and changes the demand for money; each change in the demand for money changes the interest rate, and each change in the interest rate changes investment and the level of income. The basic analysis can be adjusted for the effects of this type of feedback, but the integration of the monetary analysis with the analysis of aggregate demand is achieved more easily with the *IS-LM* analysis in the next chapter.

APPENDIX TO CHAPTER 10. SOME POST-KEYNESIAN WORK

The model in the body of the chapter presents the basic Keynesian relationships. However, the presentation of Keynesian models frequently tends to overlook the many developments in macroeconomic theory which have taken place in the post-Keynesian period. This appendix outlines some of the developments in the theories of the consumption function, investment, and the demand for money. These alternative theories are a sample of the work that has been done; a more comprehensive treatment of these and other macroeconomic concepts is covered in a course in macroeconomic theory.

Consumption

There are three major alternatives to the Keynesian absolute income hypothesis. The *relative income hypothesis,* developed by James Duesenberry,[1] asserts that the level and composition of the individual's consumption is not determined independently but is influenced by the consumption standards of the individual's peer group. This thought is a version of the well-known "keeping up with the Joneses" phenomenon. By associating with others in his peer group, the individual is exposed to new and better consumption goods (the demonstration effect) and his own self-esteem requires that he purchase these superior goods.

The second key idea of the Duesenberry hypothesis is the unwillingness of the individual to give up a high standard of living. Once an individual attains a new peak standard of living, he is reluctant to move back to a lower standard of living and is willing to sacrifice saving in order to maintain his consumption if his income falls from its previous peek level.

The second major alternative consumption hypothesis is the *permanent income hypothesis* developed by Milton Friedman.[2] This theory is developed in some detail because of its importance in Chapter 12. The first point to understand in the permanent income hypothesis is the time period for the measurement of income. Income is usually measured over a year or some division of a year. Therefore, consumption functions based on government-collected data are usually on an annual basis. This creates problems because the annual data on a person's income is not necessarily representative of the person's ability to consume. Many people have incomes that are not regular from year to year, and the selection of a given year for the measurement of their consumption may produce meaningless results. Friedman argues that consumption and income should be related over a longer period of time.

[1]James Duesenberry, *Income, Saving and the Theory of Consumer Behavior* (New York: Oxford University Press, 1967).

[2]Milton Friedman, *A Theory of the Consumption Function* (Princeton, N.J.: Princeton University Press, 1957).

TABLE 10A–3 A Hypothetical Boxer's Consumption Behavior

YEAR	*INCOME (dollars)*	*CONSUMPTION (dollars)*	*AVERAGE PROPENSITY TO CONSUME*
1	20,000	100,000	5.0
2	20,000	100,000	5.0
3	500,000	100,000	0.2
4	20,000	100,000	5.0

A simple example illustrates the measurement problem. Assume a professional boxer has the income and consumption pattern shown in Table 10A–3. In years 1, 2, and 4 his income is relatively low; he does not have any fights but picks up some income from personal appearances and product endorsements. In year 3, he has a title fight and earns a half million dollars. His consumption over the four years remains stable at $100,000 per year. In the years in which he does not fight, his *average propensity to consume*—total consumption divided by total income—is very high; in the year in which he fights, his average propensity to consume (APC) is very low.

The essence of the Friedman concept is that a year is not necessarily the best period over which to measure income and that a more representative APC for people such as the boxer would be obtained by using a longer measurement period. For example, one could assume that this boxer plans his income and consumption over the four-year period. Consumption of $400,000 from an income of $560,000 produces an APC of 0.71. Alternatively, one could say that the average income that the boxer can expect over this four-year planning period is $140,000 per year. The $140,000 per year is much more representative of his income than any of the annual income figures.

However, how is the appropriate length of the planning period determined? To establish the planning period for each individual would be an impossible job. Therefore, Friedman uses statistical techniques to obtain a measure of *permanent income*. The individual's permanent income is a weighted average of past actual incomes with declining weights assigned to incomes in the more distant past. Thus, the measure of permanent income on which a person (or a society) bases his consumption becomes

$$Y_P = a_0 Y_t + a_1 Y_{t-1} + a_2 Y_{t-2} + a_3 Y_{t-3} + \cdots + a_n Y_{t-n}$$

where $a_0 > a_1 > a_2 > a_3 > \cdots > a_n$

and $C_P = kY_P$

Y_P = permanent income

Y_t = actual income in year t

a_0 = weight assigned to actual income in year t

C_P = permanent consumption

k = proportion of permanent income spent on consumption

The individual spends a proportion k of his permanent income each year. In years in which his actual income is lower than his permanent income, his APC is high. In years in which his actual income is higher than his permanent income, his APC is low.

The Friedman permanent income hypothesis leads logically to attempts to use even longer term measures of income. The *lifetime income hypothesis,* developed by Modigliani and Brumberg,[3] is the best known of these efforts. The lifetime income hypothesis assumes that an individual of a given age rationally allocates his consumption over the remainder of his lifetime. At the point of analysis, he has an expected stream of income, an expected lifetime, and a given stock of assets. He must use this information to maximize his utility over his lifetime.

The lifetime income hypothesis points up the importance of the age distribution of the population in the determination of aggregate consumption. The ability and desire to save should vary over one's lifetime. A population with a large number of people in the 55–65 age group should save more than a population weighted heavily toward the 20–30 age group. The older group would have reached their peak earning years, have paid for their homes, and financed their children's educations. Those in the 20–30 age group are buying a home, acquiring durables, and raising children.

Investment Theory

Of the three topics covered in this appendix, investment theory, in the opinion of the author, remains the most difficult problem. In the wake of the publication of *The General Theory,* empirical studies raised questions about the effect of changes in the interest rate on the level of investment. The Oxford Studies[4] raised questions about the extent to which businessmen considered the interest rate in reaching capital investment decisions. These studies, which were later shown to have severe limitations, led many economists to believe that the interest rate had relatively little impact on capital investment, and many still hold this view. Some of the empirical work on this question is reviewed in Chapter 15.

A great deal of the more recent work on investment behavior has stressed the role of the *investment accelerator* in explaining changes in the level of investment activity, a concept developed by J. M. Clark in 1917.[5] The accelerator

[3]Franco Modigliani and Richard Brumberg, "Utility Analysis and the Consumption Function: An Interpretation of Cross Section Data," in K. K. Kurihara, ed., *Post-Keynesian Economics* (New Brunswick, N.J.: Rutgers University Press, 1954), pp. 388–436; and Albert Ando and Franco Modigliani, "The 'Life Cycle' Hypothesis of Saving: Aggregate Implications and Tests," *American Economic Review,* March 1963, pp. 55–84.

[4]H. D. Henderson, "The Significance of the Rate of Interest," *Oxford Economic Papers,* October 1938, pp. 1–31, and R. S. Sayers, "Business Men and the Terms of Borrowing," *Oxford Economic Papers,* February 1940, pp. 23–31. These are only two of several papers in what is known as "the Oxford Studies."

[5]John M. Clark, "Business Acceleration and the Law of Demand: A Technical Factor in Economic Cycles," *Journal of Political Economy,* vol. 25, no. 3 (March 1917), pp. 217–235.

TABLE 10A–4 A Simple Accelerator Model

YEAR	*DEMAND FOR OUTPUT*	*MACHINES NEEDED*	*NEW INVESTMENT IN MACHINES*
1	1,000	10	—
2	1,000	10	0
3	1,100	11	1
4	1,300	13	2
5	1,800	18	5
6	2,700	27	9
7	2,900	29	2
8	2,900	29	0

mechanism stresses the relationship between the demand for a final product and the demand for the investment goods required to produce the final product. Investment demand follows from the demand for the final product but is more volatile than the demand for the final product. Table 10A–4 illustrates the basic concept. Assume that one machine can produce 100 units of output per year and lasts forever. The number of machines can be varied instantaneously in response to changes in demand. In years 1 and 2 there is no investment, but in years 3 through 6 demand grows rapidly. The level of investment grows from one machine per year in year 3 to nine machines per year in year 6. In year 7, final demand grows at a slower pace, and the demand for machines drops off sharply. In year 8, output demand, though still at a very high level, does not increase, and the demand for new machines goes to zero. Note that the percentage fluctuations in the demand for machines were much larger than the percentage fluctuations in the demand for final output.

The use of a mechanical relationship between the demand for final output and the demand for capital investment raises several problems. First, the cost of money does not enter the accelerator mechanism. Second, there is no allowance for long-run changes in the capital/output ratio. Third, there is no allowance for excess productive capacity in the industry. If there were excess capacity at the start, the fluctuations in investment would have been reduced. Fourth, the model used in the basic example assumes away the depreciation and replacement of capital equipment. Finally, the model assumes that the producers of capital goods can always meet any new demand for machines.

A second nonfinancial model of investment is a *stock adjustment,* or modified accelerator, model. Assume that in a given period, the firm invests in order to eliminate a portion of the difference between its actual stock of capital and the desired stock of capital. Symbolically,

$$I_t = a(C_{D_t} - C_{A_{t-1}})$$

where I_t = investment in period t

C_{D_t} = desired capital stock in period t

$C_{A_{t-1}}$ = actual capital stock in period $t-1$

a = proportion of difference to be eliminated in a time period

By assuming that the desired capital stock, C_{D_t} is a simple function b of current output, O, then $C_{D_t} = bO_t$, the investment function can be written as

$$I_t = a(bO_t - C_{A_{t-1}})$$
$$I_t = abO_t - aC_{A_{t-1}}$$

The current demand for investment goods is a function of current output and the last period's capital stock. If desired capital could be based on future sales, the model would be improved but future sales are unknown.[6]

The Demand for Money

The post-Keynesian demand for money literature has centered on the resolution of the role of the interest rate in the demand for money and the empirical estimation of the determinants of the demand for money. Much of the work on the demand for money has been done by Professor Milton Friedman, and his contributions to the development of theory are covered in Chapter 12.

James Tobin,[7] in a major article on the demand for money, explores the reasons for holding funds in cash rather than in interest-bearing assets and provides added theoretical foundations for the Keynesian concept of the speculative demand for money. Tobin stresses the asset holder's desire to achieve an optimum tradeoff between return on his funds and the assumption of interest rate risk. The greater the proportion of his funds that is committed to bonds, the higher his interest income. However, the higher the proportion of bonds in his portfolio, the higher is his risk of a capital loss. Money is the risk-free asset but pays no interest; bonds pay interest but carry a risk. The investor diversifies his portfolio to balance his expected return and risk.

William Baumol[8] treats the holding of money in the framework of inventory theory. People hold an inventory of cash and demand deposits. The appropriate amount of cash to hold can be analyzed in the same manner as a business would determine its appropriate stock of a raw material. The holding of cash becomes a function of the cost of switching from other assets to cash, the lost interest resulting from holding cash rather than interest-bearing assets, and the volume of transactions to be conducted.

Baumol's model suggests that there are economies of scale in the holding of money. One's money holdings do not need to double as one's transactions per time period double. In addition, there is an interest elasticity to the demand for money. Higher interest rates induce economic units to hold less money and to make smaller

[6] A brief but comprehensive discussion of modifications of the basic accelerator models can be found in Michael K. Evans, *Macroeconomic Activity: Theory, Forecasting, and Control* (New York: Harper & Row, Publishers, 1969), pp. 80–86.

[7] James Tobin, "Liquidity Preference as Behavior Towards Risk," *Review of Economic Studies,* February 1958, pp. 65–86.

[8] William J. Baumol, "The Transactions Demand for Cash—An Inventory Theoretic Approach," *Quarterly Journal of Economics,* November 1952, pp. 545–556.

conversions from other interest-bearing assets to cash. More frequent conversions from other assets to cash are required if the amount of cash holdings is to be reduced; however, the cost of making more conversions is more than offset by the added interest income.

Much of the more recent work on the demand for money is of an econometric nature. A recent excellent study by Stephen Goldfeld[9] deals with many of the empirical issues in the quantitative evaluation of the demand for money. Goldfeld estimates that the long-run income elasticity of the demand for money is 0.68. This means that, when the economy adjusts its money holdings to a changed level of income, the demand for money increases by 0.68 percent for every 1 percent increase in the level of income. This value of income elasticity is lower than estimates of other investigators and suggests substantial economies of scale in the holding of money.

Goldfeld's estimates of the interest elasticity of the demand for money suggest a relatively low interest elasticity. A 1 percent increase in the interest rate would produce a decrease of between 0.07 and 0.16 percent in the demand for money, depending upon the interest rate used in the measurement and the structure of the adjustment process.

Research on all of these topics is an on-going process. Many basic questions remain unsettled in spite of continuous research over the past four decades. For example, the role of the interest rate in the determination of the level of investment is not certain. Likewise, the degree of interest elasticity of the demand for money is not firmly established. The exact determinants of the level of consumption, beyond the inclusion of some measure of income, remain controversial. The purpose of this appendix has been to introduce some new ideas on each of these subjects and to point out that, though all of the answers are not known, economists are continuing to search for better explanations.

REVIEW QUESTIONS

1. Assume the following basic nonmonetary model of income determination and solve for the level of income:

$$\begin{aligned} Y &= C + I + G + (X - IM) \\ C &= a + bYd \\ Yd &= Y - T \\ T &= tY \\ I &= I_0 \\ G &= G_0 \\ X &= X_0 \\ IM &= IM_0 \end{aligned}$$

[9]Stephen M. Goldfeld, "The Demand for Money Revisited," *Brookings Papers on Economic Activity,* vol. 3, 1973, pp. 577–645.

2. Using the following numerical values, calculate the level of income in the model in question (1): a = 100; $b = 0.8$; $t = 0.0625$; $I_0 = 85$; $G_0 = 62.5$; $X_0 = 15$; and $IM_0 = 12.5$. (To check your answer, consumption is 850.)

3. Using graph paper, illustrate the graphical solution to the following basic model:

$$
\begin{aligned}
Y &= C + I + G + (X - IM) \\
C &= a + bYd \\
Yd &= Y - T \\
T &= T_0 \\
I &= I_0 \\
G &= G_0 \\
X &= X_0 \\
IM &= IM_0
\end{aligned}
$$

The numerical values are $a = 100$; b = 0.8; $I_0 = 100$; $G_0 = 50$; $T_0 = 50$; $X_0 = 25$; and $IM_0 = 25$. Check your work using the algebraic solution.

4. Differentiate between the government spending multiplier, the tax multiplier, and the balanced budget multiplier.

5. Why is the tax multiplier less than the government spending multiplier?

6. Explain the derivation of the marginal efficiency of investment and the marginal efficiency of capital.

7. Explain the theoretical case behind the belief that investment is relatively inelastic with respect to the interest rate.

8. Explain the alternatives to the simple Keynesian consumption function. How do the theories vary according to the definition of income?

9. Explain the demand for money function.

10. How does the possible existence of a liquidity trap affect the ability of monetary policy to influence the level of income?

SUGGESTED READINGS

Anthony S. Campagna, *Macroeconomics: Theory and Policy.* Boston: Houghton Mifflin Company, 1974.

Thomas F. Dernburg and Duncan M. McDougall, *Macroeconomics: The Measurement, Analysis, and Control of Aggregate Economic Activity,* 4th ed. New York: McGraw-Hill Book Company, 1972.

Herschel I. Grossman, "Was Keynes a 'Keynesian'? A Review Article," *Journal of Economic Literature,* March 1972, pp. 26–30.

Lawrence R. Klein, *The Keynesian Revolution,* 2nd ed. New York: Macmillan Company, 1966.

Robert Lekachman, *The Age of Keynes*. New York: Random House, 1966.

Robert Lekachman, ed., *Keynes' General Theory: Reports of Three Decades*. New York: St. Martin's Press, 1964.

Axel Leijonhufvud, *On Keynesian Economics and the Economics of Keynes*. New York: Oxford University Press, 1968.

G. L. S. Shackle, "Keynes and Today's Establishment in Economic Theory: A View," *Journal of Economic Literature,* June 1973, pp. 516–519.

11

THE *IS-LM* ANALYSIS AND FISCAL POLICY

Chapter 10 presented the basic Keynesian model of income determination. In this chapter, a more sophisticated model, employing the basic concepts of Chapter 10 is developed and used to analyze monetary and fiscal policy. The second half of this chapter covers fiscal policy—its measurement, policy variations, and policy problems—and concludes with a discussion of wage and price controls.

The *IS-LM* Analysis

The *IS-LM* analysis is a model for the presentation of basic income determination concepts. Using the *IS-LM* model, one can analyze macroeconomic problems under a variety of possible conditions. The model assumes two equally important sectors of the economy—a money market and a goods market. Equilibrium in the money market requires equality of the supply of and demand for money; the objective is to determine alternative combinations of an interest rate and a level of income which produce equality of the demand for and supply of money. Equilibrium in the goods market requires that the aggregate demand for goods be equal to the aggregate supply of goods; the objective is to determine alternative combinations of an interest rate and a level of income which equalize aggregate demand and aggregate supply. Only one interest rate–income level combination satisfies the equilibrium conditions of both the money market and the goods market; at that interest rate and that income level, the economy is in equilibrium.

Derivation of the *LM* Curve

The *LM* curve represents the equilibrium conditions of the money market. All points on the *LM* curve represent combinations of an interest rate and a level of income which equalize the supply of and demand for money. The construction of the *LM* curve involves no new theoretical concepts but is a graphical arrangement of the ideas presented in Chapter 10.

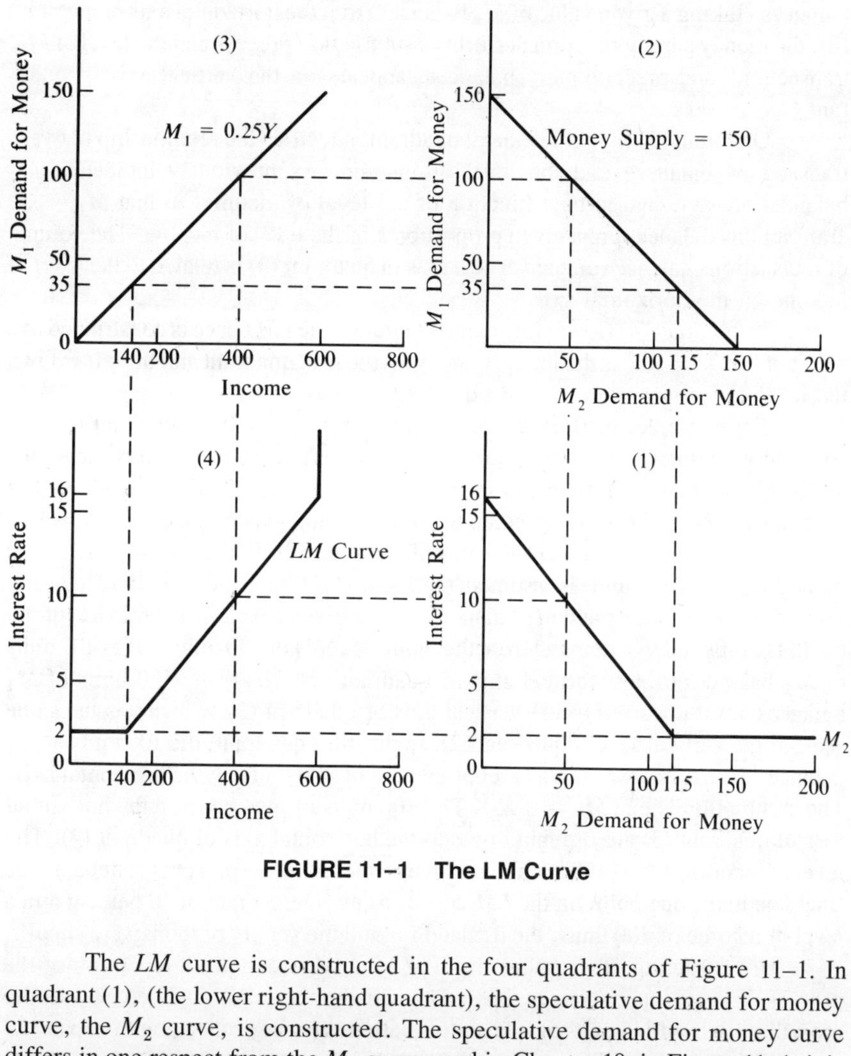

FIGURE 11–1 The LM Curve

The *LM* curve is constructed in the four quadrants of Figure 11–1. In quadrant (1), (the lower right-hand quadrant), the speculative demand for money curve, the M_2 curve, is constructed. The speculative demand for money curve differs in one respect from the M_2 curve used in Chapter 10; in Figure 11–1, it is assumed that at interest rates of 16 percent or higher the speculative demand for money is zero. At these high interest rates, the incentives for the holding of interest-bearing assets, rather than money, become so strong that the speculative demand for money is eliminated. The speculative demand increases as interest rates decrease in the normal range. Then, at a low interest rate, 2 percent, the liquidity trap appears and the M_2 curve becomes parallel to the horizontal axis.

In quadrant (2) (upper right-hand quadrant), a given money supply is assumed. This quadrant serves to divide the money supply between M_1 and M_2 balances. The money supply line indicates that the 150-unit money supply could all be held as speculative, M_2, balances or could all be held as transactions, M_1, balances. Taking a given value of M_2 balances from the horizontal axis of quadrant (2), the money supply function performs a subtraction process and the level of M_1, transactions and precautionary balances, appears on the vertical axis of quadrant (2).

Quadrant (3) (upper left-hand quadrant) specifies the relationship between transactions balances and the level of income. As previously indicated, M_1 balances are assumed to be a function of the level of income, so that $M_1 = kY$. Transactions balances are a given proportion k of the level of income. The volume of transactions balances on the vertical axis in quadrant (3) is related to the level of income on the horizontal axis.

In quadrant (4) (lower left-hand quadrant), the *LM* curve is constructed as a result of bringing across the interest rate from the first quadrant and bringing down the level of income from the third quadrant.

For example, assume an interest rate of 10 percent in quadrant (1), the speculative demand for money quadrant. At an interest rate of 10 percent, the speculative demand for money is 50 units on the horizontal axis. The 50 units of speculative demand is transferred up to the horizontal axis of quadrant (2), which has the same scale as the horizontal axis of quadrant (1). In the second quadrant, a money supply of 150 units is assumed; the 150 units of money can be divided in any proportion between M_1 and M_2 balances. In the given case, the subtraction of the 50 units of speculative demand from the money supply of 150 units leaves 100 units of M_1 balances on the vertical axis of quadrant (2). Next, the 100 units of M_1 balances are transferred to the vertical axis of quadrant (3), which has the same scale as the vertical axis of quadrant (2). In the third quadrant, the 100 units of M_1 balances are associated with a level of income of 400 units on the horizontal axis. The assumption is that $M_1 = 0.25Y$. The 400 units of income from the horizontal axis of quadrant (3) are brought down to the horizontal axis of quadrant (4). The level of income of $Y = 400$ and the initial interest rate of 10 percent produce, in the final quadrant, one point on the *LM* curve. At an interest rate of 10 percent and a level of income of 400 units, the demand for and the supply of money are equal.

Constructing other points on the *LM* curve is simply a repetition of the process. Take an interest rate of 2 percent in quadrant (1). At $i = 2$ percent, people are willing to hold 115 units of speculative balances (or any other quantity up to 150 units). Bringing the 115 units of speculative balances up to quadrant (2), 35 units are available for transactions purposes. In quadrant (3), 35 units of M_1 balances are appropriate for an income level of 140 units. Bringing the 140 units of income down to quadrant (4) and the interest rate of 2 percent over from quadrant (1), a second point on the *LM* curve is derived. At 2 percent, people would also be willing to hold 150 units of M_2 balances. Assuming 150 units of M_2 balances at an interest rate of 2 percent, income is zero and the horizontal portion of the *LM* curve, called the *Keynesian region,* is derived.

Using an interest rate of 16 percent, the M_2 demand for money is zero and the entire money supply is available for transactions purposes. With 150 units of M_1 balances, the level of income in quadrant (3) is 600 units and the point on the *LM* curve is at $i = 16$ percent and $Y = 600$. At interest rates above 16 percent, the

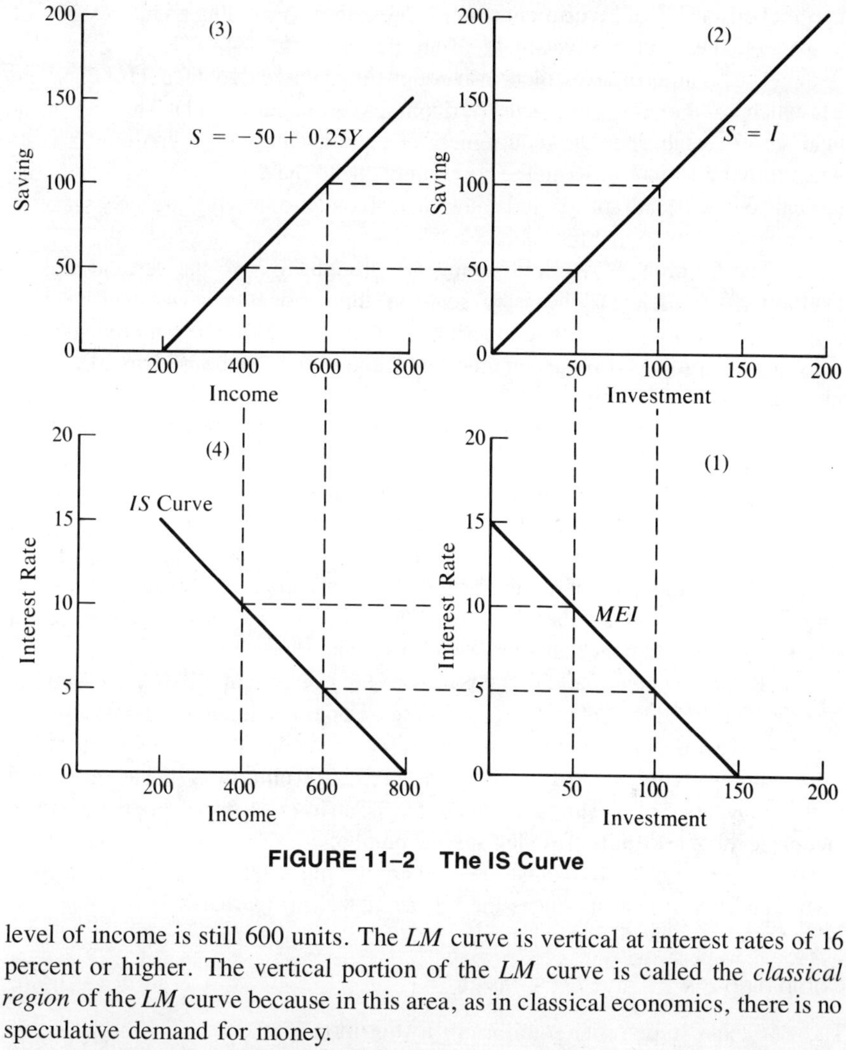

FIGURE 11–2 The IS Curve

level of income is still 600 units. The *LM* curve is vertical at interest rates of 16 percent or higher. The vertical portion of the *LM* curve is called the *classical region* of the *LM* curve because in this area, as in classical economics, there is no speculative demand for money.

By deriving sufficient additional points in quadrant (4), the complete *LM* curve can be plotted. The completed *LM* curve represents *all* combinations of an interest rate and a level of income at which the demand for money is equal to the supply of money.

Derivation of the *IS* Curve

The construction of the *IS* curve involves determining all combinations of an interest rate and a level of income at which saving and investment (or total leakages from, and additions to, the spending flow) are equal. The derivation requires the construction of a second four-quadrant model.

In Figure 11–2, the *IS* curve is constructed. In quadrant (1) a standard marginal efficiency of investment curve is presented. Assuming an interest rate of 10 percent, the level of investment would be 50 units.

The 50 units of investment are brought up to the horizontal axis of quadrant (2), which has the same scale as the horizontal axis of quadrant (1). The 45° line in quadrant (2) establishes the requirement of equality between saving and investment. Moving from $I = 50$ on the horizontal axis to the $S = I$ line and then to the vertical axis of quadrant (2) indicates that 50 units of saving are necessary to balance the 50 units of investment.

The 50 units of required saving are brought over to the vertical axis of quadrant (3), which has the same scale as the vertical axis of quadrant (2). Quadrant (3) presents the saving function, $S = -50 + 0.25Y$. The required 50 units of saving are produced by an income level, measured on the horizontal axis of quadrant (3), of 400 units.

In quadrant (4), the level of income of 400 units is brought down from quadrant (3). The horizontal axis of quadrant (4) has the same scale as the horizontal axis of quadrant (3). Next, the initial interest rate of 10 percent is brought across from quadrant (1) to the vertical axis of quadrant (4). The vertical axis of quadrant (4) has the same scale as the vertical axis of quadrant (1).

The combination of an interest rate of 10 percent and a level of income of 400 yields one point on the *IS* curve. This interest rate-income combination satisfies the requirement that saving and investment be equal.

The derivation of additional points on the *IS* curve involves a repetition of the process using different initial interest rates. For example, at an interest rate of 5 percent, investment is 100 units in quadrant (1). In quadrant (2), investment of 100 units requires saving of 100 units. In quadrant (3), 100 units of saving are produced at an income level of 600 units. In quadrant (4), an interest rate of 5 percent and an income level of 600 units provide a second point on the *IS* curve. The combination of all points at which an interest rate and an income level lead to the equality of saving and investment produces the full *IS* curve in Figure 11–2.

Combining the *IS* and *LM* Curves

The *LM* curve represents equilibrium in the money market, and the *IS* curve represents equilibrium in the product market. The *LM* curve derived in Figure 11–1 and the *IS* curve derived in Figure 11–2 are both plotted in Figure 11–3. The money market and the goods market are both in equilibrium at one point in Figure 11–3. At an interest rate of 10 percent and an income level of 400 units, both markets are in equilibrium. The equilibrium position of the economy is determined by the intersection of the *IS* and *LM* curves. At any other point in Figure 11–3, one or both of the markets are not in equilibrium and the level of either the interest rate and/or the level of income must change.

The equilibrium level of income and the equilibrium interest rate in Figure 11–3 are co-determined by the monetary forces (the supply of and demand for money) and by the real forces (the level of saving and investment). The goods

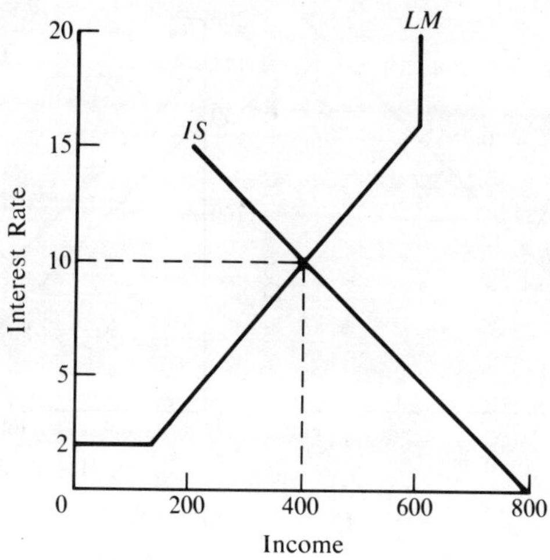

FIGURE 11–3 IS-LM Equilibrium

market and the money market are integrated and interact to determine the interest rate and income level.

A Change in the Supply of Money

The interaction of the money market and the goods market is best understood by examining the impact of a change in the supply of money on the equilibrium level of the interest rate and the income level. In Figure 11–4, the *LM* derivation from Figure 11–1 is reproduced. The *IS* curve from Figure 11–3 is added in quadrant (4), so that the equilibrium condition in Figure 11–3 serves as a starting point.

The change in the supply of money is represented in quadrant (2) by a shift to the right of the money supply line from $M_S = 150$ to $M_S{}' = 175$. With the new money supply, there are now 25 additional units of money available for either M_1 or M_2 balances. The derivation of the new *LM* curve, *LM'* in quadrant (4), is simply a repetition of the earlier derivation process, except that a new money supply line is used in quadrant (2). Note that the increase in the money supply shifts the *LM* curve to the right. The liquidity trap is extended to the right. The classical region shifts to the right but still begins at a 16 percent rate of interest.

The increase of the money supply leads to a new *IS–LM* equilibrium at $i = 8.5$ percent and $Y = 460$. Income increased by 60 units and the interest rate decreased by 1.5 percent as a result of the increase in the money supply. The 60-unit increase in the level of income required an additional 15 units of transactions balances ($M_1 = 0.25Y$), and the fall in the interest rate increased the speculative demand for money from 50 units to 60 units. The increase in the money supply was absorbed by higher M_1 and M_2 demands as the level of income and the interest rate changed.

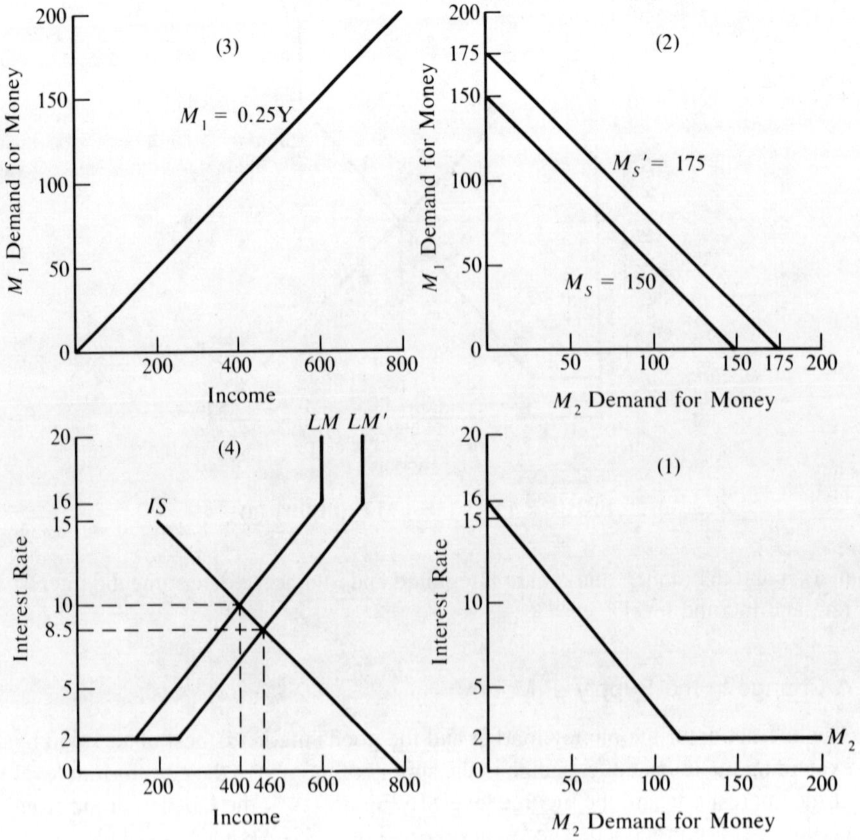

FIGURE 11–4 A Money Supply Increase

The basic multipliers developed in Chapter 10 can be used in the analysis of the change in the money supply. Refer back to the derivation of the *IS* curve in Figure 11–2. The MEI curve in quadrant (1) of Figure 11–2 indicates that a reduction of the interest rate from 10 to 8.5 percent increases the level of investment from 50 to 65 units, an increase of 15 units. The saving function of $S = -50 + 0.25Y$ in quadrant (3) of Figure 11–2 produces an investment multiplier of 4. The 60-unit income change in Figure 11–4 is the product of a 15-unit change in investment and a multiplier of 4.

A Shift of the Investment Function

Changes in the level of income can originate from the goods market as well as from the money market. A shift to the left of the investment function is illustrated in Figure 11–5; at all interest rates, the level of investment decreases by 50 units.

The derivation of the new *IS* curve is a repetition of the process by which the original *IS* curve was derived, except that the new marginal efficiency of

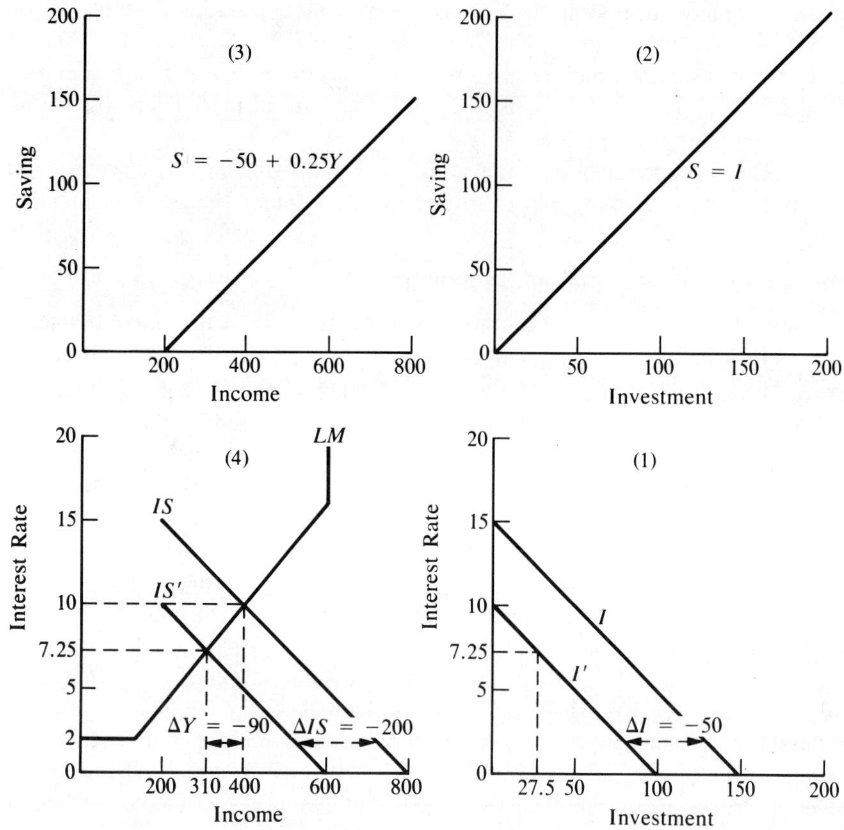

FIGURE 11–5 An Investment Decrease

investment function, I', is used as the starting point for the derivation. The new *IS* curve, *IS*′, lies to the left of the original *IS* curve in quadrant (4) of Figure 11–5. Note that the horizontal shift of the *IS* curve in quadrant (4) is equal to 200 units. The *IS* curve shifts by the amount of the horizontal shift of the investment function (50 units) times the multiplier (4).

The equilibrium level of income decreases from 400 units to 310 units as a result of the shift of the investment function. In this case, the investment multiplier is not used to determine the change in the level of income. The investment multiplier applies to the shift of the *IS* curve rather than to the change in the level of income.

Why is the change in the equilibrium level of income different from the change expected from the simple multiplier analysis? The reason is found in the interaction of the money market and the goods market. First, the shift of the investment function lowers the level of income. Second, at the lower level of income, the transactions demand for money is reduced. With a constant money supply, the supply of speculative balances increases and the interest rate falls. Third, the decline of the interest rate produces a movement down the new investment function. Fourth, the increase in investment resulting from the fall of the interest rate causes a multiplied increase in the level of income. The 50-unit decline in investment which resulted from the shift of the investment function in Figure 11–5 is partly offset by the 27.5-unit increase in investment which was induced by the fall of the interest rate.

The net decrease of investment is 22.5. Multiplying the 22.5 net change in investment times the multiplier of 4 produces the 90-unit change in income.

The Addition of Government Spending

The addition of government spending to the *IS–LM* model is illustrated in Figure 11–6. The addition of government spending begins in the first quadrant of Figure 11–6. Government spending of 100 units is added to the level of investment in quadrant (1). The investment function is shifted to the right by 100 units and becomes $I + G$. In the second quadrant, the label on the horizontal axis is changed from I to $I + G$. The appropriate label for the 45° line is $S = I + G$ because, at this point, saving must be equal to the sum of investment and government spending. In the third quadrant, the saving function determines the level of income required to generate saving equal to the sum of investment and government spending. Using these functions, an *IS* curve, IS_{I+G} is derived. The original *IS* function—before the addition of the government spending—is labeled IS_I.

The addition of government spending results in a shift of the *IS* curve from IS_I to IS_{I+G}. Note that the 400-unit horizontal shift of the *IS* curve is equal to the 100-unit change in government spending times the multiplier of 4. The actual change in the level of income from Y_1 to Y_2 is 320 units. Again, the change in the level of income is different from the change that would be expected according to the basic multiplier analysis.

Changes in the demand for money account for the difference between the actual change in the level of income and the change predicted by the multiplier. The higher level of income produced by the government spending required greater transactions balances. An increase in the interest rate was needed to release speculative balances for transactions purposes. As the interest rate increased from 2 to 10 percent, the level of investment decreased from 45 units at 2 percent to 25 units at 10 percent. The 20-unit decrease in investment (resulting from the interest rate increase) times the multiplier of 4 produced an 80-unit decrease in income. The 100-unit increase in government ding produced an income increase of 400. The net change in income is 320.

The Addition of Taxes in the *IS–LM* Analysis

The addition of taxes in the *IS–LM* analysis in Figure 11–6 requires a few basic adjustments. In quadrant (2) the notation for the 45° line becomes $S + T = I + G$ and the notation on the vertical axes of quadrants (2) and (3) becomes $S + T$. Taxes

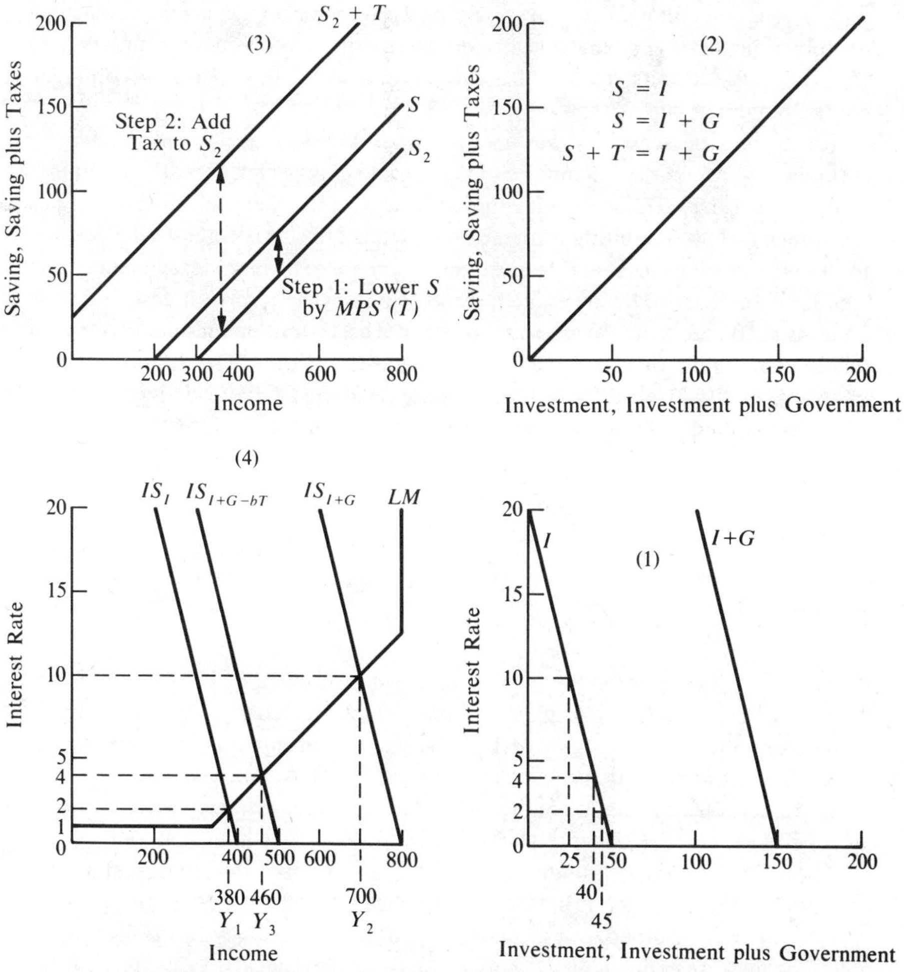

FIGURE 11–6 The Addition of Government Spending and Taxes

of 100 units are added to saving as a second leakage, just as government spending was added to investment as a second addition to the spending flow.

The addition of the tax in quadrant (3) requires two adjustments. First assume, as in Chapter 10, that the tax comes out of both saving and consumption according to the MPC and MPS. Therefore, the saving function is lowered by the MPS, 0.25, times the amount of the tax, 100 units. The adjusted saving function, S_2, is 25 units lower at all income levels than the original saving function, S. The second step is the addition of the tax to the adjusted saving function. $S_2 + T$ is 100 units higher than S_2 at all income levels.

A new *IS* curve, IS_{I+G-bT}, is derived in quadrant (4), using the new $S_2 + T$ function in quadrant (3). Note that the horizontal shift of the *IS* curve from IS_{I+G} to IS_{I+G-bT} is 300 units. This is the movement that would be expected according to the tax multiplier of –3.

Income decreases by 240 units, from 700 to 460, as a result of adding a 100-unit tax. Again, the income change is less than expected from the multiplier analysis, and the difference is again due to changes in the money market. The lower income level, resulting from the imposition of the tax, decreases the demand for transactions balances, and interest rates decrease to absorb these balances into speculative demand. The lower interest rate increases the level of investment from 25 units at 10 percent to 40 units at 4 percent. The 15-unit increase in investment times the multiplier of 4 creates a 60-unit increase in income. The 60-unit increase in income partly offsets the 300-unit decrease resulting from the tax increase. The net effect is the 240-unit income decrease derived in Figure 11–6.

The Effectiveness of Monetary Policy

The effect of a given monetary policy in the *IS–LM* model depends upon the region of the *LM* curve in which the *IS* and *LM* curves intersect. In the previous illustrations, the intersections have occurred in the intermediate region of the *LM* curve. However, the *IS* curve may intersect the *LM* curve in any of the three regions of the *LM* curve and the effect of monetary policy differs from region to region. In Figure 11–7, the original *LM* curve is intersected by three alternative *IS* curves: one intersects the *LM* curve in the Keynesian liquidity trap region; one intersects the *LM* curve in the intermediate region; and one intersects the *LM* curve in the vertical classical region of the *LM* curve. An increase in the money supply is assumed so that the *LM* curve shifts to *LM'*.

In the Keynesian liquidity trap region, the equilibrium income and interest rates, i_1 and Y_1, are the same before and after the increase in the money supply. The added money is absorbed into speculative balances without any fall in the interest rate. The increase in the money supply is used to add to speculative balances rather than being used to purchase bonds. With no fall in the interest rate, investment does not increase, and therefore income and the interest rate do not change.

In the intermediate region of the *LM* curve, the addition to the money supply is divided between transactions balances and speculative balances. The interest rate falls and investment and income increase. Income increases from Y_2 to Y_2'.

In the classical region, there is no speculative demand, and the entire increase in the money supply is available as additional transactions balances. Income increases by the amount of the increase in the money supply times the inverse of the marginal propensity to hold transactions balances. As in the earlier examples, assume that $M_1 = 0.25Y$; the increase in the level of income is 1/0.25, or four times the change in the money supply.

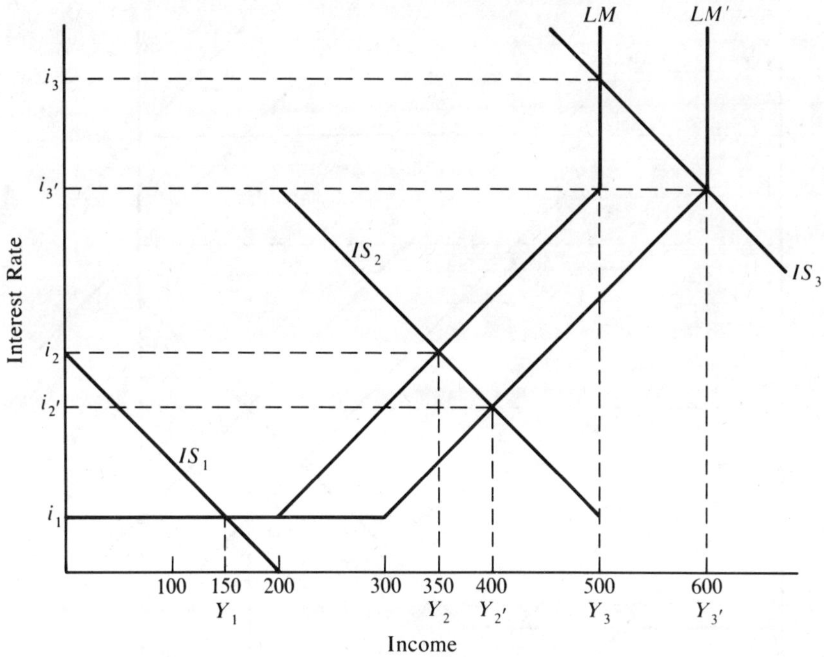

FIGURE 11–7 The Effectiveness of Monetary Policy

In summary, the impact of monetary policy becomes a function of the level of the interest rate and the level of income. In a low-interest rate and low-income period, theory would suggest that monetary policy would be the least efficient means of increasing the level of income. In a period of high interest rates and a high income level, monetary policy has its maximum effect on the level of income. Monetary policy would have some, but less than its maximum, effect on the level of income when the interest rate and the income level are neither extremely low nor extremely high.

The Effectiveness of Fiscal Policy

The effectiveness of fiscal policy also varies according to the region within which the *IS* curve intersects the *LM* curve. In Figure 11–8, each region of an *LM* curve is intersected by an *IS* curve. In each case, the *IS* curve is shifted to the right by 100 units. The *IS'* curves are the result of the fiscal policy in each case.

In the liquidity trap region, the shift of the *IS* curve results in a 100-unit increase in the income level. In this case, the full multiplier effect of the fiscal policy takes place; the change in the level of income is equal to the shift of the *IS* curve. The interest rate does not change. The reason for the full multiplier effect is

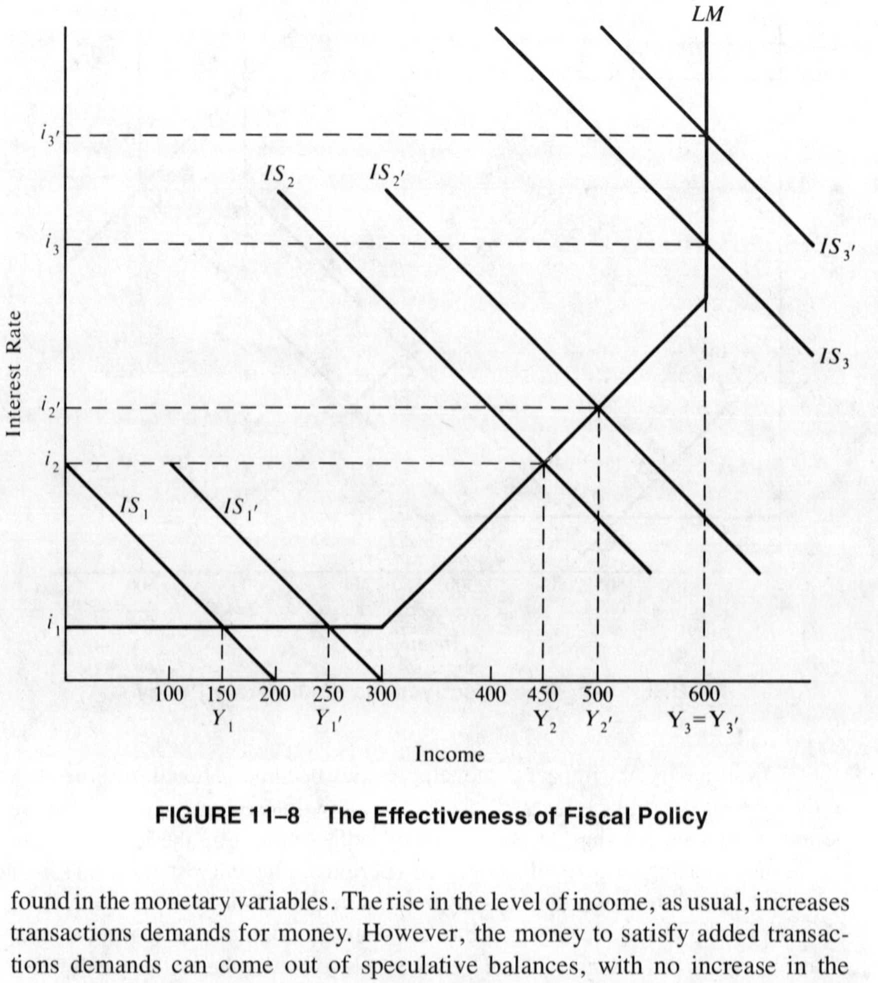

FIGURE 11–8 The Effectiveness of Fiscal Policy

found in the monetary variables. The rise in the level of income, as usual, increases transactions demands for money. However, the money to satisfy added transactions demands can come out of speculative balances, with no increase in the interest rate. The economy is in the liquidity trap region both before and after the fiscal policy. Because the interest rate does not increase, investment does not decrease, and there is no offset to the expansionary effect of the government spending.

In the intermediate region, fiscal policy increases the income level from Y_2 to $Y_{2'}$. However, the level of income increases by an amount less than the full multiplier effect. In this case, the higher transactions demands for money required a reduction of speculative balances. The increase in the interest rate, associated with the decrease of speculative balances, decreased the level of investment and income. Therefore, the fall in investment partly offsets the rise in government spending. Fiscal policy has some, but less than its maximum, effect.

In the classical region of the *LM* curve, fiscal policy shifts the *IS* curve from IS_3 to $IS_{3'}$, but the level of income remains at Y_3. In this case, fiscal policy increases interest rates but has no effect on the level of income. In the classical region, there are no speculative balances to draw upon to increase transactions balances. The added government spending bids up interest rates until the fall in investment spending is equal to the rise in government spending.

Another way of looking at this result is to assume that the government sells bonds to finance its additional spending. In the classical region, the sale of bonds drives up interest rates until businesses reduce their borrowing for investment purposes by an amount equal to the rise in government spending. In the liquidity trap region, the added bonds can be sold with no change in interest rates, so investment does not decline. In the intermediate region, the bond sale has some effect on interest rates, but the investment decline is less than the increase in government spending and income increases.

In summary, fiscal policy appears to be the most effective where monetary policy is least effective—in the liquidity trap region. Fiscal policy does not appear to have any effect where monetary policy has its maximum effect. In the intermediate region, both monetary and fiscal policy change the level of income but by an amount less than would be suggested by the basic multiplier relationships.

The Moral of the Story

In summarizing this portion of the chapter, the major point to stress is that the level of income is influenced by a large number of monetary and real factors. The level of income is determined by the interaction of the goods market and the money market. The interactions of the variables cannot always be explained by the basic multipliers developed in Chapter 10. The degree of success to be expected from a given policy may vary, according to the assumptions of the model, with the economic conditions prevailing at the time of institution of the policy.

Fiscal Policy

The remainder of this chapter deals with the use of fiscal policy as a method of producing a full employment level of income. The variations of government spending and taxes, which can be used to change the level of income, are considered and the problems encountered in the use of fiscal policy are described. In the last section, wage and price controls are examined as a supplement to, or replacement for, monetary and fiscal policy.

The Varieties of Budgetary Balance

Fiscal policy involves changing the level of government spending and/or taxes. These changes are examined in terms of their effect on the budget of the federal government. Thus, the fiscal policy discussion begins with an examination of some budgetary concepts.

The doctrine of a balanced budget—equality between government expenditures and tax receipts—has a long history and continues to have a strong hold on public and political opinion. The *annually balanced budget* was the clear goal of every American President until Franklin D. Roosevelt, and even he campaigned in 1932 on a pledge of balancing the government's budget. He probably tried, but the fall in federal revenues resulting from the Great Depression made a balanced budget out of the question.

While pre-Keynesian politicians generally argued for an annually balanced budget, three forces frequently upset their goal. First, wars increased government spending and defeated efforts to balance the budget. Second, tax revenues fluctuate with income levels and recessions produce budget deficits. The Eisenhower Administration strove for balanced budgets, but recessions produced revenue shortfalls and created pressures for greater government expenditures. Third, new government spending programs attract more votes than new tax programs. No matter how noble the concept of a balanced budget, the pressures for the government to undertake new spending activities are stronger than the pressures for new taxes.

The *cyclically balanced budget* is a second budget concept. This concept accepts the idea that the budget should be a tool of business cycle policy. The government's budget should be in balance over the course of the business cycle. Deficits can be tolerated in recession years, but there should be offsetting surpluses in good years. This concept is an improvement over the annually balanced budget but is difficult to implement because the level of business activity does not move in a consistent cycle. Thus, planning to achieve a balanced budget over the business cycle is impossible without perfect forecasting.

The *stabilizing budget* policy is a concept developed by the Committee for Economic Development, a private economic policy group. The CED proposal suggested establishing tax rates that would generate a surplus in the government's budget at a high level of employment. In a period of recession, the decline in government revenues would create a deficit in the budget and this deficit would stimulate the level of economic activity.[1]

The most recent concept of the budget is the *full employment* budget. According to this concept, the budget should be in balance at full employment, in deficit at less than full employment, and in surplus if the level of unemployment falls below the accepted measure of full employment. The tax system should be designed so that revenues would equal expenditures at full employment.

The full employment budget was developed by the Kennedy Administration as part of its efforts to sell the idea of a tax cut in 1962. The administration argued that the then-existing tax system was like tax system *A* in Figure 11–9. In tax system *A*, the budget moves into surplus as unemployment falls below 6

[1] *Taxes and the Budget: A Program for Prosperity in a Free Economy,* Committee for Economic Development, New York, November 1947. See also Walter W. Heller, "CED's Stabilizing Budget Policy After Ten Years," *American Economic Review,* September 1957, pp. 634–651.

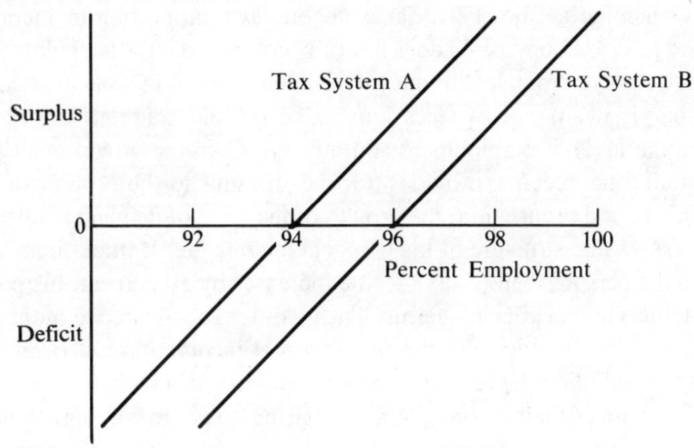

FIGURE 11–9 The Full Employment Budget

percent; the surplus depresses the level of economic activity and unemployment rises. This problem is called *fiscal drag* and was blamed for the slow growth rate and the recessions of the late 1950s. Under tax system *B,* with a schedule of lower tax rates, the budget does not come into balance until the level of unemployment declines to 4 percent. Until the 4 percent level of unemployment is achieved, the budget continues to be in deficit and continues to stimulate the economy.

The concept of the full employment budget continues to be a major consideration of fiscal policy design. The use of the concept of full employment balance should not be a static policy. Policy makers should be willing to create a full employment deficit to stimulate the economy or to create a full employment surplus to restrain the economy.

The Varieties of Fiscal Policy

The design of a fiscal policy is a complex process involving more than is implied by the theoretical models. This section describes some of the options for fiscal policy, reviews the automatic stabilizers, and considers changes in government spending and taxes.

The Automatic Stabilizers By either conscious policy design or as a by-product of other policy decisions, the American economy has a variety of built-in devices that stabilize the level of economic activity without requiring case-by-case policy decisions.

Probably the most important of these automatic stabilizers is the *progressive income tax*. The progressivity of the income tax system cushions downturns in the economy and restrains upswings. As incomes decline in a recession, people fall into lower income tax brackets. Taxes decline as a proportion of income, even though the fall in tax payments does not fully compensate for the income decline. On the macroeconomic level, the government's total income tax collections decline sharply in a period of recession; tax collections are relatively elastic with respect to the level of employment and income. Constant government spending with declining tax receipts provides a fiscal stimulus to the economy.

In a period of inflation, the growth of the level of demand is restrained by the progressive rate structure of the personal income tax. If prices increase by 50 percent and a person's before-tax income increases by 50 percent, his purchasing power declines in real after-tax terms. The income tax is geared to money income and does not take into account the fact that real income has not risen.

Thus, inflation pushes consumers into higher tax brackets and taxes take a larger proportion of their income; less purchasing power means less consumption demand. On the macroeconomic level, the tax revenues of the government grow more than in proportion to the growth of money income and restrain the rate of inflation.

The other major automatic stabilizer is the *unemployment compensation system*. As the level of unemployment grows, expenditures from the compensation fund increase. The individual recipient gains by being able to maintain at least a proportion of his former consumption level, and society gains because the level of aggregate demand is partly maintained by the expenditure of the unemployment compensation payments.

In a period of low unemployment, expenditures from the compensation fund are low, and the balance in the fund is built up by the tax levied on employers. The stabilizing impact of the tax is of less importance than the stabilizing effect of the benefit payments.

Other devices also act or have acted as automatic stabilizers. The traditional *farm price support programs* stabilized the flow of income to farmers in periods of falling crop prices and the *Social Security program* also has stabilizing aspects.

The great feature of the automatic stabilizers is that once the program is established, no policy decisions are necessary to gain the fiscal policy benefits. No policy-making lags are involved; when the need arises, the program is there. The only limitation is the inability of the automatic stabilizers to change the direction of the economy's movement. The fall in income during a recession may be lessened by the workings of the automatic stabilizers, but the stabilizers only replace a portion of lost income and cannot provide the increase in aggregate demand which is necessary to bring the economy out of the downturn.

Changes in Government Spending Consideration of a change in government spending as a fiscal policy device involves five basic questions.

First, should government spending or taxes be changed in a given situation? The theoretical analysis has indicated that either method can be used and that the only basic economic difference is that the government spending multiplier is larger than the tax multiplier. In many real-world situations, the choice is made on political, rather than economic, grounds. An increase in government expenditures expands the size of the public sector of the economy; liberals may see the need for greater government spending on social needs and favor this approach. A decrease in taxes leaves taxpayers with more disposable income and increases private, rather than public, spending. The tax decrease alternative gives conservatives the hope that the size of the government's expenditures can be permanently lowered by a decrease in the government's revenues.

Second, if added government spending is the answer, which government spending programs should be begun or expanded? This is another political decision reflecting the preferences of the Administration and the Congress.

Third, how rapidly will the spending put money into the hands of consumers? A program involving a long pre-expenditure planning period is of little use as a stabilization device. There must be some assurance that the money appropriated will be quickly used and will result in higher consumer incomes.

Fourth, will the money expended benefit business or consumers? The government can buy goods or let contracts for public works. The business firms selling the goods or receiving the contracts then employ labor and money finds its way into the hands of consumers. Critics derisively call this method of government spending, as well as business tax reductions, "trickle-down" theories—benefits are given directly to business and the income supposedly trickles down to the workers. The alternative is direct payments to consumers through welfare, public service employment, and unemployment benefit programs. In the latter case, the benefits presumably trickle up to business firms!

Fifth, if a given government spending program is instituted to fight a recession, can the program be halted once the recession is over? The benefits of government spending are not given up cheerfully. A public works program funding long-term projects may be difficult to terminate. But unless the program is to become a permanent part of government spending, plans should be made to shut off the flow of money once full employment is restored.

The use of increased government spending as a means of stimulating the economy clearly involves a variety of social choices. As long as the money is spent, the fiscal policy goal is achieved. However, the wisdom of the spending choices not only reflects on the policy maker but also influences the public's acceptance of the use of fiscal policy. Wasteful "leaf raking" projects may generate income, but they may also stiffen resistance to future fiscal policy programs.

Changes in Taxes Many options exist for the use of tax changes as a part of fiscal policy. Examples of some of the tax plans employed in the past are considered here.

The first option is a general *tax rate increase or decrease*. The general scaling down of personal and/or corporate income tax rates spreads the direct benefits of the tax reduction over a vast number of spending units. The 1964 tax reduction program is an example of this type of fiscal policy. The 1964 tax act decreased personal income tax collections by $14 billion (measuring on the basis of 1965 income and pre–tax reduction tax rates) and decreased corporate income tax collections by $6 billion. The lowest personal income tax rate was decreased from 20 to 14 percent and the minimum standard deduction was increased.[2]

A second commonly used option is the investment tax credit. The *investment tax credit* is designed to stimulate capital investment by providing business firms with a tax credit for a proportion of their investment expenditures. The first investment tax credit was enacted in 1962 and provided that business firms could deduct 7 percent of their expenditures on plant and equipment from their income tax liability. The tax credit plan was terminated in 1966, revived in mid-1967 and terminated again in 1969. In 1971, the program was reinstated and for 1975 and 1976 the rate was increased to 10 percent.

The third tax change option is a *temporary tax increase or decrease*. A temporary 10 surcharge on individual and corporate income taxes was imposed in 1968 and remained in effect, although at a 5 percent rate for part of the time, until mid-1970. In 1975, taxes were decreased. A partial rebate of 1974 tax payments was the most significant feature of the 1975 tax program. Other measures to stimulate the level of economic activity included a 5 percent tax credit on the purchase of new homes, an increase in the investment tax credit, an increase in the standard deduction on personal income taxes for 1975, and a credit against taxes for each personal exemption claimed on income tax returns. The most important of these measures were temporary changes in the tax law.

The impact of a temporary change in tax rates is less certain than the impact of other forms of tax changes. Given that the change is temporary, it may not have the same effect on spending as a permanent change in taxes. If people consume according to their permanent income, as suggested in the Friedman permanent income hypothesis, a temporary tax change will have very little effect on permanent income.

Finally, tax policy changes may take the form of *specific lower or higher taxes*—on specific industries, specific types of economic activity, or specific income groups. Passage of minimum taxes on income not subject to the regular income tax, changes in taxes on capital gains, changes in federal excise taxes on new automobiles, and changes in accounting rules for depreciation and natural resource depletion are all examples of specific types of fiscal policy measures. These policies are used not only for revenue purposes but also to provide "tax reform" or greater equity in the distribution of the tax burden.

[2]For accounts of the use and impact of fiscal policy in the early 1960s, see Arthur M. Okun, *The Political Economy of Prosperity* (New York: W. W. Norton & Co., 1970); and Walter W. Heller, *New Dimensions of Political Economy* (New York: W. W. Norton & Co., 1967).

Problems of Fiscal Policy

In the theoretical models of macroeconomics, the use of a discretionary fiscal policy appears to be very simple. Tax rates or government spending programs are changed instantaneously, and the level of income changes in the expected manner by an expected multiplier value. However, in the real world, the problems of a discretionary fiscal policy are many and varied and raise both theoretical and political questions.

The problems of fiscal policy can be discussed within a framework of lags, There are three lags involved in policy making. First, there is a *recognition lag*—time passes between the beginning of an economic problem and the general recognition of the problem by the policy makers. Second, there is a decision making, or *action lag*—having recognized a problem, the policy makers must decide upon the appropriate course of action and put the policy into effect. Third, there is a *lag in effect*—once a given course of action is begun, time passes before the policy has an effect on the variable to be changed. Within each of these lags, there are various other problems.

The Recognition Lag

The first problem in making policy is the recognition of the fact that there is a problem. This difficulty begins with the lag in the availability of data on the performance of the economy. The thermometer readings of the health of the economy are not instantly available. A given month's unemployment data, for example, are not usually available until well into the next month. GNP data are calculated only quarterly and are available only on a preliminary basis until well into the next quarter. To complicate the issue, various indicators of economic activity may be giving conflicting signals in the early stages of an upturn or downturn. Some indicators continue to fall after the economy has already turned up, and others fluctuate owing to special problems and give questionable signals about the movement of the economy. Throughout 1975, economists and politicians debated the significance of price changes, changes in measures of output, and changes in unemployment rates.

Second, even when all of the statistical evidence on the performance of the economy is available, differences in interpretation of the data continue to delay total recognition of the problem. For example, the recession of 1974–1975 was an ongoing process for nearly a year before the Administration admitted that there was indeed a recession and that recession and inflation were both problems. Political considerations may lead politicians to deny the existence of an economic problem. Few incumbent Presidents care to acknowledge the existence of a worsening recession—especially near election time.

Third, the development of the forecasting art leaves room for improvement. Every upswing or downswing in the business cycle is a unique event. While all cycles have some common features, the best indicator of one recession may not be the best indicator of the next recession.

The methods of forecasting business activity are as numerous as the forecasters. First, there are single series of data indicators. The unemployment rate, the rate of utilization of manufacturing capacity, the movement of stock prices, the volume of freight car loadings, new orders for machinery, the number of business failures, and the prices of sensitive raw materials are but a few of the commonly watched indicators of business activity. Series of leading indicators of business activity are published monthly; these indicators are chosen for their past reliability in forecasting movements of the business cycle.

A second method of forecasting economic activity is the use of large-scale macroeconomic models of the economy. Models developed by the Federal Reserve System, the Brookings Institution (an independent research and development institute concerned with economic and political studies), and others attempt to express the structure of the economy in hundreds of equations. Then, using historical data and expected values for the exogenous variables, forecasts are produced and the results of alternative policy actions are estimated. While this approach to forecasting has the greatest long run potential, results are not yet completely reliable.

The monetarists, led by Professor Friedman, argue that the analysis of the rate of change of the money supply is the most reliable indicator of future movements of the economy. This analysis is considered in the next chapter.

Given that forecasting is an inexact art, a recession or inflation may either be well underway or well under control before the need for new, or the success of past, policies is recognized.

The Action Lag

Once the data are all collected and agreed upon, the policy makers must decide upon a course of action. In the use of fiscal policy, the longest lag may occur at this point. If the President, the Council of Economic Advisors, and other economic assistants to the Administration decide upon a change in either government spending or taxes as the means of dealing with the problem, the policy must be acted upon by the Congress. When the writers of the Constitution gave the power to levy taxes to the Congress, they did not envision the need for quick fiscal policy decisions.

At the political level, action on both government expenditure changes and tax changes tends to be exceedingly slow. The proposal for a tax change comes from the President; its design is influenced by all of the expected political considerations. When submitted to the Congress, all of the political pressures on the members of the Congress influence the shape of the tax bill. If taxes are to be lowered, whose taxes should be lowered? Should a reduction in taxes be designed to stimulate consumption or business capital investment? Should reductions in tax rates lower the lowest rate in the progressive income tax schedule, or the highest rate? Should all rates be scaled down by the same percentage? Should special groups of individuals receive the benefits of lower taxes or should industries especially hard hit by the recession be given major tax concessions? Should the tax change be permanent or for only a limited period of time? While in the process of lowering taxes and writing a new tax bill, should the Congress close some of the loopholes in the tax laws? In the macroeconomic models, taxes appear simply as a lump sum or as a percentage of income; however, when the tax law is changed there are endless political controversies over the division of the pie.

A few examples of the action lag point out the problem. In 1962, President John Kennedy asked for a tax cut in order to stimulate a very slow growing economy that had suffered from several recessions in the post–World War II period. However, many of the leaders of the Congress were not convinced of the wisdom of deliberately creating a deficit in the government's budget, and so the tax changes did not go into effect until 1964.

Later in the 1960s, as expenditures for the Vietnam War increased and the cost of President Lyndon Johnson's Great Society programs increased, the need for higher taxes to avoid inflation was clear long before any action was taken to increase taxes. Politically, there was widespread opposition to the war and a proposal to raise taxes would have increased that opposition. For what many believed to be purely political reasons, wise economic policies were not followed until well after the economic damage was done.

Various methods of reducing the action lag have been suggested. The most frequently proposed idea is to delegate to the President limited authority to impose temporary changes in tax rates when he and his advisors believe that economic conditions require a quick change in fiscal policy. This proposal has been hedged in various ways to make it more acceptable to the Congress. The amount of permitted change, the duration of the change, and the right of the Congress to veto the change have all been included in proposals of this sort. However, the Congress has not accepted the idea of delegating any of its taxing powers to the President. The loss of power by the Congress to the Executive Branch, which has taken place over time, makes the Congress unwilling to give up any more of its constitutional powers. Secondly, there is the danger that a President could lower taxes for purely political motives. A tax decrease just before an election would be popular and the Congress would be hard pressed to veto the change just before standing for reelection. Third, there is a danger that tax change decisions would be made before all of the evidence was available and fully considered. The deliberative process of the Congress does have the value of preventing hasty action. Any significant reduction of the total lag would require a shortening of the action lag.

The Lag in Effect

The lag in effect is the time between the institution of a policy measure and the point at which the policy measure actually affects the target variable. In fiscal policy, the lag in effect is the time between the passage of a spending or taxing program and the point at which the level of national income is changed by the program.

The lag in effect of a spending program is longer than the lag in effect of a tax change. A change in taxes can be implemented very quickly. Revising personal income tax rates requires the production and distribution of new withholding tables. Once the withholding tables go into effect, take-home pay changes and the level of spending changes. Programs to provide tax incentives for new investment may have a longer lag because of the planning of investment projects, delays in ordering equipment, and delays in the production of the equipment.

The implementation of a new government spending program may involve a longer lag. People must be hired to administer the program, spending procedures designed, contracts sent out to bid, bids awarded, and money disbursed. Adding new money to an already existing program involves a shorter lag if the agency receiving the money has projects or programs that could easily absorb the new money.

The earliest concept of fiscal policy involved the maintenance of a backlog of public works projects that were all planned and ready for implementation. If the economy moved into a downturn, these projects would be "taken off the shelf," as it were, dusted off, and put out to bid.

In summary, the use of fiscal policy involves a great variety of economic and political problems. As will be shown in later chapters, monetary policy is also subject to lag problems. For these and other reasons, new policy measures are in demand. One policy, used during World War II and tried again in the early 1970s, is wage and price controls. This chapter concludes with a discussion of this policy option.

Wage and Price Controls

In recent years, the use of wage and price controls has gained the support of many economists (and proportionately more politicians) as a means of controlling inflation. Support for the use of direct controls resulted from persistent inflation in the late 1960s and early 1970s and from a growing impression that traditional monetary and fiscal policy either would not, or could not, stop the inflation. President Richard Nixon cited his own negative experience with controls at the Office of Price Administration in World War II and claimed he would never use his control powers. However, he eventually and reluctantly imposed first a total freeze of wages and prices and then various phases of thaws and refreezes.

Those supporting the concept of wage and price controls believe some or all of the following points:

1. Wage and price controls, if administered properly, will hold down the rate of inflation. The Nixon Administration was opposed philosophically to the controls and had no stake in the success of the control program.

2. Wage and price controls can hold down the symptoms of inflation (rising wages and prices), while the causes of inflation — excessive government spending or excessive growth of the money supply — are removed. Controls buy time until the traditional tools have their impact on the root causes of inflation.

3. Controls are necessary because monetary and/or fiscal policy have no significant effect, have been poorly administered, or cannot cope with the causes of a given period of inflation.

4. Controls are a fair method of dealing with inflation. The traditional policy tools have strong negative effects on specific groups, types of economic activity, or the level of employment. Controls spread the burden of policy more evenly.

5. Controls are necessary because of extensive monopoly power in the economy. Given monopoly power, some industries or labor groups will be able to achieve real income gains at the expense of consumers, other industries, and less powerful groups.

6. The imposition of controls leads to a reduction of inflationary expectations. The expectation of price stability will reduce hoarding in anticipation of higher prices, decrease inflated wage and price demands, and reduce any inflation premium that has been included in interest rates.

On the other side of the argument, many economists remain unconvinced by the case for wage and price controls. The major arguments on the negative side are as follows:

1. If prices are held below their equilibrium levels, there will be shortages of goods and nonprice rationing will be necessary. Controls on the price of gasoline during the 1973–1974 oil embargo led to long gas lines at filling stations, hoarding, and general consumer aggravation. Wasting hours in a gas line is not an efficient use of time and, moreover, uses up gas. Most economists prefer rationing on the basis of price.

2. Questions of allocative efficiency must be separated from questions of equity, the anticontrol group says. Much of the support for controls is based on a concern for the ability of the poor to pay higher prices. If society believes that the high price of certain goods works a hardship on the poor, the answer is not to control the price of the goods but rather to use income redistribution programs to assist the poor in purchasing the goods.

3. The anticontrol group also argues that the control of prices and wages interferes with the achievement of long-run efficiency in the allocation of resources. In simple price theory, a rise in the price of a good is a signal that more of the good should be produced. Higher prices and higher profits direct the flow of capital investment. If wages and prices are frozen, they cannot provide these signals for the allocation of resources.

4. Some argue that the imposition of controls merely postpones price and wage increases. Prices are stable during the control period, but when controls are lifted there is rapid inflation. Everyone tries to achieve the gains denied during the control period.

5. The longer controls exist, the more ways are found to circumvent the controls. For example, minimal changes can be made to products and the "improved" or "new" product can be sold at a higher price. Workers can be artificially upgraded to new job classifications so that they are eligible for higher wages. The control system creates an incentive to cheat, and to minimize that cheating requires an army of enforcement agents.

6. Some prices are difficult to control at a fair level. For example, the imposition of controls in August 1971 came at a time when, due to seasonal demand factors, home heating oil prices were low and gasoline prices were high. The oil companies had little incentive to switch to producing more home heating oil and less gasoline. Food prices are another example of the problems of imposing controls. If controls go on when agricultural commodities are abundant, the price is too low to encourage production and shortages develop. Interest rates are another example of a price that is difficult to control.

7. The opponents of control argue that even merely talking about imposing controls is inflationary because firms boost prices and unions demand higher wages in the fear that forthcoming controls will prevent them from improving their profits or incomes.

8. Finally, there is a problem of decontrol. How are the controls to be lifted without returning to the problems that caused the imposition of the controls? Once the total freeze is ended, those groups with the most market power are able to obtain income gains, while other groups do not have sufficient bargaining power to recoup their losses. The 1972 coal miners' strike in Britain demonstrated the ability of a powerful group to avoid limits imposed on wages and prices.

I encourage you to make up your own mind on the validity of the arguments about wage and price controls. However, it is fair to tell you that I am personally unconvinced as to the merits of such controls. The revival of inflation after the ending of controls in 1973, for instance, does not give me confidence in the efficiency of controls, and the advocates of control have yet to provide sufficient evidence of the success of controls in other periods or in other countries.

Having considered some of the problems involved in the making of macroeconomic policies, the following chapters consider the monetarist view of money and the use and problems of monetary policy.

REVIEW QUESTIONS

1. Using graph paper, derive an *LM* curve using the same assumptions as in Figure 11–1 except in quadrant (3) assume that $M_1 = 0.30Y$.

2. Using graph paper, derive an *IS* curve, using the same assumptions as in Figure 11–2, except in quadrant (3) use a saving function of $S = -100 + 0.30Y$.

3. Combine the *IS* and *LM* curves derived in questions (1) and (2) above and determine the equilibrium income level and interest rate.

4. Why does the intersection of the *IS* curve and the *LM* curve produce an equilibrium in both the goods market and the money market?

5. How would the equilibrium level of income in question (3) be changed by a 50-unit decrease of taxes?

6. How would the equilibrium level of income in question (3) be increased by a 50-unit increase of the money supply?

7. How are the multipliers developed in Chapter 10 applicable to the *IS-LM* analysis?

8. In Figure 11–7, how would the effectiveness of monetary policy be changed if the interest elasticity of the MEI curve were increased?

9. Why is fiscal policy less effective than monetary policy in the classical region of the *LM* curve?

10. Formulate your position relative to wage and price controls. The list of suggested readings provides a variety of recent publications on the subject.

SUGGESTED READINGS

John T. Boorman and Thomas M. Havrilesky, *Money Supply, Money Demand and Macroeconomic Models.* Boston: Allyn and Bacon, 1972.

Michael K. Evans, *Macroeconomic Activity: Theory, Forecasting, and Control.* New York: Harper & Row, Publishers, 1969.

Robert H. Floyd, "Incomes Policies: A Quick Critique," *Federal Reserve Bank of Atlanta Monthly Review,* December 1970, pp. 174-181.

Crawfurd G. Goodwin, ed., *Exhortation and Controls: The Search for a Wage-Price Policy, 1945–71,* Brookings Institution, Washington, D.C. 1975.

Carol S. Greenwald, "Deflated Leading Indicators Revisited," *New England Economic Review,* January–February 1975, pp. 3–16.

Michael C. Lovell, *Macroeconomics: Measurement, Theory, and Policy.* New York: John Wiley & Sons, 1975.

Michael J. Prell, "The Full Employment Budget—Its Uses and Limitations," *Federal Reserve Bank of Kansas City Monthly Review,* April 1972, pp. 3–12.

William L. Silber, "Monetary Policy Effectiveness: The Case of a Positively Sloped IS Curve," *Journal of Finance,* American Finance Association, New York, December 1971, pp. 1077–1082.

Arnold Weber, *In Pursuit of Price Stability: The Wage-Price Freeze of 1971,* Brookings Institution, Washington, D.C., 1973.

12

THE MONETARISTS

Beginning in the late 1950s, many assumptions and policy designs based on Keynesian analysis came under attack from a group of economists classified as *monetarists*. The best known of the monetarists is Professor Milton Friedman of the University of Chicago. The University of Chicago and the Federal Reserve Bank of St. Louis have become the leading centers of monetarist analysis. The central thesis of the monetarists is that *money matters*. In the 1940s and 1950s, Keynesian doctrine spread rapidly and the role of money in the economy was discounted; fiscal policy was considered to be the important macroeconomic policy tool. The resurgence of interest in money and the new stress placed on the importance of monetary policy stems from the challenging work of Friedman and the other proponents of monetarism.

This chapter explores the roots of modern monetarism, the analysis and the conclusions of Friedman and other monetarists, and the criticisms of monetarism.

The Origins of Monetarism

Milton Friedman represents the continuation of a long line of distinguished University of Chicago students of money. The Chicago economists are noted, first and foremost, for their attachment to the free market system. Although most economists are philosophically attached to the value of allowing the market to allocate resources, the degree of continued devotion to these ideas appears to be higher at Chicago than at most other schools. The Chicago economists are characterized by their belief that nearly all problems can be solved by the free and unimpeded operation of the forces of supply and demand.

Friedman's early book, *Capitalism and Freedom*[1] is a ringing defense of the free enterprise system and its relationship to political freedom. He cites the failure of most attempts to interfere with the free workings of the marketplace as evidence that the government should not intervene in the economy any more than is absolutely necessary.

[1]Milton Friedman, *Capitalism and Freedom* (Chicago: University of Chicago Press, 1962).

But even the most devout believers in the operation of the market system recognize the need for some governmental intervention, and the regulation of money is one of the very few areas where Friedman recognizes the need for governmental control. Still, he believes that when intervention is necessary, the rules governing intervention must be specified in detail and must allow the regulator only a minimum amount of discretion. Rules, he insists, rather than discretionary powers, should govern the actions of the regulator.

The argument for rules, rather than discretion, was best expressed by Henry Simons[2] of the University of Chicago, who said the advantages of providing the regulator with specific rules for achieving specific targets include: the certainty implied by rules, the avoidance of arbitrary action by the regulator, and the avoidance of speculation relative to the future actions of the regulator.

Friedman[3], in a 1948 paper, followed Simons and wrote:

> (1) Government must provide a monetary framework for a competitive order since the competitive order cannot provide one for itself. (2) This monetary framework should operate under the "rules of law" rather than the discretionary authority of administrators.[4]

A third distinctive feature of the Chicago tradition is the adherence to the quantity theory of money as the basic framework for monetary analysis. Friedman indicates that, though the quantity theory generally was ignored after the beginning of the Great Depression, the theory continued to be employed by the Chicago economists.[5]

Thus, the writings of Friedman are a continuation of a long tradition of economic analysis at the University of Chiago,[6] and the various portions of the Friedman monetary system are considered below.

Friedman and Monetarism

The basic monetarist theory, as developed by Friedman and his associates, is that money is of critical importance in determining the level of economic activity. Monetarism is based on a revised version of the quantity theory of money and stresses the need to control the level of, or rate of change of, the money supply.

In Friedman's system, only one macroeconomic policy is required: the

[2]Henry C. Simons, "Rules Versus Authorities in Monetary Policy," *Journal of Political Economy,* vol. 44 (February 1936), pp. 1–30. Also available in Lutz and Mints, eds., *Readings in Monetary Theory* (Homewood, Ill.: Richard D. Irwin, 1951), pp. 337–368.

[3]Milton Friedman, "A Monetary and Fiscal Framework for Economic Stability," *American Economic Review,* vol. 38 (June 1948), pp. 245–264. Also available in Lutz and Mints, eds., ibid., pp. 369–393.

[4]Friedman, op. cit., pp. 245–246.

[5]Milton Friedman, "The Quantity Theory of Money—A Restatement," in M. Friedman, ed., *Studies in the Quantity Theory of Money* (Chicago: University of Chicago Press, 1956), p. 3.

[6]The role of Friedman as part of the Chicago tradition is analyzed in Don Patinkin, "The Chicago Tradition, the Quantity Theory, and Friedman," *Journal of Money, Banking and Credit,* February 1969, pp. 46–70.

monetary authority should use open market operations to provide a stable rate of growth of the supply of money. All other monetary tools could be abandoned; the Federal Reserve System would only have to ensure that the money supply grew each year at a constant predetermined rate consistent with the long-run growth of the economy at stable prices.[7]

The argument for a constant rate of growth of the money supply is derived from a great deal of historical and empirical evidence produced by Friedman and others. In the following sections, the various parts of the Friedman work are related to the central theme of the constant rate of growth of the money supply.

Before beginning the analysis of the supporting arguments in the monetarist case, the method of defining the money supply must be re-emphasized. Friedman uses the M_2 definition of the money supply, which includes time deposits at commercial banks as well as coin, currency, and demand deposits. Thus, unless otherwise stated, all references to the money supply in this chapter refer to the M_2 definition. The major reason for the M_2 definition is rather pragmatic. The historical work done by Friedman and his associates goes back to the late 1800s, but a clear distinction between time deposits and demand deposits was not made until the mid-1930s. Therefore, the M_2 definition is used throughout the Friedman analysis.

The Theoretical Base

In monetarist analysis, the key theoretical relationship is between changes in the supply of money and changes in the level of money income. The line of causation runs from changes in the stock of money to changes in the level of money income. Monetary changes cause income changes.

The mechanism begins with the demand for money stated in terms of real balances. The real balances (M/P) held by the public are measured as the money supply (M) divided by the price level (P). The public's desired holdings of real balances are related to real income and other variables. Assume all individuals and business firms are holding the desired quantity of real balances. The supply of money is then increased by the monetary authority. The recipients of the addition to the money supply now have a greater quantity of purchasing power than they desire to hold. There is only one way they can reduce their real balances to the desired level—by spending. However, as the initial group spends and reduces its money holdings, the money holdings of others increase and they hold added balances. This second group spends its excess real balances, and the process continues.

The excess cash balances are eliminated in one of two ways. First, if real output and income increase as a result of the added spending, the demand for money increases. The excess balances are now required to meet the higher demand for money at the higher income level. Second, if prices increase as a result of the added spending, the real value of the money supply declines. Price increases

[7]Milton Friedman, *A Program for Monetary Stability* (New York: Fordham University Press, 1959), pp. 84–95.

continue until the real value of the money supply is restored to its original level. Both M and P have increased, but M/P is unchanged.

The monetary authority is able to control the nominal supply of money (M), but the public determines the real value of the money supply (M/P). Therefore, a change in the supply of money produces a change in either prices or output or some combination of a change in prices and a change in output.

A decrease in the money supply has the opposite effect. A decrease in the quantity of money lowers the public's real balances below the desired level. The only way people can restore their real balances to the desired level is by reducing spending or selling assets. The decline in spending reduces either prices or output until the desired level of real balances is again attained at a lower level of prices or output. A decline in prices accomplishes the objective by increasing the real level of the money supply to the desired level. A decline in output reduces the demand for real balances until the lowered demand for real balances is equal to the existing supply of real balances.[8]

In comparing his approach to the Keynesian model, Friedman argues that Keynesian analysis looks first at the effect of a change in the supply of money on interest rates and then at the effect of interest rates on the level of investment spending and income. By channeling the effect of changes in the money supply through the interest-rate mechanism, monetary policy affects only those forms of spending which are normally considered to be influenced by changes in interest rates. In comparison, Friedman indicates that his approach provides a more direct relationship between changes in the supply of money and changes in money income. In his approach, the increase in the money supply leads economic units to redistribute the added money throughout their balance sheets. The new funds might be used to purchase investment goods, durable goods, real estate, or financial assets. With flexible prices and flexible interest rates, changes in interest rates and prices follow from the distribution of the new purchasing power.[9]

Friedman appears to overstate the difference between his theoretical mechanism and that of the Keynesians. While the simple Keynesian model expresses the speculative demand for money in terms of money versus bonds and relates the interest rate to business capital investment, a modern Keynesian would not object to a broadening of the analysis. The inclusion of a relationship between money and all other financial assets and a relationship between interest rates and all forms of business and consumer spending presents no basic changes in the Keynesian framework. The real difference appears to be the degree to which the change in the money supply influences spending directly as opposed to affecting spending indirectly through the interest rate mechanism.

[8]Milton Friedman, "A Theoretical Framework for Monetary Analysis," *Journal of Political Economy,* vol. 78 (March–April 1970), pp. 194–195. For a more formal model, see also Friedman, "A Monetary Theory of National Income," *Journal of Political Economy,* vol. 79 (March–April 1971), pp. 323–337.

[9]Milton Friedman, "Comments on the Critics," *Journal of Political Economy,* vol. 80 (September–October 1972), pp. 906–907.

The Demand for Money Function

In the Keynesian mechanism, the demand for money is a function of the level of income and the level of interest rates. Friedman's first expression of a demand for money equation argues that the real demand for money, M/P, is a function of six factors:

1. The rate of return on bonds is important, for the higher the return on bonds, the lower the demand for money.
2. The rate of return on equities (stock) means that the higher the rate of return on stock, the lower the demand for money.
3. The rate of change of prices is influential because if prices are rising at a rapid rate, one would have an incentive to reduce his holdings of money in order to avoid a decline in real purchasing power.
4. The ratio of nonhuman to human wealth also affects the real demand for money. Human capital is embodied in the individual; your education represents an investment in the acquisition of human capital that will produce future returns. Nonhuman capital represents ownership of income-producing physical assets. A change in the proportions of total wealth held in these two forms may change the demand for money.
5. Real income, Y/P, would affect the demand for real balances, M/P.
6. Tastes and preferences, non-economic as well as economic conditions, can change the desire of the public to hold money. Friedman cites uncertainty or geographic mobility as possible causes of an increase in the public's preference for money.

Friedman considers his work in the tradition of the quantity theorists but drops the assumptions of automatic full employment and a constant value of velocity. Velocity is not constant but is a stable function of a limited number of variables.[10]

In a later, simplified version of the demand for money, Friedman draws upon his concept of a permanent income[11] and makes the demand for money a function of real per capita permanent income. In this study, the demand for money function becomes

$$M/NP_p = \gamma(Y_p/NP_p)^\delta$$

where M = the nominal stock of money
N = population
Y_p = permanent income
P_p = permanent prices

This second version of the demand for money is not as different from the first version as it would at first appear to be. The concept of permanent income is broad enough to include the several variables used in the earlier version of the

[10]Milton Friedman, "The Quantity Theory of Money—A Restatement," in M. Friedman, ed., *Studies in the Quantity Theory of Money* (Chicago: University of Chicago Press, 1956), pp. 3–17.

[11]See discussion of the permanent income hypothesis in the appendix to Chap. 10.

demand for money function. One's permanent income is affected by securities yields and human and nonhuman wealth holdings.

Empirically, Friedman finds that the demand for nominal cash balances is

$$M = (0.00323)\,(y_p/N)^{1.810}(NP_p)$$

where all variables have the same definition as previously stated, except that y_p = real permanent income. In this form, the Friedman equation indicates that (holding population and permanent prices constant) a 1 percent increase in real permanent income increases the demand for nominal money balances by 1.81 percent.[12]

Moving in the opposite direction, an increase in the supply of money of 1.81 percent should increase permanent income by 1 percent; the income increase expands the demand for money to absorb the increased supply of money. The cause-and-effect relationship in the Friedman model runs from changes in the supply of money to changes in the level of income.

The Stability of Velocity

A second part of the monetarist analysis holds that the level of velocity is more stable than the Keynesian expenditure multipliers. In this analysis it is argued that the relationship between money and income is a more stable empirical relationship than the relationship between autonomous expenditures—investment and government spending—and the level of income.

In this connection a variety of empirical evidence is offered by the Friedmanites. Central to the controversy is a series of papers published in the mid-1960s in response to a study done by Friedman and Meiselman[13] for the Commission on Money and Credit. Friedman and Meiselman compare simple monetary models and simple models of autonomous expenditures on the basis of each model's ability to predict consumption. The two basic models[14] used are (1) the Keynesian model,

$$C = a + KA$$

in which C = consumption
a = a constant
K = the Keynesian multiplier
A = autonomous expenditures $[I + G + (X - M)]$

and (2) the quantity theory model,

$$C = a + VM$$

in which C = consumption
a = a constant
V = the money multiplier
M = the supply of money

[12]Milton Friedman, "The Demand for Money: Some Theoretical and Empirical Results," *Journal of Political Economy,* vol. 67 (August 1959), pp. 327–351.

[13]Milton Friedman and David Meiselman, "The Relative Stability of Monetary Velocity and the Investment Multiplier in the United States, 1897–1958," in *Stabilization Policies,* a Series of Research Studies prepared for the Commission on Money and Credit (Englewood Cliffs, N.J.: Prentice-Hall, 1963), pp. 116–268.

[14]Ibid., pp. 170–187.

Except for the World War II period, the empirical results suggest a better statistical relationship between changes in the supply of money and changes in consumption than between changes in autonomous expenditures and changes in consumption.

This paper led to a series of papers in which Friedman and Meiselman and their critics debated theory and empirical results. DePrano and Mayer[15] found that using alternative specifications of the autonomous expenditure variable led to better forecasts of consumption than were obtained by either the Keynesian or the monetarist models used by Friedman and Meiselman. DePrano and Mayer concluded that both money and autonomous expenditures are important in the determination of income.[16]

The argument continued on the basis of methodology, data, and definitions of variables, with neither side substantially changing the opinion of the other side. The implication of this argument, from the point of view of the monetarists, is that control of the supply of money is more important than the control of autonomous expenditures.

The Failures of Past Monetary Policies

In large measure, monetarist analysis is based on the empirical study of past monetary policy. First, the monetarists claim that the Federal Reserve System has been more concerned with interest rates and the conditions of the credit markets than with control of the supply of money. In this regard, the critics of past Federal Reserve policy are probably quite correct. The Federal Reserve's analysis of the money supply and the rate of growth of the money supply is of relatively recent origin.

Second, the monetarist interpretation of history constitutes an attack on past Federal Reserve policy decisions. The Federal Reserve System's errors resulted from the failure to control the rate of growth of the money supply.

The major historical work of the monetarists is *A Monetary History of the United States, 1867–1960* by Milton Friedman and Anna Schwartz.[17] In this important piece of monetary analysis, Friedman and Schwartz trace the development of the money supply of the United States, analyze changes in the determinants and components of the money supply, and study monetary policy in terms of the effect of public policy both before and after the establishment of the Federal Reserve System.

Friedman and Schwartz study changes in the supply of money in terms of three "proximate determinants of the money stock."[18] Their system is a variation of the money supply model developed in Chapter 8. The three key variables are:

[15]Michael DePrano and Thomas Mayer, "Tests of the Relative Importance of Autonomous Expenditures and Money," *American Economic Review,* September 1965, pp. 729–752.

[16]Ibid., p. 747.

[17]Milton Friedman and Anna Schwartz, *A Monetary History of the United States, 1867–1960* (Princeton, N.J.: Princeton University Press, 1963).

[18]Ibid., p. 51.

1. The quantity of *high-powered* money—that is, the supply of currency in the hands of the public plus reserve deposits at the Federal Reserve Banks. These items are classified "high powered" because they do, or can, serve as the basis for the expansion of the money supply.

2. The ratio of bank deposits to bank reserves, which measures the extent to which the commercial banking system utilizes the available reserve assets.

3. The public's ratio of deposits to currency, which indicates that the lower the proportion of the money supply held as currency, the higher the level of bank reserves and the greater the possible expansion of the money supply.

Friedman and Schwartz use these ratios to determine the sources of changes in the money supply during the period 1867–1960.[19] Their interpretation of the events of the Depression of the 1930s is both illustrative of the Friedman-Schwartz analysis, and of general interest. Before going into the Friedman-Schwartz analysis, a nonmonetarist analysis of the Depression is useful as a comparison.

John Kenneth Galbraith, in his book *The Great Crash,*[20] discusses a variety of general factors that have traditionally been used to explain the forces leading to the crash in 1929 and the subsequent Depression. Five generally accepted explanations are worthy of note:

1. The historical instability of the banking system contributed to the collapse.

2. Excessive speculation in the securities markets and eventual panic selling of stock purchased on margin destroyed confidence.

3. The Federal Reserve was unable to control the use of credit to purchase stock.

4. The Federal Reserve was unwilling to tighten credit generally and risk contracting business activity. The Federal Reserve faced a dilemma; if it tightened credit to control speculative uses of credit, legitimate nonspeculative uses of credit would also be restrained.

5. Neither fiscal nor monetary policy was used effectively. The adherence to classical policy prevented the use of fiscal policy, and the Federal Reserve lacked the leadership, experience, and policy tools to deal with a severe decline in economic activity.

In contrast to the nonmonetarist analysis of the events of the 1930s, Friedman and Schwartz interpret events in monetary terms and place a major part

[19]Ibid., pp. 50–51. The money supply equation is

$$M = H\frac{\frac{D}{R}\left(1 + \frac{D}{C}\right)}{\frac{D}{R} + \frac{D}{C}}$$

where M = supply of money
H = supply of high-powered money
D/R = ratio of deposits to reserves
D/C = ratio of deposits to currency

[20]John K. Galbraith, *The Great Crash* (Boston: Houghton-Mifflin Company, 1954).

of the blame for the collapse on the Federal Reserve System's failure to increase the supply of money during the mid- and late 1920s. During all other periods of economic expansion, the money supply had expanded. In the latter part of the 1920s, wholesale prices declined slowly, even though prices had never risen substantially from the low levels of the 1920–1921 recession.[21]

In the work of Friedman and Schwartz, the very low growth of the money supply during the 1920s was attributed to very little growth of high-powered money combined with increases in the deposit/currency ratio and the deposit/reserve ratio. The money supply reached its peak in April 1928 and declined until the crash in October 1929.[22] Thus, the Federal Reserve, which had not supplied the high-powered money needed for growth of the money supply in the 1920s, permitted the supply to decrease in the critical months before the collapse.[23]

In the period 1929–1932, money income declined 53 percent and real income declined 36 percent. Unemployment rose to 24.9 percent of the labor force. Vast waves of bank failures devastated the banking system and led to the 1933 "bank holiday."

Friedman and Schwartz attribute the length and depth of the Depression to the failures of the Federal Reserve System. Instead of undertaking a massive expansion of the money supply, the Federal Reserve permitted the money supply to contract by 33 percent during the 1929–1933 period.[24]

The fall in the money supply from 1929 to 1933 resulted from sharp declines in the deposit/reserve ratio and the deposit/currency ratio. The Federal Reserve expanded the supply of high-powered money beginning in late 1930, but the increase was too little and too late.[25]

The Federal Reserve did not begin large-scale open market operations until early 1932, and by that time the damage had already been done to the banking system and to confidence in the Federal Reserve System. The banking system accumulated excess reserves and the Federal Reserve developed the doctrine that an expansionary monetary policy was not especially effective because the banks could not be forced to use the newly created reserves.

One does not have to be a monetarist to agree with the basic thrust of the Friedman-Schwartz analysis of the 1929–1933 period. Many would not agree that the downturn resulted from the slow growth of the money supply in the 1920s and would place less emphasis on the 1929–1933 contraction of the money supply. However, most economists would agree that the Federal Reserve System should have acted more rapidly and more aggressively to stop or shorten the decline.[26]

Friedman and Schwartz also find that the policies of the Federal Reserve

[21]Friedman and Schwartz, op. cit., p. 298.

[22]Ibid., p. 290.

[23]Ibid., p. 298.

[24]Ibid., p. 302.

[25]Ibid., pp. 333–334.

[26]For a general discussion of the Friedman-Schwartz approach, see James Tobin, "Monetary Interpretation of History (A Review Article)," *American Economic Review,* June 1965, pp. 464–485.

contributed significantly to the recession of 1937–1938. By 1935, the Federal Reserve was concerned that the large quantity of excess reserves would contribute to a massive future expansion of the money supply. Between August 1936 and May 1937, the Federal Reserve used its newly gained power to increase reserve requirements and gradually increased reserve requirements to the maximum level. The increased reserve requirements caused the supply of money to decline between March 1937 and May 1938. The economy peaked in May 1937 and entered a short but sharp recession, which reached its trough in June 1938.[27]

In summary, the monetarist interpretation of history is based on the analysis of changes in the rate of growth of the money supply; economic problems and solutions are analyzed in terms of the behavior of the money supply. Although monetary policy is important and the Federal Reserve System has not always followed the appropriate policy, the question remains whether such a univariate analysis of history can reveal all of the truth.

The Lag in Effect of Monetary Policy

A major point in the Friedman analysis concerns the lag in effect of monetary policy. Short-run monetary policy actions by the Federal Reserve System do not have a quick effect on economic conditions. What the Federal Reserve does today is not felt today but has its impact at some point in the future. The question is, when is the effect of today's policy felt? Friedman believes that the lag is both lengthy and of variable duration. He fears that today's policy measure, designed to deal with today's problems, may not have its effect until some point in the future when new problems exist. For example, the antirecession policy of one year may have its expansionary effect a year or two later, when inflation may be the problem.

Friedman's conclusion relative to the length and variability of the lag in effect of monetary policy results from his work on the Friedman-Schwartz monetary history. He finds that "On the average of eighteen nonwar cycles since 1870, peaks in the rate of change of the stock of money precede reference peaks by sixteen months and troughs in the rate of change of the stock of money precede reference troughs by twelve months."[28] The reference peaks and troughs he refers to are the official turning points of the business cycle as determined by the National Bureau of Economic Research.

The critical point in the determination of the lag in the effect of monetary policy is the measurement of the lag. The lag to which Friedman refers is the lag between the peak rate of change of the supply of money and the peak level of business activity. The peak *rate of change* in the stock of money is compared to the peak in the absolute *level* of business activity. In a fluctuating series, the rate of change of the series must be reached before the turning point of the absolute value.

[27]Friedman and Schwartz, op. cit., pp. 520–545.

[28]Milton Friedman, "The Lag in Effect of Monetary Policy," *Journal of Political Economy,* vol. 69 (October 1961), p. 457.

John Culbertson, attacking Friedman's measurement system, argues that the lag should be measured (assuming that the process is legitimate at all) either by comparing the rate of change in the stock of money with the rate of change in business activity or by comparing the absolute level of the money stock with the absolute level of business activity. Either of these alternatives would produce a much shorter lag.[29]

Friedman defends his methodology by arguing that the appropriate comparison is between the flow of two variables. He claims he is comparing two flows—the flow of output and the flow of money. Culbertson does not accept this argument and reasons that people demand absolute amounts of money determined by their absolute incomes and do not change their money holdings on the basis of the absolute level of their income.[30]

The Friedman lag argument, if accepted, would require either a switch from a discretionary policy to an automatic rule or a great improvement in forecasting techniques. The evidence to be reviewed in the criticisms of monetarism indicates that the lag is not as long as Friedman suggests.

The Effects of Fiscal Policy

If changes in the supply of money produce changes in money income, what is the role of fiscal policy? A rigid monetarist answer to this question is that fiscal policy has no effect unless the fiscal policy leads to a change in the money supply.

How can a change in the government's fiscal policy lead to a change in the supply of money? Assume that the government lowers taxes to increase the level of income and that bonds are sold to finance the resulting deficit in the budget. Through open market purchases, the Federal Reserve buys the new issue of bonds and prevents the rising interest rates that would otherwise result from the sale of the new bonds. New bank reserves are created and the money supply expands. The creation of the new money leads to a change in the level of income. From a strict monetarist viewpoint, the change in the level of income is a result of the change in the money supply and is not a result of the fiscal policy.

If the Federal Reserve had not bought the new bonds and had permitted interest rates to rise as the new government debt was sold, the reserve position of the banking system would not have changed, the money supply would not have changed, and the level of income would not have changed. If the money supply had not increased, the public debt issue would have increased interest rates and private bond issuers would have been bid out of the market. This effect is called the *crowding-out* effect because, by the monetarist analysis, private debt issuers are crowded out of the debt markets by the government's sales of new debt.

[29]John Culbertson, "The Lag in Effect of Monetary Policy: Reply," *Journal of Political Economy,* vol. 69 (October 1961), pp. 467–477.

[30]Ibid., p. 469.

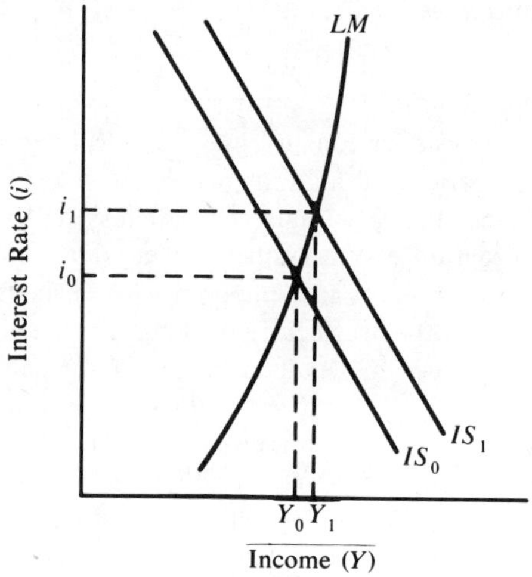

FIGURE 12–1 The Crowding Out Effect

The basic concept of the crowding-out effect can be demonstrated with the *IS-LM* analysis. In Figure 12–1, an *IS-LM* analysis is presented, with the *LM* curve having a relatively steep slope. The *LM* curve is derived on the basis of a speculative demand for money curve which has relatively little interest elasticity. At the extreme, if the speculative demand for money is totally interest-inelastic or does not exist (as in the classical region of the *LM* curves in Chapter 11), the *LM* curve becomes a straight line perpendicular to the horizontal axis.

In Figure 12–1, the effect of fiscal policy on income, shown by the shift of the *IS* curve and the change in income from Y_0 to Y_1, is relatively small. Income is changed by an amount that is less than would be suggested by the simple multiplier. In this example, crowding out has taken place. The sale of new government debt has increased interest rates and decreased the level of investment. Income increases by the full multiplier only if the central bank expands the money supply and shifts the *LM* curve to the right.[31]

The prescription of a constant rate of growth of the money supply would take the Federal Reserve's attention away from interest rates, and interest rates would be free to increase as new government debt was sold. The constant rate of growth rule would reduce the pressure on the Federal Reserve System to accommodate monetary policy to an unwise fiscal policy.

[31]For a comprehensive treatment of the crowding-out effect, see Roger W. Spencer and William P. Yohe, "The Crowding Out of Private Expenditures by Fiscal Policy Actions," *Federal Reserve Bank of St. Louis Review,* October 1970, pp. 12–24.

Monetary Policy and Interest Rates

Friedman[32] argues that the Federal Reserve System cannot maintain a given interest rate target for more than a short period of time. In fact, contrary to the short-run Keynesian analysis, Friedman argues that low interest rates are evidence of a past tight money policy and high interest rates are evidence of a past easy money policy. How does this seemingly contradictory result come about?

Assume the Federal Reserve wants to lower interest rates. It increases the rate of growth of the money supply and temporarily lowers market rates of interest. However, this is only a short-run effect. In the long run, the higher rate of growth of the money supply increases money income, so that the demand for money and interest rates rise. If rising prices are associated with the rise in money income, an inflation premium is added to interest rates, so that the rise in the money rate of interest is even higher. Thus, an easy money policy designed to lower interest rates leads to higher interest rates. If the Federal Reserve sticks to its original interest rate target, the supply of money must be expanded a second time. This action produces a second round of rising income and rising interest rates.

In the opposite direction, assume the Federal Reserve wants to raise interest rates to a higher level. The rate of growth of the money supply is decreased and interest rates increase initially as desired by the Federal Reserve. However, the lower than normal rate of growth of the money supply restricts the growth of money income, and prices and/or output decrease. The decline in output decreases the demand for money and interest rates fall. If prices fall, or rise at a reduced rate, the inflation premium on interest rates decreases and the interest rate falls.

To Friedman, this analysis of the central bank's attempt to set a given rate of interest indicates that measuring the *ease* or *tightness* of policy on the basis of interest rates is faulty and leads to wrong policy decisions. Using the rate of growth of the money supply is a superior policy measure.

The Friedman analysis of the long- and short-run effects of changes in the supply of money is not something unique. While the short-run models used in macroeconomics do not always explicitly include this extension, the effect is basically logical. If the lower initial interest rate has an effect, then income, the demand for money, and the interest rate will all increase. However, there is no obvious reason why the Federal Reserve would feel compelled to restore the initial interest rate by producing a second increase in the money supply. Presumably, they would change their target rate of interest as income increased.

Monetary Policy and the Rate of Unemployment

Friedman's analysis of attempts to change the level of unemployment by the use of monetary policy is similar to his analysis of changing interest rates.[33] The mone-

[32]Milton Friedman, "The Role of Monetary Policy," *American Economic Review,* March 1968, pp. 5–7.

[33]Ibid., pp. 7–11.

tary authority can change the rate of unemployment temporarily but cannot affect the unemployment rate on a permanent basis. A natural rate of unemployment is determined in the labor market by the real wage factors. The equilibrium level of employment in Figure 9–1 could be taken as the natural level of employment. Unemployment at this level of employment would be natural unemployment.

Assume stable prices, a given rate of unemployment, and a past stable rate of monetary growth. The Federal Reserve now decides that a lower level of unemployment is desirable and increases the rate of growth of the money supply. Money income responds to the faster rate of growth of the money supply; both output and prices increase and unemployment declines. However, the decline in unemployment is the result of a fall in real wages. Money wages are not as flexible as prices, and although money wages initially stay constant, the expansion of the money supply increases prices and lowers the real wage. At the lower real wage, the demand for labor is higher and employment increases.

The gain in employment is only temporary. In the longer run, workers react to the lower real wage by demanding higher money wages. At the lower real wage, employers demand more labor and bid up money wage rates to attract workers. These forces eventually bring the real wage and the employment level back to their original values. If the monetary authority wants to continue to hold the level of unemployment below its equilibrium value, the rate of growth of the money supply must increase a second time. However, in each case, a higher rate of growth of the money supply would be necessary to produce the temporary decline in the unemployment rate.

Friedman concludes by arguing that there is a temporary short-run tradeoff between inflation and unemployment because people do not anticipate inflation. Thus, the real wage can be lowered temporarily and employment increased. However, there is no lasting tradeoff between these two evils, and the Phillips curve is a straight line perpendicular to the unemployment axis.

Given that the monetary authority cannot change the long-run rate of unemployment, Friedman argues for a stable rate of increase in the money supply. This policy would avoid the danger that the Federal Reserve will create greater problems by following policies that it believes will lower unemployment.[34]

The Role of Monetary Policy

Friedman's view of the role of monetary policy is quite different from the general concept of monetary policy as a tool of short-run economic stabilization. What can monetary policy do? First, Friedman argues that monetary policy "can prevent money itself from being a major source of economic disturbance."[35] This point is based on the analysis of the previous two sections and the destabilizing effects of monetary policy found in the Friedman-Schwartz monetary history.

[34]Ibid., pp. 16–17.
[35]Ibid., p. 12.

Second, monetary policy should "provide a stable background for the economy."[36] Friedman argues that the stable rate of growth of the money supply would create stability of expectations with respect to wages and prices.

Third, monetary policy "can contribute to offsetting major disturbances in the economic system arising from other sources."[37] In this objective, Friedman refers to long-run problems, rather than to short-run business cycle problems.

The stable rate of growth of the money supply would naturally meet these objectives. The Federal Reserve would abandon its attempts to correct short-run business cycle problems.

Summary

The Friedman system stresses the following major points:

1. The policy actions of the Federal Reserve System should be governed by fixed rules rather than by the discretionary actions of the Board of Governors.
2. Changes in the level of money income are the product of changes in the supply of money.
3. Changes in the supply of money affect income with a long and variable lag.
4. Monetary actions are much more important than fiscal policy actions.
5. The record of the Federal Reserve System in controlling the money supply has been very poor.
6. The monetary authority can produce only temporary changes in the level of interest rates or unemployment.
7. The best monetary policy would provide a constant rate of growth of the money supply.

Monetarism in St. Louis

The Friedman ideas have not found great support within the structure of the Federal Reserve System. Given Friedman's criticisms of the methods and results of monetary policy, this is hardly surprising. However, monetarism has taken root at the Federal Reserve Bank of St. Louis, although its form of monetarism differs from that of Friedman and his associates.

The St. Louis monetarist views are stated by Andersen and Carlson,[38] the major developers of the St. Louis model, as follows:

1. Changes in the rate of growth of the money supply change total money

[36] Ibid., p. 13.

[37] Ibid., p. 14.

[38] Leonall C. Andersen and Keith M. Carlson, "A Monetarist Model for Economic Stabilization," *Federal Reserve Bank of St. Louis Review,* April 1970, pp. 7–25.

demand and production in the short run and produce changes in prices in the long run.

2. Output and employment—the real variables of the economy—are not affected in the long run by changes in the money supply. Output in the long run is determined by the supply and productivity of the factors of production.

3. Fluctuations in the economy are the result of fluctuations in the supply of money.

4. Fiscal policy has little effect on the level of economic activity unless monetary policy is also used.

5. The crowding out of private spending by government fiscal policy does take place.

6. Control of the supply of money is the most important macroeconomic policy tool.[39]

On the major points, Andersen and Carlson are in general agreement with the Friedman view of the economic world. There are important differences on two points. First, Andersen and Carlson do not find Friedman's long lag in the effect of monetary policy. Second, they do not suggest explicitly that the only macroeconomic policy should be the constant rate of growth of the money supply.

Given that the model used by Andersen and Carlson is relatively short and representative of monetarist thinking, it is produced here as an example of current monetarist analysis.

The model has eight equations:

$$\Delta Y = F(\Delta M_t \ldots \Delta M_{t-n}, \Delta E_t \ldots \Delta E_{t-n}) \quad (1)$$

This equation measures changes in income, ΔY, as a function of current and lagged changes in the supply of money, ΔM, and current and lagged changes of federal government expenditures, ΔE. The measure of government expenditures used is the level of government expenditures at a high level of employment. This measure is comparable to the high employment tax revenue function used in the full employment budget concept.

$$\Delta P_t = F(D_t \ldots D_{t-n}, \Delta P^A_t) \quad (2)$$

This is the price equation relating changes in prices, ΔP, to current and lagged demand pressures, D, and anticipated price changes, ΔP^A.

$$D_t = \Delta Y_t - (X^F_t - X_{t-1}) \quad (3)$$

D measures demand pressure and is the difference between the change in total spending, ΔY, and the difference between full employment output, X^F_t, and the level of output in the previous period, X_{t-1}.

$$\Delta Y_t = \Delta P_t + \Delta X_t \quad (4)$$

This equation is the total spending identity in which the change in total spending is the sum of the change in prices, ΔP, and the change in output, ΔX.

$$R_t = F(\Delta M_t, \Delta X_t \ldots \Delta X_{t-n}, \Delta P_t, \Delta P^A_t) \quad (5)$$

[39]Ibid., pp. 8–9.

Equation (5) determines the interest rate as a function of the change in the money supply, ΔM; current and lagged changes in output, ΔX; changes in prices, ΔP; and the anticipated change in prices, $\Delta P^A{}_t$.[40] Both a short-term and a long-term interest rate are calculated.

$$\Delta P^A{}_t = F(\Delta P_{t-1} \cdots \Delta P_{t-n}) \tag{6}$$

Anticipated price changes are a function of lagged price changes which have been adjusted for past unemployment rates. The assumption is that people form their expectations of inflation on the basis of past rates of inflation. Past rates of inflation were determined by demand pressures, which were measured by past unemployment rates.

$$U_t = F(G_t, G_{t-1}) \tag{7}$$

The unemployment rate, U, is a function of the current and past period's Gross National Product gap, G.

$$G_t = \frac{X^F{}_t - X_t}{X^F{}_t} \tag{8}$$

The GNP gap, G, is full employment output, $X^F{}_t$, minus current output, X_t, divided by full employment output. This is a measure of the shortfall of current output from the potential output of the economy.[41]

Andersen and Carlson estimate these equations statistically and study the response of the system to monetary and fiscal policy actions. They find that changes in the money supply (measured by the M_1 definition) have a large and rapid effect on total spending. Fiscal actions have some initial impact, but after a few quarters the crowding-out effect operates to minimize the net income change.[42]

In terms of timing, they find that monetary policy affects spending within two or three quarters. Output responds faster than prices to a change in the money supply. The impact of the monetary change occurs much faster than in the Friedman system. According to Andersen and Carlson, "about half of the total response to a change in monetary growth occurs in the first two quarters, and about 80 percent in the first three quarters."[43]

In comparison with other, more complex models, the Andersen-Carlson model is able to forecast and replicate past movements of the economy quite well. However, for actual policy-making purposes, it does not contain the degree of detail necessary for many decisions.[44]

[40]Monetarist analysis distinguishes between a nominal and a real rate of interest. The real rate of interest is determined by the productivity of capital and saving. The nominal rate of interest is the real rate of interest plus an inflation premium. The inflation premium is based on expectations of rising prices. Thus, the anticipation of future price changes is one of the determinants of the interest rate in this model.

[41]Andersen and Carlson, op. cit., pp. 9–10.

[42]Ibid., p. 11.

[43]Ibid., p. 15.

[44]Ibid., p. 21. See also Keith M. Carlson, "Projecting with the St. Louis Model: A Progress Report," *Federal Reserve Bank of St. Louis Review,* February 1972, pp. 20–27.

Criticisms of Monetarism

The rise of Friedman and the other monetarists has challenged the conventional Keynesian mechanisms. The concentration on the writings of Keynes and fiscal policy concepts during the late 1940s and 1950s led to a deemphasis of money and monetary policy. While the monetarists may be accused of arguing that only money matters, they were reacting to a situation in which many believed that money did not matter at all. Thus, to some extent, the conflict between the Keynesians and the monetarists is an overreaction to an overreaction.

Money is important. The conflict has certainly established that point very firmly. But how important is monetary policy relative to fiscal policy? Should the constant rate of growth of the money supply rule be adopted?

The concept of a fixed rule for the conduct of macroeconomic policy is appealing in its simplicity. All the problems and conflicts of the past would be swept away and the Federal Reserve System would be reduced to a very minor agency. Periodic reviews of the appropriateness of the rate of growth of the money supply would be necessary; a continual upward price drift would be evidence that the fixed rate was too high and continued downward price trends would suggest the rate was too low.[45] However, the simplicity of the idea must not cause one to overlook very serious questions relative to the Friedman program.

The Question of Lags

The claimed superiority of the monetary rule depends, in part, on the length of the lag in the effect of monetary policy. If the lag is as long as Friedman suggests, then a stable rate of growth policy might be an improvement. Economists cannot forecast very far into the future. If monetary actions have their effect one to three years in the future, the rule may be necessary. At least, the rule might have to be an interim policy until forecast reliability is improved.

However, Friedman's lag is longer than the lags found by others. The Andersen-Carlson monetarist model and most nonmonetarist models suggest that Friedman overstates the size and the variability of the lag; the lag is sufficiently short that today's policy measures will have much of effect within a year. Thus, unless Friedman is right and nearly everyone else is wrong, discretionary monetary policy can be successful without great improvement in forecasts.[46]

[45]Friedman, *A Program for Monetary Stability,* op. cit., p. 92.

[46]For a short review of the evidence on lags, see Michael J. Hamburger, "The Lag in the Effect of Monetary Policy: A Survey of Recent Literature," *Federal Reserve Bank of New York Monthly Review,* December 1971, pp. 289–298.

The Problem of Interest Rates

In large measure, the policy of the Federal Reserve System has been oriented toward the control of interest rates. Changes in the supply of money are used to smooth out seasonal fluctuations in interest rates, to maintain interest rate stability while the Treasury is selling new debt issues, and to induce changes in interest rates for countercyclical purposes. All of these stabilizing actions presumably would be eliminated under the Friedman plan.

The Friedman plan could cause wide swings in interest rates as a result of Treasury financing and seasonal and cyclical changes in the demand for money. A sudden rapid change in interest rates would have effects in every area influenced by interest rates — capital investment, housing, financial intermediation, saving or consumption, and asset values. These interest rate effects would be destabilizing if they were of long duration and simply disruptive if the effects were only temporary.

The implication of the Friedman plan is that the demand for money and the level of income would be more stable and interest rates would not fluctuate to the same degree as under a discretionary policy system. To an extent, this might be the case. For example, borrowers would not have to speculate about the actions of the Federal Reserve System and would not be led to borrow ahead of their needs in anticipation of a tight money, high interest rate period. However, it does not seem likely that the degree of stability that Friedman envisions is probable in an unstable world. Random shocks to the system, technological changes in the payments mechanism, foreign economic developments, and changes in the public's asset-holding tastes and preferences seem to require that the central bank have some flexibility in the control of the supply of money.

Perhaps Friedman is partly correct in arguing that the Federal Reserve has spent too much time and effort changing the supply of money in response to minor changes in the demand for money. More reliance could be placed on market mechanisms and interest rate fluctuations to adjust the demand for money to the supply of money.

Tests of Rules Versus Discretion

Various economists have attempted to use macroeconomic models to determine what would have happened if we had been using the Friedman rule in the past. Tests of this sort are very difficult; the necessary assumptions create grounds for challenging the results.

Historical models are a product of discretionary policy. Are these models sufficiently flexible to be used to test an entirely different policy structure? If the adoption of an alternative policy structure would lead to changes in public behavior or expectations, tests using existing models and past data would be unproductive.

The conclusions of these tests are mixed but seem to indicate that the use of a money supply growth rule would not represent a general improvement over discretionary policy.[47] In some cases, a rule would have prevented an excessive expansion of the money supply. However, in the cases in which an excessive expansion of the money supply is most obvious, the control of the business cycle was not the sole objective of monetary policy. During World War II and for nearly six years after the war, monetary policy was subordinated to the objective of maintaining low interest rates so that the Treasury could finance and refinance wartime debt. The rule would have produced a lower rate of growth of the money supply, but the rule could not have been maintained during this period; the national defense effort of World War II would have led to the suspension of the rule, and the need to refinance the debt after the war would have been given higher priority than a return to the rule.

The pressures that lead to an excessive rate of growth of the money supply without the rule would not go away if the rule were being used. Pressures to violate the rule, in the interest of national defense or some other good purpose, would still exist.

The Effect of Fiscal Policy

Regardless of the opinions of Friedman and the other monetarists, most economists still remain convinced of the need for a discretionary fiscal policy. Fiscal policy still matters. The evidence presented by the monetarists has not yet convinced the vast majority of students of macroeconomic policy that fiscal policy should be forgotten.

First, the crowding out of private expenditures by changes in public expenditures is a function of the level of employment. In a period of full employment, some crowding out would be expected. However, crowding out should not occur in a period of high unemployment. As the *IS-LM* analysis suggests, crowding out should increase as the economy comes closer to full employment.

Second, most economists have difficulty accepting the assumption that the money supply is the only important variable and that the line of economic causation is in only one direction — from money to income. Feedbacks from income to the demand for (and supply of) money may complicate matters more than the monetarists believe.

Third, the monetarists did not win the argument over the relative stability of velocity and autonomous expenditures. The evidence changed as the model used to specify autonomous expenditures changed. It is much easier to summarize changes in the money supply in one variable than to summarize all changes in all autonomous expenditures in one variable.

[47]See Franco Modigliani, "Some Empirical Tests of Monetary Management and of Rules Versus Discretion," *Journal of Political Economy,* vol. 72 (June 1964), pp. 211–244; and Martin Bronfenbrenner, "Statistical Tests of Rival Monetary Rules," *Journal of Political Economy,* vol. 69 (February 1961), pp. 1–14.

Fourth, most nonmonetarist macroeconomic models show a definite effect of fiscal policy independent of changes in the supply of money. Until nonmonetarists are able to find that fiscal policy has no effect, the findings of the monetarists will continue to be suspect.

Other Questions About the Rule

Beyond the basic points that have already been raised, several other shorter points can be made about the rule.

First, adoption of a rule for the growth of the money supply would be a setback in terms of the development of a more efficient discretionary policy program. The Friedman policy, rather than being used pending the develoment of a better discretionary policy, would discourage research on new policy measures.

Second, some of the past policy errors of the Federal Reserve System have been serious, especially if one accepts the supply of money and its rate of change as the key policy variable. One can hope that the Federal Reserve has learned something from the policy errors of the past and will not repeat these errors in the future. For example, few believe that the Federal Reserve would repeat the policies that allowed the money supply to decline by one third during the early 1930s.

Third, the stability of expectations that Friedman believes would result from his policies would apply only to expectations about the growth rate of the money supply. There is no basic reason that stability in the rate of growth of the money supply would produce stable growth of all variables or stability of expectations about the interest rate.

Fourth, the concept of the Federal Reserve System as a lender of last resort would be ended under Friedman's program.[48] Friedman argues that this function is no longer needed. However, flexibility in responding to the problems of individual banks or groups of banks is still required. The periods of financial disintermediation in the late 1960s and early 1970s indicate that a lender of last resort is still needed both for member banks and for all other financial institutions. Although market mechanisms such as the Federal Funds market can provide funds for the individual institution in normal times, these markets cannot create new reserves, and a lender of last resort is needed to increase liquidity in crisis periods.

Fifth, stability of the rate of growth of the money supply would not lead necessarily to price stability. Inflation can arise from causes other than excessive rates of growth of the money supply. Cagan[49] demonstrates that periods of *hyperinflation* (defined as inflation at rates in excess of 50 percent per month) are associated with excessive rates of growth of the supply of money and that the continuation of hyperinflation depends upon continuation of high rates of growth of the money supply.

[48]Friedman, *A Program for Monetary Stability,* op. cit. pp. 35–40.

[49]Philip Cagan, "The Monetary Dynamics of Hyperinflation" in M. Friedman, ed., *Studies in the Quantity Theory of Money* (Chicago: University of Chicago Press, 1956), pp. 25–120.

There is relatively little dispute over the important role of the supply of money in periods of hyperinflation. However, for inflations such as those experienced by the industrialized Western nations in the post–World War II period, the role of money is much less clear. Alternative theories of inflation are reviewed in a later chapter, but it is difficult to accept the idea that only monetary variables can cause or perpetuate inflation. Changes in conditions of supply and changes in the composition of demand are difficult to ignore, especially in an economy with less than perfect competition and considerable wage and price rigidity.

Sixth, the Friedman definition of the money supply in M_2 terms is of questionable value. A strict cash and demand deposits (M_1) definition is appropriate if one wishes to limit the definition of the money supply to include only those items serving as a means of payment. Once the means of payment test is dropped, the definition should be widened to include a variety of assets that can readily be converted to cash. The M_3 definition of the money supply (M_2 plus saving and time deposits at nonbank financial intermediaries) would appear to be superior to the M_2 definition.

What is the Resolution of the Monetarist Debate?

The debate between the proponents and opponents of monetarism is not resolved. The nonmonetarist position has softened and few would argue that money does not matter. The nonmonetarist conclusion is that both monetary and fiscal policy are important in controlling the level of aggregate demand. The monetarist position does not seem to have been modified significantly.

From the point of view of a nonmonetarist, the monetarists have made significant contributions to the development of monetary theory and policy. First, the development of monetarist thought has led to a complete reexamination of the basis for monetary and fiscal policy. The deemphasis of monetary policy associated with the spread of Keynesian macroeconomics has been checked.

Second, the conduct of monetary policy has been altered to take into account the rate of growth of the money supply. While the Federal Reserve has not indicated an abandonment of its other indicators of monetary policy—reserve levels and interest rates—attention has been focused, as never before, on the level of the money supply and the rate of change of the money supply. With this modification of emphasis, it is doubtful that the Federal Reserve would permit the large and rapid changes in the money supply found in Friedman and Schwartz's monetary history. However, the new attention to the rate of change of the money supply does not mean that the Board of Governors of the Federal Reserve System is ready to buy the concept of the constant rate of growth in the money supply.

There is some acceptance of the concept of limiting the range within which the Federal Reserve can vary the rate of growth of the money supply. Rather than being constrained by a given rate, the Federal Reserve would be given a limited range of rates within which to operate. In hearings before the Joint Economic Committee in 1968 and the House Banking and Currency Committee in 1975, some support was offered for this concept.[50] Thus, the Friedman influence forces a continuing review of the basis on which monetary policy is conducted and forces the Federal Reserve System to examine the influence of their actions on the rate of growth of the money supply.

Third, the monetarist examination of the crowding-out effect points up a basic policy problem. The analysis of crowding out was very important in the discussion of the tax cut of 1975; there was no great discussion of that subject at the time of the 1964 tax cut. In the decade between the two tax cut bills, the experience of three periods of severe disintermediation reinforced the theoretical analysis of crowding out. The financing of debt—both public and private—can lead to the attraction of funds from financial intermediaries and a contraction of those activities normally financed through intermediaries.

Finally, the monetarists, though they have not converted all their opponents to their views, have opened up new channels of inquiry and analysis which may lead to future discoveries of better means of achieving national economic objectives.

REVIEW QUESTIONS

1. How is Milton Friedman's work related to the Chicago tradition?

2. What forces determine the demand for money in the Friedman analysis?

3. Why do monetarists believe that the Federal Reserve System has failed to make its maximum possible contribution to economic stabilization?

4. Why is fiscal policy of relatively little importance in monetarist analysis?

5. How does the St. Louis version of monetarism differ from the Friedman analysis?

6. Why does Friedman believe that monetary policy can have only temporary effects on the interest rate and level of unemployment?

7. How is the problem of measuring lags in the effect of monetary policy related to the possible need for a monetary growth rule?

8. How does Friedman's quantity theory of money differ from the classical quantity theory of money?

9. In what ways is the Friedman analysis similar to and different from classical analysis? Keynesian analysis?

[50]See *Standards for Guiding Monetary Action,* hearings before the Joint Economic Committee, 90th Cong., 1968.

10. What are the criticisms of the monetarists' work? In addition to the points cited in the chapter, many economists object to Friedman's methodology—see, for instance, the articles by Friedman and Velk on this subject.

SUGGESTED READINGS

Keith M. Carlson and Roger W. Spencer, "Crowding Out and Its Critics," *Federal Reserve Bank of St. Louis Review,* December 1975, pp. 2–17.

J. Phillip Cooper and Stanley Fischer, "Monetary and Fiscal Policy in the Fully Stochastic St. Louis Econometric Model," *Journal of Money, Credit and Banking,* Ohio State University Press, Columbus, February 1974, pp. 1–22.

J. Phillip Cooper and Charles R. Nelson, "The Ex Ante Prediction Performance of the St. Louis and FRB-MIT-PENN Econometric Models and Some Results on Composite Predictors," *Journal of Money, Credit and Banking,* Ohio State University Press, Columbus, February 1975, pp. 1–32.

Milton Friedman, "The Methodology of Positive Economics" in M. Friedman, *Essays in Positive Economics* (Chicago: University of Chicago Press, 1935), pp. 3–43. Reprinted in W. Breit and H. M. Hochman, eds., *Readings in Microeconomics,* 2nd ed. (New York: Holt, Reinhart and Winston, 1971), pp. 23–47.

Stephen F. LeRoy, "Interest Rates and the Inflation Premium," *Federal Reserve Bank of Kansas City Monthly Review,* May 1973, pp. 11–18.

Robert H. Rasche, "Comments on a Monetarist Approach to Demand Management," *Federal Reserve Bank of St. Louis Review,* January 1972, pp. 26–32.

Ronald T. Teigen, "A Critical Look at Monetarist Economics," *Federal Reserve Bank of St. Louis Review,* January 1972, pp. 10–25.

Thomas J. Velk, "The Central Characteristics of Professor Friedman's Analysis and the Issue of Normalism," *Eastern Economic Journal,* January 1975, pp. 34–51.

John H. Wood, "Money and Output: Keynes and Friedman in Historical Perspective," *Federal Reserve Bank of Philadelphia Business Review,* September 1972, pp. 3–12.

13

CONTROL OF THE MONEY SUPPLY: POLICY MAKING

This first of three chapters on monetary policy concentrates on the formulation of monetary policy. The first section of the chapter describes the policy-making groups and examines some of the charges made against the organization of the Federal Reserve System. The second section covers the measurement and definition of policy and offers some guidelines for judging the Federal Reserve's policy actions.

The Policy-Making Process and Problems

The structure of the policy-making process within the Federal Reserve System involves both formal and informal decision-making groups. Some of the processes and structures have been designed and others just "grew that way."

The Policy-Making Bodies

The responsibility for the making of monetary policy is divided in principle but is more concentrated in practice. The most important policy-making group is the Board of Governors of the Federal Reserve System. The Board, appointed by the President of the United States and confirmed by the Senate, has the ultimate responsibility for monetary policy. The Chairman of the Board of Governors is clearly the most important Board member; he speaks publicly for the Board and usually represents the Board at Congressional hearings and at meetings with executive branch officials.

The Board of Governors has undivided authority in the establishment of reserve requirements. The Board can establish guidelines for the administration of the discount windows at the various Federal Reserve Banks and must approve any proposed change in the discount rate charged by the Federal Reserve Banks. The seven members of the Board of Governors constitute a majority of the voting membership of the Federal Open Market Committee. In addition, the Board establishes the Regulation Q interest rate ceilings on deposits at member banks.

The second most important group within the Federal Reserve System is the *Federal Open Market Committee,* which is composed of the seven members of the Board, the president of the Federal Reserve Bank of New York, and four other Federal Reserve Bank presidents. The president of the Federal Reserve Bank of New York is a permanent member of the FOMC because the New York Bank conducts open market operations. The other four seats for Federal Reserve Bank presidents rotate among the other eleven presidents.

The representation of the Federal Reserve Bank presidents on the Federal Open Market Committee is a by-product of the development of open market operations. In the early years of the Federal Reserve System, each bank conducted its own purchases and sales of government securities. However, these purchases and sales were not designed to influence monetary policy; the various Federal Reserve Banks purchased government securities to invest their surplus funds and earn income to finance their operations. Thus, each Bank managed its own securities portfolio. Eventually, it was recognized that the purchase or sale of government securities by the Federal Reserve Banks changed the availability of reserves to the commercial banks and that these operations were an instrument of monetary policy. A committee was established to coordinate the purchases and sales by the various Banks, and this committee became the Federal Open Market Committee. The continued representation of the Federal Reserve Bank presidents on the FOMC is a result of the origin of the committee as a coordinating body for the Federal Reserve Banks.

The Board of Governors receives policy advice from a number of other System committees. The *Federal Advisory Council* consists of one representative from each Federal Reserve District (elected by the Board of Directors of each District's Federal Reserve Bank). The Federal Advisory Council consults regularly with the Board of Governors on both short- and longer run policy problems. In addition, Conferences of Presidents of Federal Reserve Banks and Chairmen of the Boards of the Federal Reserve Banks are organized to meet periodically with the Board. These three groups are purely advisory and only indirectly affect policy decisions.

In the making of policy, the role of the staff of the Board of Governors and the staffs of the Federal Reserve Banks cannot be overlooked. The staff members conduct research on monetary matters, prepare policy alternatives for the Board, and carry out the policies selected by the Board. One need not be experienced in money and banking to serve on the Board of Governors, although some members, such as Dr. Arthur Burns, are professional economists. Given the diverse background of Board members, the maintenance of a high-quality professional staff is very important.

Beyond the policy-making groups, there is one very important person involved in conducting monetary policy—the manager of the Federal Reserve

System's Open Market Account. The manager is responsible for carrying out the open market policy established by the Federal Open Market Committee. Whereas the establishment of reserve requirements or discount rates requires only periodic decisions, open market operations are an on-going process. Therefore, the FOMC delegates the responsibility for conducting open market operations to the manager of the Open Market Account. The trading desk, supervised by the manager, is located at the Federal Reserve Bank of New York, and the manager is a vice-president of that institution.

While there are clear formal lines of authority for the use of the various monetary policy tools, the making of monetary policy does not always follow the formal lines. The meetings of the FOMC appear to be the arena for determining overall policy. The use of open market operations cannot be determined separately from decisions about all of the other components of monetary policy. Thus, the FOMN meetings, usually held every four weeks, serve as a general forum for the discussion of monetary policy. Nonvoting participants include those Federal Reserve Bank presidents not currently on the FOMC and senior staff members from the Board of Governors and the Federal Reserve Banks.

The format of the FOMC meetings consists of a discussion of current economic conditions, the outlook for the near future, and the policies that seem appropriate. The members of the FOMC vote on a directive to govern open market operations between the meetings of the committee. The policy directive is intended to guide the manager of the Open Market Account; if conditions change, the directive can be amended by special meetings or as a result of daily conference calls. A sample directive is reproduced later in this chapter.

Criticisms of the Organization of the Federal Reserve System

Many aspects of the organization of the Federal Reserve System are attacked periodically by the System's critics. The late Representative Wright Patman, former Chairman of the House Banking, Currency and Housing Committee, was a leader in formulating some of these attacks on the organization and policies of the System. Some of the critics object to the people involved in the formulation of policy, some to the orientation of policy, some to the System's traditional secrecy, and some to the policy making independence of the Federal Reserve System. While none of these objections is totally justified, problems do exist and some reforms are required.

Banker Involvement in Policy Making The first objection alleges that there is excessive banker influence on monetary policy. The ownership of the Federal Reserve Banks by the member commercial banks is one channel of possible influence. Another is via the election by member banks of six of the nine directors of each Federal Reserve Bank. The directors, as explained in Chapter 3, elect the president of each Federal Reserve Bank, and these presidents all have their turn on the Federal Open Market Committee.

On the first point, ownership of the Federal Reserve Banks by the member banks is anachronistic; the district Federal Reserve Banks should be owned by the federal government and the directors appointed by either the Board of Governors of the Federal Reserve System or by the President and the Senate of the United States. In most other countries, the government owns and operates the central bank. The current ownership system was acceptable in 1914 for an agency acting as a lender of last resort, but the role of the Federal Reserve has changed. Given the vast responsibilities of the Federal Reserve System in the American economy, the System should be owned by the public through the government.

On the second charge, the bankers do have a degree of influence on the selection of the president of each Federal Reserve Bank. However, their influence is not as broad as the critics state. Bankers are only three of the nine directors; the representatives of business—although elected by the bankers—are users of credit and should have interests different from those of the suppliers of credit. The public directors should also be independent of banker influence. Data gathered by Representative Patman indicated that many nonbanker directors had the same interests as the bankers. Significant numbers of business and public directors owned or had owned bank stock and/or served or had served as commercial bank directors.[1]

Banker influence on the behavior of the Federal Reserve System does seem to occur in one major area. Banks are not required to belong to the Federal Reserve System; the option to become a state nonmember bank is always open. The Federal Reserve appears to have been very concerned about maintaining bank membership in the System and has attempted periodically to force all banks either to join the System or hold reserves equal (in percentage terms) to those held by the member banks. These efforts to force membership have been vigorously opposed by the nonmember banks. The right not to join, or to withdraw from, the System appears to act as a constraint on reserve requirement policy, because higher reserve requirements would cause more banks to leave the System. This reluctance to increase reserve requirements has not changed monetary policy but may have changed the relative usage of the various policy tools. Less reliance has been placed on reserve requirement changes and more reliance has been placed on open market operations.

Beyond the freedom to give up membership in the Federal Reserve System, any significant banker influence that does exist tends to be at the District Reserve Bank level. Over time, the monetary policy powers have shifted from the Federal

[1]The study is summarized in *The Federal Reserve After Fifty Years: Proposals for Improvement of the Federal Reserve and Staff Report on Hearings Before the Subcommittee on Domestic Finance of the Committee on Banking and Currency,* Subcommittee on Domestic Finance, Committee on Banking and Currency, U.S. House of Representatives, 88th Cong., 2d. Sess., August 25, 1964, pp. 67–68.

Reserve Banks to the Board of Governors. Regardless of past practices and problems, the Federal Reserve System should be owned by the government and operated by people who are free from all financial attachments to the banking industry.

The *Financial Institutions and the Nation's Economy (FINE) Discussion Principles* suggested that Federal Reserve Bank stock be retired, that presidents of Federal Reserve Banks be appointed by the President of the United States and confirmed by the Senate, and that Federal Reserve Bank boards of directors be eliminated and replaced by a representative monetary policy advisory committee in each district. Federal Reserve Bank presidents would participate in the discussion of monetary policy but would not vote on policy measures; the Board of Governors of the Federal Reserve System would determine policy.[2]

The Inflation-Unemployment Tradeoff Another criticism of the Federal Reserve System is that the Board of Governor's implicit tradeoff between inflation and unemployment has been too heavily oriented toward preventing inflation. A critic could argue that the Board has sacrificed jobs for the sake of preventing inflation. The basic question is whether society's preferred mix of unemployment and inflation is the same as the Board's preferred mix. Over time, the members of the Board have probably spoken more words on the evils of inflation than they have on the evils of unemployment. However, this untested statistical assertion may not reflect the real preferred tradeoff of the Board; the Board may have been forced into the role of being the chief opponent of inflation.

By not having to respond to political forces, the Federal Reserve System may be in the best position to speak in favor of unpopular anti-inflation policies. The System itself may have assumed this position or may have been thrust into this role by those in more politically vulnerable positions. The Congress and the Administration are frequently more growth and employment oriented than is the Federal Reserve; expansionary policies are more popular than contractionary policies.

The traditional involvement of central banks in international finance may be another factor in the strong anti-inflation position of the Federal Reserve System. International central bankers are all strongly opposed to inflation because of the effect of inflation on the balance of payments. The central bank is usually charged with the protection of the nation's international reserves and with the maintenance of the exchange rate. Therefore, central bankers have been identified with price stability. The balance of payments threat may make the Federal Reserve System more willing to trade off some employment for greater price stability.

Thus, the appearance of a willingness to accept less than optimum

[2]*Financial Institutions and the Nation's Economy (FINE) Discussion Principles,* 94th Cong., 1st Sess., Committee on Banking, Currency and Housing, U.S. House of Representatives, November 1975, pp. 15–16.

employment levels in order to achieve price stability may be inherent in the nature of the independent central bank. Central bankers fear inflation, and from their point of view the evils of a slightly higher short-term rate of unemployment are less than the evils of massive inflation and the breakdown of the international monetary system.

Secrecy of Monetary Policy Traditionally, monetary policy decisions of the Federal Reserve System were made behind a veil of secrecy and were kept behind the veil forever, Brief descriptions of the policy directives were printed in the *Annual Report of the Federal Reserve System,* but these statements were not very informative. Policy secrecy increased suspicions about the actions of the Federal Reserve System.

The Federal Reserve defended its secrecy by arguing that the disclosure of its policy actions would create speculation in the market for government securities. If the public knew that the Federal Reserve intended to increase the supply of money and lower interest rates, speculators would buy securities in anticipation of a capital gain. If it were revealed that the Federal Reserve intended to push up interest rates, massive selling of government securities would take place.

The need for secrecy was overdone by the Federal Reserve. Although details of planned future policies cannot be revealed without bringing about speculation, this argument does not apply to past policy actions. The failure to reveal the basis for past policy actions merely contributed to the belief that the Federal Reserve was using the speculation argument to cover up past policy errors.

After a long conflict between the Federal Reserve System and Representative Patman, the secrecy rules were modified. Access to past records was made easier and more information was made available on recent policy actions. Currently, the policy directive that results from the meeting of the FOMC and a summary of the discussion leading to the directive are released soon after the next FOMC meeting and are published in the next edition of the *Federal Reserve Bulletin*.

Policy-Making Independence The third issue is the independence of the Federal Reserve System from other policy-making organizations. Ideally, the parts of macroeconomic policy should be consistent with each other. There is no mechanism to prevent the Federal Reserve System from using monetary policy to restrain the economy at the same time the Congress is using fiscal policy to expand the economy.

The division of macroeconomic responsibility means that the President, the Congress, and the Federal Reserve could all be moving in different directions to fight different problems. In the fall of 1974, the President and the Federal Reserve System seemed to be concerned mainly with a battle against inflation, while the Congress was growing concerned about signs of a developing recession.

In 1962, the Congress and the President were concerned with economic growth and recovery from recession, while the Federal Reserve appeared to be more concerned with possible inflation and balance of payments difficulties.

An attempt is made to coordinate monetary and fiscal policy through meetings of the Secretary of the Treasury, the Chairman of the Council of Economic Advisors, and the Chairman of the Board of Governors of the Federal Reserve System. While regular consultation between these and other officials serves to maintain communications and share information and insights, these meetings may not produce a common policy if one of the participants, the Chairman of the Board of Governors, is under no legal compulsion to agree to a common policy.

The policy coordination problems can be especially difficult for a new President. A President coming into office after a long tenure of the opposition party discovers that most of the members of the Board of Governors have been appointed by the previous administration and may be totally opposed to the goals of the new administration. President John Kennedy, for example, inherited a Board appointed by Presidents Truman and Eisenhower and headed by William McChesney Martin. Mr. Martin expressed great reservations about the Kennedy administration's plans for a tax cut. President Richard Nixon was fortunate that, early in his first administration, he was able to appoint Dr. Arthur Burns as Chairman of the Board of Governors. Dr. Burns had served as an advisor to Presidents Eisenhower and Nixon and was sympathetic to the economic goals of the Nixon administration.

Three questions arise: First, is coordination necessary? Second, is the need for coordination worth sacrificing the independence of the Federal Reserve System? Third, is there an institutional arrangement that would preserve independence while producing greater coordination?

Coordination is certainly desirable from a policy-making point of view. Any administration is elected partly on the basis of economic issues and should have some flexibility in carrying out its economic programs. Currently, the economic policies of an elected administration can be vetoed by the previous administration's appointees to the Board of Governors. However, is coordination tantamount to subservience? Does coordination mean that the Federal Reserve System must operate a permissive monetary policy to support any fiscal policy adopted by the administration?

There is one major instance of the total subservience of the Federal Reserve to the wishes of the executive branch. Upon American entry into World War II, the Federal Reserve System agreed to support the Treasury's debt financing. A target term structure of interest rates was developed and the Federal Reserve agreed to peg (or hold) the term structure at that level for the duration of the war. From the point of view of the Treasury, this procedure insured that funds could be borrowed at fixed interest rates. Government bonds would not sell at a discount because the Federal Reserve would buy bonds as necessary in order to hold bond prices up and maintain yields at the agreed-upon low levels.

Under this arrangement, the Federal Reserve was forced to buy government debt each time a new sale of debt put downward pressure on prices and pushed yields upwards. Federal Reserve ownership of Treasury debt increased from \$2.3 billion in 1941 to \$24.3 billion in 1945 as a result of price-supporting operations in the government debt markets. The fixed-yield pattern was maintained and the purchasers of government securities were assured that subsequent sales of government debt would not drive down the prices of earlier issues.

The conflict between the Treasury and the Federal Reserve began when the war ended. Both the banks and the public had purchased huge quantities of government securities during the war. Rationing, war production requirements, limitations on the production of civilian goods, and the high level of employment had produced high consumer savings and had restricted private demands for credit. Consumers desired to replenish their stock of durable goods and banks wished to reduce their holdings of government securities and return to their normal lending activities.

The Treasury wanted the Federal Reserve System to continue the policy of pegging interest rates at low levels. If interest rates rose as consumers, businesses, and banks reduced their holdings of government bonds, the cost to the Treasury of borrowing to refinance the maturing war debt would increase.

The Federal Reserve saw the problem differently. They realized that vast quantities of new bank reserves had been created as a result of supporting the government bond market during the war. By continuing to peg yields and prices, the Federal Reserve was making it easy for banks to liquidate government bonds—without taking a capital loss—and convert the funds to business and consumer loans. The Federal Reserve saw the inflationary consequences of its continued support of the government bond market and became increasingly anxious to terminate its agreement with the Treasury. The Federal Reserve wanted to sell—rather than buy—government securities and take reserves away from the banks to prevent an inflationary expansion of credit.

As time passed and inflation continued, the System became increasingly distressed by the pegging arrangement. Finally, in 1951, President Harry Truman agreed with the Federal Reserve and a Treasury–Federal Reserve Accord was reached. Under the Accord, the Federal Reserve was released from its obligation to facilitate Treasury borrowing at low interest rates.

Independence regained is independence not easily relinquished. Wars require deviations from standard operating practices; however, the fact that the Federal Reserve did not regain its independence for nearly six years after the end of the war may be a good argument for isolating the central bank from political forces.

Another danger of nonindependence is the possibility that a President could use monetary policy to ensure favorable economic conditions at election time. A sharp increase in the money supply might produce full employment before the election and inflation after the election. No President with influence over monetary policy could be expected to call for a restrictive monetary policy just before an election, even if the need for such a policy was indicated.

In the author's opinion, a high degree of independence is desirable to avoid political influence and the sacrifice of long term price stability goals for short-term employment gains. However, the coordination of macroeconomic policy could be improved without sacrificing the independence of the central bank.

One reasonable suggestion involves a change in the timing of appointments to the Board of Governors. A President must be able to make his opinions known to the Board. Therefore, a new President should be able to make an immediate appointment to the Board; the new man should be Chairman of the Board. This change would ensure a fair hearing for a new President's policies without committing the other members of the Board to any specific policy.

The *FINE Discussion Principles* suggested reducing the Board of Governors to five members, each serving 10-year terms. The Chairman would be appointed by the President for a four-year term that would coincide with the term of the President.[3]

A second reform would involve greater congressional input into the monetary policy-making process and the establishment of the ultimate goals of monetary policy. However, the proper degree of input is difficult to achieve. In 1975, the House Banking, Currency, and Housing Committee held hearings on a bill to require the Board to increase the supply of money at a rate of 6 percent per year for the first half of 1975 and to report to the committee any deviation from that target.[4]

The establishment of a congressionally determined fixed rate of increase of the money supply represents excessive intervention. Although the Congress should provide broad guidelines for monetary policy, the wisdom of congressional establishment of a target is questionable. In testimony in opposition to the bill, Chairman Arthur Burns argued[5] that giving the Federal Reserve System a specific target failed to take into account the fact that the System's policy was not formulated in terms of one rigid target, and that the relationship between the supply of reserves provided to the banks and the growth of the money supply was not so exact as to ensure the attainment of such a definite target.

The conflict between the Congress and the Federal Reserve System was resolved by congressional adoption of a nonbinding resolution calling upon the Federal Reserve System to provide sufficient monetary growth to produce a rapid recovery from the recession and to lower long term interest rates.[6]

While the merits of a specific case can be argued, clearly the Congress is not in a position to make monetary policy on a continuing basis, although some members of the Congress appear to want to do just that! Most observers would agree that the Federal Reserve does not have a very clear mandate and that the Congress should formulate more detailed objectives for the System. However, given the need for flexibility in monetary policy, directions cannot be too precise

[3]Ibid., pp. 15–16.

[4]*An Act to Lower Interest Rates and Allocate Credit,* hearings before the Subcommittee on Domestic Monetary Policy of the Committee on Banking, Currency, and Housing, 94th Cong., 1st Sess., U.S. House of Representatives, February 4–6, 1975.

[5]Ibid., pp. 200–203.

[6]*Wall Street Journal,* March 21, 1975, p. 21.

without destroying either the independence of the System or its ability to respond to new problems.

In addition, the Federal Reserve System should be required to justify its policy actions. Regular quarterly reports to the Congress were required by a joint resolution of the Congress in 1975. These reports include justification for past policies and plans for future policies. In the past, opportunities for the Congress to criticize policy came irregularly either when Federal Reserve officials testified on proposed legislation or when Congress reviewed the annual *Economic Report of the President.* Regular hearings on current monetary policy serve not only to inform the Congress but also to provide additional congressional guidance to the Federal Reserve System.

Summary By observing the actions of the Federal Reserve System, critics have not only found problems in the making of monetary policy but have reminded the policy makers that the System was created by Congress and can be restructured by Congress. The independence of the Federal Reserve System can be lost if not used wisely.

Measuring and Watching Monetary Policy

As indicated in the previous section, monetary policy is reflected in the directive issued by the Federal Open Market Committee to the manager of the Open Market Account. In this section, the policy directive is examined and the measurement of monetary policy in terms of targets and indicators is discussed. The section ends with some suggestions for students who wish to follow monetary policy.

The Policy Directive

A sample policy directive is reproduced here as an illustration of the instructions given to the account manager by the Federal Open Market Committee. Note that the first quotation is a rather general review of economic conditions and policy objectives, while the second quotation becomes very specific and quantitative.

The following domestic policy directive was issued to the Federal Reserve Bank of New York:[7]

> The information reviewed at this meeting suggests that real output of goods and services leveled off in the second quarter of the year, as consumer spending continued to strengthen. Activity in residential real estate markets has picked up in recent months. In June industrial production rose slightly, following 8 months of

[7] *Federal Reserve Bulletin,* September 1975, pp. 584–585. The quotation is from the policy directive resulting from the Federal Open Market Committee Meeting held on July 15, 1975.

decline. The calculated unemployment rate declined substantially, but this was attributed mainly to problems of seasonal adjustment. Average wholesale prices of industrial commodities rose somewhat more in June than in the preceding three months, chiefly because of increases in prices of petroleum products, but prices of farm and food products declined appreciably. From the first to the second quarter of the year, the advance in average wage rates continued to moderate.

In recent weeks the average exchange value of the dollar against leading foreign currencies has risen considerably, as interest rates on U.S. dollar assets increased relative to rates on foreign currency assets after mid-June. In May the U.S. foreign trade balance registered a substantial surplus, as imports dropped more sharply than exports. U.S. banks reported a sizable increase in claims on foreigners, while liabilities to foreigners were reduced slightly.

Growth in M_1, M_2, and M_3—which was substantial in May—was extremely rapid in June, in part because of Federal income tax rebates and of supplementary Social Security payments; beginning late in the month, after completion of such payments, the aggregates weakened. Business demands for short-term credit remained unusually weak both at banks and in the commercial paper market, while demands in the long-term market continued exceptionally strong. Market interest rates in general have risen appreciably in recent weeks.

In light of the foregoing developments, it is the policy of the Federal Open Market Committee to foster financial conditions conducive to stimulating economic recovery, while resisting inflationary pressures and working toward equilibrium in the country's balance of payments.

To implement this policy, while taking account of the forthcoming Treasury financing and of developments in domestic and international financial markets, the Committee seeks to maintain about the prevailing bank reserve and money market conditions over the period immediately ahead, provided that growth in monetary aggregates appears to be slowing substantially from the bulge during the second quarter.

Votes for this action: Messrs. Burns, Baughman, Bucher, Coldwell, Eastburn, Jackson, MacLaury, Mayo, Wallich, and Debs. Vote against this action: Mr. Holland.

Absent and not voting: Messrs. Hayes and Mitchell. (Mr. Debs voted as alternate for Mr. Hayes.)

Reading only this portion of the directive would not tell one very much about the direction of policy. The following partial paragraph provides more quantitative detail about the intentions of the FOMC:[8]

At the conclusion of the discussion, the Committee decided to seek bank reserve and money market conditions over the period immediately ahead about the same as those now prevailing, provided that growth in monetary aggregates appeared to be slowing substantially from the bulge during the second quarter.

[8]Ibid., p. 584.

Specificially, the members agreed that growth in M_1 and M_2 over the July–August period at annual rates within ranges of tolerance of 3 to 5½ percent and 8 to 10½ percent, respectively, would be acceptable. Such growth rates were thought likely to involve growth in reserves available to support private nonbank deposits (RPD's) within a range of −2 to +½ percent. The members agreed that in the period until the next meeting the weekly average Federal funds rate might be expected to vary in an orderly fashion within a range of 5½ to 6¾ percent, depending on the behavior of the monetary aggregates. The members also concluded that, in the conduct of operations, account should be taken of the forthcoming Treasury financing and of developments in domestic and international financial markets.

The policy directive contains the analysis of a great number of objectives and economic conditions. In formulating the policy directive, the Federal Open Market Committee attempts to take into account all possible macroeconomic variables. Mention is made of the ultimate objectives of policy—full employment, stable prices, economic growth, and balance of payments equilibrium. Reference is also made to the fiscal policy of the administration. All of these factors are discussed in more depth than is revealed in this summary of the meeting. A large portion of the quotation is framed in terms of targets and indicators; the next section discusses the formulation of targets and indicators with reference to the directive.

Targets of Monetary Policy

The *ultimate targets* of monetary policy—full employment, stable prices, economic growth, and balance of payments equilibrium—are long-range targets that the Federal Reserve can only affect with a long lag. The Federal Reserve does not directly affect employment or prices; direct control is exercised only over the quantity of reserves available to the banking system. Therefore, intermediate targets are necessary.

The ideal *intermediate target* variable would have several important characteristics. First, it would have a stable cause-and-effect relationship with the level of income, so that if monetary policy produced a given change in the intermediate target, a given change in income would also be produced. Second, the lag between an induced change in the target and the change in income would be short. Third, the ultimate target variable would be influenced by a minimum number of variables other than Federal Reserve policy measures; other forces that do affect the target would be predictable so that the policy tools can be adjusted for these influences. Fourth, there would be no feedback from income, the ultimate target, to the intermediate target. The line of causation would be unidirectional so that, for example, if the money supply were the intermediate policy target and income the ultimate target, changes in the money supply would change income but changes in income would not feedback and change the money supply. Finally, up-to-date data on the intermediate and ultimate targets would be available so that policy could be adjusted for differences between the actual and the desired level of the intermediate target.

The intermediate targets implied in the sample directive are the rates of growth of M_1 and M_2. The Federal Reserve wanted to produce a 3 to 5½ percent annual growth rate of M_1 and an 8 to 10½ percent annual growth rate of M_2. The FOMC was assuming that these rates of growth of M_1 and M_2 would lead to the appropriate level of income.

However, the money supply is not directly controlled by the Federal Reserve System. Thus, an *operating target* is needed. The operating target is stated in terms of the supply of reserves available to the banking system. The operating target in the sample directive is the rate of growth of reserves available to support private deposits. According to the directive, a −2 to +½ percent growth rate of reserves available to support private deposits was considered sufficient to produce the desired rate of growth of the money supply. Thus, the *operating target* is connected to the *intermediate target,* and the *intermediate target* is connected to the *ultimate target.* The wide range of acceptable rates indicates that the Federal Reserve, especially in the short run, cannot exercise exact control over the rate of growth of the monetary measures.

There are a variety of monetary and reserve measures that can be chosen as policy targets. Although the directive may state policy in terms of one of these measures, many other measures are tracked and studied for any potential contribution to policy analysis. Six of the best known reserve measures are the following:

1. *Total reserves* available to the banking system are coin and currency holdings of member banks plus reserve deposits at the Federal Reserve Banks.

2. *Required reserves* are the minimum quantity of reserves necessary to satisfy the current reserve requirement rules.

3. *Excess reserves* are the difference between total reserves and required reserves; they are a rough measure of the ability of the banking system to expand the supply of money.

4. *Borrowed reserves* are the quantity of reserves that the member banks have obtained by discounting, or other borrowing, from the Federal Reserve Banks; to an extent, the level of borrowed reserves is an indicator of the desire of the member banks to gain additional reserves and increase their lending activity.

5. *Free reserves* or *net-borrowed reserves* result from the subtraction of borrowed reserves from excess reserves. If the subtraction results in a positive number, the measure is called free reserves. If borrowed reserves are greater than excess reserves so that the subtraction produces a negative value, the measure is called net borrowed reserves. The free reserve measure was traditionally of great importance in the formulation of monetary policy; however, in recent years it has fallen out of favor because it was capable of producing misleading signals about the direction of monetary policy. In the 1950s and 1960s, free reserves were the intermediate target of open market operations, and changes in the level and trend of

free reserves were studied by observers of the Federal Reserve for indications of policy changes.

6. *Reserves available to support private nonbank deposits (RPDs)* is the most frequently employed reserve measure. The sample directive indicated that the operating target was stated in terms of the rate of growth of RPDs. Reserves available to support private nonbank deposits are the sum of required reserves for nongovernmental demand deposits, required reserves for total time and savings deposits, required reserves for nondeposit sources of funds subject to reserve requirements (Eurodollar loans, repurchase agreements, and bank holding company commercial paper), and excess reserves. The RPD measure excludes required reserves held against deposits of the federal government and other banks, since these deposits are volatile and policy should not be changed as a result of the changes in these deposits.

The monetary aggregates used in the directive are the familiar M_1 and M_2 measures of the money supply. M_3, which adds deposits at savings and loan associations and mutual savings banks to M_2, is also mentioned. Other unmentioned money supply measures are also watched by the Federal Reserve.

The other major monetary aggregate is the *adjusted credit proxy*. This is a comprehensive measure of the lending ability of the banking system and includes all bank liabilities subject to reserve requirements. Interbank deposits and government deposits are included as are nondeposit liabilities such as Eurodollar borrowings.

Indicators of Monetary Policy

The analysis of the Federal Reserve System's success in achieving its policy targets involves the study of many indicators. Observing the lagged values of the target variables is one approach. Calculating the changes in reserves available to support private nonbank deposits measures the degree to which the System is achieving the desired target and, before the actual target is known, provides some indication of the thinking of the Federal Open Market Committee.

Short-run indicators for the Federal Reserve's analysis of money market conditions include both reserve measures and interest rate measures. The most important reserve measures have already been covered. Interest rates that would indicate an easing or tightening of policy include the Federal Funds rate, the commercial paper rate, the three-month Treasury bill rate, the short-term certificate of deposit rate, and the Eurodollar rate.

These rates are all sensitive indicators of the impact of monetary policy because they represent the supply of and demand for those assets which the banks use to make short-run asset and liability adjustments. In asset management, the bank adjusts its holdings of Treasury bills or commercial paper in response to a loss of reserves. From the liability management side, a need for funds is reflected in higher rates for Federal Funds, certificates of deposit, and Eurodollars. Therefore, the rates that banks must pay to adjust their assets and liabilities indicate the impact of FOMC actions on the commercial banking system.

The indicator in the sample directive appears to be the level of the Federal Funds rate. A permitted range of fluctuation of the Federal Funds rate was specified. The FOMC assumed that if the Federal Funds rate fell below 5½ percent, the supply of reserves would be growing too rapidly, and if the Federal Funds rate rose about 6¾ percent, this would be an indication that reserves were increasing too slowly.

The desired Federal Funds rate is conditioned by a *proviso clause* in the next-to-last sentence of the directive which states that the Federal Funds rate can move within the range "depending upon the behavior of the monetary aggregates." In recent years, most directives have included such a proviso clause.

In summary, the sample directive is based on M_1 and M_2 as intermediate targets, on reserves for private deposits as the operating target, and on the Federal Funds rate as the indicator of policy. However, while policy is framed in terms of these variables, the System's emphasis is not that narrow, and all of the other variables are watched carefully.

The need for the variety of policy targets and indicators is a reflection of the fact that policy making is not an exact science and that the connections between the various measures are not perfect. It is also an indication of the difficulty of the task faced by both the FOMC and the manager of the Open Market Account.

The Sources of Information on Monetary Policy

The interested analyst of current monetary policy has access to many sources of information. Obviously, as the policy maker, the Federal Reserve System has the most detailed and current data. However, there are many publications available for those who wish to do some Monday morning quarterbacking.

The *Federal Reserve Bulletin,* published monthly by the Board of Governors, is the first source of information on monetary policy. The publication of the directive and the summary of the meetings of the FOMC, although not available immediately, provides the maximum available insight into the concerns and targets of the Federal Reserve System. Reading these statements gives one a feeling for the System's policy-making processes and decisions. Over time, the careful reader can see changes in policy taking place. The data in the *Bulletin* can be used to evaluate the degree to which the targets established in the FOMC statements were achieved and to assess the ultimate effects on the major macroeconomic variables.

The Federal Reserve System releases a variety of statements on a more frequent basis. *The Weekly Summary of Banking and Credit Measures* published on Fridays in the major financial newspapers summarizes current data on the targets and indicators of monetary policy. The observer of monetary policy can use these data to judge how well the Federal Reserve is doing in its attempts to hit the target. Table 8–14, "Changes in Member Bank Reserves," in Chapter 8, provides the data necessary for the short-term analysis of policy measures.

However, a word of caution should be added here. The linkages between variables in the monetary control process are not perfect and changes in short-run data cannot be expected to reflect accurately the intentions of the Federal Reserve System. Random variables, seasonal variables, Treasury financing actions, and any number of changes in the credit markets can affect the weekly data in ways that can confuse the interpretation of the data.

Other, less regular sources of information on current policy can be very helpful. Publications of the district Federal Reserve Banks deal with aspects of current policy. Speeches and congressional testimony by Federal Reserve System officials may yield some insight into current monetary policy thinking. However, Board members attempt to avoid revealing any information that could lead to profit-making opportunities for those possessing the knowledge.

Sources outside the Federal Reserve System are also helpful in attempting to interpret policy actions. "Bank letters" written by the economics departments of many of the major banks provide some insights into monetary policy. Some of the larger securities dealers and brokers also produce newsletters for their clients. In addition, the financial press covers daily economic news.

Nearly all of the material described above can be obtained free. Most Federal Reserve publications are made available at little or no cost. Those whose interest in monetary policy is so intense, or whose profit-making activities require a careful analysis of monetary policy trends or interest rate forecasts, can subscribe to a variety of private forecasting services that—for a price—provide general and specific types of information.

REVIEW QUESTIONS

1. Describe the organization of the Federal Open Market Committee. Should representatives of the Federal Reserve Banks be on this committee?

2. Evaluate the *FINE Discussion Principles*' recommendations for reform of the organization of the Federal Reserve System.

3. Why has the Federal Reserve System attempted to maintain policy secrecy? What rules currently apply with respect to the release of policy decisions?

4. Describe the World War II program of pegging the yields on government securities. What were the benefits and costs of this program during the war? after the war?

5. To what extent can Congress influence current monetary policy? Should Congress establish a target rate of growth of the money supply?

6. Distinguish between an operating target, an intermediate target, and an ultimate target of monetary policy.

7. What measures are the most generally watched indicators of monetary policy?

8. What is the proviso clause?

9. Briefly identify the various reserve measures that could be used as monetary policy targets.

10. Obtain the most recent copy of the *Federal Reserve Bulletin* and analyze the FOMC directive. Is the directive stated in terms of the same targets and indicators as were used in the directive quoted in this chapter?

SUGGESTED READINGS

G. L. Bach, *Making Monetary and Fiscal Policy.* Brookings Institution, Washington, D.C., 1971.

Karl Brunner, ed., *Targets and Indicators of Monetary Policy.* San Francisco: Chandler Publishing Co., 1969.

J. A. Cacy, "The Differential Behavior of M_1 and M_2," *Federal Reserve Bank of Kansas City Monthly Review,* July–August 1974, pp. 3–9.

Controlling Monetary Aggregates, Federal Reserve Bank of Boston, June 1969.

Jan Warren Duggar, "The Federal Open Market Committee's Proviso Clause: Usage and Analysis," *Journal of Finance,* American Finance Association, New York, September 1971, pp. 885–895.

Glossary: Weekly Federal Reserve Statements, Federal Reserve Bank of New York, October 1975.

Edward J. Kane, "New Congressional Restraints and Federal Reserve Independence," *Challenge,* International Arts & Sciences Press, New York, November–December 1975, pp. 37–44.

Paul Meek, "Nonborrowed Reserves or the Federal Funds Rate as Desk Targets—Is There a Difference?" *New England Economic Review,* Federal Reserve Bank of Boston, March–April 1975, pp. 31–47.

William Poole, "The Making of Monetary Policy: Description and Analysis," *New England Economic Review,* Federal Reserve Bank of Boston, March–April 1975, pp. 21–30.

John D. Rea, "Behavior of the Monetary Aggregates and the Implications for Monetary Policy," *Federal Reserve Bank of Kansas City Monthly Review,* September–October 1974, pp. 3–10.

Charlotte E. Ruebling, "RPDs and Other Reserve Operating Targets," *Federal Reserve Bank of St. Louis Review,* August 1972, pp. 2–7.

14

CONTROL OF THE MONEY SUPPLY: POLICY TOOLS AND THEIR IMPACT

The major tools of monetary policy—changing discount rates, changing reserve requirements, and open market operations—have been outlined in previous chapters. In the first three parts of this chapter, these tools[1] are considered in greater detail and their impact on the reserves available to the banking system is illustrated. The fourth part of the chapter describes the first effects of a change in monetary policy, effects that eventually lead to changes in the level of economic activity.

The Discounting Mechanism

The discount mechanism is the oldest tool of monetary policy.[2] The first function of the Federal Reserve System was to provide discounting facilities for commercial banks. Although there are variations in the procedures, discounting is the process by which the commercial bank borrows from the central bank.

In the early years of the Federal Reserve System, loans were rediscounted. Assume a merchant borrowed $100 from his bank to finance his store's inventory build-up. Typically, the bank would discount his note by deducting its interest charge from the face value of the note. Thus, if he borrowed $100 for one year at 6 percent, the discount would be $6 and he would receive $94. Naturally, he would repay $100; the bank collected its interest right off the top. Assume now that the bank wanted to borrow from the Federal Reserve Bank. The bank took the merchant's note to the Federal Reserve Bank and the bank borrowed against the

[1]Excellent sources on the tools of monetary policy include Joseph Aschheim, *Techniques of Monetary Control* (Baltimore, Md.: Johns Hopkins Press, 1961); Thomas Mayer, *Monetary Policy in the United States* (New York: Random House, 1968); and Warren L. Smith, "The Instruments of General Monetary Control," *National Banking Review,* vol. 1, no. 1 (September 1963), pp. 47–76.

[2]A comprehensive analysis of the history of the discounting function is Howard H. Hackley, *Lending Functions of the Federal Reserve Banks: A History,* Board of Governors of the Federal Reserve System, Washington, D.C., 1973.

loan. The note was discounted for the second time (rediscounted) by the Federal Reserve Bank. The rate at which the bank paid interest to the Federal Reserve was the rediscount rate.

After the first few years of the System's operation, the Federal Reserve Banks were given the right to make advances to the member banks. An *advance* is a direct loan to the bank; the bank gives the Federal Reserve Bank its own note. The assets of the borrowing bank—usually its Treasury bill holdings—are pledged as security for the loan.

The Federal Reserve System was established to provide mechanisms for averting liquidity crises and for increasing the elasticity of the money supply. Prior to 1914, the banks' attempts to increase their liquidity forced a reduction in new loans or the calling in of existing loans. (Some loans are made on a *call* basis as opposed to bearing a fixed maturity date. The lender can "call" upon the borrower to repay within a day. Security dealers and brokers are the most frequent users of these loans.) Borrowers left without a source of funds were forced to liquidate their assets rapidly and the rush to liquidity spread. The Federal Reserve System was designed to alleviate this problem. By rediscounting loans at the Federal Reserve Bank, a commercial bank could increase its cash holdings and meet deposit withdrawals. By lending to the individual bank, the Federal Reserve System could avert the spread of a liquidity crisis.

As indicated in Chapter 2, under the National Banking System the money supply did not change with the demand for money. The Federal Reserve System could permit the expansion of the currency supply by providing the banks with Federal Reserve notes as the proceeds of a rediscount loan. Thus, a bank could obtain currency to satisfy a withdrawal of deposits or could obtain added reserves to expand its lending and meet its customers' credit needs.

The establishment of the discount window was related to the commercial credit theory of bank lending. This theory, also known as the "real bills doctrine," was described in Chapter 5. By rediscounting loans, the Federal Reserve Banks would be providing for the financing of real business activity. The supply of credit would be expanded to meet the needs of business. As business credit needs increased, the banks would submit more loans for rediscounting and obtain added reserves to meet the expanded demand for credit. If the demand for credit decreased, banks would repay their rediscount loans and the volume of outstanding currency or bank reserves would decrease.

In the early years of the Federal Reserve System, the discount window was the major source of Reserve Bank credit. As Table 14–1 indicates, during the 1920–1927 period, 59 percent of total reserve bank credit was provided by the discounting mechanism. After the mid-1930s, open market operations became the most important policy tool. Now float accounts for more Reserve Bank credit than does discounting. The low level of discounting after the mid-1930s reflects the fact that open market operations had created a large volume of excess reserves and had greatly reduced the need to borrow. The expansion of reserves during the 1930s,

TABLE 14–1 Sources of Reserve Bank Credit (percent of total)

PERIOD	*OPEN MARKET OPERATIONS*	*DISCOUNTING*	*FLOAT*	*TOTAL*
1920–1927	37	59	4	100
1928–1933	65	33	2	100
1934–1944	96	1	3	100
1945–1950	97	1	2	100
1951–1953	95	2	3	100
1954–1959	95	2	3	100
1960–1966	95	1	4	100

SOURCE: "Report of a System Committee," *Reappraisal of the Federal Reserve Discount Mechanism,* vol. 1, Board of Governors of the Federal Reserve System, Washington, 1971, p.6.

the creation of new reserves in the process of financing World War II, and the Federal Reserve's support of government bond prices in the early postwar period reduced the banks' needs to borrow until well into the 1950s.

In the period after the 1951 Treasury–Federal Reserve Accord, discounting activity increased but discounting never regained its pre-Depression role.

The Discount Mechanism after the Accord

In the post-Accord period, the discount window became a source of short-term adjustment credit for the member banks. Control of the supply of credit was exercised by open market operations, the supply of currency was no longer inelastic, and the problem of liquidity crises had ended. Therefore, the original functions of the discount window had been eliminated or replaced, and discounting became a means for individual banks to obtain added reserves.

The effect of discounting on the balance sheet of the borrowing bank was illustrated in Table 8–2. The member bank has an added asset—reserve balances at the Federal Reserve. The bank has a new liability—its note to the Federal Reserve. On the balance sheet of the Federal Reserve Bank, the asset entry is the note of the borrowing bank and the liability entry is the addition to the reserve balance of the borrowing bank. The lending rate is the discount rate.

Other features of the discount process are important. First, credit is intended to be of a short-term nature. The Federal Reserve was not designed to make long-term loans to banks. The duration of the usual loan is 15 days or less. Renewals are permitted under the increasingly watchful supervision of the lending Federal Reserve Bank.

Second, access to the discount window by the member banks is a privilege and not a right. Membership in the System never guaranteed the right to borrow—only the application right is attached to membership. However, most initial applications to borrow are approved.

Third, the banks have held—and the Federal Reserve has encouraged them to hold—a tradition of reluctance to be in debt to the Federal Reserve System. This form of nonprice rationing has permitted the Federal Reserve to hold the discount rate at a low level without bringing about floods of borrowing requests. The longer a bank remains in debt, the more influence the System has on its asset management policies. The banks are reluctant to subject themselves to this supervision and are convinced that if they abuse the borrowing privilege, the discount window eventually will be closed on their fingers.

Fourth, most discount loans are for short-term portfolio adjustment purposes. Banks borrow in order to meet loan demands without liquidating securities. Banks, like other investors, do not like to sell securities at a loss. Thus, when faced with the option of either borrowing to meet added loan demands or selling government securities at a loss, many prefer to borrow and avoid or delay taking a loss in their securities account. However, the Federal Reserve does not regard the discount window as a means of allowing the banks to postpone indefinitely the realization of securities losses and attempts to limit borrowing for this purpose. Temporary credit is usually provided, but eventually the bank is forced either to restrict lending or sell securities to repay its debt.

During the 1960s, bank use of the discount window declined as the scope and volume of activity in the Federal Funds market increased. For part of the period, the Federal Funds rate was lower than the discount rate, and the banks shifted to the lower cost market. However, even when the Federal Funds rate rose above the discount rate, the banks continued to use the Federal Funds market, and other sources of funds, rather than the discount window.

The New Discount Mechanism

In the face of declining demand at the discount window, the Federal Reserve System established a committee to reappraise the functions of the discount mechanism. The 1968 report of the committee[3] suggested substantial changes in the role of the discounting function. The form and details proposed for the redesigned discount window are presented in Table 14–2.

As the table indicates, the first part of the lending to member banks was termed a *basic borrowing privilege*. Unlike the traditional lending process, the basic borrowing privilege would have made access to limited amounts of reserve bank credit automatic. This change would have represented a substantial deviation from the historical concept of borrowing as a privilege rather than a right. Note that a bank could have been drawing upon its basic line of credit at the Federal Reserve

[3]A summary of the report can be found in "Reappraisal of the Federal Reserve Discount Mechanism," *Federal Reserve Bulletin,* July 1968, pp. 545–551.

TABLE 14–2 Summary of Proposal of Redesign of Discount Mechanism

ITEM	BASIC BORROWING PRIVILEGE (1)	OTHER ADJUSTMENT CREDIT (2)	SEASONAL BORROWING PRIVILEGE (3)	EMERGENCY CREDIT TO MEMBER BANKS (4)	EMERGENCY CREDIT TO OTHERS (5)
Definition	Member bank access to credit upon request, within precisely stated limits on amounts and frequency and on specified conditions.	Supplemental discount accommodation, subject to administrative procedures, to help a member bank meet temporary needs that prove either larger or longer in duration than could be covered by its basic borrowing privilege.	Member bank access to credit on a longer-term and, to the extent possible, prearranged basis to meet demonstrable seasonal pressures exceeding minimum duration and relative amount.	Credit extended to member banks in unusual or exigent circumstances.	Credit extended to institutions other than member banks in emergency circumstances in fulfilling role as lender of last resort to the economy.
Rate	Discount rate.	Discount rate.	Discount rate.	Discount rate.	Significantly higher rate than discount rate.
Quantity limitations	___(20–40) percent of first $1 million capital stock and surplus plus ___(10–20) percent of next $9 million, plus ___(10) percent of remainder.	None specified.	Seasonal needs in excess of (5–10) percent of average deposits subject to reserve requirements in preceding calendar year.	None specified.	None specified.
Frequency or duration limitations	___(6–13) of any ___(13–26) consecutive reserve computation periods.	None specified.	Need and arrangement must be for more than 4 weeks. Maximum 9 consecutive months.	None specified.	None specified.
Administrative procedures	None other than general discouragement of net selling of Federal funds by borrowing banks.	Appraisal and, where necessary, action broadly similar to procedures developed under existing discount arrangements.	Prearrangement involves discussion between discount officer and bank management concerning amount, duration, and seasonality of need. Administrative review maintained during borrowing to prevent abuse or misuse.	Continuous and thoroughgoing surveillance. Require that bank develop and pursue workable program for alleviating difficulties.	Continuous and thoroughgoing surveillance (may have to be through conduit). Require that institution develop and pursue workable program for alleviating difficulties.
Other restrictions	Must not have been found to be in unsatisfactory condition.	None specified.	None specified.	None specified.	Required to use all other practicable sources of credit first.
Method of provision	Direct.	Direct.	Direct.	Direct.	(1) through central agency; (2) direct; (3) conduit through member bank.

SOURCE: "Reappraisal of the Federal Reserve Discount Mechanism," *Federal Reserve Bulletin,* July 1968, p. 551.

during one-half of the reserve computation periods. Under the current system, very few banks are allowed to borrow that frequently. The basic borrowing privilege concept was not adopted by the Federal Reserve System.

The second category, *other adjustment credit*, would have been the most comparable to the traditional discount window. The bank would have applied for credit and would have been subject to administrative supervision. This credit would have been in addition to borrowing under the basic borrowing privilege. Given that the basic borrowing privilege was not adopted, the changes involved in this category were not required.

The *seasonal borrowing privilege* was formally implemented[4] in 1973 and presents the opportunity for relatively long-term loans—up to nine consecutive months—for banks experiencing seasonal demands for credit and unable to obtain necessary funds in the money markets. In this case, the required quantity of borrowing from the Federal Reserve Bank is established before the need arises on the basis of past deposit and loan data. Note that the requirement for seasonal borrowing eligibility, only 5 to 10 percent of average deposits, is relatively low. A very large portion of member banks should be able to demonstrate a seasonal pattern of deposit fluctuation of at least this magnitude.

The fourth category, *emergency credit to member banks* (implemented in 1973), is limited to the (hopefully) infrequent cases in which the maintenance of the solvency of a given bank requires substantial borrowing from the Federal Reserve System. In this case, as the description indicates, surveillance is "continuous and thoroughgoing."

The final category, *emergency credit to others* (implemented in 1973), was a new concept. Traditional central banking practice limited access to the discount window to member institutions. However, during periods of financial disintermediation in 1966, 1969, and the 1970s, outflows of deposits from nonbank financial intermediaries—especially savings and loan associations—threatened the solvency of these institutions. Failures in the savings and loan industry would have increased fears about the solvency of the entire financial system and could have led to other failures.

The Federal Reserve, as the lender of last resort, recognized its ultimate responsibility for the solvency of the entire financial system. Thus, procedures were designed by which the Federal Reserve can lend to nonmember institutions on an emergency basis. This lending can be done either directly by the Federal Reserve or through a member commercial bank. Under the latter arrangement, the Federal Reserve can lend to a member commercial bank with the understanding that the borrowing bank will relend the funds to the endangered nonbank financial intermediary.

Are there merits to the new discounting proposals or do these new systems represent an attempt by the Federal Reserve System to "get back business" previously lost to the Federal Funds, Eurodollar, and other markets? There is no problem on the question of emergency credit; this is a necessary function for a central bank responsible for preserving the liquidity and solvency of the financial system. The only reservation in this regard is the extent to which the Federal Reserve System should extend credit to a bank that is in danger of failing because of poor management practices. The massive lending effort involved in the 1974 attempt to rescue Franklin National Bank is an example of this problem. Given that depositors are protected, should poorly managed banks be saved?[5]

Questions can also be raised relative to the seasonal borrowing privilege.

[4]For the change in the discounting regulations governing seasonal borrowing and emergency credit, see *Federal Reserve Bulletin,* May 1973, pp. 353–354.

[5]On this issue, see A. Dale Tussing, "The Case for Bank Failure," *Journal of Law and Economics,* October 1967, pp. 129–147.

The provision of reserves for up to nine months every year (as long as the bank can demonstrate a relatively small seasonal deposit pattern) comes very close to providing low-cost capital to the banks. A greater seasonal pattern of deposit fluctuations should be required for this type of lending by the Federal Reserve, and banks should be encouraged to meet their needs for funds in the money or capital markets. General nationwide seasonal patterns of reserve needs are met by open market operations, so there may be little need for the seasonal discounting program.

The seasonal borrowing and emergency credit provisions do not significantly affect the ability of the Federal Reserve System to control the quantity of bank reserves. Open market operations can be designed to allow for reserve lending under these programs.

Criticisms of the Concept of Discounting

Beyond the specifics of the revision of the discount window, more basic questions can be raised about the role of discounting. One could argue that the basic functions of the discount process have been taken over by the Federal Funds market, and thus discounting could be eliminated with no loss to the monetary system.

Comparison of the Federal Funds market with the discounting mechanism reveals several interesting factors. The discount window provides reserves for a longer period of time and at an interest rate that is usually lower than the Federal Funds rate (except in those now infrequent periods when reserves are very plentiful). Borrowing at the discount window requires that the bank apply for a loan and convince the Federal Reserve Bank of the need to borrow. The supervisory element involved in borrowing from the Federal Reserve Banks is considered to be one of the factors responsible for the growth of the Federal Funds market; many banks appear to be willing to borrow at the higher Federal Funds rate to avoid Federal Reserve supervision.

The Federal Funds rate is a market-determined rate that changes daily; the discount rate is an administered price that is changed infrequently. The banker's choice of the two markets may be affected by the degree to which the discount rate is out of step with other interest rates. For example, in a period of tight money and rapidly rising interest rates, the Federal Funds rate will increase along with other interest rates. Unless the Federal Reserve Banks move promptly to increase the discount rate, the advantage of borrowing at the discount window increases.

There are restrictions on the use of funds obtained at the discount window which do not apply to the use of reserves borrowed in the Federal Funds market. For example, banks are not allowed to use discount window funds to speculate on the future price of government securities and banks borrowing from the Federal Reserve Banks should not be net sellers of Federal Funds. These constraints may limit the desirability of borrowing from the Federal Reserve as opposed to the Federal Funds market.

The final difference between discounting and the Federal Funds market is the fact that discounting increases the total volume of reserves available to the banking system. The bank that obtains a loan from the Federal Reserve has greater reserves; no other bank loses reserves as part of the transaction. In the Federal Funds market, no new reserves are created. The borrowing bank has more reserves, but the lending bank has fewer reserves. Thus, although the Federal Funds market can be a lender of last resort for an individual bank, only the discount window can serve as a lender of last resort for the entire financial system. In normal times, the Federal Funds market can replace the discount window. However, if all banks desired to increase their reserves, the supply of reserves to the Federal Funds market would decrease to zero. By this line of thought, the discount window should at least be retained for emergency use.

Another criticism of the discounting process centers around the administration of the discount rate. Past levels of the discount rate appear in Table 14–3. Historically, the discount rate has been changed too infrequently and has often been too low relative to market rates of interest. For example, during 1974, the Federal Funds rate averaged approximately 10½ percent; the discount rate did not go above 8 percent. While the monthly averages of the daily Federal Funds rate ranged from a low of 8.53 percent to a high of 12.92 percent, the discount rate ranged between 7½ and 8 percent. Although this example does include a period of extremely high interest rates, the relationship of the two rates is typical of a tight money period.

From the point of view of those attempting to analyze monetary policy, changes in the discount rate are difficult to interpret. An increase in the discount rate may mean one of two things. First, a discount rate increase may signal a tightening of monetary policy; the Federal Reserve System may wish to discourage borrowing by raising the price of borrowed reserves. Alternatively, the increase in the discount rate may be a technical change intended merely to bring the discount rate into line with other interest rates. In a period of rising interest rates, there is an increase in the difference between market rates—such as the Treasury bill rate—and the discount rate. When the difference becomes too large, the discount rate is increased to reduce the gap. No change in monetary policy is intended; this is merely a technical adjustment of the discount rate.

Traditionally, the discount rate has been a "follower" rather than a "leader." Changes in the discount rate are made to bring the discount rate into closer alignment with other interest rates. In the traditional British system, *bank rate* (the term for the discount rate in England) moves ahead of other interest rates. An increase in bank rate signals the money markets that higher interest rates are desired by the Bank of England (the central bank).

From the standpoint of an effective monetary policy, discounting represents a means for some banks to regain reserves lost through open market operations. In this sense, the discount window represents slippage in the process of controlling the supply of reserves. Total reserves are not changed if the Federal Reserve Banks lend an amount of reserves equal to the reserves taken away by open market operations.

TABLE 14–3 The Discount Rate (percent per annum)

EFFECTIVE DATE	*RANGE (OR LEVEL)– ALL F.R. BANKS*	*F.R. BANK OF N.Y.*
In effect Dec. 31, 1955	2½	2½
1956—Apr. 13	2½–3	2¾
20	2¾–3	2¾
Aug. 24	2¾–3	3
31	3	3
1957—Aug. 9	3 –3½	3
23	3½	3½
Nov. 15	3 –3½	3
Dec. 2	3	3
1958—Jan. 22	2¾–3	3
24	2¾–3	2¾
Mar. 7	2¼–3	2¼
13	2¼–2¾	2¼
21	2¼	2¼
Apr. 18	1¾–2¼	1¾
May 9	1¾	1¾
Aug. 15	1¾–2	1¾
Sept. 12	1¾–2	2
23	2	2
Oct. 24	2 –2½	2
Nov. 7	2½	2½
1959—Mar. 6	2½–3	3
16	3	3
May 29	3 –3½	3½
June 12	3½	3½
Sept. 11	3½–4	4
18	4	4
1960—June 3	3½–4	4
10	3½–4	3½
14	3½	3½
Aug. 12	3 –3½	3
Sept. 9	3	3
1963—July 17	3 –3½	3½
26	3½	3½

EFFECTIVE DATE	*RANGE (OR LEVEL)– ALL F.R. BANKS*	*F.R. BANK OF N.Y.*
1964—Nov. 24	3½–4	4
30	4	4
1965—Dec. 6	4 –4½	4½
13	4½	4½
1967—Apr. 7	4 –4½	4
14	4	4
Nov. 20	4 –4½	4½
27	4½	4½
1968—Mar. 15	4½–5	4½
22	5	5
Apr. 19	5 –5½	5½
26	5½	5½
Aug. 16	5¼–5½	5½
30	5¼	5¼
Dec. 18	5¼–5½	5½
20	5½	5½
1969—Apr. 4	5½–6	6
8	6	6
1970—Nov. 11	5¾–6	6
13	5¾–6	5¾
16	5¾	5¾
Dec. 1	5½–5¾	5¾
4	5½–5¾	5½
11	5½	5½
1971—Jan. 8	5¼–5½	5¼
15	5¼	5¼
19	5 –5¼	5¼
22	5 –5¼	5
29	5	5
Feb. 13	4¾–5	5
19	4¾	4¾
July 16	4¾–5	5
23	5	5

EFFECTIVE DATE	*RANGE (OR LEVEL)– ALL F.R. BANKS*	*F.R. BANK OF N.Y.*
1971—Nov. 11	4¾–5	5
19	4¾	4¾
Dec. 13	4½–4¾	4¾
17	4½–4¾	4½
24	4½	4½
1973—Jan. 15	5	5
Feb. 26	5 –5½	5½
Mar. 2	5½	5½
Apr. 23	5½–5¾	5½
May 4	5¾	5¾
11	5¾–6	6
18	6	6
June 11	6 –6½	6½
15	6½	6½
July 2	7	7
Aug. 14	7 –7½	7½
23	7½	7½
1974—Apr. 25	7½–8	8
30	8	8
Dec. 9	7¾–8	7¾
16	7¾	7¾
1975—Jan. 6	7¼–7¾	7¾
10	7¼–7¾	7¼
24	7¼	7¼
Feb. 5	6¾–7¼	6¾
7	6¾	6¾
Mar. 10	6¼–6¾	6¼
14	6¼	6¼
May 16	6 –6¼	6
23	6	6
In effect, Nov. 30, 1975	6	6

SOURCE: *Federal Reserve Bulletin,* December 1975, p. A6.

The replacement at the discount window of reserves lost by open market operations is not a serious problem. Only a portion of the banks losing reserves will apply at the discount window. Even if the reserves are regained at the discount window, borrowed reserves are not the same as unborrowed reserves; the borrowing bank knows that the loan must be repaid. The Federal Reserve Bank would justify the loan on the basis that the borrowing bank needs time to adjust its assets and liabilities to meet reserve requirements.

A Summary Evaluation of the Discount Window

After considering the evidence on the role of the discount window, the author must conclude that substantial changes are desirable. However, the changes needed are not those outlined in Table 14–2. Except for true emergency credit, the financial system can operate without a discount mechanism. The traditional customers of the window have demonstrated that, even at substantially higher interest rates, they prefer the other markets.

The only function of discounting which cannot be taken over by the Federal Funds market is that of the role of lender of last resort. Thus, the window should be kept available for banks experiencing real difficulties. Other than that, the banks are perfectly capable of finding their own adjustment credit. Recourse to the Federal Funds market is available to all banks, either directly or through their city correspondents. The discount window was established when the banks held few highly liquid assets; the modern commercial bank can adjust its reserve position by the sale of Treasury bills. If a sale of Treasury bills requires the bank to take a capital loss, so be it. The Federal Reserve System was not established to protect the banks from ever having to incur a loss on the sale of assets.

Substantial changes in the administration of the discount rate are necessary. The discount rate should not be the "bargain basement" interest rate. If banks are to be permitted to borrow from the Federal Reserve System, they should pay a realistic price for the borrowed reserves. The discount rate should be tied to a market rate of interest. Despite contrary expressions of intent, the Federal Reserve does not keep the discount rate in line with market-determined rates of interest. With a tied rate, a rule would be established to determine the discount rate. One possible rule would be to announce that the discount rate will always be equal to the Treasury bill rate plus two percentage points. As the Treasury bill rate fluctuated, the discount rate would also change. This rule would keep the discount rate in line with other rates of interest and relieve the System of the responsibility of periodically changing the rate.[6]

If the discount mechanism were limited to lending only to those banks experiencing real adjustment difficulties and lending at rates in excess of market

[6]Warren L. Smith, "The Instruments of General Monetary Control," *National Banking Review,* vol. 1, no. 1 Comptroller of the Currency, Washington, D.C., September 1963, pp. 65–66.

rates of interest, the basic traditional function of a central bank would be preserved, the incentives to borrow would be reduced, and the efficiency of open market operations would probably be increased.

Reserve Requirements

One of the oldest features of bank regulation is the requirement that banks hold reserves against deposits. The original intention of reserve requirements was to ensure the safety of depositors' funds. The National Banking Act of 1864 established reserve requirements for the newly formed national banks.

The concept of varying reserve requirements as a tool of monetary policy was incorporated in the Banking Act of 1935. The Board of Governors of the Federal Reserve System was given the power to alter member bank reserve requirements within a fixed legal range.

Traditionally, reserve requirements varied on the basis of a geographical classification of banks. Banks in central reserve cities (New York, Chicago, and St. Louis) were subject to the highest reserve requirements. Banks in other reserve bank cities were subject to lower reserve requirement levels. All other banks, called country banks, were subject to the lowest reserve requirements. This classification system recognized the role of correspondent banking relationships. Each bank held correspondent deposits in banks in larger cities. Thus, if a country bank needed funds it drew upon its balances in a city bank, the city bank drew upon its balances in a larger city, and so on. Ultimately, the pressure was concentrated on the major banks in New York and Chicago. Therefore, because banks in larger cities tended to have large correspondent deposits, these major banks were required to hold greater reserves.

In 1962, the central reserve city designation was dropped and only two categories—reserve city and country—were used. In 1972, the system was again modified and the flat percentage reserve requirements were replaced with a graduated system of reserve requirements; as deposits increase, the reserve requirement applicable to the added deposits also increases. Under the current system, banks having in excess of $400 million of demand deposits are classified as reserve city banks. Current member bank reserve requirements are indicated in Table 14–4. The same schedule of reserve requirements, based on graduated marginal rates, applies to all member banks. A member bank must hold as reserves 7½ percent of its first $2 million of demand deposits; 10 percent of the next $8 million of deposits is held as reserves; 12 percent of the next $90 million; 13 percent of the next $300 million and 16½ percent of all demand deposits over $400 million must be held as reserve balances.

Time deposits are subject to much lower reserve requirements than demand deposits. Demand deposits are transactions balances and turn over rapidly. Time deposits represent either personal savings deposits—funds that people do not

TABLE 14–4 Reserve Requirements on Deposits of Member Banks (deposit intervals in millions of dollars; requirements in percent of deposits)

EFFECTIVE DATE	NET DEMAND					TIME					
							OTHER TIME				
	0–2	2–10	10–100	100–400	Over 400	Savings	0–5, Maturing in—		Over 5, Maturing in—		
							Less than 4 years	4 years or more	30–179 days	180 days to 4 years	4 years or more
1972—Nov. 9	8	10	12	16½	17½	3	3			5	
Nov. 16				13							
1973—July 19		10½	12½	13½	18						
1974—Dec. 12					17½				6	3	
1975—Feb. 13	7½	10	12	13	16½						
Oct. 30							3		1		3
1											
In effect Nov. 30, 1975.	7½	10	12	13	16½	3	3	1	6	3	1

Present legal limits:	Minimum	Maximum
Net demand deposits, reserve city banks	10	22
Net demand deposits, other banks	7	14
Time deposits	3	10

SOURCE: *Federal Reserve Bulletin*, December 1975, p. A7.

TABLE 14–5 Effect of Reduction of Reserve Requirement

MEMBER BANK (before)		*MEMBER BANK (after)*	
Assets	*Liabilities*	*Assets*	*Liabilities*
Reserves $16.50	Demand Deposits $100	Reserves $16.50	Demand Deposits $100
(Required $16.50)		(Required $15.50)	
(Excess $ 0)		(Excess $ 1.00)	
	Capital		*Capital*

intend to spend immediately—or other time deposits that have been placed in the bank with the agreement that they will be left on deposit for some fixed period of time. Thus, the turnover, or withdrawal rate, of time and savings deposits is lower than the turnover rate of demand deposits; the lower withdrawal rate justifies the lower reserve requirements on time deposits.

As indicated in Chapter 4, the Federal Reserve has imposed reserve requirements on sources of funds other than demand and time deposits. The use of reserve requirements against Eurodollar deposits, repurchase agreements, and holding company commercial paper is designed more to control these specific activities than as a general instrument of monetary policy. Thus, the discussion of reserve requirements in this section is confined to its traditional function.

Reserve Requirements as a Policy Tool

The balance sheet effect of a decrease in reserve requirements is easily illustrated. Actually, the entries do not change; only the breakdown of the reserve balances changes. Table 14–5 shows the impact of a reserve requirement decrease on a typical member bank. Before the decrease in the reserve requirement, the member bank is holding the required 16½ percent of demand deposits as reserves; excess reserves are zero. Assume that the reserve requirement is lowered to 15½ percent of demand deposits. The bank's reserve account does not change, but the bank now has $1 of excess reserves. As the money supply expansion examples in Chapter 8 demonstrated, the individual bank can expand its deposit-creating and lending activity by an amount equal to its excess reserves. Thus, a lowering of reserve requirements increases the excess reserves of all member banks and permits an expansion of bank lending.

In considering reserve requirements as a policy tool, the most important point is the large impact of even a small change in reserve requirements. Either liquid assets must be sold, lending activity reduced, or borrowed funds obtained to satisfy the higher requirement. Banks that do not meet the reserve requirement are fined; however, the banks are given advance notice of the change in requirements to allow time for portfolio readjustment.

A variation of the reserve requirement is the only tool of monetary policy that has a simultaneous effect on all member banks. A change in the discount rate hits only those banks that actually borrow from the Federal Reserve Banks. Open market operations affect the major money market banks first. Outside the money market centers, the reduced availability of reserves is felt with a time lag. Although every member bank is affected by a change in reserve requirements at the same time, not all banks are affected to the same degree. Many banks, especially smaller rural banks, usually have excess reserves. For these banks, the higher reserve requirements mean more required reserves and fewer excess reserves. The larger banks are more apt to be profit maximizers and hold no excess reserves; these banks are the ones that must adjust to the higher reserve levels most rapidly.

Another basic fact about variations of reserve requirements is the infrequency with which this most powerful of monetary tools is actually employed by the Federal Reserve. As Table 14–4 indicates, reserve requirements have seldom been increased or decreased. Given the power of this tool, why has it not been used more often? Actually, its power *is* the basic reason it is not used more frequently. A change of one-half of a percentage point takes away or supplies a large volume of reserves; usually the Federal Reserve does not need to change policy so drastically. However, there is no reason why changes in requirements could not be made in fractions smaller than one-half of 1 percent.

There is a desire to avoid very frequent alterations of reserve requirements. Changes could not, and should not, be made on a daily or weekly basis; bank planning would be made even more difficult. Variations of reserve requirements also clearly affect bank profitability. An increase in reserve requirements means that the bank must hold a higher percentage of its assets in nonearning deposits at its Federal Reserve Bank. A lower proportion of total assets is available for lending or investing. The effect on the profit margin of the bank is clear to the banker—much clearer than the effect of open market operations. An increase in reserve requirements creates a clear profit-making incentive for the bank to leave the Federal Reserve System and take advantage of generally lower—and seldom changed—state reserve requirements.

Given the infrequency with which reserve requirements are altered, their interpretation is very simple. A technical change is seldom necessary, and virtually all variations in reserve requirements can be interpreted as indicating significant modifications of monetary policy. Higher reserve requirements mean a significantly tighter monetary policy, and reduced requirements mean an easier monetary policy.

Reserve requirement increases or decreases are usually moderated in effect by the use of discounting and open market operations. Given that an increase in reserve requirements has such a great impact on bank reserve positions, a change in requirements is gradually eased into effect. Discounting policy is liberalized at the time of the increase of reserve requirements and open market policy supplies some added reserves to the banking system. Most banks react to the need for added reserves by selling government securities, and the Federal Reserve's failure to make open market purchases would mean sharp declines of government security prices. Therefore, the Open Market Account buys Treasury bills and supplies new reserves to the banking system. Then, after the new reserve requirements are in effect, the transition reserves supplied through the discount window and by open market operations are gradually withdrawn by not renewing discount loans and by open market sales of Treasury bills.

Finally, a change in the level of reserve requirements may have an effect on the risk-assuming behavior of the banking system. Assume that reserve requirements are increased; the bank's ratio of earning to nonearning assets decreases as a higher proportion of assets becomes nonearning deposits at the Federal Reserve Banks. If the bank is attempting to earn a given rate of return on its total assets, a higher return must be earned on the smaller volume of earning assets. To increase the rate of return on assets, a greater degree of risk must be assumed. This change in the degree of risk assumption may involve either an increase in higher risk loans or a decrease in short-term liquid assets and an increase in loans. In either event, the average degree of risk assumption increases.[7]

Alternative Reserve Requirement Systems

Various proposals have been made to change the reserve requirement system. A simple solution would be to set the reserve requirement at a given level and forget it. With reserve requirement variations seldom made, this proposal is not really very far from the present situation. The logic of this proposal is that open market operations can do anything changes in the reserve requirement can do, and open market operations can do it more efficiently.[8] This proposal, however, gives up the advantages that could be obtained by creating a better reserve requirement system.

The opposite extreme would employ more frequent, but smaller, reserve requirement changes. Even the smallest of banks can afford a calculator and could determine its appropriate quantity of reserves if the reserve requirement were stated to two or three decimal places. Small changes in reserve requirements could be used to make the major proportion of a desired change in reserve availability; then open market operations could be used to bring the level of reserves to the exact target figure. Open market operations would become the tool for fine-tuning the level of reserves. This plan can be opposed on the grounds that reserve requirements would be changing too frequently to permit efficient bank planning.

In the 1930s, some economists—mainly at the University of Chicago—proposed a plan that would have required 100 percent reserves against demand

[7]Aschheim, *Techniques of Monetary Control,* op. cit., pp. 19–32.

[8]Milton Friedman, *A Program for Monetary Stability* (New York: Fordham University Press, 1959), pp. 50–51.

deposits.[9] An institution holding demand deposit balances would have held reserves exactly equal to its demand deposit liabilities. This plan would have drastically changed the organization of banking by separating the checking account system from all other banking activities. With 100 percent reserves behind demand deposits, demand deposit accounts would have been perfectly safe. The lending, investing, and other activities of institutions offering demand deposit accounts would have been taken over by other institutions. Interest in this plan diminished with the institution of federal deposit insurance. In addition, the plan would have eliminated the multiple expansion of demand deposits and improved the Federal Reserve's ability to control the money supply.

The payment of interest on reserve deposits is an idea that appeals to member banks.[10] This change would make membership in the System more attractive to the banks. However, a significant portion of the income from the Federal Reserve System's portfolio would go to the member banks rather than reverting to the United States Treasury. Economics aside, this idea would only be popular with the banks and would stand little chance in the Congress. Nevertheless, in terms of controlling the expansion of the money supply, the idea does have some merit. By increasing or decreasing the rate paid on reserve deposits, the Federal Reserve would be better able to influence the banks' decisions on holding excess reserves as opposed to using the excess reserves to grant new loans. This system would influence the use of *excess reserves* at the cost of paying interest on *total reserves*. A better case can be made for the payment of interest on excess reserves. However, given the efficiency of the Federal Funds market, the banks can already earn interest on their excess reserves.

Proposals have been made to base reserve requirements on assets rather than on deposits.[11] This approach would argue that the need for reserves arises from the risk and degree of liquidity of the bank's asset holdings rather than from the deposits. Under a plan of this sort, each type of asset would be judged according to its liquidity and riskiness, and an appropriate reserve requirement would be imposed. As the banking system switched from liquid assets to business loans in a period of economic expansion, the average level of reserve requirements would increase, and lending activity would be gradually constrained. The complexity of the grading of assets is the greatest drawback of this plan. This proposal would not ensure the liquidity of the bank; the holding of reserves does not per se guarantee that the bank will have funds on hand to meet deposit outflows.

One suggested variant of the asset reserve plan would place reserve

[9] For a summary of this plan, see Albert G. Hart, "The 'Chicago Plan' of Banking Reform," *Review of Economic Studies,* vol. 2 (1935), pp. 104–116. The article is reprinted in F. A. Lutz and L. W. Mints, eds., *Readings in Monetary Theory* (Homewood, Ill.: Richard D. Irwin, 1951), pp. 437–456.

[10] James Tobin, "Towards Improving the Efficiency of the Monetary Mechanism," *Review of Economics and Statistics,* vol. XLII (August 1960), pp. 276–279.

[11] Jacob Viner, letter to the editor, *New York Times,* April 22, 1951, p. 10E.

requirements on the assets according to the social desirability of the particular asset.[12] The value to society of various types of lending would be used to establish reserve levels. For example, one might judge a home mortgage to a low-income family to have a higher social value than a loan to a securities dealer. Thus, the reserve requirement against the home loan would be lower than the reserve requirement against the securities loan. This plan is considered in Chapter 19 as a system for the allocation of credit.

Finally, the author's preferred system,[13] commonly used in other countries, involves both a cash reserve ratio and a liquidity reserve ratio. Under this system, the banks would be required to hold a relatively low cash reserve deposit at the central bank. This portion of the reserve requirement would be the same as under the current system except that the reserve percentage would be lower. In addition to the low cash reserve requirement, which usually would not change for monetary policy purposes, there would be a *variable liquidity reserve ratio*. In this second portion of the reserve requirement, the member bank would be obligated to hold a given proportion of deposits in the form of liquid assets. The variation of the liquidity ratio would be the monetary policy tool.

The variable liquidity reserve system would limit the bank's ability to switch from liquid assets to relatively illiquid loans during periods of high loan demand. Under the present system, the banks must hold a large percentage of their deposits as nonearning reserves. However, beyond meeting that reserve requirement, the bank is free to become as illiquid as the examiners will allow. Given its natural desire not to say "no" to a regular loan customer and the desire to expand profits, the bank sells off liquid assets in order to meet business loan demands. With the institution of a liquidity ratio requirement, limits would be placed on this temptation to switch to loans. The Federal Reserve System would vary the liquidity reserve ratio in order to protect the banking system from illiquidity and to curb the expansion of credit.

The combination of cash and liquid asset reserve requirements would strengthen monetary policy. The cash reserve requirement could be varied to change the quantity of reserves available to the banking system, and the liquidity reserve ratio could be changed to control the expansion of bank lending activity in periods of high loan demand.

In summary, the Federal Reserve has minimized changes in reserve requirements. Under a different reserve requirement system, this tool could be a much more useful and effective part of monetary policy.

[12]Lester C. Thurow, "Proposals for Rechanneling Funds to Meet Social Priorities," *Policies for a More Competitive Financial System,* Federal Reserve Bank of Boston, 1972, pp. 179–189.

[13]See Warren L. Smith, "Reserve Requirements in the American Monetary System," *Monetary Management* (Englewood Cliffs, N.J.: Prentice-Hall, 1963), pp. 175–315, especially 249–271. This source also provides significant coverage of the various other proposals for changing the reserve requirement system.

Open Market Operations

It should be clear by now that open market operations are the most important of the monetary policy tools. Open market operations are the most active policy measure both for day-to-day stabilizing purposes and for monetary policy changes.

As a by-product of open market operations, the Federal Reserve System has become one of the largest owners of federal government debt. The Federal Reserve holds $90 billion of the $567 billion of gross debt. The Treasury benefits from the use of open market operations because most of the Federal Reserve's profits—mainly interest received on federal government debt—reverts to the Treasury.

Open market operations—the purchase or sale of government securities from the portfolio of the Federal Reserve System—directly affect the supply of reserves available to the banking system.

The effect of an open market purchase was illustrated in Table 8–3. In Table 14–6, the effect of an open market sale of government securities is illustrated. In the table the Federal Reserve's sale of $1,000 of government securities decreases the supply of reserves available to the commercial banking system. The securities dealer has added government bonds, and reduces his demand deposits to pay for the bonds. The Federal Reserve's government securities account decreases, and the Federal Reserve decreases the reserve account of the securities dealer's bank. The securities dealer's bank records a reserve loss and a deposit decrease.

The commercial bank has lost reserves of $1,000 and has lost deposits of $1,000. Assuming that the bank was holding the minimum required reserves before the transaction, the bank now has insufficient reserves and must restore its reserves by liquidating securities and/or reducing loans.

In recent years, the Federal Reserve has frequently used repurchase agreements as part of its open market operations. Under the repurchase agreement, the Federal Reserve buys (sells) government securities with the understanding that the seller (buyer) will, at a fixed future time and price, buy (sell) the government securities back.

As a tool of monetary policy, open market operations are in many ways superior to the other instruments. Using open market operations, the Federal Reserve can quickly change reserve availability. The supply of reserves can be adjusted either for policy purposes or to offset factors, such as float, which vary on a day-to-day basis. Once detected, an oversupply of reserves can be quickly reversed; a shortage of reserves can be compensated for by greater purchases. None of the other instruments is as flexible as open market operations, and none can be so easily reversed if conditions change.

Open market operations have their initial impact on the money market banks, which deal in the government securities markets themselves and also hold the deposits of other government securities dealers.

TABLE 14–6 Open Market Sale of Government Securities

SECURITIES DEALER		*COMMERCIAL BANK*		*FEDERAL RESERVE BANK*	
Assets	*Liabilities*	*Assets*	*Liabilities*	*Assets*	*Liabilities*
Demand deposits −\$1,000	*Capital*	Reserves at Federal Reserve Bank −\$1,000	Demand deposits −\$1,000	Government bonds −\$1,000	Reserves of commercial bank −\$1,000
Government bonds +\$1,000			*Capital*		*Capital*

Problems in the Use of Open Market Operations

Two continuing problems complicate the use of open market operations. First, these operations are used for two purposes—defensive and dynamic. *Defensive* open market operations refer to the day-to-day purchases and sales of government securities by the Trading Desk for the purpose of preventing nonpolicy factors, such as float, from having undesirable effects on the level of bank reserves. Most Federal Reserve purchases or sales are of this nature and reveal nothing about the course of monetary policy. The second purpose, *dynamic* open market operations, represents the use of open market operations to change the availability of reserves and change monetary policy. Unfortunately, for the outside observer, these open market operations are indistinguishable from defensive operations.

The two uses of open market operations are so intertwined that the failure to conduct defensive operations may be an indication of a dynamic policy change. For example, a decline in the level of float contracts the supply of reserves; normally, this decline would be offset by Federal Reserve purchases. However, the Federal Reserve may desire to tighten policy and, rather than compensate for the change in float, will allow the change in float to decrease the availability of reserves. The interpretation of policy would be easier if the Federal Reserve System eliminated short-run defensive operations. Then the use of open market operations could be interpreted as a dynamic policy measure. However, the failure to compensate for factors such as float would cause greater day-to-day interest rate fluctuations.

The second continuing problem with open market operations is the choice of the item to be purchased or sold by the Federal Reserve System. One normally thinks of open market operations as being conducted via the purchase or sale of Treasury bills, but this restriction is not necessary. The impact of open market operations on the availability of bank reserves would be the same regardless of what the Federal Reserve System bought or sold. Open market sales of motorcycles or rabbits would change bank reserve positions just like sales of government debt. There are only two limitations on using motorcycles or rabbits: Are there organized markets in which the Federal Reserve can conduct millions of dollars of sales of rabbits on a given day? Does the Federal Reserve have an initial endowment of these items so that the first use of the item could be a sale as well as a purchase?

Only financial assets have ever been considered seriously as the instrument of open market operations. The major conflict has centered on whether the Federal Reserve should operate in intermediate and long-term government debt markets. The Federal Reserve System has, since 1953, confined its operations to Treasury bills first under a *Bills Only* policy and then under a *Bills Usually* policy. The System prefers the bill market because of the high volume of activity in this market and because this policy avoids direct Federal Reserve control of the entire term structure of interest rates. In addition, the Federal Reserve believes that market mechanisms transmit pressure on the short-term interest rate to other longer term rates. Opponents of this policy argue that the Federal Reserve should buy and sell across the full spectrum of government securities, rather than rely upon market mechanisms to transfer interest rate changes. According to this line of thought, in a period of recession, the Federal Reserve should buy long-term government securities to push down the long term rate and encourage housing and business capital investment. Obviously, the Federal Reserve and its opponents frequently hold differing theories of the term structure of interest rates. The difference between the theories presented in Chapter 5 is important in the management of open market operations.

If short-term and long-term interest rates are determined in segmented markets, the term structure can be adjusted to achieve multiple objectives. The only major attempt of this sort occurred in 1961. Two problems existed: first, business capital investment was too low, and the government desired lower interest rates to stimulate investment; second, higher interest rates were desired to decrease the outflow of short-term funds from the United States to other nations. Thus, *both* higher and lower interest rates were desirable. Theory suggested that investment would be more responsive to long-term interest rates and that the international capital flows would be more responsive to short-term rates.

The policy design, called *Operation Twist,* required that the Federal Reserve buy long-term governments—bidding up prices and pushing down yields—and simultaneously sell short-term governments to lower the price and increase the yield on these securities. Thus, with no net addition to total reserves, the term structure of interest rates could be changed to obtain two seemingly conflicting objectives. The evaluation of experiments of this sort is very difficult because no one can say what would have happened if this policy had not been tried. Many within the Federal Reserve considered the attempt a failure, while others thought that the Federal Reserve, with its attachment to the Bills Only policy, had not tried hard enough to make the policy a success.

Summary

The use of open market operations as the major tool of monetary policy seems certain and appropriate—especially given the declining role of discounting and the infrequency of changes in reserve requirements. Probably the Federal Reserve should be less concerned with day-to-day defensive operations. The money markets can—to a greater extent than the Federal Reserve seems to believe—take care of themselves. Daily fluctuations in reserve demands can be met through the Federal Funds market and small changes in interest rates. The Federal Reserve should concentrate on the use of open market operations for dynamic policy measures.

While control of the supply of reserves is the major policy objective, the Federal Reserve cannot divorce itself from responsibility for interest rates—both long and short term. He who controls supply cannot disclaim all responsibility for price! Thus, the operations of the Federal Reserve System should give more attention to the term structure of interest rates and should work toward establishing an appropriate term structure to contribute to the attainment of current objectives.

The Impact of Policy Measures

Assume that the Federal Reserve System moves to tighten credit by simultaneously increasing reserve requirements, increasing the discount rate, and engaging in open market sales of Treasury bills. What impacts would these measures have in the short run?

Impact on Prices and Yields of Securities

The first short-run impact of all of these contractionary measures would be on the prices and yields on government securities. To meet the higher reserve requirements and to reduce indebtedness to the Federal Reserve, most banks would sell short-term Treasury bills. The price of bills would decline and the yield would increase.

The interest rate effects would spread to other sources of funds, as the banks increased their search for new short-term money. The Federal Funds rate would increase as more banks entered the market as buyers and fewer reserves were made available for sale.

With a little longer lag, the increased yield on short-term securities would induce some holders of longer term securities to switch to the relatively higher yielding short-term instruments. Sales of longer term debt would lower the price of long-term bonds and increase yields on long-term bonds. A new yield curve would be formed at a higher overall level of interest rates. This analysis assumes that markets are not segmented and that the holders of longer term debt can, and do, switch to shorter term debt.

The impact of the higher rates in the government debt market is also transmitted to the private debt market. Yields on short-term, and then long-term, private debt issues would also increase.

In recognition of the higher market yields, new issues of public and private debt would be offered at higher coupon interest rates. At this point, some issuers of debt securities, unwilling to pay higher interest rates or expecting the higher rates to be temporary, would postpone debt sales.

Announcement Effects

The reaction of the market to the simulated tight money policy is composed of direct effects and announcement effects.[14] The *announcement effects* are difficult

[14]Smith, "The Instruments of General Monetary Control," op. cit., pp. 61–64.

to anticipate; they are based on the market's expectations of the future. Some of these announcement effects will strengthen the policy action, and other reactions will weaken the effects of the policy measures.

First, assume that people interpret the Federal Reserve's actions as the beginning of a long battle to lower the rate of inflation. Security holders believe that the Federal Reserve will continue to push up interest rates. Thus, the outlook is for falling bond prices; some bond holders decide to sell before prices go even lower. Bonds are liquidated, prices fall, and interest rates rise. The Federal Reserve's policy is reinforced by the announcement effect.

Alternatively, continue these assumptions and add the expectation that inflation will indeed be reduced by the tight money policy. If there is an inflation premium added to bond interest rates, the reduction of inflationary expectations should lower interest rates and bring about rising bond prices.

On the other hand, participants in the money markets may interpret all of the Federal Reserve's policy actions as either temporary or unlikely to have any effects on inflation; in that case, these anticipatory effects would either work in the opposite direction or not take place at all.

Beyond these interest rate effects, the announcement effects may change the demand for and supply of credit. For example, if interest rates are expected to continue rising, borrowers would be wise to borrow long-term funds before rates go higher. Thus, the demand for long-term credit may increase. On the other hand, banks may have the same expectations and will prefer to lend short term now so that funds will be available in the future for long-term loans at higher interest rates. By this line of thought, short-term interest rates would decline (demand would decrease and supply increase), and long-term rates would rise (demand would increase while supply decreased).

Finally, the change in monetary policy could affect spending behavior, as consumers and businesses evaluate inflation expectations and the probable effect of the Federal Reserve's anti-inflation policy.

Effects on Credit Availability

The initial reaction of the banking system to the assumed contractionary monetary policy comes in the form of changes in interest rates and security prices as banks adjust to the decreased availability of reserves. However, assuming that the banking system does not arrive at this point with large quantities of excess reserves, the decrease in the availability of reserves must affect the supply of credit.

The lowered availability of credit may be reflected by price and nonprice rationing of loans. Price rationing will be reflected in an increase in the prime rate and rates charged to the vast majority of borrowers who do not qualify to borrow at the prime rate. Nonprice rationing will produce quantity limitations on loans to individual borrowers.

The tightening of credit will be partly offset by a realignment of the bank's portfolio. As has been indicated, banks do not like to lose loan customers. Therefore, in the attempt to maintain lending activity, the ratio of loans to total assets will increase. Short-term liquid asset holdings will be reduced and longer term bond holdings will be sold. On the liability side, efforts to buy funds will be intensified. Rates on time deposits will be increased if Regulation Q ceilings permit.

Another partly offsetting effect comes about through the influence of rising interest rates on cash holdings. Corporate treasurers have an incentive to minimize the company's holdings of cash and invest funds in interest-bearing assets. Alternatively, by reducing its desired bank balance, the company is able to reduce its need for short-term borrowing. This general reduction of cash balances can be looked upon as being equivalent to an increase in the velocity of circulation, or turnover rate, of the money supply. If each economic unit holds a smaller cash balance, the same level of economic activity can be financed with the smaller money supply.

Effects on Economic Activity

Eventually, all of the contractionary forces should have an impact on spending plans. The absolute level of, or rate of growth of, output should decline. This impact on economic activity comes about either by the interest rate effects described in Chapters 10 and 11 or by the Friedman mechanism described in Chapter 12.

Through the interest rate mechanism, the higher interest rates reduce the demand for credit to finance economic activity. Among the types of borrowing that could be affected by the higher interest rate are consumer durable goods purchases, business inventory holdings, business capital investment, and state and local government borrowing. Federal government borrowing is for debt-financing and would not be sensitive to interest rates. Consumer spending on nondurable goods and services is seldom financed by borrowing; only durable goods purchases—cars, appliances, furniture, and the like—would be likely to be affected by interest rate changes. In the business sector, either working capital or long-term investment capital may be borrowed and be subject to interest rate changes. With respect to state and local governments, regular current expenditures are financed by taxes. Borrowed funds are used for the financing of capital improvements such as schools, roads, and pollution abatement facilities.

Thus, there are a few major types of spending which may be reduced as a result of the higher interest rates. Chapter 18 explores, in greater detail, the effect of monetary policy on specific types of debt-financed activity.

By the Friedman analysis, the decrease in the money supply reduces the public's real balances below the desired level. Spending units are led to reduce their level of spending in order to restore their desired real balances. They reduce spending and the level of economic activity decreases.

Thus far, the analysis of the impact of policy has been conducted in terms of a restrictive policy. However, the opposite case, an easing of policy, should also be considered. For the most part, the reasoning can simply be reversed. The major difference may occur in terms of the effects on economic activity. Conventional theory, as illustrated in the *IS-LM* analysis of Chapter 11, suggests that monetary policy does not work as well in a period of recession as in a period of high and rising levels of economic activity.

Why should the ability to encourage expansion be different from the ability to restrain expansion? In the constraining case, there is some limit to the absolute amount of monetary expansion that can be obtained from a given quantity of reserves. Even allowing for slippage, borrowed funds, higher velocity, and other factors, continued pressure on reserve positions limits the ability of the banking system to meet loan demands. However, in the attempt to expand economic activity, the Federal Reserve System cannot ensure that newly provided bank reserves will indeed be used to increase the supply of money or credit. New reserves may be used by the banks to rebuild their liquidity positions. New money is used to replace high-cost borrowed funds. Loan demand decreases as business activity declines. Even though interest rates fall, the need for business credit is lower than it was during the expansion phase of the cycle. Business inventories are being liquidated, and the need for credit to finance these inventories declines. With the lower level of output, the need for new capital investment is reduced.

During the 1974–1975 recession, the Federal Reserve System was under great pressure to create a rapid recovery. However, in spite of substantial infusions of new reserves, the growth of the money supply was less than anticipated. The factors described in the previous paragraph appear to be part of the explanation of the sluggish response of the money supply to the expansion of reserves.

The final point to be considered in this context is the question of lags in the effect of monetary policy actions. This description of policy has not indicated any time period. The use of monetary policy is subject to the same lags as were described in the section on fiscal policy. Recognition of the problem takes the same length of time. The action lag is shorter for monetary policy because Federal Reserve policies do not have to be approved by the Congress. The lag in effect, as indicated in the discussion of lags in Chapter 12, may be relatively long.

Chapter 15 examines the impact of monetary policy in terms of the ability of policy to deal with the problems of recession and inflation.

REVIEW QUESTIONS

1. How did the founders of the Federal Reserve System attempt to increase the elasticity of the supply of currency and the supply of credit?

2. Why would a member bank borrow in the Federal Funds market at a rate higher than the discount rate?

3. Explain the seasonal and emergency credit provisions of the discounting mechanism.

4. Is the discount window necessary to monetary policy? Evaluate its role.

5. Why were reserve requirements traditionally based on the location of the bank?

6. Why are all banks not subject to the reserve requirements established by the Federal Reserve System? What are the costs and benefits of this situation?

7. Why are reserve requirements on demand deposits higher than reserve requirements on time deposits?

8. Do any of the alternative reserve requirement systems appear to be more efficient than the present system? Are any more equitable than the present system? Should reserve requirements be discarded as a policy tool?

9. To what extent can open market operations replace or not replace the other two major tools of policy?

10. Differentiate between the announcement effects and the credit availability effects of a monetary policy change. To what extent are they related?

SUGGESTED READINGS

Margaret E. Bedford, "The Seasonal Borrowing Privilege," *Federal Reserve Bank of Kansas City Monthly Review,* June 1974, pp. 10–16.

Joseph M. Burns, "Academic Views on Improving the Federal Reserve Discount Mechanism: A Review Essay," *Journal of Money, Credit and Banking,* Ohio State University Press, Columbus, February 1973, pp. 47–60.

J. A. Cacy, "Determinants of Member Bank Borrowing," *Federal Reserve Bank of Kansas City Monthly Review,* February 1971, pp. 11–20.

George Garvy, "Reform of Reserve Requirements," *Federal Reserve Bank of New York Monthly Review,* August 1972, pp. 201–207.

Ira Kaminow, "The Case Against Uniform Reserves: A Loss of Perspective," *Federal Reserve Bank of Philadelphia Business Review,* June 1974, pp. 16–21.

Ira Kaminow, "Why Not Pay Interest on Member Bank Reserves?" *Federal Reserve Bank of Philadelphia Business Review,* January 1975, pp. 3–9.

Robert E. Knight, "Reserve Requirements Part I: Comparative Reserve Requirements at Member and Nonmember Banks," *Federal Reserve Bank of Kansas City Monthly Review,* April 1974, pp. 3–20.

Robert E. Knight, "Reserve Requirements Part II: An Analysis of the Case for Uniform Reserve Requirements," *Federal Reserve Bank of Kansas City Monthly Review,* May 1974, pp. 3–15.

George W. Mitchell, "A New Look at Monetary Policy Instruments," *Journal of Money, Credit and Banking,* Ohio State University Press, Columbus, May 1971, pp. 381–390.

15

CONTROL OF THE MONEY SUPPLY: RECESSION AND INFLATION

This final chapter on monetary policy considers the effectiveness of monetary policy in solving two major macroeconomic problems—recession and inflation.

Monetary Policy in Recession

The *IS–LM* analysis in Chapter 11 suggested theoretical problems relative to the use of an expansionary monetary policy in a recession. Given the liquidity trap, the use of monetary policy in a recession has been described as being equivalent to pushing on a string; monetary policy can restrain the economy in a period of expansion or inflation, but it cannot stimulate the economy in a period of recession or depression.

At first, the events of the 1930s appeared to confirm the strict interpretation of the inability of monetary policy to cope with depression. Even though some interest rates decreased drastically, the level of economic activity did not recover from its depressed state. However, in later reinterpretations of the period, analysts have decided that monetary policy was not expansionary. As noted previously, the supply of money was permitted to decline by about one third from 1929 to 1933, and long-term interest rates failed to decrease as much as did short-term interest rates.

In present terminology, the effectiveness of monetary policy in either a recession or an expansion depends upon the existence of stable cause-and-effect relationships between monetary variables and real variables. In other words, monetary policy requires the existence of channels of influence which can transmit changes in the policy variables to the real variables—output, employment, and income.

This section considers four main channels of influence between financial and real variables. The literature in each of these areas is vast, and coverage of each topic can only scratch the surface. An attempt is made to present the conventional wisdom on each topic, and the interested reader may pursue the variations, deviations, and dissents.

Monetary Policy and Velocity

A change in the money supply will affect the level of money national income, via the basic quantity theory of money, if velocity is constant. In the basic equation $MV = PO$, the quantity theorists argued that V was determined by institutional factors and would be constant in the short run. Changes in the long-run value of V would occur as the payments mechanism changed.

One of the Keynesian objections to the quantity theory centered on the stability of velocity. Velocity may decline as the money supply is increased in a recession. If velocity declines as the money supply increases and the product of M and V remains constant, national income (PO) does not change. Thus, the change in the money supply would not have any effect on the level of output or prices.

The argument relative to the stability of velocity centers on the responsiveness of velocity to changes in the interest rate. As the description of the monetarist position in Chapter 12 indicated, the Friedman-Meiselman argument is that velocity is more stable than the investment multiplier and that control of the supply of money is more important than the control of aggregate demand.

However, velocity is merely another way of looking at the public's desire to hold cash balances. Thus, from a theoretical point of view, velocity should be related to the level of the interest rate. If interest rates increase, there is a positive incentive for the public to reduce its money holdings. Idle cash holdings do not collect interest, and a rising opportunity cost of holding cash should induce reductions in cash balances. This behavior is particularly important for the managers of corporate cash balances. The astute corporate treasurer should forecast cash inflows and outflows and invest the maximum possible amount of money until the funds are needed to meet the firm's obligations. High and rising interest rates create increased incentives to behave in this manner; low or falling interest rates reduce the incentive to maximize returns on cash balances.

Table 15–1 presents the basic data on velocity; velocity is measured by dividing GNP by the M_1 measure of the money supply. The table indicates that velocity has risen over the 1953–1975 period. One could argue that the upward trend in velocity is due to long-run factors changing the payments mechanism. Alternatively, the rising interest rates over the period may have induced the increasing level of velocity.

Table 15–1 indicates that in each year in which velocity has declined, interest rates have also declined. However, in other years, interest rates have fallen, but there has been no decline in the rate of turnover of the money supply.

The range of velocity fluctuations in a recession may be different than the range of velocity fluctuations in an inflationary period. In the short run, regardless of the level of interest rates, velocity can only increase by a limited amount; there is

TABLE 15–1 Velocity and Interest Rates

YEAR	GNP (billions of dollars)	M_1 (billions of dollars)	V_1	TREASURY BILL RATE (percent)
1953	366.1	128.8	2.84	1.93
1954	366.3	132.3	2.77	0.95
1955	399.3	135.2	2.95	1.75
1956	420.7	136.9	3.07	2.66
1957	442.8	135.9	3.26	3.27
1958	448.9	141.1	3.18	1.84
1959	486.5	143.4	3.39	3.41
1960	506.0	144.2	3.51	2.93
1961	523.3	148.7	3.52	2.38
1962	563.8	150.9	3.74	2.78
1963	594.7	156.5	3.80	3.16
1964	635.7	163.7	3.88	3.55
1965	688.1	171.3	4.02	3.95
1966	753.0	175.4	4.29	4.88
1967	796.3	186.9	4.26	4.32
1968	868.5	201.7	4.31	5.34
1969	935.5	208.7	4.48	6.68
1970	982.4	221.4	4.44	6.46
1971	1063.4	235.3	4.52	4.35
1972	1171.1	255.8	4.58	4.07
1973	1306.3	271.5	4.81	7.04
1974	1406.9	284.4	4.95	7.89
1975[p]	1499.0	296.4	5.06	5.84

[p]preliminary.

SOURCE: *1976 Economic Report of the President*, pp. 171, 231, 238.

a limit to the maximum possible reduction of cash balances. However, in a period of recession and low interest rates, cash balances can be expanded without limit and velocity can decline without limit. Thus, in inflation, once the level of velocity increases to its short-term maximum, further changes in the money supply affect output or prices; in a recession, declines in velocity could continue to offset increases in the supply of money. In the short run, increases in the supply of money—intended to stimulate the economy—may be at least partly offset by velocity changes.

The effect of a change in the money supply on velocity continues to be a controversial issue. Some analysts argue that the turnover rate of money is relatively constant and presents no problem. Others insist that the rate is not constant but is a stable function of a limited number of other variables and can be predicted with a reasonable degree of accuracy. Others go so far as to argue that quarter-to-quarter changes in velocity are essentially random fluctuations and that velocity changes cannot be predicted as part of the planning of monetary policy.[1]

[1]A comprehensive bibliography on the demand for money and velocity can be found in David E. W. Laidler, *The Demand for Money: Theories and Evidence* (Scranton, Pa.: International Textbook Co., 1969).

The determination of the role of velocity as a possible connecting link between money and GNP is important. Using the 1975 figures from Table 15–1 and expressing the relationship as $M \times V = \text{GNP}$, an increase in velocity of 0.01 would have been associated with a $3 billion increase in GNP. Thus, from a practical policy-making point of view, a small, short-term change in velocity is important.

Although the empirical evidence is mixed, the theoretical arguments create substantial doubt about the short-run stability of velocity. It appears reasonable to conclude that during a recession increases in the supply of money are at least partly offset by velocity decreases. If monetary policy is to contribute to the correction of recession, the major impact of policy probably will have to come via an alternative channel.

The Wealth Effect

The wealth effect is a second possible connecting link between monetary policy and the level of output. Changes in monetary policy affect the value of wealth, and these fluctuations in total wealth could lead to changes in spending.

Assume, for example, that monetary policy results in a decline in bond interest rates. Bond yields are now relatively lower than yields on common stock. People substitute common stock for bonds and common stock prices increase. The value of the public's wealth in the form of common stock increases.

The key question is whether wealth is a component of the consumption function so that a higher value of wealth would result in a higher level of consumption. The lifetime income hypothesis cited in the discussion of consumption functions in the appendix to Chapter 10 includes wealth as one of the determinants of consumption spending. In the Ando-Modigliani study, the empirical value of the propensity to consume out of net worth was found to be relatively low.[2]

However, de Leeuw and Gramlich find that: "Although the marginal propensity to consume out of net worth is quite small—less than 0.04 in the consumption function we are presently using—consumption is so important in total final expenditures that even this response is large enough for stock market swings to have an important effect on the economy."[3]

The evidence is providing increasing support for the existence of the wealth effect as a channel of monetary policy influence. The theoretical case is strong and the empirical studies provide added support. For the wealth effect to stimulate spending by changing the value of common stocks, stock prices would have to increase during some part of the recession. The record of past stock price movements indicates that stock prices do begin to rise well before a recession reaches its

[2]Albert Ando and Franco Modigliani, "The 'Life Cycle' Hypothesis of Saving: Aggregate Implications and Tests," *American Economic Review,* March 1963, pp. 55–84.

[3]Frank de Leeuw and Edward M. Gramlich, "The Channels of Monetary Policy: A Further Report on the Federal Reserve–M.I.T. Model," *Journal of Finance,* May 1969, pp. 276–277.

low point. Thus, the wealth effect could be a channel of monetary policy in a recession.

Rationing Effects

Another possible channel of influence of monetary policy may be the nonprice rationing of credit. As previously indicated, consumer installment loans are frequently rationed; institutions establish a rate for various types of loans and accept or reject loan applications on the basis of the degree of risk presented by each potential borrower. Higher lending standards can reduce the quantity of lending to consumers.

Rationing would be likely to occur in the home mortgage lending area. Given the problem of financial disintermediation, there may be a quantitative limitation on the ability of nonbank financial intermediaries to provide funds to the potential homeowner regardless of ability to pay. Given the effect of Regulation Q on the ability of institutions to attract deposits, credit for home mortgages may be limited, and monetary policy may have its effect on this component of demand.

Business lending may also be subject to nonprice rationing. Until recent years, the prime rate for loans to large businesses was changed infrequently; when the rate was below its equilibrium level, the banks rationed credit to business borrowers. In recent years, the prime rate has fluctuated more freely and the price of credit has tended to be the more important rationing device.

The rationing of business credit can take a number of forms. First, the bank may raise its lending standards. Second, the borrower's maximum line of credit may be decreased. Third, compensating balance requirements may be increased. Under compensating balance rules, the borrower is required to leave a given percentage of the loan on deposit at the bank. This requirement increases the bank's return because a portion of the loan is held in a noninterest-bearing demand deposit account.

Many of the rationing effects change the composition of lending rather than the total quantity of lending. Deposit losses at thrift institutions result in less housing construction, but the lost funds finance other types of economic activity. Likewise, funds not loaned to one business are loaned to another business. Thus, rationing may have a much stronger effect on the distribution of spending than on the total quantity of spending. In addition, rationing should be a much more important factor in a period of expanding economic activity than in a recession. Therefore, the rationing effect probably has very little potential as a means of stimulating the economy in a period of recession.

The Interest Rate Mechanism

The major influence of monetary policy on the demand for goods and services should come through fluctuations in the price of credit. To consider the impact of changes in the interest rate on the level of aggregate demand, each of the components of aggregate demand must be examined for possible interest rate effects.

Consumption Consumer nondurable goods and services usually are not purchased on credit and thus would not be affected by changes in the cost of credit. The interest rate is most likely to affect the purchase of durable goods. In the consumer durable goods category, the most attention has been devoted to automobile expenditures.

The argument that car expenditures are influenced by interest rate changes rests on the fact that a majority of consumers finance their car purchases on the installment plan. The interest cost of installment financing adds significantly to the total cost of the automobile. The negative case rests on the fact that the consumer, attracted to a new car, may not remain a rational economic man! As long as he can meet the monthly payments, he is willing to sign the credit contract. In this context, the availability of credit and the consumer's disposable income would be the most important determinants of auto purchases.

Substantial evidence suggests that the high positive income elasticity of demand for autos is more important than the negative price elasticity.[4] Thus, a 1 percent increase in consumer income and a 1 percent increase in the price of cars would result in increased total auto sales. The interest elasticity of demand is significant but less than either of the other two elasticities.[5]

Hamburger finds that the income elasticity of demand for cars is +4.32 (for other durables +1.65), the price elasticity of demand is –1.17 (for other durables –1.81), and the interest elasticity of demand, as measured by the interest rate on AAA-rated corporate bonds, is –0.85 (for other durables –0.17). He also finds that rates charged on consumer auto loans do fluctuate in response to changes in market interest rates. However, this fluctuation occurs with a lag.[6] To maintain a constant level of demand for automobiles, the interest rate charged on car loans would have to fall approximately 5 percent to compensate for a 1 percent decline in income levels. For other durable goods, the interest elasticity of demand is less than for cars; there is relatively little hope that the demand for other durables can be stimulated by lowering interest rates.

Business Capital Investment According to the theoretical analysis of Chapters 10 and 11, the impact of changing interest rates should fall on business capital investment. However, from the earliest post-Keynesian years there have been

[4]Unless otherwise stated, elasticity measures in this section are measured as the percentage change in the appropriate component of aggregate demand divided by the percentage change in the price of the good, income, or the interest rate. Thus

$$\text{Price elasticity of demand for autos} = \frac{\%\text{ change in auto expenditures}}{\%\text{ change in price of autos}}$$

$$\text{Income elasticity of demand for autos} = \frac{\%\text{ change in auto expenditures}}{\%\text{ change in disposable income}}$$

$$\text{Interest elasticity of demand for autos} = \frac{\%\text{ change in auto expenditures}}{\%\text{ change in interest rate}}$$

[5]Michael J. Hamburger, "Interest Rates and the Demand for Consumer Durable Goods," *American Economic Review,* December 1967, pp. 1131–1153. This article provides a comprehensive bibliography of interest rate effects on durable goods.

[6]Ibid., pp. 1138–1140.

doubts about the ability of the central bank to influence the level of investment by control of the interest rate. The Oxford surveys cited in the Appendix to Chapter 10 indicated that businessmen did not give heavy weight to the interest rate in making capital spending decisions.[7]

The theoretical case for an interest rate effect is incorporated in the standard theory; at this point, some of the arguments against the interest rate effect should be cited. First, it can be argued that, in dollar terms, large business firms are responsible for most new investment. These firms have access to all business lenders in American and foreign money markets; thus, if credit is available, it will be available to these large firms.

Second, these large firms may be in a less than perfectly competitive industry and have substantial control over the selling price of their product. These firms are able to raise prices and pass the higher cost of credit on to their customers. In the ultimate case of a high degree of pass-through of costs, a study of capital investment in the electric power industry indicated that the demand for plant and equipment was a function of demand for the product and the existing degree of capacity utilization. Plant and equipment demand was not affected by the cost of capital.[8]

Third, many capital investments are not completely voluntary. Replacement of a given machine may be absolutely necessary if production is to continue. Regardless of the interest rate that must be paid, the firm must purchase the machine or cease production.

Fourth, not all firms analyze the costs and returns of an investment as carefully as basic theory requires. The firm may use simple rules of thumb to evaluate investment decisions. The payoff period rule is frequently used, and investments that provide the quickest payback of costs are selected.

Fifth, changes in sales may be the important determinant of investment. Firms may purchase new capital equipment in response to an increase in sales without adequate regard to profitability or the rate of interest.[9]

Sixth, the large firm may not be a profit maximizer in the traditional sense. The firm may be more concerned with the maximization of sales, relative standing in its industry, security of its position, or some other set of objectives. Thus, while the firm may desire to produce a sufficient level of profits to keep the stockholders happy, the managers of the firm may have goals other than strict profit maximiza-

[7]For a summary of these surveys see William H. White, "Interest Inelasticity of Investment Demand: The Case from Business Attitude Surveys Reexamined," *American Economic Review,* September 1956, pp. 565–587. This article is reprinted in M. G. Mueller, ed., *Readings in Macroeconomics,* 2nd ed. (New York: Holt, Rinehart, and Winston, 1971), pp. 95–113.

[8]Avram Kisselgoff and Franco Modigliani, "Private Investment in the Electric Power Industry and the Acceleration Principle," *Review of Economics and Statistics,* November 1957, pp. 363–379. This article is reprinted in Robert A. Gordon and Lawrence R. Klein, ed., *Readings in Business Cycles* (Homewood, Ill.: Richard D. Irwin, 1965), pp. 340–365.

[9]See A. D. Knox, "The Acceleration Principle and the Theory of Investment," *Economica,* August 1953, pp. 269–297. This article is reprinted in M. G. Mueller, ed., *Readings in Macroeconomics,* 2nd ed. (New York: Holt, Rinehart and Winston, 1971), pp. 114–133.

tion.[10] Thus, there are important theoretical reasons that suggest that the impact of the interest rate on the level of investment may not be as significant in fact as in theory.

In terms of empirical work on the elasticity of investment with respect to the interest rate, Evans,[11] after reviewing the literature on the subject and constructing an econometric model, concludes that capital investment is relatively interest-inelastic. By his elasticity measure, a 1 percent change in the interest rate will lead to a ¼ to ½ percent change in investment over a two-year period. For example, increasing the market interest rate from 5 to 6 percent (a 20 percent increase) would decrease investment by 5 to 10 percent. Evans also finds that the key interest rate is the long-term rate; changes in the short-term rate are only important if they lead to changes in the long-term rate. A change in the long-term interest rate affects the level of investment with a one-year lag. Presumably, those projects that have been financed in the past are completed, and changes in investment plans caused by changes in the interest rate affect the level of actual investment spending with a relatively long lag.[12]

Evans also finds that investment changes follow from changes in output; the response of investment to a change in output is greater than the response of investment to a change in the interest rate. Thus, if output decreases by 1 percent, investment would be expected to decrease by 1½ to 2 percent. Given the range of interest elasticity values, a fall in the interest rate of between 3 and 8 percent would be necessary to counteract the effect of the fall in output on the level of investment.[13]

Jorgenson, in a study of a large number of modified accelerator investment functions, finds that in some of the models the cost of investment funds is a significant determinant of investment. However, the role of the interest rate is less important than the role of output in determining the level of investment activity.[14]

In summary, the evidence suggests that although business capital investment is somewhat sensitive to the cost of capital, the degree of interest elasticity is relatively low, interest rate changes affect investment with a long lag, and changes in the cost of capital are relatively less important than fluctuations in output. From the point of view of control of the business cycle, the relative elasticities suggest problems in the use of monetary policy to stimulate business investment. In either a downturn or an upswing, the weight of output changes as a force encouraging or discouraging new capital investment is greater than the weight of interest rate

[10]See, for example, William J. Baumol, *Business Behavior, Value and Growth* (New York: Macmillan Co., 1959).

[11]Michael K. Evans, *Macroeconomic Activity: Theory, Forecasting, and Control* (New York: Harper & Row, Publishers, 1969), p. 138.

[12]Ibid.

[13]Ibid.

[14]Dale W. Jorgenson, "Econometric Studies of Investment Behavior: A Survey," *Journal of Economic Literature*, December 1971, pp. 1111–1147. See extensive bibliography.

changes. Very substantial changes in the interest rate are needed to offset the impact of changes in output.

Investment in Business Inventories Business inventory investment was considered traditionally as one of the areas in which monetary policy should have its effects. Many firms finance their inventory holdings by borrowing from banks. Thus, an increase in interest rates should lead businesses to reduce inventories.

For a number of reasons, inventory holdings may not be sensitive to a change in the interest rate. Inventories of goods in process and finished goods are necessary to the operation of the firm. Sales are lost if goods cannot be delivered. The cost of lost sales is greater than the increased interest cost of inventory financing.

The interest cost of financing inventories is only part of the total cost of holding inventories. Other costs of holding inventories include storage costs, theft or spoilage, and losses caused by product obsolescence.

The small firm, which finances its inventory through its bank, may be most sensitive to rising interest costs. However, the small firm may be able to transfer a part of these costs to its large suppliers; in times of tight money and high interest rates, the large firm may grant easier payment terms to its small customers. By allowing the small firm to delay payment for orders received, the financing of inventories may be shifted up the distribution line to the better financed large firm.

In addition, the holding of inventories provides protection against shortages, delivery delays caused by transportation problems or strikes, and protection against rising prices. These causes of inventory increases were clearly important in 1973–1974 as firms built up their inventories to protect themselves against shortages, lengthening delivery lags, and rising prices.

The statistical evidence on the determinants of inventory investment tends to suggest that the interest rate is not an important determinant of inventory holding behavior. Work on this topic indicates that in an accelerator model variables such as changes in sales, desired inventory/sales ratios, and unfilled orders explain inventory holdings. The Evans[15] inventory model does not include an interest rate variable. In the Brookings model, Darling and Lovell find that the interest rate is marginally significant as a determinant of retail inventories but is not a significant determinant of other types of inventories.[16]

Thus, on the basis of the evidence, interest rate variations cannot be expected to have any major effect on the level of inventory investment. Changes in inventories are a major factor in most recessions; business attempts to reduce inventories as sales decline. On the basis of the evidence, reduced interest rates cannot offset this phenomenon.

[15]Evans, op. cit., p. 219–220.

[16]Paul G. Darling and Michael C. Lovell, "Factors Influencing Investment in Inventories," in J. S. Duesenberry, G. Fromm, L. R. Klein, and E. Kuh, eds., *The Brookings Quarterly Econometric Model of the United States* (Chicago: Rand McNally & Co., 1965), p. 153.

TABLE 15–2 Effect of the Interest Rate on Home Financing Cost: A $10,000 Mortgage Paid over 20 Years

INTEREST RATE (percent)	*MONTHLY PAYMENT (dollars)*	*INTEREST PAID OVER LIFE OF MORTGAGE (dollars)*
9	89.97	11,592
8½	86.78	10,827
8	83.64	10,023
7½	80.56	9,334
7	77.53	8,607
6½	74.56	7,894
6	71.64	7,193
5½	68.78	6,507
5	66.00	5,840

Residential Construction New residential construction is the third component of total investment. There is a strong theoretical case in support of an interest rate effect on housing construction. The supply of credit problem resulting from credit rationing has already been cited. However, other problems also contribute to the theoretical relationship.

First, most homes are purchased with long-term mortgages. The monthly payment and the total amount paid over the life of a mortgage is a function of the interest rate on the mortgage. At no other point in an individual's life is shopping around for a better deal more important than in home financing. Table 15–2 demonstrates the effect of various interest rates on a 20-year $10,000 mortgage. Given the data, high interest rates may cause many potential buyers to postpone their home purchase.

A second problem is the structure of the home building industry. The industry is composed of many small firms and most of the firms are heavily dependent on bank construction financing. The builder borrows from the bank to buy materials and hire labor while a house is being built. He repays the loan when the house is sold. In periods of high and rising interest rates, credit for speculative home building becomes more difficult and expensive to obtain. Thus, the home builder, as well as the home buyer, is dependent on credit.

Third, maximum interest-rate ceilings under Federal Housing Administration and Veterans Administration loan programs create problems. If the ceiling rate of interest is below the rate being charged for conventional loans, the banks limit or eliminate lending under the FHA and VA programs. The ability to obtain the government-guaranteed (VA) or insured (FHA) mortgages may be critical to potential home buyers who would not qualify for a conventional mortgage. State usury laws may also limit mortgage lending during periods of high interest rates.

For the reasons cited, housing has traditionally fluctuated in a countercyclical manner. Periods of high levels of business activity and high interest rates have been bad for the housing industry, and periods of recession have improved conditions in the industry. However, the combination of recession and high interest rates in the mid-1970s was disastrous for the housing industry.

The statistical estimation of the effect of interest rate changes on residential construction is difficult because the interest rate affects both the demand side and the supply side of the market. In one study, Arcelus and Meltzer derive a demand for housing model and conclude that "cyclical changes in interest rates of ±0.5 or 0.6 around a mean 5 percent market rate of interest would induce changes of 15 to 20 percent in the demand for housing. Moreover, the effect on the demand for housing is reinforced by the effect on supply. The computed interest elasticities of the supply equation are also comparatively large and negative."[17] Their data imply an interest elasticity of demand of between –1.5 and –2, and a supply elasticity of about the same magnitude.

Craig Swan criticizes the Arcelus and Meltzer work on various statistical and model-building grounds, but his elasticity estimates are of about the same magnitude of those found by Arcelus and Meltzer.[18]

Although not quantified in elasticity terms, other previously-cited models, such as the Brookings Quarterly Econometric Model of the United States[19] and the Federal Reserve Board–Massachusetts Institute of Technology (FRB-MIT) Econometric Model,[20] indicate significant interest rate effects on housing.

State and Local Government Theory suggests that debt issues to finance state and local government capital spending programs would be sensitive to interest rates. Some states impose a ceiling on the interest rate that can be paid by state and local governments. If the sale of debt must have voter approval by public referenda, the voters may be sensitive to interest rates and reject more proposed bond issues as interest rates increase.

The Brookings[21] and FRB-MIT[22] models include interest rate variables in all, or a portion of, the econometric analysis of state and local government capital expenditures.

In simulations of the effects of various policies using the FRB-MIT model, de Leeuw and Gramlich find that a $1 billion increase in the supply of unborrowed bank reserves would lead, over a period of four years, to a $1.4 billion increase in state and local construction.[23]

[17]Francisco Arcelus and Allan H. Meltzer, "The Market for Housing and Housing Services," *Journal of Money, Credit and Banking,* February 1973, p. 86.

[18]Craig Swan, "The Market for Housing and Housing Services," *Journal of Money, Credit and Banking,* November 1973, pp. 960–978.

[19]Sherman J. Maisel, "Nonbusiness Construction," in Duesenberry et al., op. cit., pp. 179–201.

[20]F. de Leeuw and E. Gramlich, "The Federal Reserve–MIT Econometric Model," *Federal Reserve Bulletin,* January 1968, pp. 11–40.

[21]Albert Ando, E. Cary Brown, and Earl W. Adams, Jr., "Government Revenues and Expenditures," in Duesenberry et al., op. cit., pp. 533–585.

[22]de Leeuw and Gramlich, loc. cit.

[23]F. de Leeuw and E. Gramlich, "The Channels of Monetary Policy," *Federal Reserve Bulletin,* June 1969, pp. 472–491.

Indirect evidence on the interest elasticity of state and local capital expenditures is provided by Galper and Petersen,[24] who determined that for the period 1962–1970 a 1 percent increase in the interest rate on state and local bonds led to a 1.549 percent decrease in the supply of new state and local bonds. However, the reduction of bond sales would not produce an equivalent reduction in state and local capital construction because governments could substitute short-term borrowing for the sale of permanent long-term bonds and could temporarily draw down cash balances and postpone borrowing. However, these figures do provide some evidence on the interest elasticity of state and local capital expenditures.

Some of the best statistical data on the effect of interest rates on state and local government capital expenditures and their sensitivity to interest rates come from survey studies done by the Federal Reserve and the Bureau of the Census.[25] Since 1969, these surveys have measured planned and actual bond issues by governmental units, the reasons given for deviations between planned and actual bond issues, and the effect of borrowing problems on capital spending by governmental units.

The fiscal 1970 experience can be used to illustrate the effects of rising interest rates on state and local borrowing.[26] Yields on municipal bonds rose from 4 to 5 percent in 1968 to 6 to 7 percent in fiscal 1970. The units surveyed intended to borrow $23.13 billion in fiscal 1970. However, actual long-term borrowing was only $13.2 billion; the borrowing shortfall was nearly $10 billion. Still, only $7.4 billion of the shortfall was attributed to high interest rates; the remainder was due to failure to obtain voter approval or various administrative and technical problems. Of the $7.4 billion of debt not sold on schedule, $2.2 billion was sold later in the fiscal year, and the net borrowing shortfall was $5.2 billion. The inability to borrow, attributed in many cases to maximum interest rate ceilings, resulted in a $2.85 billion decrease in planned capital expenditures. Other sources of funds and later borrowing resulted in a net loss of capital spending of $1.6 billion. The $1.6 billion of actual reduction (or postponement) of capital spending represented an amount equal to 5.6 percent of the previous year's capital spending by state and local governments.[27]

The survey indicated that just under half of the $1.6 billion capital spending shortfall was due to interest rate ceilings and that slightly over half was due to the level of interest rates.[28] In other years studied, interest rate ceilings were of less importance and these ceilings would not interfere with attempts to stimulate the economy in a recession. However, given that the ceilings operate only in a high interest rate period, the effect of a restrictive monetary policy should be greater than the stimulative effect of a low interest rate policy.

[24]Harvey Galper and John Petersen, "An Analysis of Subsidy Plans to Support State and Local Borrowing," *National Tax Journal,* June 1971, pp. 205–234.

[25]For studies of this type see *Federal Reserve Bulletin,* March 1971, December 1971, and April 1973.

[26]John E. Petersen, "Response of State and Local Governments to Varying Credit Conditions," *Federal Reserve Bulletin,* March 1971, pp. 209–232.

[27]Ibid., p. 210.

[28]Ibid., p. 222.

Summary Monetary policy can be used to control the expansion or contraction of the level of economic activity. Although a great deal of additional work is needed to quantify the relationships, some faith in monetary policy is justified. However, monetary policy alone is probably not sufficient to bring about recovery from a recession. Monetary policy is helpful, but it appears that much of the force for recovery must come from fiscal policy.

The strongest impacts of monetary policy in a recession appear to be produced through the wealth effect and the effect of interest rates on residential construction and state and local government capital expenditures. In a period of economic expansion, monetary policy is more effective. Interest rate ceilings, velocity limitations, and credit rationing effects reinforce the interest rate effects.

The problem of inflation is examined in the next section. The control of aggregate demand is important for the prevention or termination of some forms of inflation. Thus, the analysis of the ability of high interest rates to control aggregate demand is applicable in the next section.

The Problem of Inflation

Inflation was a problem during the Revolutionary War and is still a problem 200 years later. As Chapters 1 and 7 indicated, the United States and most other nations of the world have experienced nearly continuous inflation since World War II. In some years the American inflation rate has been suppressed below 2 percent, but in 1974 the rate shot up to 11 percent per year. Of the various macroeconomic problems, inflation has proven to be the most persistent. In this section, the various theories of inflation are examined and related to the American inflationary experience.

Demand-Pull Inflation

The oldest, most dangerous, and most basic form of inflation is called *demand-pull* inflation. Most of the world's past great inflations have been demand-pull inflations. In Keynesian macroeconomic terms, demand-pull inflation results from a level of aggregate demand greater than the level of full employment output. The aggregate demand for goods exceeds the maximum supply of goods and prices rise. In the microeconomic analysis, if the quantity demanded of one good exceeds the quantity supplied of that good, the price rises. Demand-pull inflation is an extension of the micro analysis to the macro level. On the micro level, one expects the prices of individual products to rise and fall in response to changes in supply and demand conditions. However, inflation represents rising prices for the majority of goods and services.

Demand-pull inflation can, and frequently does, arise from the monetary side of the economy. An excessive rate of increase of the money supply can create an excessive aggregate demand for goods and services. Many great inflations have

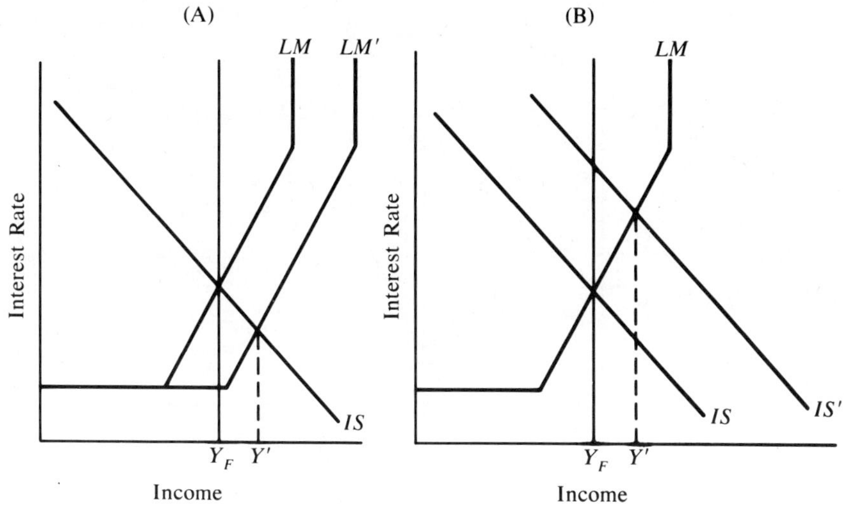

FIGURE 15–1 Demand Pull Inflation

been associated with rapid expansions of the supply of money. Particularly during and after wars, governments have attempted to maintain government spending by creating new money rather than by increasing taxes. The resulting inflation is characterized as "too much money chasing too few goods." When prices rise rapidly, people lose confidence in the ability of the money supply to serve as a store of value and attempt to dispose of their money holdings by spending. The spending creates more demand, and prices rise even faster.[29]

In the American context, the greatest single cause of inflation has been war. Current tax collections seldom pay for wars. Either the community cannot raise sufficient tax revenues to finance the war spending or the government decides that the required tax level would destroy the taxpayers' incentives to work. In the modern economy, borrowing by the sale of government debt has replaced the expansion of the currency supply as the method of financing wars.

Within the context of the *IS-LM* analysis, demand-pull inflation can be illustrated as the result of either an increase in the money supply (which shifts the *LM* curve) or as an increase in government spending or investment (which shifts the *IS* curve). In panel (A) of Figure 15–1 the money supply is increased and the *LM* curve is shifted from *LM* to *LM'*, and in panel (B) of Figure 15–1 the *IS* curve is shifted from *IS* to *IS'*. In both panels, the new income level, Y', is greater than the full employment equilibrium income, Y_F. At this point, the diagrams illustrate the existence of excess demand.

By adding a basic assumption, one point can be made about the ending of inflation. Assume in Figure 15–2 that the original money supply has a real value of

[29]For an excellent study of some of the world's greatest inflations, see Philip Cagan, "The Monetary Dynamics of Hyperinflation" in Milton Friedman, ed., *Studies in the Quantity Theory of Money* (Chicago: University of Chicago Press, 1956), pp. 25–117.

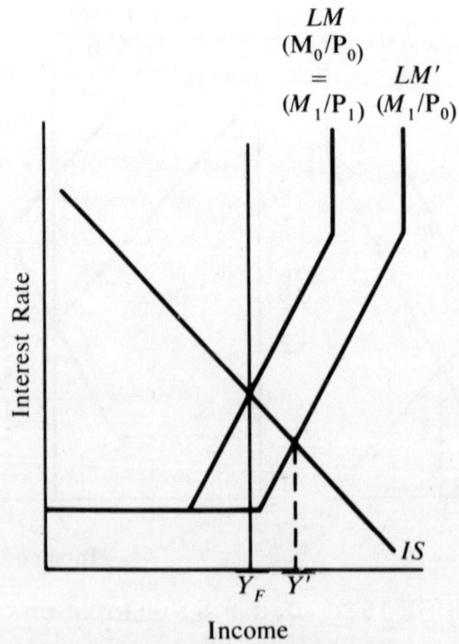

FIGURE 15–2 Demand Pull Inflation: Restoration of the Real Value of the Money Supply

M_0/P_0 (the absolute quantity of money is M_0 and the level of prices is P_0). The money supply increases from M_0 to M_1 and initially the real value of the money supply increases to M_1/P_0 and the *LM* curve shifts to *LM'*. The real value of the money supply initially increases because prices cannot increase as rapidly as the money supply can be expanded. However, the excess aggregate demand at Y' leads to rising prices. As the price level increases from P_0 to P_1, the real value of the money supply declines. As the real value of the money supply declines, the *LM* curve is restored to its original position. When the equilibrium level of income returns to Y_F, both prices and the money supply have increased in absolute levels, but the ratio of money to prices (M/P) has been restored to its original level. This restoration of the real value of the money supply is indicated in Figure 15–2 as $(M_0/P_0) = (M_1/P_1)$.

Demand-pull inflation originating in the goods market can be illustrated in the same manner. In Figures 15–3, assume the original full employment equilibrium is at Y_F, and an increase in government spending shifts the *IS* curve from *IS* to *IS'*.

Again, there is an excess aggregate demand for goods, and prices increase. The price increase lowers the real value of the money supply from (M_0/P_0) to (M_0/P_1); the money supply remained at M_0, but the price level increased from P_0 to P_1. As in the previous example, inflation comes to an end as the full employment equilibrium is restored at the higher price level P_1.

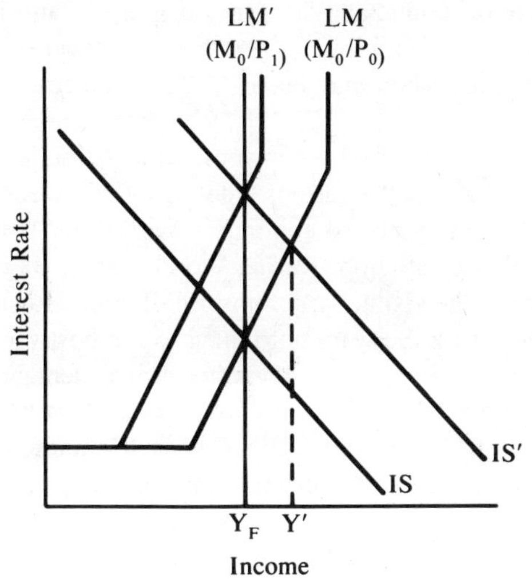

FIGURE 15–3 Demand Pull Inflation: A Decrease of the Real Value of the Money Supply

The severity of an excess demand inflation depends on a variety of factors. The major determinant is the size of the gap between the quantity of output demanded and the full employment output of the economy. The second factor is the extent to which the real demand for goods changes as prices rise. If each demander of goods maintains a constant *real* demand for goods as prices rise, aggregate demand continues to expand and prices continue to rise. If each demander of goods maintains a constant *money* demand for goods as prices rise, the real demand for goods declines until the full employment level of demand is restored at a higher price level.

Control of demand-pull inflation is easy—at least in the technical models. Given that this form of inflation is a result of excessive demand, control involves reducing the level of demand through either monetary or fiscal policy. Decreasing the money supply, increasing taxes, and reducing government spending are all appropriate policies to stop the inflationary process. Of course, these policy prescriptions are easier to describe than to carry out. If the inflation is to be ended, the policies causing the inflation must be changed. For example, halting a wartime inflation requires a change in the war financing process. If the government is financing the war effort by increasing the money supply and the rapid growth of the money supply is responsible for inflation, then controlling inflation requires the development of an alternative noninflationary method of war financing.

Ending a demand-pull inflation places burdens on those affected by the anti-inflation program. All sectors of the economy are not affected equally by a high interest rate policy; taxes are not a lump sum but are levied on particular people and types of economic activity. Once begun, the anti-inflation policy may be excessively contractionary and may reduce the level of demand below full employment. Thus, recession may become one of the costs of eliminating inflation.

Identifying periods of pure demand-pull inflation is difficult. One of the problems of inflation is that the various types of inflation tend to become blended together as an inflationary period continues. World War II and the Korean war resulted in demand-pull inflation. During World War II, wage and price controls were used to suppress the visible symptoms of inflation. However, the build-up of purchasing power during the war contributed to the postwar inflation. After the Korean war, which imposed a smaller proportional demand on the economy's resources, the wartime inflation was followed by a short recession.

The growth of American involvement in Vietnam in the mid-1960s provided a classic case of demand-pull inflation. New expenditures to finance expanded military activities in Southeast Asia were added to a nearly full employment level of aggregate demand. A tax increase or a reduction in government spending was clearly required. However, appropriate action was not taken, and the extra demand created inflation.[30]

Procedures for the prevention of demand-pull inflation should be incorporated into the macroeconomic policy-making processes. Demand-pull inflation can and must be prevented by intelligent policy decisions. Policy-making mechanisms must recognize and react to the fact that adding major new spending programs to an already full employment economy will create inflation. The congressional budget committees and the administration must be aware of the price level implications of budgeting decisions.

Cost Push Inflation

In the post–World War II period, the traditional demand-pull theory of inflation appeared to be unable to explain the continuing inflation. As an examination of the data on prices and unemployment rates in the 1950s and 1960s indicates, inflation continued during periods of relatively high unemployment. The *cost-push* inflation analysis attempts to explain the existence of inflation during periods of *no* excess demand.

Cost-push inflation,[31] in its original form, was mainly a theory of wage-push inflation. The typical explanation of the process involved the use of market power by organized economic interest groups. Assume that the steel workers receive a substantial raise in wages through the bargaining efforts of their union. The wage increase is greater than the increase in the productivity of labor and the unit labor cost of output increases in the steel industry. The steel producers use their

[30]For a discussion of this period see Walter W. Heller, *New Dimensions of Political Economy* (New York: W. W. Norton & Co., 1967).

market power to increase steel prices and pass on the higher labor cost to steel users. Both the negotiation of the higher wages and the establishment of the higher prices require the existence of market power. In perfectly competitive labor and product markets, this process would be either impossible or unlikely. However, in this case the assumptions are that the steelworkers have monopoly control over the sale of labor to the steel companies, and the steel companies are an oligopoly with price setting powers.

What are the consequences of this wage and price determination process? The price of steel is increased, and a key input to the production of all sorts of manufactured goods is now more costly. Naturally, the producers of goods containing steel will attempt to recapture their higher costs of production by increasing the prices of their products. If these firms are able to control the price of their products, the higher costs of production are passed on to the consumer. In the example, the higher price of steel would result in higher prices for cars, machinery, refrigerators, and so on. Firms without sufficient market power to pass along the higher price of steel would suffer a fall in profits.

The increase in the price of steel increases the cost of living and lowers the real income of everyone except the steelworkers. Those experiencing a loss of real income attempt to restore their purchasing power. In some cases, workers are protected by cost-of-living escalator clauses in their labor contracts. As prices rise, they will automatically receive higher pay. The firms employing these workers will attempt to pass on the higher labor costs by raising the prices of their products. Other workers will attempt to restore their lost purchasing power when their labor contracts are renegotiated. There will be some imitation effects because other unions, seeing the steelworkers receive a large increase, will attempt to do even better for their members. The union leadership will be under pressure from the membership to produce at least as good a package of wages and fringe benefits as was obtained by the steelworkers. The settlement of one collective-bargaining case becomes the precedent for the settlement of other cases.

Thus, the process continues round after round. The strong, organized workers and firms are able to restore their real wages and profits; the unorganized workers and those firms in more competitive industries are unable to maintain their relative positions.

The continuation of this cost-push process involves a reduction of the level of employment. Unlike demand-pull inflation, cost-push inflation creates less employment at higher price levels. The lower level of employment comes about through a variety of mechanisms. First, higher product prices reduce the demand for goods produced by industries subject to cost-push inflation. Less demand for an industry's output means fewer jobs in that industry and in industries that supply inputs to the affected industry. In the example, the higher price of steel reduces the

[31] A good survey of cost-push theory and general inflation theory is Martin Bronfenbrenner and Franklyn Holzman, "Survey of Inflation Theory," *American Economic Review,* September 1963, pp. 593–661.

demand for steel, iron ore, and coal. Employment is reduced in these industries, and the buying power of unemployed steelworkers, iron ore producers, and coal miners declines. Those steelworkers who are still employed have more income, but fewer workers are employed. The net effect of the higher wages on labor's purchasing power is determined by the elasticities of demand for steel and for steelworkers.

Second, jobs will be lost in the steel industry as firms attempt to replace labor with capital. The relatively higher cost of labor will create incentives to replace labor with added machinery. The addition of new machinery may make the industry more efficient and competitive in the long run; in the short run, jobs are lost. In addition, steel sales are lost to foreign steel producers, and domestic jobs and purchasing power are lost to foreign firms and workers.

Finally, those consumers who cannot restore their real incomes are able to purchase fewer goods. Thus, there is a reduction of aggregate demand. The decline in aggregate demand may affect the firms and workers responsible for the price increases or may fall on other workers and firms that have not been able to obtain higher wages and prices.

While the cost-push scenario is usually stated in terms of wage push, the theoretical framework can apply to other cost-generated price increases. The most obvious example is the inflationary spiral associated with the increased price of foreign-produced petroleum after the 1973 oil embargo. The demand is relatively inelastic because the product is a key ingredient in the production and transportation of all goods and a vital product to owners of cars and many homes. The price increases resulting from the actions of the Organization of Petroleum Exporting Countries (OPEC) spread through the U.S. economy and increased the costs of production and prices of most products. Reductions in real wages and profits, resulting from higher petroleum prices, produced the expected demands for compensatory wage and price increases.

The impact of higher costs of gasoline, heating fuels, electricity, and other petroleum-related products had the expected effects on the level of aggregate demand. Faced with rising energy and food costs, the consumer was forced to cut back on his other expenditures to pay his food and fuel bills. Although the reduction of aggregate demand had its most notable effect on the automobile industry, most industries were hurt by either the primary or secondary effects of the reduction of demand.

The reduction of aggregate demand in a cost-push inflation presents policy makers with a dilemma: prices are rising while employment is falling. In this case, the traditional tools for halting a demand-pull inflation would aggravate the employment problem without necessarily restraining the inflationary forces.

One course of action is to allow the economy to remain at less than the full employment level of output. However, this option creates all of the problems of recession without guaranteeing that the forces that generated the inflation will be affected by the slowdown of economic activity. In the petroleum case, maintaining a high level of unemployment and a low level of economic activity decreased the demand for OPEC's petroleum. In the wage-push case, the rising level of unemployment hurts the least protected members of the labor force rather than those organized groups that benefited from the inflationary process.

The use of monetary and fiscal policy to restore full employment ratifies the higher price level. Both labor and management realize that they can establish wages and prices to maximize their objectives and that the government will then create adequate demand to produce full employment at the new price level. Thus, problems are created by both the use of, and the nonuse of, policy tools.

Are other policy tools necessary? Possibly not. One can argue that if demand-pull inflation can be avoided, traditional relationships between prices and wages within and between industries will not be disrupted. The relatively good price performance of the early 1960s can be cited as evidence that, even with high degrees of imperfect competition in labor and product markets, reasonable price stability can be maintained. However, even in that relatively stable period, some Presidential persuasion was necessary to keep wage and price settlements within the established guidelines. The 1962 confrontation between President John Kennedy and U.S. Steel Corporation demonstrated that even in the best of times pressure may be necessary to prevent excessive wage and price increases.

Can the problems of wage and price escalation in noncompetitive sectors be used as a justification for wage and price controls?[32] Control may be necessary as a comprehensive measure or may be needed only in those industries in which market forces do not control wage and price determination. Controls in a few key industries, which act as pacesetters in the establishment of wages and prices, would probably be sufficient to limit the degree of cost-push inflation. The unanswered question is whether those who now have the power to control wages and prices would also be able to control the wage and price controllers!

Between the two extremes, there are a wide variety of measures available to limit the wage- and price-setting powers of organized economic groups. One possibility is greater import competition. Even though the American steel and auto industries and their unions are very powerful, they must compete with imported steel and foreign cars. The rise in the market share of foreign-produced cars serves as some restraint on the wage and price behavior of the domestic automobile industry. A rise in imports usually brings a demand for higher tariffs from both management and labor. If the Congress relents and protects the domestic industry, the market power of these industries and unions is increased.

The application of the antitrust laws against concentrated industries is a second possibility. While this option sounds reasonable, there is only a slight likelihood of the greater use of antitrust laws. The complexity of antitrust cases, the long legal battles, and the limited resources available to the Antitrust Division

[32]See John Kenneth Galbraith, *The New Industrial State* (Boston: Houghton Mifflin Co., 1967), especially chap. 22.

of the Justice Department limit the use of this potential weapon against inflation. However, if a few concentrated industries could be made more competitive, cost-push inflation would be less of a problem. If the firms could not pass on wage increases, they would be forced to bargain more aggressively with their labor unions. The unions, realizing that the firms could not pass on wage increases, would lower their demands.

A third policy prescription is the creation of greater incentives for firms to expand capital investment and increase labor productivity. If labor productivity increases, higher wages can be paid without increasing prices. To some extent, the continued pressure for higher wages has served as an incentive for productivity-increasing investments. However, in some industries, labor-management agreements on work rules have limited the ability of management to reduce the work force even though technological improvements have reduced the demand for labor.

Productivity increases in a given industry can be used to justify higher wages and profits in that industry. However, should gains in productivity be divided entirely between the workers and owners of a given industry, or should the gains be shared with society through lower prices? Allowing labor and capital to divide all productivity gains results in higher overall prices. In those industries in which productivity does not or cannot increase, wages will be pulled up by the influence of rising wages in more productive industries. Prices will rise in industries in which there are no productivity gains to absorb the higher wage costs. Thus, to achieve general price stability, falling prices in industries achieving rapid productivity gains are required to offset rising prices in those industries that are unable to achieve productivity gains.

Cost-push inflation, whether arising from wage push or raw materials push, is more difficult to control than is demand-pull inflation. However, if demand-pull inflation can be avoided, the likelihood of cost-push inflation as a "hangover" is lessened. In any event, though cost-push inflation will probably continue to be a problem, this type of inflation is at least not likely to produce hyperinflation.

Demand Shift Inflation

A third type of inflation is *demand-shift* inflation[33] or structural inflation. The basic premise of this theory is that inflation arises from changes in the composition of demand. Assume in Figure 15–4 that there are two industries, *A* and *B*. The original demand curves are labeled *D;* original prices are labeled *P.*

Because of a change in consumer tastes and preferences, the demand for product *B* increases substantially, and the demand for product *A* decreases substan-

[33]For a complete discussion of demand shift inflation, see Charles L. Schultze, "Recent Inflation in the United States," Study Paper No. 1, *Employment, Growth, and Price Levels,* Joint Economic Committee, 86th Congress, U.S. Government Printing Office, Washington, D.C., 1959.

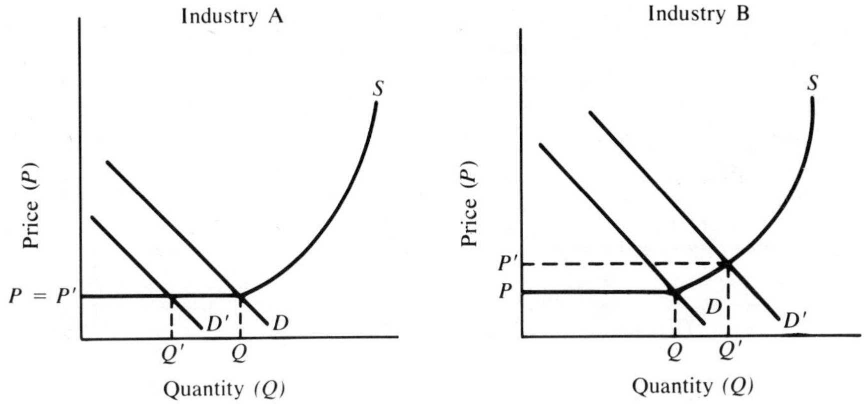

FIGURE 15–4 Demand Shift Inflation

tially. For whatever reason, consumer demand has shifted from A to B. The new demand curves (D') and the new prices (P') are illustrated in Figure 15–4. As expected, the price of the product in greater demand, product B, increases. However, the price of product A does not decrease, even though demand has decreased.

The increase in the price of product B is easily explained by basic price theory, but the failure of the price of product A to decline requires some explanation. A variety of possibilities may be cited. First, product A may be produced in a highly concentrated industry. If the producers are able to control prices, the fall in demand does not necessarily lead to a fall in price. Second, product A's unit cost of production may not have fallen as output declined. If industry A is characterized by substantial economies of scale, the output decline may have increased the per-unit cost of production. Third, the general overhead costs per unit of output may have risen as output fell. Production workers were probably laid off as output declined; the nonproduction staff was probably not decreased in proportion to the fall in output. Thus, each unit of output must bear a heavier amount of total administrative costs.

Therefore, given the growth of fixed costs of production and administered pricing, one can argue that shifts in the composition of demand may be inflationary. Assuming a constant growth in the variety of available products, this problem could become more important.

Monetary policy does not have great potential as a means of controlling demand-shift inflation. A change in the rate of growth of the money supply or higher interest rates are extremely unlikely to have any impact on shifts in consumers' tastes and preferences.

Although demand-shift inflation is not particularly susceptible to treatment with conventional policy tools, this type of inflation should not produce very rapidly rising price levels. A higher price is the initial response to an increase in demand for a product, but an increased level of profits should generate either new domestic entry (except in those industries in which barriers to entry are especially high) or should stimulate the importation of competitive foreign goods. In the industry facing declining demand, the falling level of profits should in time encourage exit from the industry and permit the remaining firms to regain the economies of scale.

The Perpetuation of Inflation

Whatever the causes of inflation, other forces that are partly separate and independent can perpetuate the inflation long after the initiating forces have had their effect.

The major force tending to perpetuate inflation is the expectation of inflation. Inflation creates forces that generate the expectation of further inflation; the expectation of further inflation causes that further inflation. In part, expectations can create the self-fulfilling prophecy. As the St. Louis monetarist model in Chapter 12 illustrated, anticipated future price changes can be based on past actual price changes and are a factor in the determination of actual future price changes.

Expectations of inflation can perpetuate inflation in innumerable ways. The expectation of price increases leads the consumer to stock up on goods and beat the expected price increases. Business firms are led to increase inventory holdings beyond the normal level. All of this anticipatory buying increases the level of aggregate demand and adds to the upward pressure on price levels.

The negotiation of contracts is also affected by the expectation of inflation. Labor unions inflate their demands for future wages or insist upon the inclusion of a cost-of-living adjustment clause in their contract. The business firm inflates its bid on a long-term project to allow for the anticipated rate of inflation.

Wise consumers attempt to invest in those items that are expected to increase in value as price levels rise. Investments, such as bonds, which do not offer inflation protection, are in lesser demand and market interest rates must increase to attract investors to accept the inflation risk.

The anticipation of inflation may contribute to the continuation of any of the types of inflation—demand pull, cost push, or demand shift—given that expected inflation distorts the normal patterns of economic behavior.

How to Have an Inflationary Recession

The first half of the 1970s appeared to deny the experience of the past. Whereas traditional theory placed inflation and recession at opposite ends of the spectrum —inflation as a symptom of too much demand and recession as a sign of deficient demand—the 1970s demonstrated that inflation and recession could occur simultaneously.

The explanation of this period involves a number of elements. Macroeconomic policy was erratic. First, inflation seemed to be the greater evil, and energies were expended to stop inflation. Wage and price controls were imposed. Then recession became the greater evil, and economic policy shifted toward halting the decline in demand. Policy did not seem to concentrate on one evil long enough to have any effect before the attack swung in the opposite direction.

The other important element was the impact of the rise in petroleum prices. Given sharp price increases for this all-important product, drastic cost and price increases were inevitable. The cost-price spiral transmitted the impact of the energy price increases throughout the entire economy. For most of the period, consumer incomes did not rise fast enough to offset the higher prices of energy and food. While the consumer may have conserved some energy and reduced food purchases, the rapid rise in energy and food prices decreased the amount of discretionary income remaining to purchase other, less vital items. Thus, demand for less critical items declined, and recession followed on the heels of inflation.

Policy probably contributed to the joint incidence of inflation and recession. The rising price level led the Federal Reserve to slow down the growth of the money supply and to permit interest rates to rise to record levels in 1973 and 1974.

In part, the recession-inflation effect was slightly different from past problems because of its international trade implications. The rising prices of food and petroleum did not have the same effect on domestic aggregate demand. Higher food prices hurt the purchaser of food but provided more income to the domestic producers of food. One group had less purchasing power and another group had more purchasing power; the income transfer was an internal transfer. The petroleum problem, however, represented an international transfer of purchasing power. Billions of additional dollars were transferred from American consumers to foreign oil producers. The oil producers did not instantly use those dollars for the purchase of American goods and services. The initial reaction of the OPEC states was to pile up bank balances and short-term securities, rather than buying goods and services. Therefore, the lost domestic demand was not offset by an increase in export demand from the oil-producing states. In the longer run, imports by OPEC nations have added to demand in the United States and other countries. However, in the short run, this did not occur, and the level of aggregate demand declined while prices rose.

Is Inflation Built into the American Economic System?

Has the United States developed a system in which inflation is and will continue to be a chronic problem? The answer to the question has to be yes. In a variety of ways, the United States has assured itself of seldom, if ever, facing a period of generally declining prices. The question for the future will be, how can the rate of inflation be minimized? Several factors suggest continued inflation in the future.

First, most past periods of falling prices (deflation) were associated with recessions or depressions. Typically, inflation occurred during periods of war; after the war, the economy suffered a serious depression and prices declined. For example, by the late 1870s, wholesale prices were back to the 1860 level. Wholesale prices dropped in 1921 and reversed most of the price increases associated with World War I.

Today, for perfectly good reasons, society does not tolerate recessions of the magnitude necessary to decrease prices. Furthermore, there are tools to put society's preferences into action and prevent very severe recessions. People are willing and able to avoid price-reducing recessions. Therefore, there have been no recessions of the magnitude necessary to reverse the inflations of World War II, the Korean war, and the Vietnam war. Since 1945, consumer prices have marched upwards annually, with only minor year-to-year interruptions in 1949 and 1955. Unless society changes its commitment to the avoidance of depression—and few would advocate this policy—past price increases will not be reversed. Even the relatively severe recession of 1974–1975, which produced an unemployment rate averaging 8.5 percent in 1975, produced only a slowdown of the inflation rate.

Second, the extent of administered pricing means that prices are unlikely to decline even with substantial reductions in demand. The price of automobiles goes up year after year regardless of the demand for cars. Price rebate programs, such as were used in 1975, were only temporary; list prices were restored later in the year in spite of the low sales volume. Food and raw material prices still appear to be responsive to supply and demand changes, but most prices do not rapidly respond to reduced demand.

Many costs of production do not decline in a period of recession. List prices for purchased inputs may be shaved a bit by suppliers, but the major costs of production, such as labor, are stable. Even in a major recession, wage rates seldom decline. Fixed costs and administered pricing keep prices constant in a recession.

Third, the economy could not afford significant deflation. A fall in prices and incomes would have severe effects on those firms and households that are relying on inflation to bail them out of their indebtedness. For example, an equal percentage fall in both family incomes and real estate prices would force many mortgage foreclosures. Houses would be difficult to sell and the solvency of the banks would be threatened. Given the high levels of consumer and business debt, a reduction of incomes and prices could create great problems.

Fourth, the expectation of rising wages creates a bias in favor of inflation. All workers—regardless of whether or not their productivity has increased—have come to expect an annual wage increase. Given that a large proportion of the population has grown to maturity in a period of rising prices and money wages, the expectation of the annual raise has become ingrained in the bulk of the work force.

Fifth, there is a reasonable expectation that declining world supplies of raw materials will increase costs of production. New sources of energy and raw materials will be produced only at higher costs. While the world may not run out of critical resources, marginal additions to total supplies will be developed at increasing marginal costs.

In summary, it appears that inflation is here to stay. The policy problem will be to minimize the rate of inflation without creating unacceptable levels of unemployment.

What Has Macroeconomic Policy Achieved?

Over 40 years have now passed since the publication of Keynes' *The General Theory of Employment, Interest and Money.* What problems still remain? To fully answer the question would require another book, but some general opinions can be presented from the analysis of the chapters in this part of the text.

First, economists have a better grasp of the forces determining the level of aggregate demand. Vast quantities of empirical and theoretical work have yielded a greater understanding of the determinants of aggregate demand.

Second, there is still a long way to go in controlling inflation and recession. While the fiscal and monetary policy tools and the built-in stabilizers have eliminated the danger of massive depressions and hyperinflations, economists have not developed the precision instruments required to produce full employment growth at stable prices.

Third, theoretical advances have moved ahead of policy making practices. A concern for macroeconomic goals is still only partly incorporated into political decision-making processes. Governmental responses to macroeconomic problems are still too slow to have their maximum effectiveness.

Fourth, monetary and fiscal policy can control demand-pull inflation but, except for wage and price controls, there are no new policy tools to control other types of inflation. The wage and price control alternative, though acceptable to many in the short run, would probably not be acceptable in the longer run.

Finally, automatic policy rules have not been perfected. Until such time as demonstrably better rules can be invented, economists will have to concentrate on improving the use of the discretionary policy tools.

REVIEW QUESTIONS

1. Explain the wealth effect on consumption spending.

2. Why would the credit rationing effect be more important in a period of economic expansion than in a period of recession?

3. Review the theoretical case for and against the interest rate effect on the level of investment. What forces would strengthen the interest rate effect in a period of expansion? What forces would weaken the interest rate effect in a recession?

4. Why does monetary policy have an exceptionally strong effect on residential construction?

5. Differentiate between the various theories of inflation.

6. Which of the various types of inflation would be most likely to be controlled by wage and price controls?

7. Why does inflation continue to be a problem long after the factors that initiated the inflation have ceased to be a problem?

8. Are there any long-run forces that would suggest that inflation will not continue to be an international problem?

9. To what extent does inflation serve to redistribute income and wealth?

10. What are the possible costs and benefits of reducing the economic power of major unions and concentrated industries?

SUGGESTED READINGS

R. J. Ball, *Inflation and the Theory of Money.* Chicago: Aldine Publishing Co., 1964.

Peter Fortune, "An Evaluation of Anti-Inflation Policies in the United States," *New England Economic Review,* Federal Reserve Bank of Boston, January–February 1974, pp. 3–27.

Robert Aaron Gordon, *Economic Instability and Growth: The American Record.* New York: Harper & Row, Publishers, 1974.

William Guttman and Patricia Meehan, *The Great Inflation.* London: Saxon House, D.C. Heath Ltd., 1975.

Robert Lekachman, *Inflation.* New York: Random House, 1973.

John M. Mason, "A Structural Study of the Income Velocity of Circulation," *Journal of Finance,* American Finance Association, New York, September 1974, pp. 1077–1086.

J. Huston McCulloch, *Money and Inflation; A Monetarist Approach.* New York: Academic Press, 1975.

John J. Seater, "A Perspective of Stagflation," *Federal Reserve Bank of Philadelphia Business Review,* May 1975, pp. 19–30.

Steven A. Seelig, "Rising Interest Rates and Cost Push Inflation," *Journal of Finance,* American Finance Association, New York, September 1974, pp. 1049–1061.

Roger W. Spencer, "Channels of Monetary Influence: A Survey," *Federal Reserve Bank of St. Louis Review,* November 1974, pp.8–26.

"The Universities—National Bureau Conference on Secular Inflation," *Journal of Money, Credit and Banking,* Ohio State University Press, Columbus, February 1973, pp. 237–593.

"World Inflation," *Federal Reserve Bank of San Francisco Business Review,* Spring 1975, pp. 1–48.

Jai-Hoon Yang, "The Case for and Against Indexation: An Attempt at Perspective," *Federal Reserve Bank of St. Louis Review,* October 1974, pp. 2–11.

PART III

THE ALLOCATION OF CREDIT

The functions of the credit-supplying institutions in the American financial structure were described in Part I. Part II examined the ability of monetary policy to control the level of aggregate demand. In Part III, the analysis focuses on the distribution of the available supply of credit among alternative uses of credit.

Chapter 16 studies the role of the market in the process of allocating credit among alternative uses and users. Theoretical and practical problems resulting from the market's allocation of credit are presented.

Chapter 17 examines the massive impact of the government on the allocation of credit. Both the demand for and the supply of credit are affected by governmental activities in the credit markets.

Chapter 18 analyzes the effect of monetary policy on the allocation of credit. Although monetary policy is a general macroeconomic tool, all sectors of the economy may not bear equal shares of the burden of monetary policy. If monetary policy effectively restrains some sectors of the economy and has no impact on other sectors, can the unequal distribution of the burden be justified in terms of equity or national economic goals? Are distributional inequities the result of the functioning of the market or do they result from other causes?

Chapter 19 concludes the examination of credit allocation. The case for and against a comprehensive credit allocation program is presented and alternative methods for the allocation of credit are reviewed.

16

THE MARKET AND THE ALLOCATION OF CREDIT

Nearly every person, business firm, and governmental unit is a user or potential user of credit, and in the American economy the market is the predominant allocator of goods and services. The first part of this chapter examines the process by which the market allocates credit. The second part describes some problems associated with the market's allocation of credit, and the third section presents the arguments for and against governmental intervention in this credit allocation process.

The Market's Allocation of Credit

In the American economy, most goods and services are rationed by the price mechanism. Those consumers willing and able to pay the price acquire new cars and other necessities and luxuries. Those business firms willing and able to purchase capital equipment obtain the most modern means of production.

The supply of credit is not limitless and, like most goods and services, is usually rationed on the basis of price. The price of credit—the interest rate—determines the distribution of credit among alternative potential borrowers. At an interest rate of 15 percent, some people are willing and able to borrow to finance a new car; others are unable or unwilling to pay that interest rate. On the supply side, lenders are willing to grant a certain dollar value of car loans at 15 percent; at 20 percent the lenders would be willing to make more car loans and at 5 percent would be willing to make very few car loans. Thus, the supply of and demand for car loans should determine the market price of car loans.

The interest rate paid by most borrowers is established by supply and demand forces. If General Motors desires to sell a new issue of long-term bonds, the supply of funds available in the market, the credit demands of other borrowers, and the market's assessment of General Motors' credit standing determine the interest rate paid by General Motors. Naturally, some credit transactions do not pass through the marketplace. For example, one may borrow from a relative or a friend without any formalities and might not be charged any interest on the loan.

A Model of Lending Behavior

The financial institution operates as a profit-making firm. Faced with alternative lending opportunities, the bank can be expected to choose that mix of loans which, after allowing for lending costs and risk differentials, maximizes profits.

Assume a hypothetical bank, Fail-Proof National Bank. Fail-Proof operates in competition with other local banks. Fail-Proof has met its reserve requirements and is holding sufficient secondary reserve assets. The bank is ready to make loans. Assume that the bank is restricted (by a law invented for the purpose of this analysis) to two alternative activities: making one-year car loans or holding one-year government bonds.

As one of thousands of purchasers of Federal government bonds, Fail-Proof National Bank has no impact on the market price or yield on government debt. Fail-Proof can buy or sell any quantity of government bonds without affecting the assumed current yield of 6 percent.

The market for car loans is different from the market for government bonds. In the local car loan market, Fail-Proof is one of a few lenders; Fail-Proof competes with a limited number of other commercial banks and thrift institutions. As Fail-Proof reduces the interest rate charged on car loans, more people are encouraged to finance new car purchases, and Fail-Proof attracts loan customers from the other lending institutions.

Table 16–1 presents a hypothetical relationship between the interest rate charged on one-year car loans and the volume of car loans which Fail-Proof could grant each month. In Table 16–1, column (1) lists alternative interest rates that could be charged to borrowers, and column (2) lists the dollar value of loans that could be made at each alternative interest rate. In column (3), the interest income that could be earned by Fail-Proof is calculated. The analysis abstracts from all operating costs and the income calculation is obtained simply by multiplying the interest rate in column (1) by the volume of car loans in column (2).

Column (4) is the marginal or added revenue that would be received by Fail-Proof as a result of lowering the interest rate by one percentage point and granting an additional $500,000 of car loans. For example, by lowering the interest rate from 16 to 15 percent, an added $65,000 of income is earned; the marginal, or additional, revenue is $65,000. In column (5), the marginal revenue in column (4) is converted into percentage form by dividing the marginal revenue in column (4) by the added volume of loans. Thus, as the interest rate is reduced from 16 to 15 percent, $65,000 of marginal revenue is earned on the added or marginal $500,000 of car loans. A marginal revenue of 13 percent is earned ($65,000/$500,000).

Note that the *marginal revenue* declines more rapidly than the *average revenue* (the price, or interest rate, charged on car loans). The bank must lower the

TABLE 16–1 Fail-Proof National Bank's Marginal Revenue from Car Loans

(1) INTEREST RATE CHARGED–PRICE OR AVERAGE REVENUE) (percent)	(2) CAR LOANS (dollars)	(3) INCOME (dollars)	(4) MARGINAL REVENUE FROM ADDED $500,000 OF CAR LOANS (dollars)	(5) MARGINAL REVENUE (percent)
17	500,000	85,000	85,000	17
16	1,000,000	160,000	75,000	15
15	1,500,000	225,000	65,000	13
14	2,000,000	280,000	55,000	11
13	2,500,000	325,000	45,000	9
12	3,000,000	360,000	35,000	7
11	3,500,000	385,000	25,000	5
10	4,000,000	400,000	15,000	3

price on all loans in order to expand the volume of loans. For example, as the price is lowered from 17 to 16 percent, the added $500,000 of loans increases revenue by $80,000. However, the first $500,000 of loans, which at 17 percent could have produced $85,000 of income, are now made at 16 percent and produce only $80,000 of income. This $5,000 revenue difference is subtracted from the $80,000 of income from the additional $500,000 of loans. The net revenue gain, the marginal revenue, is $75,000.

The critical information in Table 16–1 is plotted in panel (A) of Figure 16–1. The interest rate is the price variable on the vertical axis, and dollars of car loans is the quantity variable on the horizontal axis.

Fail-Proof now has the necessary information on the marginal revenue of alternative quantities of car loans. In panel (B) of Figure 16–1, the average and marginal revenue that would be obtained by holding government bonds is plotted. Regardless of the quantity of bonds purchased by Fail-Proof, both the average revenue (the interest rate or price) and the marginal revenue are equal to the market-determined yield of 6 percent.

The next step is the construction of a third marginal revenue curve combining the information in panels (A) and (B) of Figure 16–1. If Fail-Proof had only one $500,000 unit of funds available, the bank would invest these funds in car loans at a marginal revenue of 17 percent, which represents a higher return than the 6 percent that could be earned on government bonds. The second $500,000 unit of funds invested in car loans produces a marginal revenue of 15 percent, which is also better than the 6 percent yield on government bonds. The third, fourth, fifth, and sixth units of funds are also allocated to car loans.

After $3 million are allocated to car loans, the marginal revenue from added car loans is reduced to 7 percent. Consider the seventh unit of funds; the seventh $500,000 unit could be used to receive a 5 percent marginal revenue from

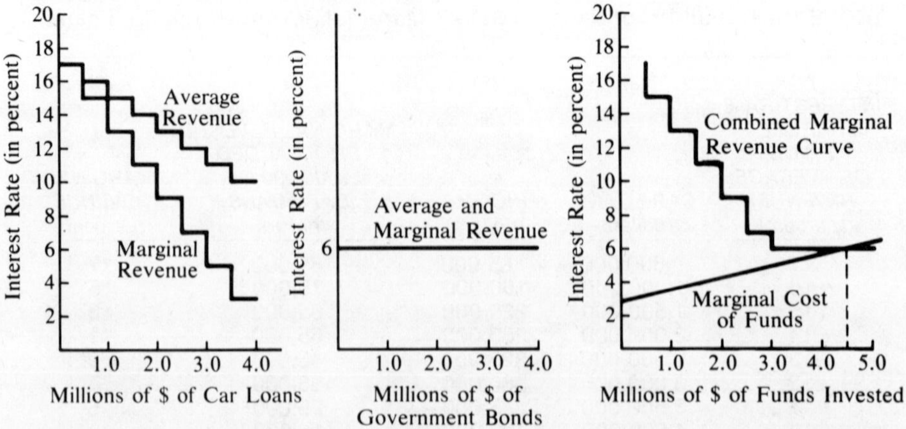

FIGURE 16–1 Hypothetical Returns from Alternative Uses of Bank Funds

car loans or a 6 percent marginal revenue from government bonds. Given that the marginal revenue of subsequent funds devoted to car loans continues to decline, 6 units of funds are used for car loans and the remaining funds are invested in government bonds at 6 percent. The combined marginal revenue curve in panel (C) of Figure 16–1 illustrates this conclusion. The marginal revenue curve becomes parallel to the horizontal axis at a marginal revenue of 6 percent.

The final necessary bit of information is the marginal cost of funds. A hypothetical marginal cost of funds curve is plotted in panel (C) of Figure 16–1. The marginal cost of funds curve slopes upwards to indicate that the bank's cost of added (marginal) funds increases.

In this example, Fail-Proof competes for $4.5 million of funds. Funds are purchased up to the point at which the marginal (added) cost of the last unit of funds is equal to the marginal (added) revenue obtained from the use of the funds.

Fail-Proof uses the $4.5 million of funds to make $3 million of car loans and to invest $1.5 million in government bonds. Note that Fail-Proof charges an interest rate (price) of 12 percent on the $3 million of car loans.

Assuming Multiple Lending and Investment Alternatives

The previous example assumed that the bank had only two possible uses for its funds. The extension of the example to include multiple lending and investing opportunities presents no new theoretical concepts. The bank again calculates the marginal revenue for each activity and engages in each activity up to the point at which the marginal revenue is equal to the marginal cost of funds.

Assume an example in which Fail-Proof has three alternatives: lending to business, lending to consumers, or purchasing government bonds. The price and marginal revenue functions for each activity are presented in Table 16–2. In this

TABLE 16–2 Credit Allocation with Three Alternatives

BUSINESS LENDING			CONSUMER LENDING			GOVERNMENT BONDS		
MILLIONS OF DOLLARS	PRICE (AVERAGE REVENUE) (in percent)	MARGINAL REVENUE (percent)	MILLIONS OF DOLLARS	PRICE (AVERAGE REVENUE) (in percent)	MARGINAL REVENUE (percent)	MILLIONS OF DOLLARS	PRICE (AVERAGE REVENUE) (in percent)	MARGINAL REVENUE (percent)
1	9	9	1	10½	10½	1	4¾	4¾
2	8½	8	2	9½	8½	2	4¾	4¾
3	8	7	3	8½	6½	3	4¾	4¾
4	7½	6	4	7½	4½	4	4¾	4¾
5	7	5	5	6½	2½	5	4¾	4¾
6	6½	4	6	5½	½	6	4¾	4¾

TABLE 16–3 Distribution of Units of Funds Between Consumers, Business, and Government Securities

UNIT (of $1 million)	*SECTOR RECEIVING FUNDS*	*MARGINAL REVENUE (percent)*
1	Consumer	10½
2	Business	9
3	Consumer	8½
4	Business	8
5	Consumer	7
6	Business	6½
7	Business	6
8	Business	5
9	Government	4¾
10	Government	4¾
11	Government	4¾
12	Government	4¾
13	Government	4¾
14	Government	4¾

case, funds are allocated in $1 million units. As in the previous example, the marginal revenues from business lending and consumer lending decrease as interest rates are lowered to attract new borrowers. The marginal revenue from purchasing government bonds is again constant because Fail-Proof cannot affect the market-determined 4¾ percent yield on government bonds.

As in the previous case, Fail-Proof allocates each unit of funds to the activity offering the highest marginal revenue. The first $1 million of funds is allocated to consumer loans because the 10½ percent marginal revenue from this use of the funds is greater than the 9 percent that could be earned from the first $1 million of business loans and the 4¾ percent that could be earned from the first $1 million of government bond purchases. Thus, consumers receive the first $1 million.

For the allocation of the second $1 million, the bank has the alternatives of a marginal revenue of 9 percent from lending to business, 8½ percent from lending a second $1 million to consumers, and 4¾ percent from purchasing government bonds. Obviously, the second $1 million is used for business lending.

The alternatives for the use of the third $1 million unit of funds are a second unit of business lending at an 8 percent marginal revenue, a second unit of consumer lending at an 8½ percent marginal revenue, and a first unit of government bond purchases at a 4¾ percent marginal revenue. Consumers receive the third $1 million unit. The process continues with each unit of credit allocated in a similar manner. The distribution of units among the various alternatives is presented in Table 16–3. Using the information in Table 16–3, a composite marginal revenue curve is presented in Figure 16–2.

The marginal revenue curve in Figure 16–2 is intersected by a rising

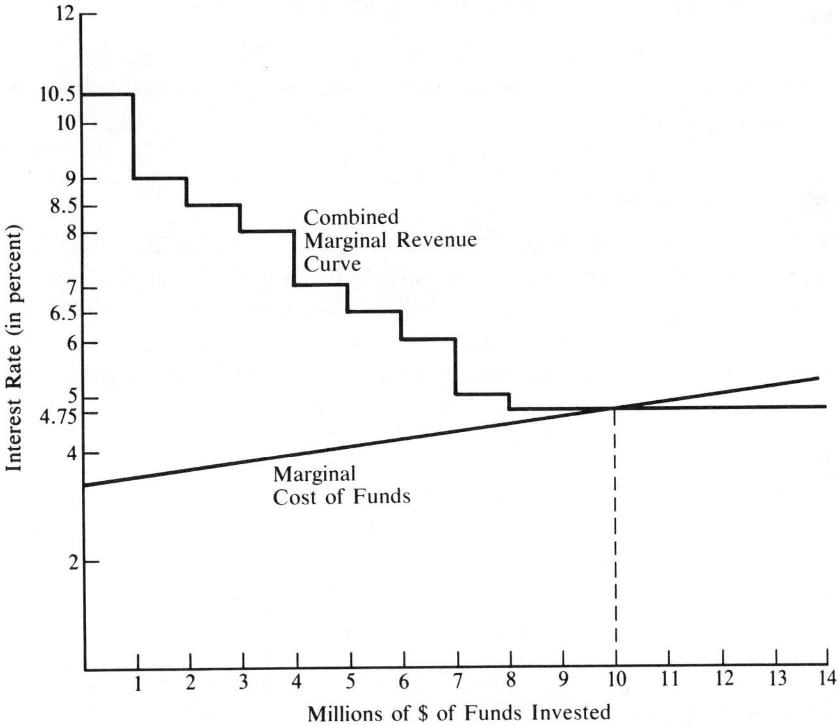

FIGURE 16–2 Hypothetical Returns from Use of Bank Funds

marginal cost function to reflect the higher cost of added funds. The bank obtains funds up to the point at which the marginal cost of added funds is equal to the marginal revenue produced by the use of the funds. In this case, the bank uses 10 units of funds of $1 million each.

Referring to Table 16–3, if only 10 units of funds are available, the bank would make $3 million of consumer loans, $5 million of business loans, and would purchase $2 million of government bonds.

Turning back to Table 16–2, the bank would charge consumers an interest rate of 8½ percent for the $3 million of consumer loans, would charge business an interest rate of 7 percent for the $5 million of business loans, and would receive a 4¾ percent return on their $2 million of government bonds. Both the quantity of credit allocated to each sector and the price of credit to each sector have been determined. The market has allocated credit.

Regardless of the number of bank activities included in the analysis, the basic procedure remains the same. The bank engages in each activity up to the point at which the marginal revenue produced by another unit of that activity equals the marginal cost of funds. Naturally, in a detailed analysis, allowance would have to be made for considerations of risk differentials, the costs of lending, and other factors. This analysis did not consider these complications.

Credit Allocation Problems in the Market Place

A variety of problems—both legal and theoretical—suggest that the market does not allocate credit perfectly. These problems are described in this section and various proposals for their elimination are considered in Chapter 19.

Legal Limitations on Interest Rates

Many types of loans are subject to interest rate ceilings. In most states, usury laws limit the interest rate that can be charged on consumer loans. Under government-subsidized mortgage lending programs, ceiling interest rates are established. Some state laws limit the maximum interest rate payable by either the state or any governmental unit within the state. All of these interest rate limitations can interfere with the market's allocation of credit. Consumers may be unable to borrow even though they are willing to pay an interest rate in excess of the usury limit. Municipal governments, although willing to pay a high market-determined rate of interest, may be prohibited from borrowing by state law.

Thus, the consumer or the governmental unit may not be able to exercise their preferences because of various legal restrictions on interest rates. To the extent that these restrictions are effective, credit is not allocated totally in accordance with the borrowers' willingness and ability to pay.

Regulation Q

Interest-rate ceilings on bank deposits change the allocation of credit. If a savings and loan association is willing and able to pay 7 percent on passbook deposits but is limited to paying 5 percent, fewer funds are available for mortgage loans.

Limits on Institutional Powers

In a completely free market, each financial institution would be able to select its preferred mix of various types of loans. Changes in relative interest rates would lead to a reallocation of the institution's funds among alternative uses. However, some institutions cannot freely move funds between various types of loans. For example, savings and loan associations normally have very restricted lending powers. The community may have a much greater need for business credit than for mortgage credit, but the savings and loan association cannot adjust its lending pattern.

Nonprice Rationing

Under the assumptions of the models of credit allocation, all credit was allocated on a price basis. However, nonprice rationing does occur. Nonprice rationing of consumer credit and business loans has already been discussed. Nonprice credit rationing can also occur on the basis of established institutional relationships. Established customers receive preferential treatment and new credit applicants are served if and when funds are available. When the supply of funds is limited, the institution has a long-run interest in meeting the credit needs of its regular customers.

In some cases, the institution may make certain types of loans only to its established customers. Education loans are frequently rationed on the basis of the student's family's ties with a given bank.

Borrowing Alternatives

All potential borrowers do not have access to all of the same sources of credit. The average consumer is usually restricted to local lending institutions. The cost of seeking a car loan in another city may be prohibitive. The outlays involved in telephone calls and traveling expense could offset any interest savings. In addition, banks in other cities would not have credit information on the loan applicant. The credit investigation costs would be very high relative to the size of the loan. The small business, like the consumer, may operate in a relatively restricted market. However, as the size of the business firm grows and the size of the loan increases, the number of potential sources of credit expands. Large nationally known firms with good credit ratings are welcome customers at any bank. If the banking system cannot meet corporate credit needs, these firms have the option of selling commercial paper or bonds.

Thus, all potential borrowers do not have access to the same number of lenders, the same types of lenders, and the same credit markets. The market's lack of knowledge of the borrower's credit worthiness, the cost of obtaining credit information relative to the size of the loan, and the borrower's imperfect knowledge of credit alternatives all may affect the allocation of credit. If all credit users were completely identical, the pattern of credit allocation might be quite different.

Discrimination

The allocation of credit may be affected by various types of discrimination. Most discriminatory effects would be between types of borrowers rather than types of credit. For example, a white middle class family might be granted a mortgage loan, while a similar black family is denied credit. Prior to the enactment of the Federal Equal Credit Opportunity Act[1] in October 1975, women often found it difficult or impossible to obtain credit. Although discrimination is illegal and immoral, it probably has relatively little effect on the total volume of mortgage credit; the impact of discrimination falls on the distribution of credit between individual borrowers.

[1] *Federal Reserve Bulletin,* November 1975, pp. 762–766.

The Ability to Shift Credit Costs

Obviously, the wealthier individual or the more prosperous business firm is better able to compete for credit and to pay higher interest rates. However, beyond this expected price rationing effect, some borrowers may be able to pass on the costs of higher interest rates. For example, the firm operating in an imperfectly competitive industry or the firm in a regulated industry may be relatively indifferent to the higher cost of credit. If the firm has control over the price of its product, the price can be increased to compensate for the higher interest rates. If the firm is in a regulated industry, the higher interest costs justify an application for higher rates. However, the consumer and the firm in a competitive industry do not have this ability to shift the higher costs of credit. In a period of high interest rates, less credit flows to those borrowers unable to shift the higher costs of credit.

The points considered in this section describe some of the ways in which the market fails to allocate credit according to consumer, business, and government preferences. The next section considers the case for and against government intervention in the allocation of credit.

Limiting the Role of the Market in the Allocation of Credit

Should the market allocate all forms of credit or should some forms of credit be allocated on a partially nonmarket basis? Society has chosen to allocate many goods and services on other than a price basis. Perhaps some forms of credit should also be distributed on a nonprice basis. This section explores the arguments for, and the problems involved in, government intervention in the allocation of credit.

Arguments for Intervention in the Credit Allocation Process

There are four arguments for instituting new governmental programs to allocate credit. First, one could argue that because of the imperfections cited in the previous section, the market does not allocate credit properly and thus intervention in the market is necessary to compensate for these imperfections.

The second part of the argument is that monetary policy discriminates against some forms of credit; therefore, a credit allocation program is necessary to correct for the effect of monetary policy on the allocation of credit. This argument is examined in Chapter 18.

Third, there is already governmental involvement in credit allocation, but these various programs, to be described in Chapter 17, have been instituted one by one on a nonsystematic basis. The consideration of an overall credit allocation program would force a comprehensive review of the present scope of governmental intervention in the nation's credit markets.

Fourth, it is argued that limited intervention in the credit markets is needed to encourage certain high-priority credit-using activities. The argument is that the market system does not recognize all of the social benefits resulting from some uses of credit; therefore, the government must intervene in the market to increase the flow of credit to certain sectors of the economy.

Regardless of the social value resulting from a given use of credit, credit is allocated on the basis of ability to pay the market-determined rate of interest. In the first chapter of this book, a student faced a credit allocation problem in which the social value of a student's education loan was not reflected in the bank's allocation of funds between tuition loans and car loans.

A student is acutely aware of the advantages of higher education and could cite the values to society of his education, including greater tax-paying ability, increased productivity as a member of the labor force, and a more diversified background for participation in society. However, other groups also see social benefits resulting from increasing the allocation of credit to alternative uses. Those lobbying for improved housing view the provision of low-cost mortgage credit as providing social benefits in the form of a reduced number of substandard housing units, fewer slum neighborhoods, and the property-maintenance incentives associated with home ownership. The hospital administrator argues that health care is of high priority and that low-cost credit should be available for the construction and equipping of modern hospital facilities. These activities are also worthwhile, according to most people's value judgments.

How does society recognize these social values and subsidize those activities that produce gains both to the individual recipient of the good or service and to the society? First, society can subsidize the price of the good or service. Providing direct governmental support for education and government-subsidized home and hospital construction reduces the direct cost to the user. In recognition of society's share of the benefits, the government can finance part of the cost of the good or service from general tax revenues.

Second, society can subsidize the individual user of a good or service. Higher education, for example, can be "sold" at a price reflecting the total cost of the education, and those who cannot afford to pay can be assisted by direct educational grants. A similar grant program can be used to assist homeowners to meet mortgage payments.

Third, a more radical alternative is to have a general redistribution of income to equalize people's ability to pay for education, homes, and medical care. However, there is little prospect for greater equality in the distribution of income in the near future.

Finally, goods and services can be provided at their full cost of production, and government-subsidized lending programs can make loans available for those unable to pay the full price of the good or service.

Thus, the provision of government-subsidized lending programs is only one of a number of alternative solutions to the problem of making certain goods available on a subsidized basis. In many cases, society has combined a number of options. For example, education is supported by government expenditures, student tuition payments, scholarships, work-study programs, and loans. Housing is subsidized by the provision of low-cost public housing and various low-interest rate lending programs. Society must decide upon both the total amount of public support for various programs and the form in which the support should be distributed. Intervention in the market's allocation of credit is only one of several options.

The use of credit allocation programs appears to have merit in a number of cases. First, if credit costs are a high proportion of the total cost of the product, lowering the cost of the credit may be the best approach to subsidizing the activity. For example, mortgage interest payments are frequently the largest portion of total monthly housing costs. Reducing the interest rate charged to the borrower substantially lowers the borrower's total expenditure over the life of the mortgage.

Second, general support for a given governmental function may still require supplementary support for particular individuals. For example, states maintain university systems and charge tuition at rates well below total education costs. However, even low tuition rates create problems for some students. Increasing general tax support for the university and further lowering tuition assists all students regardless of their ability to pay. Providing subsidized interest rate loans to those students unable to pay the tuition deals with individual financial problems, is less expensive for the taxpayers than is general tuition reduction, and leaves the ratio of tuition and public support relatively unchanged because the student must repay the loan.

Third, in some cases, the need for credit may be critical and credit may be unavailable without government assistance to the prospective borrowers. Loans to businesses and individuals in a disaster area might be placed in this category. Aid to economically depressed areas might also be included in this category.

Thus, there is a case for governmental intervention to alter the normal market allocation of credit. However, an argument can also be made that the government should not change the market's allocation of credit.

The Case Against Credit Market Intervention

There are four major arguments against intervention in credit markets. First, the credit allocation program might not achieve the social objective in the most efficient manner. Perhaps the objective could be accomplished at lower costs with an alternative method.

Second, once the allocation of credit is removed from the marketplace, the distribution process becomes more complex. There is no alternative economic methodology for assessing the relative needs of competing groups. The decision to provide more funds for student loans may mean fewer loans to homeowners. The credit distribution process becomes a function of the political process. Can the Congress make the appropriate decisions? If Congress were to delegate the responsibility to the Federal Reserve System, would the Board of Governors produce the socially optimal allocation of credit?

Third, the introduction of nonmarket credit allocation requires making value judgments on the relative merits of different activities. Throughout this discussion, the author has interjected his own value judgments by indicating that he thinks both education loans and mortgage loans are worthwhile and that both deserve to be favored in the credit allocation process. It is very difficult to discuss credit allocation problems without becoming involved in value judgments. The question is, under a credit allocation system, who should make these judgments?

As another example of the introduction of value judgments into the process of allocating credit, consider the following quotation from the late Nat Goldfinger, the former Director of the Department of Research of the AFL-CIO: "We believe that the allocation of credit on the basis of social priorities is essential to a sensible monetary policy. We'd like to see high priorities for such purposes as housing, community facilities and the normal operations of business; and the restraint of credit for such purposes as commodity market speculation, land speculation, foreign lending, foreign subsidiary operations, and so forth."[2] Mr. Goldfinger apparently did not believe that student loans are among the high priority items, yet his opinion would have been considered if additional credit allocation decisions were made outside of the normal market processes.

Fourth, government lending programs are costly, and financial institutions may not have the ability or incentive to make high-priority loans. Direct government lending involves all the normal governmental red tape. In addition, the question arises as to how the funds should be obtained. Some combination of reductions of other government spending programs, tax increases, or increased government spending is necessary. Each of these approaches involves obvious social decision-making problems.

If lending programs are to be operated through private banking institutions, the loans must be able to compete with other bank lending opportunities. If the government places an interest rate ceiling on loans of a given type, banks will not allocate funds to these loans if other alternatives offer higher rates of return. Thus, the banks must be given an incentive to lend in the desired manner. If the full cost of the loan is not to be assumed by the borrower, part of the interest cost must be absorbed by government payments to the lenders.

Summary

Programs for intervening in the market's allocation of credit involve numerous potential problems and must be evaluated very carefully. The market system may not be the best allocator of resources, but the alternatives may be much worse. The social benefits obtained by changing the market's allocation of credit could easily be offset by added social costs.

[2]Nat Goldfinger, "The General State of Affairs in the American Economy Is Very Serious and Very Dangerous," *Challenge,* November–December, 1975, p. 31.

The four policy questions to be analyzed in the following chapters continue the examination of the market and alternatives to the market as a means of allocating credit. The questions to be considered are as follows:

1. What is the current level of governmental intervention in the credit allocation process?

2. Does monetary policy have an unjustifiably large effect on certain credit-using sectors of the economy?

3. Can the market's allocation of credit be improved?

4. If the allocation of credit needs to be changed, is there a better credit allocation system?

REVIEW QUESTIONS

1. In the credit allocation examples, why did the marginal revenue from consumer and business lending decrease while the marginal revenue from purchasing government securities remained constant?

2. In the credit allocation examples, why does the marginal cost of funds increase as the quantity of funds increases?

3. The credit allocation examples assume that the bank is under no legal obligations to hold certain types of assets. How do requirements such as reserve requirements or liquidity requirements affect the basic analysis?

4. How is the market's allocation of credit affected by the existence of usury laws?

5. Explain the effect of Regulation Q on the competition for deposits and the resulting impact on the allocation of credit.

6. How would reforms such as those suggested by the Hunt Commission affect the credit allocation process?

7. What arguments could be made against a market-oriented credit allocation system? How would you respond to these arguments?

8. Should lenders be required to consider the social value of various types of loans? What would be the costs of this type of policy to the lender? to society in general?

9. Explain nonprice credit rationing. How does this promote or interfere with the optimal allocation of credit?

10. How does the ability of some borrowers to shift credit costs to others affect the allocation of credit?

SUGGESTED READINGS

David P. Eastburn, "Federal Reserve Policy and Social Priorities," *Federal Reserve Bank of Philadelphia Business Review,* November 1970, pp. 3–8.

Darryl R. Francis, "Social Priorities and the Market Allocation of Credit," *Federal Reserve Bank of St. Louis Review,* May 1971, pp. 8–13.

Ira Kaminow and James O'Brien, eds., *Studies in Selective Credit Policies,* Federal Reserve Bank of Philadelphia, 1975.

Thomas Mayer, "Credit Allocation—A Critical View," *Government Credit Allocation, Where Do We Go From Here?"* Institute for Contemporary Studies, San Francisco, 1975, pp. 39–92. (Copyright by the Center for Research in Government Policy and Business of the Graduate School of Management, University of Rochester, Rochester, N.Y.)

Bernard Shull, "Commercial Banks as Multiple-Product Price-Discriminatory Firms," pp. 351–368 in Deane Carson, ed., *Banking and Monetary Studies*. Homewood, Ill.: Richard D. Irwin, 1963.

17

THE GOVERNMENT AND THE ALLOCATION OF CREDIT

The impact of the federal government on the allocation of credit occurs through two different channels. First, the Federal Reserve System influences the quantity and allocation of credit in the process of conducting monetary policy. The effects of monetary policy on credit allocation are discussed in Chapter 18.

Second, even if the total supply of credit is held constant, the government has an impact on credit allocation. This chapter examines the following six aspects of government influence on the allocation of a given supply of credit:

1. Government is a demander of credit.
2. It is a supplier of credit.
3. It has credit guarantee programs.
4. It has credit restriction programs.
5. It has taxation power.
6. It regulates the structure and powers of the credit industry.

Government as a Demander of Credit

The federal government has not always been a major borrower. Traditionally, debt was contracted during war years and repaid after the war. Federal debt in 1929 was a mere $16.5 billion. By 1940, the debt had increased to $41.9 billion as a result of the Great Depression. Of this debt, $33.4 billion was held by the public and $8.6 billion by government agencies, government trust funds, and the Federal Reserve System. By the end of 1946, the total federal debt had increased to over $259 billion, and the portion held by the private sector was over $203 billion. The application of Keynesian economics to the business cycle problem and the Vietnam war resulted in a continued growth of federal debt. By December 1975, total federal debt was $576.6 billion, and the portion held outside of government agencies, trust funds, and the Federal Reserve was $349.4 billion.

TABLE 17–1 Total Funds Raised by the Sale of Debt Instruments in the Credit Markets, 1974

TYPE OF DEBT INSTRUMENT	*BILLIONS OF DOLLARS*	*PERCENTAGE OF TOTAL*
U.S. Government securities	33.5	15.8
State and local obligations	17.4	8.2
Corporate and foreign bonds	23.3	11.0
Mortgages	54.5	25.6
Consumer credit	9.6	4.5
Bank loans (not elsewhere classified)	39.5	18.6
Open market paper and repurchase agreements	13.6	6.4
Other loans	21.1	9.9
Total funds raised by sale of debt instruments	212.5	100.0

SOURCE: Summary of Funds Raised in United States Credit Markets, *Federal Reserve Bulletin,* October 1975, p. A56.

Two points can be made relative to the effect of federal debt on credit allocation. First, as a borrower the federal government has a major impact on the total debt market. Table 17–1 presents the 1974 data on total funds raised in credit markets through the sale of debt instruments. In 1974, the federal government accounted for 15.8 percent of all funds raised by the sale of debt instruments. Over time, the government's proportion varies, depending upon federal budgetary policy. In the first half of 1975, the federal government accounted for 49 percent of total funds raised in the debt markets (on an annual rate basis). With less borrowing by the government, interest rates would have been lower and private credit users probably would have been able to increase their borrowing.

Second, the impact of the government can be examined in terms of the distribution of the federal debt between investors. If the debt of the government were not available, individuals and institutions could hold larger quantities of private securities. Table 17–2 presents a breakdown of the ownership of the Federal debt as of December 1975. This table indicates that a large portion of the total debt, $139.3 billion, is held within the government sector by trust funds (primarily the Social Security Trust Fund) and the Federal Reserve System. Outside the government sector, individuals and commercial banks are the largest holders of federal debt. The major advantages of holding federal government debt are perfect safety, an active market for the resale of government bonds, and the wide variety of types and maturities. However, to an extent, the holding of federal government debt replaces the holding of other types of securities.

State and Local Government Debt

Although more attention is usually focused on federal government debt, the pressures for capital expenditures by state and local governments have resulted in rapid increases of outstanding state and local government bonds. The debt of states

TABLE 17–2 Ownership of the Federal Debt, December 1975

HELD BY	*BILLIONS OF DOLLARS*	*PERCENTAGE OF TOTAL*
U.S. Government agencies and trust funds	139.3	24.2
Federal Reserve banks	87.9	15.2
Commercial banks	85.8	14.9
Mutual savings banks and insurance companies	13.4	2.3
Other corporations	20.3	3.5
State and local governments	34.2	5.9
Individuals	91.0	15.8
Miscellaneous investors	104.7	18.2
Total gross public debt	576.6	100.0

SOURCE: *1976 Economic Report of the President,* p. 254.

and local governments increased from $15 billion in 1945 to over $200 billion by 1974. Throughout the period, these governmental units have been consistent demanders of new funds. As Table 17–1 indicates, 8.2 percent of funds raised in 1974 were obtained by state and local governments. The major holders of these bonds are upper income individuals and commercial banks; both groups are attracted by the tax advantages associated with state and local government bonds.

State and local government debt can be divided by term to maturity and by type of obligation. State and local governments borrow short term on a regular basis to bridge the gap between expenditures and the receipt of tax revenues. A municipality is supported mainly by property taxes and receives its income once a year. However, local expenditures continue throughout the year and the municipality may need to borrow against future tax collections. This short-term borrowing is usually from local banks and is in the form of *tax-anticipation notes.*

Longer term state and local government debt issues are designed to provide funds for capital improvements and serve to divide the payments over a multi-year period. If the public facility is to be used for many years, present users and taxpayers share the cost with future users and taxpayers.

State and local government debt can also be subdivided on the basis of legal backing; two major types of debt instruments are commonly used. The *general obligation bond* pledges the "full faith and credit" of the issuing town or state. Thus, the bonds are backed by the taxing power of the governmental body. Alternatively, *revenue bonds* may be issued to pay for specific projects or by governmental authorities. The legal security of revenue bonds consists of the income from the specific project being financed rather than the general credit of the governmental unit. Thus, a port authority, airport authority, or turnpike authority may be established by the state and may borrow without pledging the credit of the state. The bonds are secured only by the income and assets of the issuing authority. The yield on revenue bonds is usually higher than the yield on general obligation bonds because the revenue bonds are not backed by the full taxing power of the state.

The Government as a Supplier of Credit

While the government is a major demander of credit, most government units also supply credit. In some cases, the government directly provides credit to borrowers. In other cases, the government influences the terms on which borrowers can obtain credit. This section deals only with direct credit; programs influencing credit terms are examined in the following section.

Housing

A major portion of direct government lending involves support of the secondary mortgage market and government mortgage market institutions. A mortgage is a relatively illiquid instrument; the quality of a given mortgage depends upon the financial status of the debtor, the value of the property mortgaged, and other factors that vary with each mortgage loan. Assume a bank in one area has insufficient funds to meet the demand for mortgages, and a bank in another area has the funds but few mortgage lending opportunities. The system needs a secondary mortgage market that would allow the bank in the high mortgage demand area to sell mortgages to the bank having a low demand for mortgage loans. However, because each mortgage is a unique instrument, the purchasing institution's cost of evaluating each mortgage would be very high relative to the size of the average loan.

The government has tried various schemes to develop secondary market institutions and to facilitate the sale of mortgages between financial institutions. In addition, the government has attempted to add new money to the mortgage markets by purchasing existing mortgages from the lending institutions. The Federal National Mortgage Association (FNMA) was established in 1938 to accomplish these objectives.

The FNMA purchases mortgages from financial institutions with funds obtained by selling FNMA bonds in the capital markets. Thus, the credit of the government is used to obtain funds for support of the mortgage market. FNMA purchases only mortgages that are insured by the Federal Housing Administration (FHA) or guaranteed by the Veterans Administration (VA) (the distinction between the two will be clarified later) and has assisted in injecting new money into the mortgage market during periods of tight money. The FNMA has now been converted into a private corporation, but it still performs the same basic functions. Mortgages are purchased in periods of tight money and in periods of greater credit availability, FNMA sells mortgages from its portfolio.

The Government National Mortgage Association (GNMA) was formed after the conversion of FNMA and assumed some of FNMA's functions. The GNMA also attempts to increase the flow of funds to the mortgage market. GNMA purchases mortgages from financial institutions and either holds the mortgages or resells them to FNMA. In addition, GNMA guarantees debt securities sold by financial institutions and secured by the institution's FHA or VA mortgage loans.

The Federal Home Loan Bank System (FHLBS) is a government organization composed of member savings and loan associations, mutual savings banks, and insurance companies. In many ways the organization is comparable to the Federal Reserve System. The members hold stock in the FHLBS and can borrow from it. The FHLBS's funds come mainly from the sale of bonds. The FHLBS's subsidiary, the Federal Savings and Loan Insurance Corporation, insures deposits at savings and loan associations. Another subsidiary of FHLBS, the Federal Home Loan Mortgage Corporation (FHLMC), can purchase FHA and VA mortgages and issue GNMA-guaranteed bonds secured by these mortgages. Conventional mortgages can also be purchased by FHLMC, but bonds backed by these mortgages are not eligible for GNMA guarantee.

A partial assessment of the government's involvement in housing credit is obtained by examining the outstanding debt obligations of some federal housing agencies. As of August 1975, the following debt was outstanding: the Federal Home Loan Banks, $19.7 billion, and the Federal National Mortgage Association, $28.7 billion.[1]

Small Business Credit

Most business credit is obtained through the capital markets and the banking system. However, small business access to these sources of credit is often limited. A firm may be too small to have direct access to the capital markets and may not meet the credit standards of the local banks.

Government involvement in business lending began in the 1930s. Because of depressed business conditions, widespread bank failures, and the problems of the capital markets, the normal flow of credit was disrupted. The Reconstruction Finance Corporation, established in 1932 and liquidated in 1953, was designed to provide credit to firms threatened with bankruptcy and to reorganize bankrupt financial institutions and other critical businesses.

Also during the 1930s, the Federal Reserve was empowered to make direct business loans to firms unable to find credit through normal channels. This lending power has not been extensively used. The Export-Import Bank was founded in 1934 to assist firms in financing exports and imports. This credit was intended to be available only to those firms unable to finance through regular methods. Over time, the Export-Import Bank has become a means of providing credit to foreign purchasers of American goods.

The Small Business Administration (SBA) operates through Small Business Investment Companies (SBICs). The SBICs raise funds in the private capital markets and through the sale of their stock to the SBA. The funds are loaned to small businesses on a long term basis or are used to purchase stock in small businesses. As in the other cases of direct government lending, the goal is to provide funds to firms unable to obtain other financing.

A "small business" is defined as having assets less than $5 million, net

[1]*Federal Reserve Bulletin,* October 1975, p. A38.

worth less than $2.5 million, and income after taxes of less than $250,000. Alternatively, a firm may be classified as a small business on the basis of its size relative to the size of other firms in its industry.

Attempts to provide business assistance and credit to minority businessmen led to the creation of Minority Enterprise Small Business Investment Companies. These organizations operate on privately raised capital and funds provided by or guaranteed by the SBA.

Aid to Agriculture

Because of the economic importance of agriculture and the size of the farm bloc in Congress, the agricultural sector of the economy has received government credit assistance for several decades. Several direct lending programs provide the farmer with greater access to credit. Through the Federal Land Banks System, a local farm loan association can obtain credit for the purchase or improvement of a farm or for livestock or machinery. These are normally long-term loans.

The Bank for Cooperatives provides short- and intermediate-term credit to agricultural supply and marketing cooperatives. The Farmers' Home Administration assists tenant farmers to acquire farms and finances low-income rural housing. The Rural Electrification Administration lends to cooperatives that provide utility services to rural areas. Intermediate Credit Banks discount commercial bank loans to farmers and lend to other farm agencies.

While there are self-help aspects to virtually all of the agricultural lending programs, the borrowing power of government is also used to raise capital. As of August 1975, the outstanding bond issues of some agricultural agencies were as follows: Bank for Cooperatives, $3.0 billion; Federal Intermediate Credit Banks, $9.7 billion; and Federal Land Banks, $14.4 billion.[2]

Government Credit-Guarantee Programs

Although the amount of direct government lending is not large in an absolute sense, the government also acts as a financial backer for some borrowers. By guaranteeing that a financial institution will not suffer loss on a given loan, the government improves the terms on which the borrower can obtain credit. In some cases, the improvement in terms means a lower interest rate; in other cases, the guarantee means that borrowers who would otherwise be unable to obtain credit are able to find a willing lender.

The Housing Industry

The most familiar credit guarantee programs involve housing loans. The government's extensive involvement in the home financing industry began in the 1930s as

[2]Ibid.

a result of the widespread foreclosures of mortgages. Veterans Administration and Federal Housing Administration mortgages are now the most important of these programs. The VA loan, which began as part of the effort to assist veterans returning at the end of World War II, involves government guarantee of payment. The lender is protected against loss resulting from the borrower's failure to pay. The FHA program is based on an insurance principle, with the borrower paying an insurance premium. The terms of FHA and VA mortgages differ in detail, but both have the effect of reducing the risk to the lender and both permit borrowers to obtain long-term, low-down payment, low-interest loans.

At the end of 1974, $140.3 billion of FHA-insured and VA-guaranteed residential mortgage debt was outstanding. This sum represented 27.7 percent of the $507.0 billion total outstanding nonfarm, noncommercial mortgage debt.[3]

Economic Development Financing

Government guarantees also have been used to assist in the financing of local or regional economic development. In some cases, economic development is financed by direct low-interest rate state loans to private firms to aid in plant construction, capital goods purchases, and other costs of operation. In other cases, states guarantee loans made to industrial firms by private lenders. Although these programs are intended to influence firms to locate in a specific area, they probably also increase the total level of investment spending.

Ailing Industries and Ailing Cities

In 1971, the Lockheed Aircraft Company was near bankruptcy and the federal government agreed to guarantee a $250 million private loan to Lockheed. In the 1930s, the government had also made loans to ailing companies through the Reconstruction Finance Corporation, but the Lockheed loan guarantee raised substantial questions about the relationship between the government and private firms. Should the government bail out firms in danger of failing? Which firms should be eligible for these loan guarantees and which should be allowed to fail? Many questions can be raised relative to this type of lending.

In 1975, the financial problems of New York City presented demands for a new type of federal government credit guarantee, and many of the questions raised with respect to the Lockheed loan guarantee can be asked about the wisdom of federal loans to cities or states. The cases differed because some of the difficulties of New York City reflected national problems, and New York City is not a privately owned business. Again, however, the loan program was instituted on an ad hoc basis, without full consideration of the future eligibility of other cities in similar circumstances.

[3]Ibid., pp. A42, A44.

Student Loans

The loan guarantee program most familiar to students is the federal program to guarantee repayment of loans made by private lenders to students in post-secondary institutions. The government establishes a maximum interest rate on these loans and encourages the banks to make student loans by paying interest to the bank. The bank, of course, also receives interest paid by the students.

Government Credit Restriction Programs

Although the government has many programs to expand the use of credit, some government regulations restrict the use of credit or the terms on which private borrowers can obtain credit. Three types of credit restrictions are examined in this section; these programs can also be considered as tools of monetary policy, although they are less important than the major tools discussed in Chapter 14.

The Use of Credit for Stock Purchases

The longest standing program of credit restriction involves control over the use of credit to purchase common stock and bonds convertible into common stock. Investors use credit to purchase stock in order to obtain *leverage* and increase the return on their capital. Assume two possible cases. In the first case, an investor buys 100 shares of XYZ stock at $50 per share and pays for the stock with his own $5,000. If the price of the stock doubles and he sells, he has received a 100 percent profit on his funds. In the second case, the investor purchases the same quantity of stock for the same price, but he pays for the stock with $1,000 of his money and $4,000 borrowed from his bank. He uses the stock as collateral for the bank loan. In this case, when he sells the stock for $10,000 and repays the bank, he is left with a $5,000 return on his $1,000 investment. He has made a 500 percent return on his funds (before paying interest on his bank loan).

The risk of purchasing stock on margin (the margin in the example was 20 percent) occurs when the price of the stock goes down instead of up. Assume that the price of the stock in the previous example declines to $40 per share. The lender, either a brokerage firm or a bank, would be very nervous at this point. The value of the loan is equal to the value of the stock; the stockholder's margin is zero. A *margin call* would be issued even before this point is reached. The margin call requires the stockholder to increase his proportion of the value of the stock. If the stockholder cannot decrease his outstanding loan, the lender will sell the stock in order to avoid or minimize any loss to the lending institution. If the stock is sold at $40, the lender loses interest income, but the borrower loses the entire amount of his investment.

The widespread use of margin accounts is frequently cited as one cause of the severity of the 1929 stock market crash. Many investors had all their funds invested on margin. When prices declined and margin calls were issued, the investors could not raise added funds, and their stock was sold. These sales depressed stock prices and decreased the margin of other investors; more margin calls went out and more stock was sold. The selling continued and prices snowballed downwards. Some financial institutions suffered losses because the sale of stock in margin accounts was at such low prices that only a fraction of the value of the loans could be recovered.

In reaction to the excessive margin buying, the Securities Exchange Act of 1934 granted margin controls to the Federal Reserve System. Since then, the Board of Governors of the Federal Reserve System has determined the amount of margin an investor must maintain on loans against stock collateral. The requirement was later expanded to cover credit purchases of bonds convertible into common stock. The margin requirement since the Depression has ranged between 40 and 100 percent. For most of the 1970s, the requirement has ranged between 50 and 65 percent. As stock market prices have risen, the margin requirement has usually been increased.

From the point of view of the allocation of credit, the margin requirement would probably be considered an appropriate instrument. Very few individuals would consider credit for stock market speculation to be a high-priority credit use.

Credit for Consumer Durable Goods

During World War II and the Korean war, the government took actions to limit the use of credit for the purchase of durable goods, especially automobiles. This authority has now expired.

The major method of restricting consumer durable goods purchases was through the control of the terms of installment lending contracts. By increasing minimum down payment requirements and decreasing the maximum period over which payments could be extended, the government was able to discourage the installment purchase of durable goods. These controls were adopted to free production facilities for the manufacture of military goods and to encourage saving rather than spending.

Credit controls could be part of a general anti-inflation effort; however, these have never been tried in peacetime. The objections to their use center around two points. First, the use of installment credit controls forces an economic loss on the firms producing those goods normally sold on the installment plan. Naturally, those firms would object to the controls. Firms selling goods usually purchased with cash rather than credit would benefit. In addition, the control of credit terms favors those consumers who can afford to pay cash and discriminates against those who must buy on installment plans.

Second, these controls are difficult to enforce because sale terms can be changed to evade minimum down payment requirements. Given the number of automobile dealers, regulation would be expensive. The controls worked better during World War II than during the Korean war period, principally because of the general unavailability of cars during the earlier war.

In terms of credit allocation problems, the peacetime use of consumer credit controls would depend upon society's valuation of the gain to be achieved by restricting consumer credit and expanding other credit uses.

Voluntary Guidelines on Lending

Two attempts have been made in the post–World War II period to allocate credit by voluntary lender compliance. During the Korean war, major providers of credit were encouraged by the Federal Reserve to establish some priorities in the use of credit so that sufficient credit would be available to finance the war. The program was judged to be somewhat successful. However, the measurement of success was tempered by the fact that industry realized that the failure to comply would lead to compulsory controls.

A more recent effort at obtaining voluntary compliance with lending guidelines occurred in 1965. Lending by American banks to foreign borrowers had expanded rapidly because domestic policy had maintained relatively low interest rates. American banks were an attractive source of credit for foreign borrowers, and loans to foreigners increased rapidly. The Federal Reserve used its *moral suasion* (talked the banks into following a recommended course of action) to impose voluntary guidelines for the future expansion of foreign loans; the restriction on foreign lending was intended to prevent a greater deterioration of the American balance of payments.[4]

This effort at moral suasion was effective because it called only for limitations on the growth of loans to foreign borrowers and not for a cutback in the total amount of foreign loans. Also bankers feared that noncompliance would lead to more restrictive credit policies and the refusal of advances at the discount window. In this case, moral suasion had a good chance of success because the number of banks to be checked for compliance was limited to a few large urban banks.

In general, guidelines for the allocation of credit have not been used frequently in the United States. However, expanded use of this technique is a possible method of credit allocation.

Government Taxation and Credit Allocation

The taxation of economic activity and the use of tax breaks to encourage particular types of economic activity influence the allocation of credit. The impact of

[4]Arnold Dill, "Selective Credit Controls: The Experience and Recent Interest," *Monthly Review,* Federal Reserve Bank of Atlanta, vol. LVI, no. 5 (May 1971), p. 78.

taxation on the allocation of credit is particularly noticeable when specific activities are given special treatment in the tax laws. Some uses of the power of taxation are considered in this section.

State and Local Government Bonds

The ability of state and local governments to borrow is increased greatly by the exemption of the interest received by the bondholders from the Federal Personal Income Tax. This tax exemption stems from prohibitions against taxes by one governmental unit on the activity of another governmental unit. Thus, interest on federal government bonds is not taxable by the states, and interest on state and local government bonds is not taxable by the federal government. Given that the federal income tax is much higher than any state income tax, the net advantage accrues to state and local governments.

If the tax advantages of state and local government bonds did not exist, these governments would be forced to pay interest rates substantially higher than those paid by the federal government. Given the tax advantage, the smallest community in the nation may be able to borrow at a lower interest rate than the federal government.

A number of questions can be raised relative to the rationality of not taxing the interest received from state and local government bonds. First, there is the obvious problem of equity in the distribution of the total tax burden. Everyone has read about wealthy individuals who receive hundreds of thousands of dollars a year of income but who pay only the minimum income tax because their income is derived from holding tax-exempt bonds. It is estimated that the taxation of this income would produce, on the basis of projected 1976 income tax rates and income levels, an additional $4.9 billion of federal government revenue. In addition, the rest of us taxpayers would feel better about the tax system![5]

Second, the elimination of the tax-exempt status of state and local government bonds would change the allocation of credit. State and local governments would have to pay higher interest rates and, given tight budgets and taxpayer resistance, would probably borrow less. The provision of necessary public facilities would be reduced, and local property taxes and state sales and income taxes would be increased to meet higher borrowing costs. From a different perspective, how would funds now invested in state and local government bonds be reallocated if these bonds lost their tax-exempt status? There is obviously no direct answer to this question. Some funds previously invested in state and local government securities would be invested in various other debt and equity instruments; the entire flow of funds and pattern of yields would be changed.

[5]George F. Break and Joseph A. Pechman, *Federal Tax Reform,* Brookings Institution, Washington, D.C., 1975, p. 57.

Homeowners Tax Allowances

The tax deductibility of real estate taxes and home mortgage interest payments costs the Treasury nearly $12 billion per year in lost income tax revenues on the basis of the 1976 fiscal year tax and income levels.[6] The tax advantages of home ownership probably distort the allocation of mortgage credit between single-family dwellings and rental housing. The total quantity of credit flowing into the housing industry probably does not change significantly, but the proportions flowing into owned versus rented housing probably are changed. The nondeductibility of real estate taxes and mortgage interest would probably increase the demand for apartments and decrease the demand for single-family homes.

Within the single-family home market, the tax deductibility feature is of greater advantage to those in high income tax brackets because of the progressivity of the federal income tax. This factor probably increases the flow of funds to higher priced homes and away from the construction of more modestly priced houses.

The Investment Tax Credit

The investment tax credit, described in Chapter 11, is a use of tax policy to stimulate business capital investment by allowing firms to deduct a proportion of their investment expenditures from their income tax liability.

To the extent that the investment tax credit program has been successful, the amount of credit allocated to business investment has probably increased and the amount of credit allocated to other uses has probably decreased.

The Deductibility of Corporate Interest Payments

The corporation can include interest payments as a business expense in calculating its taxable income. Thus, its income taxes are reduced by nearly 50 percent of its interest payments. (For large corporations, the marginal tax rate is nearly 50 percent of income.) However, dividends to stockholders are not deductible and are paid out of after-tax profits. The large corporation has an incentive to borrow funds rather than sell new shares of stock. If the tax laws treated interest and dividends the same, the incentive to sell stock would be increased and corporate reliance on debt financing would be reduced.

The Interest Equalization Tax

The interest equalization tax was imposed to change the allocation of funds. In the early 1960s, low American interest rates made American capital markets an

[6]Ibid., p. 15.

attractive place for foreign firms to sell their equity and debt instruments. The funds raised by these security sales flowed out of the United States and contributed to the balance of payments problem.

The *interest equalization tax,* imposed in 1964 and removed in 1974, placed a 15 percent tax on the sale of foreign securities in the United States. The effect of this tax was an increased cost to foreigners of raising funds in the United States capital markets; the tax discouraged foreign borrowing in the United States. Unlike most taxes, this tax was designed to discourage a particular activity rather than to raise revenue.

In summary, taxes can be used to guide the allocation of resources by encouraging or discouraging the flow of funds to particular activities.

Government and the Regulation of the Credit Industry

The government also affects the allocation of credit through the regulation of the credit industry. Two aspects of credit industry regulation are of particular importance. The first is the preservation of competition within the credit industry; the second is government regulation of the sources and uses of funds by financial institutions.

Credit and Competition

The regulation of the structure of the banking industry was discussed in Chapter 6. The maintenance of relatively easy entry into the various sectors of the credit industry is necessary to provide a sufficient number of alternatives for the prospective borrower and to maintain interest rates at fairly competitive levels.

Regulation of Sources and Uses of Funds

To the extent that the government regulates the methods and terms on which financial firms can raise or employ funds, the government is altering the allocation of credit.

The major problem is the operation of Regulation Q, which has a major effect on the flow of credit to the housing industry. Credit that would have been used to finance home purchases is used by other borrowers for other uses.

As mentioned, the imposition of margin requirements on loans to finance stock purchases is an example of restricting the use of funds, as are the imposition of maximum interest rates on FHA and VA loans, which restrict mortgage lending activity.

Changes in the range of services that various financial institutions can provide also affect the allocation of credit. However, some concern has been expressed that allowing thrift institutions to offer expanded financial services would result in a shifting of funds away from home mortgage lending.

In a similar manner, the development of new financial instruments causes a change in credit allocation. The entry of financial institutions into the installment credit field shifted resources to the financing of consumer durable goods purchases and expanded both financial institution profits and the sale of consumer durable goods. Therefore, changes in the legal environment of financial institutions affect the allocation of credit between alternative uses.

Conclusion

The net effect of all of these governmental influences on the allocation of credit cannot be measured. However, the allocation of credit would certainly be changed drastically if all governmental bodies were to withdraw completely from the credit markets.

Although this chapter has not described all the various programs by which the government influences credit allocation, the fact remains that the influence of the government has been on an ad hoc, case-by-case basis. No government plan for overall credit allocation has ever been considered; the government's involvement is a patchwork of various programs.

This chapter has been based on the assumption of a fixed supply of credit. The next chapter examines the credit allocation effects that would result from a change in the total supply of credit.

REVIEW QUESTIONS

1. What is the difference between a general obligation bond and a revenue bond?

2. What economic units are the major holders of federal government debt? of state and local government debt?

3. What government programs are designed to increase the flow of credit to the housing industry?

4. What are the pros and cons of direct government lending to failing firms? to failing cities?

5. What costs are imposed by the use of credit restriction programs? What are the benefits of these programs?

6. To what extent can credit allocation programs be implemented through moral suasion?

7. In what ways do the tax laws favor certain uses of credit? Other than the revenue losses to the government, what are the costs of these programs?

8. How would free entry into the banking industry affect the allocation of credit in light of the credit allocation process in Chapter 16?

9. How do government credit-guarantee programs affect the allocation of credit?

10. Referring back to the case at the start of Chapter 1, what factors made the bank more willing to grant a car loan than to grant a tuition loan?

SUGGESTED READINGS

George Benston, "State Controls on Consumer Finance Company Loans: The Case of Maturity Regulation," *Government Credit Allocation, Where Do We Go from Here?*, Institute for Contemporary Studies, San Francisco, 1975, pp. 181–208. (Copyright by the Center for Research in Government Policy and Business of the Graduate School of Management, University of Rochester, Rochester, N.Y.)

Edward J. Kane, "Deposit-Interest Ceilings and Sectoral Shortages of Credit: How to Improve Credit Allocation Without Allocating Credit," *Government Credit Allocation, Where Do We Go from Here?*, Institute for Contemporary Studies, San Francisco, 1975, pp. 15–38. (Copyright by the Center for Research in Government Policy and Business of the Graduate School of Management, University of Rochester, Rochester, N.Y.)

James L. Kochan, "Federal Agency Issues: Newcomers in the Capital Market," *Federal Reserve Bank of Cleveland Economic Review,* February 1972, pp. 3–18.

Rudolph G. Penner and William L. Silber, "The Interaction Between Federal Credit Programs and the Impact on the Allocation of Credit," *American Economic Review,* December 1973, pp. 838–852.

Philip K. Robins, "The Effects of State Usury Ceilings on Single Family Homebuilding," *Journal of Finance,* American Finance Association, New York, March 1974, pp. 227–235.

18

MONETARY POLICY AND THE ALLOCATION OF CREDIT

Previous chapters described the roles of the market and of various government programs in allocating credit. This chapter examines the impact of monetary policy on the allocation of credit. The hypothesis is that three areas of expenditures—residential construction, state and local government capital expenditures, and small business investment—are affected disproportionately by a high interest rate policy. The analysis of short-term credit flows to these sectors is the basic concern of this chapter. The hypothesis does not argue that these sectors receive less than a fair share of total credit in the long run; however, in a long period of sustained high interest rates, these sectors might receive too little credit. Economic literature and empirical evidence are examined to test the validity of the hypothesis and to determine if the evidence justifies proposals for modifying the credit allocation process.

The Definitional Issue

The first problem is the establishment of guidelines for the measurement of discriminatory treatment. How does one judge whether a given type of economic activity bears an excessively large percentage of the burden of monetary policy? It is impossible to judge the effects of monetary policy on the basis of simple percentages. For example, it is misleading to argue that sector X represents 10 percent of GNP and should bear 10 percent of the restraining effect of monetary policy. All components of aggregate demand are not equally sensitive to monetary policy. Government demand is not affected by interest rate changes. Consumers do not normally purchase nondurable goods or services on credit, and these components of consumer demand would only be affected by monetary policy through wealth effects. Thus, shares of the burden cannot be compared directly to shares of total GNP.

The problem of judging the allocation effects of monetary policy is complicated by the difficulty of differentiating between demand and supply effects. A given shift of the supply of credit curve produces unequal changes in the quantity of credit obtained by various groups. Differences in the elasticities of demand for credit by various types of borrowers produce the variations in the quantity of credit received. If one group's demand for credit is perfectly inelastic with respect to the interest rate, a shift of the supply curve to the left increases the price of credit but does not change the quantity of credit allocated to that group. Alternatively, the demand curve for a second type of borrower may be highly elastic with respect to the interest rate; this group would obtain substantially less credit as the supply curve shifted to the left in a period of monetary restraint.

The credit allocation problem involves the effect of both demand and supply curves on the quantity of credit obtained. However, of the two variables determining price, more emphasis is placed on the supply factor. Is the elasticity of the supply of credit curve the same for all borrowers? In a period of credit restraint, do the supply of credit curves for some borrowers remain unchanged, while the supply of credit curves for other borrowers shift to the left toward the origin of the supply and demand model?

Given the present state of knowledge, economists do not have supply and demand models for all credit-using sectors of the economy. Thus, the credit allocation effects of monetary policy must be judged in much less specific terms.

In this analysis, credit allocation effects are judged by four standards. First, the relative effects of monetary policy on various components of aggregate demand are examined to determine which components of demand are affected by monetary policy. In addition, how is the total burden of policy divided? Does the analysis indicate that any specific component of demand bears a disproportionately large share of the impact of policy?

Second, changes in the relative shares of total credit flows are studied. How are changes in interest rates related to these changes in total credit flows? Are there obvious relationships between the flows of credit to various sectors of the economy?

The third standard is the ability of the Federal Reserve System to institute a restrictive monetary policy without being constrained by the fear of the effect of that policy on a particular sector of the economy. Regardless of other standards, a credit allocation effect that restricts the use of monetary policy requires corrective changes in the system of allocating credit.

The final standard is whether monetary policy creates credit allocation effects that threaten the stability of financial institutions. For example, the earlier discussions of financial disintermediation indicated the effect of tight money on the institutions that finance residential construction.

In this chapter, macroeconomic and microeconomic evidence is considered in an attempt to determine if monetary policy does discriminate against certain types of economic activity.

Macro Evidence on Credit Allocation

Two types of macroeconomic evidence provide some insights into the allocation of credit. The first approach employs a large econometric model to simulate the credit allocation effects of monetary policy. The second approach uses the Federal Reserve System's Flow of Funds data to study the flow of credit to various sectors of the economy.

The FRB-MIT Model

The Federal Reserve-MIT model[1] was designed to assist in the examination of monetary policy. This large macroeconomic model uses 75 equations to estimate the behavioral relationships of the economy. The model is much more complex than the simple models developed in Chapter 10; more variables are included and the relationships between the variables are derived statistically using real-world data.

These statistically estimated models of the economy are used to estimate the effect of various economic policies. In a process called *simulation,* "what would happen if?" tests are conducted. A key policy variable is changed and the values of the final output data—GNP and its components—are recomputed to measure the effect of the policy. By repeated simulations, using various policies and various size policies, the analyst can compare the relative effects of different policy measures.

The effects of various policy measures using the FRB-MIT model are estimated by Frank de Leeuw and Edward Gramlich.[2] The specific simulation of interest for the study of credit allocation is the effect of a $1 billion increase in the supply of unborrowed reserves available to the banking system. De Leeuw and Gramlich begin with data for the first quarter of 1964, increase the level of unborrowed reserves by $1 billion, and trace the effects on the level of economic activity for the next four years. The goal is to compare the difference in the output of the model after the introduction of the added reserves with the results that would have been obtained if these reserves had not been available to the banking system.

Table 18–1 presents the effects of the $1 billion increase in unborrowed reserves. The interpretation of the data in the table is not complicated. For example, in part (e), the summary data indicate that after four quarters total expenditures on consumption, residential construction, plant and equipment, and state and local construction were $3.5 billion higher than they would have been without the increase in unborrowed reserves. Of this amount, $1.7 billion was due to the lower cost of capital (various interest rate changes), $1.2 billion was due to

[1]Frank de Leeuw and Edward Gramlich, "The Federal Reserve–MIT Econometric Model," *Federal Reserve Bulletin,* January 1968, pp. 11–40.

[2]Frank de Leeuw and Edward Gramlich, "The Channels of Monetary Policy," *Federal Reserve Bulletin,* June 1969, pp. 472–491.

TABLE 18–1 The Effect of a $1 Billion Increase in Unborrowed Reserves (amounts in billions of dollars)

(a) CHANGE IN CONSUMPTION

Quarters after policy change	*Due to cost of capital*	*Due to wealth effect*	*Total change*
4	0.3	1.2	1.5
8	0.4	2.3	2.7
12	0.5	3.0	3.5
16	0.4	3.2	3.6

(b) CHANGE IN RESIDENTIAL CONSTRUCTION EXPENDITURES

Quarters after policy change	*Due to cost of capital*	*Due to credit rationing*	*Total change*
4	1.0	0.6	1.6
8	1.3	0.5	1.8
12	1.5	0.3	1.8
16	2.2	−0.8	1.4

(c) CHANGE IN PLANT AND EQUIPMENT

Quarters after policy change	*Due to cost of capital*
4	0.2
8	0.6
12	1.1
16	1.5

(d) CHANGE IN STATE AND LOCAL CONSTRUCTION

Quarters after policy change	*Due to cost of capital*
4	0.2
8	0.3
12	0.4
16	0.5

(e) TOTAL CHANGE (a + b + c + d)

Quarters after policy change	*Due to cost of capital*	*Due to wealth effect*	*Due to credit rationing*	*Total change*
4	1.7	1.2	0.6	3.5
8	2.6	2.3	0.5	5.4
12	3.5	3.0	0.3	6.8
16	4.6	3.2	−0.8	7.0

SOURCE: Frank de Leeuw and Edward Gramlich, "The Channels of Monetary Policy," *Federal Reserve Bulletin,* June 1969, p. 487.

TABLE 18–2 Percentages of Total Effects Resulting from Policy Change

QUARTERS AFTER POLICY CHANGE	*CONSUMPTION*	*RESIDENTIAL CONSTRUCTION*	*PLANT AND EQUIPMENT*	*STATE AND LOCAL CONSTRUCTION*
4	43	45	6	6
8	50	33	11	6
12	51	26	16	7
16	51	20	21	8

SOURCE: Computed from data in: Frank de Leeuw and Edward Gramlich, "The Channels of Monetary Policy," *Federal Reserve Bulletin,* June 1969, p. 487.

changes in the wealth position of consumers, and \$0.6 billion was due to credit rationing effects. After 16 quarters (four years), the total change in spending was \$7 billion.[3]

Although the model does not show all of the policy effects, the data permit some analyses of the effects on specific sectors of the economy. Table 18–2 presents a percentage distribution of the policy's total effect on each component of demand. The data in the table are derived by dividing the effect on each component of aggregate demand by the effect on total demand. Table 18–1 indicates that after four quarters the level of consumption has increased by \$1.5 billion and total demand has increased by \$3.5 billion. Dividing \$1.5 billion by \$3.5 billion reveals that 43 percent of the effect of policy was on consumption.

Table 18–2 indicates that the distribution of the impact changes as time passes. The initial impact fell on consumption (43 percent) and residential construction (45 percent); plant and equipment expenditures and state and local

TABLE 18–3 Percentage Change in Components of Demand After Four Quarters

	1964 VALUE (in billions of dollars)	*CHANGE DUE TO POLICY (in billions) of dollars)*	*PERCENTAGE CHANGE IN 1964 VALUE DUE TO POLICY CHANGE*
Consumption	401.2	1.5	0.37
Residential construction	27.1	1.6	5.90
Plant and equipment	61.1	0.2	0.33
State and local construction	16.5	0.2	1.21

SOURCES: *1975 Economic Report of the President,* pp. 263–264, 292, and Frank de Leeuw and Edward Gramlich, "The Channels of Monetary Policy," *Federal Reserve Bulletin,* June 1969, p. 487.

[3]The model in this form shows only the direct effects through the financial sector on the demand for goods and services. Including the multipliers and accelerators would produce feedback from the goods markets on the money markets. See de Leeuw and Gramlich, ibid., p. 487.

TABLE 18–4 Percentage Change in Components of Demand After 16 Quarters

	1964 VALUE (billions of dollars)	*CHANGE DUE TO POLICY (billions of dollars)*	*PERCENTAGE CHANGE IN 1964 VALUE DUE TO POLICY CHANGE*
Consumption	401.2	3.6	0.90
Residential construction	27.1	1.4	5.17
Plant and equipment	61.1	1.5	2.45
State and local construction	16.5	0.5	3.03

SOURCES: *1975 Economic Report of the President,* pp. 263–264, 292, and Frank de Leeuw and Edward Gramlich, "The Channels of Monetary Policy," *Federal Reserve Bulletin,* June 1969, p. 487.

construction changed very little. However, by the time 16 quarters passed, the level of plant and equipment expenditures responded to the change in monetary conditions; the share of the impact falling on plant and equipment rose and residential construction's share of the gain declined.

Table 18–3 is constructed by dividing the policy-induced change in each component of demand by the 1964 value of that component of demand. The table indicates that the increase in unborrowed reserves had the effect of increasing residential construction by 5.90 percent. Note in the table that only residential construction was affected significantly (on a percentage basis) by the monetary policy. Although the dollar change in consumption was nearly as large as the dollar change in residential construction, the percentage change in consumption was much smaller than the percentage change in residential construction.

Table 18–4 repeats the analysis of Table 18–3, using the results of the policy action after 16 quarters. After 16 periods, the percentage changes in the components other than housing have increased and the percentage change in housing construction has declined.

This policy simulation was conducted on the basis of an expansion of the supply of reserves available to the banking system. On this assumption, residential construction expanded by the largest percentage, and state and local construction expanded by the second largest percentage. The effects of a $1 billion *decrease* of unborrowed reserves would involve more than just a change of signs; the dollar values of the changes would be expected to be larger.

The effect of decreasing reserves available to the banking system can be inferred from the analysis of the interest rate elasticities in Chapter 15. In that analysis, Regulation Q, disintermediation, and usury laws operated to increase the magnitude of the effect of monetary restraint on residential construction and state and local government construction. Thus, the effect on residential construction in the tight money case would be substantially more than 5 to 6 percent.

The FRB-MIT model adds strength to the argument that residential construction—and, to a lesser extent, state and local construction—do bear a disproportionately large portion of the effect of monetary policy.

The Flow of Funds Accounts

The Flow of Funds Accounts, maintained and published by the Board of Governors of the Federal Reserve System, are the most comprehensive compilation of the financial relationships within the economy. The Flow of Funds Accounts are as important to financial policy as the National Income Accounts are to macroeconomic policy. Whereas the emphasis of the National Income Accounting System is on output and income, the emphasis in the Flow of Funds Accounts is on the holding of financial assets.

In the *Flow of Funds Accounting System,* the economy is divided into 11 sectors:

A. Private domestic nonfinancial sectors
   1. Households
   2. Business
   3. State and local government

B. United States Government

C. Financial sectors
   1. Federally sponsored credit agencies
   2. Monetary authority
   3. Commercial banks
   4. Private nonbank finance

D. Rest of the world

The basic objective of the Flow of Funds Accounting System is to record the stocks (absolute amounts) and the quarterly flows (changes) of financial assets and liabilities within and between the various sectors of the economy. Some of the types of questions that can be investigated by examining the Flow of Funds Accounts are as follows:

1. What is the amount and composition of household saving? What kinds of assets are held by households? How did households distribute last year's savings among the various financial assets?

2. What are the assets and liabilities of savings and loan associations? How did savings and loan associations change their asset holdings in the last quarter?

3. How did each sector of the economy change its holdings of government securities during the past year? What is the total distribution of government securities among the various sectors?

The data in Table 18–5, "Total Funds Raised in Credit Markets by Nonfinancial Sectors," from the Flow of Funds Accounting System are of interest in an analysis of the allocation of credit. The data in the table represent annual flows, or changes, in the dollar values. The table begins with total funds raised in the credit market by nonfinancial sectors. Then equity funds and government borrowing are deducted. The value of debt instruments, other than U.S. government securities, is subdivided by type of borrowing instrument and then subdivided by borrowing sector. All data are expressed in terms of billions of dollars.

TABLE 18–5 Total Funds Raised in Credit Markets by Nonfinancial Sectors, 1954–1974 (amounts in billions of dollars[a])

	1954	*1955*	*1956*	*1957*	*1958*	*1959*	*1960*
Total funds raised by nonfinancial sectors	27.5	38.1	29.8	30.5	41.8	52.9	37.6
less equity funds	1.7	2.0	2.3	2.4	2.3	2.3	1.6
Debt instruments	25.8	36.0	27.5	28.1	39.5	50.6	36.0
less U.S. Government	2.4	−0.8	−5.8	−2.2	9.3	7.1	−2.1
Debt instruments other than U.S. Government	23.4	36.8	33.3	30.3	30.2	43.5	38.0
Allocation by type of instrument (excluding U.S. Government)	23.4	36.8	33.3	30.3	30.2	43.5	38.0
State and local government securities	6.1	5.3	3.6	4.2	5.5	6.3	5.3
Corporate and foreign bonds	3.4	2.6	3.9	6.8	6.6	3.4	4.0
Mortgages	12.1	16.1	14.6	12.0	14.5	18.6	15.7
Home	9.3	12.4	10.8	8.6	9.3	12.7	10.1
Other residential	0.5	0.8	0.6	0.5	1.5	1.8	1.7
Commercial	1.7	2.0	2.4	2.4	2.9	3.1	3.2
Farm	0.5	0.8	0.8	0.6	0.7	1.0	0.7
Other private credit	1.7	12.8	11.2	7.3	3.6	15.2	13.0
Bank loans (not elsewhere classified)	0.4	5.6	6.4	2.1	1.5	6.4	3.4
Consumer credit	1.1	6.4	3.5	2.6	0.2	6.4	4.6
Open market paper	0.4	−0.4	0.3	0.4	0.1	−0.4	1.3
Other	−0.1	1.2	0.9	2.2	1.8	2.7	3.6
Allocation by borrowing sector	23.4	36.8	33.3	30.3	30.2	43.5	38.0
Foreign	0.2	0.2	0.9	1.3	2.0	0.7	1.8
State and local government	5.7	5.3	3.7	4.4	5.7	6.5	5.5
Households	11.1	19.7	16.1	12.9	11.0	21.5	17.7
Nonfinancial business	6.4	11.6	12.6	11.7	11.5	14.8	13.1
Farm	0.8	1.4	0.9	1.1	1.4	1.9	1.0
Nonfarm, noncorporate	0.8	1.7	1.1	1.0	1.5	2.4	1.6
Corporate	4.8	8.5	10.7	9.7	8.6	10.5	10.4

[a]Details may not add to totals due to rounding.

TABLE 18–5 *(Continued)*

	1961	*1962*	*1963*	*1964*	*1965*	*1966*	*1967*
Total funds raised by nonfinancial sectors	46.5	53.5	57.7	67.8	69.9	67.9	82.4
less equity funds	2.5	0.4	−0.5	1.5	0.3	1.0	2.4
Debt instruments	43.9	53.1	58.1	66.4	69.6	66.9	80.0
less U.S. Government	7.2	7.0	4.0	6.3	1.8	3.6	13.0
Debt instruments other than U.S. Government	36.7	46.1	54.2	60.1	67.9	63.3	67.0
Allocation by type of instrument (excluding U.S. Government)	36.7	46.1	54.2	60.1	67.9	63.3	67.0
State and local government securities	5.1	5.4	5.7	6.0	7.3	5.6	7.8
Corporate and foreign bonds	5.1	5.5	4.9	4.5	5.9	11.0	15.9
Mortgages	18.8	21.7	25.1	26.1	25.6	22.3	22.0
Home	11.1	12.8	15.1	15.6	15.4	11.7	11.5
Other residential	2.6	2.8	3.2	4.5	3.6	3.1	3.6
Commercial	4.0	4.8	5.1	3.8	4.4	5.7	4.7
Farm	1.1	1.3	1.6	2.1	2.2	1.8	2.3
Other private credit	7.8	13.5	18.5	23.5	29.0	24.4	21.3
Bank loans (not elsewhere classified)	2.8	4.7	6.3	9.1	14.1	10.7	9.5
Consumer credit	1.8	5.8	7.9	8.5	9.6	6.4	4.5
Open market paper	1.0	0.0	0.0	0.7	−0.3	1.0	2.1
Other	2.1	2.8	4.3	5.2	5.6	6.2	5.1
Allocation by borrowing sector	36.7	46.1	54.2	60.1	67.9	63.3	67.0
Foreign	2.2	1.8	3.6	4.9	2.4	1.8	4.0
State and local government	5.3	5.9	6.0	6.3	7.7	6.3	7.9
Households	15.3	20.8	24.8	27.8	28.3	22.7	19.3
Nonfinancial business	13.9	17.6	19.8	21.1	29.5	32.5	35.7
Farm	1.6	2.3	2.6	2.6	3.3	3.1	3.6
Nonfarm, noncorporate	2.3	3.2	4.5	5.3	5.7	5.4	5.0
Corporate	10.1	12.0	12.7	13.2	20.4	24.0	27.2

[a]Details may not add to totals due to rounding.

TABLE 18–5 *(Continued)*

	1968	*1969*	*1970*	*1971*	*1972*	*1973*	*1974*
Total funds raised by nonfinancial sectors	95.9	91.8	98.2	147.4	169.4	187.4	179.6
less equity funds	0.0	3.9	5.8	11.5	10.5	7.2	3.9
Debt instruments	95.9	88.0	92.5	135.9	158.9	180.1	175.8
less U.S. Government	13.4	−3.6	12.8	25.5	17.3	9.7	12.0
Debt instruments other than U.S. Government	82.5	91.6	79.7	110.4	141.6	170.4	163.8
Allocation by type of instrument (excluding U.S. Government)	82.5	91.6	79.7	110.4	141.6	170.4	163.8
State and local government securities	9.5	9.9	11.3	17.6	14.4	13.7	17.4
Corporate and foreign bonds	14.0	13.0	20.7	19.7	13.2	10.2	21.9
Mortgages	27.1	27.7	25.7	46.9	67.3	73.2	55.9
Home	15.1	15.7	12.8	26.1	39.6	43.3	31.6
Other residential	3.4	4.7	5.8	8.8	10.3	8.4	7.8
Commercial	6.4	5.3	5.3	10.0	14.8	17.0	11.5
Farm	2.2	1.9	1.8	2.0	2.6	4.4	4.9
Other private credit	32.0	41.0	22.1	26.3	46.8	73.3	68.7
Bank loans (not elsewhere classified)	13.1	15.3	6.4	9.4	21.8	38.6	31.9
Consumer credit	10.0	10.4	6.0	11.2	19.2	22.9	9.6
Open market paper	1.6	3.3	3.8	−0.9	−1.5	1.8	13.4
Other	7.2	12.0	5.9	6.6	7.3	10.0	13.8
Allocation by borrowing sector	82.5	91.6	79.7	110.4	141.6	170.4	163.8
Foreign	2.7	3.2	2.7	4.6	4.7	7.7	15.7
State and local government	9.8	10.7	11.3	17.8	14.2	12.3	16.6
Households	30.0	31.7	23.4	39.8	63.1	72.8	43.5
Nonfinancial business	40.1	46.0	42.3	48.2	59.6	77.7	88.1
Farm	2.8	3.2	3.2	4.1	4.9	8.6	7.8
Nonfarm, noncorporate	5.6	7.4	5.3	8.7	10.4	9.3	7.3
Corporate	31.7	35.5	33.8	35.4	44.4	59.7	73.0

[a]Details may not add to totals due to rounding.

SOURCES: Board of Governors of the Federal Reserve System, *Flow of Funds Accounts, 1945–1972,* August 1973, pp. 4–6; *1974 Supplement Flow of Funds Accounts, 1965–1973,* September 1974, p. 2; and *Flow of Funds Unadjusted,* 1st Quarter, 1975, May 9, 1975, p. 1.

The data in the "Allocation by Borrowing Sector" portion of Table 18–5 are presented in percentage form in Table 18–6. The household sector's share is subdivided into home mortgage and other household credit. A representative interest rate, the yield on three- to five-year federal government bonds, is also included in Table 18–6 to provide the basis for an analysis of relationships between the interest rate and the allocation of credit.

For the purpose of analysis, year-to-year percentage changes in the interest rate were calculated. In 10 of 20 years, the interest rate changed by 10 percent or more. Eight of these significant changes were increases and two were decreases.

An examination of the home mortgage share of funds in Table 18–6 reveals that in all eight years in which the interest rate increased significantly (by more than 10 percent), the percentage of funds allocated to home mortgages declined. In the two years in which the interest rate declined significantly, the percentage of funds allocated to home mortgages increased. Including all years, the proportion of funds allocated to home mortgages moved inversely to changes in the interest rate (funds allocated to home mortgages increased when the interest rate decreased and decreased when the interest rate increased) in 15 of 20 years. In the other five years, the interest rate change was less than 10 percent.

Examining the state and local government share of total funds, in those 10 years in which the interest rate changed by more than 10 percent, the percentage of funds flowing to state and local governments fluctuated in the expected direction (inversely to the change in the interest rate) in 8 of the 10 years. In the two years in which the share of state and local governments' funds increased as interest rates increased, the percentage increases in the interest rate were greater than 10 percent but were the smallest significant changes in the interest rate. Combining all years, the change in the proportion of funds allocated to state and local governments moved in the opposite direction to the change in the interest rate in 13 of 20 years.

Allowing the noncorporate, nonfarm, nonfinancial business sector to represent small business, the proportion of funds allocated to small business moved inversely to the interest rate in only 6 of the 10 years of significant interest rate changes. For 12 of the 20 year-to-year changes, the proportion of funds going to small business fluctuated inversely to the interest rate change.

The Flow of Funds analysis supports the argument that the proportion of funds allocated to home mortgages does indeed move inversely to changes in the interest rate. The argument with respect to state and local government borrowing is weaker, and no substantial conclusion can be reached relative to the small business share of total funds.

Micro Evidence on Credit Allocation

This section examines specific evidence relative to the three sectors—housing, state and local government borrowing, and small business borrowing—which may bear greater than proportional shares of the burden of monetary policy.

TABLE 18–6 Allocation of Funds Raised in Credit Markets, by Borrowing Sector, 1954–1974 (in percentages of total debt instruments other than U.S. Government)

	1954	*1955*	*1956*	*1957*	*1958*	*1959*	*1960*	*1961*	*1962*	*1963*	*1964*	*1965*
Foreign	0.76	0.48	2.59	4.40	6.62	1.70	4.62	5.87	4.01	6.73	8.19	3.31
State and local governments	24.57	14.36	11.00	14.52	18.80	14.87	14.42	14.47	12.73	11.00	10.42	11.29
Households	47.25	53.59	48.43	42.50	36.46	49.36	46.62	41.67	45.14	45.71	46.30	41.87
Home mortgages	39.91	33.80	32.39	28.23	30.88	29.27	26.64	30.29	27.74	27.91	26.04	22.67
Other household	7.34	19.78	16.04	14.27	5.57	20.10	19.98	11.38	17.40	17.80	20.25	19.20
Nonfinancial business	27.43	31.57	37.98	38.58	38.13	34.06	34.34	37.99	38.12	36.56	35.09	43.54
Farm	3.30	3.91	2.58	3.49	4.52	4.45	2.71	4.34	4.99	4.71	4.33	4.85
Nonfarm, noncorporate	3.55	4.70	3.35	3.16	5.01	5.44	4.18	6.26	6.99	8.37	8.80	8.47
Corporate	20.58	22.96	32.04	31.93	28.61	24.17	27.45	27.39	26.15	23.48	21.96	30.22
Interest rate (3–5 year U.S. Government securities)	1.82	2.50	3.12	3.62	2.90	4.33	3.99	3.60	3.57	3.72	4.06	4.22

	1966	*1967*	*1968*	*1969*	*1970*	*1971*	*1972*	*1973*	*1974*	*HIGH*	*MEAN*	*LOW*
Foreign	2.48	5.92	3.24	3.51	3.39	4.17	3.32	4.52	9.58	9.58	4.26	0.76
State and local governments	9.92	11.86	11.90	11.65	14.05	16.12	10.03	7.22	10.13	24.57	13.11	7.22
Households	35.75	28.43	36.29	34.62	29.36	36.05	44.56	42.72	26.56	53.59	40.92	26.56
Home mortgages	18.49	17.16	18.24	17.09	16.06	23.64	27.97	25.41	19.29	39.91	25.67	16.06
Other household	17.26	11.28	18.05	17.53	13.30	12.41	16.60	17.31	7.26	20.25	15.24	5.57
Nonfinancial business	51.86	53.78	48.57	50.22	53.07	43.66	42.16	45.60	53.79	53.79	41.72	27.43
Farm	4.92	5.41	3.43	3.47	4.02	3.71	3.46	5.05	4.76	5.41	4.11	2.58
Nonfarm, noncorporate	8.56	7.40	6.73	8.03	6.65	7.88	7.34	5.46	4.46	8.80	6.23	3.16
Corporate	38.38	40.98	38.41	38.72	42.41	32.07	31.16	35.04	44.57	44.57	31.38	20.58
Interest rate (3–5 year U.S. Government securities)	5.16	5.07	5.59	6.85	7.37	5.77	5.85	6.92	7.81	7.81	4.66	1.82

SOURCES: Computed from data in Table 18–5. Interest rate from *1975 Economic Report of the President*, p. 317.

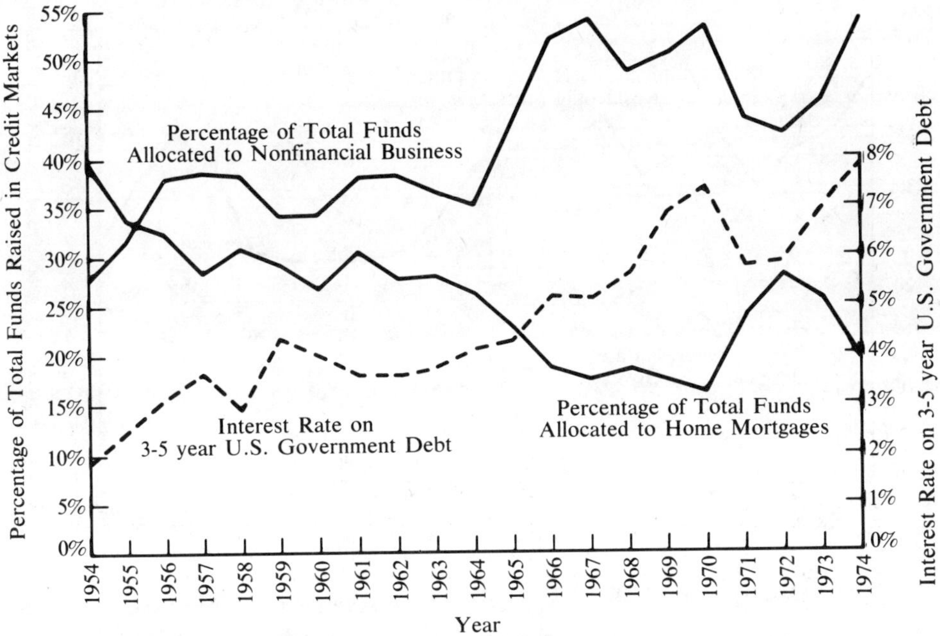

SOURCE. Data in Table 18.6

FIGURE 18–1 Percentages of Total Funds Raised in Credit Markets (excluding Equities and Federal Government Borrowing) Allocated to Home Mortgages and Nonfinancial Business, 1954–1974

Residential Construction

Residential construction and nonfinancial business are major users of borrowed funds, and in many ways these two users compete for the available supply of credit. The theoretical basis for this competition is clear. In periods of high credit demand, business borrowers bid up interest rates and funds are attracted away from the home-financing institutions. Regulation Q creates financial disintermediation and shifts funds from housing to business financing. Housing is crowded out in the competitive process.

The shares of total funds allocated to home mortgages and nonfinancial business are plotted in Figure 18–1, along with the yield on three- to five-year government securities. Even a casual examination of Figure 18–1 suggests that the percentage of funds flowing to the business sector appears to vary directly with the interest rate and inversely with the share of funds allocated to home mortgages. In 9 of 10 years of significant interest rate changes, the proportion of funds allocated to home mortgages moved inversely to the proportion of funds allocated to nonfinancial business. For all 20 year-to-year changes, in 17 years the proportion of funds allocated to home mortgages moved inversely to the proportion of funds allocated to business.

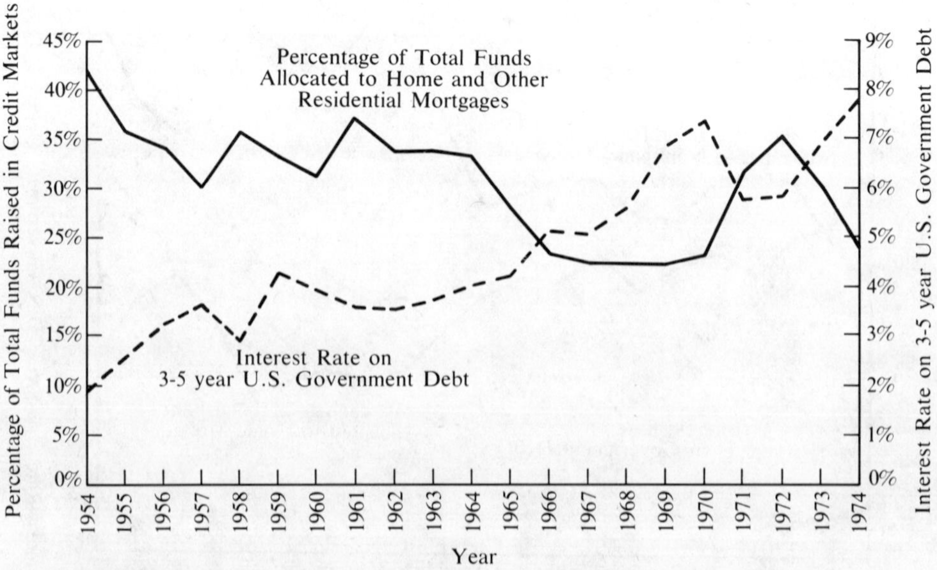

SOURCE. Computed from data in Table 18.5

FIGURE 18–2 Percentage of Total Funds Raised in Credit Markets (excluding Equities and Federal Government Borrowing) Allocated to Home and Other Residential Mortgages, 1954–1974

Limited econometric evidence also suggests that housing and business finance compete for funds. Terrance Clauretie,[4] in constructing an equation to explain the supply of mortgage funds, determined that the business demand for funds is a significant explanatory variable. There is an especially strong competitive relationship in the market for conventional, as opposed to government-underwritten, mortgages. According to Clauretie's findings, either an increase in the business demand for funds or an increase in the corporate bond rate leads to a decrease in the supply of mortgage funds.

Figure 18–2 presents the percentages of total non–United States Government debt instruments represented by home and other residential mortgages. These percentages are plotted along with the interest rate. Again, there is an apparent inverse relationship between the interest rate and the proportion of funds allocated to housing. In all 10 years of significant interest rate changes, housing's share of total funds moved in the direction opposite to the interest rate change.

While the evidence is not perfect, one can make a relatively strong case that housing does bear an excessively large proportion of the burden of monetary policy.

[4]Terrence M. Clauretie, "Interest Rates, the Business Demand for Funds, and the Residential Mortgage Market: A Sectoral Econometric Study," *Journal of Finance,* December 1973, pp. 1313–1326.

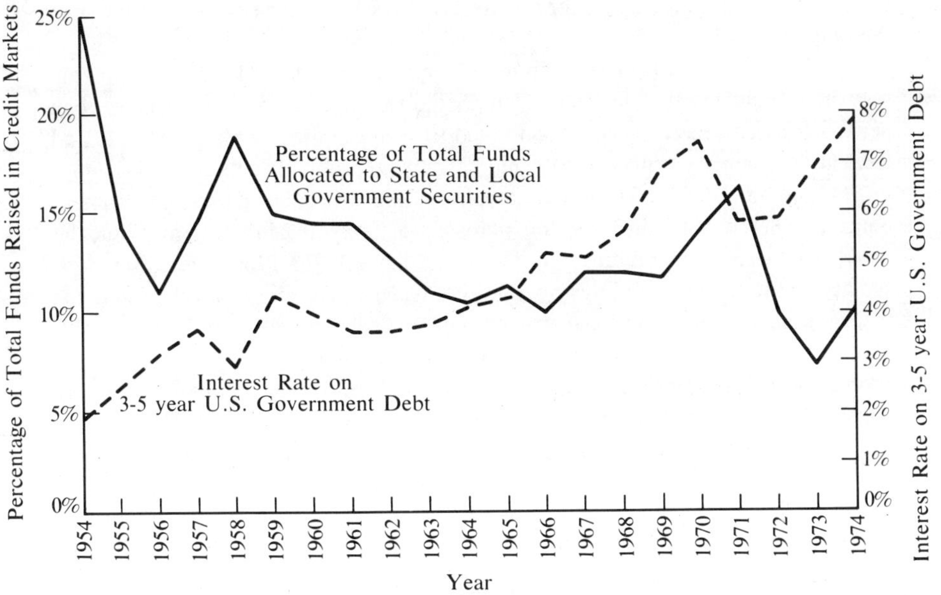

SOURCE. Data in Table 18.6

FIGURE 18–3 Percentage of Total Funds Raised in Credit Markets (excluding Equities and Federal Government Borrowing) Allocated to State and Local Government Securities, 1954–1974

State and Local Government Borrowing

The argument that state and local government borrowing receives a reduced proportion of total funds in a period of high interest rates results from the role of the commercial banking system as the major holder of this type of debt. In periods of high business demand for funds, the commercial banks would be expected to liquidate these securities and reallocate the funds to business loans.

Figure 18–3 presents the percentage of total funds allocated to state and local governments; the yield on three- to five-year U.S. government securities is also plotted in the figure. As indicated previously, in 8 of the 10 years of significant interest rate changes, the proportion of funds flowing to state and local governments moved inversely to the change in the interest rate. For 12 of the 20 year-to-year changes, the direction of change in the proportion of funds was opposite to the direction of change of the interest rate.

In 10 of the 20 year-to-year changes, the proportion of funds allocated to state and local government borrowing moved in the opposite direction to the proportion allocated to nonfinancial business. For 7 of the 10 years of significant interest rate changes, the percentages of funds allocated to the two sectors moved in opposite directions. Thus, the evidence of a competition for funds between business and state and local governments is not as strong as the evidence relative to the competition between business and residential housing.

Examination of the data on the ownership of state and local government securities indicates that in years of high interest rates and high business loan demand, the commercial banks continued to increase their holdings of state and local government securities, but the increases were relatively small. For example, in 1968, commercial banks increased their holdings of state and local government bonds by \$8.55 billion; in 1969, the increase was only \$0.2 billion. However, the small net increase of holdings by commercial banks in 1969 was offset by a substantial increase in holdings by households. In 1968, households had reduced their holdings of state and local government securities by \$0.76 billion; in 1969, they increased their holdings by \$9.61 billion. The same pattern was evidenced in 1966 and 1974; banks purchased fewer state and local government securities, but households increased their holdings.[5]

The income tax advantages of holding state and local government securities may be responsible for household behavior, or this behavior may be another example of financial disintermediation. The higher rate of tax-exempt interest on state and local government bonds may increase the general attractiveness of these securities and cause disintermediation. In any event, the behavior of the household sector partly offsets the effect of rising business loan demand on commercial bank holdings of state and local government bonds.

Small Business Borrowing

One of the many enduring questions in the economics literature is whether banks discriminate against small business borrowers in periods of monetary restraint. To be effective, a tight money policy must reduce some forms of lending; the controversy centers around whether large or small business firms suffer most at the hands of the bankers. Several factors can be cited to support the argument that small firms would receive proportionately less credit in a tight money period. First, small firms generally have lower credit ratings, and if credit standards are tightened small firms are most apt to be denied credit. Second, on the demand side, small firms may be less able than large firms to pass on higher interest costs to their customers and may be forced to reduce their credit demands in periods of tight money and high interest rates. Third, large firms are able to transfer their loan demands to other banks on a regional or nationwide basis; small firms, with no national credit reputation, are unable to find new sources of funds if the local bank is unable to meet their credit needs. Finally, the large firm may crowd out small firms; a bank may reduce lending to small firms in the hope of obtaining the larger national firm as a continuing customer.

[5]See Board of Governors of the Federal Reserve System, *Flow of Funds Accounts, 1945–1972*, pp. 48–49, and *Flow of Funds, Seasonally Adjusted 1st Quarter, 1975 (Preliminary)*, p. 18.

However, the banks would argue that small local business firms are their best long-term customers and that the banks would be reluctant to lose these established borrowers. The large firm may appear suddenly when credit conditions are tight nationally; when conditions ease, the large firm will go back to its previous sources of credit.

The Literature on Bank Discrimination against Small Business A 1960 study on small business credit, done by George Bach and C. J. Huizinga, utilized extensive bank lending data collected for October 1955 to October 1957, a period of tight money.[6] In general, Bach and Huizinga concluded that banks do not discriminate against small business borrowers in a period of monetary restraint. However, their conclusion may have been stronger than was justified by their data.

They classified banks on the basis of bank size and the extent to which each bank was affected by the tight money policy. Thus, there were "tight banks," "medium banks," and "loose banks,"[7] ranked according to their ability to expand their lending activity. The study measured the percentage increase in loans to various size borrowers, with the banks classified according to size and degree of "tightness." Bach and Huizinga found that only large and very large "tight" banks discriminated against small borrowers to a greater extent than "medium tight" banks.[8] Otherwise, they found that discrimination against small business was based on tests of credit worthiness.[9]

The general finding of nondiscrimination was not as clear to others as it was to Bach and Huizinga. Deane Carson[10] pointed out that the "loose" banks, which had the ability to expand their lending activity, increased loans to large firms by much larger percentages than they increased loans to small businesses.[11]

William Silbert and Murray Polakoff[12] utilized the Bach-Huizinga data to test the same hypothesis, using econometric techniques. They criticized the earlier study on several grounds but principally for not specifying demand and supply functions for the various size borrowers. The Bach-Huizinga findings demonstrated the outcome of supply and demand, but it did not specify the extent to which the banks accommodated various borrowers' demands for loans.

Silbert and Polakoff constructed loan supply functions and compared loan allocations from added deposits in 1957 to loan allocations from added deposits in 1955. They concluded that banks desired to discriminate against small business (firms with less than $5 million of assets) during periods of tight money.[13] In a tight

[6]George L. Bach and C. J. Huizinga, "The Differential Effects of Tight Money," *American Economic Review,* March 1961, pp. 52–80.

[7]Ibid., pp. 56–59.

[8]Ibid., p. 68.

[9]Ibid., p. 79.

[10]Deane Carson, "The Differential Effects of Tight Money: Comment," *American Economic Review,* December 1961, pp. 1039–1042.

[11]Ibid., p. 1040.

[12]William L. Silbert and Murray E. Polakoff, "The Differential Effects of Tight Money: An Econometric Study," *Journal of Finance,* March 1970, pp. 83–97.

[13]Ibid., pp. 92–93.

money period, banks were less willing to use added deposits to make added loans to small businesses and preferred to use added deposits to make added loans to large businesses.

Duane Harris[14] provided some additional evidence on the subject of discrimination against small business borrowers. In a survey of bank reactions to tighter credit conditions, Harris found that banks tended to give the best treatment to established local borrowers, especially those who maintained deposit accounts at the bank and used various other bank services. By these standards, the large firm would be favored over the small firm because the large firm would hold greater deposits and would be most likely to use other bank services.

Dudley Luckett[15] also found that established low-risk customers would be given preferential treatment in a period of tight credit. New customers and those with poor credit credentials are the first to be refused.

In summary, the literature seems to indicate some tendency toward discrimination against small business during periods of monetary restraint. However, at this point, the evidence from the literature does not justify suggesting a program of credit reallocation.

The Flow of Funds Data The nonfarm, noncorporate business borrowing percentage of total debt instruments (other than United States Government borrowing) is plotted in Figure 18–4, along with the yield on three- to five-year U.S. Government securities.

In four of the eight years of significant interest rate increases, the share of noncorporate, nonfarm business increased; in four years the share decreased. In both of the years in which the interest rate decreased significantly, the share of funds allocated to small business increased.

For 14 of the 20 year-to-year changes, the proportion of noncorporate, nonfarm business funds moved inversely to the proportion of corporate funds. In six years of rising interest rates, the share of noncorporate and corporate funds moved in the same direction.

The Flow of Funds data do not provide solid evidence to prove or disprove the issue of discrimination against small business, although the studies cited in the review of the literature provide limited support for the discrimination argument.

Conclusion

The review of the literature and the empirical evidence on the effect of high interest rates provides varying degrees of support for the hypothesis that three sectors of the economy bear a disproportionately large part of the burden of monetary policy. The

[14]Duane G. Harris, "Some Evidence on Differential Lending Practices at Commercial Banks," *Journal of Finance,* December 1973, pp. 1303–1317.

[15]Dudley G. Luckett, "Credit Standards and Tight Money," *Journal of Money, Credit and Banking,* November 1970, pp. 420–434.

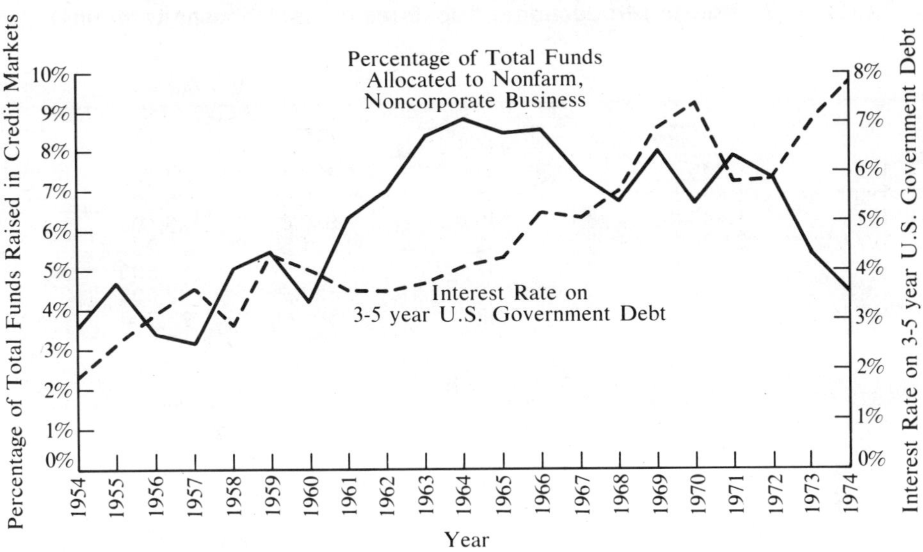

SOURCE. Data in Table 18.6

FIGURE 18–4 Percentage of Total Funds Raised in Credit Markets (excluding Equities and Federal Government Borrowing) Allocated to Nonfarm, Noncorporate Business, 1954–1974

residential housing case seems to be the strongest. The FRB-MIT model, other studies cited in Chapter 15, and the Flow of Funds data confirm the impact of monetary policy on housing. If any form of expenditure is subject to the crowding-out effect, residential construction is the most likely candidate. A comparison of the evidence on the burden of monetary policy on borrowing by state and local governments with the evidence on small business borrowing indicated that more of the burden is placed on state and local government borrowing. However, for these two sectors, neither case is extremely strong. The final section of this chapter considers the value of permitting residential construction to bear the largest proportion of the effects of monetary policy.

The Value of Protecting Housing

The analysis indicates that housing, more than the other components of aggregate demand, is affected by interest rate fluctuations. Yet the government has been concerned with the housing problem for a long time.

The National Housing Act of 1968 established housing goals. Achievement of the objective of providing everyone with adequate housing required that 2.6 million new housing units be produced each year for 10 years. Even with the redefinition of the goal to include mobile homes, the objectives of the Housing Act

TABLE 18–7 Housing Production and Costs (amounts in thousands of units)

YEAR	*PUBLIC AND PRIVATE HOUSING STARTS*	*MOBILE HOME SHIPMENTS*	*TOTAL UNITS*	*MEDIAN PRICE OF NEW HOMES SOLD (dollars)*
1968	1,545.4	318	1,863.4	24,700
1969	1,499.5	413	1,912.5	25,600
1970	1,469.0	401	1,870.0	23,400
1971	2,084.5	497	2,581.5	25,200
1972	2,378.5	576	2,954.5	27,600
1973	2,057.5	567	2,624.5	32,500
1974	1,352.5	329	1,681.5	35,900
1975	1,172.4	216	1,388.4	39,200

SOURCES: *Federal Reserve Bulletin,* March 1976, p. A51, and *1976 Economic Report of the President,* p. 214.

were not met. Table 18–7 provides data on new housing starts, mobile home shipments, and the price of new single-family homes.

The high interest rates, characteristic of the period since 1968, are not totally to blame for the failure to achieve the goal. The price of housing has increased rapidly, as indicated in Table 18–7. Rising costs of land, labor, and materials have combined with high interest rates to restrict housing production.

To an extent, housing has become a sacred cow; however, the sacred cow has not fared very well. Before considering added assistance to the housing industry, it is necessary to question why housing receives so much attention.

In economic terminology, adequate housing is believed to have significant positive externalities. Slums breed crime and other social problems. Substandard housing has negative external effects on adjacent good housing. The run-down house is not just an eyesore; it reduces the value of better housing and encourages the process of neighborhood decay.

In more sociological or humanitarian terms, it can be argued that in a nation as wealthy as the United States all individuals should be able to obtain good housing at a reasonable price. Perhaps housing should be allocated on the basis of need rather than the ability to pay.

The goal of adequate housing creates a definitional problem. What is satisfactory housing? Does the provision of simple but clean and safe housing meet the requirement? Or does this standard require the provision of suburban single-family homes? Obviously, the answer lies at some undefinable point between these two extremes.

The next major question is whether housing should be exempted from the effects of monetary policy. It is clear that housing bears the heaviest burden of monetary policy. Should society isolate the housing industry from the impact of monetary policy? On the basis of humanitarian and general social goals, the answer would be yes. However, the economic objections to "exempting" housing from restrictive monetary policies must be considered.

William Gibson[16] challenges the value of protecting the housing industry from monetary policy for several reasons. First, he argues that protecting the housing industry would reduce the efficiency of monetary policy. Residential construction is sharply and quickly affected by increasing interest rates. The FRB-MIT model demonstrated that the initial impact of policy falls on housing and that other components of aggregate demand are affected with longer lags.

If the housing industry were exempt from the effects of high interest rates, monetary policy would be less effective. To compensate for the exemption of housing, even higher interest rates would be required to reduce other components of aggregate demand. In addition, longer periods of high interest rates would be necessary for monetary policy to affect aggregate demand.

On the question of the effectiveness of policy, Gibson is correct. Monetary policy would be less effective. However, should the effectiveness of policy depend upon its ability to severely disrupt production in one small sector of the economy? One could argue that more reliance should be placed on fiscal policy and that efforts should be made to increase the short-term interest elasticity of the other components of aggregate demand.

Gibson's argument that higher interest rates would be necessary also has merit. Higher interest rates would be necessary to bring about cutbacks in other areas and would create more problems of financial disintermediation and greater decreases in the market value of bonds.

A greater reliance on longer term deposits in thrift institutions and the elimination of Regulation Q ceilings on interest rates should reduce the disintermediation problem. The wealth effects of greater declines in the value of fixed interest rate securities are uncertain.

The longer lag in the effect of monetary policy would be a problem. Unless methods could be developed to make consumption and capital investment more interest-elastic, longer periods of high interest rates would be required to meet stabilization objectives.

Gibson[17] also discusses the factors of production employed in the housing industry. To an extent, the workers released by a decline in residential construction are absorbed into nonresidential construction. Thus, unemployment created by a housing decline may be less than the unemployment that would be created if other sectors of the economy were to bear a heavier share of the monetary policy burden. However, there are limitations on the transferability of skills within the construction industry.

A further problem is the effect of instability on the price and supply of entrepreneurial services to the housing industry. The high risk and high degree of instability in the industry should permit potential home-building firms to demand and obtain a higher rate of return on their capital. In the long run, instability may

[16]William E. Gibson, "Protecting Homebuilding from Restrictive Credit Conditions," *Brookings Papers on Economic Activity* Vol. 3 (1973), pp. 647–691.

[17]Ibid., pp. 667–673.

keep firms from entering the industry. Gibson[18] found that the cost of capital to the residential construction industry is increased by the sensitivity of home building to money market conditions.

Gibson also considers the short production period for housing and the relatively small loss of housing services associated with a decline in output. Capital investment projects, once started, are difficult and expensive to interrupt. However, it does not take long to build a house and the house not built this year can be built next year. Once a house is begun, production does not have to be stopped in midstream.[19]

While the flow of housing can be more easily stopped and started than the flow of capital investment, this does not mean that housing should bear the burden of monetary policy. The production of all consumer durable goods can be stopped and started as easily as the production of housing; most of these consumer durables are less critical than housing.

Although the housing industry has many characteristics that increase the efficiency of monetary policy, the sensitivity of housing to interest rates hampers the use of monetary policy. The Federal Reserve System, in determining the degree of restraint, may be forced into a less than optimal policy because of the feared effect of the optimal policy on the housing industry.

Sherman J. Maisel, a former governor of the Federal Reserve System, indicates in discussing the tight money period of 1966 that "the housing industry accounted for up to 90 percent of the deflationary impact of monetary policy during this period. The effect was equivalent to a high tax on one industry for the purpose of cutting spending. Congress would never have chosen this type of fiscal policy to pay for the war."[20]

In discussing monetary policy during the 1966 credit crunch, Maisel describes the Federal Reserve's actions and the concern for the housing industry and the thrift institutions. Clearly the problem of homebuilding and home financing complicated, and may have constrained, the making of policy decisions.[21] Perhaps, in this one case, monetary policy is too efficient.

While efficiency arguments indicate the need for the perpetuation of monetary policy's impact on residential construction, the ultimate question is an equity issue. Does an equitable policy place the major portion of the burden of stabilization on one small sector of the economy? If this policy is indeed inequitable, it should be changed. Chapter 19 examines some optional systems for allocating credit.

[18]Ibid., pp. 675–682.
[19]Ibid., p. 664.
[20]Sherman J. Maisel, *Managing the Dollar* (New York: W. W. Norton & Co., 1973), p. 100.
[21]Ibid., pp. 86–105.

REVIEW QUESTIONS

1. Why would one expect that the business sector and the residential construction industry would be competitors for the available supply of funds?

2. Appraise the evidence relative to the effect on each major credit-using sector of changes in the rate of interest.

3. How does the literature evaluate the effect of tight money on small business investment? Why would small business be affected more than large business if the supply of credit is decreased?

4. What are the costs and benefits of protecting housing from the effects of a high interest rate period?

5. The numerical results in Tables 18–1 and 18–2 are based on an expansionary monetary policy. Which of these results would be changed the most (other than expected changes in signs) if the policy measure had been a reduction of the supply of reserves?

6. Why does the distribution of the effect of the policy action in Table 18–2 change as additional time periods are studied?

7. Why would one expect state and local government capital expenditures to be affected by interest rate changes? What theories could be offered to explain the fact that in some years in which banks reduced their purchases of state and local government bonds individuals increased their purchases of these bonds?

8. What problems are involved in determining whether or not a given sector receives an adequate supply of credit?

9. A greater familiarity with the Flow of Funds Accounting System can be obtained by working with some of the data. Updating the data in Tables 18–5 and 18–6 would be one way of working with the data.

10. After reading the evidence within the chapter, could you argue that substantial changes are necessary in the process of credit allocation?

SUGGESTED READINGS

Consumer Spending and Monetary Policy: The Linkages, Federal Reserve Bank of Boston, 1971.

Robert Moore Fisher and Charles J. Siegman, "Patterns of Housing Experience During Periods of Credit Restraint in Industrialized Countries," *Journal of Finance,* American Finance Association, New York, May 1972, pp. 193–205.

Housing and Monetary Policy, Federal Reserve Bank of Boston, October 1970.

Dwight M. Jaffee, "Housing Finance and Mortgage Market Policy," *Government Credit Allocation, Where Do We Go From Here?*, Institute for Contemporary Studies, San Francisco, 1975, pp. 93–122. (Copyright by the Center for Research in Government Policy and Business of the Graduate School of Management, University of Rochester, Rochester, N.Y.)

Allan H. Meltzer, "Credit Availability and Economic Decisions: Some Evidence from the Mortgage and Housing Markets," *Government Credit Allocation, Where Do We Go From Here?*, Institute for Contemporary Studies, San Francisco, 1975, pp. 123–150. (Copyright by the Center for Research in Government Policy and Business of the Graduate School of Management, University of Rochester, Rochester, N.Y.)

Lawrence S. Ritter, "The Flow of Funds Accounts: A Framework for Financial Analysis," *The Bulletin,* No. 52 (1968), Institute of Finance, Graduate School of Business Administration, New York University, New York.

19

CREDIT ALLOCATION SYSTEMS

The three previous chapters described the influences of the market, the government, and monetary policy on the allocation of credit. By applying value judgments, it is possible to conclude that certain sectors of the economy do not receive the appropriate amounts of credit and that other, less deserving sectors have easy access to low-cost credit. The social benefits resulting from some uses of credit are not reflected in the price of credit.

In addition, the analysis in Chapter 17 indicated that the government is already involved in an ad hoc system of intervention in credit markets. Comprehensive modifications of the credit allocation system would eliminate the need for the existing intervention and consolidate governmental credit allocation activities into one rational program.

Finally, the impact of monetary policy on the allocation of credit creates problems for some important credit users. This chapter considers the wisdom of changing the credit allocation process and examines alternative allocation systems.

The Hunt Commission, The Fine Discussion Principles, and the Credit Allocation Problem

The Report of the President's Commission on Financial Structure and Regulation[1] presented a case against greater intervention in the market's allocation of credit. The report contained some points that are reminders of problems to avoid in designing a credit allocation system.

The Hunt Commission's first general objection rested upon the theoretical value of the free market system of resource allocation.[2] Clearly, the free market has great virtues for resource allocation; many cases can be cited to demonstrate that government intervention has not improved the allocation of resources. The counterarguments are that credit is not allocated in perfectly competitive markets and that the market does not recognize the social benefits of certain credit uses.

[1]The major recommendations of the Hunt Commission were presented in Chap. 3.

[2]*The Report of the President's Commission on Financial Structure and Regulation,* U.S. Government Printing Office, December 1971, p. 9.

Second, the Hunt Commission argued that adoption of its recommendations would improve the allocation of credit.[3] Allowing a freer flow of funds between institutions, removing interest rate ceilings on various types of loans, phasing out Regulation Q, providing more liberal chartering of financial institutions, and expanding powers for thrift institutions would all improve the allocation of credit. However, the recommendations of the Hunt Commission would not achieve the objective of providing specific assistance to high-priority uses of credit.

Third, the Hunt Commission, after considering the question of the social value of some uses of credit, concluded that a system of subsidies to high-priority borrowers would be preferable to a credit allocation system operating through the credit markets, because the cost of a borrower subsidy system would be more obvious than the cost of a system working through financial institutions.[4] This conclusion does not mean that borrower subsidies are the best or only possible plan.

A system based on borrower subsidies would increase the demand for certain types of credit. However, would there be an increased supply of these types of credit at constant interest rates? Assume a program of subsidies to assist low-income families to meet mortgage payments. The program would increase the demand for mortgage funds. However, if the demand for business loans is interest-inelastic and, as former Federal Reserve Governor Andrew Brimmer[5] argues, business loans are given high priority by the financial institutions, would added funds be allocated to home mortgages or would interest rates simply increase?

Fourth, the Hunt Commission argued that the costs of achieving social objectives should not be placed upon depositors and the owners of financial institutions.[6] Some of the schemes for the reallocation of credit would put the cost burden on financial institutions. The Commission was correct in arguing that social objectives should be financed by the entire society.

Fifth, a system of credit allocation could result in financial disintermediation. A program that lowered the return on an institution's assets would reduce the institution's ability to compete for funds and would lead to deposit outflows. This argument is also correct and imposes a constraint on the design of a credit allocation system.

The *Financial Institutions and the Nation's Economy (FINE) Discussion Principles* are more oriented toward credit allocation systems than the report of the Hunt Commission. Increased aid to the housing industry is suggested. The first form of aid would be a mortgage interest tax credit for institutions holding mortgages on low- and middle-income housing. Second, institutions would re-

[3]Ibid., p. 8.

[4]Ibid., pp. 17–18.

[5]"Commercial Bank Lending and Monetary Management," remarks by Andrew F. Brimmer, member of the Board of Governors of the Federal Reserve System, before the 57th Annual Fall Conference of the Robert Morris Associates, Los Angeles, Calif., October 25, 1971.

[6]*The Report of the President's Commission on Financial Structure and Regulation,* op. cit., p. 118.

ceive a credit—equal to a percentage of their mortgage holdings—against their required reserves at the Federal Reserve Banks.[7]

Both sides in this argument present good cases. The ultimate question becomes, can an alternative allocation system do a better job? In the next section, the criteria for a credit allocation system are examined.

Criteria for a Credit Allocation System

This section sets forth some general criteria for a credit allocation system, and the next section applies these criteria to various credit allocation systems.

The first criterion requires that any alternative credit allocation system should, to the maximum extent possible, rely on market incentives. The ideal system would influence the forces of the market to produce the appropriate allocation of credit. The evidence in the previous chapters does not suggest the need to abandon the market and allocate all credit according to a government plan.

Second, any credit allocation system should be flexible. Social priorities change over time, and a credit allocation system should be able to accommodate change without major disruptions of financial markets or lengthy administrative lags.

Third, a system of credit allocation should not interfere with the conduct of monetary policy. However, the desirable restraining effects of monetary policy should not impose disproportionately large burdens on high-priority credit uses.

Fourth, the system should not cause or aggravate conditions of financial disintermediation. Adjustments in rates of return on various financial instruments would be required, but the system must maintain the ability of financial institutions to attract funds.

Fifth, the system should operate with a minimum of administrative complexity. The costs of conducting the programs of credit allocation should be as low as possible relative to the gains.

Sixth, decision making—with respect to the selection of high- and low-priority uses of credit and the administration of the allocation plan—must be vested in an appropriately selected public body. Congressional guidelines would probably be provided, but the Congress could not administer the system. Congressional vesting of the allocating powers with the Board of Governors of the Federal Reserve System is one possible solution. Most Federal Reserve officials would disagree with this solution and would argue that the Congress should make allocation decisions.[8]

These conditions for a credit allocation system are rather strict. The next section considers various credit allocation systems in terms of these conditions.

[7]*Financial Institutions and the Nation's Economy (FINE) Discussion Principles,* 94th Cong., 1st Sess., Committee on Banking, Currency and Housing, U.S. House of Representatives, November 1975, pp. 5–7.

[8]On this issue see Donald R. Hodgman, "Selective Credit Controls," *Journal of Money, Credit and Banking,* May 1972, p. 357.

Credit Allocation Systems

The Credit Control Act of 1969 authorized credit allocation control. Several formal systems for this allocation of credit are discussed in this section. Some of these systems have been studied in the past and some are new. Informal credit allocation plans based on moral suasion are not covered; because of the number of financial institutions in the United States, plans based on attempts to convince institutions to follow a certain course of action are usually effective only in the very short run.

Quota Systems

A quota system for the allocation of credit would force each institution to hold a given percentage of its assets in loans or other assets judged to be of high social value. For example, the credit-allocating authority could decide that the residential mortgage market should have highest priority and that each bank should hold at least 50 percent of its assets in home mortgages. Presumably the quotas would not be the same for all types of financial intermediaries, and some allowance would be made for the historical differences in asset holdings of various institutions.

The principal advantage of this system is its basic simplicity. The total number of dollar value of mortgages necessary to meet housing objectives would be determined and converted into appropriate quotas. The establishment of a high quota, relative to the current outstanding supply of mortgages, would increase the financial institutions' demands for new mortgages and would lower mortgage interest rates.

The problems with this system are numerous. First, the system would not operate through normal market processes. Second, lowering the yield on a high-priority credit instrument would lower the ability of financial intermediaries to compete for funds. This system would act as a tax on the depositors and owners of the banks. However, this income loss might be partly offset by increased yields on the remainder of the institution's asset portfolio. The yield on those assets not accorded high priority would be expected to increase.

Third, if a financial institution were forced to hold part of its assets in certain types of assets and were free to allocate its remaining assets as it wished, the net impact of the plan would depend upon the allocation of the uncontrolled portion of the portfolio. Low yields on the controlled portion of the portfolio would raise the institution's desire for income and the natural response would be an attempt to increase the yield on the remainder of the portfolio. This action might encourage more risk-taking, or a movement of funds from one type of asset (possibly of some social value) to another type of asset (possibly of lower social value). For example, assume that commercial banks were forced to hold a higher than desired portion of their assets in home mortgages at low interest rates. The uncontrolled portion of the portfolio might be reallocated to add more high-risk loans. Alternatively, the holding of state and local government bonds (assumed to be of high social value) might be reduced and the holding of car loans (assumed to be of low social value) increased. In the process of aiding the mortgage market, the allocation plan would hurt the state and local government bond market.

The Hunt Commission, as would be expected, took a dim view of the quota system. Its report argued that "to require specific types of institutions to invest percentages of their portfolios in particular types of investments is the equivalent of a special tax. The initial effect would be to move funds in the desired direction, but eventually as other institutions offered savers better terms than the 'taxed' institutions could afford, there would be a loss of support for the favored programs."[9] The Hunt Commission's argument is correct unless the assumption is made that all institutions would be placed under similar allocation quotas. However, even with equity between institutions, problems would not be avoided. Even if returns were decreased equally and no institution suffered a relative income loss, financial disintermediation would still be a problem.

On the basis of the stated criteria and the objections to the plan, the quota system does not appear to be an appropriate mechanism for the allocation of credit.

Asset Reserve System

A second possible system for controlling the allocation of credit would base reserve requirements on the social value of each institution's assets. The asset reserve system is not a new idea; the plan was proposed as a means of adjusting reserve requirements to take into account risk differentials between various types of assets.[10]

The *social value* version of the asset reserve plan would base the reserve requirement for a given class of assets on the degree of social value assigned to that asset. Thus, institutions would be required to hold high reserves against assets of low social value and would be required to hold only minimal reserves against assets of higher social value.[11]

This system would increase the effective rate of return on socially desirable forms of investment and decrease the effective rate of return on less socially desirable investments. For example, assume that the market return on mortgages is 7 percent and no reserve requirement is imposed; the yield is 7 percent. However, for car loans (assumed to be less desirable) the market rate is 12 percent and the institution must hold a 100 percent reserve against these loans. Thus, each dollar of car loans would require that one dollar be held as nonearning reserves. Allowing for the nonearning reserves, the yield on car loans would be only 6 percent. To equalize its yield on various loans, the bank would either decrease its volume of car loans or increase the price of car loans. As the interest rate charged on car loans increased, fewer car loans would be made (assuming that the demand for car loans responds to interest rate changes).

[9]*The Report of the President's Commission on Financial Structure and Regulation,* loc. cit.

[10]See the discussion of asset reserve systems in Chap. 14.

[11]For a more complete discussion of this option, see Lester C. Thurow, "Proposals for Rechanneling Funds to Meet Social Priorities," *Policies for a More Competitive Financial System,* Federal Reserve Bank of Boston, June 1972, pp. 179–189.

The first problem with this system results from differences in the interest elasticities of demand for the various types of loans. To continue the previous example, assume that the demand for car loans is highly interest-inelastic (a change in the interest rate leads to relatively little change in demand) and the demand for mortgage loans is relatively interest-elastic (a change in the interest rate leads to a large change in demand). A given institution specializing in these two types of loans is faced with the yields and reserve requirement levels stated above. As the institution expands its holdings of mortgages, the return declines very little and as holdings of car loans contract, the return increases significantly. To push the case to an extreme, assume that the mortgage yield declines to 6 percent and the car loan rate increases to 18 percent. The yield on car loans is now higher than the yield on mortgages even after allowing for the effect of the 100 percent reserve requirement on car loans. Thus, the difference in elasticities could have a perverse effect and lead to the shift of funds from mortgages to added reserves against an expanded portfolio of car loans.

Second, the asset reserve system would suffer from a possible inflexibility. Once the reserve requirement on a particular asset had been established, the rate could be increased only with great difficulty. An increase in the social priority level of a given asset would not present any special problem (other than the need to redistribute portfolios), but a lowering of the social priority level of an asset and the accompanying increase in the reserve requirement would place a heavy cost on institutions with large holdings of that particular asset. There would always be great pressures against lowering the priority level of any type of asset.

Finally, the usefulness of reserve requirements as a means of monetary control would probably be eliminated. Even though changes in reserve requirements are seldom made under the present system, the dislocations that would be produced under the asset reserve system would mean that reserve requirements could not be changed for monetary policy purposes.

Given the problems of the asset reserve system, this scheme does not meet the criteria for an efficient credit allocation mechanism.

Multi-Asset Open Market Operations

Under the multi-asset open market operations system, the Federal Reserve System would abandon its policy of conducting open market operations exclusively in short-term government debt and would conduct its operations both to control the supply of bank reserves and to influence the allocation of credit. If, for example, the market interest rate on state and local government bonds were relatively high and it were determined that the rate should be lowered, the Federal Reserve would buy municipal bonds. If an expansion of the money supply were desired, no offsetting action would be required; if no expansion of the money supply were thought desirable, the Federal Reserve would sell an equal amount of Treasury bills. A similar operation to lower mortgage interest rates would presumably require the Federal Reserve to purchase FNMA or GNMA bonds as part of its open market operations.

In 1973, the majority of the Joint Economic Committee (JEC) of the Congress appeared to favor this approach. The JEC Report on the *1973 Economic Report of the President* states:

> The Administration and the monetary authorities should move at once to establish a stand-by credit allocation system. The Federal Reserve authority should establish a set of guidelines for the banking community to assure those who are most likely to be cut off from credit sources in a period of tight money—builders, home buyers, local government, and small business—are provided adequate access to credit. The central bank can and should move directly to provide more funds in these areas by stepping up sharply its purchases of securities of State and local governments and mortgages and by indicating in its discount policy due regard for the credit needs of small business.[12]

Although the basic simplicity of a system that would rely on the Federal Reserve's portfolio as the balancing factor in the credit allocation process is attractive, this system of credit allocation has several deficiencies.

First, this plan could only be used to favor certain groups of borrowers. The Federal Reserve could purchase "socially desirable" securities but would have no "socially undesirable" securities to sell. Thus, while the mechanism would improve the market position of those securities selected for preferential treatment, the market for government securities would be injured by the plan. If the Federal Reserve sold government debt each time it purchased the favored debt instruments, the cost of financing the government's debt would increase. The burden of this plan would fall on the taxpayer rather than on the issuers of lower priority securities. A more attractive alternative would provide a method by which the Federal Reserve could buy high-priority securities and sell lower priority securities. However, given that the Federal Reserve does not hold a portfolio of lower priority securities, this option could not be implemented.

Second, if the return on socially desirable assets were lowered by the Federal Reserve's actions, the return to private holders of these assets would also be lowered and they would be induced to switch to other assets. Also, disintermediation problems would be expected to arise, as institutional holders of the low-yielding favored assets became less able to compete for funds.

The third problem, which follows from the second, is the extent to which the reallocation of institutional portfolios would negate the effect of the Federal Reserve's change in the relative yields on securities. Assume that the Federal Reserve purchases municipal bonds and lowers the yield. At a lower interest rate, the supply of new municipal bonds should increase. However, the lower yield on

[12]*Report of the Joint Economic Committee, Congress of the United States, on the January, 1973 Economic Report of the President,* March 26, 1973, p. 27.

municipal bonds would decrease lender demand. The greater supply and lower demand for municipal bonds would at least partly offset the initial decline in yield; the degree of offsetting yield change would be determined by demand and supply elasticities. To hold the yield at the initially desired level, the Federal Reserve would have to continue purchasing municipal bonds.

Although multi-asset open market operations do not violate many of the criteria for an efficient allocation control system, the dangers of distinermediation remain. In addition, the monetary authority is unable to place some of the program's cost on the issuers and holders of the less desirable forms of credit use.

Government Subsidies to and Taxes on Lenders

A credit allocation system could be based on the taxation of low-priority credit users or the subsidization of high-priority credit users.

The effectiveness of this system would again depend on the interest elasticity of demand for the various types of credit. If the demand for automobile financing were very inelastic, the imposition of a tax on the lender would increase the cost of car loans but would not significantly decrease the volume of car loans. The tax approach would work best if it were determined that the demand curves for the low-priority forms of credit were relatively elastic. However, there is no evidence that this is the case; more likely, the forms of credit, which would normally be considered as less desirable, would have relatively inelastic demand curves.

The use of lender subsidies raises eligibility questions. For example, if a subsidy were to be given to those institutions making home loans, would this apply to all loans granted, or would the subsidy be paid only on loans to specific borrowers? Would the subsidy extend for the life of the loan or for a certain period of time? Would the subsidy level be sufficiently flexible to allow for changes as market interest rates changed? Would the tax approach increase or decrease the ability of institutions to attract funds?

The tax and/or subsidy approach appears to have merit, but the elasticities of demand and supply for each type of credit must be known. The final system to be considered appears to be a better method of utilizing the tax and subsidy concept.

The Variable Portfolio Change Subsidy and Tax Plan

A variation of the tax and subsidy idea would subsidize or tax changes in bank loan portfolios. At the beginning of each time period, the level of the subsidy for each high-priority use of credit and the tax on each low-priority use of credit would be announced. At the end of the time period, each lender would receive a subsidy for each dollar of *increase* in his holdings of the high-priority assets and would be charged a tax on each dollar of *increase* in his holdings of low-priority assets.

There are five main advantages to this plan:

1. Incentives would be provided at the margin to encourage some types of lending and discourage other types of lending.

2. Rates and asset classifications could be changed from year to year or quarter to quarter.

3. The program would not have to be permanent but could be maintained on a standby basis.

4. The competitive position of those institutions distributing their funds in the "socially desirable" manner would be enhanced by the receipt of the subsidies.

5. The plan would be, at least in part, self-financing because the tax on the less desirable loans would contribute funds for the subsidization of the more desirable loans.

On the negative side, the variable portfolio change subsidy and tax plan would require considerably more knowledge of demand elasticities than would some of the other plans. However, the operation of the plan and the ability to change subsidy and tax rates from period to period would provide the flexibility for change as additional data became available.

The problem of forecasting becomes more critical under this plan. The need to establish rates for the next period requires the authorities to have prior knowledge of the future demand for and supply of various types of credit.

Under this program, a given type of credit could be eligible for a subsidy payment at the time the loan was granted but could become ineligible in subsequent time periods. To avoid creating an institutional preference for short-term loans, the level of the subsidy payment would probably have to be geared to the term of the loan. The institution's subsidy would become a function of the subsidy payment level for that type of loan, the size of the loan, and the term of the loan. In addition, recovery procedures would be needed to cover early repayment of loans.

The variable portfolio change subsidy and tax plan appears to meet all the stated criteria for an efficient credit allocation plan. However, this plan also requires the highest degree of knowledge of the credit markets. Implementation of this plan would require answers to many questions that have not yet been conclusively answered.

These various plans for controlling credit allocation indicate the range of possibilities and number of problems involved in attempting to reallocate credit. A great deal more work would be necessary before any of these plans could be put into effect, but the problems and alternatives should be considered.

A Conclusion on the Credit Allocation Process

There is pressure to change the credit allocation process. The passage of the Credit Control Act of 1969 and the quotations in this part of the text demonstrate the desire of many responsible individuals and groups to revise the credit allocation system.

The author has attempted to present the issues involved in this examination of credit allocation systems as objectively as possible. Examples of "socially desirable" uses of credit have been used but these should not be interpreted as being more than just convenient examples.

Before the author would recommend additional intervention in the market's allocation of credit, several conditions should be met:

1. More convincing evidence is required to demonstrate that the market is not properly allocating credit. At this point, one can conclude that monetary policy does place an excessive burden on residential construction. However, for other types of credit, the evidence is not strong and does not justify additional government intervention in the credit markets.

2. A relatively strong case must be made to demonstrate that greater intervention in the credit markets would indeed produce an improved allocation of credit. The weight of the evidence in favor of a credit allocation system must be substantial.

3. Standards for the selection of "socially desirable" and "socially undesirable" uses of credit must be developed. Objective criteria are required to select the credit uses that would be assisted or restricted by a credit allocation program.

4. An appropriate public body must be selected to assume responsibility for the credit allocation program. Can a method be devised to select a group that will reflect the long-run interests of the entire society? Can society be assured that the group will operate objectively rather than on the basis of their value judgments?

In conclusion, the author has strong reservations about the expansion of government intervention in the credit allocation process. The suggested course of action includes implementation of the recommendations of the Hunt Commission, further research on methods of stabilizing the flow of credit to housing, and a comprehensive study of the entire credit allocation process.

REVIEW QUESTIONS

1. Evaluate the Hunt Commission's case against a greater degree of government involvement in credit allocation.

2. How would a system of quotas for the holding of specific types of assets work? What would be the problems with this approach?

3. In what ways would financial disintermediation be a problem in each of the credit allocation plans discussed in the chapter?

4. What guidelines would you suggest for the selection of those uses of credit that would be favored by a credit allocation system and those uses of credit that would be restricted by a credit allocation system? Who should make these choices?

5. How should the costs of a credit allocation system be divided between bank depositors, bank owners, and society in general?

6. What potential problems exist in the use of open market operations in socially desirable assets as the method of influencing the allocation of credit? While the Federal Reserve has no undesirable assets to sell, the money supply is growing over time and purchases of assets other than Treasury bills would be possible. What limitations would exist in this case?

7. How could taxes and subsidies be used to influence the allocation of credit? Should the taxes or subsidies fall on the lender or the borrower?

8. How would the variable portfolio change tax and subsidy plan operate to influence the allocation of credit?

9. How would the asset reserve system operate to influence the allocation of credit? What effect would this use of reserve requirements have on the use of reserve requirements as a tool of monetary policy?

10. After studying the material in this section of the book, would you agree or disagree with the author's conclusions relative to the use of greater credit allocation controls?

SUGGESTED READINGS

Credit Allocation Techniques and Monetary Policy, Federal Reserve Bank of Boston, September 1973.

Ira Kaminow and James M. O'Brien, "Selective Credit Policies: Should Their Role Be Expanded?" *Federal Reserve Bank of Philadelphia Business Review,* November 1975, pp. 3–22.

PART IV

THE INTERNATIONAL MONETARY SYSTEM

The various domestic economies of the world are linked together by the international monetary system. A smoothly operating system permits nations to cooperate in the solution of their domestic economic problems. As world trade and international financial relationships expand, the efficient operation of the international monetary system becomes of increasing importance to all national economies.

Events in recent years have produced great changes in, and pose future problems for, the organization of international financial relationships. The basic areas covered in this final part of the book are the following:

1. The balance of payments statement, which is an accounting record of the international trade and financial transactions between one economy and all other economies, is examined.
2. The alternative methods for determining exchange rates between national currencies are studied.
3. The problems of correcting a balance of payments deficit and dividing the burden of international adjustment between deficit and surplus nations is examined.
4. International organizations developed to promote cooperation in the solution of international economic problems are studied.
5. The American dollar's role and problems as a major international currency are explained.
6. Finally, several continuing problems that must be solved as part of the future development of the international monetary system are analyzed.

20

THE INTERNATIONAL FINANCIAL SYSTEM AND THE BALANCE OF PAYMENTS

This chapter begins by describing the process of trading national currencies in the foreign exchange markets. In the second section the Balance of Payments Accounting System is presented and the complexities of selecting the appropriate measure of surplus or deficit are explored.

The Foreign Exchange Markets

Each nation maintains its own national currency system and controls its own supply of money. International finance is concerned with the financing of trade and other transactions between nations that have different monetary units and monetary systems. The English exporter of goods wants to receive pounds sterling; his suppliers and workers expect to be paid in pounds (£). The French importer of the English goods prefers to pay in his nation's currency, the French franc. Thus, markets must be provided so that the Frenchman can sell his francs for pounds and make payment. Alternatively, if the Englishman accepts francs, he needs a market in which the francs can be sold for pounds sterling.

International trade provided the original need for the exchange of national currencies, but other types of international transactions have grown in importance as the world's economies have become increasingly interdependent. The major sources of American demand for foreign currencies are:

1. the financing of American imports of goods and services from other nations;
2. the financing of American foreign travel;
3. the transfer of gifts by individuals and foreign economic and military aid by the United States Government;
4. the purchase of foreign securities from foreigners;
5. the purchase of foreign plant and equipment;
6. the transfer of funds to foreign banks as foreign interest rates increase relative to American interest rates;

7. speculation on movements of exchange rates between currencies; and

8. the holding of working capital in foreign currencies by multinational corporations.

The foreign demand for American dollars arises from these same factors. Individuals, business firms, and governments demand foreign currencies for all of the same reasons that they demand their own nation's currency.

The foreign exchange market provides the mechanism for the trading of currencies. The foreign exchange market does not have a central trading place comparable to the floor of the New York Stock Exchange; rather, the participants in this worldwide market are linked together by telephone and cable communications systems. The major dealers in the foreign exchange markets are the large banks in the world's trade and financial centers. The dealers in foreign exchange maintain an inventory of foreign currencies and sell to, or buy from, their customers at the current market price. Their inventories of various currencies are adjusted by buying from, of selling to, other dealers.

The dealer's holdings of a currency (or of bank deposits denominated in that currency) are referred to as his *position* in the currency. The dealer's position in a currency depends upon his expectations of customer demand and his forecast of the currency's future price movements. The expected future price is a very critical criterion; the foreign currency dealer does not want to be caught holding a large inventory of a currency when its price is declining in terms of other currencies.

The currency dealer may be either *long* or *short* in a given currency. If a trader thinks that the price of the German mark is going to rise, he will hold a long position in marks. A long position means that the dealer either owns marks or has contracts that require others to deliver marks to him in the future at a fixed price. Being long in a currency means that the dealer has a positive inventory of that currency. If the dealer thinks that the British pound is going to decline in price, he may be short pounds; he holds a negative inventory of pounds. Going short in pounds means that he has promised to deliver pounds at a given price at some future time; he does not now own those pounds.

For example, assume the current price of the British pound sterling is 1£ = \$2. The dealer believes that in 60 days the price will be 1£ = \$1.98. He sells 1,000 £ short at the current price of 1£ = \$2. He is betting that in the next 60 days, the price of the pound will decline and he can buy at \$1.98 per pound sterling. He buys at \$1.98 and sells for \$2. He makes a small profit on each pound sterling, but by dealing in very large quantities he makes a good return on his funds. Of course, if his expectation of the future price of the pound is wrong and the price increases to \$2.02, he must buy at the higher price in order to make his promised delivery of 1,000£ at \$2 = 1£. He loses on the transaction.

The prices of foreign currencies are quoted to four or more decimal places. The price of the pound sterling may be \$2.0016. A movement of one cent in a given day would be a major change. Fortunes can be made or lost on very small price fluctuations.

Arbitrage

The existence of instantaneous communications systems linking foreign exchange dealers keeps the price of a currency the same around the world. If the price of a currency differs between places, arbitrage will eliminate the variation. *Arbitrage* is simply the simultaneous buying and selling of a currency in order to take advantage of a price differential. For example, the dealer notes that Swiss francs are selling at $0.40 in New York and at $0.41 in London. He buys in the low price market, New York, and sells simultaneously in the high price market, London; thus, he gains $0.01 per Swiss franc. The dealer's arbitrage transaction helps to eliminate the differential because he is increasing the demand for Swiss francs in New York and bidding up the price. He is increasing the supply in London and pushing down the price. The dealer's arbitrage helps keep the price of the Swiss franc, relative to the dollar, the same in all markets. When price differentials do exist, they are small and are rapidly eliminated if markets are free and uncontrolled.

The Forward Markets

Currency exchange may be either on a *spot* or a *forward* basis. The spot market is the market for immediate delivery of the currency purchased or sold. The forward market deals in contracts for the future delivery of currency. The most important forward markets are contracts for 60-, 90-, and 180-day delivery periods. The forward market provides the opportunity to avoid the risk of a currency price change. One can *hedge* against a loss by giving up the possibility of a profit.

Assume an American exporter agrees to sell machinery to a British manufacturer. Delivery of the machines is to be made in 90 days and payment is to be made when the machines are delivered. The price of the machines is $100,000. The exporter arranges to be paid in dollars and will receive the $100,000 regardless of changes in the price of the pound and the dollar.

The British purchaser is bearing the exchange rate risk of the transaction. In 90 days, he must make payment in dollars. He can buy dollars now or buy dollars when payment is due. Assume the present exchange rate is 1£ for $2. If he waits, his pound sterling may be worth $2.10 or it may be worth $1.90. There is an exchange-rate risk. The British importer is a manufacturer and not a currency speculator; he would like to obtain a low price on his purchase of dollars but fears that he may have to buy dollars when the price is high.

To avoid the exchange-rate risk, the Englishman buys dollars for *forward delivery*. He agrees to accept delivery of $100,000 in 90 days at the current forward price of 1£ = $2.01. He has shifted the exchange rate risk to someone else. He knows that he will have to pay 1£ = $2.01 when the dollars are delivered. He no longer has to worry about the future price of dollars.

The same transaction would be possible with the American agreeing to receive payment in pounds and to accept the exchange rate risk. The American would be uncertain of the number of dollars he would obtain for the pounds. Thus, he arranges to sell the pounds for forward delivery at a fixed price. He will obtain a known number of dollars for the pounds. He gives up both the hope of a profit (if the price of the pound is high when the sale is finalized) and the risk of a loss (if the price of the pound is low when the transaction is completed). However, the American is a machine manufacturer, not a currency trader; he is willing to sacrifice the hope of a profit on the currency transaction in order to avoid a possible loss.

Forward markets do not exist for every currency, but most international transactions are conducted in a few major currencies, and so most international transactions can be hedged through the forward market.

The example assumed that both the Englishman and the American could find a customer for their forward contract. The other party to the transaction could have been another firm with a similar hedging objective or could have been a currency dealer or speculator. The English importer needed to make payment in dollars. His forward contract could have been with a second English firm that would be receiving dollars in 90 days and was selling the dollars in the forward market. Or the forward contract might have been with an American who was hedging against exchange rate fluctuations by buying pounds for future delivery.

In summary, the foreign exchange markets act as the means by which national currencies are traded and payments are made between economies. The growth of international trade and other international economic relationships depends upon the ability of the financial markets to provide for the smooth and efficient conversion of national currencies.

The Dollar As an International Medium of Exchange

Since World War II, the American dollar has played a special role in the world monetary system. While international trade is conducted in all currencies, some currencies are more important than others. For most of the postwar period, the dollar has been the most important currency.

The dollar, as the strongest currency for most of the period, has become an international medium of exchange. Transactions are conducted in dollars even though no Americans are involved in the transaction. Dollar deposits in foreign banks (Eurodollars) are exchanged in the course of international trade and finance.[1] In recent years, other currencies have also become international mediums of exchange.

The Balance of Payments Accounts

Each part of this book has involved a basic accounting system. The understanding of international finance requires an examination of the Balance of Payments Accounts.

[1]See the discussion of Eurodollars in Chap. 4.

The Balance of Payments statement is a summary of all of the transactions, private and public, between one nation and the rest of the world. The transactions include not only exports and imports but also the acquisition or sale of all varieties of assets and liabilities. By working through the accounts, the types of transactions involved and the various measures of Balance of Payments surplus or deficit become clear.

The full Balance of Payments Summary is presented in Table 20–1. The items in the accounts are marked with a plus or minus sign. A *plus* sign represents an American claim on the rest of the world; a *minus* sign represents a foreign claim on the United States. Alternatively, the signs can be regarded in terms of foreign demand for and supply of dollars. A plus sign represents a foreign demand for dollars to make a payment to Americans. A negative sign represents a supply of dollars by Americans to foreigners.

The Merchandise Trade Balance

The first three columns of Table 20–1 represent the American merchandise trade balance. Exports and imports of goods and the net export or import balance are included in these columns. American exports of goods represent a foreign demand for dollars to pay for these goods. The foreign buyer of American goods must sell his own currency on the foreign exchange market in order to obtain dollars to pay the American exporter. American importers of foreign goods must sell dollars in order to make payments to foreign exporters.

Note that except for 1971, 1972, and 1974, the United States maintained a merchandise balance of trade surplus in all post–World War II years. Except for those three years, exports exceeded imports and created a net foreign demand for dollars.

The rate of growth of both exports and imports has been high in the 1970s, but the international sector is still small relative to total American output. In 1974, merchandise exports represented less than 7 percent of total American GNP.

Of 1975 American exports, 15.7 percent were food, beverages, and tobacco; 14.4 percent were crude materials and fuels; and 66.2 percent were manufactured goods. Of 1975 imports, 10.5 percent were food, beverages, and tobacco; 33.9 percent were crude materials and fuels; and 53.2 percent were manufactured goods.[2]

In terms of geographical distribution of 1975 exports and imports, 60.2 percent of American exports went to developed nations and 36.5 percent went to developing nations; 58.3 percent of American imports came from developed nations and 40.8 percent came from developing nations. Western Europe, Asia, and Canada are the major American trading partners.[3]

The United States imports goods because of consumer tastes and preferences for foreign-made goods, because of price and quality differentials between

[2] *1976 Economic Report of the President,* p. 276 (based on January–November data).
[3] Ibid., p. 277.

TABLE 20–1 United States Balance of Payments, 1946–1975 (in millions of dollars)

Year	Merchandise			Military transactions			Net investment income		Net travel and transportation expenditures	Other services, net	Balance on goods and services	Remittances, pensions, and other unilateral transfers	Balance on current account	Long-term capital flows, net		Balance on current account and long-term capital	Nonliquid short-term private capital flows, net	Allocations of special drawing rights (SDR)	Errors and omissions, net	Net liquidity balance **	Liquid private capital flows, net	Oficial reserve transactions balance **	Changes in liabilities to foreign officla agencies, net	Changes in U.S. official reserve assets, net	U.S. official reserve assets, net (unadjusted end of period)
	Exports	Imports	Net balance	Direct expenditures	Sales	Net balance	Private	U.S. Government						U.S. Government	Private										
1946	11,764	−5,067	6,697	−493		−493	554	6	733	310	7,807	−2,922	4,885	......	......	......	−253	......	155	......	......	......	......	−623	20,706
1947	16,097	−5,973	10,124	−455		−455	807	50	946	145	11,617	−2,625	8,992	......	......	......	−236	......	861	......	......	......	......	−3,315	24,021
1948	13,265	−7,557	5,708	−799		−799	975	85	374	175	6,518	−4,525	1,993	......	......	......	−131	......	1,115	......	......	......	......	−1,736	25,758
1949	12,213	−6,874	5,339	−621		−621	989	73	230	208	6,218	−5,638	580	......	......	......	158	......	717	......	......	......	......	−266	26,024
1950	10,203	−9,081	1,122	−576		−576	1,146	78	−120	242	1,892	−4,017	−2,125	......	......	......	75	......	−124	......	......	......	......	1,758	24,265
1951	14,243	−11,176	3,067	−1,270		−1,270	1,317	151	298	254	3,817	−3,515	302	......	......	......	−227	......	354	......	......	......	......	−33	24,299
1952	13,449	−10,838	2,611	−2,054		−2,054	1,267	140	83	309	2,356	−2,531	−175	......	......	......	−41	......	497	......	......	......	......	−415	24,714
1953	12,412	−10,975	1,437	−2,615	192	−2,423	1,283	166	−238	307	532	−2,481	−1,949	......	......	......	183	......	220	......	......	......	......	1,256	23,458
1954	12,929	−10,353	2,576	−2,642	182	−2,460	1,594	213	−269	305	1,959	−2,280	−321	......	......	......	−556	......	60	......	......	......	......	480	22,978
1955	14,424	−11,527	2,897	−2,901	200	−2,701	1,775	180	−297	299	2,153	−2,498	−345	......	......	......	−328	......	371	......	......	......	......	182	22,797
1956	17,556	−12,803	4,753	−2,949	161	−2,788	2,054	40	−361	447	4,145	−2,423	1,722	......	......	......	−479	......	390	......	......	......	......	−869	23,666
1957	19,562	−13,291	6,271	−3,216	375	−2,841	2,174	4	−189	482	5,901	−2,345	3,556	......	......	......	−174	......	1,012	......	......	......	......	−1,165	24,832
1958	16,414	−12,952	3,462	−3,435	300	−3,135	2,008	168	−633	486	2,356	−2,361	−5	......	......	......	−145	......	361	......	......	......	......	2,292	22,540
1959	16,458	−15,310	1,148	−3,107	302	−2,805	2,147	68	−831	573	310	−2,448	−2,138	......	......	......	−89	......	260	......	......	......	......	1,035	21,504
1960	19,650	−14,758	4,892	−3,087	335	−2,753	2,270	17	−964	612	4,073	−2,300	1,774	−885	−2,100	−1,211	−1,405	......	−1,060	−3,677	273	−3,403	1,258	2,145	19,359
1961	20,108	−14,537	5,571	−2,998	402	−2,596	2,832	105	−978	628	5,563	−2,514	3,048	−885	−2,182	−20	1,200	......	−1,032	−2,252	904	−1,348	742	606	18,753
1962	20,781	−16,260	4,521	−3,105	656	−2,448	3,177	134	−1,155	845	5,074	−2,628	2,446	−882	−2,606	−1,043	−657	......	−1,165	−2,864	214	−2,650	1,117	1,533	17,220
1963	22,272	−17,048	5,224	−2,961	657	−2,304	3,227	98	−1,312	996	5,930	−2,742	3,188	−1,151	−3,376	−1,339	−968	......	−406	−2,713	779	−1,934	1,557	377	16,843
1964	25,501	−18,700	6,801	−2,880	747	−2,133	3,926	9	−1,149	1,078	8,533	−2,769	5,764	−1,352	−4,511	−100	−1,643	......	−954	−2,696	1,162	−1,534	1,363	171	16,672
1965	26,461	−21,510	4,951	−2,952	830	−2,122	4,143	26	−1,284	1,426	7,140	−2,841	4,299	−1,539	−4,577	−1,817	−154	......	−506	−2,478	1,188	−1,290	67	1,222	15,450
1966	29,310	−25,493	3,817	−3,764	829	−2,935	3,543	55	−1,332	1,404	4,552	−2,917	1,635	−1,478	−2,778	−2,621	−104	......	575	−2,151	2,370	219	−787	568	14,882
1967	30,666	−26,866	3,800	−4,378	1,152	−3,226	3,865	41	−1,751	1,652	4,380	−3,107	1,273	−2,337	−2,909	−3,973	−522	......	−189	−4,683	1,265	−3,418	3,366	52	14,830
1968	33,626	−32,991	635	−4,535	1,392	−3,143	3,941	63	−1,548	1,671	1,620	−2,933	−1,313	−2,164	1,190	−2,287	231	......	446	−1,611	3,252	1,641	−761	−880	15,710
1969	36,414	−35,807	607	−4,856	1,528	−3,328	3,471	156	−1,763	1,878	1,020	−2,976	−1,956	−1,949	−44	−3,949	−640	......	−1,492	−6,081	8,820	2,739	−1,552	−1,187	16,964
1970	42,469	−39,866	2,603	−4,855	1,501	−3,355	3,631	−112	−2,023	2,220	2,966	−3,248	−281	−2,045	−1,434	−3,760	−482	867	−476	−3,851	−5,938	−9,839	7,362	2,477	14,487
1971	43,311	−45,579	−2,268	−4,819	1,926	−2,893	5,659	−956	−2,315	2,537	−237	−3,642	−3,879	−2,376	−4,383	−10,637	−2,347	717	−9,698	−21,965	−7,788	−29,753	27,405	2,348	12,167
1972	49,388	−55,797	−6,409	−4,784	1,163	−3,621	6,208	−1,888	−3,024	2,803	−5,930	−3,779	−9,710	−1,334	−69	−11,113	−1,542	710	−1,884	−13,829	3,475	−10,354	10,322	32	13,151
1973	71,379	−70,424	955	−4,658	2,342	−2,317	8,188	−3,009	−2,862	3,222	4,177	−3,841	335	−1,490	177	−977	−4,238	......	−2,436	−7,651	2,343	−5,308	5,099	209	14,378
1974	98,309	−103,586	−5,277	−5,103	2,944	−2,158	13,351	−3,229	−2,692	3,830	3,825	−7,182	−3,357	1,119	−8,463	−10,702	−12,936	......	4,698	−18,940	10,543	−8,397	9,831	−1,434	15,883
1975	107,184	−98,139	9,045	0,000	0,000	−819	6,030	0,000	−1,968	4,211	16,500	−4,583	11,916	−1,726	−8,789	1,401	−2,819	......	4,556	3,138	−5,601	−2,463	3,070	−607	16,226

SOURCES: *1976 Economic Report of the President,* pp. 274–275; *Federal Reserve Bulletin,* April 1976, p. A58.

TABLE 20–2 The Merchandise Trade Balance, 1975

	MILLIONS OF DOLLARS	
Exports	+107,184	
Imports	− 98,139	
Merchandise trade balance		+9,045

American and foreign goods, and because of the need for products and raw materials that are not domestically produced. Other nations purchase American goods for the same reasons.

In the short run, the levels of American exports and imports depend upon current relative prices and income levels. In the long run, relative prices and income levels change. Other factors, such as consumer tastes and preferences, availability of supply, technological advances, tariffs and other barriers to trade, currency exchange rates, and relative costs of production of goods also affect trade levels.

Reorganizing the 1975 data in Table 20–1 produces Table 20–2. Exports in 1975 were $9,045 million greater than imports.

The Balance on Current Account

Besides merchandise, other current transactions in both goods and services must be entered into the accounts. Table 20–3 presents the balance on goods and services and the balance on the current account.

In Table 20–3, the merchandise trade balance is adjusted first for the provision of other goods and services during 1975. Foreign military expenditures by the United States are listed as a negative item and the sale of military goods to other nations as a positive value. The net value in this category is −$819 million. In other words, American foreign military expenditures were $819 million greater than American sales of military goods to other nations.

Net investment income includes the payment of interest and dividends to Americans by foreigners less payments of interest and dividends to foreigners by Americans. The data for the private sector indicate that, excluding the government, Americans receive more interest and dividends from foreigners than they pay to foreigners. The U.S. government account is the payment of interest by the United States government on foreign holdings of American government debt minus interest paid to the U.S. government on its holdings of foreign assets. In recent years, foreigners have acquired a larger proportion of U.S. government debt, and the payment of interest on this debt is of increasing importance in the balance of payments.

Net travel and transportation measures expenditures on tourism and shipping. Your trip to Europe is a negative entry and a foreigner's trip to the United States is a positive entry. The income from other services provided to foreigners by Americans minus the expenditures on all other foreign services provided to Americans is the other services net entry.

TABLE 20–3 The Balance on Current Account, 1975[a]

	MILLIONS OF DOLLARS	
Exports	+107,184	
Imports	− 98,139	
Merchandise trade balance		+ 9,045
Military transactions, net	− 819	
Direct expenditures	—	
Sales	—	
Net investment income	+ 6,030	
Private	—	
U.S. government	—	
Net travel and transportation	− 1,968	
Other services, net	+ 4,211	
Balance on goods and services		+16,500
Remittances, pensions, and other unilateral transfers	− 4,583	
Balance on current account		+11,916

[a]Detail may not add to totals due to rounding.

Adding and subtracting the values of military transactions, net investment income, net travel and transportation, and other services net from the merchandise trade balance yields the balance on goods and services. The balance on goods and services indicates a 1975 surplus for the United States. This figure is comparable to the net export figure used in the National Income Accounting System.

Continuing in Table 20–3, the final adjustment is for remittances, pensions and other unilateral transfers. If you send a gift of money to a relative in another country, the present is included here. If you retire and live in another country and receive a pension from an American firm, this is included. Foreign aid grants from the United States government are also included. All of these expenditures are payments for which no current goods or services are furnished; they are transfer payments. Subtracting the value of these transfer payments produces a current account surplus of $11,916 million.

The current account balance reflects the balance of all trade and transfer payments. This measure reflects *current* economic activity and transfers but does not cover changes in the holdings of various assets or long term investment.

The analysis continues with the addition of long-term capital movements. In Table 20–4, an American loan to a foreign government would have a negative sign because this would represent an outflow of dollars from the United States. If an American firm buys a foreign company, this would be an outflow of dollars from the United States and would have a negative sign. Likewise, if an American purchases stock on the Zurich stock exchange, he must sell dollars (an outflow) to obtain Swiss francs; the transaction would have a negative sign. Conversely, if foreign investors purchase American factories or securities, the transaction represents an inflow of dollars (an increased demand for dollars) and has a positive value.

TABLE 20–4 Current Account and Long-Term Capital Balance, 1975

			MILLIONS OF DOLLARS
Balance on current account			+11,916
Long-term capital flows, net		−10,515	
U.S. government	−1,726		
Private	−8,789		
Balance on current account and long-term capital			+ 1,401

Table 20–4 indicates that American investment in other countries was significantly larger than foreign investment in the United States. Table 20–1 indicates that the 1975 figure is typical of most years. This outflow of dollars creates a deficit in the long-term capital account but produces future earnings for American investors and an American surplus on net investment income. Thus, the act of investing abroad creates a current deficit but contributes to future surpluses.

The balance on current account and long-term capital is also called the *basic balance*. A case can be made that this measure reflects all the basic trade, transfers, and long-term capital investment decisions and that the remaining items in the accounts describe the methods of financing the resulting surplus or deficit.

The Net Liquidity Balance

The next measure of the balance of payments position of the economy is the net liquidity balance. Three adjustments are made to the balance on current account and long-term capital to obtain the net liquidity balance in Table 20–5. The nonliquid short-term private capital flows in the table are short-term claims that cannot be readily transferred. For example, a loan by an American bank to a foreign borrower would be an outflow of funds from the United States and would have a minus sign. A loan by a foreign bank to an American corporation would be an inflow of funds to the United States and would have a positive sign. Like most bank loans, these would be short-term loans and would be relatively nonliquid.

The allocation of Special Drawing Rights refers to the International Monetary Fund's distribution of newly created international reserves. No new reserves were created by the IMF in 1975. The role of Special Drawing Rights is discussed fully in Chapter 23.

TABLE 20–5 The Net Liquidity Balance, 1975

		MILLIONS OF DOLLARS
Balance on current account and long-term capital		+1,401
Nonliquid short-term private capital flows	−2,819	
Allocation of Special Drawing Rights	0	
Errors and omissions	+4,556	
Net liquidity balance		+3,138

TABLE 20–6 Official Reserve Transactions Balance, 1975

		MILLIONS OF DOLLARS
Net liquidity balance		+3,138
Liquid private capital flows, net	−5,601	
Official reserve transactions balance		−2,463

The net liquidity balance excludes liquid short-term private capital flows such as bank deposits; these flows are considered to be a means of financing the deficit or surplus. As indicated in the previous section, the basic balance considers all liquid and nonliquid capital flows as a means of financing a surplus or deficit. The basic balance yields a 1975 surplus of $1,401 million. Including the −$2,819 million net outflow of nonliquid short-term private capital (representing mainly an increase of foreign indebtedness to American banks) would have created a deficit, but the positive allowance for errors and omissions offset the capital outflows and increased the surplus to $3,138 million.

The Official Reserve Transactions Balance

The final measure of the balance of payments, which is used by most nations, is the official reserve transactions balance. This balance is derived in Table 20–6. Liquid private capital flows consist mainly of changes in American deposits in foreign banks and foreign deposits in American banks. These flows may be a result of speculation on future exchange rates or may be transfers for the purpose of obtaining a better interest rate.

An increase of liabilities to foreigners by United States banks and a decrease of foreign bank liabilities to Americans have a positive sign. An increase of foreign bank liabilities to Americans and a decrease of American bank liabilities to foreigners have a negative sign. In 1975, foreigners reduced their deposits in American banks, and net liquid private capital flows recorded a net outflow of funds.

Financing the Deficit

Using the official reserve transactions balance as the measure of the deficit, the $2,463 million deficit must be financed. If a consumer spends more than he earns during the year, he can finance his deficit in one of two ways. First, he can issue claims to his creditors for future payment; second, he can reduce his asset holdings. In other words, he borrows or he sells his worldly goods.

The columns in Table 20–1 entitled Changes in liabilities to foreign official agencies and Changes in United States official reserve assets indicate the methods of financing the 1975 deficit. Liabilities to foreign official agencies, either central banks or government treasuries, increased by $3,070 million and American reserves increased by $607 million. Netting the two changes produces the $2,463 million needed to finance the deficit. The changes in United States official reserve assets have signs contrary to what would be expected; an increase in reserve assets has a minus sign and a decrease has a positive sign! The decrease is represented by a positive sign because if foreign central banks converted dollars to American gold, there would be an inflow of dollars to the United States.

The changes in liabilities to foreign official agencies represents increases in dollars held by foreign monetary agencies and increases in holdings of American government debt by foreign central banks. While foreign central banks were allowed to convert dollars into gold (prior to August 1971), this account represented the dollars that could potentially be converted to gold.

The change in the United States official reserve assets is the sum of the changes in American gold reserves, the American government's holdings of foreign currencies, Special Drawing Rights, and the American gold deposits at the International Monetary Fund. All of these assets could be transferred to other nations in the settlement of balance of payments deficits. The function of these assets as international reserves is considered in Chapter 21.

How Large Was the American Surplus or Deficit in 1975?

After all of the descriptions of the balance of payments statement, the question remains, was there a deficit or a surplus? The person who wants a single number will be frustrated, because the analysis has produced six different measures of surplus or deficit; these measures range from a surplus of $16.5 billion for 1975 to a deficit of over $2.4 billion for 1975.

The first answer to the question depends on the interests of the analyst. If one is concerned with the maintenance of the American competitive position in world export markets, one would look at the merchandise trade balance.

The basic balance position includes all current account items and long-term investment. This measure is free from the influence of short-term capital flows caused by trade financing, foreign borrowing, interest rate differentials, and exchange rate speculation. For an overall analysis of nonfinancial transactions, this is a good measure.

If the analyst is concerned about America's reserve position and the growth of foreign claims against American reserves, the official reserve transactions balance would be the appropriate measure to examine.

A second basis for selecting a balance of payments measure is based on a definitional issue of distinguishing between causes of the deficit and the methods of financing the deficit. There are three definitional options.

Option 1: Basic Balance Definition The items in the basic balance—trade, long-term investment, and transfer payments—are cited as the causes of the surplus in this option. The American trade surplus and net investment income were sufficiently large to offset deficits in remittances, travel, grant, and foreign

TABLE 20–7 Financing the Basic Balance, 1975 (millions of dollars)

CAUSE OF SURPLUS		*FINANCED BY*	
Basic balance	+1,401	Nonliquid short-term private capital flows	−2,819
		Liquid private capital flows	−5,601
		Changes in liabilities to foreign official agencies	+3,070
		Changes in U.S. reserve assets	− 607
		Errors and omissions	+4,556
		Total financing	−1,401

investment accounts and leave a surplus on current account and long-term capital. All the other items are classified as financial flows resulting from the surplus. The right-hand side of Table 20–7 lists financial flows equal to the basic balance surplus.

Option 2: Net Liquidity Definition In this option, the nonliquid short-term private capital flows are classified as an additional cause of the surplus or deficit. In this case, American interest rates are lower than foreign interest rates, so foreigners borrow from American commercial banks; there is an outflow of funds. In Table 20–8, nonliquid short-term private capital flows are listed as a cause of the surplus, and the remaining items on the right-hand side of the table are the financial flows associated with the surplus.

Option 3: Official Reserve Transactions Definition In this option, the flow of deposits between nations, which result from interest rate differentials or foreign exchange speculation, are classified as a cause of what is now a deficit. These deposits are unstable; if relative interest rates change, these deposits will be moved to another country. These deposits, called *hot money,* are not a stable method of financing a deficit. This option is illustrated in Table 20–9.

TABLE 20–8 Financing the Net Liquidity Balance, 1975 (millions of dollars)

CAUSES OF SURPLUS		*FINANCED BY*	
Basic balance	+1,401	Liquid capital flows	−5,601
Nonliquid short-term private capital flows	−2,819	Changes in liabilities to foreign official agencies	+3,070
Errors and omissions	+4,556	Changes in U.S. reserve assets	− 607
Net liquidity balance	+3,138	Total financing	−3,138

TABLE 20–9 Financing the Official Reserve Transactions Balance, 1975 (millions of dollars)

CAUSES OF DEFICIT		*FINANCED BY*	
Basic balance	+1,401	Changes in liabilities to foreign official agencies	+3,070
Nonliquid short-term private capital flows	−2,819	Changes in U.S. reserve assets	− 607
Liquid private capital flows	−5,601		
Errors and omissions	+4,556		
Official reserve transactions balance	−2,463	Total financing	+2,463

Thus, the appropriate measure of the deficit depends upon the definition of "cause" and "financing." Those who favor the official reserves measure and those who favor the net liquidity measure conflict on the basis of total claims against American reserves. Those favoring the official reserves definition argue that only claims held by foreign official agencies result in reserve losses by the United States. Those favoring the net liquidity basis argue that liquid private capital flows are also a threat to American reserves because these dollar holdings can flow to a foreign central bank and become an official holding of claims against American reserves. The moral of the story is that the increase of both private and public foreign claims against the dollar are threats to American reserves.[4]

The balance of payments may be in surplus and deficit simultaneously if one looks at two different measures. For example, the 1969 figures in Table 20–1 indicate a deficit according to the net liquidity balance and a surplus according to the official reserve transactions balance. Liquid capital flows were large enough to offset the liquidity balance deficit and create a surplus in official reserves transactions.

A deficit in the balance of payments is financed by decreases in those items classified as financing the deficit. International reserves are drawn down in years of deficit and built up in years of surplus. The reserve assets provide a short-term method of dealing with a balance of payments deficit. The supply of reserves is finite; a nation cannot finance continual deficits from reserves because reserve positions would eventually be exhausted. Thus, although short-term balance of payments deficits can be financed by the reduction of reserves, in the long run, other measures must be employed to deal with the causes of the deficit. A balance of payments surplus can be enjoyed indefinitely because there is no limit on the holding of reserves; a deficit cannot go on forever.

A balance of payments surplus or deficit can be eliminated by a change in the market value of the nation's currency or by other policy measures. The next chapter begins the examination of exchange rate systems by describing the present system of floating currency prices.

[4]See Mark H. Willes, "Balance of Payments—in Surplus or Deficit?" *Business Review,* Federal Reserve Bank of Philadelphia, November 1969, pp. 26–31.

REVIEW QUESTIONS

1. List the transactions that influence the nation's balance of payments.

2. Distinguish between the spot market for a currency and the forward market for the currency.

3. How would an importer use the forward market to hedge against changes in the value of foreign currency to be received in the future?

4. What mechanisms ensure that the exchange values of two currencies remain the same in foreign exchange markets around the world.

5. What is the difference between a long position in a currency and a short position in a currency?

6. Why did the American dollar become an international medium of exchange in the post–World War II period?

7. What is the difference between the merchandise balance of trade and the balance on current account?

8. Define the basic balance. Why is this measure generally used as a measure of the nation's competitive position in world markets?

9. What is the difference between the net liquidity balance and the official reserve assets balance?

10. Why are there several measures of the nation's balance of payments?

SUGGESTED READINGS

Clay J. Anderson, "Balance of Payments," *Federal Reserve Bank of Philadelphia Business Review,* June 1970, pp. 17–29.

Gerald H. Anderson, "The Nature and Use of Forward Exchange," *Federal Reserve Bank of Cleveland Economic Review,* April–May 1972, pp. 7–15.

Norman S. Fieleke, "Exchange-Rate Flexibility and the Cost of Using the Foreign-Exchange Market," *New England Economic Review,* Federal Reserve Bank of Boston, July–August 1972, pp. 18–26.

Patricia Hagan Kuwayama, "Measuring the United States Balance of Payments," *Federal Reserve Bank of New York Monthly Review,* August 1975, pp. 183–194.

John Pippenger, "Balance-of-Payments Deficits: Measurement and Interpretation," *Federal Reserve Bank of St. Louis Review,* November 1973, pp. 6–14.

21

THE FLOATING EXCHANGE RATE SYSTEM

This chapter and Chapter 22 examine alternative systems for determining the rate of exchange between national currencies. This chapter describes the current system of floating exchange rates, which began informally in 1973 and was adopted formally by the International Monetary Fund in 1976. Chapter 22 analyzes the pegged exchange rate system, which prevailed from the end of World War II until 1973, and describes other exchange rate systems that combine aspects of both the floating and the fixed exchange rate systems.

Supply and Demand in Currency Price Determination

The first step is to construct a basic supply-and-demand model. A currency price model differs from other supply and demand models in only one respect—the price of one currency must be stated in terms of another currency. Supply and demand curves for the British pound sterling are shown in Figure 21–1. The price of the pound is stated in terms of the number of American dollars that must be paid for one pound sterling.

The supply curve in Figure 21–1 represents the quantity of pounds sterling that would be supplied in exchange for dollars at each exchange rate. Pounds are supplied to the foreign exchange markets for many reasons. Englishmen exchange pounds for dollars to buy American goods, to travel in the United States, to buy American securities, and for all the other types of international transactions cited in Chapter 20.

The quantity of sterling offered for sale in the foreign exchange market increases as the number of dollars that can be obtained for one pound sterling increases. Holders of pounds sterling are willing to sell more pounds if the selling price is \$3 per 1£ than if the price is \$1 per 1£. The supply of pounds sterling curve also can be thought of as a demand for dollars curve. At an exchange rate of \$3 = 1£, American goods are relatively inexpensive for British purchasers and the

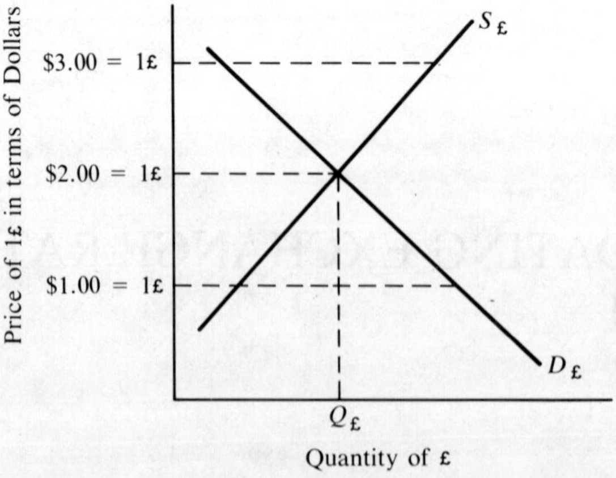

FIGURE 21–1 Exchange Rate Determination

demand for dollars is high. At an exchange rate of $1 = 1£, American goods are expensive for British buyers; only a small quantity of pounds is offered for sale in exchange for dollars.

The demand curve in Figure 21–1 indicates that the quantity of pounds demanded varies inversely with the price of the pound in terms of dollars. As the price of the pound declines, in terms of dollars, the quantity of pounds sterling demanded increases. The lower price of the pound makes British goods less expensive for American purchasers. The demand for sterling in the foreign exchange market reflects many factors. Holders of dollars demand sterling to pay for British goods, to travel or invest in Britain, and to make all other types of payments in sterling.

The demand curve for pounds sterling can be regarded as a supply of dollars curve. Those holding dollars will supply increasing quantities of dollars to the market as the price of the dollar, in terms of the pound, increases. A large quantity of dollars is supplied when $1 can obtain one pound; the quantity of dollars supplied decreases as the number of pounds obtainable for $1 decreases. At $2 = 1£, only 0.5£ can be obtained for $1; at $3 = 1£, only 0.333£ can be obtained with $1. As the number of pounds that can be obtained for $1 decreases, the quantity of dollars supplied decreases.

In Figure 21–1, the demand for and supply of pounds sterling determine the equilibrium price of the pound, $2 = 1£. This is a market-determined equilibrium exchange rate. As in other supply and demand diagrams, at an exchange rate above the equilibrium price—such as $3 = 1£—the quantity supplied exceeds the quantity demanded. If the quantity of pounds supplied exceeds the quantity of pounds demanded, the price falls until the quantity demanded equals the quantity supplied at the equilibrium price of $2 = 1£. At a price below the equilibrium—such as $1 = 1£—the quantity of pounds demanded exceeds the quantity supplied and the price of the pound increases. As the price increases, the quantity demanded decreases and the quantity supplied increases until the two quantities are equal at the equilibrium exchange rate of $2 = 1£.

As in the normal supply and demand analysis, shifts of the demand or supply curves change the equilibrium price. A sudden increase in the popularity of British goods in the United States or an increase in the desire of Americans to travel in Britain would shift the demand curve for pounds to the right and increase the equilibrium rate of exchange. Alternatively, if more Englishmen desire to visit the United States or purchase American goods, the supply curve in Figure 21–1 would shift to the right and the price of the pound would decrease.

Fluctuations in supply and demand produce a market determined exchange rate between the two currencies. However, there are variations in the extent to which the market is permitted to establish the exchange rate. Under a system of *pure* or *clean floating,* supply and demand are the sole determinants of the exchange rate; there is no governmental intervention in the foreign exchange market. Figure 21–1 presents a system of pure floating.

The alternatives to pure floating are managed floating and dirty floating. Both of these alternatives involve government intervention in the foreign exchange market. The distinction between managed and dirty is made on the basis of the motives for intervention. *Managed floating* permits government intervention to smooth out movements in the exchange rate, to offset erratic day-to-day changes in the exchange rate, or to prevent excessive sudden increases or decreases in the price of the nation's currency. *Dirty floating* is an artificial lowering of the exchange rate in order to make the nation's exports more competitive in world markets.

The current floating exchange-rate system is a system of managed floating, but the objective of floating is best illustrated by beginning with a pure floating rate system.

The Pure Float

A *pure floating rate system*[1] is one in which the market forces of supply and demand determine the exchange rate. Floating exchange rates allow currency price changes to assist in correcting a balance of payments surplus or deficit. If a nation has a deficit in its balance of payments, the value of its currency declines (either the demand for the currency decreases or the supply increases), and the lower price of the currency stimulates exports and decreases imports. If a nation has a surplus in its balance of payments, the value of its currency rises (either the demand for the currency increases or the supply decreases), and the higher currency price decreases exports and increases imports.

[1]Milton Friedman was a leading advocate of pure floating exchange rates. See his "The Case for Flexible Exchange Rates," in Milton Friedman, ed., *Essays in Positive Economics* (Chicago: University of Chicago Press, 1953), pp. 157–203.

A Change in the Exchange Rate and the Balance of Payments

The effect on the nation's balance of payments of a change in the exchange rate depends upon the elasticity of the foreign demand for the nation's export goods and the domestic elasticity of demand for imports.[2] Some examples illustrate the conditions necessary for the balance of payments to be improved as a result of a change in the exchange rate.

Assume a mythical country, Urgo, with a currency called the urg. The exchange rate between the urg and the dollar is 1 urg = $1. Urgo trades only with the United States; exports to the United States consist of 1 million pounds of coffee and imports from the United States are 250 cars. Coffee costs 1 urg per pound and cars cost $4,000 per car. Americans spend $1 million to purchase 1 million urgs to buy coffee. Urgians spend 1 million urgs to obtain $1 million to buy 250 American cars. Assuming no other trade or financial transactions between the two nations, Urgo has a balance of payments equilibrium. Assume Urgo's currency declines in value by 50 percent, so that 2 urgs = $1. The urg now buys the Urgian only half as many dollars as before the price decline. (Urgo's currency should not fall in value while Urgo is in balance of payments equilibrium. However, for the example, a currency price decrease is necessary to illustrate the effects of a currency price change on the balance of payments.)

Assume that at the new exchange rate Americans still buy the same 1 million pounds of coffee and Urgians still buy 250 cars. The elasticity of demand for Urgian coffee in the United States is zero, and the elasticity of demand for American cars in Urgo is zero. Americans now spend $500,000 to obtain 1 million urgs for the purchase of 1 million pounds of Urgian coffee. Urgians give up 2 million urgs to obtain $1 million for the purchase of 250 American cars. The Urgian balance of payments is in deficit by 1 million urgs; Urgo exported 1 million urgs worth of goods and imported 2 million urgs of goods. In terms of dollars, Urgo earned $500,000 from exporting coffee and spent $1 million importing American cars. The decrease in the price of the urg created a balance of payments deficit because the quantities of goods exported and imported did not change.

In a second example, assume the same fall in the price of the urg but assume that at the lower dollar price of Urgian coffee, Americans purchase 5 million pounds of coffee at 1 urg per pound. The coffee costs Americans 5 million urgs or $2.5 million. Urgians continue to purchase 250 cars from the United States at $4,000 per car; Urgians spend $1 million or 2 million urgs on American cars. The Urgian balance of trade has improved. In terms of the urg, Urgo exported 5 million urgs of goods and imported 2 million urgs of goods. The exchange rate decrease created a surplus in the Urgian balance of payments because of the high foreign elasticity of demand for Urgian coffee.

[2]For the purposes of this analysis, exports and imports are assumed to be the only items in the balance of payments. The elasticity of export demand can be interpreted as the percentage change in exports divided by the percentage change in the foreign currency prices of the nation's exports. The elasticity of import demand can be interpreted as the percentage change in imports divided by the percentage change in the price of imports. For a technical analysis of the elasticity conditions, see Leland B. Yeager, *International Monetary Relations: Theory, History, and Policy,* 2nd ed. (New York: Harper & Row, Publishers, 1976), pp. 158–181.

In a final example, assume that Americans continue to purchase only the original 1 million pounds of coffee after the currency price change. Urgian exports are equal to 1 million urgs. However, at the higher price for American cars (8,000 urgs per car, rather than the previous 4,000 urgs per car), Urgians purchase only 50 American cars. Fifty American cars at $4,000 per car cost $200,000 or 400,000 urgs. Urgian exports are 1 million urgs and imports are 400,000 urgs. Urgo has a balance of payments surplus because of the high Urgian elasticity of demand for American cars.

It should be clear that the effect of the change in the exchange rate on the balance of payments depends upon the elasticity of demand for exports and imports. The technical condition for an improvement in the nation's balance of payments is called the Marshall-Lerner condition.[3] The *Marshall-Lerner condition* specifies that the sum of (forgetting plus or minus signs) the foreign price elasticity of demand for a nation's exports and the price elasticity of import demand must be equal to, or greater than, one. In the first example, both elasticities were zero; the fall in the exchange rate led to a deterioration of the balance of payments. In each of the other two cases, the elasticity of demand for one commodity was held at zero, but there was a large percentage change in the demand for the other commodity. Thus, in the second and third examples, the currency price decrease had the desired effect on the balance of payments.

The effect of a currency price change is illustrated by the American devaluations. The combined effects of the 1971 and 1973 American devaluations reduced the foreign value of the dollar by approximately 17 percent. From the fourth quarter of 1971 to the fourth quarter of 1974, American exports increased at a compound annual rate of nearly 40 percent. In absolute terms, American merchandise exports increased from slightly less than $43 billion in 1971 to $96.5 billion in 1974, and the American balance of trade improved.[4] However, the combined impacts of the embargo by the Organization of Petroleum Exporting Countries (OPEC), the oil price increase, inflation, and recession make an exact interpretation of the effects of the currency price change very difficult.

Under a pure floating exchange rate system, currency price fluctuations should move both the surplus and the deficit nation toward balance of payments equilibrium without government intervention in the foreign exchange markets. In the next section, government intervention is introduced.

Managed Floating

Under the current system, nations allow currency prices to float but reserve the right to intervene in exchange markets. Why would nations interfere with the workings of the market? First, a nation may intervene to smooth out day-to-day

[3]See Alfred Marshall, *Money, Credit and Commerce* (New York: Macmillan Co., 1924), Appendix J; and Abba P. Lerner, *The Economics of Control* (New York: Macmillan Co., 1944).

[4]*U.S. Balance of Payments Trends,* Federal Reserve Bank of St. Louis, April 24, 1975, p. 11.

fluctuations in the price of its currency. This action would be comparable to the Federal Reserve System's stabilization of interest rates by defensive open market operations to counteract the effects of changes in float.

Second, a nation may intervene in the market for its currency to offset the effects of speculation. Speculative selling of the currency may be driving the price below the level necessary for balance of payments equilibrium or speculative buying may be pushing the currency price above the level required for balance of payments equilibrium.

Third, the nation may intervene in the market to reduce the rate of currency price change. The market determined exchange rate may decline suddenly, and the government may desire to permit the currency price to fall to its new equilibrium level at a slower rate over a longer period of time. Thus, the government acts to delay temporarily the movement to the new equilibrium exchange rate.

Why doesn't the nation simply allow the pure floating system to operate? The reason is that currency price changes affect exports, imports, and domestic price levels. Assume the exchange rate declines. Exporters are happy; assuming the demand for the nation's exports is elastic, foreign sales should increase. However, importers find that all imports rise in price. Imported raw materials, capital goods, and consumer goods are more expensive. To the extent that imported goods are included in the consumers' market baskets, the cost of living increases. As the cost of living increases, workers demand higher wages. Inflation becomes a greater problem and some of the export markets that were gained as a result of the fall in the currency value are lost as a result of inflation. Through intervention in the exchange markets, these effects on imports, exports, and price levels can be temporarily postponed or gradually accepted over time. The impact is less than if the exchange rate were permitted to change suddenly.

In addition, the nation may believe that a long-run balance of payments equilibrium can be attained at the old exchange rate and that the currency price decline is only temporary. Thus, the government intervenes to restore the exchange rate to its original level.

Government Intervention in the Foreign Exchange Market

Assume that a nation wants to hold its exchange rate at a given level. However, the exchange rate fluctuates on both a day-to-day basis and on a long-term basis. To hold its currency at the desired level, a nation uses its *exchange stabilization account*. The exchange stabilization account of a nation consists of the nation's *international reserve assets*. The managers of the exchange stabilization account use the international reserve assets to intervene in the foreign exchange market.

International Reserve Assets The nation's international reserve assets consist of those items generally acceptable as a medium of exchange in the settlement of balance of payments deficits. Note that the definition of international reserve assets is very similar in substance to the definition of the domestic money supply.

Historically, gold was the basic international reserve asset. While the world operated on a pure gold coin standard, gold served as both the national and the international medium of exchange.

Gold continued to play a major international role after domestic gold convertibility was terminated. However, the American dollar became the major international reserve asset in the post–World War II period. The United States Treasury was willing to convert dollars held by foreign central banks into gold at the option of the foreign central bank. As long as the United States held sufficient gold to meet all likely conversion demands, holding dollars was equivalent to holding gold. In fact, most central banks preferred to hold dollars because dollars could be invested in interest-bearing assets.

If the foreign central bank desired to convert its dollar holdings to gold, the securities were sold and the dollars were converted. The suspension of the gold convertibility of the dollar in August 1971 was the end of an era and the end of the absolute supremacy of the dollar as an international reserve asset.

The newest international reserve asset is the *Special Drawing Right* (SDR). Special Drawing Rights are a reserve asset created by the International Monetary Fund to supplement gold and national currencies as reserve assets. The SDRs are transferable between member nations in the settlement of balance of payments deficits.

A nation's international reserve assets normally include gold, Special Drawing Rights, dollars, and other convertible foreign currencies. (In this context, convertible means that the currency can be freely bought and sold in the foreign exchange markets.) Dollars, German marks, French and Swiss francs, Japanese yen, and the British pound sterling are the major currencies held as reserve assets. A nation's currency will become an international reserve asset if central banks believe that the currency will continue to be traded freely in world money markets and will maintain or increase in market value relative to other major currencies. Managers of exchange stabilization accounts do not want to hold their nation's international reserves in any currency that is expected to decline in market value.

Using the Exchange Stabilization Account The international reserve assets in the exchange stabilization account are used to maintain the price of the nation's currency in the foreign exchange markets. Assume, in Figure 21–2, that Britain desires to maintain the price of the pound sterling at \$2 = 1£. The original supply curve ($S_£$) and demand curve ($D_£$) determine a market price that is equal to the desired price.

Assume that the demand curve for pounds sterling shifts to the right to $D_£'$. Any number of factors can be responsible for the shift of the demand curve. American demand for British goods may have increased, and at all exchange rates Americans desire to obtain more English products. As another possibility, foreign exchange dealers may believe that the British balance of payments is improving and that the price of the pound will increase. For whatever reason, the demand curve shifts and the new supply and demand equilibrium would tend to be at \$2.10 = 1£.

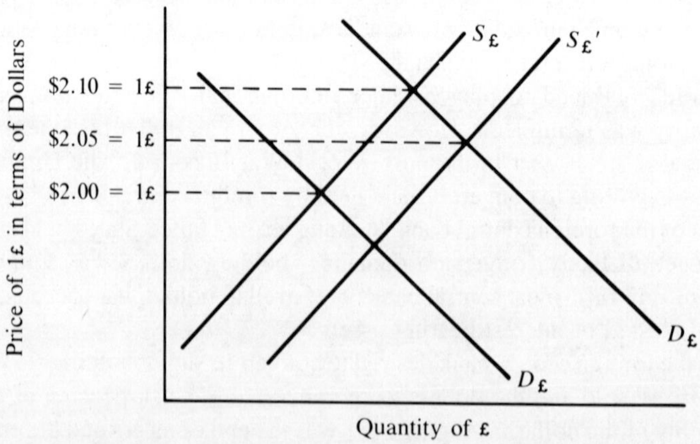

FIGURE 21–2 Managed Floating Decreases the Price of the Pound Sterling

The \$2.10 = 1£ exchange rate is higher than desired by the British government. The government fears that at \$2.10 = 1£ the nation will not be able to expand exports sufficiently to attain a balance of payments equilibrium. However, some concession is made to market forces and the exchange stabilization account manager is instructed to bring the price of the pound down to \$2.05 = 1£. The exchange stabilization account adds to the market supply of pounds by selling pounds for dollars. The actions of the exchange stabilization account shift the supply curve to the right to $S_£'$, so that the exchange rate (determined at the intersection of $D_{£'}$ and $S_{£'}$) is \$2.05 = 1£.

In the process of increasing the supply of pounds on the foreign exchange market, the exchange stabilization account adds to its dollar holdings. British international reserve assets increase as a result of lowering the price of the pound.

The managers of the exchange stabilization account may also act if the price of the pound tends to decline. In Figure 21–3, assume the same initial conditions as in Figure 21–2. However, in Figure 21–3, the demand for pounds shifts to the left from $D_£$ to $D_{£''}$. The American demand for pounds sterling decreases at all exchange rates. The exchange rate falls toward a new equilibrium at \$1.90 = 1£. The government decides this price is too low and would cause too drastic an increase in the price of imported goods. The exchange stabilization account adds to the demand for pounds sterling by purchasing sterling and selling dollars. The exchange stabilization account's purchases increase the demand for sterling from $D_{£''}$ to $D_{£'}$, and the price of the pound rises to \$1.95 = 1£. Part of the market determined price change is offset. The cost of bringing the market price of the pound up to \$1.95 = 1£ is the loss of a portion of the exchange stabilization account's limited dollar reserves.

Note the difference between the cases in Figures 21–2 and 21–3. The rising price of the pound reflected a rising demand for pounds and indicated the

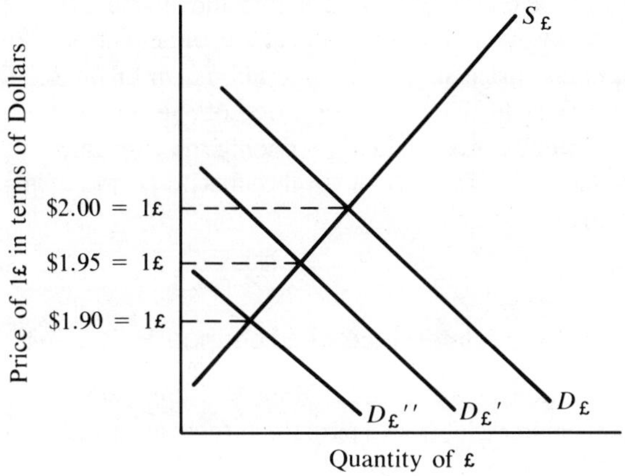

FIGURE 21–3 Managed Floating Increases the Price of the Pound Sterling

market's confidence in the future value of the pound. In addition, the rising price of the pound probably also indicated an improvement in the British balance of payments. Either a balance of payments deficit was being reduced or a balance of payments surplus was being enjoyed. The British reserve position is improved as dollars are purchased by the exchange stabilization account.

The falling price of the pound in Figure 21–3 presented a much less pleasant situation. Americans were not demanding sufficient pounds sterling to maintain the price of the pound near the desired level. The low demand for pounds may have reflected pessimism about the future price of the pound or may have reflected a deficit in the balance of payments. The exchange stabilization account decreased its dollar holdings in the process of partly restoring the desired market value of the pound.

The British can increase the supply of pounds sterling to hold down the price of the pound, but they cannot increase the supply of dollars. The limited British holdings of dollars acts as a constraint on the ability to support the price of the pound. As long as price fluctuations are equally distributed above and below the desired price, there is no problem. Some days dollars are added to reserves and other days dollars are used in support operations. The real problem arises from a consistent downward pressure on the price of the pound, which requires continuous support operations and drains the exchange stabilization account's holdings of dollars.

A persistent decline in the nation's reserves sets in motion forces that tend to produce even greater reserve decreases. Continued reserve decreases are an indication that the nation may be attempting to hold its currency value at too high a level. If the market fears that the government will be forced to permit the price of the currency to float to a lower level, all holders of the currency have an incentive to sell before the price decline.

The selling of the currency by speculators and business firms pushes down the price of the currency and requires that the nation either accept a lower price for its currency or continue price supporting operations. In this case, Britain either could allow a pure float to determine the price of the pound sterling or could continue a managed float while gradually reducing the exchange rate to the level that would be produced by a pure float. In the interim period of managed float, Britain may seek international assistance.

International Aid in the Maintenance of Exchange Rates

If a nation is losing reserves in the process of maintaining the price of its currency above the price that would result from a pure float, there are a variety of methods of obtaining additional reserves.

Borrowing from the International Monetary Fund The International Monetary Fund, established as a result of the 1944 meeting of experts in Bretton Woods, New Hampshire,[5] provided the organizational framework for international monetary cooperation in the post–World War II period. The participants in the formation of the IMF attempted to develop a monetary system within which trade could expand, competitive currency price decreases could be avoided, and nations could assist each other in solving balance of payments problems and maintaining currency exchange rates. Earlier international monetary organizations, such as the Bank for International Settlements, had met with only limited success; in 1944, the need for greater cooperation was more evident than in the past. With the exception of neutral Switzerland and the Soviet Union and its satellite nations, all of the major allied nations joined the International Monetary Fund. New nations continue to join the Fund.

The IMF has become the major forum for the discussion of international financial and monetary problems; the Fund also provides training programs for central bankers and monetary advisory services. The basic purpose of the Fund is to assist nations in maintaining the price of their currency. The IMF obtains funds from the payment of quotas by member nations.

[5]The Bretton Woods conference also resulted in the formation of the International Bank for Reconstruction and Development, better known as the World Bank, to provide capital for the reconstruction of the war-torn economies of Europe and the less developed nations of the world. The World Bank obtains funds through bond sales in the developed nations and from donations by member nations. These funds are loaned to less developed nations on a long-term basis at rates below those the recipient nations would normally pay. The World Bank also provides technical assistance in the planning of economic development projects. For a comprehensive analysis of the activities of the World Bank, see Edward S. Mason and Robert E. Asher, *The World Bank Since Bretton Woods,* Brookings Institution, Washington, D.C., 1973.

Each nation joining the Fund is assigned a quota. The quota is paid into the Fund partly in foreign currencies and partly in the new member's own currency.[6] Quotas are determined on the basis of the nation's income, reserve holdings, imports, ratio of exports to income, and the variability of imports. The payment of quotas into the Fund creates a pool of national currencies from which members can borrow under prescribed rules.

In the years 1948–1974, the Fund provided over $31 billion of loan assistance to member nations.[7] Quotas have been increased periodically to provide added funds for lending activities. The 1976 Jamaica Accords called for over $11 billion of quota increases so that added loans could be made available to deficit nations. Special lending programs to provide assistance for nations experiencing sharp export declines were developed and loan programs have been designed to assist nations in paying the increased costs of petroleum.

Each nation can easily borrow 25 percent of its quota from the Fund. Borrowings beyond that level are subject to greater Fund supervision and increased borrowing charges. Pending approval of the new higher quotas recommended in 1976, members were temporarily permitted to borrow higher percentages of their old quotas.

Since World War II, most loans have been made in dollars because the dollar was the currency used by exchange stabilization accounts. However, in recent years, the lending of currencies of both other developed nations and of the less developed nations has become more common.

Swap Agreement A second source of funds for the country experiencing difficulty in maintaining its exchange rate is its network of *swap agreements*. The major nations of the world have developed a series of bilateral swap agreements. Under these agreements, two countries agree that each can draw upon the other to provide a given amount of the lending nation's currency in exchange for an equal amount of the borrowing nation's currency. For example, Britain has an agreement with the United States which permits Britain to swap a given number of pounds for a given number of dollars. Any time Britain experiences difficulty, Britain can draw upon this prearranged swap agreement to obtain dollars for currency support operations. If the United States has a problem, it can swap currencies with Britain and obtain pounds. In addition to the American-British swap agreement, Britain would be able to draw against swap agreements with other major nations. Once the exchange rate problem passed, the British would return the dollars to the United States and the United States would return the British pounds.

[6] Prior to the 1976 changes, new members were required to pay part of their quota in gold or American dollars.

[7] *1974 Annual Report of the International Monetary Fund,* Washington, D.C., p. 93.

Additional Loans In addition to IMF loans and the use of swap agreements, a nation may be able to obtain funds through bilateral or multilateral loans from other nations. These agreements to lend and borrow are made on a case-by-case basis and may be critical to maintaining the value of the nation's currency. During the 1964 exchange rate crisis, Britain was depleting its international reserves at the rate of $100 million per hour. At this rate, a nation's international reserves can be exhausted very quickly. However, a group of nations arranged a $3 billion multilateral loan to Britain. The important feature of the loan was not the size of the loan; at $100 million per hour, $3 billion can go fast. The important factor was the psychological impact on the currency speculators. The announcement of the loan convinced the speculators that the lending nations did not want the price of the pound to decrease and that other nations were determined to assist Britain. In June 1976, foreign nations loaned Britain $5.3 billion so that Britain could support the pound and reverse a downward price trend that had driven the pound from 1£ = $2.40 down to 1£ = $1.71.

Thus, managed floating involves the use of domestic reserve assets and borrowed reserve assets to establish a given value for the nation's currency. Pure floating would not require any of these steps and would allow the value of the currency to fall to whatever level is dictated by supply and demand. Each nation can choose between pure floating and managed floating.

Other Balance of Payments Measures

Under the floating exchange rate system, a change in the currency price is the primary method of dealing with a disequilibrium in the nation's balance of payments. However, if the nation is operating under a managed float and is attempting to hold its exchange rate above the pure market price, other measures may help to maintain the currency value and reduce the need for exchange stabilization account activity.

Deflation Deflation is one option for attempting to correct a balance of payments deficit. Deflation, a lowering of prices, should have the same effect on the balance of payments as a currency price decline—an expansion of exports and a reduction of imports.

An absolute decline in price levels is difficult to achieve. The overall price level in the United States, as well as in most other nations, could only be reduced at the cost of unacceptably high unemployment rates.

Deflation in the modern world is more appropriately described as experiencing less inflation than other nations. The nation that can maintain a consistently low rate of inflation gradually gains a price advantage over its competitors. For example, West Germany's export success is generally attributed to its ability to maintain relatively low rates of inflation.

What level of unemployment must the nation accept in order to maintain a relatively low inflation rate? The West Germans have been able to maintain very low unemployment rates, but most nations would have to accept higher rates of unemployment than would be politically feasible. Nations that export only a small proportion of total output may be unwilling to suffer unemployment for the sake of balance of payments equilibrium and may prefer to allow an exchange rate decline to correct the balance of payments deficit.

Recession and Unemployment Recession and unemployment attack the balance of payments problem through income and output effects as well as through the price effects described in the previous paragraphs. If the demand for imported goods is income elastic (a given percentage change in income leads to a greater percentage change in imports), the demand for imports declines more than proportionately as income declines. Alternatively, if the nation's imports are basic necessities, the demand for imports is less income elastic, and an income reduction produces a proportionately smaller import decline.

The declining level of economic activity decreases the demand for imported raw materials and semifinished goods. On the export side, declining domestic sales may encourage business firms to push foreign sales more vigorously.

There is a danger that the recession will spread to other nations. A decline in one nation's imports is a decline in another nation's exports. Declining export sales mean declining employment, output, and income. The exporting nation has an incentive to restrict imports to restore its trade balance. Thus, the contractionary forces spread from one nation to another.

Declining currency prices, deflation, and depression all spread around the world during the 1930s; each nation tried to use trade policy as a method of stimulating its own economy. Each nation thought it could expand its exports (creating domestic production and employment) and contract its imports (creating domestic employment in the production of goods that were previously imported). But all nations cannot simultaneously decrease imports and increase exports, and during the 1930s, these attempts led to a great decline in international trade and the breakdown of the international financial system. One nation can use these corrective measures; however, if all nations attempt to use these solutions simultaneously, the problems of all nations increase.

Monetary Policy Other than assisting in a general reduction of aggregate demand, monetary policy does not affect the balance of trade. By increasing the rate of interest, monetary policy can influence international short-term capital flows. Higher interest rates attract funds into the nation's money markets. The capital inflows improve the balance of payments but not the balance of trade.

Higher interest rates are only a short-term policy measure unless they decrease imports by reducing domestic income. Most short-term capital inflows resulting from high interest rates will become capital outflows if interest rates fall or if interest rates rise in other nations.

Trade Controls, Foreign Exchange Controls, and Wage and Price Controls The final options for dealing with a balance of payments deficit consist of various trade controls, monetary controls, and wage and price controls. These options also have substantial costs and pose threats to the world's economy.

The quickest way to improve a nation's balance of trade is to limit imports by imposing higher tariffs or quantity limitations on imports. If the tariffs are high enough or the quantity limitations are low enough, imports will decline and the balance of trade will improve. The complication in this seemingly easy solution is that exporters in other nations will be injured by the higher tariffs and will demand that their governments retaliate and increase tariffs. Thus, increasing barriers to free trade leads to retaliation and a reduction of total world trade without necessarily improving any nation's balance of payments.

During the Great Depression, the United States and most other nations increased tariffs in an attempt to improve their balance of payments and create domestic employment. American tariffs reached their peak in 1930 with the passage of the Smoot-Hawley Tariff Act. In the post–World War II period, the *General Agreement on Trade and Tariffs* (GATT) has provided the framework for international agreements to reduce tariffs and other barriers to trade. Except on a very temporary basis, nations have reduced their reliance on tariff adjustments as a means of resolving balance of payments difficulties.

Various exchange control systems are another option for the treatment of balance of payments difficulties. A complete exchange control system would require that all foreign currency receipts be surrendered to the government. The government would then determine the allocation of the available supply of foreign exchange among the potential importers of goods. The government could decide that certain imports (such as capital equipment) should have first claim on the available foreign exchange and other imports (such as luxury consumer items) should receive low priority in the use of foreign exchange. Alternatively, the available supply of foreign exchange may be sold to importers at prices reflecting the nation's priorities. Dollars would be sold to capital goods importers at a low price (in terms of the nation's own currency) and would be sold to consumer goods importers at a high price (in terms of the nation's own currency).

Like most control systems, exchange controls invite attempts to evade the regulations. In addition, the international trend has been in the direction of eliminating exchange controls and improving the free flow of funds between nations.

Wage and price controls, or some form of incomes policy, may also be used to assist in correcting the balance of payments deficit. If these controls can be used to restrain domestic inflation, the nation may be able to increase exports and decrease imports. The advantages and disadvantages of wage and price controls were discussed in Chapter 11.

Short-Term and Longer Term Solutions All of the policy options discussed thus far have two things in common—they are short-run measures and they are politically unpopular. These are short-term measures because they only temporarily improve the nation's balance of payments. Deflation and depression can suppresss the demand for imports in the short run; however, once the economy recovers from its depressed state, the demand for imports will revive. Decreased currency prices work until domestic prices rise and offset the gains from the fall in the value of the currency. Exchange and trade controls lead to efforts to evade the controls.

Politically, none of these measures is apt to win friends or votes for the governing political party. A declining exchange rate increases the prices of imported goods and raises the cost of living. The falling currency value is an admission of economic failure and an issue for the opposition parties in the next election. Deflation and recession create unemployment; the unemployed tend to vote against those politicians perceived to be responsible for their unemployment.

Fundamental changes in a nation's balance of payments are brought about in the long run. The development of a competitive position in world export markets is the ultimate solution. The key to a balance of payments surplus is the production—at competitive prices—of goods and services desired by residents of other nations.

For a few fortunate nations, a balance of payments surplus results from being located over a large pool of petroleum. For most nations, the production of goods and services is the objective. Even the resource-rich nations realize that their mineral wealth will one day be exhausted and that they will have to find new ways of earning foreign exchange.

Competition in world markets is subject to most of the same conditions of competition in domestic markets. The firm must produce a better product at a lower per unit cost than its competitors. In many cases, world markets are more competitive than domestic markets. Although the American automobile industry is highly concentrated, the variety of imported cars adds to overall competition.

In some highly labor intensive industries, low labor costs provide the nation with a competitive advantage. However, in the longer run, the productivity of labor (measured by the unit labor cost of production) is more important than the wage level. Although one nation's wage rates may be less than those of another country, the higher wage country may have more efficient capital equipment and be able to produce the goods at a lower per unit cost.

The development of more efficient methods of production is of critical importance. The technologically innovative nation will increase its role in world markets. The English domination of world textile markets in the early stages of the Industrial Revolution was in part attributable to the development of better methods of production. Research and development are keys to the retention of export markets by the developed nations. A large percentage of American exports result from a continuing high level of research expenditures. Computers and aircraft are examples of products with a high research and development component. The maintenance of a balance of payments equilibrium requires that the nation's products become and remain competitive in world markets.

Summary

Under a system of pure floating, supply and demand determine exchange rates between currencies. Fluctuations in currency prices should lead to balance of payments equilibrium.

Managed floating allows for government intervention—through the use of exchange stabilization accounts—to stabilize day-to-day currency price fluctuations or to establish the exchange rate at a level other than the level that would be determined by a pure float. In attempting to support the price of its currency, the nation relies on its international reserve assets and various sources of international assistance.

Although currency price fluctuations are the primary method of restoring a balance of payments equilibrium, other policies—deflation, recession, and various control systems—also can be used.

In the next chapter, the pegged exchange rate system is examined and compared with the floating rate system. Other exchange rate systems are also studied.

REVIEW QUESTIONS

1. Explain the forces determining the demand for and supply of a currency in the foreign exchange market.

2. Why is the price of one currency stated in terms of another currency?

3. In the examples in Figure 21–1, why does the demand-for-sterling curve represent the supply of dollars? Why does the supply-of-sterling curve represent the British demand for dollars?

4. Describe the difference between pure floating, managed floating, and dirty floating.

5. Explain the Marshall-Lerner condition and its relationship to the effect of a currency price change on the nation's balance of trade position.

6. What is an exchange stabilization account?

7. How is the exchange stabilization account used to increase the market price of the nation's currency? to decrease the value of the nation's currency?

8. Describe the organization of the International Monetary Fund. What are the functions of the IMF?

9. What forms of international assistance are available to help a nation maintain the value of its currency?

10. Why do nations attempt to influence the price of their currency rather than allow the market to determine the price?

SUGGESTED READINGS

Robert Z. Aliber, "Monetary Interdependence Under Floating Exchange Rates," *Journal of Finance,* American Finance Association, New York, May 1975, pp. 365–376.

Charles P. Kindleberger, *International Economics,* 5th ed. Homewood, Ill.: Richard D. Irwin, 1973.

The International Adjustment Mechanism, Federal Reserve Bank of Boston, 1969.

Ronald I. McKinnon, "Exchange-Rate Flexibility and Monetary Policy," *Journal of Money, Credit and Banking,* vol. III, no. 2, part II, Ohio State University Press, Columbus, pp. 339–355.

Delbert A. Snider, *Introduction to International Economics,* 5th ed. Homewood, Ill.: Richard D. Irwin, 1971.

Leland B. Yeager, *International Monetary Relations: Theory, History, and Policy,* 2nd ed. New York: Harper & Row, Publishers, 1976.

22

ALTERNATIVES TO THE FLOATING EXCHANGE RATE SYSTEM

This chapter examines the pegged exchange rate system—the system of currency price determination employed prior to the establishment of the floating exchange rate system—and compares floating and pegged exchange rate systems. The last section of the chapter discusses other exchange rate systems that have been proposed in recent years.

The Pegged Exchange Rate System

The *pegged exchange rate system* was devised at the 1944 Bretton Woods conference. The plan was designed to provide the exchange rate stability considered conducive to the post–World War II growth of international trade. The designers of the system realized that the exchange rate between two currencies could not be held constant forever, but they hoped that changes would be infrequent and would be made for valid reasons under controlled circumstances.

Under the pegged rate system, each currency was defined in terms of gold or the United States dollar. Each nation was required to maintain (to peg) the market value of its currency within ± 1 percent of the defined (the par) value. The American dollar was defined in terms of gold—at a rate of $1 = 1/35 ounce of gold—and other currencies were defined in terms of the dollar. The United States maintained the pegged value of the dollar by buying or selling gold at the fixed price of $35 per ounce.

The pegging of the price of the British pound—representing a typical foreign currency—is illustrated in Figure 22–1. The supply and demand curves for pounds sterling in Figure 22–1 determine the equilibrium exchange rate. The equilibrium exchange rate of $2 = 1£ is selected as the par value of the pound and the price is pegged at this value. Naturally, no one can see the real-world supply and demand curves, but the experts agree that the equilibrium price is at $2 = 1£; in this case, the experts are correct and the pegged value is set at the equilibrium price.

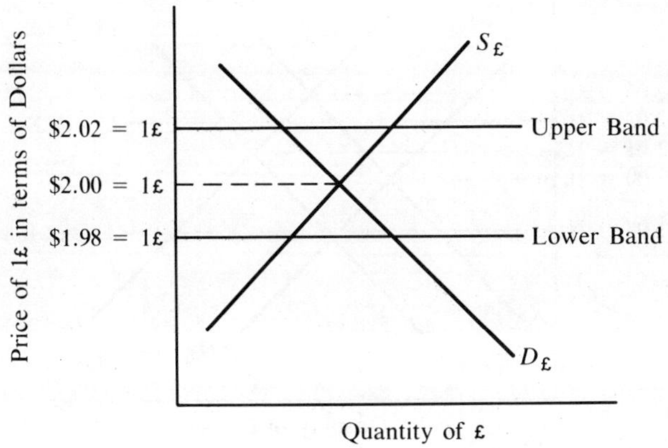

FIGURE 22–1 Exchange Rate Determination with Pegged Rates

Under the pegged rate system, Britain maintained the market price of the pound within ± 1 percent of the pegged rate. The upper limit on exchange rate fluctuations, the *upper band* in Figure 22–1, is $2.02 = 1£, and the lower limit on price fluctuations is at the *lower band* exchange rate of $1.98 = 1£. The ±1 percent bands were in effect from the end of World War II until the 1971 Smithsonian Agreements widened the bands to ±2¼ percent of par value. The range between the upper and lower bands is not drawn to scale but is magnified for purposes of illustration.

Maintaining a Pegged Value

Once the pegged value of a currency was established and the upper and lower bands were in place, the nation attempted to hold the market price of its currency within the bands. Figure 22–2 illustrates intervention to hold the exchange rate below the upper band. The original equilibrium is at $2 = 1£. The demand curve for pounds shifts to $D_{£}'$, and the price rises above the upper band to $2.03 = 1£. The exchange stabilization account buys dollars and sells pounds. The added supply of pounds shifts the supply curve to $S_{£}'$, and the price of the pound decreases to $2.01 = 1£, a price within the bands.

In Figure 22–3, a fall in the demand for pounds, from $D_{£}$ to $D_{£}'$, lowers the price from $2 = 1£ to $1.97 = 1£. The new equilibrium price is below the lower band, and the exchange stabilization account must buy pounds and sell dollars. The added demand for pounds shifts the demand curve from $D_{£}'$ to $D_{£}''$, and the price of the pound rises above the lower band to $1.99 = 1£.

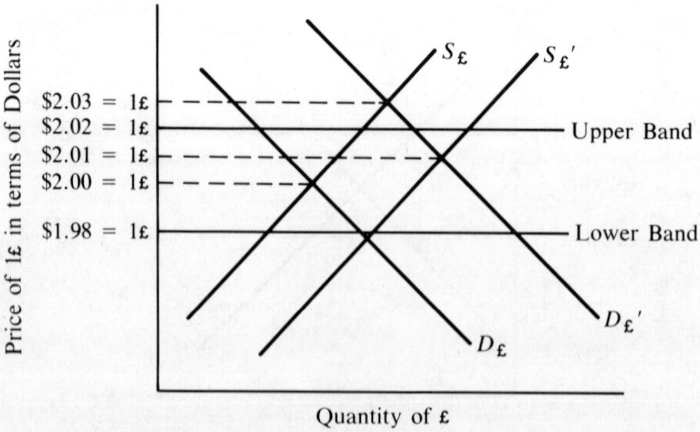

FIGURE 22–2 Maintaining Exchange Rate Below Upper Band

The nation needing assistance in maintaining the price of its currency had access to all of the forms of international aid listed in Chapter 21. International Monetary Fund loans, swap agreements, and other loans were all devised as methods of assisting nations to maintain their pegged exchange rates. These loan mechanisms were carried over into the managed floating rate system.

The basic difference between exchange rate stabilization under the pegged rate system and stabilization under the floating rate system is in the degree of commitment to a given exchange rate. Under the floating rate system, the nation may intervene to support a given exchange rate or may choose to let the rate float to a new level. Under the pegged rate system, the nation was committed by international agreement to maintaining a certain rate and was expected to make a determined effort to maintain the pegged value of its currency.

Under the pegged rate system, the nation attempted to restore a balance of payments equilibrium without changing the value of its currency. High interest rates were used to attract funds into the nation, and contractionary monetary and fiscal policies were used in attempts to reduce imports. The currency price was changed as a last resort if international assistance and the domestic policy measures listed in Chapter 21 did not succeed in convincing the foreign exchange markets that the nation could achieve a balance of payments surplus at the existing exchange rate.

Pegged Versus Floating Rates

Although many academic economists long favored a floating exchange rate system, the world's central bankers traditionally favored a system of pegged exchange rates. Many meetings of academicians and central bankers ended in spirited

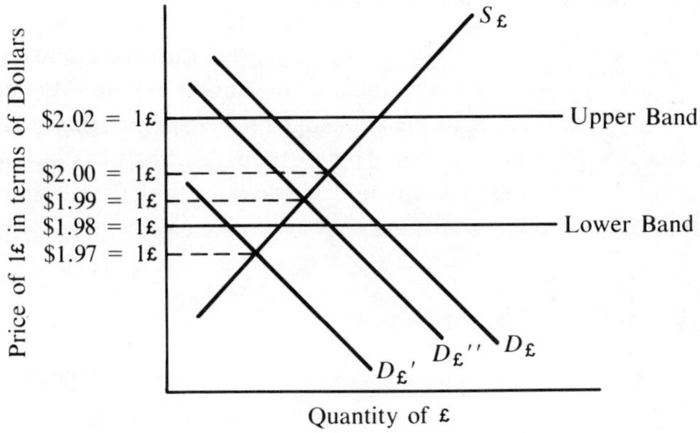

FIGURE 22–3 Maintaining Exchange Rate Above Lower Band

arguments over fixed versus floating exchange rates. The following sections present some of the frequently heard arguments.

The Method of Changing Currency Prices

Under the pegged rate system, a change in the value of the nation's currency, other than within the narrow bands, required a formal devaluation of the currency. *Devaluation* in a pegged rate system meant that the pegged value was reduced to a lower level. For example, the British devaluation of 1967 reduced the pegged value of the pound from $2.80 to $2.40. The dollar value of the pound was moved from one fixed level to another fixed level. Upper and lower bands were placed around the new pegged value and the exchange stabilization account maintained the value of the pound within the new bands.

The decision to devalue was usually made after consultation between the officials of the nation, the central bank officials of other major nations, and the executives of the International Monetary Fund. Devaluations of more than 10 percent of the value of the nation's currency were supposed to be approved by the IMF, although in the final analysis only the devaluing nation could make the ultimate decision.

The changing of pegged values by devaluation was accomplished only in a crisis atmosphere and was accompanied by large speculative currency flows. The devaluation of one currency encouraged speculators and transferred devaluation pressures to other relatively weak currencies.

Under the floating rate system, the market price of the nation's currency is adjusted daily by fluctuations in supply and demand without any governmental action being required. Changes in currency values come about more gradually and without the sudden large speculative flows of funds.

Correcting a Balance of Payments Deficit

The pegged rate system did not allow currency price movements to assist in the correction of balance of payments problems. Assuming that the Marshall-Lerner conditions are met, the floating of the exchange rate can contribute to the elimination of a balance of payments deficit. Under the pegged rate system, a currency price change could not be used as a method of correcting a deficit until the nation's problems became so great that a large formal devaluation was required.

Freedom of Domestic Economic Policy

The floating exchange rate system frees domestic economic policy from the constraints imposed by the pegged rate system. Under the pegged rate system, a nation experiencing unemployment feared that expansionary policies would generate a higher rate of inflation, worsen the balance of trade position, and cause an exchange rate crisis. The exchange rate crisis might force a devaluation. Therefore, under the fixed rate system, the nation might choose to accept a relatively high rate of unemployment in order to avoid an exchange rate crisis. Under the floating rate system, the nation can move ahead with its domestic employment policy, accept the higher rate of inflation, and permit the exchange rate to decline. The fall in the exchange rate would be part of the cost of reducing the level of unemployment. The nation's currency would be gradually devalued by the market without an exchange rate crisis.

The Burden of Balance of Payments Adjustment

The pegged exchange rate system placed nearly all of the burden of balance of payments adjustment on the deficit nation. The deficit nation was forced to devalue and take other measures to correct its deficit. The surplus nation was able to hold its currency below the upper band and add to its international reserve assets. The only real pressure on the surplus country was the obligation to assist the deficit nation by lending reserves during the exchange rate crisis. However, these loans presented no problem because the flight from the weak currency was a flight to the strong currency.

During the 25 years of the fixed rate system, the only major upward revaluations were made by West Germany; those revaluations increased the pegged price of the mark but did not produce any significant reduction in that nation's balance of payments surplus. Most other changes in pegged values involved devaluations.

Under the floating rate system, the burden of balance of payments adjustment is divided between the deficit nation and the surplus nation. The price of the deficit nation's currency decreases and the price of the surplus nation's currency increases. Under a pure float, both nations bear a part of the burden of international adjustment. However, under a managed float, the surplus nation may hold down the value of its currency and preserve its balance of payments surplus. This action is a form of dirty float and shifts the burden of adjustment on to the deficit nation.

Speculation in Foreign Exchange Markets

The central bankers feared that floating rates would encourage currency speculation. The advocates of floating answered that speculation was not absent in the pegged rate system. In the pegged rate system, speculation was very important during exchange rate crises. During an exchange rate crisis, the speculation was destabilizing because most speculators were betting on devaluation. But currency speculation does not have to be destabilizing; speculation can help to stabilize the value of an asset. There is speculation on a stock exchange, but stock prices do not fluctuate wildly from minute to minute; most day-to-day stock price changes are relatively small. Speculation tends to stabilize the market value in the short run by adding to the volume of trading and reducing the amount of price movement necessary for a seller to attract a buyer. In addition, speculators hold differing opinions relative to the future price of a stock or a currency. While one speculator is gambling that the price of a stock is going to rise, another speculator is equally convinced that the price is going to decline. Speculation is a problem only if all speculators have the same expectations of future price movements.

Foreign Trade and Investment

Central bankers also believed that floating exchange rates would discourage foreign trade and investment. Under a fixed rate system, the exporter or importer could be relatively certain of the domestic currency value of foreign currency receipts. Price fluctuations occurred within the bands, but unless a currency was devalued, the trader or investor could not gain or lose a great deal as a result of currency fluctuations.

Under a floating exchange rate system, the foreign trader or investor is subjected to a much higher degree of exchange rate risk. To central bankers, the higher exchange rate risk meant less incentive to export, import, and invest abroad. However, academicians pointed to the forward markets as a means of hedging against the exchange rate risk.

The central bankers responded that the forward markets were relatively undeveloped and did not even exist for many currencies. The academic answer was that the need for forward markets was relatively low under a fixed rate system and that floating rates should encourage the development of the forward markets. As the range of possible currency price fluctuations is expanded, the cost of hedging might increase, but the opportunity to hedge should be provided by a market system. Furthermore, it was pointed out, forward markets are not required between all currencies because most trade is conducted in a relatively few major trading currencies. If there was a need to develop a forward market between two currencies, it was suggested, the profit motive should lead to its development.

International investment presents a different problem than does international trade. Investment is a long-term activity. The purchaser of a foreign factory expects to recover his investment and earn a profit over a period of many years. How can he hedge against changes in exchange rates? What certainty does the investor have that his profits, in terms of a foreign currency, will not become worthless in terms of his own currency? Actually, the investor has little protection under either a pegged or a floating exchange rate system. In the long run, currency prices change under both systems; no private forward market can be developed to protect the investor against currency price changes over decades.

Exchange Rate Systems and Inflation

Central bankers traditionally argued that a floating exchange rate system would not provide the same degree of protection against inflation as would a pegged exchange rate system. The fear of reserve losses and a currency crisis was supposed to provide an incentive for the avoidance of inflationary domestic economic policies. Under the floating rate system, the bankers said, there would be no pegged rate to defend, and so one more barrier to inflationary policies would be removed.

But did pegged rates really provide a defense against inflation? Actually, at best pegged rates encouraged each nation to hold its inflation rate below inflation rates in other nations. And even this degree of anti-inflation policy existed as a matter of choice. If a nation was willing to accept higher rates of inflation as the cost of avoiding unemployment, the country could devalue frequently. In practice, inflation is prevented by appropriate national economic policy decisions, and not by the actions of an exchange rate system.

Flexibility in Dealing with Worldwide Crises

The fixed rate system could not adjust easily to worldwide changes in the relative economic strength of groups of nations. The system was designed to deal with the problems of one nation at a time. If the pegged rate system had been in effect when petroleum prices increased so rapidly and drastically, large numbers of devaluations would have been required and the impact would have been devastating. So many nations were affected to such differing degrees that many devaluations would have occurred simultaneously.

Under the floating rate system, the market evaluated the relative energy independence of each nation, the ability of the nation to meet the higher costs of petroleum, and the effects on the nation's balance of payments. Then, exchange rates floated to new levels without the crises that would have been likely under the pegged exchange rate system.

Devaluing the American Dollar

The pegged exchange rate system limited the ability of the United States to devalue its currency, because the American dollar was the key currency, and other currencies were pegged to the dollar. Other nations could devalue by changing the price of their currency in terms of the dollar, but how could the United States devalue? An American devaluation required that other nations cooperate and revalue their currencies upwards against the dollar. The value of the common denominator, the American dollar, could only be changed by international agreement.

Under the floating rate system, the dollar is more like other currencies. The market values the dollar in terms of other national currencies on a day-to-day basis. On a given day, the dollar may appreciate in value in terms of the British pound and depreciate in terms of the Swiss franc. The value of the dollar can change without an international conference.

Summary

All of the points raised in this section were debated for many years by the advocates of alternative exchange rate systems. While many points were made against the fixed exchange rate system and in favor of floating rates, the fixed exchange rate system did work reasonably well. The basic objectives of those who established the system were accomplished; trade grew rapidly from its prewar lows, and all other forms of international economic relationships expanded. Although there were devaluations, they were not massive in number. Now that the world has switched to floating rates, time will be the judge of the performance of this system.

Between the Two Extremes

The narrowly banded pegged rate system and the floating exchange rate system represent extremes of control and noncontrol. In recent years, various other systems have been proposed. Some of these systems combine features from both of the two extremes.

Wider Bands

By increasing the width of the bands, the basic pegged exchange rate system can be modified to permit more currency price fluctuations. The 1971 Smithsonian agreements, which realigned pegged rates after the first American devaluation, increased the bands around par value from ±1 percent to ±2¼ percent. This widening of the bands had two effects. First, it reduced the need for exchange stabilization account intervention in the currency markets. Currencies could move further away from their par values without official action being required.

Second, the wider bands permitted greater price effects on exports and imports. If one currency appreciated to its upper band and a second currency depreciated to its lower band, the total currency price change could be a maximum of 4½ percent. A change of this magnitude should have some effect on trade levels between the two nations.

The 1971 wider band decision produced an interesting variation. The European Common Market nations decided that their currencies should be more closely linked together; thus, these nations agreed to retain the ±1 percent bands between their currencies. (This agreement is referred to as "the European snake in the Smithsonian tunnel.")

A wider bands system would employ substantially wider bands than the ±2¼ percent bands employed between 1971 and 1973. Bands of ±10 percent of par value would allow a much greater degree of currency price fluctuation.

The wide bands proposal, as a pegged value system, would place the major burden of adjustment on the deficit nation. With wider bands, the surplus nation would make some added sacrifice because its currency could rise to a higher price. If this higher permitted degree of appreciation led to some deterioration of the surplus nation's balance of payments, the surplus nation would bear a greater portion of the burden than it would under the narrow band system.

Crawling Pegs and Gliding Bands

Another proposed system would use bands and exchange rate stabilization but would provide for the periodic adjustment of each currency's par value. The slow periodic changes in the par value produce the term *crawling peg*.[1] Or, because the bands would change as the pegged value changed, the term *gliding bands*[2] is used. Several options exist for determining the rules by which the peg would crawl or the bands would glide.

One option would be to allow each deficit nation to preannounce small periodic changes in its par value. These changes would take place according to a schedule until an exchange rate compatible with balance of payments equilibrium was attained.

A second option would permit the market to determine the pegged value of each currency. The pegged value for a given day would be calculated as the moving average of daily market values of the currency. In the case of a depreciation in the market value, the operation of the moving average would gradually reduce the level of the pegged value. Daily decreases in the price of the currency would

[1]See John Williamson, "The Crawling Peg," *Essays in International Finance,* No. 50, Princeton University Press, Princeton, N.J., December 1965.

[2]A good discussion of this option is George N. Halm, "The Gliding Band for Variations of Exchange Rates," *New England Economic Review,* Federal Reserve Bank of Boston, November–December, 1971, pp. 2–17.

gradually decrease the pegged value as lower prices were added to the moving average and higher prices dropped from the calculation of the moving average. Under this plan, the bands around the par value would have to be sufficiently wide to allow the market value to fluctuate. If the market price were not allowed to deviate from the par value, the moving average would always have the same value and the peg would never crawl.

Most versions of the crawling peg plan include a limitation on the amount of crawl permitted in a given year. Once the moving average had allowed the par value to crawl by the maximum amount for the year, the price could not continue to change in that direction. However, there is no theoretical need for a limitation on the permitted amount of crawl.

This system would allow for some market determination of currency values while also providing short-term price stability through the use of the exchange stabilization account. Over time, the price of a currency would appreciate or depreciate slowly.

As with so many of the other systems, the adjustable band concept would allow the surplus nation to avoid balance of payments adjustment. The surplus nation could use its exchange stabilization account to prevent the value of its currency from crawling upwards.

Reserve Tests

Under the fixed exchange rate system in effect for most of the post–World War II period, the burden of balance of payments adjustment was placed mainly on the deficit nations. The reserve test plans[3] would incorporate a more even distribution of the adjustment burden into a pegged rate system. The reserve test plans were popular with many American officials as an alternative to greater floating of exchange rates.

The reserve test concept recognizes that reserve changes are the best measure of balance of payments problems and policies. A nation experiencing reserve increases is in a strong position, and a nation losing reserves has a balance of payments problem. The reserve test plan would use reserve changes as an indicator of the need to increase or decrease pegged currency values.

Under this plan, each nation would be assigned a base level of reserves determined by its need for reserves and past reserve experience. Rules would then be established to deal with significant deviations from the base level. On the downside, a lower warning level of reserves would be established. If reserves fell below this level, the nation would be permitted to undertake small devaluations. If reserves fell to an even lower level, the *low point,* the nation would be required to undertake adjustment policies. Failure to follow appropriate policies to rebuild reserves would bring international sanctions, including denials of SDR allocations and reserve loan refusals.

[3]The details of reserve test plans are presented in the *1973 Economic Report of the President,* pp. 160–174.

On the upside, an upper warning point would be established above the base level. If reserves reached this level, the nation would need to take action to reduce its reserve inflows. A small upward revision of the pegged rate of exchange might be required. Above the upper warning level would be an *outer point*. Once reserves had reached the outer point, more drastic action would be necessary. If the nation did not take action, international sanctions could be applied to reduce the nation's surplus. A tax on excess reserves or increased tariffs against the nation's exports could be used to force action.

The reserve test concept would require the surplus nations to share some of the burden of adjustment, but it would also raise four principal questions. First, how much international cooperation could be forced upon sovereign nations? Would all IMF members agree to a plan of this type?

Second, how would base levels of reserves be determined? There is no general rule that determines a nation's need for reserves. Can the special problems of each nation be given adequate recognition in the development of the base level reserves?

Third, how much reserve fluctuation should be permitted between the base level and the warning level? How much additional variation is to be permitted between the warning level and the outer point? Again, the answers are unknown.

Finally, can effective sanctions be developed and imposed? The deficit nations might be forced to comply eventually, but unless the sanctions were strong, the surplus nations might be able to avoid adjustment.

Summary

All of these alternative exchange rate systems have their strengths and weaknesses. Ultimately, the selection of an exchange rate system depends not only on economic factors but also on the system's political acceptability to the members of the International Monetary Fund.

A conversion from the current system of managed floating to any of the systems described in this chapter would depend upon the future assessment of the performance of managed floating. Various other international monetary questions may also influence the future of the exchange rate system. Some of these continuing questions and problems are discussed in the next chapter.

REVIEW QUESTIONS

1. Explain the pegged exchange rate system. What were the reasons for its adoption?

2. How did each nation maintain the price of its currency within the bands under the pegged exchange rate system?

3. What arguments are made in favor of pegged as opposed to floating exchange rates?

4. If each nation manages its exchange rate, how different is a system of floating rates from the pegged exchange rate system?

5. How is the freedom of domestic policy makers greater under a system of floating exchange rates than under a system of pegged exchange rates?

6. How has the role of the dollar changed as floating rates replaced the fixed exchange rate system?

7. Explain the advantages of a system of wide bands. How would such a system differ from floating exchange rates?

8. Explain the concept of a crawling peg.

9. What problems are involved in the concept of measuring changes in par values by measuring reserve levels?

10. Review each of the exchange rate systems and determine the probable distribution of the burden of adjustment between the deficit and the surplus nation.

SUGGESTED READINGS

J. Herbert Furth, "International Monetary Reform and the 'Crawling Peg'—Comment," *Federal Reserve Bank of St. Louis Review,* July 1969, pp. 21–25.

Donald L. Kohn, "Capital Flows in a Foreign Exchange Crisis," *Federal Reserve Bank of Kansas City Monthly Review,* February 1973, pp. 14–23.

Lawrence B. Krause, "Fixed, Flexible, and Gliding Exchange Rates," *Journal of Money, Credit and Banking,* vol. III, no. 2, part II, Ohio State University Press, Columbus, pp. 321–338.

George W. McKenzie, "International Monetary Reform and the 'Crawling Peg,' " *Federal Reserve Bank of St. Louis Review,* February 1969, pp. 15–23.

George W. McKenzie, "International Monetary Reform and the 'Crawling Peg'—Reply," *Federal Reserve Bank of St. Louis Review,* July 1969, pp. 26–31.

23

CONTINUING INTERNATIONAL MONETARY PROBLEMS

The chapters in this last part of the book have pointed out some of the remaining unsettled international monetary issues. The major question, covered in Chapter 22, is the controversy between pegged and floating exchange rates. This chapter describes other continuing problems and discusses the post–World War II history and problems of the American dollar.

The IMF and the Reserve Creation Issue

One of the first controversies over the design of the International Monetary Fund centered on the question of the expansion of world monetary reserves. Should the IMF be able to create new reserves, or should it merely lend existing reserves? Keynes argued at Bretton Woods that IMF loans should increase total world monetary reserves, just as discounting at a national central bank increases reserves available to the domestic banking system. The Keynes plan would have created a true international central bank rather than a lending agency. Each member nation would have been assigned a borrowing quota in terms of a new reserve asset called *bancor*. Each nation could borrow bancor from the international central bank and use the bancor to settle balance of payments deficits. Under the Keynes plan, surplus nations would have been required to accept unlimited quantities of bancor and there would have been no limits on the ability of the international central bank to create bancor. The granting of bancor loans would have added to world monetary reserves.

The Keynes plan was not acceptable to the United States. As the major surplus nation in the immediate postwar period, the United States would have received large quantities of the newly created bancor from the deficit nations. Keynes argued that if the United States did not want to hold large quantities of bancor, American trade barriers could be lowered to permit greater imports and reduce the American surplus. However, a reduction of American trade barriers might not have decreased the American surplus because at that time other developed nations were recovering from the war and did not have the productive capacity to expand their exports significantly.

As a result of American opposition, the less innovative lending plan was accepted as the basis for the International Monetary Fund. The politics of the situation required acceptance of the American plan. The United States held most of the world's monetary gold and was the major economic power in the world; a monetary system not supported by the United States could not have survived. In addition, IMF voting power was distributed in proportion to quotas, and the United States had nearly 25 percent of the votes.

The issue of expanding the supply of world monetary reserves, put aside after the rejection of the Keynes plan, arose again in the early 1960s. The primary impetus for the revival of interest in the expansion of reserves was provided by Robert Triffin's book, *Gold and the Dollar Crisis.*[1] Triffin recognized that the expansion of world trade would increase the need for reserves and that gold supplies would not expand to fill this need. Thus, national currencies would have to serve as reserve assets. Triffin's solution was the creation of a new international reserve asset—IMF balances—to replace gold and foreign currencies in national reserve accounts.

Triffin's plan, although not adopted by the IMF, did lead to the creation of Special Drawing Rights (SDRs) by the IMF in the late 1960s. The creation of a new reserve asset by the IMF was opposed strongly by French President Charles de Gaulle. The French have traditionally preferred gold as a reserve asset, and the final design of the SDR plan was influenced by French opposition. The desire to limit the creation of new reserves persisted and influenced the design of the SDR plan.

The Special Drawing Right

The SDR was defined in terms of gold so that 1 SDR equaled 0.888671 grams of fine gold. At the time of the inauguration of the SDR system, 1 SDR was equal to \$1 in terms of gold content. Given that other currencies were defined either in terms of gold or the American dollar, each currency received an SDR value based on gold.

The creation of new SDRs requires a prior determination that total world monetary reserves should be increased. Expansion of the supply of SDRs is not automatic; an 85 percent affirmative vote by the Board of Governors of the IMF is necessary. Because the voting power is distributed according to IMF quotas, the United States can block an expansion of SDRs. The high vote required for SDR creation was a concession to France in the negotiations leading to the plan's adoption.

Once the creation of a given amount of new SDRs has been approved by the IMF, each member nation's reserve account receives a credit for its share of the new reserves. The SDRs are distributed on the basis of national quotas in the Fund; each

[1]Robert Triffin, *Gold and the Dollar Crisis* (New Haven, Conn.: Yale University Press, 1961).

nation receives a percentage of the SDRs equal to its percentage of total IMF quotas. In the first allocation of SDRs on January 1, 1970, 3.5 billion SDRs were allocated and the United States received 867 million SDRs.[2]

The method of distributing SDRs was one of the controversial points in the negotiations on the creation of SDRs. (Any plan for the distribution of a free good is apt to be controversial!) Proposals for the distribution on the basis of quotas and proposals for the distribution of SDRs as economic aid to the less developed nations were both considered. The concept of distribution according to quotas was accepted. Many participants believed that aid to the less developed nations should be kept separate from the reserve growth issue and that the developed nations had as great a need for the new reserves as the less developed nations.

Only IMF member nations can own SDRs. SDRs cannot be directly used by exchange stabilization accounts to maintain the value of a nation's currency; a nation's holdings of SDRs must be converted into currency. The nation that needs dollars for its exchange stabilization account buys the dollars from another nation and transfers its SDRs to the selling nation. The buying nation trades SDR balances for dollars and the selling nation trades dollars for SDR balances at the IMF. The dollars are then used to support the nation's currency.

To encourage the holding of Special Drawing Rights, each nation is paid a small amount of interest on its SDR holdings in excess of its total past allocations of SDRs. Over a five-year period, each nation's SDR holdings must average at least 30 percent of its total allocations. Thus, a nation can temporarily use all of its SDRs, but over the long run it must reconstitute its holdings to meet the 30 percent requirement.

The devaluations of the dollar in 1971 and 1973 changed the one-to-one relationship between the dollar and the SDR. After the second devaluation, $1 was equal to 0.828948 SDR. The fluctuation of currency values also creates problems for the valuation of the SDR. For purposes of member transactions in SDRs, the SDR is valued on the basis of a weighted average of the market values of 16 currencies.[3]

The Reserve Expansion Issue

Thus far, SDR allocations have been limited in quantity and the SDR accounts for only a small proportion of total monetary reserves. The need for growth of total reserves has not been met by SDR expansion. Gold cannot meet the need for added reserves and the dollar and other national currencies should not become the basis for reserve expansion. Thus, either SDRs or some other newly invented international reserve asset must be expanded. Otherwise, the problems involved in past reliance on the dollar will be repeated.

[2]"Experience with Special Drawing Rights," *Economic Review,* Federal Reserve Bank of Cleveland, March 1971, pp. 3–14. This article provides a clear and comprehensive explanation of the SDR.

[3]For a list of currencies and their weights in the determination of the SDR value, see *1974 Annual Report of the International Monetary Fund,* p. 117.

However, the expanded use of SDRs as a reserve asset presents at least three problems. First, the appropriate rate of growth of the supply of SDRs must be determined. If SDRs were to grow very rapidly, all deficit nations would be able to settle by using their SDR allocations and would never have to eliminate their deficits. At the other extreme, a slow rate of growth of SDRs would mean that national currencies or gold would have to fill the gap between desired reserve growth and the creation of SDRs.

Unfortunately, there is no simple rule for determining the appropriate rate of growth of international reserves. The most commonly used guide to reserve adequacy is the ratio of total reserves to total imports. However, this is a very rough guide to the overall need for reserves. In a period of floating exchange rates, the total need for reserves is less than that during a period of pegged exchange rates. Under a system of pegged exchange rates, the need for reserves depends upon the potential variability of a nation's balance of payments. If each nation's balance of payments were in perfect equilibrium, the need for reserves would be low. Alternatively, if each nation's balance shifted sharply each year, the demand for reserves would be very great.

Second, SDRs cannot be directly used to intervene in currency markets. SDR holdings must be converted to dollars. If dollars can be used directly while SDRs must be converted, there is little incentive to hold SDRs. The development of a system in which SDRs could be used to intervene in currency markets appears necessary if the role of the SDR is to increase.

The incentive to hold SDRs would also be increased if the IMF paid a higher interest rate on SDR holdings. A nation can invest its holdings of dollar reserves and receive a much higher rate of return than is paid on SDRs.[4]

Third, there is the issue of control of SDR creation. Under the present requirement of an 85 percent affirmative vote, a relatively small number of nations can block a proposed SDR expansion. A lowering of this requirement would be the most desirable long-run solution, but those favoring limited IMF powers would oppose this change.

In spite of the problems of increasing the use of SDRs as an international reserve asset, the trend probably will be in this direction. The flaws in both the gold standard and the dollar standard would appear to make the SDR alternative inevitable.

The Role of Gold

For most of recorded history gold was the cornerstone of the international monetary system. However, the role of gold declined in the post–World War II period, and gold has now been almost totally demonetized.

[4]In this connection, see Michael W. Keran, "An Appropriate International Currency—Gold, Dollars, or SDRs," *Federal Reserve Bank of St. Louis Review*, August 1972, pp. 8–19.

Under the pegged rate system in effect prior to 1973, gold was the asset behind the American dollar and the dollar was the major reserve asset held by other nations. Although the dollar was convertible into gold by foreign central banks, most nations held dollars in preference to holding gold. Only the French, with their traditional preference for gold and gold-based systems, converted a large proportion of their dollar holdings into gold. However, the volume of dollars convertible into gold eventually grew so large that convertibility had to be suspended in 1971.

When the United States suspended the gold convertibility of dollars held by foreign central banks, the last major link between money and gold was broken. American increases in the price of gold in 1971 and 1973 did not have any real economic meaning because the United States was no longer willing to sell gold at either the old price or the new price.

The divergence between the official price of gold ($42.22 per ounce after the second American devaluation) and the market price of gold (currently $130 per ounce) created the ultimate pressure for the reduction of the role of gold in the international monetary system. The producers of gold did not want to sell newly mined gold to central banks at $42.22 per ounce while the free market price of gold was nearly four times the official price. In addition, those central banks holding gold desired to value their gold on the basis of the free market price rather than on the basis of the low official gold price.

Two events in 1975 indicated the changing role of gold. First, the United States considered auctioning off part of its gold holdings. Second, Italy, in need of a foreign loan, pledged part of its gold holdings as security for the loan, and the pledged gold was valued at the free market price rather than at the official central bank price.

The Jamaica Accords of 1976 continued the gradual process of reducing the importance of gold. The official price of gold was eliminated; all gold holdings can now be valued at the free market price. In addition, the IMF decided that one-sixth of its gold holdings should be sold and the proceeds used to establish a trust fund to provide aid to the less developed nations.

Although gold will be sold by some central banks and by the IMF, some nations will continue to hold a portion of their international reserve assets in gold. However, the primary determinant of the price of gold will be the commercial and industrial demand for gold. The reserves of those nations continuing to hold gold reserves will fluctuate in value as the free market price of gold changes.

The International Transmission of Domestic Policy

Under all exchange rate systems, the domestic monetary and fiscal policies of any major nation have impacts on other nations. As economic relationships between nations increase, as knowledge spreads, and as communications improve, the maintenance of total economic policy independence becomes more difficult. From one point of view, the international transmission of policy is a desirable part of the mechanisms working to produce balance of payments equilibrium. From another point of view, the transmission of economic policy may force a nation to accept inflation or other economic ills as the result of another nation's economic policies. In this case, the policy transmission is unwelcome.

Under the gold standard, inflationary policies led to gold outflows. Those nations gaining gold experienced imported inflation unless they were able to offset the effects of the gold inflows.

The post–World War II pegged exchange rate system also had the effect of transmitting monetary policy between nations—especially between the United States and other nations. The floating rate system can also transmit domestic policy, but nations affected by foreign economic policies can simply allow their currencies to float. Assume that, under a pegged rate system, the United States expanded its money supply at a relatively high rate and lowered interest rates in order to increase capital investment and domestic employment. Assume, as was the case, that West Germany, on the other hand, maintained a conservative monetary policy and high interest rates.

Given the high German interest rates, there was an incentive for the transfer of funds from the United States to Germany. Savers sold dollars for marks and received interest from either deposits in German banks or the purchase of German securities. German interest rates tended to fall and American interest rates tended to rise as funds were shifted.

The conversion of dollars into marks increased the price of the mark in terms of the dollar. Under the pegged rate system, the German authorities had to sell marks for dollars in order to hold the price of the mark below the upper band. In the process of supplying marks to the foreign exchange market, the German government expanded the German money supply. Thus, maintaining the pegged exchange rate required a greater than desired rate of growth of the German money supply. While the United States continued to lower its interest rates and encourage the shifting of funds to Germany, the German money supply continued to grow. Germany and all nations pegging their currency to the dollar were subject to these same pressures. To an extent, Germany's choice of a domestic monetary policy and its preferred inflation-unemployment tradeoff was influenced by American domestic monetary policy.

What could the Germans do to prevent this interference with their domestic policy goals? A number of options were available. First, domestic monetary policy could be used to decrease the money supply as rapidly as the use of the exchange stabilization account increased the money supply. Open market operations, the discount rate, and reserve requirements could be used to offset the internationally imposed increase in the money supply. However, most other nations do not have all of the monetary policy tools that are available to the Federal Reserve System. The market for government securities may be much less active than that in the United States; open market operations are not as easily conducted in other nations.

Second, Germany could place a tax on deposit inflows. A tax on foreign-held balances or on new foreign balances could offset the interest rate differential and/or any expected increase in the price of the mark. However, this policy would work against the longer term goal of permitting freer international flows of funds.

Third, Germany could attempt to divide the foreign exchange market into a pegged rate market for normal import and export transactions and a floating rate market for all other transactions. If the two markets could be kept separate, the increased price of the floating mark would not affect domestic price levels. However, it is difficult to maintain two separate markets in the same currency.

Finally, Germany could break away from the pegged rate system and allow the price of the mark to float upwards under a pure float. The conversion of dollars into marks would no longer affect the domestic supply of marks, and Germany would be free to follow its own policy. However, there is a cost to this policy. As the price of the mark increases, German goods would become more expensive in world markets and exports would decline. Foreign goods would become less expensive in Germany and imports would rise. The balance of payments position would deteriorate and employment would decline. Under a managed float, Germany could allow some increase in the price of the mark and also use some of the other policy options.

Thus, under any exchange rate system, domestic policy is influenced by international forces. The problem was especially acute under the pegged rate system, and many nations complained that the United States was exporting inflation. The transition to managed floating in early 1973 reduced the problem, but the flow of funds between nations continues to affect export competitiveness. However, under the floating rate system, the United States is as vulnerable to the problem as are other nations.

In the long run, an exchange rate system is evaluated on the basis of the degree of domestic policy-making freedom accorded to national governments.

Food and Energy Crises and the International Monetary System

In the 1970s, shortages and rising prices of energy and food placed new strains on an international monetary system already suffering from widespread inflation and recession. The food problem represented the continuing difficulty of assisting the food-short nations of the world; the energy crisis created problems for both the developed and the less developed nations.

American food surpluses, which had been sold on easy terms or given to poor nations, suddenly evaporated in the face of increased sales to the Soviet Union and other nations. Those who could afford to pay absorbed the surplus.

The petroleum price rise caused a massive shift of funds from the oil-importing to the oil-exporting nations and created balance of payments problems for all energy-importing nations. Currency prices fluctuated as the foreign exchange markets assessed each nation's relative energy independence and the impact on each nation's balance of payments.

The first problem was the necessity of recycling the surplus revenues of the oil exporters into world money markets so that the funds could be borrowed by the oil importing nations. Nations belonging to the Organization of Petroleum Exporting Countries (OPEC) preferred to hold their revenues as relatively short-term deposits. The oil-importing nations desired to finance their deficits by borrowing long term. Banks receiving short-term petrodollar deposits (dollar deposits received from selling petroleum) were reluctant to lend the funds on a long-term basis because they could not be certain of the continued availability of the OPEC deposits. Time and the general improvement of the liquidity positions of the banks reduced the seriousness of this problem.

Second, while the developed nations had stronger reserve positions and could maintain their oil imports, the less developed nations were in a weak reserve position and needed assistance to continue both oil and food imports. The IMF developed an oil facility to provide assistance to nations having financial difficulty in meeting the higher costs of petroleum imports.[5]

Third, the OPEC nations are using their higher export earnings to finance added imports, but the less developed nations are not likely to benefit from this spending. The OPEC countries are not highly industrialized nations, and a high proportion of their imports will be capital goods purchased from the developed nations. The OPEC countries realize that they have only a limited quantity of oil under their lands, and that this may be their only chance to come up to the income levels of the affluent nations.

Faced with higher food and fuel bills, the less developed nations need added foreign development assistance. The developed nations, attempting to meet their higher fuel bills, are less willing to provide the necessary aid to the poor nations. The OPEC nations are being called upon to finance the development efforts of those unfortunate nations not located over oil deposits. The OPEC nations have loaned some funds to the less developed countries, but these loans must increase in number and size if the poorer nations are to increase per capita income levels.

Lending by the OPEC nations will probably be determined by both political considerations and the speed with which the OPEC nations can absorb capital into their own development efforts. In nations such as Iran and Venezuela, large-scale development plans were underway before the increase in petroleum prices; thus, the new funds can easily be absorbed by an acceleration of existing plans. In other OPEC countries, the ability to absorb new capital is restricted by lack of an on-going development plan. Some small and underpopulated OPEC nations may be unable to absorb all of their oil revenues. These latter nations may be the best source of longer term loans to the less developed nations.

[5]For a discussion of the problems of the less developed nations, see Constantine Michalopoulos, "Financing Needs of Developed Countries: Proposals for International Action," *Essays in International Finance,* No. 110 (June 1975), Princeton University Press, Princeton, N.J.

Fourth, the receipt of huge revenues by one unified group creates the danger of disruptive shifts of funds between currencies. Assume, for example, that the OPEC nations decided to hold all oil revenues and to receive all oil payments only in German marks. The demand for marks would increase and the demand for dollars would decrease as oil importers sold dollars to purchase marks. Under a pegged rate system, Germany would have to hold down the price of the mark and would have to accumulate great quantities of dollars. Under the floating exchange rate system, the dollar would depreciate and the mark would appreciate. The decline in the value of the dollar would improve the United States' trade position and the increase in the price of the mark would lead to a deterioration of the German trade position.

The international payments system managed to accommodate the shifts in wealth associated with the petroleum price increases. Many OPEC nations responded to the higher value of their exports by increasing their imports. Some OPEC nations turned their surpluses into deficits as imports expanded rapidly and the recession decreased oil revenues. More funds from the surplus nations were loaned to the less developed nations. The worldwide recession of the mid-1970s decreased petroleum demands and demands on international capital markets; both of these changes allowed policy makers time to adjust to the new conditions of the petroleum market.

For the long run, there are three continuing problems in this area:

1. The poorest nations must be helped to expand their export markets so that they will not have to borrow continuously to obtain petroleum imports.

2. Mechanisms must be provided to rechannel OPEC surplus funds into the money markets on terms acceptable to both OPEC and the borrowing nations.

3. Extreme changes in currency values must be avoided as OPEC nations shift their balances between currencies.

The American Dollar: Its Problems and Its Future

At the end of World War II, the American dollar was clearly the strongest currency in the world. American gold reserves were over $20 billion. The large American gold holdings resulted from a number of factors. First, the American gold supply was large as a result of American gold production during the 19th century. The 1933 calling in, or nationalization, of gold centralized most American gold in the United States Treasury. Second, in 1933 and 1934, the price of gold was increased to $35 per ounce. As expected, the higher price of gold created gold inflows. Third, in the later 1930s, American gold stocks were increased as Europeans foresaw the coming of World War II and transferred some of their gold holdings to the United States. Finally, American military sales to the allied nations in World War II created a balance of payments surplus and provided added gold inflows.

As a result of the strength of both the American dollar and the American economy, the postwar pegged exchange rate system was based on the dollar and the gold behind the dollar. This decision was the basis for the future problems of the dollar.

The United States ran balance of payments deficits during most of the 1950s and 1960s. These deficits were welcomed because they provided additional reserve assets for other nations. If the United States had not run deficits, other nations would have been unable to build up their international reserve assets. Most nations were happy to hold added dollars because the dollar was convertible into gold and the dollars could be invested in interest-bearing assets until the holder desired to convert to gold.

During the period in which all nations were attempting to add to their dollar holdings, the United States was free from the normal pressures to eliminate its balance of payments deficit. General de Gaulle, while president of France, was opposed to the idea that one nation should be free to run deficits without being subjected to the same limitations as were imposed on other nations. His solution was to refuse to build French dollar reserves. By converting dollars into gold, he attempted to force the United States to eliminate its balance of payments deficit. However, most nations were willing to continue adding dollars to their reserves.

During the early and mid-1960s, the United States did take some measures to reduce its deficits. The Interest Equalization Tax and the Voluntary Foreign Credit Restraint program attempted to reduce foreign borrowing in American credit markets and from American financial institutions. Attempts were made to encourage other nations to pay a greater share of Western defense costs so that the drain of American foreign military spending could be reduced. However, deficits continued and, as indicated in Table 20–1, United States official reserve assets declined while liabilities to foreign official agencies increased.

In 1970 and 1971, conditions worsened for the dollar. American inflation was accelerating and the balance of payments deficit was increasing. The 1971 net merchandise balance of trade recorded a deficit for the first time in the post–World War II period.

The deteriorating absolute and relative strength of the dollar led to speculative selling of the dollar and purchases of other currencies such as the German mark. Speculators hoped that the mark would be appreciated, and the German authorities absorbed billions of dollars into their exchange stabilization account as they attempted to maintain the pegged value of the mark relative to the dollar. Other strong currency countries also absorbed large dollar inflows. In 1971, United States liabilities to foreign official agencies increased by $27.405 billion. These liabilities would have increased even more if the Germans had not stopped supporting the dollar and allowed the mark to float upwards.

The American government used foreign exchange reserves and currency swaps to absorb dollars from the foreign exchange markets. While some $600 million of gold was sold, the demand for the conversion of dollars into gold was much less than would be expected. By this time, foreign central banks recognized that the United States could not come close to converting into gold all outstanding convertible dollars. A rush to convert into gold by foreign dollar holders would have destroyed the entire system.

By August 15, 1971, domestic inflation, the deteriorating balance of payments, and the continued flight from dollars required decisive action. President Nixon announced the suspension of the convertibility of dollars into gold, the first wage-price freeze, a temporary 10 percent surcharge on import duties, and the decision to devalue the dollar by increasing the price of gold from \$35 per ounce to \$38 per ounce.

The problems resulting from basing the international monetary system on the dollar were now obvious. The strength of the dollar, measured as the ratio of dollars held by foreign central banks to the value of American gold, was unquestioned at the end of World War II. Few dollars were held by foreign central banks and the American gold stock was huge. Over time, the supply of dollars convertible into gold grew and the gold stock declined. The early attractiveness of the dollar had produced such great dollar holdings that dollar claims against American gold became larger than the stock of gold. The initial popularity of the dollar led to its eventual difficulties.

Many nations responded to the American devaluation of August 1971 by allowing their currencies to float until the Smithsonian Institution meetings in December 1971. At these meetings, new pegged rates were established. The realignment of pegged values, rather than the decision to increase the price at which gold would not be sold, represented the real devaluation of the dollar. Some relatively weak currencies, such as the British pound, were not appreciated against the dollar; the stronger currencies were appreciated substantially. The Japanese yen was appreciated by nearly 17 percent, and the mark was appreciated by over 13 percent. The Smithsonian agreements also expanded the bands around par values to ±2¼ percent, so that currency prices could move over a greater range without requiring exchange stabilization account activity. Many speculators and central bankers believed that these revisions were not sufficient, and in time they were proved correct.

The economic problems of the United States continued through 1971 and 1972; prices continued to rise in spite of alternating programs of wage and price freezes and thaws. The 1972 balance of merchandise trade was in deficit by nearly \$7 billion, and liabilities to foreign official agencies increased by another \$10 billion as foreign nations attempted to maintain the Smithsonian rate structure.

By February 1973, none of the causes of the continuing problems of the dollar had been eliminated and the dollar was devalued a second time; the second devaluation of 10 percent followed the 8.57 percent devaluation of 1971. Subsequent to the second devaluation, most currencies were allowed to float, and most nations adopted a policy of managed floating.

As a result of the two formal devaluations and the adoption of floating rates, the dollar has lost a considerable portion of its pre-1971 value. Table 23–1 presents some data on the number of units of various foreign currencies which could be obtained for an American dollar. The decrease in the foreign exchange value of the dollar has not been the same from currency to currency. Between 1970 and 1975, the number of Italian lira and British pounds which could be obtained for \$1 increased. These two currencies depreciated in market value even more than the dollar.

TABLE 23–1 Number of Units of Various Foreign Currencies Obtained for $1

	1970	*1971*	*1972*	*1973*	*1974*	*1975*
France (franc)	5.529	5.510	5.044	4.437	4.806	4.282
Germany (mark)	3.646	3.476	3.188	2.648	2.582	2.455
Japan (yen)	358.153	347.476	303.076	270.892	291.528	296.692
Switzerland (franc)	4.311	4.111	3.818	3.154	2.968	2.581
United Kingdom (pound)	0.417	0.409	0.400	0.408	0.427	0.450
Norway (krone)	7.147	7.040	6.588	5.745	5.519	5.214
Italy (lira)	627.156	618.276	583.703	581.666	650.533	652.401

SOURCE: *Federal Reserve Bulletin,* various issues.

Subsequent to the February 1973 devaluation of the dollar, the value of the dollar continued to decline in terms of many major currencies. The OPEC oil embargo and the drastic increase in world petroleum prices affected the value of the dollar less than the value of many other currencies, because the United States was less dependent on imported oil than were many other Western industrialized nations.

In spite of a near doubling of the dollar value of American exports between 1972 and 1974, imports also increased rapidly. The merchandise trade deficit, which had been eliminated in 1973, reappeared in 1974. In 1975, the trade balance again swung into surplus and the dollar revived in international money markets.

The dollar probably cannot recoup all of the losses experienced since the 1971 devaluation. Most observers believed that the dollar was overvalued long before the devaluation. However, some improvement can be reasonably expected. Continued significant trade and payments surpluses would reduce foreign dollar holdings and restore confidence in the future value of the dollar. Control of the rate of inflation is the key to achieving this objective.

The value of the dollar will continue to be depressed by the *overhang* of dollars acquired by foreign central banks prior to the suspension of gold convertibility. Foreign central banks are holding more dollars than they care to hold. Increases in the dollar's value are apt to encourage central banks to ''cut their losses'' and switch from dollars to other stronger currencies.

By the end of 1975, total American reserve assets were lower than at the end of 1946, and the American gold supply had declined by $9 billion from its 1946 level. Total reserve assets are presented in Table 23–2. While total American reserve assets are relatively high, the supply of gold is insufficient to permit a resumption of gold convertibility.

The future role of the dollar will differ from its past role. The dollar will never again be the cornerstone of the international monetary system. No one currency will ever be accorded, or forced into, that position, However, as the currency of a major economic power with substantial reserve assets, the dollar will continue to be one of a group of major currencies.

An Evaluation of the International Monetary System

Two points must be stressed in the evaluation of the performance of the international monetary system. First, the pegged exchange rate system must be given all due credit, even though the system contained serious faults. From 1945 to 1971, the system worked reasonably well and was associated with a high level of world economic performance. International trade and investment expanded rapidly, barriers to free trade and the free movement of capital were reduced or eliminated, and the number of major currency devaluations was relatively small. The system provided the exchange rate stability conducive to recovery from the Depression of the 1930s and from World War II.

TABLE 23–2 American Reserve Assets, 1975 (millions of dollars)

Gold	11,599
SDRs	2,335
Convertible foreign currencies	80
Reserve position in the IMF	2,212
Total reserve assets	16,226

SOURCE: *1976 Economic Report of the President,* p. 279.

The pegged rate system, based on the dollar as the key currency, did contain serious flaws and these flaws produced its eventual downfall. The system did not allow for crisis-free changes in exchange rates and did not provide a method for changing the value of the key currency. The dollar could not be devalued unless other nations agreed to appreciate their currencies. While other nations were willing to add to their dollar holdings, there was no pressure on the United States to reduce its deficits. The accumulation of deficits eventually weakened the dollar, reduced its desirability as a reserve asset, and forced the suspension of convertibility. If another currency were to be placed in the role of the dollar, the same problems probably would be repeated.

Second, an evaluation of managed floating would be premature. Some believe that changes in currency prices have been in excess of the changes necessary to restore balance of payments equilibriums. Others argue that the new freedom for domestic policy makers is worth the price in terms of currency fluctuations and that market forces will correct excessive rate changes.

The disasters that central bankers once feared would result from floating rates have not occurred. Of course, Utopia has not arrived yet either. However, given the world economic conditions at the beginning of general floating in 1973, the managed float seems to have coped with a vast number of problems in a reasonably smooth manner.

REVIEW QUESTIONS

1. Explain the Keynes plan for the creation of an international central bank. In what ways has the IMF become the type of institution Keynes desired?

2. What are Special Drawing Rights? How are these assets used between central banks?

3. What factors must be considered in determining the appropriate rate of growth of world monetary reserves?

4. Why has gold gradually lost its position in international monetary economics?

5. How do exchange rate systems transfer economic problems between nations?

6. What problems would have been created if the United States had not run balance of payments deficits in the first decade after World War II? What problems were created by running continued deficits?

7. How has the position of the American dollar changed since the latest data included in Table 23–1?

8. What is meant by an overhang of dollars?

9. Why did the food and energy crises present unique problems for the international monetary system?

10. Given the performance of the floating exchange rate system thus far, have the fears of its opponents been justified?

SUGGESTED READINGS

C. Fred Bergsten and Lawrence B. Krause, eds., *World Politics and Industrial Economics*. Washington, D.C.: Brookings Institution, 1975.

Norman S. Fieleke, "Oil and International Payments," *New England Economic Review,* Federal Reserve Bank of Boston, November–December 1974, pp. 29–40.

Fred Hirsch, "An SDR Standard: Impetus, Elements, and Impediments," *Essays in International Finance,* No. 99, (June 1973), Princeton University Press, Princeton, N.J.

Donald L. Kohn, "Interdependence, Exchange Rate Flexibility, and National Economies," *Federal Reserve Bank of Kansas City Monthly Review,* April 1975, pp. 3–10.

Ronald A. Krieger, "The Monetary Governors and the Ghost of Bretton Woods," *Challenge,* International Arts & Sciences Press, New York, January–February 1975, pp. 33–39.

Adrian W. Throop, "Bicentennial Perspective—Decline and Fall of the Gold Standard," *Federal Reserve Bank of Dallas Business Review,* January 1976, pp. 1—11.

Marina v.N. Whitman, "The Current and Future Role of the Dollar: How Much Symmetry?" *Brookings Papers on Economic Activity,* vol. 3 (1974), Brookings Institution, Washington, D.C. pp. 539–583.

Thomas O. Willett and Edward Tower, "The Welfare Economics of International Adjustment," *Journal of Finance,* American Finance Association, New York, May 1971, pp. 287–302.

INDEX